Contents

Environmental Science for Environmental Management

Edited by
TIMOTHY O'RIORDAN

School of Environmental Sciences, University of East Anglia

LONGMAN

This book is dedicated to the memory of Lord Zuckerman, OM FRS, who did so much to promote the cause of interdisciplinary environmental science both by example and by visionary leadership.

Addison Wesley Longman Limited
Edinburgh Gate, Harlow
Essex CM20 2JE, England
and Associated Companies throughout the world

© Longman Group Limited 1995

First published 1995
Reprinted 1995 (twice), 1996, 1997

British Library Cataloguing in Publication Data
A catalogue entry for this title is available from the British Library

ISBN 0-582-21889-6

Library of Congress Cataloging-in-Publication data
A catalog entry for this title is available from the Library of Congress.

Set by 14B in 10/12 pt Times

Produced by Longman Singapore Publishers (Pte) Ltd.

Printed in Singapore

List of contributors

All contributors are at the University of East Anglia and are listed below in order of contribution together with their positions and main areas of research.

Professor Timothy O'Riordan, School of Environmental Sciences (Environmental policy)

Professor Kerry Turner, School of Environmental Sciences (Environmental economics)

Dr Ian Bateman, School of Environmental Sciences (Environmental economics)

Dr Alastair Grant, School of Environmental Sciences (Marine sedimentology and chemistry)

Dr John Barkham, School of Environmental Sciences (Ecology and ethics)

Professor Keith Clayton, School of Environmental Sciences (Applied environmental management)

Dr Richard Hey, School of Environmental Sciences (Environmental geomorphology)

Dr Karen Heywood, School of Environmental Sciences (Physical oceanography)

Professor Mike Stocking, School of Development Studies (Soil erosion and land use management)

Dr Kevin Hiscock, School of Environmental Sciences (Environmental geohydrology)

Dr Tim Jickells, School of Environmental Sciences (Biogeochemistry)

Dr Peter Brimblecombe, School of Environmental Sciences (Environmental chemistry)

Frances Nicholas, School of Environmental Sciences (Environmental science)

Dr Simon Gerrard, School of Environmental Sciences (Risk analysis)

Dr Gordon Edge, School of Environmental Sciences (Energy policy)

Dr Keith Tovey, School of Environmental Sciences (Environmental engineering)

Dr Robin Haynes, School of Environmental Sciences (Epidemiology and health sciences)

Foreword

In June 1992 at Rio de Janeiro in Brazil, about 25 000 people gathered for the world's largest conference ever. Often known as the Earth Summit because of the large number of world leaders and heads of government who attended, it was held under United Nations' auspices and was concerned with Environment and Development. It considered such questions as, 'how can the right balance be struck between our need to develop and to improve human quality of life and the important imperative to preserve the environment' and 'how can the goal of sustainable development be achieved?'

Not only was the conference an important milestone for the environment; that environmental considerations have firmly entered the political arena could not have been more clearly demonstrated. But it was also an event of large significance in the relationship between science and politics. Because of the clear presentation by the world scientific community of the problem of Global Warming (including the uncertainties involved) to the world's politicians and policymakers, it proved possible at the conference for nearly all countries to agree to the signing of the Framework Convention on Climate Change.

The Earth Summit at Rio was only a beginning. Agreement was not reached on issues like forestry and biodiversity. The Climate Convention is a big step forward but specific and binding action has yet to be specified.

In all these areas of concern the outcome of the Summit presents an enormous challenge to the world's scientists. For instance, the Objective of the Climate Convention speaks of the requirements to stabilize the concentration of carbon dioxide in the atmosphere, to avoid unacceptable damage to ecosystems, to ensure that global food supply is not threatened and to provide for sustainable economic development. To address these requirements demands that the very best particular expertise be brought to bear in complex areas of natural science, economics, risk analysis and human behaviour. But it demands more than that. It is also necessary that expertise is linked right across the disciplines of the natural and the social sciences.

It is this urgent need for a multidisciplinary approach which is the burden of the book. If such an approach is to be adequate it not only requires very good understanding and communication between the disciplines, but a degree of interchange and integration beyond what is normally available or considered necessary. The coverage of the different chapters is aimed at illustrating how such interchange and integration can be realized.

Because of its broad coverrage and integrated style, the book will find particular value in the training of environmental scientists and managers. A question which is continually posed when science courses are being planned is how to balance the need for a broad coverage against the equally strong need for knowledge in depth. That students should study a particular scientific problem to its full depth is essential if they are to understand what science is about. Because in environmental science many particular problems possess a fundamental multidisciplinary character, their study can bring about an in-depth understanding of more than one discipline.

Many environmental issues raise questions of value, which go far beyond considerations of economic or utility value. To what features of our environment, for instance, should most value be attached? A lot of attention is being given to such questions; it is easy to pose the questions, it is far more difficult to find adequate answers. When it comes to how to value the Earth, the broadest possible view coupled with a multidisciplinary scientific approach is essential if a balanced perspective is to be realized. This book will help in generating such a perspective.

Sir John Houghton
Chairman, Royal Commission in Environmental Pollution

Acknowledgements

In March 1990 I gave a lecture on the theme of this book in the marvellous Wren-designed church of St James Picadilly. At the conclusion of the talk an exceedingly lively gentleman asked me if I would be prepared to convert this into a book to help the citizens of the future to fully appreciate environmental science. This individual was Isador Caplan, former Secretary to the Hilden Trust, a charitable foundation that sponsors, amongst other things, the pursuit of education. Subsequently the Hilden Trust financed the preparation of this book, and my colleagues and I are immensely grateful to both Mr Caplan and the Trust for their support. In addition I would like to thank the staff of Longman Higher Education for backing the project and for being so helpful in its preparation. Finally to all my colleagues here at UEA I owe an enormous debt of gratitude. They have patiently and willingly prepared their chapters when other even more pressing demands failed to distract their attention.

We are grateful to the following for permission to reproduce copyright material:

Academic Press (London) Ltd. for Fig. 14.2 (Hamilton & Clifton, 1979); American Society of Civil Engineers for Fig. 7.10 (Paice & Hey, 1993); Annual Reviews Inc. for the second figure in Box 16.3 (Rasmussen, 1990); R P Ashley for Figs 13.1 and 13.2; Blackwell Scientific Publications for Figs 14.3 (Ruivo, 1972) and 5.5 (Newman, 1993); Butterworth Heinemann Ltd. for the first figure in Box 16.3 (Carter, 1991); Cambridge University Press for Figs 6.1, 6.2, 6.3, 6.4, table in Box 6.1 (Houghton, Jenkins and Ephraums, 1990), Fig. 6.8 (Warrick & Rahman, 1992), the second figure in Box 17.3 and Table 17.1 (Holdern & Pachauri, 1992); Defence Research Agency (Space and Communications Department) for Fig. 11.8 (Curran, 1985); Earthscan Publications Ltd. for Fig. 6.6a (Parry, 1990); Elsevier Science for Fig. A.1 Reprinted from *The Science of the Total Environment*, 108, O'Riordan, The new environmentalism and sustainable development, 5–15, Copyright (1991) with kind permission from Elsevier Science Ltd., The Boulevard, Langford Lane, Kidlington, OX5 1GB, UK, Fig. 14.8 Reprinted from *Marine Pollution Bulletin*, 12, Fonselius, Oxygen and hydrogen sulphide conditions in the Baltic Sea, 187–194 Copyright (1982) with kind permission from Elsevier Science Ltd, The Boulevard, Langford Lane, Kidlington, OX5 1GB, UK and for Fig. 18.5

Reprinted from the *Journal of Chronic Diseases*, 9, Cobb, Miller and Wald, on the estimation of the incubation period in malignant disease, 385–93, Copyright (1959), with kind permission from Elsevier Science Ltd., The Boulevard, Langford Lane, Kidlington, OX5 1GB, UK; Engineering Surveys Ltd (Incorporating Clyde Surveys) for figure in Box 11.6 (Curran, 1985); The Geographical Journal for Fig. 6.6b (Hulme, Hossell & Parry, 1993); Dr M. George for figure in Box 5.2 (George, 1992); Harvard University Press for Fig. 18.4 Reprinted by permission of the publishers from *AIDS in the World* edited by Jonathan Mann, Daniel J M Tarantola and Thomas W Netter, Cambridge, Mass. Copyright © 1992 by the President and Fellows of Harvard College; Helgolander Meeresuntersuchungen for Fig. 14.4 (Ernst, 1980); Her Majesty's Stationery Office for table in Box 17.2 (Warren Spring Laboratory, on behalf of the DOE, first published in the Digest of Environmental Protection and Water Statistics no. 15 Reproduced with the permission of the Controller of HMSO) and Fig. 18.3 (HMSO, 1952) Crown Copyright. Reproduced with the permission of the controller of Her Majesty's Stationery Office; Hodder and Stoughton Ltd. for Fig. 4.1 (Anderson, 1977); Institute of Fisheries Management for Figs 7.13, 7.14, 7.16 and 7.17 (Hey, 1992); IOP Publishing Ltd for figure in Box 14.2 (Wood, 1982); Kluwer Academic Publishers for figure in Box 6.8 (Pittock and Nix, 1986) Reprinted by permission of Kluwer Academic Publishers; Longman Group Ltd. for Figs 11.1, 11.3, 11.4, 11.9 and 11.10 (Curran, 1985); National Radiological Protection Board for Fig. 18.6 (Hughes and O'Riordan, 1993); Nature for Fig. 6.5 and Table 9.1 (Wigley & Raper, 1992) Copyright (1992) Macmillan Magazines Ltd; National River Authority Thames Region for Fig. 9.5; OECD for Fig. 3.1 (Bateman, 1992); Oxford University Press for Fig. 3.5 and Tables 3.2 and 3.3 (Willis & Benson, 1989) and for Fig. B in Box 17.2 (from *World Resources 1992 – 1993* by World Resources Institute. Copyright © 1992 by the World Resources Institute. Reprinted by permission of Oxford University Press, Inc.); Research Institute for Agrobiology and Soil Fertility (AB-DLO) for Fig. 14.1 (Salomons & de Groot, 1978); Routledge Kegan Paul for Fig. 11.2 (Harris, 1987); The Royal Society for Fig. 14.6 (Royal Society, 1983); Scientific American, Inc. for Fig. 17.4 (Goodman, 1990); Springer Verlag GmbH & Co. KG for Fig. 7.12 (Brookes, 1987); Verlag Heinz Heise GmbH & Co RG for Fig. 13.3 (Foster, 1985); John Wiley & Sons Inc. for Fig. 7.5 and Table 7.1 (Winkley, Reponse of the lower Mississippi to river training and realignment. In Hey, Bathurst and Thorne (Eds) *Gravel-bed Rivers*) Copyright © 1982 John Wiley & Sons Inc.; World Health Organization for Figure in Box 18.1 (Beaglehole, Bonita and Kjellström, 1993); Worldwatch Institute for Table 1.1 Reprinted from *State of the World* 1988, edtied by Lester R Brown *et al.*, with the permission of W W Norton & Company, Inc. Copyright © 1988 by Worldwatch Institute.

Whilst every effort has been made to trace the owners of copyright material, in a few cases this has proved impossible and we take this opportunity to offer our apologies to any copyright holders whose rights we may have unwittingly infringed.

Environmental science on the move

TIMOTHY O'RIORDAN

Science does not need qualifiers like 'good' or 'green', or suffixes like 'ism'. Adding the -ism is designed simply to bring science down to the level of the pseudo sciences such as Marxism or Creationism. People who do so think it a ticket of entry: actually it is a rejection slip.

Alex Milne writing in *New Scientist*, 12 June 1993

A challenge to science

Alex Milne speaks for many scientists who see their culture threatened by a wave of populist criticism. The claim of the non-conformists is that the established ways of conducting science act against sensitive and precautionary environmental management by reflecting and reproducing the élitist and exploitative aspects characteristic of all instruments of power. For example, Brian Wynne and Sue Meyer (1993) echo the environmental activist when they argue that research seeking a high degree of control over the system being studied, and which enables precise observations of the behavioural correlations between a small number of variables, draws the regulator into restricting only those relationships where cause and effect can either be proved or shown to be reasonably unambiguous.

This practice tends to place the regulator on the defensive. There may be a great number of inter-correlating factors that are not measured with equivalent diligence, due to lack of resources or inadequate recording equipment. But in a democratic political culture, the regulator has to justify the level of protection being sought. A challenge by a discharger can result in a costly and time-consuming appeal. So it is possible that the regulator plays safe and determines the environmental standard or the permitted level of discharge on the basis of the evidence that can stand up in court. That in turn will rely on the conventional scientific method. Hence the very essence of the scientific technique becomes a political weapon in the legal culture of appeal and ministerial determination of environmental quality.

Science is value-laden, as are the scientists who practise their trade. That is to be expected, though it is not always recognized. We shall see that the process of peer review is designed to iron out the obvious ideological wrinkles. More important is the belief that the practice of science may reinforce a non-sustainable economic and social culture. Because we do not know where the margins of sustainability are, the scientific approach may provide a justification for pushing the alteration of the planet beyond the limits of its tolerance. Even by playing safe, the scientific approach may, quite unintentionally, create a sense of false security over the freedom we have to play with the Earth. The critique, therefore, is directed at the role and self-awareness of science in a world that is grappling for the first time with seeking to restrain human aspiration and imposing global obligations on self-fulfilling private enterprise.

Until now those qualities have been the very essence of progress and material security. To challenge them requires boldness and a cast-iron justification.

Science is under fire, but it remains for the most part true to its traditions. Yet there is also change. It is the creative relationship between retaining the basic principles of the scientific method and adapting to fresh realities of the role of science in human affairs that is shaping modern environmental science. This is the context for the chapters that follow.

Environmental science and interdisciplinarity

It has long been held that environmental science equates with 'earth science', namely that it is the study of the atmosphere, the land, and the oceans and the great chemical cycles that flow through the physical and biological systems that connect them. For the most part this is still the case in the content of environmental science courses in higher education in the UK. It is becoming less so in continental Europe and especially in the US, where broad-based and more interdisciplinary courses are more commonly found.

A study for the UK Department for Education (1993) found that in 1988 only 21 higher education institutions offered environmental sciences or environmental studies courses, with a further 27 providing specialist professional programmes in environmental health, technology and engineering. By 1992 a total of 35 institutions were offering environmental science or related courses, with 71 providing specialist environmental training. Nowadays the subject matter is of great interest and much in demand, but the validation of what is properly environmental science needs to be better justified. It is becoming fashionable to label any science-based course as 'green', much to the annoyance of Mr Milne and the traditions for which he so vehemently stands.

The UK Department for Education study took a narrower view of what constitutes a specialist environmental programme. These are courses primarily designed

- to develop students' understanding of the environment, drawing upon a range of disciplines from the natural and social sciences, and/or
- to provide vocational education for various kinds of environmental practitioner.

We see that modern environmental science is increasingly becoming *interdisciplinary*, preparing people for *global citizenship*, and training them to be flexible, yet competent, *analysts and decision takers*. These are not objectives that are easily reconciled in one degree course, and certainly not in one subject area.

Interdisciplinarity differs from multidisciplinarity in that it draws upon common themes of process and evolution that embrace both physical and social systems, and usually requires team work and close collaboration between teachers, students and the phenomena being studied. Multidisciplinarity draws upon a variety of disciplines for information, analysis and insight, but does not seek to create a broader and more integrated understanding of what and why. It is administratively easier to carry out, and less dependent on the good will and tolerance of the practitioners.

As can be seen from the discussion in Box 0.1, interdisciplinarity is much more than a meshing of disciplines. That would be multidisciplinarity as illustrated in the overlap zones between the established disciplines. Interdisciplinarity means taking a more negotiated science into the policy realm and engaging with the public. This is because societal understanding is vital to the conduct of science under conditions of great uncertainty, value conflict and data ambiguity. As we shall often see in this text, actual collection of evidence is a function of the outlook of the scientists, the research environment and nationalist perspectives. Evidence of methane production from rice paddies varies by a factor of over 200. How is a figure going to be arrived at to measure a given country's contribution to greenhouse warming potential? Similarly the allocation of say carbon taxes, or sulphur dioxide emissions permits depend critically on credible data gathering and negotiation. Interdisciplinarity is therefore 'outreach' science or 'civic science', as well as multidisciplinary science.

Interdisciplinarity is truly difficult to put into effect because:

- the modern scientific tradition does not readily share its culture with other cultures of knowing and understanding;
- career advancement in science tends to be accelerated if peer review accepts the basis of research and the consistent high quality of the research method;
- though multiple authorship is slowly becoming a more recognized basis for career promotion, multiple authorship involving the integration of many disciplines can be stressful and time-consuming, even though ultimately rewarding;

Box 0.1 Interdisciplinarity and multidisciplinarity

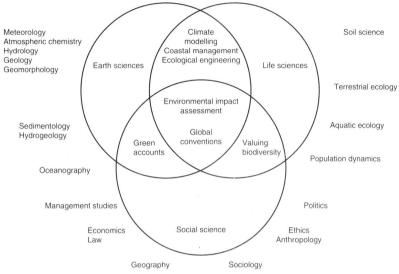

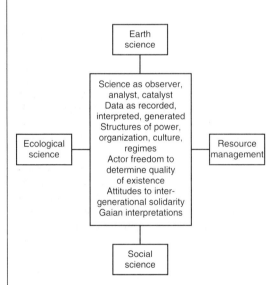

The two diagrams portray in a highly simplified fashion the distinction between interdisciplinarity and multidisciplinarity. In the latter case, the three branches of science, namely physical, life and social sciences, rarely interact. Each has its own developmental arena, and the attractive research areas are by no means found only on the margins where an element of joint disciplinarity takes place. But it is possible for the climate system to be studied this way, with much success, and for the emerging field of environmental economics to flourish in the inter-stices between economics and ecology. A more formal multidisciplinarity is often found in the ever-widening area of environmental impact assessment (EIA). Admittedly even today, almost a quarter of a century after the Americans first introduced the approach in the 1969 National Environmental Policy Act, this technique is more an amalgamation of mini reports based on predetermined approaches than a truly integrative document.

But for EIA to flourish it needs not just to integrate the disciplines. It also needs to provide regular guidance over how a project should evolve. Interdisciplinarity recognizes that power is shared when information exchange is open, when those likely to be affected by change actually negotiate their values and reactions from the outset, and that data are a function of knowledge, experience and power. In other words, the vital ingredients for the EIA have to come from the people on the ground whose interests are directly affected. This is not just a matter of well-intentioned liberalism: it is a recognition that those who have used a resource for generations are the best judge of how impacts of change can be evaluated.

This interdisciplinarity goes well beyond environmental assessment, even of policy, let alone projects. It covers a fresh approach to the gathering and interpretation of data, it recognizes the need to weigh information according to various parameters of political and ethical norms, and it creates an extension of power for those who are not always recognized as being of importance.

- many established higher education institutions find it difficult to create interdisciplinarity out of long-serving single-discipline departments, especially those with high research ratings and a steady flow of research funding.

This means that interdisciplinarity has not in the past attracted the best and brightest scholars, nor has it flourished even in environmental sciences departments. Interdisciplinarity is not just a matter of integration. It is the basis for a fresh way of identifying, defining, interpreting, analysing and solving environmental problems. It involves not just the academic researcher, but also a creative relationship between those who have to act and be responsible for their deeds, and those who prepare the evidence and offer advice on the basis of various methods of enquiry.

Take, for example, the vexed issue of environmental taxation. We shall see in Chapters 2 and 3 and also in Chapters 1 and 19 that there is an overwhelming case for 'paying our way' in determining, literally, the full cost of living. To the economist, this means creating an extension of the market to take into account the benefits of protecting environmental services that make our lives survivable or enjoyable. Examples include safeguarding the soil-stabilizing role of vegetation-covered slopes and organic rich topsoil, or stopping commercial whaling in favour of whale watching. Similarly it means penalizing those who do not pay for using these environmental services, either in the form of a tax or in the form of a permit that can be traded.

It is possible for economists, combined with bio-geo-chemists, or ecologists, or hydrologists, etc., to come up with a reasonable estimate of what these services are

---

Box 0.2 On the nature of interdisciplinarity

Children under the age of 5, we are told, think holistically, as do many people who do not have the advantage of a structured scientific education. Interdisciplinarity is the merging of knowledge into common concepts, and the application of ideas in the round for real-world problem solving. True interdisciplinarity has probably never existed, because, by definition, the phenomenon involves the unification of concepts that are designed to be conceived as separate entities. A simile is trying to create an orange from segments and pith separated out. With skill, and with some adhesive, a plausible orange will appear, but it will be a contrivance, not a living entity. Thus we can distinguish between multidisciplinarity or pluridisciplinarity, and true interdisciplinarity. The first two are essentially synonymous: the last is fusion *ab initio*. This is why there is confusion around the term. The common way out is for multidisciplinarity, the coordination of specialisms, based on framework, but with integration only occurring by effort and often by chance. True interdisciplinarity is a fundamentally unique approach to total science.

It is, however, possible to identify some common concepts that embrace both the social and natural sciences. Here are four that look promising:

1. *Chaos* is a concept that enables dynamic systems to be understood for their unpredictability and patterns of indeterministic behaviour. Chaos takes place as much in governing institutions as it does in the worlds of quantum physics or hurricane formation. The point is to learn from the principles involved as they apply to various circumstances.

2. *Social learning* is the process by which organisms 'see' their environmental circumstances by intelligence gathering, and act with foresight or prepared adjustment. This principle of precautionary but evolutionary adjustment may be a vital one for responding to environmental stress.

3. *Dynamic equilibria* abound in nature, but usually in an entropic sense, namely that over time equilibria may shift to new sets of dynamically stable relationships. Just as this may be the case for oxygen, or sulphur fluxes, so too it may be for carbon and the human population.

4. *Carrying capacity and evolutionary adjustment.* This is another version of (3) above. Carrying capacity is akin to sustainability, and involves the application of cooperation, competition, justice and respect from individuals as well as group welfare. Enshrined in these principles are also those of reciprocity, sharing to ensure that adequate conditions of survival are maintained. Carrying capacity must be linked to physical and ecological parameters such as tolerance and adaptability.

This in turn may require the rethinking of approaches to research training and the connections between educational institutions and industry, commerce and government. There should be scope for the university and college to collaborate with organizations engaged in policy analysis and environmental problem solving. There is also the probability of joint PhDs, partnerships between university and a supportive institution. Such PhD schemes would provide both training and problem-solving skills.

worth, how much it would cost society to find substitutes, and hence how much the user should pay to purchase the right to use some of those services. But such calculations can never be 'right': they can only be approximations based on the best evidence available. If the price is too low, the penalty will not have the desired effect. Even though subsequent polluting or safeguarding behaviour adjusts to the new market conditions, a systematic underestimate of the possible losses of environmental services could result in further destruction. Because the tax is imposed, the subsequent shift in behaviour is somehow more justified (or legitimate), and hence far more difficult to regulate further by additional, and correctional, increases in taxation.

If the price is too high, on the other hand, not only would there be a real social cost in terms of excessively diverted investment towards environmental clean-up where the net improvements would not be justified. There could also be a huge row at the supremacy of the environmental scientist not properly consulting and empathizing with those who have to bear the burden.

This happened in Norway. A high carbon tax was imposed to reduce carbon dioxide emissions, the main source of greenhouse warming (see Chapter 6), to the outrage of the shipping and transport industries. They felt unduly penalized in a predominantly hydroelectric power-using electricity economy, where neighbouring countries did not impose a carbon tax at all. Eventually the carbon tax was lowered, and Norway plans to buy out some of the carbon dioxide emissions of other countries at a lower cost than to remove its own. In global terms as well as in economic terms this is a more cost-effective tactic. But it could have been established at the outset if the analysts had consulted more widely with those whose livelihoods they were about to savage in the name of the noble objective – the polluter pays.

The Norwegian case here is usually referred to as *joint implementation*, namely a bilateral trade between two CO_2 emitters both seeking to minimize the costs of joint action. From a global viewpoint there is nothing wrong with this approach. After all, one molecule of CO_2 is radiation forcing wherever it is emitted. But from an ethical and political vantage point, joint implementation could be regarded as backsliding. Norway is anxious to be an environmental leader: this policy of offsetting the majority of her CO_2 via joint implementation may be economically efficient but politically dangerous.

Interdisciplinarity is not just a matter of more integrated theories and greater gelling of disciplines. It applies to the style of research, in terms of being more consultative, pro-active and participatory. It must also be sensitive to the institutional settings in which research and analysis are conducted. The phrase 'institutional settings' applies to processes of learning and communicating and norms about how to behave and make judgements, as well as to the organizations involved and their interrelationships.

For example, in certain institutional settings participation can be self-serving and illusory, maintaining the status quo yet giving the impression of accommodation. This happens when information is not freely available, where communication programmes are run by hired consultants, and where there are no accountable mechanisms to show that there is real responsiveness. In the US, chemical companies are required to consult with their communities as to the toxic emissions that should be tolerated. In the UK this information is only passed on to those whom the chemical companies feel ought to be informed. In the US there are legal sanctions against non-compliance with the public involvement programme. In the UK the arrangements are discretionary.

Environmental science, as a form of analysis, therefore needs to see itself in the structures of pressure, power, lobbying, prejudice and dispute resolution. No 'problem' will be seen by key participants in the same way. Inevitably there will be disagreement about the need for and nature of solutions. For example, most coal, oil and gas producers do not fully accept the mainstream science of global warming. They believe that more time should be given to improve scientific prediction while they have longer to create profit, some of which can be diverted into renewables, energy conservation and wholly different product lines. They might accept a carbon tax, but only if that tax could be recycled through them into finding non-greenhouse gas-emitting substitutes. Yet there is much disagreement amongst finance ministries over the practice of 'earmarking' revenue for particular ends. This is not a universal position: in the US and Germany, as well as more recently in Japan, directional spending out of specified tax revenue is permitted. But in the UK and France, as well as in Italy, this is not the case.

Directional taxation is bound to grow in importance as the whole issue of environmental taxation blossoms. While the UK has no specific policy in this regard, in the 1993 autumn budget the Chancellor channelled £1.25 billion of the VAT on domestic fuel back to those most vulnerable to the higher changes, in the form of tax rebates and domestic insulation subsidies. In addition he raised £70 million for an extension to the home energy efficiency scheme from either this fuel tax or the extra £1.6 billion he raised from petrol prices, car road tax and car insurance premium tax.

The politics of environmental taxation will probably dominate the fiscal scene for quite a time to come. Yet even a simple economic and ethical issue such as environmental taxation stumbles against scientific uncertainty, organizational bias and political manipulation. Yet it is precisely all those relationships that represent what is meant by 'interdisciplinarity'. That is why mod-

ern environmental science is both very challenging and very exciting when well done.

Broadening the scientific tradition

There has always been a lively debate about the objectives and definitions of science. A flavour of the dispute was provided at the outset. Opinions die hard and views are strenuously defended. Part of the problem lies in the misinterpretation by the various antagonists of

---

Box 0.3 Scientific advice and political decisions

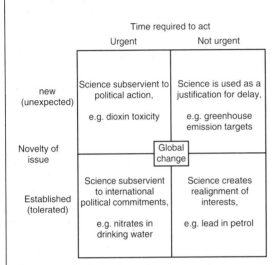

The diagram provides one characterization of the relationship between scientific advice and political decisions. Before we analyse these relationships, the role of scientific advice depends enormously on the openness of information to wide public access, the broadening of the membership of advisory committees to include a wide array of interests whose views are designed to be heard, and some sort of science and technology review office in the national legislature, the reports of which are commissioned and run by the legislators themselves. The reports of this office should also be available to the public (Jasanoff, 1992).

The diagram chooses only two axes, namely the perceived urgency of the issue, and its relative novelty. Politicians love to buy time, because this puts off the discomfort of making a decision, takes the heat out of a controversial issue, and allows for some sort of scientific review to legitimize any final decision taken. Where urgent action is desperately

needed, then scientific advice is often subservient to political expediency. For example, the reputed carcinogenic properties of dioxin are probably less serious than originally claimed. But any dioxin scare (around a chemical plant, linked to pulp and paper and printing industries because of the bleaching process) tends to create a high risk adverse reaction. Only the very highest standards of dioxin removal are now permitted on incinerators, and the ratio of cost to environmental benefit is heavily stacked in favour of the costs. Similarly if a problem is seen to be urgent and a country is forced by international agreements to treat it in the same way as other countries are, then science becomes subservient to these commitments. A good example in the US is the grudging recognition of the need to remove sulphur dioxide and nitrogen oxides from coal-burning stations in order to save Canadian forests and wildlife. A similar example is the decision by the UK government to stop dumping of sewage sludge in the North Sea even when the scientific evidence suggests that the UK contribution is both economically and ecologically marginal.

Where a problem is not perceived as urgent, no scientific advice is welcomed as a justification for delay. The function of the Intergovernmental Panel on Climate Change was influenced in part by the need for formal justification of the international measures inflicted on nation states to get rid of excess CO_2 and methane emissions. To do this is both costly and potentially labour-shedding. So a science justification was considered vital.

Finally, under the right conditions of time and established public acceptances, scientific advice can be used to realign interests. This is the active role of interdisciplinarity and science in the 'open classroom' that is very much the aim of applied environmental sciences. The conditions noted at the outset of this box have to hold for this to be a successful arrangement.

each others' positions. Science certainly seeks to move forward on the basis of broad principles, theories, laws and hypotheses, namely statements of interpretation that apply to a broad array of circumstances, and which are subject to continuous scrutiny through experiment, observation, verification and replication.

These are proper procedures. They form the basis for both the social and natural sciences. As we have seen, the problem is not so much whether these approaches are necessary, because they are. The issue is whether they should be extended by other forms of judgement and dialogue to create a partnership with society on a broader front. This would allow science to be more aware of its scope for misdirecting human development even when it is sincerely searching for the truth.

Let us look first at the scientific method as it is commonly understood (de Groot, 1993, provides a good review). Science evolves by *theory building, theory testing* and *normative evaluation*. The basic theories themselves are examined for their *correctness* in terms of their internal logicality, and for their *consistency*, that is their inherent plausibility.

These theories in turn are converted into hypotheses or propositions whose truth or applicability to a given set of circumstances is subjected to analysis. Normally that analysis relies upon *observations* and meticulous recording; *experimentation*, also with meticulous recording; or *modelling*, through which representations of 'reality' are created to provide a more manageable basis for examination and prediction. Where there is a historical record, the model can be calibrated against measured output to test its *robustness* and *accuracy*. Where there is no historical record, or where the model is essentially designed to depict the future, the only test for reliability is *peer group criticism* of the model's assumptions, interactions and sensitivities to relationships between cause and outcome which are uncertain or simply not known.

Peer review is the combined judgement of those who are both knowledgeable and experienced, and who sincerely wish to retain the credibility of their collective profession by maintaining the very highest standards of excellence. This is the vital basis of predictive science. We shall see that the great global change issues – climate change, ozone depletion, biodiversity loss, tropical forest removal, microtoxicological disturbance of ecosystems – cannot be predicted with absolute certainty. All are therefore subject to networks of peer scientific review with the aim of generating consensus as a basis for political conviction and action. This prediction is followed for both the social and the

natural sciences. For interdisciplinary science the task is more difficult and less successful, but the principle of retaining authoritative professionalism remains.

So much for the fundamental principles of *corrections of theory* and *faithfulness of the empirical method*. There is a third aim of science, namely to provide a background of advice as to what is good practice. This is known as its *normative role*, which can only be conducted through evaluative criteria based on socially agreed norms. Such norms are usually controversial, and certainly ambiguous. They apply to principles of justice, fairness, efficiency and whatever else is deemed to be morally right. Clearly the definitions of these principles will vary from political culture to political culture, and will even be disputed by scientists themselves. For example, economists regularly battle over which should have supremacy, efficiency or equity. We shall see in Chapter 2 that this is by no means a clear distinction any longer. Politicians prefer to think in terms of fairness or evenness of treatment, even when this means a more costly (i.e. less efficient) solution.

It is wise not to assume that there is a single normative criterion. Different circumstances will throw up varying yard sticks;

- *Efficiency in the form of least-cost solutions* is fine where there is something close to a functioning market which manages to incorporate environmental side effects into price.
- *Fairness or equity* for all concerned tend to operate where rights are universally shared between present and future generations, and where collective action, usually involving many nation states acting together, is necessary to produce a desired outcome.
- *Paying for past debts* (i.e. differential equity) is applied for issues such as the clean-up of contaminated land, the reduction of greenhouse emissions (where some countries have emitted over longer periods), and (increasingly) the reallocation of water rights. However, such a norm is very contentious politically; usually those first in, and/or politically the most powerful, have to be persuaded by the collective weaker (usually victimized) interests to pay up. Yet in modern environmental science this normative principle is an important one.
- *Equivalence of treatment* may not be very cost-effective, but it applies to the principle of burden sharing. This is commonly found in circumstances where a number of countries are contributing to environmental degradation, and even when some are creating more damage than others, everyone is expected to

pull their weight simply because it is seen as socially responsible and a statement of collective solidarity. In such circumstances, 'scientific' justification of contribution and removal is by no means the basis for negotiation. It is primarily a matter of being part of the whole commitment. Such shared action helps to keep all the concerned countries involved.

We shall see in the chapters that follow how all these evaluative criteria apply to environmental problem solving. Efficiency issues tend to dominate economic analysis (Chapters 2 and 3) while equity considerations strongly influence collective agreements (Chapters 1 and 19). Paying for past debts appears in risk management matters while equivalence of treatment turns up in ethical approaches to ecosystem management for the good of the planet as a whole (Chapter 5) and in health and environment issues (Chapter 18).

The precautionary principle

One of many themes of the text that follows is the endless search for better understanding of environmental processes. This is the basis on which to make sound models and reliable predictions of what may happen if various policy measures, including doing nothing, are put in place. Clearly we are nowhere near that state of certainty with regard to all environmental systems. Indeed there is a vigorous debate as to whether we know enough to make any sensible predictions at all, let alone predictions that can guide and justify political action.

One should distinguish three levels of uncertainty in environmental science:

1. *Data shortage.* Often there is neither the historical record nor the comprehensiveness of monitoring to form a reliable picture of what is happening. Take the case of nutrient enrichment of the North Sea (see Chapter 14). There is good evidence of great fluctuation in phytoplankton (microscopic plant life), normally a sign of high nutrient status. But there is no accurate historical trend, so we do not know if these fluctuations are unusual. Also, from time to time, nutrient-rich water from the North Atlantic sweeps in to the North Sea, carried by currents and driven by wind. This may be a prime natural factor in altering the nutrient status. But so could be the nutrient-rich discharge from the major rivers fed by municipal sewage treatment waste, industrial dis-

charges and agricultural wastes. It is possible to generate the data over time, but no amount of new data will make up for the lack of historical record in the medium term.

2. *Model deficiencies.* Models of global climate change (see Chapter 6) and associated sea-level risk (Chapter 9) rely on an understanding of the links between atmosphere, ocean, biota and ice that are still being generated. Scientists can test their models for the sensitivity to input parameters, but any model will be limited by ignorance of these highly complicated but little-understood relationships. Here is where peer review and networks of scientists both collaborating and criticizing each other act as the safeguard, but the models are still highly imperfect. Arguably such models can only be refined, not made representationally accurate.

3. *Beyond the knowable.* Both data limitations and model imperfections can be overcome with time and effort. But there is a school of thought which claims that certain natural processes are indefinable and indeterminate because they operate in mysterious ways that can never be fully understood. Just as stars and galaxies undergo seemingly chaotic phase changes and comprehensive chemical transformations apparently without warning or in relation to any known laws, so earthly systems appear to act chaotically (randomly) and catastrophically (flipping into new phase states or exhibiting huge but transitory turbulence). These are not essentially modellable, and by definition, data sets do not provide any great insight. In the foreseeable future, the predictive pathways of such intricate systems seem beyond comprehension. Can anyone really tell us just what would happen to climate, rainfall and the Earth's species mix if nine-tenths of the world's tropical forests were to be removed in the next half century?

Each of these three qualities of uncertainty places potentially very great strains on environmental science. We cannot follow the practice of utilizing the natural assimilability of environmental services, the so-called *critical load* approach, because we cannot be certain where these thresholds are. Nor can we use population dynamics, predator – prey relationships or indicator species theories of ecosystem change, because we do not know enough about these phenomena to do justice to our judgement of what is tolerable. We can and must improve our theoretical models and empirical designs, but that will not provide us with robust interpretations of disturbance and consequence.

So we are beginning increasingly to fall back on the *principle of precaution*. This is still a much misunderstood notion that is held in deep suspicion by some scientists and developers. This is because the application of precaution changes the balance of power between science and the community, between developers and environmentalists, and between those who exploit the environmental services that the vulnerable depend on for their survival.

The concept of precaution will emerge throughout the text that follows. Put at its simplest, it can be regarded as having four meanings:

1. *Thoughtful action in advance of scientific proof* of cause and effect based on the principles of wise management and cost effectiveness, namely better to pay a little now than possibly an awful lot later. In this sense, precaution is a receipt for action over inaction where there is a reasonable threat of irreversibility or of serious damage to life-support systems.

2. *Leaving ecological space as room for ignorance.* This means quite deliberately not extracting resources even when they are there for the taking, for example fish or whales, or even mineral ores, simply because we do not know what will be the longer-term consequences of virtually total removal. This also applies to levels of development. It is a moral responsibility of wealthy nations to allow room for the poorer nations to develop unsustainably for a while just to grant them time to make any transition towards a more sustainable economy less painful.

3. *Care in management.* Because it is not possible to forecast all the possible consequences of altering a habitat, or manipulating an ecosystem, or cleaning up a waste dump, so it is necessary to carry the public through the trial and error of experiment and adjustment. This calls for focused and creative participation in the very process of management, and is particularly relevant in the control of hazardous activities such as nuclear stations, incinerators and the release of genetically modified organisms.

4. *Shifting the burden of proof from the victim to the developer.* This is by far the most controversial aspect of the precautionary principle, for it signifies the power shift mentioned earlier. In the past, development has operated on the basis of risk-taking, environmental assessment and compensation out of the proceeds of growth. Arguably, many innovations and explorations would not have taken place if risks were not accepted as a necessary element of progress. Similarly where damage has occurred, it is customary to pay the victims out of the gains and profits associated with the damage-creating scheme. Growth is the basis for subsequent redistribution. Environmental impact assessments were designed to list the likely consequences of a proposed course of action in a reasonably formal and public manner and this was deemed sufficient prudence.

The precautionary principle seeks to change all this. It aims to place much more emphasis on the responsibility of those who seek to improve things to show that they will not cause harm, or at least will put up a performance bond to provide a fund for possible compensation to subsequently proven victims.

This is the *public trust doctrine*, namely a commitment to put back into the Earth at least the equivalent of what is being removed in any particular development. Clearly this compensatory investment does not necessarily mean replacement. But it does mean providing the equivalent of the environmental services that have been expropriated. So profits from non-renewable resource use should, in part, be directed at providing renewable substitutes. Removal of tropical forests or coral reefs should be limited by punitive requirements for guaranteeing protection of sizeable remaining amounts of these resources, possibly by payment into a global heritage fund, or via royalty payments for taxonomic research so we know more about what species are remaining, or by tradeable development rights whereby rights to develop are denied in sensitive zones but can be purchased in less sensitive spots. These are speculative ideas, and quite contrary to established ways of doing things. Hence the controversy and resistance from powerful development interests.

Precaution should be distinguished from prevention in that the latter is applied to eliminating known hazards, such as toxic substances, or at least reducing noxious materials at the point of production and/or use. Thus prevention is simply a regulatory measure aimed at an established threat. Precaution is a wholly different matter. It introduces the duty of care on all actions, it seeks to reduce uncertainty simply by requiring prudence, wise management, public information and participation, and the best technology. It also propels action across nations even when some countries are obviously going to be inconvenienced more than others as a result. This is why the international interpretation of precaution suggests that it should be applied *according to capabilities*, that is with due regard for the ability of a country to take advance action, and *in proportion to the likely benefits*. At present, therefore, the concept is held in check by the principles of ability (or reasonableness of treatment) and proportionality (or cost of advance action in relation to likely benefits). In the latter case, as we shall see in Chapter 19, side payments, or inducements, have to be made to poorer or disadvantaged countries to compensate them for investing in courses of action more expensive than they would otherwise have spent resources on, in order to meet a global benefit (such as reducing or substituting for ozone-depleting products, or greenhouse gases).

Environmental science as seen from the outside

Environmental science is evolving internally by becoming more problem-focused, policy-relevant, interdisciplinary and self-critical. These are healthy developments, but in no way do they remove the fundamentals of the scientific tradition. Yet to accommodate the needs of uncertainty, indeterminacy, public outreach and political manipulation requires a wariness, an openness and a refreshing frankness that will stand this science in good stead.

Interestingly, both industry and non-governmental organizations (NGOs) are also adapting to the new look of environmental science. Industry has become overwhelmed by the plethora of international treaties, regulations and codes of practice that are demanded of it by international government organizations such as the United Nations, the North Sea Basin States, the European Community and the various trading blocks. In addition, much modern national legislation is influenced by these international agreements as well as by forceful public opinion. Admittedly that opinion is fluctuating but it still places a great deal of reliance on science and independent analysis, as well as on cleaner and safer living conditions. In the pecking order of public credibility, scientists remain near the top, close to medical practitioners and clergy: journalists and politicians foot all tables of believability.

So industry is beginning to forge alliances with environmental scientists across a wide array of themes – cost benefit analysis, environmental impact assessment, risk management, eco-auditing, life cycle analysis and trouble shooting new regulations, especially covering the use of

---

Box 0.4 Science for sustainability

In their follow up to the famous *Limits to growth*, Meadows *et al.* (1992) looked at the conditions for a creative dialogue between the sciences and the community of nations to generate a sustainable future. They identified five key parameters:

1. *Visioning or imagining* what you really want, and not what someone has told you you should want, or what you have learnt to settle for. Visioning means taking off all the impediments to treasured dreams and uplifting future states. This is the basis for the new institutions of sustainability based on paying one's way, sharing, identifying with the totality of creation and acting out of commitment, not duty or loyalty.
2. *Networking* or community groupings. Informal networks convey both information and values, often very effectively. Networks are also connections among equals: they allow everyone to have a legitimate say, and to feel genuinely part of the whole, no matter how complex the whole might be. This is the one arena where the modern world of frightening information overload and social alienation is most oppressive.
3. *Truth telling* or devising a language that beckons, not frightens or divides. Truth telling generates a sense of commitment and vitality as well as honesty, and it allows communications to function far more effectively. So the language should be open, not closed. For example, do not say that change is sacrifice, but that change is a challenge that opens up new potentials: sacrifice is a misnomer because giving to future generations is an act of sharing, not loss.
4. *Learning* means acting locally but in a global context. Each molecule of CO_2 or CFC saved is a contribution, as is the skill to enable others to take such action. Governments can only create the conditions for citizen action: that should be extra-governmental or anarchic.
5. *Loving* means extending solidarity of the joy of creation to all humans and to all life on Earth. Loving means friendship, generosity, understanding and a real sense of empathy with life before, during and beyond temporal existence. It is unfashionable to act in such ways beyond 'church'; but loving is the essence of religion, and religion is the very basis for bonding people together. Sadly the majority of religious fundamentalists have forgotten the very basis of their faith.

---

new products and the responsibility for cleaning up waste. This is allowing environmental scientists to find new job opportunities as managers, public relations specialists, ethical investment analysts and environmental assessors. At the same time industry is providing very fertile ground for environmental science research. It creates case studies, good data sets and interesting problems that can only be solved by creative interaction.

Meanwhile the environmental pressure groups are also hiring scientists and liaising with research institutions. All the major international groups such as Greenpeace, Friends of the Earth and the World Wide Fund for Nature have a science group responsible for reviewing scientific information and spotting gaps or flaws. Campaigners in these organizations are usually found at major science congresses, and are actively connected to computerized science information flows. It is not wise for the modern pressure group to be scientifically illiterate. Equally it is not wise for the group to be too conventional and uncritical over the role of science in environmental problem identification, analysis and solution. Nowadays there is a formative debate between the NGOs, industry, government and academia that is pushing the whole of environmental science forward. The net result is an extension of science into the world of politics, commerce and social change.

This extended science has been termed 'civic science' by the American political analyst Kai Lee (1993). Civic science is the process through which scientific analysis, threading its way through uncertainty and vast areas of unchartered territory called 'social judgement to future options' opens up its work to public involvement and responsiveness. In almost all the major environmental issues touched on in this book – toxic waste management, radioactive waste disposal, carbon taxation, widening the basis of property rights to global commons and reallocating developmental and consumption priorities between north and south – environmental science has a vital role as guide and commentator for public response and approval. This is the interdisciplinary science for the next generation.

It is a wonderful time to be an environmental scientist. You can be sure that, whatever your views on the subject matter now, you will have changed your stance in a decade or so. Such is the dynamism of the subject matter and its methods of enquiry.

References

de Groot, W.T. (1993) *Environmental science theory: concepts and methods in a one-world, problem-oriented paradigm.* Dordrecht: Elsevier.

Department of Education (1993) *Environmental responsibility: an agenda for environmental education in higher education.* (Toyne Report) London: HMSO.

Jasanoff, S. (1992) Pluralism and convergence in international science policy. In IIASA (Ed.) *Science and sustainability: selected papers on IIASA's 20th anniversary.* Laxemburg, Austria: International Institute for Applied Systems Analysis, pp. 157–80.

Lee, K. (1993) *Compass and gyroscope: integrating science and politics for the environment.* New York: Island Press.

Meadows, D.H., D.L. Meadows and J. Randers (1992) *Beyond the limits: global collapse or a sustainable future.* London: Earthscan.

Milne, A. (1993) The perils of green pessimism. *New Scientist,* 12 June, 31–7.

Wynne, B. and S. Meyer (1993) How science fails the environment. *New Scientist,* 5 June, 33–5.

Further reading

For those who like to start at the beginning there are two major books on the changing nature of science, namely:

Kuhn, R. (1970) *The structure of scientific revolutions.* Chicago: University of Chicago Press.

Merton, R. (1973) *The sociology of science.* Chicago: University of Chicago Press.

Two more recent works that are well worth consulting are:

Latour, B. (1987) *Science in action.* Cambridge MA: Harvard University Press.

Ezrahi, Y. (1990) *The descent of Icarus: science and the transformation of contemporary democracy.* Cambridge MA: Harvard University Press.

For a review of the precautionary principle, see:

O'Riordan, T. and J. Cameron (Eds) (1994) *Interpreting the precautionary principle.* London: Cameron and May.

Costanza, R. and L. Cornwell (1992) The 4P approach to dealing with scientific uncertainty. *Environment* 34 (**9**), 12–20, 42.

For a broader look at the possible role of environmental science, see:

O'Riordan, T. (1992) Towards a vernacular science of the environment. In L.E.J. Roberts and A. Weale (Eds) *Innovation in environmental management.* London: Belhaven, pp. 149–61

The success of environmentalism is the loss of its special identity. Think about that. For the past 20 years or so environmentalists have been trying to bully or scare us into reforming our conscience, our behaviour, our society and our economy. They have done this by trying to make environmentalism not a separate science, or teaching material, a political party or social ethos, but a companion in our day-to-day existence. The so-called 'greening' of society is the attempt to incorporate the cost of living into our economics, the totality of existence into our ethics, and the sharing of the living world into our politics. When that is properly achieved, we should be emancipated. There should be no separate environmentalism.

Needless to say it is not as simple as that. Figure A.1 suggests that humans relate to the environment in three distinct ways:

1. By putting science first, in the sense of relying on scientific credibility before taking definitive action, and by utilizing the best of modelling techniques to make believable predictions.
2. By designing with nature in recognizing that natural processes actually do us a great service and that we should appreciate that inestimable benefit by adjusting to it and nurturing it. This opens up the pathways to ecological economics, ecologically based ethics and eco-auditing of industrial activity.
3. By giving way to gaia. The concept of gaia is covered in Chapter 19, especially Box 19.3, but it symbolizes the immersion of human life within the totality of life-maintaining creation.

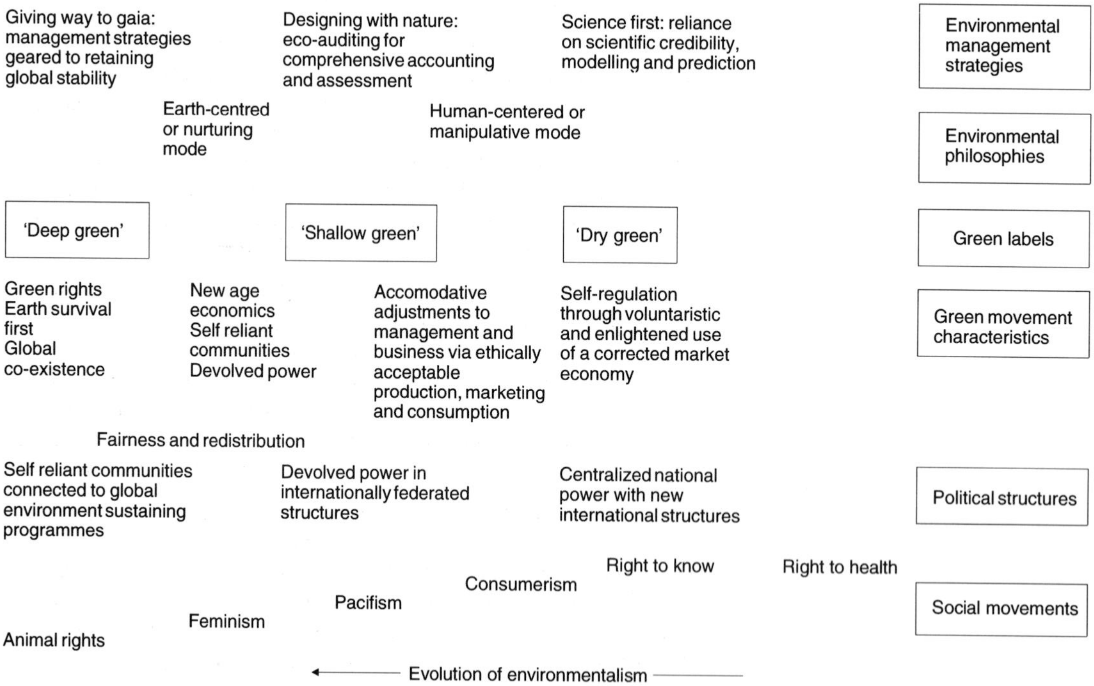

Giving way to gaia: management strategies geared to retaining global stability	Designing with nature: eco-auditing for comprehensive accounting and assessment	Science first: reliance on scientific credibility, modelling and prediction	Environmental management strategies
Earth-centred or nurturing mode		Human-centered or manipulative mode	Environmental philosophies
'Deep green'	'Shallow green'	'Dry green'	Green labels
Green rights Earth survival first Global co-existence	New age economics Self reliant communities Devolved power	Accomodative adjustments to management and business via ethically acceptable production, marketing and consumption	Self-regulation through voluntaristic and enlightened use of a corrected market economy	Green movement characteristics
Fairness and redistribution			
Self reliant communities connected to global environment sustaining programmes	Devolved power in internationally federated structures	Centralized national power with new international structures	Political structures
Animal rights	Feminism	Pacifism	Consumerism	Right to know	Right to health	Social movements

← Evolution of environmentalism

Fig A.1 Modes of greenness. None of these represents a given individual, but each is a reflection of a way of looking and feeling about the world, society and politics. (Source: O'Riordan, T., 1991, The new environmentalism and sustainable development. *The Science of the Total Environment*, **108**, 5–15.)

These three approaches to environmental management have always been inherent in the human condition. All societies model, negotiate and succumb to their natural worlds: it is essentially a matter of degree. Various authorities agree too that humanity is born with a desire to manipulate the world to make it a more certain and secure place in which to live, meanwhile helping nature along as well. Yet humanity also accepts that the Earth nurtures our existence, so should be regarded with humility and respect. This tension is healthy so long as it is roughly evenly split. The two modes of thought are sometimes referred to as *technocentrism* and *ecocentrism* (O'Riordan, 1981). We shall see in the chapters that follow how both of these perspectives can be incorporated into economics and ethics in a most lively and exciting way.

The connection between the three ways of knowing about the world, and feeling about our relationship to nature, produces three qualities of 'greenness'. These are political or value-shaped orientations to environmental management, and lie at the heart of this text. Each is a condition, not a person: no one is a pure type. At various times of our lives, our days, our circumstances one or other of these orientations rise to the surface.

1. *Dry greenness* is broadly a right-of-centre orientation, rooted in scientism and technocentrism. It favours self-regulation through enlightened conscience, sufficient information for one's needs, and appropriate manipulation of markets to create efficient, that is cost-effective, solutions to environmental improvement. Such orientations tend to be associated with centralized national governments coupled to benign international institutions brought to heel by benevolent sovereignty.

2. *Shallow greenness* splits the technocentrist – ecocentrist philosophies but takes its cue from designing with nature. It favours ecologically biased management and evaluative tools such as extended cost benefit analysis and comprehensive policy-integrated environmental appraisal. It is becoming the flagship of sustainable development and is to be found, amongst various places, in the Fifth Environmental Action Plan of the European Community. Shallow greenness is federalist by political structure both regionally (i.e. sub-nationally) and internationally.

3. *Deep greenness* is altogether more radical and more demanding on traditional viewpoints. It is given greater coverage in Boxes 19.1 and 19.2. It is both deeply radical in favouring violence in the name of ecological peace and also transformational in seeking to convert the 21st century-designed economy into self-reliant, service-sharing communities. By definition it supports devolved, anarchic, political structures espousing the principles of fairness and redistribution across all generations.

This triple alliance of environmental management orientations is fed in turn by a series of social movements that are energized by environmentalism, but which have their roots in other areas of social and political life. It is this infusion of vitality that gives environmentalism its encompassing and adaptive characteristics, qualities that in turn enable it to evolve and to endure. These movements are rights to basic health, to freedom of information and to eco-consumerism – all of which seek to empower people with control over their lives as consumers and citizens. At the more radical end are the peace, security, feminist, animal and ecological rights movements which seek to

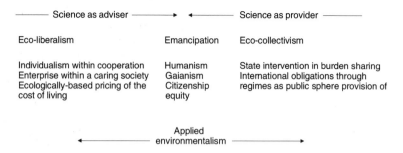

Fig A.2 Different conceptions of environmental management and politics rooted in various degrees of radicalism.

empower groups and organisms which simply do not yet have adequate rights.

Figure A.2 puts these relationships in another frame, namely the struggle between two strands of radicalism. On the one hand there is the radicalism of neo-liberalism, the freeing of economies to adopt an ecological framework. On the other is the radicalism of collectivism, the greening of the soul from the asphyxiation of capitalism, state or privately run, with its subtle controls over the hearts and minds of citizens as consumers and householders. Lined up in the middle is the pluralist and emancipatory line of humanism, education and citizenship creation, the incorporation of environmental ethics into all aspects of society and the economy without going the whole hog of anarchism, yet recognizing that market reformation under capitalism is impossible.

This is the route adopted in this book. The extension of science into wider ways of believing and knowing, the ecoliberalization of economics and financial accounting, and the incorporation of a fundamental transcendental solidarity with the majesty of creation. The chapters that follow carry these ideas into the pragmatics of economics and ecology, the two all-embracing perspectives on the earthly household that should never have been separated.

Further reading

If you are interested in green political theory, the early material is covered by O'Riordan, T. (1981) *Environmentalism* (Pion, London). Subsequently, you should read Pepper, D. (1986) *The roots of modern environmentalism* (Croom Helm, London) for a sound analysis of ecocentrism and technocentrism. Weston, J. (1986) *Red and green* (Pluto, Nottingham) is an excellent critique of socialist perspectives on environmentalism. This is superbly balanced by Dobson, A. (1990) *Green political thought* (Unwin Hyman, London), which provides a comprehensive analysis by a first-rate political theorist. For those of you who would like to see a more Marxist statement, read Dickens, P. (1992) *Society and nature: towards a green social theory* (Harvester Wheatsheaf, Hemel Hempstead). Finally, for an excellent review of various eco-movements see Eckersley, R. (1992) *Environmentalism and political theory: towards an ecocentric approach* (UCL Press, London). Any one of these books should encourage you to read the rest. Also recommended is Emel, J. and R. Peet (1989) Resource Management and natural hazards. In R. Peet and N. Thrift (Eds.) *New models in geography*, Volume 1. London; Unwin Hyman, 49–76. Three recently published books add to the literature on green politics. Dobson, A. and Lucardie, P. (Eds.) (1993) *The politics of nature: explorations in green political theory.* (Routledge, London) provides a wide perspective on various aspects of green ideologies. Pepper, D. (1994) *Ecosocialism: from deep ecology to social justice* (Routledge, London) reviews the post-Marxist literature on anarchism and green socialism. Finally, Sachs, W. (Ed.) (1993) *Global ecology: a new arena for political conflict* (Zed Books, London) provides the most comprehensive post-Marxist critique of the Rio Conference and of the politics of sustainable development.

CHAPTER 1

The global environment debate

TIMOTHY O'RIORDAN

The global environment debate is a mixture of worry for the planet Earth as a whole, and concern for the billions of less fortunate humans whose children face a possible future of desperate choices – between dying and staying alive by destroying the fabric of existence that will keep their children alive in 10–20 years' time.

There are literally thousands of reports and books published by knowledgeable individuals and organizations which point to the need for greater sharing between the rich and the poor to help all of us create a sustainable future. That sharing goes well beyond money, to include scientific know-how, technology, management and adaptation skills and informed understanding of each other's predicament. This flow of 'knowledge for survival' must move in all directions.

Yet too little is being done at a rate that is necessary to permit a peaceful transition. Any talk of transfers or sharing arouses anger on the part of those who are expected to donate without conditions of good management attached, and equal anger on the part of the recipients, who dislike being told how to run their affairs by those with a long history of environmental and social injustice to their name. Of much interest is the changing perception of the balance of power. The Group of 77 (in actuality 130 poor countries) feel that, for the first time, the rich countries actually need their resources and earth-sustaining biological and bio-geo-chemical mechanisms – attributes that could be undermined by resource depletion, war or persistent degradation. It is likely that local wars, of which there are over 40 in the world today, could have a very serious effect on ecological stability and the essential civil rights prerequisites for the transition to sustainability. It is no wonder that global ecological security is now high on the international agenda. Humanity does have the livelihoods of its members in its hands. This is why the global environment debate will dominate economic and political affairs – not to mention military analysis – for the foreseeable future.

This chapter discusses Agenda 21, the blueprint for a sustainable society on Earth which contains important material on science. This provides a basis for an interdisciplinary environmental science, for improved scientific capacity building the world over, and for a regular global audit. The prospects for extending and empowering environmental science are very exciting indeed.

If current predictions of population growth prove accurate and patterns of human activity on the planet remain unchanged, science and technology may not be able to prevent either irreversible degradation of the environment or continued poverty for much of the world.

National Academy of Sciences, Royal Society 1992

According to a distinguished meeting of a cross-section of the world's scientists

highest priority should be given to reducing the two greatest disturbances to planet Earth: the growth of human population and the increase of resource use. Unless these disturbances are minimised, science will become powerless to assist in responding to the challenges of global change, and there can be no guarantees of sustainable development (Dooge et al., 1992, p. 7).

Both these statements, from the pinnacle of the scientific profession, conclude that humanity has the power to disturb, but not destroy, the life-support systems of a globe that may be unique in the universe, and which has maintained life for at least 3.5 billion years. What is really threatened is humanity itself, or at least the two-thirds of the population which is vulnerable even to relatively modest reductions in basic resources such as fertile land, fuel, water and waste disposal capability.

Evidence from the fossil record suggests that the Earth itself is staggeringly resilient. The biosphere – the living envelope of air, water and land that maintains life – has endured volcanic 'blackouts' and huge meteorite collisions which have drastically altered climates and caused catastrophic species kills (Wilson, 1989). But, given time, the Earth has not only restored its equilibrium, it has actually increased the diversity and complexity of species, not least evolving *Homo sapiens*.

However, these periods of restoration have always been very long in human time-scales, and in the interim there were undoubtedly wholesale changes to chances of survival on a regional scale. The Earth itself has no feeling for its species: species reproduce and die according to the mysterious processes we call creation and evolution. Until humans appeared there was no sentient being to mourn loss or to welcome birth. It is we, as a species, who care about life on the Earth as a whole. As the historian Arnold Toynbee (1976) observed, humanity is both good and evil; it destroys but it can create and restore. Alone amongst all living beings, humans have rational minds and emotional souls: humans have a conscience, so are capable of reflective

Box 1.1 Demands on planet Earth
- World population is 5.5 billion and increasing by 100 million annually or about 270 000 per day.
- World economic activity has grown by 3 per cent per year since 1950. If this continues, total world output will be five times larger in 2050 than today.
- One billion people presently do not have enough food to eat, yet 1.2 billion hectares have been seriously degraded by over-cultivation since 1950.
- Annual marine first catch in 1990 was 84.2 million tonnes, 35 per cent more than in 1980 and 400 per cent more than in 1950. In 8 of the world's 17 major fisheries, catches exceeded the lower levels of sustainable yield.
- In 70 years almost all the oil that is realistically recoverable will have been used up at current rates of growth in consumption, allowing for price rises and increases in recoverability efficiency.
- In 150 years all the remaining natural gas reserves will be exhausted, again assuming appropriate changes in price and reserve recoverability.
- Given current increases in energy consumption, total energy demand in 2010 will be equivalent to 17.5 trillion watts or 92 billion barrels of crude oil. This is 50 per cent more than is used today, yet 85 per cent of this would still be fossil-fuel generated: 35 per cent more fossil fuels than burnt today. Even with 2 per cent per year improvements in efficiency, 15 trillion watts of energy will be needed by 2010.
- Over 1 billion people have no access to safe drinking water, and 1.7 billion people (about half of the developing world's population) have no access to adequate sanitary facilities. Over 60 countries world-wide irrigate less than 10 per cent of their cropland. All of Israel's post-1967 water demand growth is met by supplies from former Arab territories and 95 per cent of the Nile waters used by Egypt flow in from other territories – 9 countries now use more water than falls annually on their lands.

judgement. Throughout history, humans have been troubled by knowledge of their ability to undermine their livelihood and an awareness that only they can stop themselves from doing so.

Report after report, book upon book, conference following conference, all conclude that humans are in trouble and that the Earth is severely stressed.

There are three annual reports that should be consulted if you wish to remain up to date with the scale and extent of global environmental change. These are *World Resources*, published by Oxford University Press and produced by the US World Resources Institute; the *State of the World*, published by Earthscan and written by the US Worldwatch Institute; and the UNEP *Environmental Data Report* published by Blackwell. Box 1.1 summarizes the evidence as it has accumulated over the past 20 years. Such is the ubiquitousness of the media and the widening of the school curriculum that much of this is well known to the reader.

The following conclusions reveal the severity of the crisis:

- Already about 5000 children per day die because of avoidable lack of food, water, sanitation and basic health care.
- About 900 million people live in circumstances where their established means of producing food and gathering fuelwood and clean water are no longer sufficient to keep them or their families alive.
- Currently about 15 million people have been displaced from their homelands because of the inability to keep alive where they once lived, or because of oppression or military insurrection. About another 10 million people are displaced within their own borders into marginal lands or already highly stressed regions.
- Loss of protective soil cover, and forest cover generally, is now so widespread that erosion of land exceeds the creation of new food-producing areas. The introduction of high yield varieties and improved marketing and storage have maintained overall per capita food production, but in parts of Africa and in south-east Asia, per capita food production has dropped for over a decade, as populations catch up with productivity increases.
- Population growth, compulsory migration, landlessness forcing people to move and road schemes that improve accessibility to previously uninhabited areas all contribute to the loss of tropical forests, as do national economic policies that even today subsidize the removal of hardwood despite the calamitous environmental consequences.
- Possibly as many as two-fifths of the world's peoples live under conditions where small changes to climate, water availability and access to fuelwood will have disproportionate effects on their chances of survival. Climate change may be a century away in terms of truly noticeable departures from temperature norms. But relatively small fluctuations as precursors to that change will almost certainly adversely affect many millions of people.
- For the great majority of the world's poor, the killer is not environmental degradation on a global scale. It is the common scourges of disease, inadequate sanitation and nourishment, and localized pollution from cars, household and industrial waste, and domestic fuel burning. For this beleaguered group, global environmental politics are effectively the same as polishing the brass on the *Titanic*.

Environmental stress and social deprivation are with us already. Television footage shows us that every day. The problem, as everyone knows, is to try to move development into an environmentally sustainable path in such a way as to make it as painless as possible for the already deprived whose poverty and local indebtedness drives them to destroy the very land upon which their survival depends.

Much of the debate so far has emphasized the priority that should be given to food security, land stabilization, energy availability and civil rights for minorities and women generally if the basic preconditions for sustainable development are to be met. The richer nations of the Organization for Economic Cooperation and Development (OECD), however, tend to emphasize instead the 'big' global issues that appear to threaten them directly. These are *climate change* with its imponderable implications for agriculture, water supply and coastal protection, *ozone depletion* with its equally uncertain implications for skin cancer, eye cataracts and the functioning of phytoplankton on the surface of the sea, and *loss of species and habitats* with its attendant waste of potentially vital genetic resources for pharmaceuticals, food technology and pest control.

For the poor South these are potentially devastating dangers, but they are not so clearly a matter of priority given the day-to-day requirement of survival that affects so many of its peoples.

It is tempting to conclude that wealthy nations worry about global changes whose consequences may be two or more generations away, while poor nations do not have the cash to provide clean water and proper waste removal in desperately polluted towns filled with toxic dust and fumes. In a global survey of heavy metal pollution, Nriagu (1990) concluded that over 150 million people experienced elevated lead in their blood, 250 000–500 000 suffer renal failure due to cadmium poisoning and another 500 000 are believed to have skin cancer as a result of arsenic poisoning. In developing countries generally, Nriagu (1990, p. 32) concludes

Table 1.1 One set of estimates for converting the Earth to health. This is a best guess but is based more on standardized and somewhat simplistic calculations than on 'ground truth' evidence. Much now needs to be done in applied environmental science to gather better calculations, related to actual conditions region by region (figures in US $ billions)

| Year | Stabilizing population | | | Reducing deforestation and conserving biodiversity | Forest and tree planting | Energy conservation | | Protecting topsoil on debt | Retiring Third World | Total |
	Family planning services	Education and health improvements	Financial incentives			Increasing efficiency	Developing renewables cropland			
1991	3	6	4	1	2	5	2	4	20	47
1992	4	8	6	2	3	10	5	9	30	77
1993	5	10	8	3	4	15	8	14	40	107
1994	5	11	10	4	5	20	10	18	50	133
1995	6	11	12	5	6	25	12	24	50	151
1996	6	11	14	6	7	30	15	24	40	153
1997	7	11	14	7	8	35	18	24	30	154
1998	7	11	14	8	8	40	21	24	20	153
1999	8	11	14	8	8	45	24	24	10	152
2000	8	11	14	8	9	50	27	24	10	161
Total	59	101	110	52	60	275	142	189	300	1288

Source: Brown and Wolf (1993), p. 183.

the people are much more predisposed to being poisoned by toxic metals in their environment: poor nutrition and health, high population density, poor hygienic conditions, and a preponderance of children and pregnant women – who are considered to be most at risk – all enhance the susceptibility to environmental metal poisoning.

So it should not be surprising that a 22-nation poll prepared specially for the Rio Summit showed a widespread concern over environmental contamination, with a majority of all people sampled placing environmental protection and restoration in the top three issues for governmental attention (Dunlap *et al.*, 1992).

Table 1.1 summarizes the details of global environmental concern. When environmental issues are not specifically mentioned, only a few spontaneously mention this item as a priority issue. Nevertheless over a fifth did so in the Netherlands, Mexico, Finland, India, Switzerland and Chile. Most significant are the relatively comparable responses of anxiety about environmental degradation for all countries, irrespective of their wealth. This suggests a ground base of permanent concern for environmental improvement the world over.

But even more insidious in terms of real livelihoods is the very subtle but persistent erosion of freedom, denying people any vestigial ability to cope with the slow but steady loss of health, nutrition and wealth. This is the issue of creeping powerlessness and exclusion.

Excluding the commons

The *Ecologist* magazine was one of the first to champion the cause of sustainability, long before it was fashionable in UN circles. Its pioneering issue, 'Blueprint for Survival' (1972), presaged the first UN Conference on the Human Environment in Stockholm in 1972. Much of that text was rubbished by commentators at the time, but the majority of its analysis and prescriptions has subsequently appeared in various official reports, not least that of the World Commission on Environment and Development, usually known as the Brundtland Report (1987), of which more later. Let us look at the argument for the restoration of 'the commons' put forward in the 20th anniversary edition of the *Ecologist* in June 1992.

'The commons' is not so much an amalgam of collectively owned resources, as a form of communal existence where reciprocity is the order of the day. In the commons, people recognize their dependence on each other and on the Earth that supports them. In the commons, people aid those who are in distress, because they know they in turn will be assisted when times are hard. In the commons, wealth is shared as a recognition of social responsibility and veneration. In the commons, services are exchanged rather than commodities sold for money.

The commons is therefore a particular form of social

and cultural organization: 'local or group power, distinctions between members and non members, rough parity among members, a concern with common safety rather than accumulation, and an absence of constraints which lead to economic scarcity' (*Ecologist*, 1992, p. 125). In this context, 'power' may refer to the right to exclude outsiders or to punish anyone who abuses the commons. It may further mean an additional structure of internal rules, rights, duties and beliefs that allow the commons to become the 'owner' of human behaviour. Thus the commons becomes a metaphor for a sustainable economy in an equitable and attentive society that almost without the need for recordable communication knows why and how to co-exist.

According to this analysis, the true global dilemma lies in the steady enclosure of the commons – by multinationals, by nation states, by intergovernmental organizations and by thieves. In the words of the *Ecologist*: 'Development can never benefit more than a minority; it demands the destruction of the environment and of peoples. It attempts to dominate, fragment and dispossess – in a word, enclose. The challenge is to reject development and reclaim the commons' (front cover). Enclosure means to open up the commons to materialism, individualism, dependency and oppression. It means denying people the rights to survive and to earn a sustainable living in the name of progress and trickle-down profit dissemination. It means demeaning traditional norms by punishing those who cling on to past ways, eventually to eliminate what they stand for. Enclosure is the process of non-sustainability. According to the US commentator, Ivan Illich, enclosure is the 'new ecological order': its most insidious quality is to create structures of control that reinforce its authority. For example, the green revolution not only created dependency on fertilizers and pesticides: it created commercial alliances between seed manufacturers, agrichemical firms and pharmaceutical corporations (Shiva, 1991).

This analysis is radical but problematic. It is based on an assumption that frugality, self-restraint and the joy of minimalism are somehow an ideal human condition, the natural end state of a creative culture. It suggests that maintenance of such conditions by barring entry into commons of developmental activities such as more open markets, health care, literacy and credit can become culturally eroding and ultimately destructive. This is dangerous rhetoric: it implies that retaining a self-reliant barrier to external influence is somehow the best path for sustainable development.

There is a touch of well-meaning élitism about this perspective. Surely there must be, and should be, almost as many paths to sustainability as there are communities. Yet it is troubling in that there is more of a grain of truth in the proposition that the endeavours of those who preach sustainable development are proposing reforms that could well further enclose the commons.

The UN Conference on Environment and Development

This famous conference, referred to as UNCED, or the Earth Summit, produces strong and opposing reactions amongst commentators. Needless to say, much of this has to do with the position on the sustainable development spectrum, the experience of the pre-Rio bargaining period, and the dashing of exaggerated expectations but genuine demands.

Possibly of greatest significance for public opinion was the devastating critique offered by the non-governmental organizations (NGOs) almost before the Summit was finished (see Box 1.2). This created a huge 'turn-off' in the minds of the public and much of the media. Interestingly, almost every major newspaper and some television news companies have laid off, demoted or changed the mandate of their environment correspondents. Specialist environmental reporting is no longer as assured as it was a decade ago.

The Conference itself was designed to take stock of the state of the world 20 years after the first major Earth Summit, the UN Conference on the Human Environment held in Stockholm in June 1972. That Conference was noted for the suspicion, held by many Third World countries, of the motives of the developed world. The view was that somehow the rich nations wanted to limit development for the sake of the Earth (or their aesthetic sensibilities), or at least to control future aid and trade on environmentally conditional terms. This led to charges of environmental colonialism and subjugation of the poor to the whim of the wealthy, much of whose riches were earned on the backs of the impoverished.

The Stockholm Conference produced an uneasy relationship between North and South, tempered by the establishment of the UN Environment Programme aimed at monitoring environmental change and championing the cause of directed assistance to alleviate environmental damage and resource exploitation. Subsequent conferences on desertification, women's

We have to climb a mountain, and all governments have succeeded in doing here is meander in the foot-hills having barely established a base camp.

Jeremy Leggett, Scientific Director, Greenpeace, *Sunday Times*, 14 June 1992

We need a paradigm shift. I saw no sign of that happening in Rio. Of course we have to welcome any progress, but it has been microscopic.

Jeremy Leggett, Scientific Director, Greenpeace, *Independent*, 15 June 1992

The Earth Summit has exposed the enormous gulf that lies between what the public want and what their leaders are willing to do. The North has done little to signal let alone address, the issue of its over-consumption. Much of the burden of the environment and development crisis has been left on the shoulders of ten of the world's poorest countries in the South.

Andrew Lees, Campaigns Director, FoE, *Independent*, 15 June 1992

It's all generalities. We need to know specifically what is going to be done and by when.

Charles de Haes, Director General, WWF-International, *Financial Times*, 15 June 1992

The Earth Summit was a failure. The words were there but the action was lacking.

Chris Rose, Campaigns Director, Greenpeace, *Guardian*, 15 June 1992

I came here with low expectations and all of them have been met.

Jonathon Porritt, *Guardian*, 2 June 1992.

As the text suggests these were hip-firing reactions partly to meet the needs of media seeking instant and memorable summaries. The trouble with the media craving for simplicity and 'one liners' is that no service is provided for thoughtful and considered debate.

rights, population and urban settlements achieved little of note except plenty of rhetoric and grand promises of aid, few of which added new money. The UN Conference-go-round was regarded as an expensive circus of little relevance to the needs of those most desperate.

As is well known, the World Commission on Environment and Development was formed under UN auspices in 1983, under the Chairmanship of Mrs Brundtland, the Norwegian Prime Minister. This Commission was charged with the task of identifying and promoting the cause of *sustainable development*. This is a phrase that remains mysterious in application (see Box 1.3). Its very ambiguity enables it to transcend the tensions inherent in its meaning. It has staying power, but no one can properly put it into operation, let alone define what a sustainable society would look like in terms of political democracy, social structure, norms, economic activity, settlement geography, transport, agriculture, energy use and international relations. Arguably, the Earth Summit was convened around a mystery.

The Brundtland Commission declined to elucidate this, but it did provide a powerful analysis of what was wrong about human occupancy of the Earth, and what should be done about it. Its key proposals for institutional reform were as follows:

1. The creation of a Board of Sustainable Development to ensure that all UN agencies co-ordinate to promote the cause of sustainable development.

2. The production of national sustainable development strategies monitored for their comprehensiveness and effectiveness by an independent UN agency.

3. Financial support for and political recognition of national and local NGOs to promote the cause of community action and emancipation from non-sustainable forces.

4. To strengthen the monitoring and technical assistance programmes of the UN Environment Programme with a view to strengthening the science capacity in every country in order to produce a regular 'global audit'.

5. To establish a global risks assessment programme to identify threats and critical zones of environmental and social vulnerability, and to cooperate with local communities in building the capability of overcoming these threats sustainably.

6. To increase the role of the international scientific community to ensure that a sound scientific basis is in place for any switch to sustainable development.

7. To improve cooperation with industry so that industry takes a lead in auditing the performance

Box 1.3 What is sustainable development?

According to the Brundtland Commission, sustainable development is 'development that meets the needs of the present without compromising the ability of future generations to meet their own needs.' This automatically subsumes some notion of fairness of access to basic resource needs for all populations, both in the present day and in the future. This means transferring the opportunity of sustainable livelihoods to the very poor, through appropriate transfers of technology, capacity building in science and management, and in correct prices for resource use. It also means ensuring that the additional costs of doing this compared with 'normal growth' should be borne by the wealthy nations, and that resources should be safeguarded as 'compensation' for future generations to use should we have made reasonable errors of judgement.

Economists define three levels of sustainability:

1. *Very weak sustainability* requires that the overall stock of capital assets (natural, man-made and human) should remain constant. This assumes that substitutes for one or other of these sets of capital can be found, and sufficient income is diverted to pay off any depreciation.
2. *Weak sustainability* assumes that the world cannot guarantee the constant stock position because of constraints imposed by assimilative capacity. This critical natural capital has to be preserved to ensure life support for all species (i.e. ecological room for manoeuvre). This stock of critical capital becomes all the more important as evidence of irreversibility or catastrophe becomes apparent.
3. *Strong sustainability* takes into account the primacy of ecosystem functioning to maintain life on Earth in the most cost-effective and 'natural' manner. Nature is enabled to do its job, partly for utilitarian reasons but equally for precautionary and ethical reasons. Indicators of existence value, bequest value, irreversibility, aversion to uncertainty and critical tolerance to depletion are all required, as are indices of the environmental well-being. The last not only means reduction in life-threatening stresses, but also places a premium on the peace of mind in knowing that one is living in a truly sustainable world.

Sources: Turner (1993); Pearce and Warford (1993).

8. To commit the General Assembly of the UN to a universal declaration and subsequent convention on environmental protection and sustainable development.

9. To reorganize all of the international lending and development agencies to ensure a fundamental commitment to sustainable development, with similar commitments by bilateral aid agencies, both subject to independent audit.

10. To create new funds to finance the transition by creating a revenue from the extraction of global commons (shipping, fishing, seabed mining, the use of space) from trade which is demonstrably exploitative and from special international financing measures.

11. Guarantees of regional follow-up conferences and a major international conference 'to review progress made and promote follow-up arrangements to set benchmarks and to maintain human progress within the guidelines of human needs and natural laws' (p. 343).

This list is given in full, for it provides a useful basis for the assessment that follows. The Rio Conference did take place as requested by the Brundtland Commission, and regional conferences (11) were held in 1990. The one applying to the rich industrialized countries of the North took place in Bergen. Its significance did not lie in its conclusions, which were largely unexceptional except perhaps for the endorsement of the precautionary principle.

The Bergen process created the legitimacy of NGOs in national delegations, by permitting NGOs to participate on the pre-ministerial bargaining sessions (3, above). This in turn enabled NGOs to organize Bergen gatherings in science, industry, environmental groups, youth and trade unions (7, above). The significance of this should not be underestimated. The groups created global networks of colleague organizations to produce exuberant solidarity in their fields of endeavour and concern. The Vienna global science congress of 1991 (Dooge *et al.*, 1992) was a direct result of the Bergen science meeting, as was the creation of the Business Council on Sustainable Development. So two more of the Brundtland recommendations were at least attended to, namely the organized call for scientific capacity building (6) and the provision of international good practice for multinational industry (7). These are only very tentative initiatives, hardly beginnings even, but something has happened that would not otherwise have taken place.

controlling the development and transfer of inappropriate technology, and co-operates with the local community in maintaining sustainable economics.

If nothing else, the Rio Summit was a triumph of organization. It was presaged by four two-week preparatory conferences each involving up to 170 countries and each attended by NGOs representing nine 'stakeholder groups' – indigenous peoples, environmental organizations, science, local government, business, farmers, trade unions, women and youth. These were hard-fought occasions focusing particularly on financing mechanisms, North – South technology transfers, international conventions and overconsumption of resources (i.e. waste or inefficient use). In the event, UNCED attracted 110 world leaders, representatives from 153 countries, 2500 non-governmental groups, 8000 accredited journalists and over 30 000 associated hangers-on. Many leaders had never addressed the twin theme of environment within development before, few countries had embarked on any organized environmental plan, and even fewer had created any sort of mechanism to generate the dialogue amongst the stakeholder groups that was regarded as a prerequisite for any kind of strategy inching its way towards sustainable development.

The good points about Rio were the following:

- The excitement of the event itself, the feeling of international solidarity amongst activists, the tremendous surge of self-belief and support for groups who, before Rio, had struggled with an unreceptive culture to try to organize civil rights in depleted commons. That green networking should never be underestimated. Nowadays there are 25 000 NGOs active in the post-Rio scene. Representatives met in two follow-up conferences hosted in Manchester in September 1993 and 1994. The NGOs are coalescing around environment and development issues. There is at least a recognition that the poverty groups in the developed world and the aid charities in the developing world should form some sort of accommodation with environment groups as well as civil rights organizations such as Amnesty International. This coalescence of action at international, national and local levels is mobilized by a real momentum of 'grass roots enthusiasm'. Because the groups are formally part of all negotiating parties, Rio has electrified the NGO world. Of course, these are early days, and even the most effective of NGO co-ordination can do little if governments do not listen, international financing bodies remain unresponsive and unhelpful, and party political ideologies refuse to embrace the social and egalitarian aspects of sustainable development.

- Two global conventions were signed, one on climate change and one on biodiversity (see Chapter 19). These are based on 'soft law' or flexible wording which steadily commits all parties (including non-signatories) to international obligation. Both conventions will be overseen by a conference of parties (the signatory nations) backed by scientific and technological assessment committees and a small but significant secretariat. Both expect nations to produce annual reports of performance aimed at reaching agreed targets of commitment. Lack of these reports should, in turn, be subject to legislative surveillance and NGO politicking. In some countries this will be the case; in others not. But the effort of meeting similar norms of performance may well spur on the laggards.

- Agenda 21 was the centrepiece of the meeting, a 40-chapter report on what is wrong and what should be done to correct it. Each chapter deals with goals, priorities for action, a programme of follow-up and a cost estimate. These form the basis of sustainable development strategies that are now sent annually to the UN Commission on Sustainable Development (2, above). Chapters 23–32 deal with strengthening the role of the nine stakeholder groups mentioned earlier. Chapters 35–37 cover science, public awareness and education and capacity building for both science and technology transfer in developing countries. We shall see below that cash for capacity building is bound up with global financial transfers. But the concept of a global audit as outlined by Brundtland (4, above) is contained in Chapter 35. This would upgrade the existing database on global change, tie it to models of criticality on a regional basis and connect it to strategies for survival, hopefully with targeted international cash. These are long-distance objectives, but at least the concept is laid down. These chapters are fundamental for the future of active environmental science and the promotion of global citizenship – a community that is both knowledgeable and has the tools to alter its societies and economies towards greater sustainability. The political self-awareness mentioned in the introduction is vital here. The success of Agenda 21, in essence, hinges on the willingness of governments to create both the educational and political conditions for global citizenship to flourish. The test of Agenda 21 is to see how far these take place in the sustainable development strategies that each nation has to prepare as their contribution to meeting Agenda 21.

These are significant achievements. The implications for global governance will be discussed in Chapter 20. It is important to stress here the phenomenon of momentum and inbuilt expectation. Rio will be judged by the degree to which the institutions it creates or strengthens at all levels of human endeavour actually deliver an accountable transition to something akin to sustainability. So the extent to which the reformulated institutional structures change attitudes, alter priorities, loosen prejudices, integrate thinking, combine budgets and action, co-ordinate departmental policies and, above all, programme a persistent conscious and democratically accountable set of pathways to more sustainable development will be the crucial test of their long-lasting and life-saving achievement.

The disturbing aspects of Rio, paradoxically, lie in the failure to create international financing and organizational arrangements that should deliver Agenda 21 effectively. This was due in part to the exceeding complexity of devising the most suitable structures, in part to the unwieldiness and rigidity of the organizations already in place, and in part to the not insignificant matter of overcoming the deep mutual suspicion between the rich and the poor countries that sustainable development is a huge confidence trick. That suspicion extends to the belief that neither the rich nor the poor can be trusted to deliver sustainability within their own borders, and that any cash transfers, whether flowing North or South, will end up far from the excluded and enclosed commons dwellers whose livelihoods are seeping away in every part of the globe.

Financing sustainable development

Various estimates have been made as to how much the transition to sustainability might cost. For the most part these are creative guesswork, because no one can know the full figure. To begin with we have no idea *in detail* just what needs to be done – in provision of clean water, in reforestation, in education, in primary health care, in waste treatment, in land remediation. This is why the capacity building element of Agenda 21 is so important (5, above). Local knowledge needs to be amalgamated into local, regional and national accounts to build up a picture of restoration and protection.

In time, this will become a key component of all national sustainable development strategies (2, above). Environmental science in the round will be of crucial importance in linking the natural sciences to cultures and ecologically based accounting. This kind of assessment cannot be tackled in a strict disciplinary sense. For the actual 'cost' will depend on how it is done, through what basis of national accounting (see Table 1.1), and by whom the task is completed. For example, Holmberg (1992) would lower these estimates considerably if the job was done by community-led schemes, or by redeploying military personnel into sustainability schemes, and by diverting aid money into socially constructive projects rather than more wasteful and non-sustainable prestige investments, such as large dams, hospitals and nuclear power stations.

Another controversial aspect of international financing for sustainability concerns how far international money is necessary to pay for the extra expenditure required to meet a global commitment rather than a national priority. This is known as the *incremental cost*. In UN terms this figure, which applies only to developing countries, is defined as *either* the cost of meeting a global obligation that would not otherwise be undertaken by a nation in its own defined interest, *or* the extra amount added to a scheme to meet the requirements of a global convention. An example of the first would be the cost of replacing ozone-depleting chemicals with ozone-friendly substitutes. A case of the second would be a switch from, say, coal to gas-fired electricity production because gas produces about 40 per cent less CO_2 than coal on a heat-for-heat basis, as well as virtually no SO_2 and about half the nitrogen oxides. So the additional costs of using gas rather than coal, or renewables rather than fossil fuels, would be classified as an incremental cost and subject in principle to any sustainability account. This is relatively new thinking, so to produce a country-by-country statement of incremental costs will take many, many years.

Nevertheless, various analysts have attempted to calculate a figure for costing the transition to sustainability. Table 1.1 provides one such estimate from the Worldwatch Institute in Washington. This suggests a figure of around $150 billion annually from 1991 through to 2000, so would be closer to $200 billion in 1995 dollars if a serious start was to be made in 1995. This figure contrasts with $1000 billion annually spent on arms (Brundtland, 1987) and $127 billion spent on aid to the developing countries in 1991 (Holmberg, 1992). Agenda 21 came up with a figure of $600 billion annually for the period 1993–2000, but this was estimated sector by sector, largely on the basis of special pleading by lobbies. It is grossly exaggerated, and probably did more harm than good, because it frightened some potential donors, beset as they are by structural recession.

Taking a more dispassionate view, Grubb (1993) and his colleagues recalculated the implementation cost of Agenda 21 at $130 billion per year. The UNCED secretariat's estimate of the incremental costs for the climate and biodiversity conventions range from $30 to $70 billion.

All these estimates should be treated with a pinch of salt. Until the national sustainable development strategies come on-stream, and environmental science in the round is deployed in a rigorous manner, calculations of the costs of the sustainable transition have to be regarded as political statements. This is evident from the subsequent battles over any additional financing following Rio.

Before and during Rio, the developing countries asked for new and additional resources that would be legally enforceable obligations. This was rejected by the rich nations as being unrealistic and too committing. In the event, promises rather than cash were delivered. There is to be no increase in bilateral aid, even though the target of 0.7 per cent of GNP remained: current aid disbursements are about half this. The much-promised 'Earth increment' to the soft loan International Development Agency, originally believed to be $3–5 billion or 15 per cent of new funding for specific projects, has largely evaporated.

The one financing institution that has come out of this moderately well is the *Global Environment Facility* (GEF). This was created in 1991 as a three year pilot scheme to pay for selected incremental costs in the area of greenhouse gas emission reductions, biodiversity protection, international water management and energy conservation generally. The GEF is jointly run by the World Bank, the UN Development Programme and the UN Environment Programme and is advised by a scientific and technical advisory panel.

The use of the World Bank as the main funding body was highly controversial because most developing countries and the environmental NGOs regard the World Bank as the worst form of non-sustainable capitalism. They claim that it props up non-democratic and corrupt regimes in the Third World with prestige projects for which the recipient countries are expected to pay back the loan with interest. Many of these interest payments are met by exploitative resource mismanagement schemes that leave many destitute and dismayed. It has to be said in fairness to the World Bank that such methods of repayment are primarily for the recipient country to determine: there is no reason

in principle why the system should be exploitative. The fact that they are, and that the Bank appears to condone this practice, when it is quite prepared to impose conditionality in other aspects of its lending programme, is what gives it such a bad press in many countries.

The GEF, for better or for worse, has become the institution around which North – South transfers are occurring. In its pilot phase, it was granted $1.6 billion. From mid-1994 to 1997 it could well be given an additional $3–4 billion, by far the most significant element of additional funding to emerge from UNCED. But both the climate and the biodiversity conventions demand that the GEF should be restructured to be more accountable to funders and beneficiaries. The South would like an arrangement of one member, one vote: the North prefers voting power to reflect donor investment. This is an important issue because there is no other effective mechanism for transfers of this magnitude, unless either a whole new financing scheme is put in place, which is most unlikely, or existing multilateral banks and aid institutions are regionalized and reoriented to deal with incremental cost funding. The most likely bet is a reorganized GEF, more free standing with diplomatically created mechanisms for greater accountability. This in turn would be linked to other post-Rio institutional changes requiring a more formal commitment to more sustainable development policies and practices. These points will be given further airing in Chapter 20; see also Jordan (1993).

Before we leave the theme of international financing it must be made clear that much of the existing flow of $125 billion from the North to the South could be better spent. This would require policies to target the poorest countries, the poor in those countries, and sustainable development schemes to upgrade their livelihoods (Holmberg, 1992, p. 307). At present only about a third of all aid is free to be targeted in this way, while meeting basic needs for the poorest groups utilizes only about 10 per cent of the funds. Sadly much is either siphoned off to the rich or to the military, or it is used to subsidize energy and raw material prices to keep the urban middle classes relatively content. The majority of developing countries actively subsidize resources that should bear at least a 'normal' market price, and arguably a full environmental cost (Boxes 1.4 and 1.5). For a variety of domestic political reasons this is not the case, so precious resources are squandered and much collateral environmental damage takes place as a result. Also, as much as 40 per cent of technical aid to developing countries goes to ex-colonial civil servants or

Box 1.4 Natural resource accounting

The system of national accounts is the basis for establishing national income accounts as agreed by the UN Statistical Office. This takes into account the depreciation of capital stock (houses, roads, reservoirs, etc.). But it places into satellite accounts any depreciation of natural resources such as forest plantations or soil, and even then only covers a few resources. The main trouble is that these accounts do not systematically show the loss of natural resources through degradation or removal, nor do they provide any indication of the loss of income as a result of the loss of productivity this withdrawal of resource base creates. Thus the current arrangements are doubly misleading. On the one hand they seriously underestimate the removal of productive assets, as well as the 'downstream' adverse effects of soil erosion, siltation or species loss. On the other, they count pollution control and clean-up expenditures as increases in national income, while ignoring the costs of ill health or ecosystem destruction caused by production.

Economists are seeking to create a system of green accounting that would separate the side-effects of natural resource losses, the economic and health effects of pollution and the 'make up' expenditures of environmental repair. A study of Costa Rica indicates that forest losses account for $4.1 billion in depreciation over the past 20 years – equivalent to one year's total wealth creation. This depreciation could well cost the Costa Rican economy up to 2 per cent per year, or about one-third of net growth. Soil erosion losses were calculated to be equivalent to 9 per cent of net agricultural output per year.

It is evident that the current system of accounting seriously misleads nations into underestimating the catastrophic effects on their economies of losses of natural assets. Yet the calculations of national resource accounting still do not cover all the social and environmental aspects of soil erosion and forest removal. Here is a clear case of applied environmental science in the round. The basis of total environmental accounting has to be widened so that proper resource depreciation estimates can be made, and the costs of protection and restoration fully justified.

Source: Repetto (1992).

non-local consultants. Far too little is directed to indigenous capacity building in the basic environmental sciences of monitoring, mapping, analysing and evaluating resource management schemes.

The population question

There is a vexed and endless argument as to what precisely causes environmental degradation on such a vast scale. Some argue that the main culprit is population growth, others over-consumption by the rich, others blame ill-advised transfers of technology, and yet others look to distortional pricing leading to misuse of commons resources and gross wastage of privately owned resources. Some blame the lack of legally protected international property rights in nature and in human dignity. An extension of these rights into formal law, would, they argue, force nations, corporations and individuals the world over to recognize such rights in all aspects of development. Critics counter that such formal legal arrangements would stifle creativity and initiative, and encourage legalistic bureaucratic arrangements. Others see a malaise of ethics corroding the soul into materialism and self-centred acquisition.

In point of fact all these forces are at work. A truly sustainable society has characteristics that would be intolerable to any modern population, except those wholly untouched by western 'civilization'. Such a society would not exhibit any population growth, so there would have to be restraint on child bearing, or high birth – death rates, or quasi-voluntary euthanasia. These are slippery paths, which require very careful exploration. There would be no innovation in technology that would lead to non-replenishable resource use or to excessive acquisition of wealth. Where accumulation did take place, this would be shared with those less fortunate on the presumption that the flow of aid would be reversed if fortunes also reversed. Such a society would also only operate within the limits of replenishability, or it would work to create new resources and habitats out of the profits of removing existing non-renewable or non-substitutable resources; the public trust doctrine as summarized in the Introduction. It would be built on egalitarian and socially just lines, with communally based democracy and a plethora of codes of considerate behaviour of the kind outlined for the time 'commons' earlier in this chapter. Social control would have to come from within, via a form of egalitarian communal structures freely accepted. Such conditions do not fit with the dominant ideologies of any ruling political party at the present time.

So let us instead turn to the population question and ask, in the light of a sustainable society scenario, what can and should happen to population growth. As the reader will know, the world's population is currently doubling every 40 years, adding a billion every 10 years

Box 1.5 The costs of cleaning up

In general, the cost of reducing pollution, or more accurately, not letting it get any worse, lies between 1 and 2 per cent of GDP. In household terms in the USA this is one-third of the cost of food, one-fifth of the cost of energy, or about one-tenth of the cost of medical care. But a calculation by German economists suggests that the total expenditure on environmental protection and restoration amounted to 6 per cent of GDP for West Germany alone in 1989 and may be 10 per cent of GDP for Germany as a whole. A recent US Environmental Protection study estimates future costs of environmental regulation to exceed 2.5 per cent GDP, at an annual cost of some $150 billion.

None of these calculations covers anything like the true cost of environmental damage in terms of corrosion, waste disposal, leakage of toxic substances endangering health, the viability of ecosystems and the general aesthetic distaste over hazy vistas and yellowing trees. This has been estimated by Daly and Cobb to be so great as virtually to stabilize American 'real' income, i.e. environmental well-being as people actually want it. Growth is a very relative term. Sustainable growth would appear to mean a drop in income – but an improvement in health and happiness.

Sources: Carlin *et al.* (1992); Daly and Cobb (1989).

or so (100 million per year on average), and the children already born will create a future population of 8 billion by 2020 (cf. 5.5 billion in 1994) irrespective of any foreseeable outcome except quite horrendous calamity.

This weight of childbearing youngsters is the key to future population growth. To take an extreme example, if the onset of low fertility (say 2.2 children per childbearing woman) was delayed in Africa by 25 years from 2025 to 2050, the net difference in the African population in 2100 would be 1.5 billion, or more than three times the total African population of today (Arizipe *et al*, 1992, p. 63). Figure 1.1 reveals the possible range of population projections on various assumptions of birth and death rates for 2100. The most realistic curve is no. 2, with a strong decline in both birth rates and death rates to 2025 then constant fertility, or zero net growth. Even that puts the global population at twice the present numbers. Yet it has been calculated that for a sustainable economy at present western levels of consumption, a population of 2.5 billion would be the maximum, and 5.5 billion is the most tolerable for an average standard of living equivalent to that found in Spain today.

But fertility and mortality decline brings with it other problems such as ageing and disease susceptibility. Models show that the mean age would rise from about 35 years in the modern industrialized nations and 25 in the poorer countries to around 50 years for all countries by 2100. This will have enormously significant consequences for labour to dependency ratios, for health care and for pension provision. As Arizipe and her colleagues conclude 'either the population explodes in size or it ages to an unprecedented extent'. The explosion will sooner or later result in higher mortality levels [of which AIDS could be a major factor afflicting nearly 1 in 10 women in Thailand and central Africa already] or ageing will make painful social adjustment processes necessary, and a complete remodelling of both family and state support systems for the elderly. Whatever the outcome, those in work will have to bear a disproportionate share of the total economic burden, but there is no guarantee that more than four-fifths of any employable population will be in work to bear this awesome burden of economic responsibility. Such is the nature of labour shedding technology and the inflexibilities of labour mobility and retraining in most economies.

It would appear that the definition and practice of 'work' 'social or community service', 'salary' and 'exchange value' will have to undergo a profound evolution in the next century. The informal economy that already props up the 'commons' of poverty in most Third World cities and villages will have to become more ubiquitous, though no one knows what will happen to the tax-gathering arrangements and the financing of the sustainable transition (see *Ekins and Max-Neef*, 1992, for a good discussion).

The causes of high population growth are as varied as are the conditions that limit it. Cultures are by definition extremely heterogeneous. There is no simple package of measures that will produce the flatter curves in Figure 1.1. Minimal conditions include:

- access to safe and socially acceptable contraception delivered in a culturally appropriate manner that links birth control to family and community health generally;
- access to basic and reliable livelihoods of food, energy, water, healthcare, education and community support so that families have a stake in their future without excessive dependence on child labour;
- reform of landownership, and local indebtedness structures that free the poor from tenancy or worse and penury caused by usury;

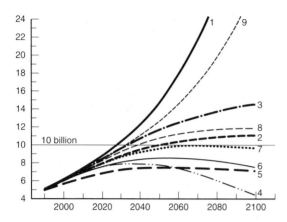

Fig 1.1 Population projections for the year 2100 based on various assumptions about the timing and rates of fertility decline and mortality. The very high rate (1) is simply an extension of existing trends for 1985–90, and the next highest (9) assumes constant birth rates in Africa and Asia, but a 10 per cent increase in mortality. The lowest projection (4) assumes rapid fertility decline to 1.4 by 2025, and the next two up (5 and 6) relate to the rapid onset of replacement fertility at 2.1 beginning in 1990 (5) with medium mortality or in 2025 (6) with constant mortality. The rest (2, 3, 7, 8) are variants of fertility and mortality rates (2, strong fertility and mortality decline until 2025, then constant; 3, UN fertility decline 25 years delayed, UN medium mortality; 7, UN mortality decline 25 years delayed, fertility rate of 2.1 in 2025; 8, life expectancy of 80/85 years and fertility rate of 2.1 in 2025). The chances of having a population lower than twice that of today in a hundred years' time are less rather than more likely, depending, of course, on the success of Agenda 21. (Source: Arizipe *et al.*, 1992, p. 63.)

- improvement of the education, social opportunities and credit rating of women to allow them to control those parts of their lives where currently they are over-dependent on others;
- reduction in the over-consumption and profligate waste of the world's rich to set an example and leave ecological space for developing nations;
- creation of genuine democracies and peace-maintaining security to allow all peoples to determine the character of their local economies and societies.

Such solutions can only be put into effect at a community level. This is why population stability is such a difficult transition to attain. It cannot be done by blueprints, or technology, or bureaucratic regulation. It must take place through peaceful revolution of the very essence of power and social relations throughout the world. This is why self-reliant sustainable economies and societies are such an important ideal. We may never reach them: indeed we may never get near to reaching them. But their wispy image is all we have got to put the human house in order. Environmental science in the round can crucially play its part in this profoundly important journey of survival.

References

Arizipe, L., R. Costanza and W. Lutz (1992) Population and natural resource use. In J. Dooge *et al.* (Eds) *An agenda of science for environment and development into the 21st century*. Cambridge: Cambridge University Press, pp. 61–78.

Brown, L.C. and Wolf, E.C. (1988) Reclaiming the future. In Brown, L.C. (Ed.) *State of the World*. New York: Norton, pp. 170–89.

Brundtland, G.H. (Chair) (1987) *Our common future*. Oxford: Oxford University Press.

Carlin, P., P.F. Scodari and D.H. Garner (1992) Environmental investments: the cost of cleaning up. *Environment*, **34** (2), 12–20, 38–44.

Daly, H.E. and J. Cobb (1989) *For our common good: redirecting the economy towards community, the environment and a sustainable future*. Boston: Beacon Press.

Dooge, J.C.I., G.T. Goodman, J.W.M. la Riviere, J. Marton Lefevre, T. O'Riordan, F. Praderie and M. Brennan (Eds.) (1992) *An agenda for science for environment and development into the 21st century*. Cambridge: Cambridge University Press.

Dunlap, R.E., G.H. Gallup jr and A.M. Gallup (1993) Of global concern; results of the health of the planet survey. *Environment*, **35** (9), 6–15, 33–9.

Ecologist (1972) Blueprint for survival. *Ecologist*, **1** (1).

Ecologist (1992) Whose common future? *Ecologist*, **22** (4).

Ekins, P. and Max-Neef, M. (1992) *Real life economics: understanding wealth creation*. London: Routledge.

Grubb, M. (1993) *The Earth Summit agreements: a guide and assessment*. London: Earthscan.

Holmberg, J. (1992) Financing sustainable development. In J. Holmberg (Ed.) *Policies for a small planet*. London: Earthscan.

International Union for the Conservation of Nature (1992) *Caring for the earth: a strategy for sustainable living*. Gland, Switzerland: IUCN.

Jordan, A. (1993) The infunctional organisational machinery for sustainable development: Rio and the road beyond. Norwich, CSERGE working paper GEC 13–93, University of East Anglia.

Nraigu, J.O. (1990) Global metal pollution: poisoning the biosphere? *Environment*, **32** (7), 6–12, 28–33.

Pearce, D.W. & J.J. Warford (1993) *World without end: economics, environment and sustainable development.* Oxford: Oxford University Press.

Repetto, R. (1992) Earth in the balance sheet. *Environment,* **34** (7), 13–20, 43–5.

Shiva, V. (1991) *The violence of the green revolution.* London: Zed Books.

Toynbee, A. (1976) *Mankind and mother earth.* Oxford: Oxford University Press.

Turner, R. K. (1993) Sustainability: principles and practice. In R.K. Turner (Ed.) *Sustainable environmental economics and management.* London: Belhaven Press, pp. 3–36.

Wilson, E.O. (1989) Threats to biodiversity. *Scientific American,* **261** (3), 60–70.

Further reading

There are three regular reports on the state of the globe. They provide indispensable reading for any assessment of the global predicament: World Resources Institute (annually) *World resources* (Oxford University Press, Oxford); Worldwatch Institute (annually) *State of the World* (Earthscan, London); United Nations Environment Programme (annually) *Environmental Data Report* (Blackwell, Oxford).

For an accessible guide to UNCED see Grubb, M. (1993) *The Earth Summit agreements: a guide and assessment* (Earthscan, London); *Environment* (1992) Earth Summit: judging its success. *Environment,* **34** (4). Holmberg, J. (1993) *The road from Rio* International Institute for Environment and Development, (London).

CHAPTER 2

Environmental economics and management

R. KERRY TURNER

Environmental economists can be characterized into three broad groups, though many individual economists would claim membership of two or all three. The first are essentially extensions of conventional neo-classical economic theorists who apply their trade to non-market phenomena, such as commons resources or public goods, as identified in the previous chapter. They do not seek to create any fundamental new theory, but rather prefer ingeniously to extend the existing theories of welfare economics and neo- classical economics by constructing 'surrogate' markets and demand curves.

The second group term themselves ecological economists. They seek to marry the underlying processes of ecology and economics into a new discipline. They try to find some estimate of the value of ecosystems or ecosystem processes in providing beauty and inspiration, in cleansing, assimilating or buffering. They also look at replacement costs – how much it might cost to substitute a naturally occurring cleansing function with an artificially created substitute. This is a very innovative discipline in resource management and dominates much of the chapters that follow. Ecological economists seek to extend cost benefit analysis, using the imaginative techniques developed by environmental economists, to search for most effective, long-lasting and naturally supportive measures for retaining soils, water flows, nutrient removal, wave protection or pleasant beaches.

The third group are sometimes referred to as humanistic economists. They tend to regard themselves as a race apart from their brethren in the economics trade. They claim to look at humans as creative and communal creatures, full of spirituality, tolerance and altruism so long as they are allowed to live in ways that are supportive, non-violent and only partially materialistic. Humanist economics is the economics of the small scale, of self-reliance, of service sharing and of mutual obligation. It is the economics of living within nature's bounds in social structures that are loving and caring. The first two groups of economists would claim that they see no difference between their view of society compared with the humanists. But the latter aim to identify and espouse a higher spirituality in humanity that, they claim, is not found in the materialism and greed of societies that can still live by environmental pricing.

The difference between the camps is less noticeable than many would want to believe, but there is no doubt that sparks can fly amongst the protagonists. At the root of the distinction is the view on society and the world. Humanistic economists take a moralistic, almost eco-fascist line on what is good for people and how they should structure their societies. The others are more anxious to ensure that the process of achieving sustainability decouples growth from environmental decay, thereby letting societies look after themselves, based on the economic signals they have created for more sustainable use of environmental resources.

In this chapter Kerry Turner teases further the various distinctions of sustainability, pointing out that economists have to take welfare and equity considerations even more seriously, possibly more so than efficiency if uncertainty over future states, the precautionary principle, and the moral needs of maintaining the welfare of our descendants are to be properly taken into account.

This suggests that the economics of resource pricing can never be simply a technical exercise, even though few economists claim that it could ever be such. There is bound to be a significant dose of politics, law and ethics in the determination of resource prices. Take, for example, a wetland in a rich country with a powerful environmental movement, open government, and a diminishing supply of such areas. The price put on safeguarding that wetland from any wetland-destroying development will be much higher than the price for an identical wetland in a poor country with impoverished local people and an opportunity to make foreign exchange out of tourism. The wetland is the source of both freshwater and effluent disposal for the tourist development. This price will be even lower if the country is run on closed government lines, where environmental impact assessments are not legally required, and where public involvement in resource management simply is not part of the accepted culture.

One can see that the price of a natural asset is not absolute. It is a product of knowledge, science, cause-championing groups, pluralistic political cultures and societal expectations over future patterns of growth and the relative role of nature in the pathways to more sustainable futures. Rounded environmental science can help the analyst to understand how the price of nature is derived, and how it can be manipulated to provide society with a survivable future.

Introduction

This chapter reviews the main ideas, concepts and methods utilized by economists who are concerned with environmental resource management issues. The analysis that they deploy is not, as is often supposed by non-economists, a form of financial accounting. As is discussed in Chapter 3, financial analysis deals with flows of money (costs and revenues) linked to an individual, firm or some other agency. To use the jargon, financial accounting deals with 'private costs and benefits'. Economic analysis, on the other hand, is not just about money. Any change in human well-being is an economic effect and is measured in terms of so-called 'social costs and benefits'. These effects are made up of 'external' costs and benefits ('externalities') as well as 'private' costs and benefits. Pollution is a typical external cost item, as are virtually all 'environmental' effects.

An external cost exists when two conditions prevail:

1. An activity by one agent (say a firm discharging effluent to a river) causes a loss of well-being (welfare) to another agent (say an angler downstream of the discharging plant) because any decline in river water quality spoils the enjoyment of the river amenity.
2. Secondly, the loss of well-being incurred by the pollution sufferer remains uncompensated.

The difference between social costs and social benefits is net social benefit. Economists attempt to measure and value all relevant social costs and benefits of projects, policies or courses of action. In the net social benefit valuation exercise, money does play a role because it is a convenient measuring rod of what people want and do not want with respect to the environment. The economic argument in favour of greater protection for the environment does not deny any moral case that individuals may wish to put forward on behalf of nature. It is simply a different argument.

The economic case may well be more powerful and more easily understood because of its familiar measuring tools than the moral case, especially where that case is, as often happens, not clear-cut. This kind of dilemma occurs, for example, when an area that is inhabited by poor people contains habitat that is prized by the wealthy who live somewhere else. Here there is a clash of rights – the property rights of the local people to have access to sustainable livelihoods (food, shelter and employment) and the wider property rights of the global community who want to save the habitat and its endangered species. As we shall see in the next chapter, it is possible for economists to examine both the valuation of these different positions, and to argue for different interpretations of these two property rights. Systems (i.e. international agreements) for a fair appropriation of the 'global value' of habitat and species are, however, much more difficult to design and implement.

We now turn to the underlying principles of environmental economics in order to argue the case in favour of an economic approach to resource management.

Scarcity and efficiency

At a fundamental level, economics is directly concerned with the concept of scarcity and with the mitigation of scarcity-related problems. Economics is the study of the allocation of scarce means (total resources, man-made and natural) towards the satisfaction of the maximum number of human ends (wants and needs) as is feasible with prevailing technology and knowledge. Given this fundamental preoccupation with scarcity, economics defines the most efficient allocation of scarce resources in a variety of contexts. It emphasizes that all projects, policies or actions have opportunity costs (see Boxes 2.1 and 2.2) which are foregone once decisions are implemented. The principle of opportunity cost therefore emphasizes that nothing, including environmental resources, is free. Using the environment to produce boating marinas or commercial port facilities, for example, may mean foregoing all the benefits (opportunities) that such natural systems can provide, e.g. pollution buffering zones, storm protection zones, wildlife habitat.

Applied economists operate with the principle and method of cost benefit analysis (we investigate this in detail in Chapter 3). Under the cost benefit principle and the criterion of economic efficiency, no project, policy or course of action is chosen unless social benefits (B) exceed social costs (C). The optimal scale of a project or activity is the point where the difference between benefits and costs is maximized. More formally[1]:

1. accept an option potentially if

$$B > C, \text{ i.e. net } B > 0$$

2. choose that option such that

$$\max [B{-}C], \text{ i.e. max net } B$$

Box 2.1 Market mechanism

Buyers (demand) and sellers (supply) coming into contact via a voluntary decentralized exchange process can, given the right conditions determine an equilibrium price and an efficient allocation of resources (i.e. there is no alternative allocation that leaves everyone at least as well off and makes some people better off).

The figure illustrates a situation in which the price of a good is taken to be of primary importance in determining just how much of a good people are prepared to buy and conversely how much of the good firms are prepared to offer for sale. All other factors which could influence demand and supply are assumed constant (income, price of substitute goods, etc.):

$$\text{so } Q_d = f(P)$$
$$W_s = f(P)$$

at position e, $Q_d = Q_s$ given a market price P.

At e, the marginal willingness to pay of consumers (their valuation of the good) is just equal to the marginal costs (labour, raw materials, energy, etc.) of producing that good and efficiency is maximized as long as the structural conditions for perfect competition are satisfied:

- large numbers of buyers and sellers;
- perfect information;
- goods being exchanged can in principle be individually owned;
- the full costs of production and consumption are reflected in market prices.

Price has adjusted until at e the amount that people demand of something is equal to the amount that is supplied. Resources are allocated sufficient to produce an amount OQ. There is no alternative allocation that leaves everyone at least as well off and makes some people better off.

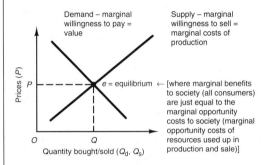

Demand – marginal willingness to pay = value

Supply – marginal willingness to sell = marginal costs of production

e = equilibrium ← [where marginal benefits to society (all consumers) are just equal to the marginal opportunity costs fo society (marginal opportunity costs of resources used up in production and sale)]

Prices (P)

Quantity bought/sold (Q_d, Q_s)

Economists have also spent much time and effort studying measures designed to increase the overall rate of economic activity in an economic system. Government policy has been, and continues to be, dominated by the goal of maximum economic growth (conventionally defined in terms of gross domestic product (GDP) or gross national product (GNP) generated per annum). The rationale for this policy objective has been that increased economic growth brings increased material standards of living and increased consumer choice. For a reinterpretation of this position see Chapter 5.

Ecological limits on the economy

Environmental economists have more recently (since the late 1960s) emphasized the fact that economic systems depend on ecological systems (plants, animals and their interrelationships) and *not* vice versa. The scarcity concept is also relevant in this environmental context. The laws of thermodynamics lay down that economic production and consumption do not result in the complete destruction of matter and energy, merely its transformation. In order to function (i.e. the production of private goods and services or wealth for its human operators) the economy must extract resources (raw materials and fuel) from the environment, process these resources (turning them into end-products for consumption) and dispose of large amounts of dissipated and/or chemically transformed resources (wastes) back into the environment. This so-called *materials balance* view of an economy demonstrates that during the growth process more and more useful (low entropy) matter and energy are drawn into the system (e.g. mining and harvesting activities) only to be discharged/emitted from the system at a variety of locations, and over a period of time, as useless matter and energy (high entropy residuals and wastes); see Box 2.3. This has led some economists to study not just the efficiency of existing economic activity but potential future 'scarcity' limits on the growth and overall scale of economic activity. The term *sustainable economic growth* has now become fashionable in the face of mounting concern over the pollution pressures on the assimilative capacity of ecosystems and the depletion of the natural resource base provided by the biosphere. The natural goods/services

Box 2.2 Pollution externality: the case of a recycled paper production plant

Market failure is related to the absence of the fourth structural condition listed in Box 2.1. In the real world all markets are not freely competitive and the structural conditions necessary for perfect competition are not present. In the case of the recycled paper plant in the figure, the price that would operate if there were no government controls (laws, regulations or taxes) on pollution would be P and the amount of the good bought and sold would be OQ.

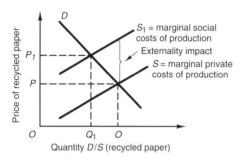

Now this position would not represent an efficient allocation of scarce resources if externalities also existed. It is likely that a pollution externality (social costs) would exist in this situation. Unfortunately, recycling paper and board plants produce a potentially damaging liquid waste as well as the 'environmentally friendly' paper products.

In the absence of pollution control regulations or some other official control instrument let us assume

the plant discharges its liquid effluent straight into the local river. Assume further that downstream of the recycling plant another plant takes water out of the river in order to process food products, and further downstream again a nature reserve and recreational swimming and boating areas also exist. The downstream users (e.g. the food plant, the birdwatchers and recreationalists) suffer costs due to the water pollution caused by the recycling plant. The food plant has to install more expensive water purification equipment and the boating and swimming enthusiasts have to put up with a poorer quality experience or even have to give up swimming in that location altogether. If the pollution is particularly severe, wildlife may disappear altogether from the nature reserve areas.

The full costs of producing and consuming the recycled goods were not reflected properly in the price level P. The recycling plant's private costs of production should be augmented by the extra social costs (in monetary terms) involved, shifting S to S_1. Once the social costs have been internalized and the supply curve shifted to S_1, a new price is determined at P_1. The efficient allocation of resources (properly reflecting the waste assimilation service of the environment) required a higher price of P_1 and a lower output level of Q_1.

Correcting for externalities in practice requires a set of government interventions in the market system via some combination of regulations and pollution taxes.

(landscape and amenity) provided by ecosystems may also face either a quality deterioration or complete destruction.

The principles of scarcity and opportunity cost, as well as the objective of an efficient allocation of scarce resources, can now be applied to the complete collection of environmental goods and services – waste assimilation functions, peace and quiet, clear air and water, unspoilt landscapes and life-support systems. If environmental resources are becoming more scarce then economic analysis can play a role in devising and justifying strategies to reduce future scarcity. A balance will be required between the interests of people wishing to use the environment in a consumptive manner (e.g. as a source of raw materials or a waste sink) and those wishing to enjoy it in an aesthetic or non-consumptive manner (e.g. to watch whales rather than to kill them, or to revel in the thought that a rich tropical forest is being kept in as natural a state as possible). This is referred to as *psychic benefit* and has real economic

value in the sense that people are prepared to pay and forego other pleasures to enjoy that particular benefit. Further, the needs of the present generation of people will have to be considered against future generations' needs. This was discussed in Chapter 1.

The question of how, and under what conditions, free markets can help achieve this balance has spawned a long and extensive literature. Economic theory demonstrates that given certain assumptions, the market is capable of achieving efficient resource allocations, provided that externalities are not present – see Box 2.4. When externalities are present and/or when public type goods (to be defined below) require allocation, markets usually fail the efficiency test and have to be corrected.

The crucial feature of externalities is that there are goods people care about (for example, clean air and water, beautiful landscapes) that are not sold on markets. The majority of environmental goods fall into a category in which market values are not available.

Box 2.3 Materials balance model

In this model the economy is portrayed as an open system pulling in materials and energy from the environment and eventually releasing an equivalent amount of waste back into the environment. Too much waste in the wrong place at the wrong time causes pollution and so-called external costs (exter-nalities). A certain amount of recycling of wastes is both possible and practicable, but 100 per cent recycling is physically impossible and economically undesirable.

Source: Adapted from Turner *et al.* (1993).

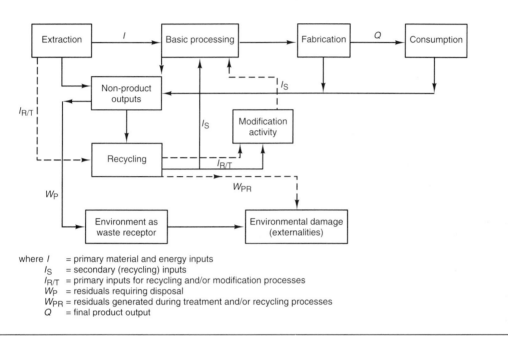

where I = primary material and energy inputs
I_S = secondary (recycling) inputs
$I_{R/T}$ = primary inputs for recycling and/or modification processes
W_P = residuals requiring disposal
W_{PR} = residuals generated during treatment and/or recycling processes
Q = final product output

These are referred to as public-type goods. Public goods generally have the characteristics of joint consumption and non-exclusion. What this means is that when the good is consumed by one person, it does not diminish the amount consumed by another person. So, for example, one person's consumption of clean air does not diminish any other person's consumption. Non-exclusion means that one person cannot prevent ('exclude') another from consuming the resource, because the resource is freely accessible to all. This is the case for clean air; it is also the case for the atmosphere into which anyone can emit carbon dioxide.

The very characteristics of many environmental goods have meant that their 'true' value (total economic value) has been underestimated or ignored altogether. They have remained unmeasured and unpriced and have therefore been inefficiently exploited. It is also the case, however, that by no means all negative externalities are due to market failure. Think about the damage (loss of habitats and landscapes and water pollution due to fertilizers and pesticides) done by agricultural practices to the environment. In this context it is the failure to regulate properly that is significant. The Common Agricultural Policy (CAP) of the European Community (EC) allows member states to intervene in agricultural markets by excluding agricultural products from beyond the EC by tariff barriers and by subsidizing crop and livestock production even when in surplus. One of the consequences has been massive over-production and unintended agricultural pollution in the form of fertilizer and pesticide residues.

Many environmental goods are also 'common property' and/or 'open access' resources. The combination of weak property rights with inadequate legal protection against overuse (or complete open access) together with free or cheap usage of these resources has inevitably led to over-exploitation, sometimes to the point of destruction of the stock. Tropical rainforests, marine fisheries and the waste assimilation capacity of seas are all examples of such over-exploited resources.

Box 2.4 Opportunity costs and resource allocation

Consider a beautiful river valley that is about to be dammed to provide hydroelectric power for a community downstream. Once the dam is built, the natural and unspoilt qualities of the river valley, including the way of life of people living by that river, will be lost. These are the costs foregone as a result of the dam construction and are part of the concept of opportunity cost. But the money spent to build the dam could have been spent to construct a coal-burning power station, or a local hospital. This diversion of resources away from one area to another is also an opportunity cost. The rule in economics is to optimize the allocation of resources, i.e. to make the most efficient use of scarce resources by choosing options which yield maximum net benefits.

The economist seeks to limit the openness of such property rights and to set prices for resource of usage so as to correct for this particular form of market failure. These points are developed in the next chapter.

To summarize the discussion so far, we have argued that environmental economists have been at pains to emphasize that at least one class of negative externalities – those associated with the disposal of wastes generated by economic systems – are not isolated and rare events but inevitable and commonplace. Further, their economic significance tends to increase as economies develop (industrialize and support larger populations) and the ability of the environment to receive and assimilate them is reduced (increasing scarcity) thereby increasing the value of remaining natural assimilative capacities.

From a theoretical viewpoint it has also been shown that if the capacity of the environment to assimilate wastes is scarce, the normal market mechanisms cannot be free of externality effects (and therefore do not provide an efficient resource allocation mechanism) unless:

- the material and energy drawn into an economy via production activities produce no waste (100 per cent recycling efficiency) and all final outputs are eventually destroyed by consumption; and
- property rights cover all relevant environmental goods, placing them in private ownership and allowing them to be exchanged in competitive markets.

The first condition contravenes the fundamental physical (thermodynamic) law of conservation of mass/energy and the second is impossible or impracticable given the characteristics of many environmental goods.

Since the essence of environmental issues is that they inevitably involve, among other things, externalities and public-type goods, the market mechanism cannot be relied upon to provide efficient levels of environmental goods and services. But this leaves us with a fundamental question – how can and how should society decide what amount of environmental quality it should purchase? One possible approach which has received most support from economists is to rely on cost benefit analysis (see Chapter 3). Nevertheless, the conventional economic approach tends in practice to be rather narrow and dominated by the economic efficiency objective (i.e. using scarce resources in such a way as to get maximum benefits net of any costs). By their very nature, environmental issues raise a broad set of scientific, political, ethical and economic questions. Thus while it is important to investigate ways of using our environmental resources as efficiently as possible, it is also vital, for example, to monitor the fairness of the resulting distribution of benefits and costs. This is known as the economic equity objective – see Box 2.5.

Box 2.5 Efficiency and equity in environmental economics

In the past the economist has generally regarded efficiency as the yardstick for optimal allocation of resources, and assumed that equity considerations can be dealt with via side payments or compensation agreements. The fact that there are sufficient gains from a given resource use to allow for this and still generate real benefits satisfies the efficiency criterion. But consider the case of increased greenhouse gas emissions raising sea-levels sufficiently to flood low-lying island states and eliminate them entirely. (Chapters 1, 6, 9 and 19 also touch on this issue.) It may not be good enough just to compensate the islanders financially for moving to higher ground elsewhere. There is a real distributional loss if the islands disappear. The economist can point out a least-cost solution, but the politician and diplomat may have to judge whose rights are paramount – those of the greenhouse gas emitters to discharge beyond the point of inundational sea-level rise, or those of the small islanders. It is cases such as these that intertwine economics and ethics.

Sustainable economic development

Questions concerning 'fair' distributions of resources can quickly become complicated and, in the environmental context, will involve fairness not just between individual people alive now but also between them and future generations. To take just one illustrative example, the exploitation of the assimilative capacity of the world's terrestrial ecosystems, oceans and atmosphere means that less of this life-saving capability is left for future generations. Arguably this capability is non-renewable beyond a certain point of exploitation. Other resources (renewables) such as fisheries and forests may also be over-exploited and not given enough time to regenerate. Again the stocks of such assets for future generations will be reduced. The question can then be posed, is this fair? Is it 'right' that those of us alive now should essentially destroy assets (and the economic opportunities that they yield), even though gaining benefits in the process, while passing on the costs to people not yet alive and who have had no say in the matter? Now, this argument has been deliberately set up in a simple way in order to provoke the reader into thinking about a number of important and tricky problems that are involved in the use and abuse of our environment.

The position taken in this chapter is that economic efficiency – getting the most 'welfare' (benefits net of costs) out of a given collection of resources – is vitally important. But the very nature of environmental issues requires an extension (a 'greening') of the conventional economic approach to encompass, among others, distributional equity and environmental quality objectives.

In terms of the economic dimension there seem to be three main features in a green agenda:

1. A rejection of the idea that economic systems should be deliberately designed to satisfy the unlimited wants of the 'rational economic person' (*Homo economicus*) – the archetypal selfish (greedy) inhabitant of the unfettered market economy. We need to think more about people's (collective) needs and less about their individual wants. Human behaviour must be modified to some extent and greed constrained.

2. A green economy is also one that has the capability of replicating itself on a sustainable basis. We will take a detailed look at sustainability and sustainable economic development later in this chapter. Many definitions of sustainable development have been put forward, but for now we will limit ourselves to thinking about this concept simply in terms of economic development that endures over the long run.

3. A green economy must over time evolve in such a way as to decouple the growth in economic output (activity) from the environmental impacts of that activity. On the basis of the materials balance principle, decoupling will involve technical changes such that our use of resources is made more efficient, and our output of pollution less and less damaging. Total decoupling is thermodynamically impossible yet some environmentalists argue that decoupling, though necessary, is not a sufficient condition for a green economy. They would go further and either freeze the scale (i.e. size of economic output, its rate of change and the level and rate of change in population) of the economy, or actually reduce it.

The most publicized definition of sustainability is that of the World Commission on Environment and Development (1987; the Brundtland Commission). The Commission defined sustainable development (SD) as: 'development that meets the needs of the present without compromising the ability of future generations to meet their own needs' (p. 43). On the basis of this SD definition both intragenerational equity (fairness among individuals currently alive) and intergenerational equity (fairness among generations of individuals) concerns must be met before any society can attain the goal of sustainability. Social and economic development must be undertaken in such a way as to minimize the effects of economic activity (on resource sources and waste assimilation sinks) whenever the costs are borne by future generations. When currently vital activities impose costs on the future (e.g. mining of non-renewable minerals), full compensation must be paid (e.g. performance or assurance bonds yielding financing aid, or new technologies allowing resource switching say from fossil fuels to solar power).

The Commission also highlighted 'the essential needs of the world's poor, to which overriding priority should be given'. In other words, SD must allow for an increase in people's standard of living (broadly defined) with particular emphasis on the well-being of poor people, while at the same time avoiding uncompensated and significant costs on future people. The Commission also took a fairly optimistic view of the possibilities for decoupling economic activity and environmental impact.

SD, it is generally agreed, is therefore economic development that endures over the long-run. Economic development can be measured in terms of GNP (i.e. the annual output for goods and services adjusted for exports and imports) per capita, or real consumption of goods and services per capita. So SD is defined as at least non-declining consumption, GNP, or some other agreed welfare indicator. The next chapter covers this point in more detail.

A more difficult task is to determine the necessary and sufficient conditions for achieving SD. Fundamentally, how do we compensate the future for damage that our activities today might cause? The answer is through the transfer of capital bequests. What this means is that this generation makes sure that it leaves the next generation a stock of capital no less than this generation has now. Capital provides the capability to generate well-being through the creation of goods and services upon which human well-being depends.

Some analysts argue that it is not necessary to single out the environment (natural capital) for special treatment, since it is simply another form of capital. They argue that what is required for SD is the transfer of an aggregate capital stock no less than the one that exists now. We can pass on less environment so long as we offset this loss by increasing the stock of roads and machinery, or other human-made (physical) capital. Alternatively, we can have fewer roads and factories so long as we compensate by having more wetlands or mixed woodlands or more education. This position is based on a very strong assumption, that of perfect substitutability between the different forms of capital.

Other analysts believe that this is not a valid assumption to make. Some elements of the natural capital stock cannot be substituted for (except on a very limited basis) by human-made capital. Some of the functions and services of ecosystems are essential to human survival; they are life-support services because they are essential for the great chemical cycles that maintain life on the planet and cannot be replaced. Other ecological assets are at least essential to human spiritual well-being if not exactly essential for human survival – landscape, space and relative peace and quiet. These assets are critical natural capital and since they are not easily substitutable, if at all, the sustainability principle requires that we protect them.

If we accept the latter position then a sustainability strategy involves the satisfaction of an intergenerational social contract via the constant capital rule and capital bequests. The current generation could rule out in advance, depending on the social opportunity costs involved, development activities that could result in natural capital depreciation beyond a certain threshold of damage cost and irreversibility (i.e. loss of critical natural capital, life-support services, keystone species and processes).

Any sustainable strategy for the future will also have to confront the question of how much larger the global population can be to guarantee at least a basic livelihood in a manner that can be sustained. For the people of the South, many of their livelihoods are already endured in environments that are fragile, marginal and vulnerable. Sustainable livelihoods can only be promoted via policies that reduce vulnerability, e.g. flood protection to guard against sea level rise induced by climate change due to global warming; measures to improve food security and to offset failures in markets; and in regulatory intervention such as inappropriate resource pricing and uncoordinated development policies.

A number of rules (which fall some way short of a blueprint) for the sustainable utilization of the natural capital stock can now be outlined:

- Market and intervention failures related to resource pricing and property rights should be corrected.
- Maintenance of the regenerative capacity of renewable natural capital (RNC), i.e. harvesting rates should not exceed regeneration rates, and avoidance of excessive pollution which could threaten waste assimilation capacities and the life-support system.
- Technological changes should be steered via an indicative planning system such that switches from non-renewable (NRNC) to RNC are fostered; and efficiency-increasing technical progress should dominate throughput-increasing technology.
- RNC should be exploited, but at a rate equal to the creation of RNC substitutes (including recycling).
- The overall scale of economic activity must be limited so that it remains within the carrying capacity of the remaining natural capital. Given the uncertainties present, a precautionary approach should be adopted with a built-in safety margin. This point was covered in the Introduction.

It can be seen that all these conditions require a mix of natural and social sciences. The failures of markets and property rights cannot be estimated without some measure of the externalities that are created by such failures – loss of forest cover means soil erosion (see Chapter 12), excess water abstraction means depleted water in rivers and lakes for ecological survival (see Chapter 13), and removal of tropical forests means loss of livelihoods for indigenous peoples (see Chapter 4). Likewise, the harvesting rates for fish and for forests require a knowledge of the regenerative capabilities of these resources, and an understanding of thresholds of tolerance. All of this provides a basis for sound science based on good data, local knowledge and regular monitoring – all leading to improved predictive models. Inevitably this knowledge will never be complete – hence the significance of the precautionary principle. But that principle should not be used wantonly: it should, as far as possible, be an adjunct to sound science and thoughtful valuation.

The issue of valuation

Economists emphasize that it is necessary to value those environmental functions and services which are generally unpriced in order to correct decisions which treat natural environments as if they were free goods. To the economist, economic value arises if someone is made to feel better off in terms of their wants and desires. Positive economic value – a benefit – arises when people feel better off, and negative economic value – cost – arises when they feel worse off. What economic valuation does is to measure human preferences for or against changes in the state of environments. It does not 'value the environment'.

Objections to economic valuation must mean one of the following things:

- The methods and techniques deployed by economists to measure preferences (e.g. willingness to pay for environmental quality) are unreliable and not valid. We examine these techniques and their limitations in Chapter 3 and conclude that reliable estimates of the value of a wide range of environmental goods and services are possible.
- The fate of environments should not be determined by human wants at all. This we consider unacceptable on democratic grounds.
- Human wants matter, but are not the only source of value. There is 'intrinsic' value in nature. The debate between human use (or instrumental) value and innate intrinsic value in nature is a sterile one.

Economists do not deny the possibility of intrinsic value but choose to apply instrumental value via willingness to pay. The debate is unresolvable because it is not possible to show empirically what intrinsic value in nature is. It has to be accepted or rejected intuitively.

Nevertheless there is a sense in which economic valuation of the environment will represent only a partial value. This is a criticism long held by scientists. Taking a 'systems' perspective, i.e. including as many economy/environment interrelationships as is practicable, it is possible to argue that healthy ecosystems have to exist prior to the existence of individual functions and services such as watershed protection, storm buffering, waste assimilation, etc. In Chapter 3 we shall see that total economic value, namely, a combination of use value and non-use or passive use values relates to these individual functions and services (called secondary values). But total secondary value does **not** encompass the primary value of the system itself, its life-supporting functions and their 'glue value' that holds everything together that also has economic value. We cannot directly estimate primary value but it serves to remind us that total economic value is an underestimate of the 'true' value of the environment.

The methods and techniques developed by economists in order to value environmental assets in monetary terms are reviewed in more detail in the next chapter. In practice, the valuation process has two main uses: first to integrate the unpriced but valuable functions of natural environments into cost benefit analysis of real world projects and, second, to illustrate the kinds of economic damage done to national economies by resource depletion and pollution.

Once society has decided on an 'acceptable' level of environmental quality assisted by, among other factors, economic cost benefit analysis there are still further problems to be resolved. To transform the decision into reality requires a change of behaviour on the part of producers and consumers. Again a continuing debate exists in environmental economics concerning the relative merits of command and control regulations (CAC) and market-based incentives to control pollution[2].

Pollution control policy

In choosing a pollution control policy, we need to determine:

- what policy instruments and technologies for reducing of pollution are available;
- what the objectives of the pollution control policy are, with particular reference to the type of pollution and the degree of environmental risk posed, the extent and reliability of pollution control methods, the full social costs of pollution control, and the actual distribution of the costs and benefits across society;
- how cost effective are the different policy instruments with respect to these objectives; and how

'politically' acceptable are certain instruments.

The regulatory approach is based on the issuing of a licence by some government agency to do or not to do something (i.e. install and operate a piece of equipment or new process), or to meet a predetermined target of performance (e.g. energy-efficiency standard). The basis of such a licensing regime is usually a matter of judgement as to what is optimal for the discharge concerned, depending on the level of technology and the shape for its future development, and the degree of investment broadly in relation to the social gains of production removal. In practice these licences are founded on decision rules. In the US the rule is best available control technology, in the UK it is best practicable means (BPM) or best available technologies not entailing excessive cost (BATNEEC), or as low as

---

Box 2.6 What are economic instruments?

The incentives that economic instruments (EIs) provide can take the following forms:

- direct alteration of price or cost levels, e.g. emission changes;
- indirect alteration of prices or costs via financial or fiscal means, e.g. subsidies or fiscal incentives to encourage the adoption of 'cleaner technologies';
- market creation, e.g. emission permits (tradeable).

Charges

These instruments represent a straightforward way to price the use of the environment.

Emission charges are charges on the discharge of pollutants into air, water or on the soil and on the generation of noise. They are related to the quantity and quality of the pollutant and the damage cost inflicted on the environment.

User charges have a revenue-raising function and are related to treatment cost, collection and disposal cost, or the recovery of administrative costs depending on the situation in which they are applied. They are not directly related to damage costs in the environment.

Product charges are levied on products that are harmful to the environment when used in production processes, or when consumed or disposed of. The charge rate is related to the relevant environmental damage costs linked to the target product.

Marketable permits are environmental quotas, allowances or ceilings on pollution levels. Initial allocation of the permits is related to some ambient environmental target, but thereafter permits may be traded subject to a set of prescribed rules.

Tradeable emission permits

- Tradeable resource and pollution permits offer an innovative and challenging way of tackling many environmental problems. Because they leave the polluter with the flexibility as to how to adjust to the environmental standard, they make compliance with regulations less expensive than would be the case with CAC.
- They do not sacrifice environmental quality because the overall level of quality is determined by the overall number of permits, and that is set by the regulatory authority.
- They appear to be more acceptable to resource users and polluters, at least once they have been in operation for a while and bureaucratic control is minimized.
- They have significant potential for controlling carbon dioxide emissions. Indeed, it is quite widely suggested that there could be *internationally traded* carbon dioxide permits. The attraction would be that countries that find it costly to reduce CO_2 emissions would buy permits, while those finding it easy to cut back emissions could sell permits. There may also be some attraction to 'over-issuing' permits to poor countries who could then sell them to richer countries.

reasonably practicable (ALARP). The regulations may also cover the following issues:

- limits in terms of maximum rate of discharge from a pollution source;
- pollution discharge bans related to pollution concentration measures or damage costs;
- specification of inputs or outputs from a given production process.

Economic incentives require not action but payments and, in principle, encourage the economically rational polluter to change behaviour by balancing reduced payments (of, say, a pollution tax levied on the waste discharged or emitted into the environment) against increased costs incurred in reducing pollution discharges. Early economic work in the field of pollution control stressed the desirability of the economic incentive approach. Given certain assumptions it can be shown that the most efficient (strictly the most cost-effective) way of achieving some predetermined level of environmental quality is via the imposition of a pollution tax or related economic incentive instrument. However, when some of these assumptions are relaxed and criteria such as distributional equity and ethical considerations are introduced, the case in favour of the incentive approach is much less clear-cut; see Boxes 2.6–2.9.

Each approach has its advantages and limitations and a combined approach has much to commend it. Since the environment should not generally be left to unfettered markets (or highly subsidized markets), regulations will be required to underpin most economic incentive and property-right systems.

Conclusions

In this brief overview of some of the main principles and practice of environmental economics we have sought to emphasize the following points:

- Economic analysis is not equivalent to financial (monetary) accounting. It is much more comprehensive and encompasses the full range of social costs and benefits related to some resource allocation decision.

Box 2.7 Selection criteria for policy instruments

- Economic efficiency.
- Low information requirements – minimal amounts of accurate information are required and the costs of updating it should not be prohibitive.
- Administrative cost – complex, highly technical schemes requiring large amounts of information run a high risk of failure or very limited effectiveness.
- Equity – heavily regressive schemes are to be avoided.
- Dependability – environmental effectiveness of the scheme should be as reliable as possible given the inevitable uncertainties.
- Adaptability – the system should have the capability to adapt to changing technology, prices and climatic conditions.
- Dynamic incentive – the system continues to encourage environmental improvement and technical innovation – beyond policy targets if this is feasible.
- Political acceptability – does not represent too radical a departure from prevailing and likely future practices and underlying philosophies.

Box 2.8 Pollution taxes

Relative advantages of taxes (charges) over regulation

- More cost-effective (i.e. lower-cost) method of achieving a given ambient quality standard.
- Incorporates a dynamic incentive for polluters to continue to reduce emissions below the regulatory standard.
- Incentive for firms to commit funds towards longer-term R & D investment in pollution control.
- 'Broader' pollution spectrum effect.

Limitations of taxes

- Uncertainty, especially over pollution damage costs and therefore over the 'optimal' level of tax.
- Regressive effect of some pollution taxes, e.g. increased VAT on domestic fuel; mitigation available via tax revenue redistribution (fiscal neutrality).
- International implication, e.g. carbon tax is likely to be introduced on a significant scale some time in the future *only* if it is introduced by a number of countries acting together. This, however, requires an international agreement ('free-rider effect' problem).

Box 2.9 Pollution control and uncertainty

Given that a great deal of uncertainty surrounds real-world pollution problems, the regulatory agency often has to try to weigh the risk of polluting too much against the risk of putting an excessive cost burden on industrial polluters. In the top section of the figure we have assumed that there is no uncertainty and in such circumstances the economic rule is to equate marginal pollution damage costs with marginal abatement costs. The regulatory agency could then set a charge OA and achieve an efficient level of pollution reduction ER^*.

If there is uncertainty but it is suspected that there is a threshold effect in the pollution damage function (i.e. pollution becomes very damaging above a certain level), then it seems sensible to be most cautious about emission reduction. The permit instrument works best in such a situation since it controls the quantity of emissions that are allowed. In contrast a charge set at level C produces a wide range of uncertainty $ER_1 - ER_2$ – see middle section of the figure.

Alternatively if it is suspected that there are no threshold effects in the damage function but that costs of controlling pollution are likely to rise sharply as emissions are reduced, then the worry will be more about excessive costs damaging industry and employment. So if a permit system is used to set emissions at level ER^* and costs of controlling pollution actually turn out to be MC_1 then industry would have wasted a substantial amount of expenditure (spending C_3). Charges would be a better instrument in these circumstances (error range $C_1 - C_2$) – see bottom section of the figure.

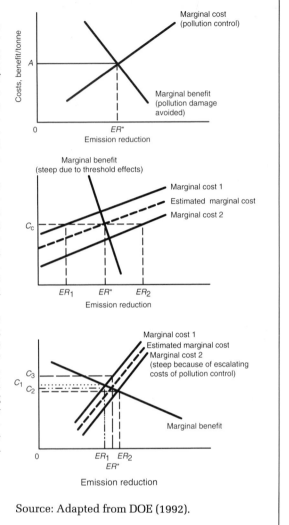

Source: Adapted from DOE (1992).

• The economic approach utilizes money only in so far as it is a convenient measuring rod of what people want (preferences) or do not want with respect to the environment. It is concerned with people's economic well-being (welfare) but does not deny the possible existence of a separate moral case in favour of nature conservation.

• Environmental resource management issues have at their core a 'scarcity' problem. Therefore the economic efficiency criterion will have an important (though not an exclusive) role to play in the mitigation of resource use conflict. Few resources possess infinite value and resource allocation decisions always involve opportunity costs. Cost benefit analysis can play a valuable role in the assessment of such allocation decisions.

- The Laws of Thermodynamics serve to emphasize that ecological systems underpin economic systems and not vice versa. Waste disposal and related pollution impacts (externalities) are inevitable and commonplace in economic activities. Because the capacity of the environment to assimilate wastes is not unlimited (i.e. it is scarce), the economic market mechanism cannot be free of externality effects. The unfettered market is therefore likely to lead to environmental degradation and loss (i.e. inefficient use of environmental resources).

- The sustainable economic development concept combines both an efficiency and an equity principle. It is economic development that endures over the long run. We have argued that one interpretation of sustainable development relies on the notion of capital bequests across generations. The passing on over time of a constant stock of capital is both a necessary and sufficient condition for sustainability.

- Analysts continue to debate the extent and degree of substitutability that may be possible (via technical change) between the different elements of the total capital stock (man-made capital, human capital and natural capital). We have also highlighted the potential importance of 'critical' natural capital which by definition is non-substitutable and therefore must be conserved.

- The monetary valuation of environmental functions and services (which provide both use and non-use values) which are generally unpriced is necessary in order to correct for decisions which treat such assets as if they were free goods. Such a situation, uncorrected, inevitably leads to resource degradation and/or complete loss.

- Once society has decided on an 'acceptable' (quasi-sustainable) level of environmental quantity and quality there are still problems to be resolved – in particular, how to transform that 'political' decision into practice and reality. So-called enabling policy instruments are required. Such instruments fall into two general categories – regulation and economic incentives. Regulatory measures are often not very efficient in the sense that they incur more costs than market-based measures, while, in principle, economic incentive approaches, if they were adopted, would increase the efficiency of the policy. The real world pollution control policies are currently based mainly on regulatory measures, although the use of economic incentive instruments is increasing. This trend is strongly supported by economists. In the end a combined package of measures will have to be deployed in order to meet as many of the multiple decision criteria as society demands in its policy-making and implementing process. The criteria list includes economic efficiency but also equity, environmental effectiveness, 'political' acceptability, and administrative convenience.

Notes

1. In certain situations some level of an activity, e.g. waste disposal, is unavoidable and in these cases efficiency is increased when the net social costs of that activity are reduced (perhaps minimized) by a project, policy or course of action (which reallocates resources).

2. In fact there is a third approach called the property (resource) rights approach which is based on the prevailing legal ownership compensation system and its possible amendment to better protect resources.

References

Costanza, R.E. (Ed.) (1992) *Ecological economics*. New York: Columbia University Press.

DOE (1992) *The potential role of market mechanisms in the control of acid rain*. London: HMSO.

Ekins, R. and M. Neef (Eds) (1992) *Real life economics: understanding wealth creation*. London: Routledge.

Turner, R.K., D.W. Pearce and I.J. Bateman (1993) *Environmental economics: an elementary introduction*. Hemel Hempstead: Harvester Wheatsheaf.

World Commission on Environment and Development (1987) *Our Common Future*. Oxford: Oxford University Press.

Further reading

The following books represent essentially non-technical/introductory treatments of the principles of environmental economics: D.W. Pearce, E. Barbier and A. Markandya (1989) *Blueprint for a green economy* (Earthscan, London). D. W. Pearce, (Ed.) (1991) *Blueprint 2.* (Earthscan, London); Turner *et al.* (1993).

For a more advanced treatment of the subject see D.W. Pearce and R.K. Turner (1990) *The economics of natural resources and the environment* (Harvester Wheatsheaf, Hemel Hempstead).

CHAPTER 3

Environmental and economic appraisal

IAN BATEMAN

Ian Bateman provides a comprehensive account of the various ways in which economists strive to put a price on resources or natural processes that have social value, but that are not normally costed when used or protected. There are critics who dislike the idea of placing prices on nature. They argue that this is simply an extension of the very capitalist system that created the environmental mess we are now in. They believe most sincerely that mone-tizing the environment is merely a further step in global degradation of the human spirit, let alone the natural world. They also claim that to tackle valuation in this way confuses the vital distinction between the individual as consumer and the individual as citizen.

This is an important point, and one that underlies much of the chapter that follows. It has a lot to do with property rights, introduced in Chapter 1. As a consumer, the individual seeks to expropriate a good for private personal use. This need not be confined to material objects, such as boats or shoes. It could well be 'positional goods' such as beautiful landscapes, clean air, peace and quiet, or interesting sculptures. In all these cases, the individual as consumer aims to buy a property right which cannot be taken by anyone else. In a sense, this is the basis of hedonic, or property, price variations that Ian Bateman discusses.

The individual as citizen sees the world rather differently. The citizen cares more about sharing, about responsibility for others, for the future and for nature. The citizen regards property rights as jointly owned between self and others. The citizen is prepared to accept social controls over consumption, exploitation and private acquisition. The citizen is both self-aware and communally engaged or grounded.

These two perspectives can be muddled when individuals are asked to respond to a contingent valuation exercise, especially if the nature of the 'pricing' game gives them nothing other than a take it or leave it figure on an escalating scale. It is hardly surprising that eco-specific contingent valu-ation studies can give a very distorted view of what the respondent as a consumer might accept compared with the respondent as citizen.

For example, it is fairly obvious that the value of a whale will depend on whether the whale is to be watched or killed. Possibly less apparent is the likelihood that the consumer will value the whale to be watched differently from the value the citizen would apply to the same whale that may never be seen, but which gives satisfaction simply in the knowledge that it is alive. Which value would be higher and which lower would depend in part on the ethical stance of the person *vis-à-vis* deep ecology (Box 19.1), and on the adjudged property rights of the whalers.

The theme of differential valuation is always evident when property rights are regarded as universal rather than personal. Hence the wide discrepancy between estimates of willingness to pay to avoid a nuisance or protect beauty compared with willingness to be bribed to accept destruction. This problem is well known amongst economists. But the world outside sometimes too glibly takes the results of quantified benefits calculations as too close to gospel truth. Ian Bateman makes no such claims. The techniques he summarizes are a contribution to better resource management and project justification – no more, no less.

Nevertheless there is an element of power in the quantified valuation of an environmental good or bad that may well distort justice if translated too naïvely into cost benefit analysis or policy. Take, for example, the carbon tax, discussed in Chapters 1, 6 and 18. To most economists one molecule of CO_2 is the same as any other when it comes to valuing the damage, or social costs, associated with an additional tonne of the gas. Estimates range from \$10 to \$30 for such a tonne. As we note in Chapter 18, to reduce CO_2 emissions to the point where there is no anthropogenic interference with the ecosystem could mean taxes of up to \$300 per tonne at the low end and five times that for developing countries about to burst into a coal-fired economy. Yet surely an additional tonne of CO_2 is not the same for a country squandering fossil fuels as it is for one with a large impoverished population still to develop. The same could be said for additional increments of ozone-depleting gases between countries basking in air conditioning and those nations where a privately owned refrigerator is as rare as rain in the Sahel.

Development does not begin from an equitable basis. Yet in physical science terms a pollutant is the same, measure for measure. In legal, political and, above all, ethical terms it is not. So the tax regime ought to be modified for distributional reasons. There is no reason why it cannot be: this can be done by some form of income equalization, or by income transfers to take account of incremental costs. The point is the transfers must be made if environmental economics is to meet its established aim of welfare maximization. Once again science provides only part of the answer, and interdisciplinary environmental science a lot more of it.

What is common to the greatest number gets the least amount of care (Aristotle)

Introduction

This chapter discusses the ways in which economists analyse a development proposal. These proposals can be as diverse as a scheme to build a new motorway, to reassess the ways in which electricity is generated or to examine the desirability of coastal defence works. As noted in the previous chapter, when assessing these projects a private company would undertake a 'financial appraisal'[1] to estimate whether the project is likely to yield a large enough profit to justify the necessary investment. However, it is the job of the economist to assess these proposals from the standpoint of society as a whole. In such an 'economic appraisal' the economist examines the total costs to society entailed in developing the project and compares these with the benefits that the project provides to society; consequently this technique is known as cost benefit analysis (CBA).

CBA economic appraisal helps politicians and planners to allocate resources between different investment options so as to maximize social welfare. In theory, CBA can be used to appraise projects (individual investments), policies (a course of action encompassing some number of projects) or programmes (a scheme which may in turn consist of a number of policies). However, since its origin in the 1950s CBA has been subject to several criticisms.

The most powerful criticism is the apparent unfairness in the way practical applications of the technique take into consideration the environmental impacts of economic developments. We can identify two major issues which have been raised concerning this traditional or conventional CBA approach[2]:

1. Conventional CBA does not assess all items in the same manner. In particular, whereas most cost or benefit items are represented by their money value, the environmental impacts of a project are often given non-money descriptive evaluations which may, in turn, not be given equal weight by decision makers.

2. Conventional CBA does not have a 'sustainability criterion', i.e. it does not have an inbuilt mechanism to ensure the preservation of environmental services between generations (intergenerational equity).

This chapter opens by considering recent approaches addressing the former problem; the evaluation of environmental goods and services in money units. This is followed by a brief discussion of some options regarding practical rules for sustainability in project appraisal.

However, before we turn to consider these approaches in detail it is useful firstly to consider the complexity of costs and benefits which need to be appraised if we are to move from a simple financial appraisal of a project to a full CBA.

The appraisal framework

To illustrate the differences between the financial appraisal of a project and economic appraisals of the same project we shall now consider a real-world example.

Figure 3.1 illustrates various frameworks for appraising a forestry company's proposal to plant trees on an area of land. The afforestation project yields both benefit and cost items. These items can in turn be subdivided as either 'internal' (those that accrue to the private company) or 'external' (those that flow to the rest of society).

The private forestry company will want to know if it is likely to make a profit from the woodland. To do this it conducts a 'financial appraisal' by comparing the internal benefits it receives with the internal costs it has to pay for (shaded boxes in Figure 3.1). If internal benefits outweigh internal costs to the extent that the company would not make more money from investing elsewhere, then it will go ahead with the project and start planting trees.

All types of CBA are concerned with the wider social value of a project and so consider both the internal and external benefits and costs listed in Figure 3.1. The interesting question for CBA analysts is, how are these items to be evaluated?

In a CBA, the internal costs and benefits of a project (shaded boxes) can usually be evaluated by reference to their market prices[3]. Some of the external items are also related to market prices (the broken line unshaded boxes of Figure 3.1). For example, if the land was previously being used to grow crops then planting trees will obviously mean that these crops are lost (the 'alternative output' in the external cost column). This is a loss to society, i.e. an external cost, which can be evaluated by looking at the market price of the lost crops. However, many items do not have market prices (e.g. amenity, recreation, wildlife habitat) and cannot be readily valued by such an approach (those items in the solid-line unshaded boxes in Figure 3.1). Until recently many CBA studies had no method for placing prices on (monetizing) externalities which have no connection with market prices. As many of the environmental externalities of a project fall into this category (benefits such as the creation of recreation, amenity and wildlife habitat, and costs such as pollution and

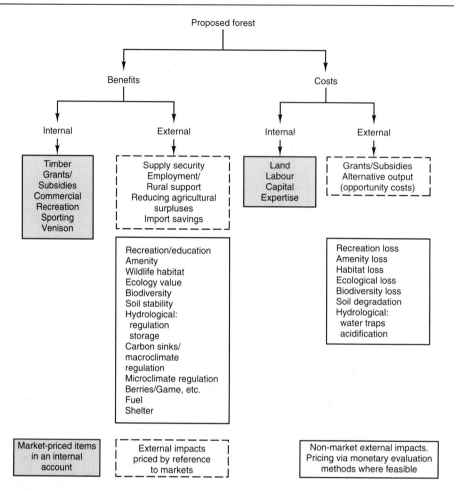

Fig 3.1 An extended cost benefit framework for appraising a proposed forest. Note that 'internal' refers to the private forestry company's costs and benefits, while 'external' refers to costs and benefits accruing directly to society. (Source: Bateman, 1992a.)

loss of habitat) this meant that the money sums resulting from such CBAs were under-representative of environmental impacts. This in turn led to decisions being taken under at best imperfect, and at worst biased, information. In practice, the traditional answer to such problems has often been to include some written qualitative environmental assessment of the project along with the CBA. However, because decision makers tend to work with monetary measures these non-monetary assessments have tended to be overshadowed by the former.

Monetary assessment methods

Overview

Often the services of the environment, whether it be as a provider of outdoor recreation, landscape amenity or pollution assimilator, are treated as 'free' goods. This arises from the common and persistent confusion over prices and values. Even the earliest economic commentators recognized that the price of a good need not correspond to its value. Adam Smith, writing more than 200 years ago, noted the extreme disparity between the (very low) price of water and its (very high) value. Yet even today the use of environmental goods and services is commonly dictated by their price rather than their value. A contemporary example of such use is the dumping of UK sewage sludge in the North Sea. In so doing, the sea provides highly valuable but virtually zero priced waste assimilation services. These are only now becoming apparent because the phasing out of such dumping (MTPW, 1990) has forced the dumping companies to find costly incineration and landfill alternatives.

This example also serves to show one route by which such environmental goods can be priced: by examining the market price of alternative goods. Such an approach belongs to a wider group of 'pricing' techniques which attempt to put monetary assessments upon environmental goods and services by reference to other goods which do have market prices. Such approaches are often relatively simple to operate and can provide a perfectly adequate evaluation. However, while some price is often better than no price, they may considerably understate the full value of a good and may therefore still allow considerable resource misallocation.

Economic theory shows that the full value of any good can only be calculated by examining demand for it, i.e. estimating the so-called demand curve showing how much of the good people would use at varying prices. Such an approach would show the disparity between the price of water and its value, as the demand curve would show that people would pay almost any amount to ensure a basic supply of water.

Figure 3.2 shows the demand curve for open-access recreation in a wood. The curve shows how much an individual values these visits as expressed in the amount he/she would be willing to pay (WTP) for them. We can see that the individual would be willing to pay a relatively high price for his/her first visit (£15.00) compared with a second (£8.50) and successive visits (£4.00; £2.00; £0.50; £0.00). The number of visits taken is determined where the WTP equals the market price of the good. Here, because this particular wood is open-access, the market price is zero so the individual makes six visits. The value of all these visits can be found by summing the WTP for all visits (£30.00), i.e. the value

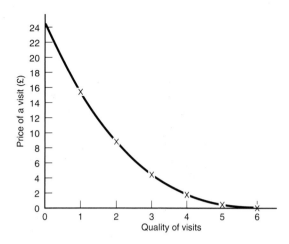

Fig 3.2 The demand for recreation visits to a wood.

of the good is given by the area under the demand curve (this rule holds for all goods both marketed and non-marketed). Clearly, as for many environmental goods, we can see that the value of woodland recreational visits is considerable. However the market price of these visits is zero.

Various demand curve 'valuation' approaches have been developed. Although generally more complex in implementation than the non-demand 'pricing' approaches, demand curve methods are useful where a large disparity between price and value seems likely. Figure 3.3 outlines the various monetary assessment evaluation techniques available, each of the which is discussed in the following sections.

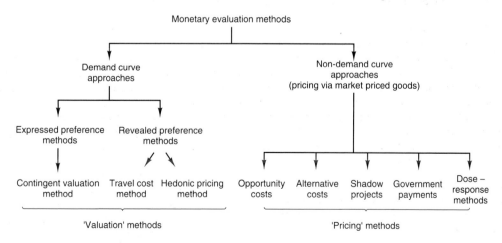

Fig 3.3 Methods for the valuation and 'pricing' of environmental goods and services. (Source: Adapted from Bateman, 1992b.)

'Pricing' methods

Opportunity costs

One approach is to examine what market value would have to be foregone in order to, say, enhance a particular environmental asset. A contemporary UK example is the on-going creation by the Countryside Commission of a 'New National Forest' between Leicester and Burton-on-Trent in the English Midlands (Countryside Commission, 1990). The site, which comprises nearly 40 000 hectares, includes a large area of quality arable land, the loss of which represents an opportunity cost.

Strictly speaking that opportunity cost should be the net market price for the crop and livestock products of the land 'lost' to the new forest. But because these products are subsidized by the Common Agricultural Policy (CAP) of the EC, the compensation paid to landowners would be the lost subsidized value of production minus the costs of input. This is a distortion in economic terms, but is politically necessary on the basis of fairness. Resource prices are more a function of the *structure* of markets and the political weight of major interest groups, rather than competitive relationships. And compensating arrangements reflect these distorted prices. Yet this 'value' sets the lower limit of the environmental benefit of the new forest.

Costs of alternatives

Where an environmental resource is being used (or its use is planned) as part of some development or production project, then one strategy for evaluation is to calculate the cost of using some alternative resource. One example is the sewage treatment alternatives to North Sea dumping discussed above. A second example arises from plans to extend the M3 motorway via a cutting through Twyford Down, a recognized area of outstanding natural beauty in mid Hampshire, UK. Here an alternative scheme for running the motorway through a tunnel under the Down was costed at just under £70 million (Medley 1992), a cost which the Department of Transport clearly felt outweighed the environmental benefits of preserving the area.

Shadow projects

Another 'pricing' option is to look at the costs of providing an equal alternative environmental good elsewhere. One study (Buckley, 1989) examined such possibilities for a development project that threatened an existing wildlife habitat. Here three options were highlighted: asset reconstruction (providing an alternative habitat site); asset transplantation (moving the existing habitat to a new site); and asset restoration (enhancing an existing degraded habitat). The costs of the preferred option can then be entered into the project appraisal as the 'price' of the threatened habitat (further details of the shadow project approach are presented later in this chapter).

Government payments

The Government, as arbiters of public preferences, occasionally directly value environmental goods and services by fixing subsidies paid directly to producers (particularly farmers) for adopting environmentally benign production methods. Such values have been used as part of project appraisals, a recent case being that for the Aldeburgh sea wall in Suffolk (southeastern England) where the costs of wall renovation were assessed against various items, one of which was the environmental value of protected land as proxied by ESA (Environment Sensitive Area) subsidies to local farmers (Turner *et al.*, 1992).

The dose – response method

Statistical techniques can be used to relate differing levels of pollution (the 'dose') to differing levels of damage (the 'response'). In an interesting recent study the environmental costs of a coal-fired power station were assessed by examining various dose – response models relating acidic and photo-oxidant emissions to their impacts upon forest, crops, fisheries, etc. (Holland and Eyre, 1992). Once the physical impact of these emissions upon, say, crops has been calculated in terms of tonnes per annum lost then this can be given a monetary evaluation by multiplying this damage by the market price per tonne. Box 3.1 illustrates this particular case study.

Summary: 'pricing' methods

Non-demand curve 'pricing' approaches can be useful in providing rough evaluations for environmental goods and services that might otherwise be treated as free. However, they are not without flaws and limitations. The 'opportunity cost', 'cost of alternatives' and 'shadow project' approaches provide monetary benchmarks against which the value of the environmental

Box 3.1 Applying the dose – response method to pricing the cost of sulphur emissions upon cereal crops

Panel A shows sulphur emissions (measured in parts per billion) from a coal-fired power station. The environmental impacts of such emissions are initially appraised in a simple scoping study, such as that shown in Panel B, where experts identify broad areas of concern. Panel C focuses in on just one of these impacts; damage to crops. The dose – response curve illustrated in this panel shows that, as the concentration of airborne sulphur increases (from C_0 to C_1), so crop yield falls (from Y_0 to Y_1). Panel D prices the overall annual quantity of SO_2 emissions from the power station but reading off the quantity loss relating to those emissions (from Panel C) and then multiplying the number of tonnes lost by the market price per tonne. Finally we have produced an estimate of the social value (or 'shadow price') of those losses taking into account the value of subsidy saving and other relevant issues.

Panel A Emission source: annual mean rural SO_2 concentration for the West Burton 'B' power station.

Panel B Scoping report: impacts matrix

Pollu-tants	Impacts				
	Forest	Crops	Wild Plants	Animals	Fisher-ies
SO_2	2	2	2	1	0
NO_2	1	1	1	1	0
NH_3	1	1	1	1	0
O_3	3	3	3	1	0
Total acid	3	1	3	2	3
Total N	3	0	3	2	2

Impact: 0 = low/no impact 1 = some impact 2 = severe impact 3 = very severe impact

Panel C Typical sulphur – crop dose – response relationship.

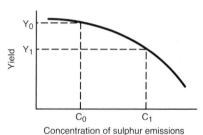

Panel D Impact pricing matrix. Scenario: Impacts of SO_2 emissions upon selected crops arising from the construction of a 1800 MW coal fired power station at West Burton

Crop	Impact[1] (tonnes lost)	Market value[2] (£)	Shadow price[3] (£)
Wheat	1 471	161 810	151 253
Barley	1 258	138 380	129 352

Source: Holland and Eyre (1992).
[1] Uses the dose response function given by Baker *et al.* (1986), adapted for stimulation of growth at very low SO_2 levels.
[2] Prices are those estimated for 1994 in Nix (1993), namely £110/tonne for both milling wheat and malting barley
[3] Shadow price adjustments are from Bateman (1994) which takes into account EC price subsidies detailed in OECD (1992) and EC (1992) and the price impacts of subsideries estimated by Roningen and Dixit (1989).

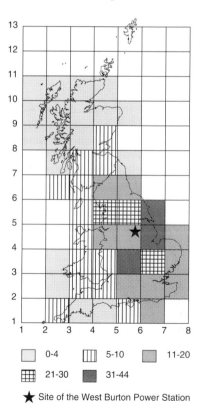

▦ 0-4	▥ 5-10	▨ 11-20
▦ 21-30	■ 31-44	

★ Site of the West Burton Power Station

good in question can only be subjectively judged. These are not true valuations since the assessment only considers whether the environmental good is of greater value than the opportunity cost. This criticism also applies to the 'government payments' approach but here we have the additional problem that the benchmark value used is set not by the market but by government.

The dose – response approach does have potential for wide application (Schultz, 1986; Barde and Pearce, 1991), although some doubts have been raised concerning the complexity of some dose – response relationships and consequent problems of statistical estimation (Turner and Bateman, 1990).

Demand curve 'valuation' approaches

The following methods all centre on the estimation of a demand curve for the environmental good in question. As such they provide true valuations rather than simple 'pricing'. Figure 3.3 indicates that there are two basic types of demand curve evaluation methods: firstly, demand can be measured by examining individuals' stated (*'expressed'*) preferences for the environmental good (elicited via questionnaires); and secondly, demand can be *revealed* by examining individuals' purchases of market-priced goods which are required in order to enjoy associated environmental goods. However, before considering these valuation methods in detail we first need to consider the more fundamental question concerning what it is we mean when we say that something is of value.

What is value?

The differing appraisal frameworks of what we have referred to as 'conventional' CBA and 'extended' CBA arise from differing specifications of what constitutes value. Traditional economic thought sees value as a 'utilitarian' concept. Here items only have value because of the functions or services they provide for humans, i.e. values in use or, more simply, use values. 'Primary' use values include the intended objective of the project, for example, in appraising the forestry project discussed earlier a 'primary' benefit would be the timber value of the forest. 'Secondary' use values include the associated uses generated by the project,

e.g. in our forestry example this would include the value of the employment and recreation created.

An important extension to utilitarian, or instrumental, use value is the notion of an 'option' value (Weisbrod, 1964; Bishop, 1982; Kriström, 1990). This recognizes that individuals who do not presently use a resource may still value the option of using it in the future. For example, they may be willing to subscribe towards the maintenance of local recreational parks, which they have not previously visited but may wish to use in the future.

A major difference between use-based utilitarian value theory and that espoused by environmental economists (and underpinning extended CBA analysis) is the inclusion of 'non-use' values. Such a theory contends that an individual may value something without ever personally using it or intending to use it.

Two subdivisions exist here. Firstly, the ability to pass assets on to future generations represents a 'bequest' value. For example, an individual who does not personally enjoy forest walks may recognize that his/her children (or others) may feel otherwise and so wish to preserve such forests for future generations. Such a concept is still based upon human use although not by the individual expressing the value. However, the second non-use category is strictly different in this respect: 'existence' values refer to the value that an individual places upon the preservation of some asset which will never be directly used either by him/herself or by future generations. For example, individuals may feel that it is important to protect Antarctica from contamination by pollution even if they can be convinced that such pollution would be of no detriment to any humans either now or in the future. Similarly, regarding our forestry example, individuals may value the preservation of remote forests for the wildlife habitat they provide.

Pearce and Turner (1990) bring together these subdivisions of use and non-use value in the concept of Total Economic Value (TEV). Figure 3.4 summarizes the parts of TEV together with illustrations from an appraisal of a forestry project.

In moving from utilitarian to TEV concepts of value (i.e. from conventional to extended CBA) we are allowing for a considerable widening of people's attitudes towards the evaluation of assets. In so doing we are recognizing that human values reflect a complexity of underlying motivations. Utilitarian value theory sees people as being basically motivated by individual gain (private preferences). TEV recognizes that people are not only individuals but also members of society and

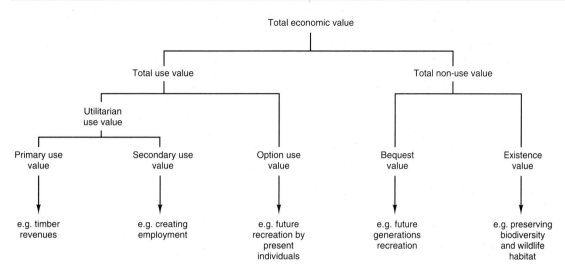

Fig 3.4 Total economic value (with examples from the appraisal of a forest project).

that, alongside individualism, people may also have altruistic motivations (public preferences). These motivations may well be in conflict. As an example of this consider the case of planning for transport demands. Individuals' private preferences may highlight the use-value of using cars for transport irrespective of the damage caused to the atmosphere. However, public preferences may be influenced by bequest and existence values to prefer the expansion of lower-pollution public transport systems. The various parts of TEV may therefore be in conflict. In the transport example the development of an expanded trunk road system may be associated with positive use-value (benefits) but negative existence/bequest values (costs). Environmental economists have therefore been concerned to extend the conventional CBA framework so as to capture both the use and the non-use values of environmental goods. This is the problem addressed by our so-called 'valuation' methods.

The 'valuation' methods refer to people as the arbiters of value. Because of this, such techniques are termed 'preference' methods and two basic variants exist:

1. *Expressed preference methods.* These directly ask people about their valuation of environmental goods. The most prevalent of these is the contingent valuation method (CVM). Because people are both individuals and members of society, their stated evaluations are likely to be a mixture of individual (private) and public preferences regarding these externalities.

2. *Revealed preference methods.* These ascertain individuals' valuations of environmental assets by observing their purchases of market-priced goods which are necessary to enjoy the environmental good in question (e.g. purchasing petrol so that a day trip to the country can be enjoyed). These methods include the 'travel cost method' (TCM) and the 'hedonic pricing method' (HPM).

We shall first consider the expressed preference, contingent valuation method.

The contingent valuation method

Here environmental evaluations are obtained by using surveys to directly ask people what they are willing to pay (WTP) for an environmental benefit or what they are willing to accept (WTA) for its loss[4]. In a recent example (Willis and Garrod, 1993) visitors and residents in the Yorkshire Dales were asked to state whether they preferred to protect the existing landscape or to have the landscape changed according to various options. Respondents were then asked their WTP for their chosen option. Table 3.1 reports results from this study showing that both visitors and residents who preferred a wild landscape had a higher WTP to those preferring the present day, whilst this group had a higher WTP to those preferring a planned and managed environment. However, whilst those visitors who preferred an abandoned landscape to that of today were WTP more than any other visitor group, few

Table 3.1 Willingness-to-pay (£ per person) for various landscapes

Landscape option chosen	Visitors (£)	Residents (£)
Today's	22.12	26.03
Wild landscape	34.20	29.75
Planned landscape	18.18	13.38
Abandoned landscape	23.75	7.67

Source: adapted from Willis and Garrod (1993).

residents liked such an option and even those who did had only a low WTP.

By multiplying the WTP for a particular landscape option by the proportion of users choosing that option we can obtain an estimate of the total use value for such a landscape option.

Surveying visitors at a site therefore gives an estimate of user values. However, CVM has the advantage that non-users can also be interviewed at points away from the site so that option, bequest and existence values can also be incorporated into the appraisal, i.e. CVM studies allow us, in theory, to estimate the full TEV of an environmental asset.

Box 3.2 illustrates a good example of a study analysing both use and non-use values.

We now turn to consider the revealed preference valuation methods.

The travel cost method

TCM uses the costs incurred by individuals travelling to reach a site as a proxy for its recreation value, i.e. values are revealed from individuals' purchases of marketed goods.

In effect the travel costs incurred by an individual in visiting a site represent the vertical 'price' axis on a conventional demand curve diagram such as that shown previously in Figure 3.2. As we can see the visit price (travel costs) determine the number of visits (horizontal axis, Figure 3.2). In effect, by surveying visitors to a site and asking them for their travel costs and frequency of visits we can map out the demand curve for the site. As with any good, the value of the site will be equal to the area under this demand curve.

The demand curve is expressed as a 'trip-generating function' which simply explains the number of visits[5]

Table 3.2 Trip generation functions: visits to four UK forests.

Forest	Constant (α)	Travel cost (TC) (b_1)	Cars (X) (b_2)
Thetford	−10.5	−0.4	6.2
Hamsterley	−11.6	−0.6	13.6
Clatteringshaws	− 7.4	−0.4	5.1
Symonds Yat	−12.4	−0.5	9.4

All results are significant ($p < 0.05$).
All functions have $R^2 > 85\%$. $n = 21$ in all cases.
Source: Willis and Benson (1989).

(V) as a function of a constant (α), the travel cost (TC) and any other relevant explanatory variables (X) as shown in Equation 1:

$$V = \alpha + b_1 TC + b_2 X \qquad (3.1)$$

Here the coefficients b_1 and b_2 show the nature and strength of the relationship between the explanatory variables (TC and X respectively) and the dependent variable (V). A good example of such trip generating functions is provided Table 3.2 which comes from a TCM study of the recreational value of visit to UK forests (Willis and Benson, 1989).

Table 3.2 shows the values of α, b_1 and b_2 for four forests. As we can see, the coefficient b_1 has (in all cases) a negative sign showing that as travel costs (TC) increase (i.e. as we consider people who live further and further away from the forest), the number of visits expressed as a visit rate (V) falls. This negative relationship confirms the downward slope of the demand curve shown in Figure 3.2. We also have a second significant explanatory variable (X) which here is the number of cars in an area. The positive sign on this coefficient (b_2) shows that as the number of cars rises so does the number of visits made. Both of these relationships are highly logical[6].

Because we now know the shape of the demand curve (the slope being given by b_1) we can find the area under this curve, i.e. we can determine the value of visits to the forest (see Bateman, 1993). Table 3.3 records results from this calculation adjusted to show the per visit value of visiting the forest (column 2, where column 1 is the forest name). Multiplying this value by the number of visitors per year (column 3) gives the total recreational value of each forest (column 4).

Dividing the total recreational value of each forest

Box 3.2 The use and non-use value of improving river water quality

This example is taken from Desvousges *et al.* (1987) who examined both the use and non-use value of improving water quality in the Monongahela River, a major river flowing through Pennsylvania, USA. Analysts asked a representative sample of households from the local area what they would be willing to pay in extra taxes in order to maintain or increase the water quality in the river. The analysts conducted several variants of the CVM survey. In one variant, households were presented with three possible water quality scenarios and simply asked how much they were willing to pay for each:

Scenario 1 Maintain current river quality (suitable for boating only) rather than allow it to decline to a level unsuitable for any activity (including boating).

Scenario 2 Improve the water quality from boatable to a level where fishing could take place.

Scenario 3 Further improve water quality from fishable to swimmable.

A number of interesting conclusions can be drawn from these results. Considering the results for the whole sample we can see that the stated willingness to pay sums draw out a conventional demand curve for water quality, i.e. people are prepared to pay a relatively high amount for an initial basic level of quality, but they are prepared to pay progressively less for increases to that water quality. The figure draws out the demand curve indicated by the results for the whole survey, i.e. for the average household.

Notice that the willingness to pay of non-users is not zero. This is due to the fact that such households, while not personally wishing to visit the river, nevertheless do value its continued existence and even upgrading so that others can enjoy its benefits. As indicated previously, this non-use, 'existence' value derives from people's altruistic 'public preferences' showing that the concentration upon people's 'private preferences' as indicated in the prices of marketed goods, does not always fully capture the entire range of values (TEV) which people have for goods, particularly those provided by the environment.

Willingness-to-pay (WTP) for river quality scenarios

Water quality scenario	Average WTP of whole sample ($)	Average WTP of users' group ($)	Average WTP of non-users' group ($)
Maintain boatable river quality	25.50	45.30	14.20
Improve from boatable to fishable quality	17.60	31.30	10.80
Improve from fishable to swimmable quality	12.40	20.20	8.50

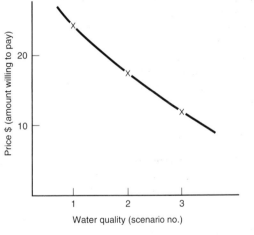

Demand curve for water quality.

Table 3.3 Value of recreational visits to four UK forests (1987 prices)

Forest	Recreation value per visitor	Annual visitor numbers	Total recreational value	Area (ha)	Recreation value (£/ha)
Thetford	2.51	102 000	256 020	20 000	12.80
Hamsterley	1.69	122 000	206 180	2 086	98.84
Clatteringshaws	2.27	32 000	72 640	5 870	12.37
Symonds Yat	2.11	158 000	333 380	1 440	231.51

Source: Willis and Benson (1989).

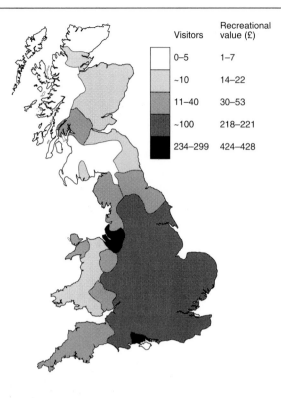

Visitors	Recreational value (£)
0–5	1–7
~10	14–22
11–40	30–53
~100	218–221
234–299	424–428

Fig 3.5 Forestry recreational values (£/ha/year). (Source: Benson and Willis, 1991.)

(column 4) by forest size (column 5) allows us to calculate the recreational value per hectare of each forest (column 6). Mapping these values (as shown in Figure 3.5) allows us to see where recreational values are highest. Figure 3.5 shows the map thus produced showing, not surprisingly, that higher values are recorded near areas of high population where visit numbers are greater. Such information can be used to help the planning of recreational resources.

Unlike CVM, the TCM can only capture the user value of those people visiting the site. Option values and non-user (bequest and existence) values are not captured and therefore TEV cannot be estimated. However, user recreation values are often a very significant part of TEV, so the TCM has received world-wide application.

The hedonic pricing method

Another revealed preference method, in practice the HPM has typically been applied to the valuation of environmental goods such as landscape amenity, noise and air quality as reflected in local house prices.

The HPM requires a two-stage analysis. In stage one the price paid for the environmental good is estimated by statistical analysis of variations in house price in relation to changes in the amount of the environmental good in question. This provides observations along the vertical axis of a demand curve graph. For example, suppose that we were interested in estimating the amenity value of broadleaved trees. Our first-stage analysis would be to see how house price (Hp) varied according to the numbers of broadleaved trees (B) near houses as well as other relevant explanatory variables such as structural characteristics (S; e.g. house size), neighbourhood characteristics (N; e.g. accessibility to workplaces) and other relevant explanatory variables (X). To do this we need to estimate the statistical function shown in Equation 2[7].

$$Hp = \alpha + b_1 B + b_2 S + b_3 N + b_4 X \qquad (3.2)$$

where

α = constant
b_1 = coefficient on number of broadleaves (B)
b_2 = coefficient on structural characteristics (S)
b_3 = coefficient on neighbourhood characteristics (N)
b_4 = coefficient on other explanatory variables (X)

We are interested in b_1 the coefficient on the 'focus' variable B. Analysis of this equation indicates the part of the house price which was paid in respect of the presence (or absence) of broadleaved trees near the house[8]; i.e. the 'price' of broadleaves (P_B).

Using this information, stage two of the HPM maps out the demand curve for the amenity value that broadleaved trees create. To do this we relate the number of broadleaves (B) around houses to the price paid for them (P_B) and any other relevant variables (which we can denote as Z to avoid confusion with X in the previous equation). This gives our demand curve equation (Equation 3):

$$B = \alpha + B_1 P_B + B_2 Z \qquad (3.3)$$

where

α = constant
B_1 = coefficient on the price paid for broadleaves (P_B)
B_2 = coefficient on other explanatory variables (Z)

Analysis of Equation 3.3 maps out the demand curve as the relationship between the price of broadleaves (P_B) and their quantity (B). This relationship is shown by the coefficient B_1 in Equation 3.3. Analysis of Equation 3.3 shows that $B_1 < 0$, revealing that the characteristic negative relationship between price and quantity demanded is true for amenity views as for other goods. Figure 3.6 shows the demand curve estimated from Equation 3.3.

Garrod and Willis (1992) undertook just such a study of the amenity value of broadleaved trees in Britain. They found a significantly higher price being paid for houses with views of broadleaved trees (i.e. $b_1 > 0$ in Equation 3.2), and estimated a characteristic downward sloping demand curve for this amenity (i.e. $B_1 < 0$ in Equation 3.3). Summing the area under this demand curve they duly estimated the value for a variety of scenarios such as planting broadleaved trees around houses or replacing conifer with broadleaved trees. The HPM can also be used to evaluate environmental costs and Box 3.3 presents results from a variety of such studies examining air pollution impacts.

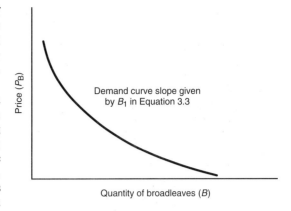

Fig 3.6 Demand curve for the amenity value of broadleaved trees.

Box 3.3 HPM studies of air and noise pollution

The majority of HPM studies carried out to date have examined either air or noise pollution in US cities. Indeed the HPM is most generally used to value environmental costs rather than benefits. However, studies of, in particular, air and noise pollution are sensitive to the extent to which individuals can perceive such costs. For example, gases such as carbon monoxide, whilst potentially very harmful (even lethal in exceptional circumstances) are imperceptible to individuals without sensitive monitoring equipment. Furthermore the occurrence of one air pollutant (or noise source) very often coincides with the incidence of others. This latter point creates problems for analysts attempting to distinguish one pollutant from another. A common solution to these problems is to focus upon a single pollutant but recognize that people's perceptions may actually refer to the wider set of pollutants which occurs with it. This factor should be borne in mind when discussing HPM results such as those for air pollution detailed in the table.

City	Year of: (a) property data (b) pollution measure	Pollution	% fall in property value per % increase in pollution
St Louis	1960	Sulphation	0.06–0.10
	1963	Particulates	0.12–0.14
Chicago	1964–67	Particulates and sulphation	0.20–0.50
Washington	1970	Particulates	0.056–0.12
	1967–68	Oxidants	0.01–0.02
Toronto/	1961	Sulphation	0.10
Hamilton	1961–67		
Philadelphia	1960	Sulphation	0.10
	1969	Particulates	0.12
Pittsburg	1970	Dustfall and sulphation	0.09–0.15
	1969		
Los Angeles	1977–78	Particulates and oxidants	0.22

Source: Pearce and Markandya (1989).

Conclusions: monetary appraisal methods

Whilst empirically the 'valuation' methods are sometimes more problematic to apply than the simpler 'pricing' approaches discussed earlier, they do have both wider applicability and the ability to estimate values rather than prices (which as we have seen may diverge considerably). Extending CBA by reference to such approaches allows us a greater theoretical ability to incorporate, via a common money unit, those environmental goods and services which otherwise would go unvalued and often by default zero-valued.

Sustainability constraints

Global environmental changes: the need for a sustainability constraint

Since the 1960s concern has been expressed that present rates of economic growth may threaten the longer-term availability of resource stocks and so endanger the well-being of future generations. This *'Limits to Growth'*[9] debate has been simmering away, albeit with a changing focus, for more than two decades. Currently, concern is primarily directed towards potential 'global environmental changes' (as outlined in Chapter 1) that may already be taking place, or are likely to take place in the future, as a direct result of the economic activities engaged in by humans and because of the growing pressures generated by the continued expansion of the global population.

There is a very real possibility that continued unrestrained economic growth may severely or even catastrophically damage the life-support services of the natural environment and thereby drastically reduce the welfare of future generations. Consequently there are strong arguments for imposing constraints upon CBA appraisals to recognize this possibility and to ensure that only proposals that use natural assets in a manner that is sustainable are allowed, i.e. to ensure that CBA studies require the imposition of a sustainable development constraint. The remainder of this chapter discusses the necessary constituents, formulation and application of such a constraint. To avoid repetition, the following symbols are used:

K_N = Natural capital; natural resources, e.g. air, water, mineral stocks.
K_M = Man-made capital; manufactured resources, e.g. buildings, machinery, finished goods.

Conventional CBA: the lack of a sustainability constraint

The objective of any CBA is to allocate resources so as to maximize human welfare. A simple maximization rule is that of 'Pareto optimality'. Here a proposed project is only allowed to proceed if it improves the welfare of some individuals in society without reducing the welfare of others. If carried out rigorously, this rule would stultify development, e.g. motorways could not be built because of the welfare loss to those near the road. Pareto optimality has therefore been qualified by the 'Hicks – Kaldor potential compensation criterion' which states that projects are allowable as long as the gainers from the project could *in theory* fully compensate the losers and still be better off, i.e. total benefits exceed total costs. Note that this only requires that the *potential* for compensation be established, not that such compensation actually take place. The possibility of there being actual losers from a conventional CBA decision is therefore not ruled out (i.e. intragenerational equity[10] is not guaranteed).

This potential compensation rule also leads to problems for safeguarding essential environmental functions. Conventional CBA has no 'sustainability theorem' to guarantee that a constant stock of environmental resources will be passed between one generation and the next. This arises because no distinction is drawn between natural capital (K_N, as defined above) and man-made capital (K_M). This means that the development by manufacturing of a specific value of K_N into an equal value of K_M is considered as an equitable exchange under conventional CBA rules.

A major problem arises from this latter view. Because of the unique attributes of K_N an increase in K_M may not in fact always be adequate compensation for using K_N. For example, the production of tropical hardwood timber (K_M) may not be adequate compensation for losing the corresponding area of rainforest (K_N) because of the variety of attributes which the latter forest provides (other output, habitat, biodiversity, etc.). This problem is often compounded, in that the decision to develop natural resources (K_N) is often irreversible (once the rainforest is logged it is lost

Box 3.4 The sewage treatment works at Stalham in the northern catchment of the River Bure in the Broads

The River Bure feeds Barton Broad, which is rapidly silting up from the detritus of algae generated by the phosphate enrichment of the sewage works. The ecological aim is to reduce phosphate concentrations in the Broad to below 100 mg per litre. This is regarded as the trigger level to re-establish large-leaved water plants and a more ecologically diverse biota. To achieve this the sewage works' effluent has to be stripped of its phosphorus down to 2 mg per litre. This can be done by adding iron sulphate. The cost annually is £150 000. The benefit is the plausible, but as yet uncertain, improvement in a recreational lake and an important conservation site. This decision requires the backing of the National Rivers Authority as the regulatory agency, and the willingness of the Office of Water Supply (OFWAT), the tariff regulatory body, to allow Anglian Water Services Plc to raise water changes above the level of inflation to pay for such schemes. In a recessionary climate with political furore over the high process and taxes on utilities generally, this is not a straightforward matter. But Barton Broad is to be restored by the NRA and the Broads Authority at a cost of £1.5 million so the pressures on Anglian Water Services are considerable.

Box 3.5 Halvergate Marshes, Norfolk

These marshes are now protected by the Environmentally Sensitive Area designation. Through this measure the Ministry of Agriculture, Fisheries and Food pays farmers up to £2 million annually to retain their marshes in grazing, and to flood their fields in the winter to encourage migratory birds. The drainage mill in the foreground is managed by English Heritage. The marshes are worth around £2–4 million per year, according to contingent valuation studies carried out at the University of East Anglia. This work forms the basis of the benefit valuation for flood protection of surplus agricultural land against North Sea storm surges and rising sea-levels. Without the evidence of contingent valuation, it is doubtful whether any improved level of flood protection would be realizable.

The constant natural assets rule

One proposed sustainability criterion is the constant natural assets (CNA) rule (Turner and Pearce, 1990). This states that: 'Compensation requires the passing-on to future generations a stock of natural assets no smaller than the stock in the possession of current generations.' (Turner and Pearce, 1990). Therefore, extending CBA to take account of the need for sustainable development entails that the Hicks – Kaldor *potential* compensation rule be extended in favour of an *actual* compensation rule for natural resources, stating that the use of K_N assets must be compensated for by creating equal substitute quantities of K_N.

So if a project wishes to use K_N (e.g. building a road across wildlife habitat land) then the compensation should be in the form of similar replacement K_N (e.g. reclaiming waste land for habitat purposes). Similarly,

forever). In the long run, by 'developing' K_N into K_M we risk eroding the environmental resource base underpinning the economy to the extent that both ecosystem and economic system can no longer function. Environmental economists have tackled this problem by explicit incorporation of a sustainability criterion into extended CBA analyses.

use of forestry for timber should be accompanied by adequate replanting programmes to ensure a constant stock is transferred into the future, so ensuring intergenerational equity.

Critics have argued that the CNA rule may slow conventional economic growth (the growth of K_M) to some extent. However, because the stock of K_N is now made secure, the CNA rule ensures that economic growth is now sustainable (K_M grows without depleting K_N) rather than unsustainable (K_M growing at the expense of K_N). Furthermore, because of the positive attributes of K_N this is likely to lead to an increase in the quality of life.

The CNA rule ensures that the analysis of economic efficiency is now complemented by considerations of equity:

- Equity for this generation (intragenerational) is enhanced by abating natural asset loss and pollution. This will improve living standards, especially for the poorer sections of society who may (arguably) suffer disproportionately from these losses.
- Equity between generations (intergenerational) is enhanced by ensuring that a constant stock of natural assets is preserved for the future.

Regarding this second point, critics may comment that the present natural asset base needs enhancement rather than preservation. While this is so, and accepting that future projects should be bent towards rebuilding the K_N base, for the moment the problem of stemming the flood of K_N depletion must take priority.

Putting the CNA rule into practice: capital substitutability and the shadow project approach

Within the CNA rule, extended CBA still retains the perspective of economic efficiency when considering how resources should be best allocated between competing uses. It therefore recognizes that where compensation (in the form of replacement K_N) is possible, then development (substitution of K_N into K_M) is permissible and should aim to maximize social welfare. The CNA rule ensures that actual compensation will keep the stock of K_N constant, whilst economic efficiency rules ensure that the input of K_N which is sustainable is put to best use.

This substitution between K_N and K_M will of course contravene the CNA rule if adequate actual compensation is not feasible. This will occur in the case of irreplaceable natural assets for which no K_N compensation is possible[11]. Thus, for example, whilst projects which use up recreation land could quite feasibly be compensated for by refurbishing degraded land, the destruction of the ozone layer or burning of the rainforests cannot be compensated for. Such items define a set of 'critical natural capital' (K_N^C) assets which cannot be considered for 'development' because their use cannot be adequately and sufficiently compensated for.

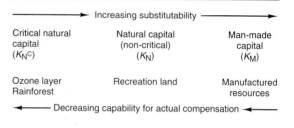

Fig 3.7 Potential for substitution between natural and man-made capital.

In practice there will be a continuum of substitutability ranging from pure critical natural capital, for which no compensation can be made, up to the purest form of man-made capital, money, which is completely substitutable. Figure 3.7 illustrates this continuum.

The K_N^C subset of natural assets can be identified by the 'shadow project' approach outlined earlier. This looks at the feasibility of actual K_N compensation for K_N use. As noted earlier there are three variants of shadow project, namely:

1. Asset reconstruction, i.e. providing an alternative habitat site.

2. Asset transplantation, i.e. moving existing habitat to a new site.

3. Asset restoration, i.e. enhancing an existing degraded habitat.

In each case, the acceptability and feasibility of such an option is assessed via an environmental impact assessment (EIA). Here environmental scientists working with environmental economists become the arbiters of the environmental acceptability of project decisions. The cost of the shadow project saluted is not a valuation of the asset involved, but it does provide a monetary cost representation of it in the CBA. Furthermore, providing the CNA actual compensation principle is adhered to, such an approach guarantees non-degradation of the environment without abandoning the social welfare advantages of economic efficiency analysis.

Non-renewable resources and the CNA rule

The CNA compensation rule is most obviously applicable to 'renewable' resources such as forestry and fish stocks which, after development, can regenerate themselves, if allowed, up to some naturally determined level. However, not all resources have this regenerative capacity. For example, coal or oil stocks are finite and therefore any use will deplete the natural capital stock in a manner which is ultimately non-sustainable. Use of such resources cannot be compensated for in the form of replacing identical natural capital. Does this then classify such items as critical natural capital ($K_N{}^C$) and forbid their use? Does the CNA rule mean an end to the pumping of oil or mining of coal?

To answer this we need to consider more carefully the meaning of 'actual' compensation. This refers to a replacement of all the *values* which environmental resources give to us. The value of the ozone layer is not that it is made up of O_3 molecules, but that it protects us from the harmful effects of ultraviolet (UV) radiation. If we could replace it with a substitute which provided the same protective power with equal absolute certainty of longevity and no adverse side-effects, then actual compensation would be feasible and the ozone layer would no longer qualify as critical natural capital. It is precisely because we cannot provide such a substitute world UV screen that the ozone layer remains critical natural capital and off-limits for natural resource development.

Does this mean that oil should be left untouched in the ground? Oil is a vital part of the world economy without which a complete economic reordering would be necessary entailing a massive loss in human welfare. What the CNA rule means is that the *services* which oil supplies must be preserved for the future, if not the black liquid itself. CNA actual compensation entails a completely new approach to the use of vital non-renewable non-critical natural capital. Actual compensation for the services of oil (i.e. energy) means that those services must be preserved for future generations. Therefore from the profits generated by producing and using oil there should be a requirement to support investment into the creation of alternative energy sources for the future.

This can take two forms, either investment to find new sources of non-renewable energy resource (e.g. finding new oil or mining for uranium), or investment into sustainable energy resources (windpower, wavepower, etc.). For compensation to be actual and sufficient this must provide at least the same quantity of future annual energy flow as do present oil stocks without burdening the future with new costs. This latter point clearly holds a question mark against investment in nuclear energy options based on depletable uranium studies. Sustainable energy options are obviously to be preferred as they prevent the necessity of repeating the actual compensation exercise (with all its associated technology costs) when the next non-renewable source of energy begins to run out.

Conclusions

Environmental economics is an extension to, rather than a rejection of, conventional economic theory. As such, it builds upon the basic economic analysis of attempting to enhance social welfare by maximizing the efficiency with which scarce resources are allocated between alternative proposed projects. Environmental economists have attempted to incorporate the environment into economic appraisal through two major extensions to conventional CBA:

1. The environmental impacts and natural resources used in a project have been given money values using a variety of techniques. This allows their common unit comparison with the other (market-priced) cost and benefit items arising in such projects and ensures that environmental assets and impacts are no longer treated as unpriced or free items.

2. The concerns of sustainable development are also incorporated into extended CBA by the imposition of a constant natural assets rule ensuring the sustainable maintenance of a constant stock of environmental goods and services into the future.

These revisions constitute a major and necessary extension to traditional project appraisal encouraging the adoption of a long-term perspective in such analyses.

Notes

1. For quick reference a short glossary of terms is included at the end of this chapter.

2. This is not in any sense an exhaustive list. Other important issues include the treatment of delayed benefits and costs (discounting); present generation (intragenerational) equity issues; and others. See the further reading section at the end of this chapter.

3. In any CBA market prices are adjusted so that they represent the true value of an item to society, e.g. the approximate social value of timber could be taken as its market price minus any subsidies (as society has to pay for these through taxes). This process is called 'shadow pricing'. See Pearce (1986) for a fuller discussion.

4. Other scenarios can be constructed; see Bateman and Turner (1993).

5. This can either be expressed as the number of visits an individual makes per annum or as a visit rate, i.e. number of visits divided by local population.

6. We have no prior expectations regarding the sign on the constant (a_0) which is here negative.

7. In reality there may be several relevant measures of S, N and X. See Bateman (1993) for further details.

8. The determination of this 'implicit price' is detailed in Bateman (1993). If the coefficient b_1 is not significant this would indicate that the presence of broadleaves did not significantly affect house price. The work of Garrod and Willis (1992) indicates that this is not the case, i.e. people do pay more for houses near broadleaved trees.

9. *Limits to Growth* is the title of a famous report by the Club of Rome (Meadows *et al.*, 1974) which first drew public attention to the potential for unsustainable growth rates and claimed that available stocks of natural resources would soon run out.

10. Notice the difference between intragenerational equity and intergenerational equity; see Glossary for definitions.

11. Note that this is not strictly true in the case of certain non-renewable resources. For example, the use of oil cannot be compensated by replacement oil. However, it can be compensated by the replacement of the services of oil, i.e. sustainable energy. This theme, as well as the entire concept of sustainability, is discussed further in Turner, Pearce and Bateman (1993).

References

Baker, C.K., J.J. Colls, A.E. Fullwood and G.G.R. Seaton (1986) Depression of growth and yield in winter barley exposed to sulphur dioxide in the field. *New Phytologist*, **104**, 233–41.

Barde, J.-P. and D.W. Pearce (Eds) (1991) *Valuing the environment*. London: Earthscan.

Bateman, I.J. (1992a) The United Kingdom. In S. Wibe and T. Jones (Eds) *Forests: market and intervention failure*. London: Earthscan.

Bateman, I.J. (1992b) The economic evaluation of environmental goods and services. *Integrated Environmental Management*, no. 14, 11–14.

Bateman, I.J. (1993) Valuation of the environment, methods and techniques: revealed preference methods. In R.K. Turner (Ed.), *Sustainable environmental economics and management: principles and practice*. London: Belhaven Press, pp. 192–267.

Bateman, I.J. and R.K. Turner (1993) Valuation of the environment, methods and techniques: the contingent valuation method. In R.K. Turner (Ed.) *Sustainable environmental economics and management: principles and practice*. London: Belhaven Press.

Bateman, I.J. (1994) Shadow prices for UK agricultural output. Mimeo, School of Environmental Sciences, University of East Anglia.

Benson, J.F. and K.G. Willis (1991) *Valuing informal recreation on the Forestry Commission estate*, Forest Bulletin No. 104. London: HMSO.

Bishop, R.C. (1982) Option value: an exposition and extension. *Land Economics*, **58**, 1–15.

Buckley, G.P. (Ed.) (1989) *Biological habitat reconstruction*. London: Belhaven Press.

Countryside Commission (1990) *A Countryside for the 21st Century*. Cheltenham: Countryside Commission.

Desvousges, W.H., V.K. Smith and A. Fisher (1987) Option price estimates for water quality improvements: a contingent valuation study of the Monogahela River. *Journal of Environmental Economics and Management*, **14**, 248–67.

European Community (1992) *CAP monitor: 24.6.92*. EC, Brussels.

Garrod, G.D. and K.G. Willis (1992) The environmental economic impact of woodland as two stage hedonic price model of the amenity value of forestry in Britain. *Applied Economics*, **24**, 715–28.

Holland, M.R. and N. Eyre (1992) Evaluation of the external costs of a UK coal fired power station on agricultural crops. In *Proceedings of the 2nd International Conference on the External Costs of Electrical Power*, September 1992, Racine, Wisconsin.

Kriström, B. (1990) W. Stanley Jevons (1888) On option value. *Journal of Environmental Economics and Management*, **18**, 86–7.

Meadows, D.H., D.L. Meadows, J. Randers and W.W. Behrens (1974) *The limits to growth.* London: Pan.

Medley, G. (1992) Nature, the environment and the future, paper presented to the U3A International Symposium, Cambridge University.

MTPW (Ministry of Transport and Public Works) (1990) *Formal declaration of the Third International Conference for the Protection of the North Sea: The Hague 1990.* The Hague, The Netherlands: MTPW.

Nix, J. (1993) *Farm management Pocketbook.* 24th ed. Kent: Wye College.

OECD (1992) *Tables of producer subsidy equivalents and consumer subsidy equivalents 1978– 1991.* Paris: OECD.

Pearce, D.W. (1986) *Cost benefit analysis.* London: Macmillan.

Pearce, D.W. and A. Markandya (1989) *The benefits of environmental policy.* Paris: OECD.

Pearce, D.W. and R.K. Turner (1990) *Economics of natural resources and the environment.* Hemel Hempstead: Harvester Wheatsheaf.

Price, C. (1993) *Time, discounting and value.* London: Blackwell.

Roningen, V.O. and P.M. Dixit (1989) Economics implications of agricultural policy reforms in industrial market economics. *Staff Report No. AGES 89–36*, Agriculture and Trade Analysis Division, Economics Research Service, United States Department of Agriculture.

Sagoff M (1990) *Ecology and economy.* Cambridge: Cambridge University Press.

Schultz, W. (1986) A survey on the status of research concerning the evaluation of benefits of environmental policy in the Federal Republic of Germany. OECD workshop on the benefits of environmental policy and decision making, Avignon.

Turner, R.K. (1988) Sustainability, resource conservation and pollution control: an overview. In R.K. Turner (Ed.), *Sustainable Environmental Management: Principles and Practice.* London: Belhaven Press.

Turner, R.K. and I.J. Bateman (1990) *A critical review of monetary assessment methods and techniques.* University of East Anglia: Environmental Appraisal Group.

Turner, R.K. and D.W. Pearce (1990) *The ethical foundations of sustainable economic development,* LEEC Paper 90–01. London: International Institute for Environment and Development.

Turner, R.K., I.J. Bateman and J.S. Brooke (1992) Valuing the benefits of coastal defence: a case study of the Aldeburgh sea defence scheme in A. Coker and C. Richards (Eds), *Valuing the environment: economic approaches to environmental evaluation.* London: Belhaven Press.

Turner, R.K., D.W. Pearce and I.J. Bateman (1993) *Environmental Economics: an elementary introduction.* Hemel Hempstead and Baltimore: Harvester Wheatsheaf and John Hopkins University Press.

Weisbrod, B.A. (1964). Collective-consumption services of individual-consumption goods. *Quarterly Journal of Economics,* **78,** 471–7.

Willis, K.G. and J.F. Benson (1989) Recreational values of forests. *Forestry,* **62** (2) 93–110.

Willis, K.G. and G.D. Garrod (1993) Valuing landscape: a contingent valuation approach. *Journal of Environmental Management,* **37,** 1–22.

Further reading

Further details regarding all the issues raised in this chapter are available at an introductory level in Turner, Pearce and Bateman (1993). More advanced material is as follows.

Cost benefit analysis

The best introduction to the subject is provided by Pearce (1986) after which a variety of texts is available, for example, R. Sugden and A. Williams (1978) *Practical cost benefit analysis* (Oxford University Press, Oxford) or, more recently, E.M. Gramlich (1990) *A guide to benefit-cost analysis,* 2nd ed. (Prentice Hall, New Jersey). Owing to space constraints and a decision to focus upon the monetary assessment issue, only the bare bones of CBA have been presented. One important omission that the interested reader is strongly advised to address is the issue of discounting (the appraisal of delayed costs and benefits). Again the basics of discounting are presented in Pearce (1986). However, the recent review by Price (1993) is highly recommended for further reading.

Externalities

The CBA approach to externalities is not the only way in which the allocation of environmental goods may be assessed. Importantly the 'Coase theorem' proposes an approach wherein the property rights of such goods are emphasized so that competitive market trading leads to their optimal use. For an introduction see Pearce and Turner (1990), then see the original paper; R. Coase (1960) The problem of social cost, *Journal of Law and Economics,* **3,** 1–44.

Prices versus values: the demand curve

There are innumerable microeconomics texts that are suitable. At an introductory level, my personal favourites are J. Hirschleifer (1991) *Price theory and applications* (Prentice Hall, New Jersey) and P-O. Johansson (1991) *An introduction to modern welfare economics,* (Cambridge University Press, Cambridge). At an intermediate level see H. Varian (1992) *Intermediate microeconomics* (Norton, New York and London).

Monetary Evaluation Methods

Relatively few texts examine 'pricing' approaches in any great detail. However, an introduction with numerous examples is provided by J.A. Dixon and P.B. Sherman (1990) *Economics of protected areas: a new look at benefits and costs* (Earthscan, London). Recent years have seen a considerable rise in texts examining the 'valuation' methods described. Introductory texts include D.W. Pearce, A. Markandya and E.B. Barbier (1989) *Blueprint for a green economy* (Earthscan, London); Pearce and Turner (1990); and the recent book by R.K. Turner, D.W. Pearce and I.J. Bateman (1993) *Environmental economics: an elementary introduction* (Harvester Wheatsheaf, Hemel Hempstead). Applications can be found in Barde and Pearce (1991) and in S. Navrud (1992) *Pricing the European environment* (Scandinavian University Press and Oxford University Press). At a more advanced level an excellent account of CVM, TCM and HPM is given in M.M. Hufschmidt, D.E. James, A.D. Meister, B.T. Bower and J.A. Dixon (1983) *Environment, natural systems and development: an economic valuation guide* (Johns Hopkins University Press, Baltimore and London): More readily available may be the chapters by Bateman and Turner in R.K. Turner (Ed.) (1993) *Sustainable environmental economics and management: principles and practice* (Belhaven Press, London) which also cover all three methods. The CVM is most thoroughly presented in R. Mitchell and R.T. Carson (1989) *Using surveys to value public goods: the contingent valuation method* (Resources for the Future, Washington, DC).

Sustainability

Reviews of the literature include J. Fernie and A.S. Pitkethly (1985) *Resources: environment and policy* (Harper and Row, London) and chapters in R.K. Turner (Ed.) (1993) *Sustainable environmental management* (Belhaven Press, London). An easily readable and important report is that of the World Commission on Environment and Development, *Our common future* (the 'Brundtland' report) (Oxford University Press, Oxford). An economic analysis of the problems of using standards is given by W.J. Baumol and W. Oates, originally in the *Swedish Journal of Economics* (1971, **73**, 1) but recently reprinted in A. Markandya and J. Richardson (1992) *The Earthscan reader in environmental economics* (Earthscan, London). Finally a recent analysis of sustainability is given by Turner in Turner (1993).

Glossary

Constant natural assets (CNA Rule) The idea that we should preserve the environment (or rather the services provided by the environment) for future generations.

Contingent valuation method (CVM) An expressed preference method for obtaining a monetary evaluation of an environmental asset which asks individuals what they are willing to pay (WTP) to preserve the site or willing to accept (WTA) in compensation for its loss.

Cost benefit analysis (CBA) *see* Economic appraisal.

Critical natural capital ($K_N{}^C$) A subset of natural resources that, once used by man, can neither adequately self-regenerate nor be properly recreated by man, e.g. the Amazonian rain forest; the ozone layer.

Dose-response method (DR) A non-preference method for obtaining a monetary evaluation of an environmental impact by calculating a statistical relationship between a pollution dose (e.g. air pollution) and the consequent response (e.g. increased respiratory disease) using market prices (e.g. costs of additional health care) to obtain the monetary evaluation of this pollution dose.

Economic appraisal An analysis of the allocation of available resources between competing development proposals, the objective being to maximize social welfare (economic efficiency).

Environmental impact assessment (EIA) A statement detailing the effects of a project/economic development upon the environment. The statement is non-monetary and concentrates upon the physical aspect of environmental changes.

Expressed preference value Value of some asset that is obtained from individual statements regarding their valuation of that asset.

Financial appraisal An analysis of the allocation of available resources (usually investment funds) carried out by a private firm, the objective being to maximize profit.

Global environmental change (GEC) Changes induced by economic growth that affect the world-wide environment, e.g. ozone depletion, global warming, sea level rise.

Hedonic pricing method (HPM) A revealed preference method for obtaining a monetary evaluation of the environment by using fluctuations in house prices to gauge the value of either an environmental asset (e.g. local woodland) or an environmental impact (e.g. local smog levels).

Intergenerational equity The equitable distribution of welfare between present and future generations.

Intragenerational equity The equitable distribution of welfare within existing society.

Man-made capital (K_M) Resources that have been manufactured from natural capital by man, e.g. cars; steel; buildings; artificial fertilizer; electricity.

Natural capital (K_N) Resources that are endowed by nature, e.g. land, water, air, minerals, fossil fuels.

Non-preference value A value that arises because of some physical property or circumstance without some human preference being ex-

pressed for it, e.g. the UV protection qualities of the ozone layer have a value quite separate from any human preference/valuation of it.

Non-renewable resources Any natural resource (K_N or $K_N{}^c$) that does not have the capacity for regeneration, therefore it can only be used once, e.g. coal; oil stocks.

Physical value see Non-preference value.

Private preference (private value) The value that an individual acting in his/her selfish personal interests has for a particular item or happening, e.g. an individual's preference for retaining their own income rather than giving it to others.

Public preference (public value) The value that an individual acting as an altruistic member of society has for a particular item or happening, e.g. an individual's preference for giving some of their income to others.

Renewable resources Any natural resource (K_N or $K^c{}_N$) that, if allowed to, has the capacity to grow to a naturally determined level, e.g. fishery stocks; temperate woodlands etc.

Revealed preference value A value of some asset that is obtained by examining those purchasing decisions of individuals which are in some way reflections of that asset's characteristics.

Sustainability constraint see Constant natural assets rule.

Sustainable development Economic growth that does not reduce or degrade the environment. Many definitions exist. Turner (1988) defines a sustainable development policy as one that 'would seek to maintain an "acceptable" rate of growth in per-capita real incomes without depleting the national capital asset stock or the national environmental asset stock'.

Travel cost method (TCM) A revealed preference method for obtaining a monetary valuation of a recreational site by examining the costs which individuals incur to visit the site.

CHAPTER 4

Human impacts on terrestrial ecosystems

ALASTAIR GRANT

It is very easy for humans to harm the Earth: they may profess otherwise, but they still do so. Word and deed rarely match. Some of the most atrocious acts are made in the name of peace and divine love. So it should not be surprising to learn that from the time of entry, humans have used simple but voracious tools, namely fire and the axe, to establish settlement, clear away enemies, frighten game or produce charcoal. The chainsaw and the bulldozer are admittedly quite a step up in the technological ladder, but the net result is approximately the same.

Alastair Grant reveals lucidly how science can tell us just what our forefathers did to the landscape and to species diversity long before the industrial revolution. It is not by any means a matter of brutality or mendacity. Ignorance of outcome, the loss of any sense of commons, the aggregation of microbehaviour into macro-adverse outcomes: these are the order of environmental change throughout the ages.

Science and biodiversity

Nowadays many are obsessed with the potential loss of species and habitats – so much so that the UN framework Convention on Biodiversity was signed in Rio and duly ratified in 1994 to try to put a legal stop to unrestrained damage. The term 'biodiversity' applies to the variety and variability of living organisms from genes to elephants. The evaluation of biodiversity is not so much a matter of numbers as of *functional redundancy*. The loss of one species upon which others critically depend is far more serious than the removal of a species whose ecological niche can readily be replaced by other species. So a major task for scientific enquiry is not just to record, but also to establish the genetic functional significance of species in a variety of ecosystems. This is why the analogy of losing a library without even cataloguing the books is only partially correct. Of much greater interest is the relative importance of each species for the resilience and robustness of genetic stock to enable them to survive against human-caused and natural stress. It is therefore not a matter of how many species the earth can afford to lose, but how many critical species must be retained.

The total number of known species or organisms is about 1.4 million, of which about 250 000 are plants, 44 000 are vertebrates and 750 000 insects. But of the fungi, so crucial for decomposition and resistance to disease, only about 69 000 of an estimated 1.5 million species are known about. Arroyo and his colleagues (1992) estimate that about 10 million different species probably exist. Less than 20 per cent of freshwater species are recorded, and less than 1 per cent of marine organisms, a group that plays a critical role in biogeochemical recycling. As Arroyo *et al.* (1992, p. 208) ruefully conclude:

> There are clearly few areas of science about which so little is known, and none of such direct relevance to human beings. One evident challenge . . . will be to devise a theoretical basis for biodiversity . . . and to develop realistic sampling procedures to collect the additional data that is so badly needed.

Various estimates put the probable loss of global plant species over the next 30 years as 20–25 per cent with over 35 per cent in the tropics at risk. For South America, using the principles of island biogeography as a guide to the vulnerability of species when habitats are disturbed and key dependent species lost, about 15 per cent of plant species and 2 per cent of bird species could be lost. Myers (1990) believes that about 20 per cent of all species are to be found on 0.5 per cent of the Earth's surface – the so-called 'hot spots' for maximum protection. Ehrlich and Ehrlich (1992, p. 225) report that between 10 000 and 60 000 species per day are being lost – over 10 000 times the removal rate following the onset of sedentary agriculture.

Why worry about biodiversity losses?

The consequences of the loss of up to a third of all living species within a stretched generation sobers the mind. This is a scientific, ethical, political and economic issue that is of profound significance to the future of humanity. Plants and organisms provide the essential basis for many medicines, genetic strains of food crops, and industrial products. The Chinese utilize 5000 of the estimated 30 000 plant species for medicinal purposes. Yet today only about 110 plant species provide virtually all the world's food. Clearly, loss of potential scientific knowledge which can subsequently be put to the good of the world is one of the many reasons why we should mourn.

The other reasons are just as powerful. *Moral concern* and *aesthetic pleasure* are two more. We ought to be worried if we are caring humans, one of many millions of different genetic constellations. The American biologist Ehrenfeld (1978) argues that species and their habitats should be preserved

> because they exist and because this existence is itself but the present expression of a continuing historic process of immense antiquity and majesty.
> Longstanding existence in Nature carries with it the unimpeachable right to continual existence.

This point is taken up in the chapter that follows. To care either comes internally from a personal conscience that is directed by cultural norms, or it may be imposed externally by legal duties or by granting rights of existence to living organisms – rights that provide statutory backing to protection. At present neither stricture is well developed in modern society.

Not to care reveals a poverty of spirit and an absence of a sense of trusteeship and solidarity with the universality of creation. In an ironic way, we should worry more that most people still appear to be unconcerned about species loss, and the values and alienation that anaesthetize them, as we should do about the disappearance of species themselves.

As whole populations disappear, another threat looms. This is the removal of the capacity to be resilient, to breed out of danger, to mutate genetically so as to evolve to cope with a changing world. Just at the time when maximum stress is placed on the Earth, so we are losing inherent capabilities of populations to adapt. Also there is the loss of the ecosystem functions that keep us all alive – on the cheap.

Forests recycle water and ocean phytoplankton play a crucial role in cycling sulphur and carbon. Estuaries lock up sediment and nutrients, releasing the latter to create ecological paradises for a host of food chains. Soils absorb toxic rain and release water in a controlled fashion, meanwhile converting minerals into essential plant nutrients. A single gram of soil may contain over 1 million bacteria, 100 000 yeast cells and 50 000 strains of fungi. Without these, nitrogen could not be fixed, nor soil minerals made into the essential building blocks for healthy humans. Remove all this and we would have to try to survive with extremely expensive substitutes.

Possible solutions

What can be done? The answer is plenty, apart from improving our science.

Debt for nature swaps appear to be on the wane, but still have merit. The idea is to trade the writing down of an unpayable Third World nation debt for local cash, bonded by a rich country organization, so as to fund the conservation and protection of genetic reserves. To date only a small amount of debt has been written off – about $1 billion for some million hectares of reserves. The main problem lies in the guarantee of sound cash flow and of good local management. Many impoverished nations resent the whole idea of ecological conditionality to a system of indebtedness which they feel is the product of a greedy capitalist world (Patterson, 1991).

Biodiversity prospecting is a variant of North – South technology transfer. Here the idea is to finance a local conservation agency, with the help of local folk knowledge of ethnobiology, to prospect for plants or organisms that could be of value for genetic modification into pharmaceuticals or disease-resistant strains, or biological pesticides. In one famous example, the US pharmaceutical giant Merck pays a Costa Rican organization INBio both to look for species of potential value, and to conserve precious habitat (Blum, 1993; Reid, 1993). Any profit from a successful formulation would be shared with INBio. Such an arrangement is fine so long as at least one jackpot drug is hit, and there is an endless supply of cash to finance ever more sophisticated medical technology.

Transferable property rights are an ingenious idea that has not yet been properly tried out. The purpose is to protect a critical ecosystem by transferring the loss of the right to develop, say for minerals or hydropower, or for forest products, to another site, possibly in another country, where such development is environmentally more tolerable. Clearly there would have to be some compensation for the transfer of development rights, but the conserver economy should not be any worse off. The conserved area might still benefit from controlled 'green tourism' by charging an entry permit for visitors to film or simply experience the retained biological diversity.

Paying for intellectual property rights (IPRs) – the rights of knowledge capable of being privatized and sold commercially or catalogued in the public interest – operate in two ways. A commercial company that fashions a drug out of a plant holds an IPR on the patent. Yet so too should the native population who successfully practise ethnobiology. Their knowledge is also an IPR and is worth a varying amount to a scientist, a tourist or a biochemical corporation. But capturing IPRs is not easy. It requires conscientious legal innovation, essential to enclosing the intellectual commons. So far little legal progress has been made, but the field is ripe for the creative union of the ecologist, the lawyer, the anthropologist and the economist. Very early studies suggest that the value of medicinal plants could be of the order of $10–60 per ha, while a low estimate of the pharmaceutical value of a rich tropical forest could be $20 per ha. Total value of tropical forest, both in terms of its role in absorbing carbon dioxide, and in its bequest status for future generations could lie between $550 and $2200 per ha – four times nominal commercial value (Brown and Moran, 1993; Brown and Adger, 1993).

This translates into an interesting calculation. Right now land prices in tropically forested countries are about $300 per ha. The conservation value of the trees storing carbon could be as much as $1000 per ha. Then it would pay the rich world to buy the development rights for the most prized of forests for any sum between these two figures. To do so would mean a transfer in property rights – both developable, and intellectual – to some global trusteeship agent. At present there is no such arrangement, but it should come now that the real 'global' price for a tropical forest is in our sights (Swanson, 1992; Pearce, 1993).

The UN Convention on Biodiversity

This important convention establishes the principle of sustained management or protection of biological reserves, seeks adequate financial measures, guarantees access to IPR, and encourages appropriate technology transfers. Every nation has to prepare a national plan for conserving and sustaining biodiversity, and to monitor its genetic stock. Also, every nation has a responsibility to safeguard key ecosystems, the indigenous knowledge of ethnobiology, and to be protected from the entry of biotechnology products that might undermine or endanger the raw genetic stock. Crucially, the convention protects the rights of nations to 'enclose' their biogenetic commons but also to share their IPR – at a price. This is why the INBio – Merck agreement is viewed as such an important precedent.

The convention also grants the conference of the signatory parties the authority and guidance to determine financial measures to facilitate all this effort. This last point is very controversial, as the UK and the US in particular saw it as a means of by-passing the Global Environment Facility (see Chapter 1) or similar donor-controlled financial instrument. To date, the matter remains vague until the Conference of the Parties to the convention meet. At present, a number of commentators worry that the convention is long on technological biodiversity via genetic engineering, and too short on natural biodiversity via adequate protection of ecosystems and ethno-knowledge. Financial transfers to ensure their rights of sustained existence may prove very difficult to guarantee – or indeed to implement – over the next few years. Yet this is a crucial period for biodiversity protection.

The current 'ecological crisis' has two interlinked strands – the large-scale destruction of complete habitats and the imminent danger of extinction for many species of animal and plant. The latter is often summarized by the term 'biodiversity loss' – the extinction of individual species as a consequence of habitat destruction and a multitude of other human impacts. Most notable amongst the destruction of terrestrial habitats are the deforestation of large areas of the humid tropics and increasing land degradation in semi-arid zones as a result of overgrazing. The best known examples of species extinctions are the elimination of species of bird and large mammal such as the dodo or the great auk as a result of hunting by humans or the introduction of predators such as rats and dogs. But mammals and birds make up a small proportion of the total species on our planet. The majority of species extinctions are the result of habitat destruction (see below).

These processes are often viewed as a peculiar feature of recent human history, the results of modern Western man being 'out of harmony' with the environment. This is contrasted with 'primitive' societies which are said to have 'established a balance' with nature. In one form, this is seen in the popular mythology of the environmental movement which sets cattle ranchers supplying the global hamburger market against the indigenous tribes of Amazonia, and views North American and Australian aboriginal cultures as living in ecological and spiritual harmony with nature. In a more sophisticated form, we have a more carefully worked out philosophy which attributes environmental degradation to a defective world view, with pagan or pantheist world views providing a sounder basis for environmental protection than the predominant world view of the developed world with its Judaeo-Christian roots. Probably the best known statement of this argument is an article by Professor Lynn White entitled 'The historical roots of our ecologic crisis' published in the journal *Science* in 1967, and still widely quoted:

> Especially in its Western form, Christianity is the most anthropocentric religion the world has seen. In absolute contrast to ancient paganism and Asia's religions, it not only established a dualism of man and nature but also insisted that it is God's will that man exploit nature for his proper ends.

It is not appropriate to examine here the environmental implications of particular theological or philosophical commitments. Bradley (1990) addresses this in a readily accessible way; O'Riordan (1981) gives a more technical discussion. It is appropriate, however, to examine the extent to which environmental degradation and human-induced species extinctions are recent phenomena and thus to evaluate whether there is any evidence that pre-modern societies actually have lived, and still do live, in harmony with nature. This chapter does this by surveying human impacts on the biosphere over the last 12 000 years. This date is chosen as representing the end of the last glaciation and the beginning of the current geological era, the Holocene. The chapter first outlines the methods used to study human impacts on past environments. It then examines structural adjustments to entire ecosystems, followed by a discussion of anthropogenic changes which influence only a subset of the species in an ecosystem.

Methods of study

The geological era which preceded the Holocene, the Pleistocene, was characterized by an alternation between glaciations and warmer interglacial periods. The last of these glaciations is known as the Weichselian in Europe, the Devensian in the UK and the Wisconsin in North America. The end of this glaciation, about 14 000–12 000 years ago seems to have been a period of rapid amelioration of the climate. As the glaciers retreated, substantial areas of land became available for colonization. There have also been climatic fluctuations since, involving changes in annual mean temperature of up to several degrees centigrade. Such climatic changes in themselves are sufficient to induce changes in the distributions of animals and plants. There are therefore two separate stages in determining human impacts on vegetation. The first is to determine states of vegetation and species distributions in the past. The second is to infer the degree to which any changes are due to human influence.

For recent changes in flora and fauna, information is sometimes available from historical records. This includes old maps, mention of species or areas of forests in books and other written records and reports of explorers. Because of the importance of wood as a building material, historical records often give good information on forest clearances. For example, historical records tell us that before 300 BC the kings of Cyprus took forests under their protection in response to their large-scale clearance. In some cases, the historical record is remarkably detailed. The Domesday book, for example, gives good information on types of land use in the 11th century in England. Similarly, the causes and timings of events leading to the extinction of the great auk (*Pinguinus impennis*) can be followed in great detail, exact dates of significant kills on particular islands being known from the logs of ships as early as the 16th century, ending with the killing of the final pair of the species by two fishermen at Eldey Rock off Iceland on 3 June 1844. Inevitably though, as one moves back into the past the record becomes more fragmentary. In consequence, the longest records of ecological change come from pollen, wood, animal bones and other materials preserved in sedimentary deposits. Plant material is preserved best in water-logged conditions such as lake muds and peat bogs and animal bones are preserved best in arid or alkaline conditions. These deposits yield information on plant and animal abundances and distribution in the past. The presence of human artefacts, butchery marks on skeletons and the contents of kitchen middens and latrines allow inferences to be made about the extent of human activities.

A pollen record which began during the retreat of glaciers would show a temporal sequence of vegetation development which is similar to the spatial gradients that occur today with latitude or altitude. The first vegetation was tundra, followed by the development of forest, which in Europe was initially of birch (*Betula* spp.), then pine (*Pinus sylvestris*). This was followed by the entry of deciduous species, particularly oak (*Quercus*), elm (*Ulmus*) and lime (*Tilia*). Forest clearance can be inferred from a decline in tree pollen, and increases in species characteristic of disturbed woodland such as alder (*Alnus*), hazel (*Corylus*) and heather (*Calluna*). Pollen from species which require open ground such as plantains (*Plantago*) and bracken (*Pteridium*) also appear. When these changes in flora are associated with the presence of charcoal and human artefacts, they are interpreted as indicating that the clearance resulted from human activity, including the use of fire. Indirect evidence of changing vegetation and its consequences is also provided by the study of soil profiles preserved under earthworks. Rates of sediment deposition in lakes, wetlands and on valley floors give information on the occurrence of soil erosion.

Evidence of this sort is inevitably fragmentary and indications of human impacts may be circumstantial rather than conclusive. However, comparison of the impacts of current activities with the fossil record helps to clarify this ambiguity. One can, for example, make inferences about the consequences of hunting, forest clearance or species introductions in the past by examining historical records of comparable events. Boxes 4.1 and 4.2 take particular case studies and show in some detail how human impacts may be elucidated.

Impacts on vegetation

Environments can be categorized as natural, subnatural, seminatural or cultural, depending on the extent of human impacts on their vegetation. In natural environments, human influence is negligible or zero. All others are impacted to a greater or lesser extent.

Natural environments

Over much of the world the natural vegetation would be forest, except where conditions are too cold or too arid. These original forests are now greatly reduced in area, either by felling or by the prevention of regeneration through fire or grazing. The largest areas of natural vegetation are probably in those areas that are inhospitable to humans or their domestic animals, such as deserts and tundra.

Except where there is no human population, it can be difficult to determine which habitats are truly undisturbed. In the UK, the original vegetation over much of the country would have been deciduous woodland. However, 14 million ha of an original 16 million ha have been cleared, and all of the remaining area has been cut at least once so there is likely to be little left which is genuinely natural. Modification of the vegetation seems to have begun quite early. There are some suggestions that, during the last (Hoxnian) interglacial, deforestation may have been caused by human use of fire, perhaps for herding animals during hunting. This is based on co-occurrence of stone hand axes and evidence of deforestation. However, there is evidence for contemporary deforestation at other sites, perhaps suggesting a large-scale fire with a natural cause, rather than controlled burning. In the Holocene, there is evidence for tree felling more than 8000 years ago, and large-scale replacement of forest by blanket mire was occurring by 5000 BP (see Box 4.1). By the time of the Norman invasion, only 15 per cent of the land in England was wooded; 25 per cent had been converted to pasture; 30 per cent was moorlands and heaths; and approximately 30 per cent used for arable farming. The English landscape has been far from natural for a long time. Large-scale replacement of forests with other

Box 4.1 Blanket mire development

Blanket mires occur at altitudes which are suitable for tree growth. Many of these blanket mires overlie quite well-developed soils, often with tree stumps and other remains indicating that the site was wooded before mire development. Clearly some change has taken place which has led to the initiation of soil waterlogging and peat accumulation. At least three possibilities have been identified – climatic change, natural soil development or human intervention.

Climatic deterioration

In the UK, it has been suggested that a short cold period between 5400 and 5000 BP may have reduced evaporation and led to soil waterlogging. But this interpretation is based, at least in part, on the initiation of peat development, and convincing independent evidence for such a climatic change is lacking.

Soil development

In areas of high rainfall, particularly under coniferous forests, the soils that develop are known as podzols. In these soils, iron is dissolved from surface layers and leached downwards. The iron may then be redeposited lower down the soil profile as an 'iron pan' – a hard impermeable layer, which can impede drainage. Perhaps soil development in high rainfall areas leads to the development of such an iron pan, impeding drainage and in time leading to soil waterlogging. This is not a satisfactory explanation of the development of blanket mires. Soils that underlie the peat may be only poorly developed, and certainly do not always show well-developed podzol characteristics or evidence for intense leaching.

It is possible that development of a shallow pan just below the depth of ploughing may have initiated mire development on land in Ireland previously used for agriculture. This explanation however requires prior human intervention.

Human intervention

The third, and most probable, explanation seems to be that human clearance of forests changed the hydrological regime sufficiently to initiate peat deposition. Once this had occurred waterlogging of soils prevented tree- re-establishment. Trees have a large surface area of leaves, and consequently relatively high rates of transpiration. A forest canopy also intercepts rainfall and, while much of this will eventually reach the ground, at least some will evaporate from the leaf surfaces. If trees are cleared, the combination of these two processes decreases evaporative water loss. The increase of water availability may produce waterlogging and consequently initiate mire development. After modern boreal or temperate forest clearance, stream discharge increases by between 8 and 40 per cent after tree felling. Studies of water interception by forest canopies and of soil – water relationships in different vegetation types indicate an increase of 10–20 per cent in water availability as a result of forest clearance, so this third explanation is entirely plausible. Perhaps the most convincing evidence comes from a number of recent examples where forest clearance has led to a raising of the water table, sometimes with soil waterlogging and killing of remaining trees. The pollen record provides evidence that is consistent with the occurrence of human interference with vegetation at the time of mire development.

---

forms of vegetation occurred in New Zealand soon after the arrival of Maoris, and certainly well before European settlement (see Figure 4.1). In the Mediterranean, most of the area of the original evergreen oak forests has been replaced with maquis (a community of woody shrubs with small, stiff evergreen leaves which form dense thickets) or more severely degraded habitats, so truly natural environments are rare here too.

Taking the world as a whole, some 8 or 9 million km^2 out of an original 45 million km^2 of forest and wood-

land have been cleared, with approximately half of this clearance taking place since 1850 (Williams, 1990). We shall see below that there is some dispute about the extent to which some environments are natural or the result of human disturbance, particularly in the case of the prairies and pampas. We *can*, however, say that much of the vegetation which is popularly viewed as natural actually results from human interference with forests. This includes much grassland and heathland, as described in the following text.

Box 4.2 'Overkill'

During the last interglacial period around 120 kyr BP, the large mammal fauna was much richer than it is at present. Those that survived the last glaciation then rapidly became extinct. At the beginning of the Holocene, the Americas had a fauna that included mammoths, mastodons and giant ground sloths. Australia had more than 12 genera of giant marsupials. In New Zealand the megafauna was represented by moas and on Madagascar by elephant birds and large lemurs. In North and South America and Australia between 70 and 80% of large animals became extinct (the figure for Australia includes large reptiles and birds).

The main extinctions did not occur simultaneously across the world. Australian extinctions occurred more than 15 000 years ago. Extinctions on New Zealand and Madagascar occurred more recently; probably between AD 1000 and 1600 in New Zealand and between AD 500 and 1100 in Madagascar. In New Zealand, more than 40 species of bird became extinct after the arrival of Maoris a little over 1000 years ago. The most notable of these extinct species were the moas – 13 or more species of flightless bird, closely related to the kiwi. The largest had an estimated live weight of 230 kg and a maximum reach of 3 m, with the most common species being between 25 and 60 kg in weight. Analogy with the densities at which the emu and cassowary occur in Australia suggests that the total population is unlikely to have been more than a few tens of thousands. Skeletons of moas occur in large butchery sites, indicating killing of several hundreds of thousands of individuals by Maoris on South Island alone. There is also evidence for extensive exploitation of eggs. The moas survived the climatic fluctuations of the ice ages and the bulk of the Holocene, but then rapidly became extinct after the arrival of the first Polynesians. The evidence that extinction was a direct result of human hunting seems strong, perhaps with some contribution from habitat destruction and predation by introduced dogs.

In North America, the majority of megafaunal species became extinct in the period 12 500–11 500 BP. This may have coincided with a time of extensive climatic change, but it is also the period when the first extensive signs of human occupation occur. The route of entry is assumed to have been the land bridge over the Bering Strait. Remains of megafauna are often associated with Paleoindian artefacts of the Clovis culture. Evidence for human occupation before this time is fragmentary and disputed, and if there was a human population before this time it must have been small. This temporal coincidence of human arrival and megafaunal extinctions is again suggestive of cause and effect, although the evidence is less conclusive than in New Zealand.

A number of strands of evidence argue against a climatic cause for these megafaunal extinctions. As noted above, the timing of extinctions varies from place to place, and in many cases is correlated with the first signs of human populations. Large mammals suffered extinctions selectively, with no corresponding evidence for contemporary extinctions in vascular plants, beetles, marine phytoplankton or even small mammals. It is difficult to see why large mammals should be unusually vulnerable to climatic fluctuations, particularly as they seem to have coped well with previous glaciations and deglaciations.

Subnatural environments

In these habitats, human influence has caused some change to the vegetation, but the structure of the vegetation is essentially the same – so forests are still forests and grassland is still grassland. As noted in the previous section, many existing forests in temperate latitudes have experienced some human disturbance, so would constitute subnatural environments.

Initial human impacts on forests appear to have created a subnatural ecosystem, rather than leading immediately to complete clearance. In the methods section I have noted the way in which forest clearance produces a decline in tree pollen and an increase in the pollen of species that are not tolerant of competition with trees. Typically, the first signs of clearance involve only a relatively small decline in tree pollen and are followed by forest regeneration. This implies that clearance may have been of small areas (perhaps camp sites) or have involved controlled burning aimed at opening up the forest canopy and encouraging the growth of young shoots to provide more food for herds of grazing ungulates, particularly deer. However, each time an area is burnt, some nutrients are lost through leaching, and repeated burning eventually impoverishes the soil. Evidence of this is provided by buried soil profiles in areas where soils were initially base-poor. After initial forest clearance, these soils became acidic. This was followed by mire development in wet areas (see Box 4.1) and the development of podzols in drier areas. In either case, woodland regeneration was eventually prevented, and on the drier soils *Calluna* heath frequently developed.

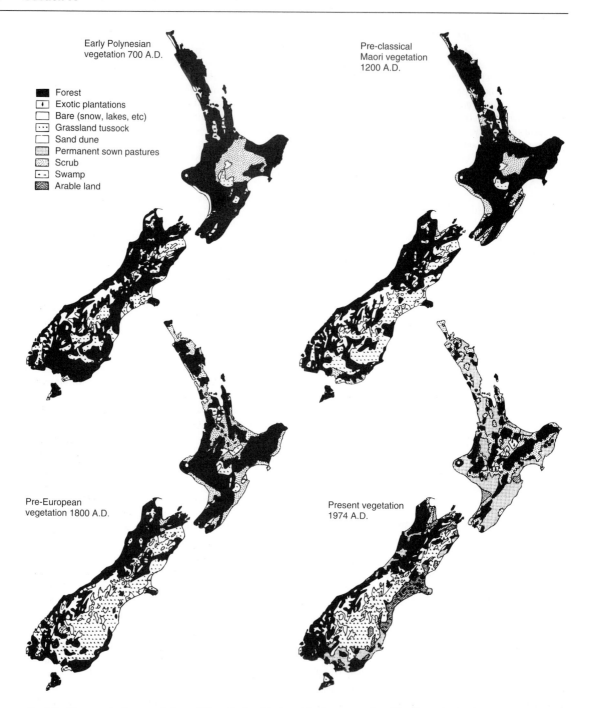

Fig 4.1. Changes in the vegetation of New Zealand induced by human action. The first map indicates the pattern of vegetation shortly after human arrival. Even at this early date, some of the coastal grasslands on the east and northeast of South Island are the result of human activity. Extensive forest clearance and the seeding of permanent pastures have taken place since the arrival of European settlers, but before this large areas of forest were replaced by scrub and grassland as a result of the activities of Maoris. (Source: Anderson, 1977.)

Seminatural environments

Here the basic type of vegetation has been altered, but there has been no intentional alteration of the species' composition: the species that occur are there spontaneously. Large areas of non-arable land would fall into this category. By far the most common alteration to vegetation structure is deforestation, resulting in a range of vegetation types. These include the sclerophyllous scrub known as maquis or chapparal in areas with a Mediterranean climate; blanket mires in upland areas with high rainfall; and a range of grasslands and heathlands elsewhere. Some of the new ecosystems which have been created, such as chalk grasslands, heathlands and grazing marshes can support diverse communities and have high conservation value. They are in most cases, however, not natural, although heathland develops naturally in the landward part of some sand dunes, and chalk grasslands may have developed from tundra on soils too thin to support tree growth. But other seminatural environments are severely degraded, and support rather few species of animal or plant – these would include the vegetation that develops on the impoverished soils left after the clearance of tropical rain forests (see Box 4.3) and arid areas that have suffered soil erosion as a result of overgrazing.

The first step in the development of grasslands and other seminatural environments is usually forest clearance, which began quite early in the Holocene. There is, for example, evidence of tree felling in the Yorkshire Wolds at 8300 BP, probably indicating the beginning of the creation of chalk grasslands there. If we classify an area as deforested when tree pollen is present at less than 50 per cent of its peak abundance, we obtain dates for forest clearance which range from 3700–3900 BP for much of northwest Scotland to 300–400 BP for the Grampians and the Cairngorms. This point was reached in much of England and Wales by 2100–2600 BP. Elsewhere in the world, substantial forest clearance dates from 3000 BP in Africa, 7000 BP in South and Central America and perhaps as early as 9000 BP in India and New Guinea.

In some cases there is dispute as to the importance of human influence, and thus scope for debate as to whether a vegetation type is natural or seminatural. Extensive areas of upland Britain and Scandinavia are covered by deposits of peat several metres thick known as blanket mires. The accumulation of peat indicates that dead vegetation is being deposited faster than it is decaying, and this is in turn a consequence of waterlogging. Superficially, it appears that waterlogging is a result of high rainfall and that this in turn prevents tree growth. Certainly high rainfall predisposes a site to blanket mire development, but there is considerable evidence that human intervention is necessary too (see Box 4.1).

The most disputed role for human intervention concerns grasslands such as the American prairies, South American pampas and African savannah. Typically, forest gives way to grassland as rainfall declines. The proximate cause of this change is not the level of rainfall in itself, but the influence of fire. In the central plains of the United States, isolated natural patches of woodland occur within the prairies, particularly on escarpments and other sharp breaks in topology. When trees of a wide range of species are planted in plantations or shelter belts, they are able to survive for several decades, including periods of drought, and are also able to reproduce in wet years. The crucial factor is that the occurrence of regular fires favours the growth of grasses over shrubs and trees. The above-ground parts of trees and shrubs represent several years' growth and although some species are able to regrow after burning, their size is restricted and, when kept small, they may be unable to reproduce.

The arguments centre on the extent to which these fires are the result of human action. In African savannahs, there is clear evidence for the deliberate starting of fires by pastoralists to maintain grasslands. There is at least some evidence that the areas covered by the American prairies and pampas may have been increased by similar deliberate burning in the pre-European period. Magellan named Tierra del Fuego from the great number of fires that he observed burning. Fire also plays a role in the conversion of forest to maquis in Mediterranean climates. This has occurred in historical times on the island of Madeira, which was uninhabited until relatively recently. The island was originally forested, but for several years after settlement uncontrolled fires burned throughout the island and the vegetation was quickly altered from forest to brush and grass. Land degradation as a result of overgrazing, particularly by sheep and goats, dates back to the very early days of farming in the Middle East, at about 10 000 years BP.

Although human populations have been very effective agents of forest clearance for thousands of years, the rate of clearance has speeded up recently. After European colonization, North America lost more woodland in 200 years than Europe lost in 2000 years.

Box 4.3 Biodiversity and tropical rainforests

The number of species that have been scientifically described is in the region of 1.4 million. The majority of these species are terrestrial, just over half are insects and about 250 000 are higher plants (Wilson, 1988). We do not know the exact number of species of living organisms on the Earth, even to the nearest order of magnitude. Intensive collections in small areas of tropical rainforests reveal large numbers of previously undescribed species, again with insects dominating. Estimates based on the extrapolation of this type of work indicate that there could be as many as 30 million species in the world, whereas the most conservative estimates put this total at about 3 million. There is concern that many species may become extinct before they have even been described – so-called biodiversity loss. Tropical rainforests have been the focus of concern about biodiversity. Although these cover only 7% of the land surface of the planet, they are biologically very rich and are estimated to contain at least 50% of the world's species. Tropical forests are also being cleared very rapidly (1% of the area is being cleared each year and more than another 1% is being significantly degraded). The number of species being lost as a result of these clearances is unknown.

Why should we worry about species extinctions?

1. *Existence value.* Here, the existence of each species is viewed as good in itself. Views of this sort range from the 'deep green' view that each species is of equal value, and that humans have no right to eliminate any other species, to the more utilitarian view that each species can potentially generate welfare benefits to humans who derive pleasure from ornithology or visits to nature reserves. The latter end of this range places a higher value on the larger and more exciting species, particularly birds, mammals, butterflies and flowering plants.
2. *Economic value.* Other concerns about species extinctions are more explicitly utilitarian, viewing biodiversity as a potential source of economic benefits. Many drugs such as aspirin and penicillin were originally extracted from plants or fungi. Only a small proportion of species have been screened for useful properties, and coverage of tropical plants is particularly poor. If many of these species become extinct before being assessed, we will almost certainly lose a number of useful pharmaceuticals. This concern has spawned the discipline of ethnobotany, which seeks to identify those plants that are used for medical purposes by indigenous people as these are the species most likely to yield useful chemicals.

There is a good economic argument against the clearance of rainforests, as they make very poor agricultural land. Heavy rainfall combined with high temperatures mean that dead organic matter is broken down rapidly and leaching and weathering are very intense. Soils are typically acidic and nutrient-poor. As little as 0.1% of nutrients reach deeper into the soil than 5 cm and the great majority of nutrients are locked up within the tissues of living plants. If the forest is cut down and the vegetation burned, the nutrients released allow crops to be grown. But the nutrients are rapidly leached from the soil and cultivation is only possible for a few years, after which the land is at best suitable for low-density cattle ranching. Regeneration of the forests is very slow both because nutrients have been lost and because many rainforest trees are rather poor at dispersal. Some attempts have been made to compare the economic benefits of clearance with the benefits from sustainable use including collection of fruits, nuts and latex with perhaps limited felling of individual trees. One estimate of the economic benefits from forest clearance (Peters *et al.*, 1989) indicated an initial gain of $1000 per hectare for timber followed by $150 per year for cattle ranching. This compared with an annual income of $700 per annum from sustainable exploitation. However, the financial benefits from clearance usually accrue to a different group of people from the benefits of sustainable exploitation, and it is a very difficult task to devise political or economic mechanisms to prevent the suboptimal path from being followed.

An original area of 170 million hectares of forest, stretching more or less continuously from the east coast of the US to the Mississippi has now been reduced to 10 million hectares. Currently tropical rainforests are being cleared at a rate of about 1 per cent of their existing area per year (see Box 4.3 and Chapter 5).

Cultural environments

This category covers artificial systems, such as arable land, in which the vegetation type is deliberately determined by man. This involves the loss of a previous habitat, which may be natural, subnatural or seminatural. The new system usually has fewer species of plant than the system it replaces and, in consequence, is likely to have a less rich fauna too. In its extreme form this involves the creation of areas dominated by a single species of plant, as takes place when a prairie ecosystem with perhaps 100 species of grass is replaced with a monospecific stand of wheat. The fauna of such environments may be further impoverished by the use of chemical pesticides to control herbivorous insect pests, although it is being increasingly realized that the indiscriminate use of such pesticides also kills the insect predators that help keep pest species in check. 'Improved' grassland spans the borderline between seminatural and cultural. A hay meadow that is cut late in the season supports many species of flowing plant. These are able to persist because the annual cutting prevents encroachment of scrub, but the plants are able to grow to a substantial size and set seeds before being mown. Improvement that simply involves the addition of fertilizer will cause some reduction in diversity as faster-growing plants are able, through competition, to eliminate other species. This is often accompanied by mowing more frequently, and earlier in the season, for silage. This prevents many plants from completing their annual cycle of growth and producing seeds, and reduces the diversity still further. When the meadow is ploughed and planted with ryegrass, we have clearly made the transition to a cultural environment.

Domestication of animals and plants started around 10 000 years ago and the creation of cultural environments presumably began at this time. Approximately 1.5 billion hectares of land are now used for crop production (out of a global total of 14.5 billion hectares). The rate of conversion of land to arable use has accelerated rapidly during the last two centuries – in AD 1700 the estimated area of land used for crop production was only 265 million hectares (Richards, 1990).

Agricultural systems usually involve plants that depend upon human intervention for their successful reproduction. This dependence is a result of both unintentional and deliberate selection. Selection for improved yields has taken place deliberately, but will also take place unintentionally as the strains with the highest yields under a particular set of growing conditions will contribute more seeds to the next generation. There has also been unintentional selection against traits which may be favourable in wild populations but lead to reduced survival in cultivated conditions. These include seed dormancy and spontaneous shedding of seeds. In many cases this has led to the evolution of what are in effect new species – there is, for example, some dispute as to which species is the wild ancestor of maize. A number of other plant species have become

dependent upon human intervention and occur primarily as weeds of agricultural land. These include what are known as crop-seed mimics which have seeds similar in size and shape to particular crop plants. The seeds are collected with the crop at harvest then replanted at the start of the next growing season. They have been subject to the same unintentional selection as occurred during domestication of crop plants. Such species have become much less common in recent decades as a result of the use of selective herbicides, development of mechanical threshing and reliance by agriculture on commercially produced seeds rather than seeds collected from the previous year's crop.

Species extinctions

We now turn from wholesale habitat change to the consequences of anthropogenic changes in terrestrial ecosystems for individual species. Large-scale habitat destruction will lead to local elimination of plant species and of animals which are dependent upon those plants or the habitat type. Even if small reserves of the habitat are left undisturbed, some loss of species diversity will occur – the small area can support only a relatively small population, at least of larger species, and these smaller populations are more vulnerable to extinction as a result of random fluctuations. Smaller populations also have a lower genetic diversity, so may be less well equipped to respond to rare events such as climatic fluctuations or infectious diseases. Research on oceanic islands indicates that the number of species in a particular taxon is proportional to the fourth root of the area of the island (area$^{0.25}$) and a similar relationship holds for islands of tropical forest surrounded by cleared areas. In addition to this species–area effect, it is common for species to be endemic to single islands, and not uncommon, particularly in the tropics, for species to be restricted to a single area of forest. In this case local extinction from this single place represents complete extinction of the species. Even where this is not the case, a series of local extinctions can lead to complete extinction of species.

Extinctions of large mammals

Large mammals and birds have been particularly vulnerable to human hunting, and have often become extinct over large areas as a result. In the UK for example, the aurochs, wolf, wild boar, brown bear and the beaver have all been eliminated in historical times and many other species have had their geographical distributions substantially curtailed. There is also considerable evidence for extinction of many species of animals in prehistoric times as a result of human actions. This is particularly true of the so-called 'megafauna' – usually interpreted as those animals larger than 44 kg (100 lbs). In many cases, particularly on islands, but probably also in North and South America, extinction of large mammals rapidly followed the arrival of human populations, a phenomenon that has been labelled 'overkill' (see Box 4.2).

Species introductions

Species extinctions also occur as a result of introductions of exotic species from other geographical areas. These introduced species then either outcompete native species or, in the case of animal introductions, eat or overgraze them. The influence of the introduction of exotic animals is particularly clearly demonstrated by examples on islands where species introductions have taken place in historical times, as such events are often well documented. Many islands lack large predators, so the introduction of a predator from elsewhere can have severe effects. Flightless and ground-nesting birds are particularly vulnerable. Introduced rats have led to the extinction of a large fraction of bird species on several Pacific islands including Hawaii and Lord Howe Island, and in some cases these introductions were by Polynesian colonists in the pre-European period. On other islands, such as Fiji, Tonga and Samoa, and the Galapagos, the introduction of rats has had little effect, apparently because these islands already supported either indigenous rats or land crabs. On other islands, introduced cats and foxes have been responsible for faunal extinctions. In 1894, the world's only flightless songbird, the Stephen Island Wren, was eliminated by the efforts of a single cat owned by the lighthouse keeper. There have also been extinctions of snail species as a result of predatory snails which were introduced to control another introduced pest, the giant African snail *Achatina fulica*. Introduced species also have deleterious effects on plants. Grazing by goats has had a particularly severe effect on island vegetation, but pigs, sheep and cattle are also responsible for the elimination of plant species. The introduced grass

Imperata cylindrica is currently preventing regeneration of cleared rainforests in Indonesia and Java.

Conclusions

We have seen that as a result of human actions the vegetation of much of the Earth has been altered and many species have become extinct. It is certainly true that increased technological development and an exponentially increasing human population have enabled our species to degrade the environment at a much greater rate in the last few centuries than previously. However, the material presented here demonstrates that human societies with even the simplest of technology are capable of large adverse impacts on the environment. These may take place either accidentally (as with transport of exotic species) or as a result of deliberate actions (forest clearance and megafaunal extinctions). There have, no doubt, been times and places when human populations have exploited the resources of the environment in a sustainable way. The broad picture, however, is that our species has been a substantial and effective agent of environmental change throughout most of the Holocene. The image of primitive societies living in harmony with nature is clearly seen to be a myth. Ancient paganism and Eastern pantheism do not seem to have prevented large-scale environmental degradation in the past. It is wrong to try to promote such world views with arguments based on some lost unity of man with nature for which there is little scientific evidence.

References

Anderson, A.G. (1977) *New Zealand in maps*. London: Hodder and Stoughton.

Arroyo, M.T.K., P. Raven and J. Sarukhan (1992) Biodiversity. In J.C.I. Dooge *et al.*, *An agenda for science for environment and development into the 21st century*. Cambridge: Cambridge University Press, pp. 205–222.

Blum, E. (1993) Making biodiversity conservation profitable: a case study of the Merck INBio agreement. *Environment*, **35** (4), 16–20, 38–45.

Bradley, I. (1990) *God is green*. London: Darton, Longman and Todd.

Brown, K.R. and N. Adger (1993) Forests for international offsets: economic and political issues of carbon sequestration. Norwich, CSERGE Working Paper GEC 93–15, University of East Anglia.

Brown, K.R. and D. Moran (1993) Valuing biodiversity: the scope and limitations of economic analysis. Norwich, CSERGE Working Paper GEC 93009, University of East Anglia.

Ehrenfeld, D. (1978) *The arrogance of humanism*. Oxford: Oxford University Press.

Ehrlich, P. and A. Ehrlich (1992) The value of biodiversity. *Ambio*, **21** (3), 219–26.

Myers, N. (1990) The biodiversity challenge: expanded hot spots analysis. *The Environmentalist*, **10** (4), 1–14.

O'Riordan, T. (1981) *Environmentalism*, 2nd Edn. London: Pion (particularly Chapter 6).

Patterson, A. (1991) Debt for nature swaps and the need for alternatives. *Environment*, **32** (10), 4–13, 31–2.

Pearce, D.W. (1993) Saving the world's biodiversity. *Environment and Planning A*, **25** (6), 755–60.

Peters, C.M., A.H. Gentry and R.O. Mendelsohn (1989) Valuation of an Amazonian rainforest. *Nature*, **339**, 655–6.

Reid, W.V. (Ed.) (1993) *Biodiversity prospecting: using genetic resources for sustainable development*. Washington, DC: World Resources Institute.

Richards, J.F. (1990) Land transformation. In B.L. Turner, W.C. Clark, R.W. Kates, J.F. Richards, J.T. Mathews and W.B. Meyer (Eds) *The Earth as transformed by human action*. Cambridge: Cambridge University Press, pp. 163–78.

Swanson, T. (1992) Economics of a biodiversity convention. *Ambio*, **21** (3), 250–8.

Williams, M. (1990) Forests. In B.L. Turner, W.C. Clark, R.W. Kates, J.F. Richards, J.T. Mathews and W.B. Meyer (Eds) *The Earth as transformed by human action*. Cambridge: Cambridge University Press, pp. 179–201.

Wilson, E.O. (Ed.) (1988) *Biodiversity*. Washington, DC: National Academy Press.

Further reading

Bush, M.B. and J.R. Flenley (1987) The age of British chalk grasslands. *Nature*, **329**, 434–6.

Folke, C., C. Perrings, S.A. McNeeley and N. Myers (Eds) (1993) Biodiversity: ecology, economics, policy. *Ambio*, **22** (2–8) 62–172.

Mannion, A.M. (1991) *Global environmental change*. Harlow: Longman.

Martin, P.S. and R.G. Klein (1984) *Quaternary extinctions: a prehistoric revolution*. Tuscon: University of Arizona Press.

Moore, P.D. (1975) Origin of blanket mires. *Nature*, **256**, 267–9.

CHAPTER 5

Ecosystem management and environmental ethics

JOHN BARKHAM

John Barkham discusses the obvious but often ignored point that nature exists everywhere – even where humanity has apparently taken over. The wonder of nature lies not just in its beauty and unpredictability, but in its resilience and scope for renewal. A spoil tip, unless wholly toxic, will slowly be covered with weeds. Careful design can camouflage almost any eyesore. There is a valuable job market in ecological restoration of the unsightly, or in the transfer of whole habitats to newly restored sites. The ash fields of Mount St Helens are steadily coming alive again through the miraculous process of colonization. Just as the seemingly devastating fire at Yellowstone National Park cleaned the ground for a new cycle of regeneration, so each catastrophic disaster becomes a living classroom for ecologists. To study the re-establishment of a disturbed habitat is an exercise in exciting discovery. Conservation need not be practised only in the high profile areas of protected sites and game reserves.

If humanity is to survive in anything like a contented state it will have to come to terms with the rights of nature and the responsibilities of ecosystem care. It is not necessary to be a professional ecologist to marvel and to fight for nature's rights. Citizens with conscience and a video camera can do wonders when organized and articulate. The modern environmental revolution will only run its course when the ethic of natural companionship, travelling on the same journey of birth and death in the endless life cycle, surfaces in the consciences and in the behaviour of us all. It is not just a matter of fabulous wildlife films or glossy coffee-table books. They have their place, but they become entertainment rather than a call to act.

The ethic of natural companionship will emerge as people learn to recognize what nature is doing in all aspects of their surroundings and leisure fields, when the cost of living begins to reflect the myriad of indispensable services that tie economy to ecology through its common root 'ecos' – the management of the household, and when laws are developed to extend a philosophical ideal of transpersonal ecology (see Boxes 19.1 and 19.2) into a statutory right of existence. These ecological and legal reformations must, however, be preceded by an extension of our own consciences and self-awareness of the uniqueness of the world we are lucky enough to inhabit.

Three vignettes

Entering the tropical moist forest on the edge of the River Amazon in the southernmost tip of Colombia (Figure 5.1) is a profound experience. The oppressive heat, stillness and gloom, the silence broken only by the periodic high-pitched whine of unseen cicadas in the canopy, reinforce the knowledge that this is a natural ecosystem, developed over thousands of years. It is not untouched by people. There is a long history of Indian occupation – small numbers of people living beside the creeks and, with their intimate knowledge of the plants and animals of the forest, using and affecting its component species.

However, as I walk slowly along the indistinct trail among what feels like an endless collection of dark green house-plants, all looking much alike to the untrained eye, I am aware that despite the Indian knowledge, no one from our scientific culture knows what plants are here. A very few specialist botanists, if they were brought here, might be able to identify possibly a majority of

Fig 5.1 Creek edge, forest trees and lianes in the Amacayacu National Park, Colombia.

plants. An inventory of trees in similar forest 1000 km down the Amazon in Brazil suggests we should expect to find up to 200 different species in any single hectare. A similar count of butterflies just upstream in Peru yielded some 1200 species in only 55 km^2 – more than in the whole of North America. Over 400 species of bird have been recorded along just this 2 km of trail here in the Amacayacu National Park. The thousands of beetles, spiders, flies and other invertebrates are unknown. I am aware that I am certainly seeing species that have never been recorded, whose names and ecological attributes are unknown even to a single specialist.

Between the neighbouring Kings Cross and St Pancras Stations in the heart of London, a noisy and dusty street leads northwards between Victorian walls, warehouses and gasometers. On the left side of Camley Street a refuse collection site emits deafening noise and clouds of dust. Opposite, behind substantial wooden palings, between the street and the Grand Union Canal, lies the 0.9 ha Camley Street Natural Park. Posters and graffiti on the palings leave no one in any doubt that this is a threatened place. It is proposed as part of the terminus for the new rail route to the tunnel linking France and the UK beneath the English Channel, to be developed by the ironically named 'London Regeneration Consortium PLC'.

Inside the palings, beyond the wooden chalet, with its little chairs for children and walls covered with wildlife posters and information, there lie flowery banks, developing woodland and a large pond with reed, iris and teaming insect life. Over 5000 schoolchildren, mainly from the inner city, visit this special place each year to experience a tiny bit of wild nature, often for the first time.

Camley Street Natural Park was developed from an abandoned coalyard by a band of volunteers and staff of the London Wildlife Trust in 1983. The small site was landscaped, the pond dug and some species introduced to give shape and shelter. Most plants and animals, however, have arrived naturally and now there are more than 150 species of flowering plant, 18 fungi and even 70–80 species of spider.

This is a wild place created by human beings in the heart of a city, a sanctuary within which wildlife is protected and children may touch, feel and smell living things. Camley Street symbolizes the need for natural places in a city, something that every developer is expected to provide under modern planning guidelines, yet few do, and even fewer do well because they are often inexperienced and ill-advised.

Fig 5.2 Recent coppice management in an 'island' ancient woodland, Honeypot Wood, Norfolk, England.

I am driving through the intensively farmed arable land of East Anglia. On top of the rather flat boulder clay landscape there is a small bunch of low trees giving a bit of shape to an otherwise undistinguished landscape. What is special about Honeypot Wood?

It is surrounded by cornfields, its isolated 10 ha dissected by a network of old concrete rides – the legacy of its use as a bomb store for the nearby airfield during the Second World War. At this time almost all the trees were felled. Nevertheless, as far as we know, there has never been anything other than woodland here since prehistoric times. Honeypot Wood owes its survival for at least 700 years to its usefulness, supplying round-wood for local farm and garden use, together with building timber from trees cut on a longer rotation.

Honeypot Wood provides a direct link with the *wildwood* which used to cover the whole of eastern England before its clearance for agriculture. Many of its species of plant and insect are known only from places such as this with their long continuity of history.

Now, with most of the surrounding hedges removed, which once linked the wood with other similar sites, its flora and fauna are more isolated than ever before (Figure 5.2).

There are other sorts of linkage though. Its value to the local community is not primarily through its wood products any more – though these are still marketed – but rather through its accessibility to everyone as a nature reserve owned and managed by the county nature conservation organization, the Norfolk Naturalists' Trust. It is a haven, like Camley Street, surrounded by human-altered land uses inimical to most plants and animals, accessible to all people, its continuing existence justified by something more than the value of its wood products. The inexorable march of 'progress' has stopped just short of destroying this remarkable little echo of wildwood. This is the same march magnified a thousand times over which, more than a millennium later than at Honeypot, threatens to reduce the great Amazonian moist forest to a scatter of similar isolated sites. Honeypot Wood and the Amacayacu National Park are similar in their historical continuity, similar too in being examples of forest ecosystems; but very different in almost all other ways, not least because the tropical forest stretches unbroken at present some 700 km to the north.

What is ecosystem management?

Ecosystem management is more than safeguarding a handful of isolated remnants of natural plant and animal communities or looking after newly created ones. It is also very much more than a series of approaches and techniques used to produce particular desired outcomes. The word *ecosystem* is a useful shorthand word meaning the plants and animals living on land and in water, interacting together and with the inanimate substances of air, water and soil. *System* indicates that these are dynamic interactions, constantly changing, with each element and species having an impact on the others, either directly or indirectly. The idea of the *global ecosystem* is an acknowledgement of the fact that, taken to its limits, everything in the natural world is mutually dependent – and of course human beings are part of this system too.

It is an inescapable fact that human beings are dependent upon the working of the global ecosystem, or the *biosphere* as it is sometimes called. It is also obvious that the human species has developed a capacity to change the dynamics of ecosystems at a pace and scale surpassing any previous organism on Earth. There are two points worth making about this capacity which are fundamental to our understanding of current dilemmas in managing the global environment:

1. Human consciousness and achievement, in apparently freeing us from the largely deterministic controls that the environment exerts over wild animals, seem to have endowed us with an arrogance which equates with the idea that we are free to *exploit* the environment, at least to the point when it manifestly harms our interests. Uncomfortable consequences of overuse or abuse may be overcome through technological development and better management, particularly if market-based pricing approaches are applied.

2. We are animals, with the same basic biological limitations of birth, growth, reproduction and death as other animals and with the same basic competitive drives towards the acquisition of material resources. *Co-operative behaviour*, where it is shown to occur in the natural animal world, is generally interpreted as behaviour most appropriate for *individual* survival. For human beings, the competitive instinct, both at the individual level and at community and national levels, emphasizes short-term gain, threatening long-term survival. Keeping humanity alive depends upon the evolution of new levels of co-operative behaviour in relation to the use of natural resources and the plight of the less fortunate.

These two points are uncomfortable. Challenging the first is unpopular; suggesting the second draws attention to an unwelcome confrontation with our unconscious competitive drives for individualistic survival. Recognizing these and raising awareness of the implications for each of us and our children's children are essential prerequisites for enabling us to move from environmental understanding and good intentions to the necessary action that will generate sustainable development.

Exploitation and its consequences for ecosystems

The word exploitation means to employ to the greatest possible advantage, to turn to maximum commercial advantage, or to make use of, selfishly or unethically. This combined definition takes no account of the status of the resource being used. It means using it even though it is not known for certain whether what is taken can be naturally replaced. If we use and manage a resource in this way there can be no guarantee of its continuing availability. The trouble is that we know the maximum sustainable yield of very few living resources, because the long-term population dynamics of wild species of natural forests, coral reefs or oceans are as yet rather little understood. Despite very hard work at improving population models, ecologists are sure in very few cases of the proportion of a living resource that can be culled. This is why the *precautionary principle* discussed in Chapter 1 has to be invoked.

Further, if management of a species is based solely upon market forces, rather than upon a flexible and regulated response to sustainable yield, the population may eventually become extinct. This simple model (Figure 5.3) applies for two reasons:

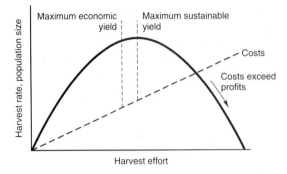

Fig 5.3 The relationship between population size, harvest size and catching effort. For further explanation, see text. (Source: After Clark, 1976.)

1. As long as there is profit to be made, it is worth further investment in the business. Once invested, loss on capital is discounted into the future, so the longer operators stay in the business, the smaller the loss written off.

2. As effort increases beyond maximum sustainable yield, the harvest decreases, and the price per unit rises. The alternatives here are to switch to another resource or, if there is none available, to pursue it to extinction, unless measures are introduced to save the remaining few.

There is now just one individual of the beautiful grey-blue Spix's macaw living wild in a closely guarded valley of NE Brazil. This species has been reduced to the edge of extinction through illegal trapping for the captive bird trade. The fact that determined efforts are being made by trappers to circumvent the protection afforded to this last wild individual by local people, illustrates the escalating monetary value for a rare living commodity. The future of the species now depends upon international co-operation bringing together some of the 22 captive individuals for breeding, with later re-establishment of offspring in the native habitat. It also depends upon fostering among local people the sense of pride and prestige in safeguarding a celebrated internationally rare species. Finally, it relies upon the removal of the market for the species – in effect, for *everyone* to agree that it has no value as a caged bird. If even a few do not accept that, the species could once again be threatened with extinction. Hence the importance of ethics in ecosystem management.

Similarly, several of the great whales have been pursued relentlessly near to extinction (Figure 5.4). Two

Box 5.1 The international regulation of whaling.

The International Whaling Commission (IWC) is a body of 37 countries, all of which have a direct interest in whaling, but not all of which actually catch whales. Each country has a single vote and any decision must be carried by a two-thirds majority. At present, three countries – Norway, Iceland and Japan – actively catch whales: the remainder have a veto over their wishes. In 1983 the IWC banned all commercial whaling, though the ban took three years to implement. In 1993, the three whaling nations tried to resurrect the catching of minke whales and to re-establish the aboriginal catching of whales by native peoples. Both proposals were blocked on the following grounds:

• The actual number of minke whales is not known. The best guess for the North Atlantic is 53–139 000 and for the South Atlantic 0.5–1 million.

• Only when recovery of stocks approaches 75 per cent of original stocks could whaling be contemplated. Since neither of these figures can be guaranteed, the moratorium will continue indefinitely.

• Whales have been exploited for a century. They need a rest from exploitation. In any case, more money can be made from whale watching than whale catching.

factors have so far prevented actual extinction. Firstly, the whaling industry has switched its attentions to alternative more abundant species – from larger ones to smaller ones (blue to fin to sei, Figure 5.4(a)); secondly, the increasing effectiveness of the International Whaling Commission intervened in the otherwise inexorable march of economic logic leading at least to commercial extinctions (see Box 5.1).

These examples illustrate the operation of an outdated and crude economic logic and one that fails to take into account both the long-term costs and those borne by people not directly involved in the market. Such costs *are* taken into account by modern environmental economists (see Chapter 2) who favour the operation of the *precautionary principle* in the management of natural resources. This means that where there is uncertainty about the long-term consequences of current resource use, we should err on the side of caution.

Nevertheless, outlooks stemming from short-term market economics underpin the prevailing attitude to-

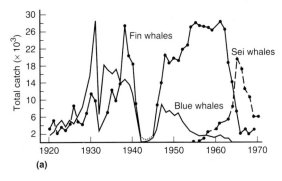

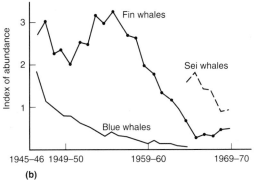

Fig 5.4 The whaling industry: (a) total catches of major species in Antarctic waters, 1920–70; (b) changes in the index of abundance of the same species, 1945–770. (Source: After Gulland, 1971.)

wards the management of our natural resources. They are founded in competitive materialism, itself in part the product of the basic biological drives referred to above. So we are observing, for example, the destruction of tropical forests on the basis of economic incentives that are much to do with brute political power. As noted in the Introduction, economics are not separable from political structures and the abuse of power. Markets do not operate freely: they are heavily influenced by the structure of the economy, the number of firms in competition, the support or hostility of governments and the state of environmental science to guide correctional pricing for natural resource losses. Thus variations of the so-called *free market* promote forest clearance, the disappearance of sea fisheries in various parts of the world, the degradation of marginal grasslands as these are overstocked with domestic grazing animals, and the annual loss of soil eroded from inten-

sively cultivated land managed in the most profitable way.

Another way of describing this approach to managing ecosystems is that it is based on short-term self-interest – blundering along the track until we hit the buffers, then changing direction to repeat the process. The inexorable logic of this process is fuelled by two further factors:

1. The demand for higher standards of living.
2. Increasing numbers of people.

The consequences for ecosystems are:

1. Loss of species, therefore of genetic diversity. Together this amounts to a loss of *biodiversity* (see Chapter 4).
2. Loss of productive capacity: not as much plant and animal material – *biomass* – can be produced.

Ecosystems are remarkably resilient. All of them are subject to natural disturbance. This may be as small as a raindrop sufficient to kill a newly emerged seedling, or as large as a volcanic eruption resulting in the partial or total destruction of hundreds of square kilometres of forest. Disturbance is followed by regeneration – the growth of new individuals or the regrowth of survivors. A rubber band stretched or compressed returns to its original shape. These *negative feedback* mechanisms illustrate the capacity of ecosystems to return towards their state prior to disturbance, to a point where they are similar, if never exactly the same as before. If, however, you stretch or scrumple the rubber band beyond its capacity to return to its original shape, the damage is permanent. So it is with ecosystems.

Populations of the great whales have so far shown no indication of returning to levels similar to those prior to the Second World War (Figure 5.4(b)). Similarly, the Peruvian anchoveta fishery catch (Figure 5.5), having peaked in 1970, shows signs of only partial recovery. It appears that overexploitation of the anchoveta reduced the population to a level from which it has, so far, been unable to recover. It is possible, with the sudden removal of such an important component part of the marine foodweb, that the *structure* of the ecosystem has changed permanently so that return of anchoveta populations to their pre-exploitation levels is prevented by competition from other species or by limitations of resources for growth and reproduction (see Box 5.2 for another example).

These examples demonstrate further fundamental principles of ecosystem management:

Box 5.2 Crossing the ecological threshold: eutrophication

The shallow water lakes arising from medieval peat workings in England called the Broads provide an example of where changes wrought in the structure of the ecosystem have become permanent. Enrichment by phosphorus (P) largely from domestic sewage but, in the case of Hickling Broad, from roosting gulls as well, has stimulated the growth of phytoplankton at the expense of submerged higher plants like water lilies. This change appears to be permanent, even if levels of P input are reduced, and can only be reversed by providing new structures to enable the survival of zooplankton in the face of increased predation. *Sources*: George (1992); after Moss and Leah (1982).

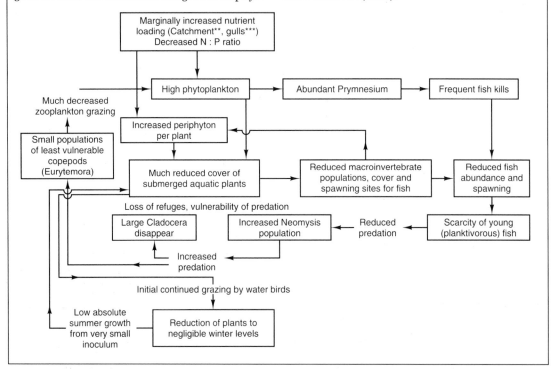

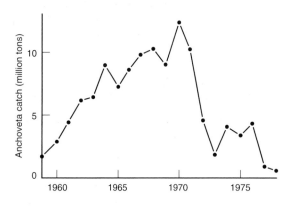

Fig 5.5 The rise and fall of the Peruvian anchoveta (*Cetengraulis mysticetus*) marine fishery off the coasts of Peru and Chile. (Source: After Newman, 1993.)

- Exploitative use of ecosystems reduces options for their future use, either temporarily or permanently.
- The attempt to restore damaged ecosystems is either expensive, or takes a long time, or may never have the required basis of scientific knowledge to achieve it, or all three.

It is not sensible to 'bash on regardless', treating our ecosystems as inexhaustible resources, hoping that 'something will turn up to solve the problem', relying on the 'technological fix' and the ingenuity of humankind to wriggle out of a tight corner. Any businessman with minimal financial acumen knows that to spend capital to cope with rising recurrent expenditure can only be a temporary expedient during a process of cost reduction. It was encouraging to note the establishment of a Business Council for Sustainable Development at

---

Box 5.3 Peat – a sustainable resource?

There are approximately 1.5 million hectares of peatland in the UK, mostly in the uplands. The amount of deep peat in the lowlands is a small proportion of this (4.5 per cent), and only about 3.3 per cent of this remains in a natural state. Most of what has been lost resulted from drainage for agriculture in the 19th century and for forestry in the 20th. In recent years, however, most losses have been due to commercial peat extraction. Peat, used widely in horticulture, is a commercially successful product of the last 30 years, and its extraction leaves interesting areas of wetland and open water with possibilities for a wide variety of recreational uses.

On the face of it, peat might be considered to be a renewable resource and, therefore, that sustainable use of it would be possible. However, the rate of renewal, perhaps about 2 mm/yr, is so slow that commercial extraction far exceeds this limit. The very recent technology of peat-milling means that the rate, and particularly the scale, of extraction is far greater than the capacity of bogs to regenerate. Changes in the hydrology of bogs following extraction, together with doubts about the capacity of the rarer and more sedentary plants and animals to recolonize, mean a permanent loss of biodiversity.

It is doubtful even if small-scale indigenous extraction is consistent with sustainable use. Recent research into the implications of peat extraction for the storage and release of carbon dioxide, one of the greenhouse gases, questions whether any use of peat bogs which disturbs the carbon pool is sustainable.

The nature conservation value of specific bogs is of great significance but the value of all bogs lies in their contribution towards the stabilizing mechanisms of world climate.

Source: Barkham (1993).

Box 5.4

Brazil

Approximate original area of Amazon Basin forest (km^2)	4 550 000	
Approximate present area (km^2)	2 200 000	
Approximate area destroyed so far (%)	52	
Recent rates of destruction (%/yr)	0.4%	1981–85
	2.1%	1987
	1.3%	1988
	2.3%	1989
	0.8%	1990
Approximate area destroyed 1981–91	9%	

United Kingdom

Seminatural ecosystem type	approximate area destroyed 1945–80 (% total 1945)
Lowland neutral grassland	95
Lowland raised mires	96
Lowland calcareous grassland	80
Ancient deciduous woodland	30–50
Lowland heaths	40
Upland moorland and grassland	30

English county	Date	Estimated % loss of number or area of seminatural habitat
Shropshire	1979–89	10.3 (area)
Cornwall	1980–88	11 (number)
Surrey	1975–85	25 (number flower-rich grasslands)
		16 (number heathlands)
Hampshire	1984–89	24 (area chalk grassland)
Gloucestershire	1977–85	33 (area limestone grassland)

---

the United Nations Conference on Environment and Development (the Rio Conference) in June 1992 which gave a powerful message to the Conference that firms that were not *eco-efficient* would not remain in business for long.

The recent popularity of the notion of *sustainable use* of living resources should not disguise its revolutionary nature. It cuts across widely accepted practice, and challenges fundamental tenets of Western culture, society and organization.

Sustainable management of ecosystems

Sustainable use is the opposite of exploitation and embraces a number of interlinked themes:

- Maintaining the productive capacity of ecosystems: this means neither removing organisms nor soil, water or nutrients to such an extent that the weight of living matter produced each year is significantly reduced. It also means not introducing elements into the environment, such as a wide range of pollutants, that have the same effect.

- Using ecosystems in such a way as to keep options for future use open: this means managing as above but, in addition, ensuring that species richness, the number of species per unit area, is maintained. Those that are of no economic value now may become so later.
- Maintaining crop systems without recourse to resources acquired at the expense of maintaining other ecosystems elsewhere – not robbing Peter to pay Paul. Thus to mine peat in order to maintain urban, garden and greenhouse ecosystems is unacceptable (see Box 5.3).

It is common sense to maintain the productive capacity of ecosystems and to keep management options open for future generations. Why this has not in general happened and how economists are now incorporating the future costs of present activity is explained in Chapters 2 and 3.

Here is where the economist and the ecologist need to co-operate further. Right now, the ecologist tries to tell the economist when a maximum sustainable yield is reached and what functions ecosystems play in, say, acting as sinks for gases and pollutants. Are these real utilities for which society should be prepared to pay – for the cost of losing these functions and trying to replace them artificially could be far greater. Thus the economist can place a value on the very usefulness of ecosystems and help society to manage them sustainably.

Global issues and local action

Global issues of ecosystem management now figure so prominently in the media that it is easy for us to be caught believing that *our* house is in order and that we need to tell other countries what to do. So we find Norway pressing the United Kingdom to reduce power station sulphur emissions which have resulted in the acidification of their lakes and rivers, while at the same time supporting efforts at re-establishing the whaling industry. Similarly, the UK, along with other Western nations, is putting pressure on Brazil to halt tropical forest destruction and to introduce measures for its sustainable use; at the same time (Box 5.4), latest figures show that in the UK remaining seminatural ecosystems are being destroyed at a rate at least comparable to the Amazonian forests of Brazil.

The immensity, seriousness and urgency of the global issues of ecosystem management that confront

us collude with our hypocritical attitudes towards the activities of other people so that it is easy to fall prey to feelings of despair and powerlessness. In fact, of course, good housekeeping begins at home. In relation to ensuring the sustainable management of ecosystems there is plenty for us to do at three different levels in our own day-to-day living:

1. Changes to personal lifestyle and consumption patterns consistent with sustainable use of natural resources rather than following the prevailing pressures of competitive materialism.

2. Local action to influence community decisions concerned with land use and waste disposal.

3. Government action to provide the legislative and organizational framework and financial incentives necessary to enable and encourage people to take personal and local action towards sustainable use.

These three levels are interdependent. Changes in direction result from an interplay between the individual and the community (Figure 5.6). This cycle of change is already progressing, at different rates in different places. In Box 5.5, some current Western European management problems, responsive actions and their results are recorded. This information illustrates three important points:

1. There is a considerable depth of awareness both at governmental and grassroots levels of ecosystem management problems.

2. Action is being taken to solve a wide range of problems, each important in itself but viewed in isolation from the others; there is attention to detail but no commitment to a radical change of direction,

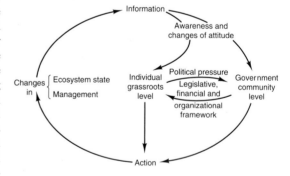

Fig 5.6 Towards sustainable ecosystem management: the interplay between the individual and the community. Arrows indicate effects and changes.

no defined goal or comprehensive strategy which recognizes the *interdependence* of all the components of the living and abiotic environment.

3. Government commitment to international action through binding conventions is weak or non-existent. Global environmental problems by definition require a level of human co-operation for which there is no precedent. This point is covered in Chapter 20.

Ecosystem destruction or changes in approach

The inertia of the predominant ethos of human culture is enormous. It is difficult at present to see how changes will come about which will be radical enough to halt, let alone reverse, the rapidly increasing rate of destruction of the biological resources upon which human civilization is built and will always depend. The human population is rising at present by about 100 million each year, will rise by about 1 billion by 2000 and probably will have doubled by the middle of the next century. This represents huge additional pressures on limited resources. In addition, higher standards of living are demanded by all.

In Box 5.6, two extreme scenarios are outlined. They are drawn together as theoretical endpoints to two different pathways which society might follow. Neither as displayed will come about: elements of both will emerge. There will always be people whose situation and personal psychology lead them more towards one than the other. Furthermore, each of us may behave in ways that are in tune with both scenarios; each of us is full of conflicts. This is why environmental abuse and degradation are so difficult to tackle. So, the words *prevailing ethos* are extremely important. At present, the prevailing ethos is in tune with Scenario 1. To move to a situation where it is more in tune with that of Scenario 2 requires a prodigious change in *attitude.* Attitudinal change in turn depends on awareness- and consciousness-raising, and all of those things on education.

Most important to recognize is that we are able to exercise *choice.* However, as long as we stay on the route towards Scenario 1, we are foreclosing choices all the time as land is degraded, living resources are impoverished and species become extinct. The extent to which global environmental disaster will be in the forefront of awareness-raising will be a measure of how far

we have to move towards Scenario 1 before there is international commitment to the ethos underpinning Scenario 2. Nothing less than a truly international commitment will allow the change. This of course was why the Rio Conference was convened, and why international governmental agreements are so important.

There is no doubt that for the great majority of people in the world, Scenario 2 is preferable, but for a minority, it means very substantial sacrifices of power, prestige and resources. There is no indication yet of a collective or individual preparedness to make such a sacrifice: there are strong psychological underpinnings for this. Alice Miller has vividly demonstrated the links with early childhood experience. Many individuals who have been unloved or emotionally abused in early childhood seek at an unconscious level to satisfy their unmet infantile needs in inappropriate ways during adulthood. One of these is through the acquisition of more material resources than are necessary for healthy fulfilment; another is through attempting to exercise power and control over the lives of others.

This is problematical because at the other end of the scale there are hundreds of millions of people whose basic needs for living are not being met because of starvation, homelessness, lack of parental care and basic civil rights. We know from the work of psychologists and sociologists that the horror and despair of this experience in early childhood provide the roots of violence. A life begun in these conditions is not conducive to the development within an individual of a respect for life, for living things and for natural resources. Those whose childhoods were marked by satisfaction of basic physical and emotional needs behave as adults with genuine caring and compassion towards people and all living things. This ethos is not predominant in the world. It is readily apparent that Scenario 1 is predominant, and that it is the product of a collective and largely unconscious philosophy of violence.

The global priority for ecosystem management is, therefore, to attend with the greatest urgency to the real basic needs of ordinary human beings. Until these are met, action to maintain the structure and diversity of the biosphere can only be locally effective. It is a holding operation and it may not be sufficiently secure for the future because of regional and global environmental changes arising from such phenomena as climatic change and sea level rise. Nevertheless, the need has never been greater for the continuing development and application of sound

Box 5.5 Examples of current strategic problems of ecosystem management in Western Europe, government and non-government agency actions, and changes in management and state of ecosystems reported or expected.

Problem	Action	
	Government	Grassroots
Overproduction of temperate crops	Reduced financial support through Common Agricultural Policy Financial support for Set Aside	
Overdependence of agriculture on chemical fertilizers and pesticides	Research extensification	Demand for organic produce
Reduced farm income	Diversification	Call for environmental subsidies
Continuing destruction of wildlife habitat on farmed land	Financial support for landowners in Environmentally Sensitive Areas Countryside Stewardship Scheme (England)	Farming and wildlife advisory groups Survey and inventory of key wildlife habitats
Low world timber prices, resulting in:		Media interest and popular concern
tropical forest destruction	Beginnings of international discussion	WWF, FoE, Plantlife campaigns
lack of temperate deciduous forest management	New management grants	Development of local timber markets
decline in temperate forest wildlife value		Use of volunteers to reduce management costs
Marine, near-coast nature conservation	Legislation for establishment of marine nature reserves	Campaigning by conservation organizations Resistance of fishing and navigation interests
Habitat on farmed land	Landowners in Environmentally Sensitive Areas Countryside Stewardship Scheme (UK)	Groups Survey and inventory of key wildlife habitats
Road developments	Promotions of new road schemes Statutory protection of special wildlife sites	Anti-road campaigns by conservation bodies Road promotion by road transport and development lobbies

Box 5.5 (cont.)

	Changes taking place
Management	Effect on ecosystem state
Alternative uses Reduced intensity	Little change at present. If long-term commitment, grass monocultures will increase in species richness
Increased organic farming	Reduced chemical residues Increased wildlife capacity, though diversity depends on other land management policies too
More sensitive and appropriate management of farm marginal habitats Priority targeting chalk and limestone grassland, lowland heath, waterside, coastal land, and upland	Maintenance of hedges, ditches, verges, old grassland, small woods, ponds Improved protection of informal fabric of countryside and features not offered statutory protection
Little change. Re-valuation of tropical timber necessary before any significant move towards sustainable logging	Slight slowing of rate of tropical forest destruction in Brazil. No impact on increased rate of destruction world-wide due to Japan
Encouragement of traditional woodmanship; re-establishment of coppice regimes	Direct benefits to a range of forest wildlife favouring short rotation
Little change; largely ineffective Road construction continues	Little change except a few small sites Valuable crop land and wildlife sites destroyed

Box 5.6

Scenario 1: Business-as-usual

	Further implications
Predominant ethos: Competitive materialism Concentration of power among few people, few multinational companies, and few nations Technological development used to reinforce the present distribution of power and resources	
Distribution of resources: Increased inequality:	Rich/poor gap increases Indebtedness increases Famine and social strife increase
Ecosystem consequences: Increased rate of tropical deforestation	Decreased availability and rise in price of wood fuel Increased drought
Increased output of greenhouse gases	Sea-level rise Decreased food output in marginal lands
Desertification of marginal crop and grazing land	Increased soil erosion Increased chemical pollution
Increased intensity of crop production in temperate lands	Increased rate of species extinction
Progressive destruction of marine fisheries	Disruption of marine food chains
Loss of biodiversity	Wildlife increasingly restricted to small and isolated nature reserves

Scenario 2: Change of direction

	Further implications
Predominant ethos: Co-operative; respect for life, empowerment of individual human-scale development Technological development environmentally friendly, in the service of all people	
Distribution of resources: Decreased inequality	First World/North develops massive aid programme in co-operation with Third World/South Financial incentives for resource conservation programmes Community care and maintenance of local natural resources
Ecosystem consequences: Environmental costs of development proposals taken fully into account	Rational planning of natural resource use
Maintenance and re-establishment of tropical forests	Conservation of fuelwood resources
Restoration of degraded land	Re-establishment of diverse and useful plant and animal communities
Conservation of marine communities	Maximum sustainable fisheries yield
Low inorganic input agricultural systems	Minimizing chemical pollution
Maximum ecological diversity consistent with efficient crop production	Diverse and interesting productive landscapes providing links between national parks and wildlife reserves
No human-induced progressive change in world climate	Maintenance of biodiversity and current status of species in existing sites

management based upon scientific ecological principles and knowledge.

Management to maintain biodiversity

Aims and strategies

The goal of the World Conservation Strategy is to find means of satisfying genuine human needs in ways compatible with the healthy survival of the biosphere. The principal objectives are:

- to maintain essential ecological processes and life-support systems;
- to preserve genetic diversity, which is being dangerously impoverished;
- to ensure sustainable use by us and our children of species and ecosystems.

In practice this means that the productive capacity of ecosystems managed for producing food and materials for our use has to be maintained. Overfishing, soil erosion, degradation resulting from pollution, regional climatic changes resulting from forest destruction all result in failure to ensure sustainable use.

Alongside crop and forest ecosystems managed intensively for particular products, it is essential to have natural and semi-natural ones for the maintenance of the resource of wild plant and animal species and the genetic diversity they contain. Managing for biodiversity is variously called *wildlife conservation, nature conservation* or just *conservation*. Central to this work is the attempt to create conditions in which populations of plants and animals are *self-sustaining*. This means that they are able to survive and reproduce naturally, without the aid of re-introduction. The maintenance of species under artificial conditions – animals in zoos, plants in botanical gardens, plant seeds in cold storage – is generally regarded as a last resort from a conservation point of view, performing a potentially valuable role if there is a threat of extinction in the wild (see Box 5.7).

Appropriate strategies for the maintenance of biodiversity need to be considered at a variety of scales. If we start at the world scale, some startling realities emerge (see Box 5.8). Birds are helpful indicators because we know more about their status and distribution than for any other group of organisms. The information in Box 5.8 shows us that by far the greatest diversity of species are dependent upon tropical ecosystems,

---

Box 5.7 The Californian condor

This magnificent scavenging bird was once widespread from British Columbia to Baja California. Its population increased during the period of Spanish cattle ranching during the 18th century. During the 19th century there were reports during the gold rush of settlers shooting 'giant buzzards' and its decline probably began at this time, continuing during the present century until the number of breeding pairs in the wild by 1981 had been reduced to just three, rising to five in 1984. However, during the winter of 1984–85, four of the five remaining breeding pairs were lost. Despite trenchant opposition, it was decided that on balance all remaining birds, including all the unpaired individuals, should be brought in from the wild to support a captive breeding project involving 16 birds already in captivity. This exercise was completed in 1987, resulting in 27 birds being held in captivity in Los Angeles Zoo and San Diego Wild Animal Park. In the following years, chicks began to be produced in captivity – 1988 one, 1989 four, and in 1990 ten. By the end of 1991, there were 52 condors in the two zoos, enough to support an attempted re-establishment in the wild. Thus plans to return individuals to the wild are presently coming to fruition with a number of releases. Unfortunately, three of these have died – one from poisoning, the others colliding with power lines. Re-establishments will, however, continue until there are at least two self-sustaining groups, each of which will contain about 100 birds.

This particular story may have a successful outcome. However, the cost of such an exercise is prodigious and cannot possibly by entertained for more than a very few species. Further, the project will only succeed if the causes of the rapid decline to extinction are reversed in the wild. For most species threatened with destruction this is due to habitat loss through human activity. This means that unless the appropriate habitat is restored, re-establishment becomes impossible. In the case of the Californian condor, almost 100 000 ha of habitat are being protected as a result of the release programme.

The costs of species decline and extinction should be brought into the cost benefit analysis of any development proposal which involves ecosystem change or destruction.

Sources: Birds and *BBC Wildlife* magazines; Gallagher (1990).

---

that most of these are forests, and almost all of them are in Third World countries. Their protection is

---

Box 5.8 Indicators of the importance of the living resources of tropical forests

- 70 per cent of the world's vertebrates, Papilionidae (the swallowtail butterfly family), and higher plants occur in just 12 tropical countries;
- tropical forests contain 155 000 of the 250 000 known plant species;
- 700 tree species were found in ten 1 hectare plots in Borneo, a number equivalent to the total number in North America;
- 90 per cent of all primates are found only in tropical forest regions of Latin America, Africa and Asia;
- one-fifth of all bird species are found in Amazon forests;
- about three-quarters of all Endemic Bird Areas identified by the International Council for Bird Preservation (ICBP) as priority areas for species conservation are within the tropics.

Sources: Lean *et al.* (1990); Bibby *et al.* (1992).

---

crucial and will only be achieved as a result of these countries being able to meet their legitimate aspirations for higher standards of living. This in turn demands changed attitudes of First World countries towards aid. The failure of the Rio Conference to reach agreement on a Forest Convention shows how far there is still to go in developing the political and economic framework that is a prerequisite to the conservation of biodiversity on a global scale. Though there were faults on both sides, a crucial factor in stopping this agreement was the wish of some developing countries to maintain the right to exploit their forests in ways that met their domestic political needs. The conservation of tropical forests is one of the most crucial environmental issues facing mankind during this decade. By the end of it, the die will have been cast and we will have a measure of the extent to which current rates of forest destruction continued and will have reduced global biodiversity for all time.

Despite the overriding importance of tropical forests at the global scale, it is important not to lose sight of the need to safeguard biodiversity both at regional and local scales and away from the tropics. The recently instituted Habitats Directive of the EC is an illustration of essential political and administrative action to enable and to ensure that natural and seminatural ecosystems and the species they contain in 12 European countries are safeguarded. This Directive demands that

each country establishes its own legislative framework to prevent the destruction of areas vital for the conservation of the resource of wild plants and animals within its territory.

At the national and local scale, there are two very different sorts of problem to be addressed if ecosystems are to be managed effectively and the safeguard of species is to be achieved. The first is to determine appropriate organizational and administrative structures. The second, where ecological science makes its crucial contribution, is to determine the management required to ensure the survival of species.

Organizational and administrative structures

Regulatory agencies geared to nature conservation vary strikingly in structure and power in different countries around the world (Box 5.9). This variation often has roots deep in past cultural traditions and attitudes towards the environment. For instance, in the Latin countries of Europe, there is no tradition at a local level of care for local wildlife. Voluntary organizations concerned with the conservation of even popular wildlife such as birds are still in the earliest stages of development in countries such as France and Italy. Attitudes have been traditionally, and remain, exploitative. Wild birds are regarded primarily as free food or sport in the countryside and get shot. By way of contrast, in Britain, a non-governmental organization, the Society for the Protection of Birds, was founded in 1889 and now, with royal patronage, has 880 000 members, owns 120 nature reserves totalling 75 000 ha, and is successful in influencing government and international conservation policy.

The most effective way of developing the administrative and organizational structures necessary to ensure species safeguard is for ordinary people and government to work in partnership. Without the grass-roots support of local communities nothing will succeed in the long term. Similarly, without the protective and facilitative umbrella of government legislation and financial assistance, local community commitment and effort will founder in the face of development pressures. This requires a sophisticated level of communication, a delicate and co-operative dance, rather than an adversarial model involving a constant struggle for power and supremacy either of government over people or *vice versa*. The Groundwork Trusts in Britain are an

Box 5.9 A comparison of approaches to environmental conservation in Britain and Sweden.

Sweden is about three times the size of Great Britain in terms of land area, with about one-sixth the number of people. On the face of it, much greater problems might be expected in relation to conservation in a country as crowded as Britain. However, whereas there are very large areas with very few people in Sweden, the problems of decline and disappearance of key habitats and species are very similar. The wolf (*Canis lupus*) is on the verge of extinction, while other predatory mammals such as the wolverine, lynx and brown bear have also much declined. Conflicts between agricultural and commercial development and the conservation of habitats are similarly commonplace. Furthermore, changes in land use traditions, such the drainage of wet meadows and the abandonment of coppice management (Britain) and wooded pasture (Sweden) have resulted in the decline of important ecosystems.

Legislation for nature protection in the two countries is broadly comparable. However, the way it is administered is different. In Britain, nature reserves are established largely by national agencies, whereas in Sweden local government is responsible for them. However, decisions to establish national parks are taken directly by Parliament in Sweden whereas in Britain the Secretary of State for the Environment is advised by three national agencies, the Countryside Commission (England), the Countryside Council for Wales and Scottish Natural Heritage. The concept of the national park is different in the two countries – that in Sweden being in line with most of the rest of the world, while that in Britain, since it is such a crowded country, embraces areas with long-established agriculture, settlement, roads and industry.

The biggest contrast between the two countries is, however, in terms of the relative importance of voluntary conservation organizations. In Britain, these are of great significance, acquiring nature reserves, influencing land use policy, campaigning for environmental improvement. Many of these bodies are membership organizations. The total number of members of such organizations is believed to be in the region of 4 million, a very substantial political lobby. In Sweden, the government has been traditionally viewed as responsible for environmental protection and for safeguarding the interests of ordinary people. It may be that the need there for a strong voluntary movement has not been so urgent.

example of this kind of development (Box 5.10), as also is the way in which the Amacayacu National Park in Colombia is being protected with the co-operation and full involvement of the local village communities. Setting aside national parks and nature reserves in the teeth of local opposition is not a recipe for success; nor are policies that exclude people from areas whose primary purpose is the safeguard of species in their habitats.

There is a major educational job still to be done and, in most parts of the world, still to be begun in raising the awareness both of national and local governments and of ordinary people, not only about the significance of living resources, but of personal, local community and governmental responsibilities towards them.

Habitat management

Different cultural traditions and different environmental conditions are intertwined to result in differing attitudes towards wild nature. For instance, in North America where there are large, relatively unpopulated areas of dry, cold and mountainous ecosystems, and where for the most part land is publicly owned, there is a strong tradition of protecting *wilderness*. In the UK, on the other hand, densely populated and with hardly a square metre of ground unaffected by human endeavour over centuries and almost all land in private

Box 5.10 The work of the Groundwork Trusts

Groundwork is committed to bringing about the sustained regeneration, improvement and management of the local environment in England and Wales by developing partnerships which empower businesses, local people and organizations to maximize their contributions to environmental, economic and social well-being.

Its small teams of trained environmental specialists act as catalysts and enablers in helping whole communities achieve environmental improvements. The present network of 30 Groundwork Trusts should grow to 50 within the next few years. Most of these are situated in old-established industrial regions where there are significant areas of derelict land and industrial buildings.

Source: Birmingham, the Groundwork Foundation.

hands, there is an equally strong tradition of intervention in and manipulation of semi-natural ecosystems – *semi* because, although they may consist of native species which have arrived naturally, such communities only have tenuous links with those *natural* ones present before the arrival and direct influence of human beings.

To enable organisms to sustain themselves in the wild, it is essential that their *habitat* is maintained. Habitat consists of both the living and non-living components of the environment essential to the life and reproduction of the species in the area in which it lives (Box 5.11). Not surprisingly, therefore, priority is frequently given in nature conservation to the establishment of protected areas, variously called *nature reserves, game reserves* or *national parks* – areas whose primary purpose is the maintenance of natural processes and in which human intervention is minimized. The ideal would be a world-wide network of such areas covering the full range of terrestrial, freshwater and marine habitats to ensure the maintenance of biodiversity.

The Amacayacu National Park, Camley Street Natural Park and Honeypot Wood Nature Reserve are three very different examples of protected habitat, illustrating different objectives and different appropriate management strategies. From an ecological point of view, a crucial difference between the sites is the way in which the process of natural succession needs to be managed. *Succession* is the sequence of changes that take place in plant and animal communities as they develop over a period of time in one place. These changes are responses to a changing environment, largely due to the establishment, growth, reproduction and subsequent death of the plants and animals arriving and living there.

Ecosystem managers have a fundamental choice over whether or not to intervene in the natural process of succession in a particular place. Non-intervention management is appropriate in situations where the end-point of the succession is the desired plant and animal community. This may often be so in relation to forest and marine habitats. In relation to others which are early successional or man-induced, such as most grasslands and heathlands, their maintenance will depend upon human intervention.

The Amacayacu National Park is a large (3000 km^2) area of tropical moist forest, contiguous with a very much larger area of as yet continuous forest in the western Amazon Basin. Forest clearings, varying in size and therefore in the environment they create, are constantly and randomly appearing as a result of fall-ing trees. Despite the unchanging appearance of the forest, probably about 2 per cent of the forest is affected by treefalls each year. They are colonized naturally by species characteristic of early stages of succession, offering temporary opportunities to species requiring direct sunlight at the forest floor. This means that the forest is a constantly changing mosaic, with different parts of it representing different lengths of time since the last major disturbance. No management is required to achieve this. Human impact in the form of the small number of local people dependent upon forest products and making temporary, but larger, clearings for crops is additional to natural disturbance, but affects only the riverine margins of the forest. The management required to maintain biodiversity at Amacayacu is effective protection which involves secure political and administrative status and wardening sufficient to prevent illegal use or clearance of the forest and poaching.

The isolated 10 ha of Honeypot Wood would become very different in the absence of habitat management. Coppice management – the practice of rotational, regular cutting of the straight-growing understorey woody stems developing from long-lived stumps beneath a low-density scatter of large timber trees (Figure 5.7) – was the standard way of treating woods in lowland Britain for hundreds of years, resulting in collections of species particularly well adapted to the regular cycle of light and shade. This is similar to the tropical forest at Amacayacu, but different in terms of the regularity of clearance and the regular appearance of stands of different age moving round the wood, however small. Many characteristic woodland butterflies, for instance, depend entirely upon sunny clearings. The development of the coppice management system may have fortuitously coincided with a deteriorating climate, providing sunny, sheltered clearings in woodlands which, if they had been largely undisturbed, would have become too cold to sustain these species. To break this now long-established pattern of management means to lose the species that have become adapted to it (Figure 5.8). Foxley Wood, a 120 ha wood 16 km away, has lost all four of its fritillary butterfly species in the last 40 years due to the cessation of coppicing (Box 5.12). They have also been lost from Honeypot at times unrecorded and have no chance of re-establishing themselves at either site without the aid of human intervention because of the present isolation of these woods. These butterflies, similar, we may suppose, to so many species about whose ecology we yet know little, have very exacting habitat requirements and have little capability of moving

Box 5.11 Conservation management and the life cycle and habitat of the large blue butterfly (Maculinea arion)

This species illustrates the level of detailed ecological knowledge and understanding that is sometimes required for successful management for the maintenance of a self-sustaining population.

History

It is a handsome, blue butterfly with a wingspan of nearly 4 cm. It was always rather rare in southern England, occurring in isolated colonies on steep, dry, south-facing grasslands, mainly close to the sea. Many colonies were lost to agricultural change during the first half of the 20th century. Then, in 1954, populations of rabbits which were crucial to the maintenance of the short grasslands upon which the large blue depended were wiped out by the disease myxomatosis. Large blue colonies were reduced to a handful. By the early 1970s only a single colony remained and, despite strenuous attempts to maintain the conditions thought to be necessary for its survival, extinction followed in 1979.

Life cycle

The female lays eggs singly in the flower heads of wild thyme (Thymus praecox). The caterpillar emerges after 5–10 days and feeds on the pollen and seeds of thyme for 2–3 weeks during which it completes its skin changes but adds little weight. At this stage it drops to the ground and is found by a red ant which is attracted by a gland which, on stimulation by the ant, exudes a honey-like substance enormously attractive to the ant. The ant then picks up the caterpillar and takes it down into its nest where it becomes cannibalistic of the ant grubs and grows rapidly to nearly full size before hibernating for the winter in the ant nest. After final feeding in the early spring it pupates, still within the ant's nest, only emerging above ground after hatching as the adult butterfly.

Habitat management

It was well known for a long time that flowering wild thyme only thrives in very short grassland turf. What did not become apparent until research in the late 1970s was completed was that, of the several species of red ant that may occur in the sorts of places frequented by the large blue, only from the nests of one species, *Myrmica sabuleti*, do adult large blues emerge successfully. This species of ant requires particularly warm, dry positions for its nests. These result from the bare patches created as a result of intensive grazing and trampling activities of rabbits or domestic grazing animals. As soon as the grass grows long, shade is cast and near-surface soil temperatures drop dramatically. The key, therefore, to successful management is the maintenance of short turf with plenty of bare patches both for wild thyme and for the red ant upon which the large blue is dependent. Failure, for even one year, in maintaining these conditions can result in the extinction of both species from a site.

Source: Thomas and Lewington (1991a).

between isolated sites. As ecologists we have to discover the mysterious and often exquisite life histories, adaptations and responses of species to changing environments. If we know what these are, we can ensure that in what may often be tiny remnants remaining of their natural habitat, we can maintain or re-create the conditions necessary for their survival into the future.

A coppice rotation is a much shortened and modified secondary succession following woodland clearance. This succession is called *secondary* because many of the species involved in the redevelopment of the ecosystem following cutting are already present as cut stumps or growing herbs of the ground layer, and there is a soil with its organic matter and associated decomposer organisms and viable dormant seeds. Intervention management of ecosystems involves initial disturbance, following which the secondary succession has to be managed in such a way as to achieve desired objectives. In the coppiced woodland case, this involves intervention every ten years or so. Heathland may require periodic burning, combined with regular grazing by sheep, while maintaining species-rich grassland demands a mosaic of areas subjected to different combinations of grazing and cutting in order to be managed successfully for different kinds of plant and insect (Box 5.13). This is complex work, dependent upon finely tuned management action, which itself depends upon understanding the complex habitat requirements of a range of species, each with its unique attributes. This illustrates the essential link between successful management and adequate ecological research.

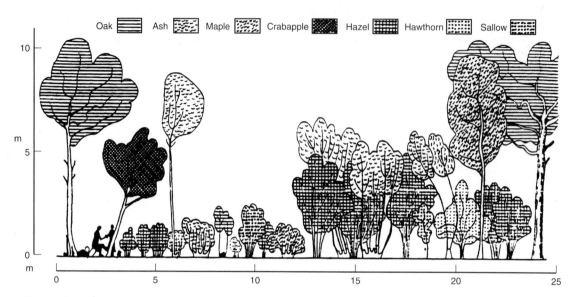

Oak ▤   Ash ▨   Maple ▨   Crabapple ▨   Hazel ▦   Hawthorn ▦   Sallow ▨

Fig 5.7 Coppice-with-standards management—the traditional form of woodmanship in parts of Western Europe in medieval and early modern times. (Source: After Rackham, 1975.)

Box 5.12 The violet-feeding fritillaries of ancient woodland in Britain.

The five species of these attractive orange-brown butterflies, all of which have declined dramatically in abundance during the last 50 years, at first acquaintance provide something of a puzzle in that the caterpillar food plant of each is the violet (*Viola* spp.). It might be expected, therefore, that competition between them would mean the elimination eventually of all but the most dominant. However, in practice, recent research has shown that the conditions under which females successfully lay their eggs and the habitats required by the adults are subtly different for each species. The traditional practice of coppice management provided a rotation around the woods of these micro-habitats which successful conservation management now has to mimic.

All species are absent from mature coppice or shady, unmanaged woodland.

Species	Habitats used	Principal breeding sites
Small pearl-bordered (*Boloria selene*)	Woodland clearings, damp grassland, damp moorland, bracken	Patchy grassland where violets grow in clumps, lush violets in woodland regrowth, 3–4 years after clearing
Pearl-bordered (*Boloria euphrosyne*)	Woodland clearings, dry grassland, bracken slopes	Violets growing in warm ground, 1–2 years after clearing
High brown (*Argynnis adippe*)	Bracken slopes, woodland clearings limestone rock outcrops	Violets growing in warm ground, 1–2 years after clearing
Dark green (*Argynnis aglaja*)	Rough grassland, scrub edges, dunes and woodland clearings	Patchy grassland where violets grow in clumps
Silver-washed (*Argynnis paphia*)	Deciduous woodland with broken canopy and sunny glades	Sunny woodland with an open canopy

Sources: Thomas and Lewington (1991); Warren (1992).

Fig 5.8 Male silver-washed fritillary *Argynnis paphia*—the most shade-tolerant of the five violet-feeding fritillary butterflies of ancient woodland.

Habitat creation

Camley Street Natural Park, where site conditions were created entirely by human intervention, illustrates the principle that what we manage for at the level of the individual site is a matter for *choice*. Some people feel passionately about birds, others about plants or dragonflies or reptiles. Others are not much concerned with rare or unusual species but are more interested in the atmosphere created by living things, a sense of *naturalness*. For this and for specifically educational purposes, for experiencing growing wild plants and moving animals, it is sufficient to have communities of common organisms. These include bacteria and other micro-organisms about which few people get passionate and yet these are important to learn about as they are most crucial in maintaining the structure and functioning of ecosystems through the work they do in energy transformation and nutrient cycling. Thus

Box 5.13 The management of chalk grassland at Old Winchester Hill National Nature Reserve, Hampshire.

The grassland part of the site shown covers about 34 hectares and, like so many nature reserves in England, is an isolated remnant of a once extensive habitat. It consists largely of short grassland on chalk – the white limestone of southern England. This was traditionally maintained by extensive sheep and rabbit grazing. Changing agricultural practice, together with the introduction of the rabbit disease myxomatosis in 1954, resulted in the loss of over 80 per cent of this habitat which is exceptionally rich in invertebrate and plant species. There may be up to 45 species per m^2 of plants. The important communities of invertebrates at Old Winchester Hill include a rich butterfly fauna. There is some conflict of interest between management for plants and for invertebrates. Maintenance of species richness in the former demands regular heavy grazing, while maintaining the latter for many species requires the development of a longer, ranker sward.

To overcome the problem of conflicts of objectives, the reserve is divided into compartments to allow seasonal, rotational sheep grazing to maintain a mosaic of sward heights. The compartment management prescriptions are as follows. They will change as more is discovered about what is most appropriate for particular groups of plants and animals from a continuing programme of long-term monitoring and research.

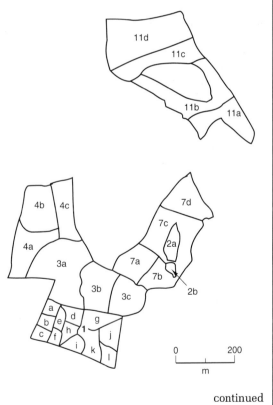

continued

Box 5.13 (Cont.)

Area regarded as grazing unit	Grazing regime	Relevant factors
Compartment 1	A small-scale rotational regime – a little grazing to be carried out in most months of the year on some areas of the slope. Hence division into sub compartments a-1	Need for a mosaic of very short, short and medium length swards. Numerous conservation features requiring conflicting management
Compartment 2a	Occasional short period winter grazing, every 3rd to 5th year	Man orchid and longer sward species
Compartment 2b	Leave to rabbits	'Rabbit-type' turf
Compartment 3	Moderate grazing pressure under a year round rotation	Botanical and butterfly interest of south rampart. Save part as emergency winter grazing
Compartment 4	Moderate grazing pressure under a year round rotation	Cowslip and early purple orchid slope Enough grazing pressure to control dogwood scrub
Compartment 7a, b	July/August (September) grazing on a 2 year rotation	Mossy, damp, north-facing slope with marbled white butterflies. Maintain proportion of fine grass and herbs amongst ranker species
Compartments 7c, d and 11a, b	Winter grazing on 2 year rotation	Naturally short sward butterfly interest on lower slope areas
Compartment 11c, d	Mid-winter graze every year	Keep short for chalk heath vegetation and adonis and chalk hill blue butterflies. Summer grazing very harmful
Compartment 11d	Moderate to heavy grazing pressure with some grazing winter and summer; mosaic of turf heights produced by electric fencing divisions	Control dominant grasses to prevent rankness; good for invertebrates; save part as emergency winter grazing

Source: Courtesy of David Henshilwood, English Nature, Newbury.

newly created habitats are capable of performing important functions, particularly in giving people in urban areas, who are otherwise deprived of it, access to ordinary wildlife.

Habitat creation is a new field stimulating considerable ecological research and experimental management. Not surprisingly, it has developed strongly in developed, heavily populated countries such as the UK and the Netherlands where much seminatural habitat has been destroyed, particularly in the last 50 years. The most important principle to recognize is that the loss of ancient seminatural habitats cannot be replaced by newly created ones. The best that can be achieved is some semblance of what was there before. We now have the ecological know-how to create interesting and attractive flower-rich meadows and lowland heathlands which look to the non-specialist eye indistinguishable from their long-established counterparts. However, we also know from research that there are no short-cuts yet devised for the development of species-rich swards of, for instance, grassland on calcareous soils. The developing and interactive relationship between plant species, and between them and the soil, is a long-term process, enabling us still to distinguish between recent and long-established grasslands after more than a hundred years.

Not surprisingly, therefore, as one cannot yet create or re-create an ancient, species-rich community, there is a developing interest in habitat transplanting – the digging up of a community threatened with destruction and transporting it to a new safe site elsewhere. The ability to do this is obviously attractive to interests faced with valued habitat in sites intended for development. On the positive side, some success has been achieved with grassland plant communities, but less so with their associated insect fauna. A colony of the increasingly rare silver-studded blue butterfly (*Plebejus argus*) was lost in one such attempt at transplanting heathland in southern England. There is no evidence to suggest that something as complicated as an ancient woodland could be transplanted. Its young trees and ground flora pose some technical difficulties which can be overcome, but the soil, developed naturally over thousands of years, poses an intractable problem. Moreover, many of the rarest lichens, bryophytes and insects are associated only with the bark and wood of the biggest, oldest trees.

Even supposing such problems could be technically overcome, there are two further difficulties, either of which may be insurmountable. The first is the unquantifiable dimension of something that is ancient and living. Can it ever be the same once moved? Secondly, the cost is likely to be so enormous that such efforts are likely to be applied only at a very small scale and under very exceptional circumstances.

However, whereas ecological research into the feasibility of habitat transplanting may be regarded as both of marginal importance and politically dangerous in relation to current needs, which are primarily to do with safeguarding what we have, there may in the mid-term be a crucial need for expansion of this sort of research in order to acquire the ability to safeguard biodiversity world-wide. If the threat of global warming becomes a reality, the survival of species now restricted to small islands of seminatural habitat in seas of intensively farmed, forested or urban-industrial land may come to depend upon whether or not they can be moved to new sites where climatic conditions are appropriate. This emphasizes the fact that large numbers of species are relatively immobile, like the fritillary butterflies (Box 5.13), and others are unable to move across large areas of land or water inimical to their needs. Birds are most mobile, while mammals, insects and plants vary enormously according to species.

Externalities in habitat management

The spectre of climate change reinforces the importance of *externalities* in tackling the problems of ecosystem management. These are factors beyond the control of the manager or her/his organization. At present, they are generally features associated with the management of the surrounding land, such as pesticide and fertilizer use on farmland and the drift from these beyond their targets. Such problems can sometimes be overcome by the establishment of *buffer zones* – areas of lesser ecological value surrounding the core of particular interest. In the case of wetland nature reserves, it is not often that management control includes water quantity and quality of the whole catchment area upon which the specific site is dependent. Similarly, air pollution is not contained within the area of source. The effects of acid rain on sites far distant from the source of NO_x and SO_2 are now well established.

Global warming poses an even more intractable threat. A rise of 1.2 °C by 2050 is now being confidently predicted. This means a northward shift in climatic belts of some 200–300 km in the northern hemisphere. Mobile species, such as birds, some insects, and plants producing large quantities of wind-dispersed seeds, may be able to keep up with the rate of change and migrate accordingly. However, for long-lived species such as trees, and more sedentary species of all kinds, the rate of climatic change predicted is far in excess of anything comparable in geological history. Species most endangered now may find themselves imprisoned in nature reserves from which no natural escape is possible. Such externalities threaten to a greater or lesser extent the success of a site-based strategy for safeguarding biodiversity. This has two implications. Firstly, there is real danger in isolating natural and seminatural ecosystems in small island areas from which immigration and emigration is rendered impossible or unlikely for substantial numbers of species. The growing interest in establishing *green corridors* or *networks* of habitats such as hedges and road and motorway verges as part of the fabric of *ordinary countryside* may prove vital in enabling a more natural, flexible response of organisms to changing conditions in the future, to add to the existing value of such linear habitats for the wealth of wildlife interest they already contain.

At an international level, however, this is going to pose some formidable difficulties. It is important to note that the establishment of specifically defined areas as national parks and nature reserves is politically and administratively very convenient. It is a solution to a problem that any politician can understand even if s/he understands nothing about ecosystem management. The establishment of an adequate world-wide network of biosphere reserves is both attractive and, in principle, administratively feasible. It also allows the perpetuation of the dangerous idea in a politician's head that the ecological lobby can in this way be bought off as a special interest group. The idea that the management of both crop and natural ecosystems and natural resources *as a whole* has to be carried out in a sustainable way is much more difficult to put into practice, because it involves the whole of every landscape, ocean and fresh water, and fundamental changes in attitudes towards the natural world.

Species conservation

If we look after the full range of habitats – forests, rocky shorelines, grasslands, rivers, mountains, and so on – across the world, we might expect species to look after themselves. However, we need to check not only that we have an adequate representation of the places where species live, but also that the status of individual species is not a cause for concern.

It is clear that habitat destruction is the single most important factor bringing about the decline of most species and, therefore, that safeguarding habitat is the highest priority for action around the world. There are, nevertheless, other sorts of pressure on particular species arising from human activity in the form of direct exploitation and persecution. Reference has already been made to the economic forces of exploitation that can lead to extinction, for instance of rare birds or whales. Fisheries are examples of the most widespread case of where the habitat needs to be protected principally from pollution and, in shallow waters, from the destruction of the sea-bed by modern trawling methods, but the key action that needs to be taken is to regulate the catch sensibly. The ecological data and predictive models generated from it are becoming available to provide the information necessary for sensible management of most major fisheries, so long as caution is also provided.

There is plenty of breeding habitat in northern Europe for the large numbers of birds that spend the winter south of the Sahara. However, we also have to attend to the habitats used by them in winter and during their extraordinary migration. Particularly important for the insectivorous birds is the semi-arid scrub zone in the Sahel zone south of the Sahara where they 'fuel up' with insect food prior to making the non-stop crossing of the desert. Desertification of this zone as a result of overuse may be having profound effects on the capacity of these birds to make the crossing. Habitat conservation here is as imperative to their survival as are their breeding and wintering places. If they do survive the Sahara crossing, they have to run the gauntlet of the trigger-happy people of southern Europe. The spring and autumn mass slaughter of migratory birds has still to be brought under control.

Migrating animals are inconvenient and expensive to conserve. They do not stay neatly within areas designated to conserve them. The Bonn Convention (Convention on the Conservation of Migratory Species of Wild Animals, 1979) endeavours to provide protection for animals crossing national boundaries. It is not yet very effective because only a minority of nations – and few African ones – have signed it. But it is indicative of the principle that it is only through international agreement that the future of both species and their habitats can be secured.

Rare species have proved very important and successful *flagships* for conservation. The panda logo for the World Wide Fund for Nature is an example of the way an individual species, generally considered cuddly and warm, can be used to promote conservation and raise public awareness. In a more general way birds are used by the British Royal Society for the Protection of Birds as a flagship for their much more general concern for both national and international conservation of biodiversity. Sometimes, as in the case of Spix's macaw, the threat of the imminent extinction of an attractive species can be used to generate action for conservation, not just of that species, but also for other similar ones, together with their habitats.

Conclusions

What then is the overall collective significance of the Amacayacu National Park, Camley Street Natural Park and Honeypot Wood?

Firstly, they are all symbols of that ethos underpinning Scenario 2 – a respect for life – Amacayacu, the wilderness; Honeypot, the fragile, tenuous link with prehistory in a highly developed landscape; Camley Street, the newly created space for life in the middle of urban dereliction.

Secondly, they are places where we can conserve biodiversity, demonstrate appropriate sustainable management practice, and carry out the essential ecological research that underpins successful management, all of which prepare us for a time when sustainable use of natural resources will be closer to common practice. In Amacayacu we are protecting the natural, phenomenally complex, largely unknown web of life of the tropical moist forest; in Honeypot Wood, maintaining a low-intensity management system that is protective of biota associated with ancient woodlands; at Camley Street, creating a rich ecosystem accessible to city people whose immediate environment is otherwise impoverished.

Thirdly, we have to feel that we are capable of doing something, changing something. Without this, we decline into despair and cynicism. The well-known exhortation, 'think globally, act locally' might now be reframed to read 'act globally, act locally'. We have to act locally because that is all most of us can do. We also have to believe that the combined weight of local action – attending to the 'minute particulars' in the words of Norman Moore – brings about significant global improvement. In essence, it will only be through local initiatives that the international, intergovernmental effort to manage ecosystems in a sustainable way can be made to work. Ecosystem management is something each of us must be involved with on our own doorstep.

References

Barkham, J.P. (1993) For peat's sake: conservation or exploitation? *Biodiversity and Conservation*, **2**, pp.556–66.

Bibby, C.J., N.J. Collar, M.J. Crosby, M.F. Heath, Ch. Imboden, T.H. Johnson, A.J. Long, A.J. Stattersfield and S.J. Thirgood (1992) *Putting biodiversity on the map: priority areas for global conservation.* Cambridge: International Council for Bird Preservation.

Clark, C.W. (1976) *Mathematical bioeconomics: the optimum management of renewable resources.* New York: Wiley.

Clark, C.W. (1981) Bioeconomics. In R.M. May (Ed.) *Theoretical ecology: principles and applications.* Oxford: Blackwell, pp. 387–418.

Gallagher, T. (1990) The dawn of recovery. *Birds*, **13** (4), 55–9.

George, M. (1992) *The land use, ecology and conservation of Broadland.* Chichester: Packard.

Gulland, J.A. (1971) The effect of exploitation on the numbers of marine animals. In P.J. den Boer and G.R. Gradwell (Eds) *Dynamics of populations.* Wageningen, The Netherlands: Centre for Agricultural Publishing, pp. 450–68.

Lean, G., D. Hinrichsen and A. Markham (1990) *Atlas of the environment.* London: WWF/Arrow Books.

Moss, B. and R.T. Leah (1982) Changes in the ecosystem of a guanotrophic and brackish shallow lake in Eastern England: potential problems in its restoration. *International Review of Hydrobiology*, **67**, 625–59.

Rackham, O. (1975) *Hayley Wood: its history and ecology.* Cambridge: Cambient.

Thomas, J. and R. Lewington (1991) *The butterflies of Britain and Ireland.* London: Dorling Kindersley.

Warren, M. (1992) Britain's vanishing fritillaries. *British Wildlife*, **3**, 282–96.

Further reading

Barkham, J.P. (1991) Personal psychology and the environmental crisis. *International Minds*, **3** (1), 12–15.

Barrett, S. (1980) Conservation in Amazonia. *Biological Conservation*, **18**, 209–35.

Brennan, A. (1988) *Thinking about nature: an investigation of nature, values and ecology.* London: Routledge.

Elkington, J. and J. Hailes (1989) *The green consumer guide.* London: Gollancz.

Gibson, C.W.D. and V.K. Brown (1992) Grazing and vegetation change: deflected or modified succession? *Journal of Applied Ecology*, **29**, 120–31.

Green, B. (1985) *Countryside conservation*, 2nd Edition. London: Allen & Unwin.

Henderson, N. (1992) Wilderness and the nature conservation ideal: Britain, Canada and the United States contrasted. *Ambio*, **21** (6), 394–9.

International Union for Conservation of Nature and Natural Resources (IUCN) (1980) *World Conservation Strategy*. Gland, Switzerland: IUCN.

King, A. and B. Schneider (1991) *The first global revolution*. New York: Simon and Schuster.

Lovelock, J.E. (1987) *Gaia: a new look at life on earth*. Oxford: Oxford University Press.

Maslow, A.H. (1970) *Motivation and personality*, 2nd Edition. London: Harper & Row.

Meyer, A. and A. Sharan (1992) *Equity and survival: climate change, population and the paradox of growth*. London: Global Commons Institute.

Miller, A. (1990) *Banished knowledge*. London: Virago.

Moore, N.W. (1987) *The bird of time*. Cambridge: Cambridge University Press.

Nature Conservancy Council (1984) *Nature conservation in Britain*. Peterborough: Nature Conservancy Council.

Newman, E.I. (1993) *Applied ecology*. Oxford: Blackwell.

Pearce, D., A. Markandya and E.B. Barbier (1989) *Blueprint for a green economy*. London: Earthscan.

Royal Society for Nature Conservation (1989) *Losing ground: habitat destruction in the UK: a review in 1989*. Lincoln: RSNC.

Sayer, J.A. and T.C. Whitmore (1990) Tropical moist forests: destruction and species extinction. *Biological Conservation*, **55,** 199–213.

World Commission on Environment and Development (1987) *Our common future* (the report of the Brundtland Commission). Oxford: Oxford University Press.

The Earth appears to be a very sophisticated self-regulating organism which functions to create and maintain life. Life is not a by-product, it is an active ingredient in the planetary gyroscope. Natural processes driven by the laws of chemistry, physics and biology seem to operate in extraordinary ways to adjust to the inevitable vagaries of shifts in the Earth's axis, fluctuations in solar radiation, the occasional meteorite impact and convulsive volcanic eruptions. How much these bio-geo-chemical processes actually 'respond' to absorb shock and disturbance remains a mystery over which few scientists are prepared to speculate. But even if the 'responses' are primarily random and unpredictable it looks as if the planetary life-support systems propel creative and adaptive forces that both transform and equilibrate in the fascinating process known as evolution.

Two contrasting views of the evolutionary process are available, views that are less at cross purposes than would appear on first reading. One is that espoused by the evolutionary biologist Richard Dawkins; the other is pursued by the supporters of the 'gaia' idea whose chief advocate is James Lovelock. Dawkins contends that evolution has no particular directional purpose. Chance selection coupled to comparative advantage fashions adaptation and adjustment in genetic traits and behavioural patterns. This is fairly straightforward Darwinism. Selectiveness can operate in a variety of directions, sometimes producing qualities of physiography that go well beyond utilitarian purpose, e.g. antler length and weight, attractive feathered extensions to bird heads and tails. Dawkins and his followers suggest patterns of evolution based on game-playing computer models. These indicate that pure randomness is not necessarily the dominant element in evolutionary development. Organisms both co-operate and compete. Co-evolution means that species adapt in relation to each other, as well as to changing environmental circumstances. Territorial 'fit' is a conscious adaptive mechanism that allows groups of species to co-ordinate to their mutual advantage via a series of collaborative and predatory techniques. Genetic alterations could well be both pro-active and reactive. Species may be able to 'plan' their futures. This could occur with increasing ability to simulate the outside world in a form of internally devised virtual reality. This could develop in an accelerating fashion by building highly sophisticated software and hardware in devising negotiated futures with life forms that, too, are ever more capable of interactive behaviour.

All this is still very speculative, but rather fun. The so-called 'new evolutionary theory' is really a throwback to 19th century ideas first articulated by Lamarck who drew his inspiration from the Dutch philosopher Spinoza. Their view was that evolution is essentially a negotiative process whereby species test out the limits of tolerance of the bio-geo-physical systems which they are both adjusting to and in turn altering by their presence and behaviour. Sometimes they go 'too far' and perish; sometimes they leave too much 'room' and are threatened by other species who enter the niches that remain. Sometimes they possibly 'consciously' adapt their surroundings so as to be better suited to survival and further adaptation. Whatever the mechanism, evolution seems to be most successful when it is co-operative as well as competitive, adventurous as well as precautionary, anticipatory as well as responsive. For the most part, this interaction takes place at the local level. Lovelock believes that it can also take place at the planetary scale.

The gaia idea and its attendant ethics are covered more fully in Chapter

19, and especially Boxes 19.3 and 19.4. At this point it is only necessary to indicate that Lovelock and his followers regard gaia as a scientific notion. They do not visualize the Earth as intelligent or teleological with some sort of divine purpose. They sincerely believe that the Earth is a phenomenal organism in which inanimate and animate processes interact, reinforce and reorganize according to mechanisms that are at best self-regulatory, but certainly not preordained. Hence the sulphur cycle involves physical weathering of rock, volcanic chemistry of gases and lava, biological uptake of marine sulphur salts by algae and precipitation of sulphur-rich aerosols over the land, so continually recreating the inorganic element.

Either way, the Earth functions both organically and inorganically in a truly extraordinary manner. Its biological and physiochemical function are of enormous significance to humanity. No one knows what is the full life-serving value of stratospheric ozone, and hence what would be the 'cost' of depleting it by a quarter or more in net terms. Present net depletion of ozone over the Antarctic is about 7 per cent, hence the significance of the precautionary principle in the international effort to safeguard this sensitive zone over 50 km above the surface of the Earth.

Lovelock has recently speculated that the 'value of the tropical forest' could be as much as the equivalent of the global economy, because of its unique role as an 'air conditioner' cooling the over-heated tropics via the latent heat of evaporation and energizing the weather patterns of the temperate latitudes where so much of global wealth and innovation takes place. Lovelock may be out by one or many orders of magnitude, but his point is still pertinent. Tropical forests are economic assets, far more in their planetary role of regulating of the water cycle and energy patterns, not to mention their unknown species mix, than in their highly short-term commercial timber value.

All this suggests that we need to know far more about the functioning of planetary processes, so that we can be clearer as to their operational role and scope for absorbing the inevitable transformational effects of the colonizing human race. This is the message of the chapters that follow. Climate change is significant because it may alter the capacity of bio-geo-chemical mechanisms to respond to what is relatively speaking very rapid temperature change. Paleoclimatic studies of the fossil record and of the composition of earlier atmospheres as revealed by chemical analyses of fossilized air trapped in ice covers and ancient sediments suggest that there is a close link between carbon dioxide concentrations and global temperatures. Indeed the ice ages fluctuated in association with CO_2 levels, though what exactly caused these variations is still not fully understood. Volcanic activity may have been partly responsible, as might have been changes in photosynthetic activity itself brought on by temperature rise. Chapters 6 and 9 by Keith Clayton – on climate change and sea-level rise – summarize the state of the scientific knowledge and the possible implications for societies and economics of these potentially long-range convulsions in global conditions.

The lesson of Lamarck, Lovelock and Dawkins is that species adapt, compete and co-operate. Humans are the classic embodiment of these facilities. One of the adaptive qualities is the changing role of science in the management of natural resources. The application of science improves understanding and provides markers for adaptive response through monitoring, modelling and the use of indicators.

One of the messages from the chapters that follow is that natural processes are not truly independent of human purpose or intervention. Ecological engineering is a good illustration. It represents the recognition that geomorphological and biological functions can and should be sensitively incorporated into the management of rivers, coasts and hazardous areas such as landslide zones, avalanche areas and seismic traps. Rivers can be left alone, eco-designed or reconstructed depending on their vulnerability or resilience. Similarly, coasts can be reassembled in numerous ways – by building offshore 'reefs' to break the force of waves and to dissipate sediment, by deliberately allowing soft headlands to erode so as to nourish beaches downcurrent, or by recreating sand dunes and their binding vegetation for both recreation and coastal protection. Whereas a decade or more ago engineering tended to be in the form of physical structures that modified natural processes, nowadays engineering is far more ecologically and geomorphologically friendly. In its small way this is a true revolution in both outlook and practice. This is very much a matter of environmental science in action.

At one level this is good news for the environmental scientist looking for a job. Engineering consultancies are looking for ecologists, geomorphologists and economists to expand their areas of competence. Similarly the planning profession is slowly becoming aware of the need to introduce a greater range of environmental sciences into the professional curriculum. The job market is expanding, but more through the wider training of established professions than the broader base of the environmental scientist turned engineer or planner. It is likely that this fairly conservative response to professional 'greening' will expand into a number of applied environmental science management courses at the Masters degree level. The first degree is neither sufficiently broad nor fully sensitized to the intricacies of the law, policy, ethics, economics and planning that is now being called by the participatory version of science introduced in the first chapter. This breed of Masters students hardened in case-studies should be in a far better position than their predecessors to manage the kinds of issue raised in the section that follows.

All this has profound implications for training the environmental managers of tomorrow. Right now there are few truly interdisciplinary courses of the kind outlined in the Introduction. This is easy to understand. Interdisciplinarity is hard work, slow in maturing and very team-dependent. These are not the routeways to individual excellence and established career paths in the reorganized disciplines. Even today, there is a mistaken belief that 'mainstream journals' apply primarily if not exclusively to the description-bound sciences. There is a lot of work to be done in shaping the scientific perspective for today's problem solving.

Within the next five years it is likely that the major research councils of North America, Europe and Australasia will combine to create more specific interdisciplinary training programmes across a range of subject areas. This may emerge as focused methodology-development schools with plenty of illustrative case-study material and access to decision makers. Also, specific interdepartmental research programmes with studentships will probably become more popular. The key to all this is the co-operation between academia, industry, government and the NGOs. We are some distance away from establishing such interdisciplinary problem-solving partnerships. But in the spirit of science capacity building under Agenda 21, their time should come.

The greening of the educational curriculum will slowly span all subjects and all educational establishments. Much can be done by adopting the myriad of pathways towards the great variety of legitimate sustainable development futures, exemplified and revealed through partnership case-studies.

Meanwhile the planning, engineering and financing institutions, along with their regulatory colleagues, will also have to respond to this, largely unnoticed, revolution in resource and environmental management. For the most part, rivers are still being straightened or dammed, coasts skirted by concrete and soil erosion controlled by artificial physical structures at the

---

Box B.1 The 1993 Mississippi floods

By any standards the Mississippi is a mighty river. Like all great rivers, flooding is an intrinsic feature of its existence. For over 150 years US engineers have sought to tame the river and its great tributaries by dams, levees and channel straightening. In 1927, 200 people died and 700 000 were displaced by floods that were worsened by artificial manipulation of the river flow. Major floods on the Ohio River in 1936 and the Missouri in 1957 increased the effort at river conquest, but made more people and property vulnerable behind levees and below dams whose design capacity could always be exceeded.

Between January and July 1993 precipitation in the upper Mississippi Basin was 1.5 to 2 times the norm. In June a stalled depression filled the system to overflowing. In 73 of the 154 recording sites flood peaks exceeded all previous records. More than 1000 levees stretching nearly 6000 miles were either breached or overtopped. The American Red Cross estimated that 56 295 homes were affected by flooding with total property damage estimated at $12 billion. Possibly less than a fifth of the affected properties were covered by insurance, and only half the inundated farmland. Numerous roads, bridges and telecommunications lines were destroyed, together with water treatment plants, propane gas storage deposits and chemical repositories, all lying behind the ephemeral shelter of the floodwalls.

This flood has begun to change the whole approach to flood plain management in the US. Mitigation, in the form of relocating damaged property, is coupled to opportunities for increasing wetland and recreational areas in vulnerable flood plains. Emergency repair is slowly being tied in with long-term avoidance and flood proofing, though this is not always possible in the rush to return to normality. Emergency preparedness, and better siting of hazardous storage areas are being coordinated, as is improved community education programmes and more adventurous use of land use conditions for insurance cover.

Ultimately the Mississippi is untameable. Any levees-only policy of flood protection is bound to fail. The task will not be easy because of the sheer organizational complexity and inter-agency coordination that will be required. Local cooperative ventures linking private initiative to collective action may emerge as a feasible alternative. Meanwhile the Mississippi should be given some room to flow naturally: after all that is what it is designed to do.

Source: Myers and White (1993).

expense of helpful natural processes and supportive local traditions. When these sympathetic and supportive allies are thwarted, they turn hostile. Rivers flood because they are too channelized – witness the mighty Mississippi floods of June 1993 (see Box B.1). Coasts erode because engineered footwalls are undermined by drainage systems on the cliffs. Well-intentioned soil conservation schemes are destroyed because local people are not motivated to remove the sediment or maintain the pumps.

The institutions that manage vulnerable resources are not always designed to permit participatory environmental science. This is partly a product of institutional history – the agencies were staffed by an 'old guard' mentality. But equally it is an outcome of budgetary procedures and cost benefit analysis that tend to favour capital expenditure over recurrent expenditure (dams over tree planting schemes) and definable projects over soft manipulative engineering. As we noted in Chapters 2 and 3, ecological economics is coming of age as a technique, but it is still making slow headway in the cost benefit analysis of river restoration or coastal protection schemes. Finance ministries are wary of the economist's claims of contingent valuation studies, and, if not environmentally trained, suspicious of soft engineered schemes that may not work for ever, or are at least very labour-dependent for their maintenance. So it is not by any means plain sailing. These new approaches still have to prove themselves.

References

Myers, M.F. and G.F. White (1993) The challenge of the Mississippi floods. *Environment*, **38** (10), 5–9.

National Research Councils (1992) *Restoration of aquatic ecosystems: science technology and public policy*. Washington, DC: National Academy Press.

Further reading

The so-called new biology can be visualized in E. Goldsmith (Ed.) (1990) *Gaia and evolution* (Ecologist Publications, Wadebridge, Cornwall). See also D. Dickson (1984) *The new politics of science* (Pantheon Books, New York) and B. Latour (1987) *Science in action: how to follow scientists and engineers through society* (Harvard University Press, Cambridge, MA). James Lovelock's work is best summarized in J. Lovelock (1992) *Gaia: the practical science of planetary medicine* (Gaia Books, Stroud). The Dawkins ideas are found in R. Dawkins (1978) *The selfish gene* (Paladin, London) and in *The Economist* (1993) *The future surveyed* (Economist Books, London). This is a particularly good anthology of futurist writings, admittedly heavily biased in variants of business as usual. The Spinoza connection can be found in P. Wienpahl (1979) *The radical Spinoza* (New York University Press, New York). For a good review of modern environmental philosophy see W. Fox (Ed.) (1991) From anthropocentrism to deep ecology, *Revision*, **13** (3), 107–52.

CHAPTER 6

The threat of global warming

KEITH CLAYTON

In an interesting analysis of how the science of acid rain, ozone depletion and global warming evolved, Kowolak (1993) reached the following conclusions:

- The discoveries evolved over a number of years, in the case of acid rain almost a century, climate warming over three quarters of a century, and ozone depletion over a decade.
- The breakthroughs come almost by accident, but always from a pool of data based on historical trends and supported by boring but vital monitoring and recording.
- Scientists learnt through networks of communication and experimentation. None of these great global problems was diagnosed by a single individual, though in the history of discovery one or two names stand out. In every case it was multidisciplinary workshops and communities of scientists that fully unravelled the mystery.
- Most, if not all, of the science was only partially funded by governments. A substantial part was privately paid for, and some even was done at the scientists' personal expense. Mega-buck science tends to follow rather than precede great discoveries.

On this basis it is a fair bet that the global worries of the next generation have already been discovered. What is missing is the painstaking collection of evidence, the formation of unusual collectivities of scientists, the steady incorporation of the nine stakeholder groups that should dominate the global debate from now on (see Chapter 1), and the reformed role of the media. The media have to act more as lubricators and synthesizers, providing a basis for reaching agreement over common positions, not scaremongers or the peddlers of micro-stories of transient human interest. Curiously it is because environmental matters are diffusing into shapeless topic areas, that environmental journalists are losing out to their agricultural, business or even religious brethren. One of the great paradoxes of environmentalism is its search for integration with daily existence, yet its desire for a sharp focus so as to maintain its momentum.

The climate debate is important in that, along with ozone loss, it is the embodiment of global environmental change. A molecule of greenhouse gas emitted anywhere becomes everyone's business. CO_2, CH_4 and CFCs remain as atmospheric warming agents for 60 years, 10 years and 100 years respectively. So each additional molecule is not just everybody's concern: it is the headache for four generations to come. The fascinating aspect of this globalization of atmospheric warming is that to find a solution, any nation or economic activity need not stop at its own borders. There is every incentive for an emitter to find either a sink elsewhere in the world, or to finance a reduction of future greenhouse gas output from another country if it is to become more efficient at the point of production. These are so-called *offset* (i.e. buying out someone else's greenhouse gases) or *joint implementation* (i.e. investing in greenhouse sinks).

Both of these approaches are enshrined in the UN Framework Convention on Climate Change (see Chapters 1 and 20). In principle, they should become among the most novel and exciting aspects of interdisciplinary environmental science. Any offset or joint implementation scheme requires a knowledge of the radiative forcing role of each gas, of the sequestration rates of various organic systems, of the possible costs of additional amounts of the gas, discounted over four generations, and of the politics and legal aspects of actually ensuring the outcome is beneficial to all parties concerned and the world as a whole.

Such a marvellously interdisciplinary opportunity will not be easy to fulfil. Take, for example, the furore over the measurement of the radiative forcing or global warming potential (GWP) of various gases. This matter was looked at by the Intergovermental Panel on Climate Change (IPCC) in both its 1990 and 1992 reports, but has been subject to a lot of further analysis by Allan Hammond and his associates (1992) at the World Resources Institute in Washington, DC. They tried to produce an index of greenhouse-forcing contributions based on the warming potential of current emissions. This in turn was related to residence time in the atmosphere.

So far, so good. The real trouble arises with estimates of actual emissions. National inventories of CO_2 have been developed but are still guesswork for many countries, notably where deforestation and soil disturbance rates are not known. For methane, the calculation is even more awkward, for rice paddies can emit anywhere from 25 to 170 million tonnes per year, and cattle 35 to 50 kg per year per animal depending on what they eat and how much work they do. In a similar vein, the forcing potential of halogenated substances is very varied depending on composition.

The third difficulty is the ethical question of historical emissions versus current emissions. The Hammond index does not take into account the legacy of emissions over the past 200 years, nor does it try to anticipate the future warming potential of the current crop of emissions. This means that Indonesia and Brazil come high up the index because of deforestation and rice production (Indonesia), most of which is relatively recent, while the contributions of Western Europe and Japan, which includes demand for food and forest products that have increased CO_2 and CO_4 releases over many years, only include current emissions. Furthermore, the index does not take into account the scope for removal by sinks such as biomass, and bio-geo-chemical cycling generally. Part of this process lies in national resources, but an unaccountable element lies in the international commons (see Chapter 19). This poses extremely awkward questions for those looking for tradeable permits or negotiating positions for greenhouse gas removal and burden-sharing, not just because sequestration rates are still not known, but also because of the very great political sensitivities over rights to continue to develop, using the global commons as a free access sink.

On another tack, recent studies suggest that sulphate aerosols, caused by emissions of SO_2 in the troposphere, help to cool the lower atmosphere by reflecting solar radiation before being absorbed and re-emitted by the Earth in the longer and atmospheric-capturing wavelengths (Wigley, 1989). This could depress future warming by about 0.2–0.4 °C over the next hundred years, significant enough for some to talk of future 'cold pools' of differential atmospheric warming. What this does is of course to credit science with thoughtful analytical modelling in the search for greater accuracy of prediction. But for the politician, faced with a possible clamour over carbon taxation or burden-sharing higher emission removal rates to let poorer nations develop non-sustainably for longer, such calculations are unsettling and liable to encourage nitpicking diplomacy and procrastination.

One can see very quickly how science can be ambushed for ideological and political purposes. There will never be a satisfactory and independent greenhouse index. But that does not mean that the effort should not be made to construct one. The fact that the world now has a climate change convention that provides a framework for greenhouse gas inventories and removal tactics means at the very least that thoughtful science has an accommodating institutional framework in which to be of service.

Future global warming: how likely is it?

Global warming is what most scientists currently think will happen as the effect of the additions humans have made to the natural mixture of 'greenhouse gases' in the atmosphere. The greenhouse gases are those that allow the short-wave radiation from the sun to penetrate the atmosphere, but absorb the lower wavelength energy which is re-radiated from the Earth's surface. The process is not really that which occurs in a greenhouse, but the term remains an effective one in public communication. We are unlikely to be able to demonstrate the reality of this warming for another one or two decades, but the predictions of an 'enhanced greenhouse effect' are taken seriously and are the starting point for efforts to bring about international action even before proof is established. If we do not act to reduce emissions promptly, we leave a much more serious problem for the next generation, and were there no action at all, the eventual amount of warming might be enough to threaten not simply our lifestyle, but perhaps even the survival of people in some areas.

As I write in 1993, that is still a statement with which the majority of scientists interested in this topic would agree. But it is not so certain that every scientist supports these views, whilst the implications for how we ought to behave (especially when it comes to burning fossil fuel and perhaps also burning rainforests) are so considerable that many governments are reluctant to concede that anything drastic should be done. Indeed, we have a contrast with the response to the 'ozone hole' in the stratosphere, where scientific proof of change convinced governments enough to bring about an international agreement to reduce the threat, known as the Montreal Protocol. Because both the amount, and especially the timing, of global warming are still uncertain, and the economic effects and the social changes required to limit CO_2 emissions are much greater than those involved in limiting CFCs and halons, it is easier for our opinion leaders to suggest that we may be able to adjust to global warming and indeed that it may be a cheaper and less disruptive option than reducing fuel use.

One particular feature of the debate about the reality of future global warming is the role played by the IPCC, the Intergovernmental Panel on Climate Change. This distinguished panel of international scientists has worked hard over the past few years to produce a series of carefully researched and clearly presented reports on the mechanisms of climate change and the likely rate of future warming. In particular, many of the inconsistencies in the different computer models used to forecast the effects of increased CO_2 levels have been reduced through the international co-operation achieved by the IPCC, so presenting a more convincing case that warming is probable. On the other hand, as we learn more about the very complicated feedbacks within the Earth/atmosphere system, scientists are finding that the rate (though not as yet the long-term amount) of change is likely to be considerably slower than the early reports suggested. This has the dual effect of reducing the apparent certainty surrounding the scientific predictions and also apparently allowing a longer delay before action must be taken. This is not strictly true: slower warming also means slower response to palliative measures, but that's not an easy message to get across.

Box 6.1 The greenhouse gases and their change in quantity since pre-industrial times.

	Carbon dioxide	Methane	CFC-11	CFC-12	Nitrous oxide
Atmospheric concentration	ppmv	ppmv	ppmv	ppmv	ppmv
Pre-industrial (1750–1800)	280	0.8	0	0	0.288
Present day (1990)	353	1.72	0.00028	0.000484	0.31
Current rate of change per year	1.8 (0.5%)	0.015 (0.9%)	0.0000095 (4%)	0.000017 (4%)	0.0008 (0.25%)
Atmospheric lifetime (yr)	50–200	10	65	130	150

Source: Houghton *et al.* (1990).

Box 6.2 The greenhouse effect and the concept of climatic forcing

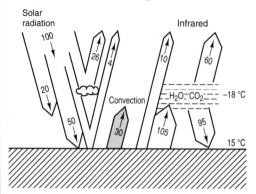

The global heat balance in space.
(Source: Jäger and Ferguson, 1991, p.53.)

This simplified diagram shows that there are two immediate controls on the temperature of the Earth, the incoming solar radiation and the insulating effect of the gaseous atmosphere and its clouds. Although not invariable, the energy from the sun is almost constant and the main climatic changes today are the result of changes in the composition of the atmosphere. The diagram shows the incoming short-wave solar radiation set at 100 units, and 30 per cent of this is reflected by clouds or the Earth's surface. Half the incoming radiation warms the Earth's surface, and this then radiates long-wave radiation (infrared) which passes less readily through the atmosphere, leading to the warming of the lower atmosphere, so that there is a difference in temperature shown here as the 'greenhouse' effect of 33°C. If the absorption by the greenhouse gases increases, this differential will increase. Thus we can build up a warmer surface (including the oceans) and lower atmosphere, which can only occur if the outgoing energy is less than that arriving from the sun. Thus currently the balance shown here is not present, and in energy units, the earth in space receives 240 Watts for each square metre of the earth's surface (W/m^2) and radiates about 236 W/m^2. The surplus of about 4 W/m^2 of absorbed over emitted radiation (the calculated value for a sudden doubling of CO_2) is called the radiative forcing. Over time, the warmer surface will cause a sufficient increase in emitted infrared energy to bring the earth back into balance with the incoming solar radiation – but with a warmer surface than before.

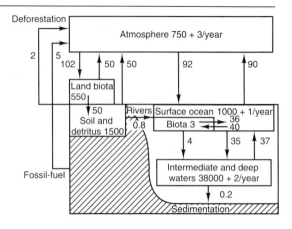

Fig 6.1 The global carbon budget.
The figures show the fluxes between reservoirs and the estimated amount of carbon within each reservoir in gigatonnes (10^9 tonnes). It will be noted that the fluxes balance – this is, however, not easy to achieve and requires a fairly high sink to the oceans and an uptake of CO_2 by increased photosynthesis by land vegetation to balance the estimated loss due to deforestation. Many estimates show a net loss from land vegetation and soils due to forest clearance and desertification. Although it may seem surprising that we cannot accurately account for the fate of the huge amount of fossil carbon burnt each year, it will be seen that the quantity is a small proportion of the total flux and a very small proportion of the carbon tied up in the major reservoirs. In addition, fluxes across the ocean and the land surfaces are extremely difficult to measure on a global basis. (Source: Houghton *et al.*, 1990)

Greenhouse gases and the 'greenhouse effect'

The Earth is in long-term heat balance, receiving radiation from the sun and losing the same amount of heat to space. If there were no 'greenhouse effect' from the atmosphere, the average temperature of the Earth's surface would be –18 °C, but the current average global temperature is close to +15 °C, a difference of 33 °C. This difference is caused by the presence of our atmosphere and is called the 'greenhouse effect' (see Box 6.2). The atmosphere is mainly composed of nitrogen and oxygen, but it is the small traces of some other gases, notably carbon dioxide and water vapour, that are responsible for the insulating effect of the atmosphere.

The flow of carbon dioxide to and from the atmosphere is controlled by a complex series of largely biological processes on Earth and can be represented as a carbon budget (Figure 6.1). The main flows of

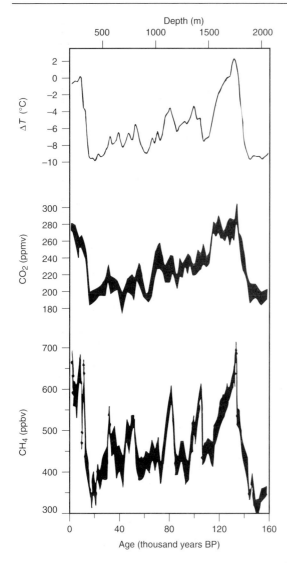

Fig. 6.2 Global ice volumes and CO_2 and methane levels, past 150,000 years.
The values for atmospheric carbon dioxide and methane were measured from bubbles of air trapped in the ice. The ice volumes are derived from measurements of ocean oxygen isotope values, but can be broadly checked from measurements of past sea-level. It will be seen that they move in sequence, but complex feedbacks are involved (larger areas of ice in glacial periods correspond with reductions in the area of tropical rainforest; cold periods mean less active vegetation; for example), so it would be unwise to regard the correlation between atmospheric carbon dioxide levels and temperature as one of simple cause and effect. Thus it may not be used to predict future global temperatures. (Source: Houghton *et al.*, 1990)

carbon are exchanges between the atmosphere and the biosphere, that is to say the plants and animals that live on land and in the sea. Plants consume carbon dioxide in photosynthesis as a source of carbon to grow, emitting oxygen. Animals consume oxygen to live and grow, emitting carbon dioxide (CO_2). Other natural sources of carbon dioxide include gases from erupting volcanoes and natural fires, as well as the decay of plant and animal material. Long-term sinks of carbon dioxide include the fixing of carbon as calcium carbonate in the shells of marine animals which accumulate on the ocean floor as limestones and chalks and the accumulation of plant and animal materials to form peat, coal and oil. In addition, ocean water itself is an absorber of carbon dioxide and it is gradually dispersed throughout the ocean as surface water sinks and moves to great depths as deep ocean currents.

The natural balance of the carbon cycle has changed greatly over the Earth's history, perhaps especially during the ice ages of the last few hundred thousand years. We can study these natural changes by measuring the carbon dioxide in air bubbles trapped in ice deep in the polar ice sheets. This shows that if we plot past atmospheric carbon dioxide levels against past temperature there is a close correlation (Figure 6.2). We might be tempted to argue that these changes in CO_2 in the atmosphere were causing the changes in ice volume, but we believe that the effect of changing global temperature on the biological activity on Earth and on the rate at which ocean waters took up or gave out carbon dioxide (which is linked with the sinking of cold, saline water and the upwelling of deep water to the surface elsewhere) was at least of equal importance. This is supported by the fact that another greenhouse gas, methane, also varies with the same pattern, suggesting that all three curves are being driven by an external factor, in this case the pattern of warming and cooling triggered by the Earth's orbital variations (the Milankovitch effect) and amplified by changes in the bio-geo-chemical cycling of these gases.

Ice cores from the 18th century show carbon dioxide levels of about 280 ppm. The level today (1991) is about 25 per cent higher than this (350 ppm) and measurements made on Mauna Loa, the extinct volcano of one of the Hawaiian Islands, since 1950 show a persistent upward trend (Figures 6.3 (a) and (b)). Hawaii is a good location for such measurements as there are few local sources of CO_2 and the relatively high altitude allows air typical of much of the northern hemisphere to be sampled. Inspection of the Hawaii curve shows a constant seasonal fluctuation, up every northern

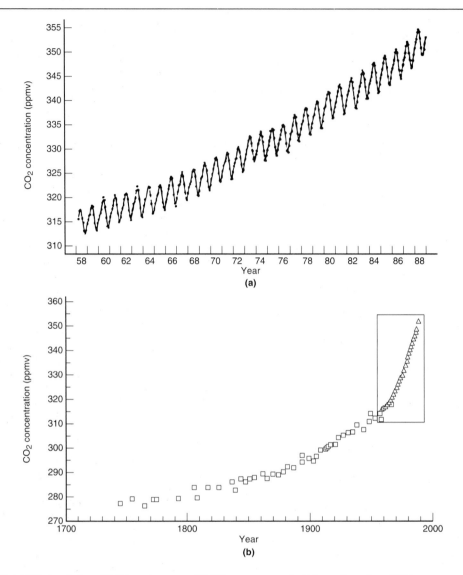

Fig. 6.3 (a) CO_2 level since 1750 from ice cores; (b) CO_2 as measured at Mauna Loa since 1950.
As in the case of Figure 6.2, past levels of atmospheric CO_2 are derived from measurements made on bubbles of air in ice of known age. Direct measurement of CO_2 in the atmosphere has only been made since 1950 at a high altitude site on the island of Hawaii in the middle of the Pacific. This shows both seasonal changes (largely due to the varying seasonal activity of vegetation since most of the world's land is in the northern hemisphere, though with some reinforcement from the burning of more fossil fuel in the northern hemisphere winter) and the long-term trend which is due to the annual addition of CO_2 derived from fossil fuel. (Source: Houghton *et al.*, 1990)

hemisphere autumn/winter, down every spring/summer. This reflects the importance of the land area of the world in the carbon balance, most of the world's land is in the northern hemisphere and the vegetation is more vigorous in spring and summer (so fixing carbon by photosynthesis) and an additional contribution is made by human societies (at least in Europe) burning more carbon in winter to keep warm; again, most of this activity is north of the equator. When the seasonal fluctuation is averaged out, the rise is persistent year on year with the only obvious hesitation in 1974. This was the result of the high price of oil following the

Box 6.3 Sequestration of CO_2 by afforestation

The estimated annual addition of carbon to the atmosphere is 5.4 gigatonnes (10^9 tonnes) from fossil fuel burning and 1.6 gigatonnes from deforestation, though these figures are subject to a margin of error of around 20 per cent. Afforestation of 450 million hectares would lock up 2.9 gigatonnes of carbon annually while it grew in total biomass, this net addition allowing for various related changes in related sinks such as the soil. To plant trees on such a vast area would be an enormous task and certainly more costly than efforts to reduce fossil fuel use through more efficient production and use of energy from fossil fuel and the substitution of energy from renewable sources such as wind and water power. If the UK were to plant 1 million hectares of three-year rotation poplars (as a fuel source) this would only account for 3 per cent of the UK total CO_2 emissions and a mere 0.01 per cent of global CO_2 emissions. These figures also help to emphasize that despite the vast amount of forest clearance that has gone on, and continues today, it is the burning of fossil fuel by the industrialized world that has been the main factor in driving up atmospheric CO_2 concentrations.

Organization of Petroleum Exporting Countries (OPEC) action of 1973: for a time we used over 6 per cent less of such costly oil, and this lower use of fossil carbon was at once reflected in the level of CO_2 in the atmosphere. There could hardly be a more dramatic indication of the role of fossil fuel in contributing carbon dioxide to our atmosphere, indeed this is the kind of evidence on which science thrives. Proof is never absolute, but good measurements applied with sound theory (i.e. a secure understanding of the processes involved in the flows and transformations of carbon) can give us the ability to predict future changes. It is on this basis that public policy can be made with confidence, though inevitably not all environmental science can give such clear and well-found forecasts of future environmental change.

Thus a significant contributor to the increased level of carbon dioxide in our atmosphere is the burning of fossil fuel. Carbon time-warped in oil and coal millions of years ago is being returned to the atmosphere at a rapid rate as we use fossil energy to power our factories, heat our homes and drive our cars. Thus it is the annual transference of some 5 billion tonnes of CO_2 each year from this store sequestered by life on Earth hundreds of millions of years ago, which is now stressing the biosphere to the extent that it cannot quickly adapt. Year by year we transfer more additional carbon into the atmosphere than natural processes can remove, so the proportion of carbon dioxide rises. We also contribute to the present imbalance by clearing vegetation, especially that great sink for carbon dioxide, the tropical rainforest. Disturbance and clearance of forest and the underlying soil releases carbon through burning or natural decay (oxidation), and the reduced area of natural forest reduces the amount of tree growth and thus the uptake of CO_2 from the atmosphere by the natural vegetation. The IPCC estimate that 10–15 per cent of the increase in atmospheric CO_2 is caused by forest clearance, and that almost all the rest is due to the use of fossil fuel.

So far we have concentrated on carbon dioxide as the most important of the world's greenhouse gases. However, although naturally it contributes almost

Box 6.4 The Copenhagen package of the Montreal Protocol

In October 1992, signatory nations to the Montreal Protocol (1987) met in Copenhagen to review the status of phase-out periods for the various ozone-depleting gases. Because further scientific evidence indicated that as much as 40 per cent of ozone over the Antarctic and 12 per cent over the Arctic was being lost during the early spring (when sunlight returns to stimulate photochemical activity) the phase-out was accelerated as follows:

- CFCs – January 1996 from January 2000, with 75 per cent reduction from 1992 levels by January 1994.
- Carbon tetrachloride – January 1996 from January 2000, with 75 per cent reduction from 1992 levels by January 1994.
- Halons – January 1996 from January 2000.
- Methyl chloroform – January 1996 from January 2005 with 50 per cent reduction to 1989 levels by 1994.
- HCFCs – Consumption to be capped in 1996 at 1989 levels plus 3.1 per cent of CFC use in 1989.

Despite these tough measures, ozone depletion will be speeded up in the short term because HCFCs are actually more rapid depleters than CFCs for the first few years of their life. Ozone depletion will continue well into the next century because CFC molecules are active for up to 75 years. It is also important to remember that many of the chlorine- and bromine-free substitutes for existing CFCs may not attack stratospheric ozone, but they remain very powerful greenhouse gases.

Box 6.5 Global warming potential

The global warming potential is a calculation of the possible warming effect on the lower atmosphere of each of the greenhouse gases relative to CO_2. There is also an indirect effect which follows from the reactions within the atmosphere as some of these gases are removed by chemical processes only to form other greenhouse gases. Measurements are still uncertain, but for methane, for example, the indirect effect is certainly positive and may well equal its direct impact. The calculation of future effects is influenced by the lifetime of these gases in the atmosphere – it is rarely the case that they are being added at the same rate as they are removed, and where inputs fall, for example as a result of the Montreal Protocol, the method of removal and their chemical stability will influence the time they stay in the atmosphere (their residence time). These figures are continually being revised as our knowledge improves, and as our sample of the atmosphere improves our knowledge of the dispersal and distribution of some of the relatively rare gases. These uncertainties have implications for policy since it makes it harder for scientists to agree on the extent to which emissions of particular gases need to be reduced if we are to reduce the concentration to some predetermined level.

	Direct global warming potential	Sign of indirect global warming potential	Long lifetime?
Carbon dioxide	1	None	Yes
Methane	11	Positive No	
Nitrous oxide	270	Uncertain	Yes
CFC-11	3400	Negative	Yes
CFC-12	7100	Negative	Yes
HCFC-22	1600	Negative	Mainly no
HFC-134a	1200	Non	Yes?

Sources: Houghton *et al.*, 1992, p. 15; and Houghton, 1991, p. 33.

80 per cent of the effect, other gases are also effective in trapping heat in the lower atmosphere and some of these have been increasing as a result of human activity. Most obvious are the CFCs, chlorofluorocarbon compounds, manufactured to provide stable gases for many purposes including refrigeration coolants, insulation foams, fire-fighting gases and the cleaning of electronic components, as well as the better known use as propellants in aerosols. As recently as 1986, aerosol propellants accounted for about 25 per cent of CFC use, but this has been almost entirely eliminated as substitutes have been introduced. However, their use as solvents and in insulating foam will take time to achieve, though the Montreal Protocol has set out a firm timetable for their elimination. These gases have become notorious through their damaging effect on the stratospheric ozone layer, but they are also very powerful greenhouse gases. Indeed, molecule for molecule they can be around 16 000 times as effective as carbon dioxide, so it is fortunate they remain relatively rare in the atmosphere. Nevertheless, they account for almost 20 per cent of the greenhouse effect (Box 6.4).

Other gases with similar properties include methane and nitrous oxides. Methane is produced by many natural process and increased animal populations on the world's farms are one source, but it also comes from the decay of vegetation, from the release of gas as frozen arctic soils thaw, and from leaks in gas pipelines. Nitrous oxides are produced by a wide variety of biological sources in soils and water. Thus many of these gases too are being produced in increasing quantities as the human population of the world increases and makes ever-greater use of farm animals, motor cars and natural gas. The current contribution to temperature forcing for all 'greenhouse gases' is shown and compared with 19th century levels in Box 6.5.

Predicting the impact of enhanced levels of 'greenhouse gases'

In order to try to predict the effect of increased levels of these 'greenhouse gases' on the world's temperature balance, that future point when all the gases contribute the equivalent of double the effect of the pre-industrial revolution value of 280 ppm is often chosen. This is usually expressed as doubling of CO_2, though in fact by that time the CO_2 level will be about 410 ppm, and it is the additional effect of CFCs, methane, etc, which bring the 'CO_2 equivalent' concentration to 560 ppm. When will this occur?

The prediction of future increases requires assumptions about the continuing rate of economic growth in the world, which in turn drives the use of fossil fuel. Less critical for the calculation are estimates of the future rate of forest clearance. There are problems about our incomplete understanding of the global carbon balance. The IPCC used a budget which does not actually balance, as Figure 6.1 explained. For some time it has been suggested that our estimates of the amount taken up by the oceans was at fault, but this now seems less probable as improved measurements of air – sea exchange and other oceanographic observations increase our understanding of the processes at work. Another possibility is the increased uptake of CO_2 by vegetation as its vigour increases with higher CO_2 levels. It has been suggested that this may be an important part of the full explanation for the missing carbon. However, the IPCC set these unresolved problems aside and adopted a future growth rate which assumes that recent increases in the atmospheric concentration of carbon dioxide will continue (known as 'business as usual' scenario, often shortened to BAU). On this basis, doubling of CO_2 equivalent will occur at about 2030, consequently this date appears in many analyses of future change.

The prediction of the warming to be expected by that date is not a simple matter. Were there no complications, the increased CO_2 would bring about a reduction in the energy loss to space to 236 W/m^2 and this would require a 1.2 °C increase in surface temperature to bring it back up to the balancing figure of 240 W/m^2. However, there are many complications, including the atmospheric global circulation and changes in cloud cover (water vapour is a greenhouse gas, but this is closely balanced by the clouds which it forms which reflect heat from their upper surfaces) and in the albedo (reflectivity) of the Earth's surface as warming reduces the area of snow and ice.

To bring these factors into the reckoning, it is necessary to use the huge computer models known as global circulation models based on the same principles as the numerical models used to forecast the weather. These can be run for long periods on powerful computers to simulate the effects of changed CO_2 levels. Different models give different predictions of temperature rise, so some effort has gone into securing convergence and an internationally agreed estimate of future warming. The publications of the IPCC predict a figure of 1 °C above the present value by 2025 and by then an increase of 0.3 °C each decade, a rate well in excess of anything experienced throughout the natural changes of the last

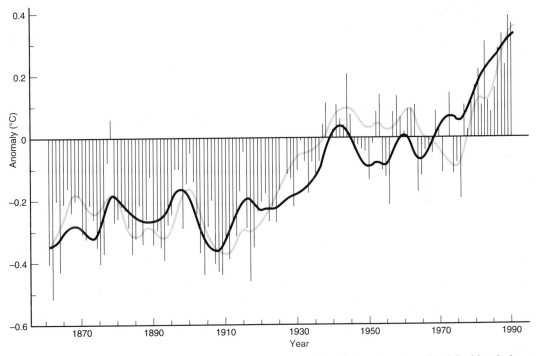

Fig. 6.4 Mean temperature observed over the last 150 years, northern (grey line) and southern (black line) hemispheres. The carefully constructed record of past hemispheric temperatures shows broad agreement between the two hemispheres, though the southern hemisphere is dominated by the oceans, the northern by land and the main area of anthropogenic output of both CO_2 and such pollutants as SO_2. The overall pattern of warming shows complex patterns of cyclical warming and cooling which can be simulated in models which include random elements. If all we had to go on was the past record of global temperature, there would be no basis on which to forecast future trends, up or down. (Source: Houghton *et al.*, 1990)

10 000 years. This would bring total warming since the beginning of the industrial revolution to about 4 °C by the end of the next century. If the figure (a global average) seems small, it is worth noting that the minimum during the last Ice Age was about 5–6 °C cooler than today, and that the warming which has occurred over the last 100 years is a rise of no more than 0.5 °C in the global average temperature (Figure 6.4).

One check on the assumptions made and the techniques used to model future change is to look at the known changes over the last 150 years and to see whether these are 'forecast' by the model when run from a pre-industrial revolution state. When this is done we discover that the predicted rise in temperature is rather higher than that observed, though the match is well within the range of natural variability and thus not inconsistent with the model. Broadly the model predicts a little more than 1 °C warming and the observed amount to date is about 0.5 °C. It is known that the southern hemisphere has warmed more than the northern and it would be encouraging if we could fully understand this. There is more ocean in the southern hemisphere and the land in the northern hemisphere carries the bulk of the world's industrial activity. It has been suggested (Wigley, 1991) that the increase in temperature in the northern hemisphere has been reduced by pollution, the SO_2 produced when coal and oil are burnt offsetting to some extent the effect of the CO_2. The SO_2 produces sulphate aerosols (small particles in the atmosphere) which have a direct effect on the radiation balance, but also an indirect effect through their modification of the albedo of clouds. This makes the forecasting of the effect of increased SO_2 burden complex, but it is thought that this may be the cause of the lag in warming observed when the northern hemisphere is compared with the southern and perhaps also that this century observed warming falls below that predicted from the increase in CO_2 and other greenhouse gases. It also has the implication that current attempts (as a consequence in part of the 'acid rain' problem) to reduce SO_2 emissions (without reducing fossil fuel use) could bring a phase of more rapid warming as we catch up with the model.

Recently, within a set of studies discussing the risks and implications of climatic change, Wigley and others (1992) have discussed the problem of detecting climate change. They note that despite the absence of any evidence that warming is occurring, already many policy makers are moving towards global action. This is the result of the general air of confidence in the public

---

Box 6.6 Climate sensitivity

Climate sensitivity is a measure of the response of global average temperature to a change in the carbon dioxide concentration in the atmosphere. For a doubling of CO_2 equivalent from its pre-industrial levels (which will be reached by about 2030) the range in the early models was from about 1.5 °C to 6.0 °C, though the highest value has now been rejected following IPCC discussions. In the case of the former value, we could burn even more fossil carbon in future years than at present between now and 2030, yet atmospheric warming would not exceed 2.5°C. If the higher values apply, then even if no more carbon were to be added between now and 2030, the temperature rise could still reach 2.5 °C as the world comes into equilibrium with current warming. This measure of climate sensitivity is thus the most critical variable in our estimates of future warming, certainly far more important in the short term than any range of estimates of future carbon dioxide output, and current research is attempting to acquire evidence for the best value to use in our calculations. Most projections show several outcomes utilizing different sensitivities; currently typically the following values are used: low (1.5 °C), best guess (2.5 °C) and high (4.5 °C). Sensitivity is affected by such issues as the increased cloudiness of a warmer Earth and the time it will take to warm the deep ocean. It is also strongly affected by the cooling role of sulphate aerosols; a substantial cooling results in a low figure for sensitivity, a limited cooling effect moves the value towards the high end of the range.

---

statements of the climatic modellers (though the scientific literature is full of caveats), and the chance (for it seems unlikely to be much more than that) that the instrumental record shows irregular but real warming though the past hundred years. So they conclude that detection may well follow decisions to act, but that it could still be helpful in suggesting *how* to act. The key issue is the climate sensitivity, for this will determine both the amount of future change and the effect of various mitigating actions. After discussing many aspects of prediction and detection they conclude that one essential is to improve the present observational network, moving away from a pattern designed to help in weather forecasting to observations of more value to the long-term study of climate. These will include not only the maintenance of long-term data sets, but also the collection of data that define other external forcing factors such as solar output and sulphate aerosol concentrations.

Box 6.7 Triad strategy for improving climate prediction

As discussed in the Introduction science proceeds by trial and error, by testing hypotheses, and by simplifying reality in the form of models verified by observations and by peer review where observations are insufficient. The search is now on to improve the global climate models so that more reliable predictions can be given to policy makers and to economists, lawyers and environmental activists. This lengthy task is moving ahead in three ways:

1. Process studies of cloud feedback, pollutant aerosol feedback, air–ocean gas exchange, ocean mixing and land–air gas exchange. This is fundamental empirical science, and absorbs much of science budgets in global change programmes.
2. Model improvement by relating prediction to the evidence from these detailed process studies, by diagnosing model validation to provide inputs, and by applying satellite observations to estimate cloud – ocean – land variables (e.g. changes in surface vegetation);
3. Model adaptation by assessing the quality of modelling the actual climate variables as these are generated by observational data. This is a continual activity.

The IPCC will update its predictions every 3–5 years. In turn these predictions will be applied to the Conference of the Parties of the UN Framework Convention on Climate Change mediated by its science and technology subcommittee. Thus the very best of the interdisciplinary environmental sciences forms the basis for productive and continuous global policy making.

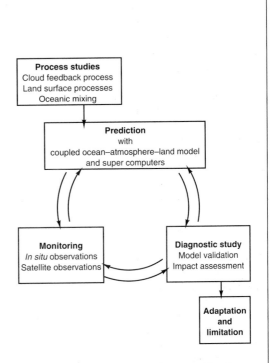

The basis for modelling global climatic change. The diagram shows the mix of simplified models, judgement on the workings of the system, monitoring and observation and evaluation using peer review.

Source: Manabe (1990).

The impacts of future warming

Sea-level rise

The IPCC has indicated one likely result of global warming, an increase in the rate of sea-level rise (Figure 6.5). This is not the result of melting of the major ice sheets in Greenland and Antarctica), but of the melting of smaller glaciers in mountains such as the Alps and the Himalayas and, of equal importance, the thermal expansion of the warming oceans (see Table 9.1). These two effects will cause the sea-level to rise by about 5 mm/yr in future compared with a rate little more than 1 mm/yr today. The predicted contribution from the melting of the large (and thus slow to respond) Greenland ice sheet is only about 12 per cent of the total estimated rise and this is offset by the forecast that at first the Antarctic ice-sheet will actually remove water from the oceans in roughly the same proportion. The reason for this prediction is that at present the Antarctic continent is a cold desert with very low snowfall. As the world warms, so the Southern Ocean will warm, allowing increased evaporation from the ocean and hence greater precipitation in high latitudes. This will increase snowfall on the Antarctic ice-sheet, especially around the margins, but with time even far into the interior. This snow will not melt but will compact to form ice. Only when the slow movement of the ice-sheet has transported it down to the ice margin will it be returned to the ocean. Undoubtedly, this will take

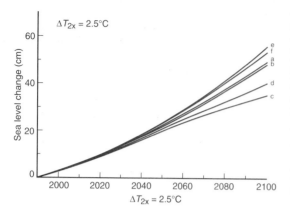

Fig. 6.5 Predicted rise in sea-level as a consequence of global warming.
The forecasts from a to f involve different assumptions about future population growth, economic activity, policies on fossil carbon use, etc. It will be noted that even quite an extreme range of policies produces little difference in the rate of future sea-level rise until after 2040. This half-century lag is both a reason for worry if modified policies are not adopted in the near future and a basis for arguing that, since there are no short-term effects, we can safely delay decisions without incurring early sea-level impacts. Nonetheless, the policies we follow in the first half of the next century will have a major impact on the amount of sea-level rise experienced in the following century – by which time the absolute amount of rise will begin to cause major problems for many coastal communities. The lags in the response of sea-level to changes in atmospheric composition will last for two or three successive generations (see also Figure 6.8). (Source: Wigley and Raper, 1992)

several hundred years, perhaps more. There has also been much discussion about the possibility that the West Antarctic portion of this great ice-sheet might be invaded by the rising sea and melt relatively quickly. This is indeed possible, but again on a timescale of many hundreds of years; it cannot contribute to sea-level rise over the next few generations. Despite scientific confidence about these lags in the huge Antarctic system, there remain individuals who persist in presenting a real long-term risk as a potential threat over the next two or three generations. They emphasize the risk of a large sea-level rise, and neglect the timescale of the lags involved, in order to add to the demand for the precautionary removal of greenhouse gases.

The cumulative predicted sea-level rise of about 30 cm by 2050 is not large, but it will make the problems of erosion and tidal flooding experienced along coast-

Table 6.1 Reductions required to eliminate forcing, 1990

Greenhouse gas	Reduction required (%)
Carbon dioxide	>60
Methane	15–20
Nitrous oxide	70–80
CFC-11	70–75
CFC-12	75–85
HCFC-22	40–50

Source: Houghton and Mers, 1990.

lines all over the world more difficult. The issues are explored in Chapter 9.

Water balance

Although changes in sea-level have received much publicity, problems of water availability (in the ground and at the tap) are likely to be more serious and perhaps more expensive to solve. Here we move from the relative certainty of predictions about future temperature and sea-level to great uncertainty. We can be sure that on average, the future world will be wetter than today, probably by between 3 and 15 per cent. This is because warmer seas will mean greater evaporation and as moisture cannot be stored in the atmosphere for long, more evaporation will mean more rain. However, our general computer models (GCMs) are unable to agree on the distribution of the extra rain in time or space. If areas with too little rain get less than is needed to offset the higher evaporation and plant transpiration (evapo-transpiration) which will be the result of warming, then summer droughts will be more severe. On the basis of current estimates the most likely outcome will be increased aridity in the deserts and desert margins, drier summers in the temperate latitudes, but a general tendency towards a more thundery and erosive rainfall (Gleich, 1992). It is not surprising that the major global conference to establish an international convention to combat desertification was held in 1994. This is when the environmental sciences can come into their own. Hulme and Kelly (1993) suggest that about 20 per cent of the increase of the Sahel is due to factors other than the change in annual rainfall – possibly a combination of overgrazing and the loss of vegetation (and thus change of albedo) due to drying and warming. In short, it is possible that desertification has a feedback effect and reduces regional rainfall, so exacerbating the effects of drought. As yet the models are too primitive to prove this, and much more work has to be done to accumulate further data on rainfall, evapotranspiration, vegetation change and temperature. Hence the urgent need to improve the scientific capacity of the Third World.

As it is, nearly 20 countries in Africa have no irrigation schemes of any size, so future climatic stress will cause many problems and much hardship. This could obviously spell long-term disaster for such drought-prone areas as the African Sahel and perhaps lead to migrations into wetter areas with the threat of increased tension and perhaps local armed conflict. This threat of instability in the Third World may prove to be the strongest pressure on the developed world to adjust its use of fossil fuel, though the arms trade which is already worth over $500 billion annually to the rich world, will doubtless get bigger as a result. Such a conclusion may sound cynical, but intelligence services the world over are interested in GCM predictions, as are the finance ministries.

But many developed countries have demands on water supply that are close to the normal available local rainfall surplus and that already have difficulty meeting needs at time of drought. New York City reservoirs have been very low at times over the last three decades; much of England suffered serious drought in 1975–76 and again in 1990 and 1991. In most areas, abstracted water is stored above ground in reservoirs and more frequent drought will increase the pressure to build more large reservoirs, expensive to build and often resisted by those who lose land. In other areas, aquifers below ground form natural stores, as in England where much of East Anglia, Lincolnshire and the Thames valley depends on water in the chalk aquifer, which is normally recharged for a few months each winter. Dry winters and the increasing water demand of hot and dry summers have led to hosepipe bans in the early 1990s and the threat of worse to come if winter rainfall (and snowfall) should fail again. In the western USA, water allocation is based on the principle of prior appropriation, namely first come, first allocated. Generally this has benefited the agricultural industry at the expense of urban and industrial supplies, as well as the wildlife of rivers and lakes now over-abstracted to meet legal requirements. In the USA there is already a growing battle over the proper price to charge for water to reflect these crucial amenity and wildlife losses. The kinds of calculations discussed in Chapters 2 and 3 reveal that wholesale allocation of water rights and major shifts in prices will be required before too long.

This will no doubt involve lengthy and expensive legal battles.

In a warmer world, summers will not only be hotter, but longer, shortening the period available for winter recharge. Thus even if rainfall does increase by 15 per cent as some models predict, and even if it increases in winter at least as much as in summer, there may be too brief a period for sufficient recharge to meet the increased summer demand. Those living in drought-prone areas will then wish that plans to import water from wetter areas with surplus yield had been implemented more rapidly. Others will demand the kind of reallocative water pricing forthcoming in the USA, coupled with the metering of domestic supplies and social valuation of the minimum flows of freshwater in streams and the conservation of groundwater to maintain discharges at natural springs. It is hardly surprising that there is such an interest in the ecological economics of water charging throughout the world, though it cannot produce surplus water for redistribution where this is unavailable from the climatic water balance. Some areas that currently just make do are going to find themselves short, whatever the cost of water to the consumer.

Natural areas and land use

The uncertainty that surrounds regional forecasts of future precipitation – and especially future seasonal patterns of precipitation and temperature – makes it difficult to forecast the effects of global warming on natural vegetation and fauna. Many nature reserves have been established to preserve plants and animals near the limit of their range, so in future they may either fall well within the natural range, or so far outside it that species that the reserve was designed to conserve will die out. It seems that the bluebell, surely that most English of spring woodland flowers, may well disappear and no doubt many other less showy species near their southern limit will go too. They will be replaced by the immigration of new plants or the increasing dominance of others already here. Bird migration patterns will change and some of our common winter visitors will stay further north than now.

However, our worst problems are trying to forecast the future of agriculture in a warmer world. This matters a great deal, since any major effects on the principal grain-producing regions of the world will have serious implications for world food supply. This would be

Box 6.8 The interrelationship of temperature change, rainfall changes (including seasons) and water availability

In a warmer world more water will evaporate from the oceans and since storage in the atmosphere is not possible, it will fall within a few days as rain. But its spatial and seasonal distribution cannot yet be forecast by GCMs. However, in a warmer world, evapotranspiration on land will increase in the growing season(s).

In tropical and sub-tropical areas, the climate is warm enough for plant growth all year, but savanna and monsoonal areas have restricted growth in a dry season, winter in the tropics and monsoonal zones, summer in the western margin subtropical 'Mediterranean' climates. Temperature change will be less in the tropics and subtropics than in higher latitudes, so the seasonal quantity of rainfall will control future water availability rather than temperature change.

In higher latitudes plant growth is restricted in the winter months by cold temperatures. Growth in the summer season depends on water stored in the soil from the winter season supplemented by rainfall during the summer. Some summers see little rain, and plant growth may be restricted by drought, but in most years the plants are able to survive relatively short periods of water stress. The winter season allows recharge of the soil moisture store, recharge of the groundwater in aquifers and refilling of any man-made surface reservoirs. These stores are drawn on for summer water supply, including irrigation.

If in a warmer world more rain falls evenly across the year, it will allow some increase in winter recharge of storages and thus help to offset the increased demand from a warmer and longer summer. This happy outcome could be offset by the shortening of the winter recharge season as spring comes earlier and autumn is prolonged. But if the rainfall is stable or declines in summer, then the need for increased irrigation to maintain agricultural crops and for all the other demands on water may lead to shortages and the increased frequency of drought. Currently smaller streams can dry up in summer in the dryer areas of the eastern USA and eastern England, this could happen in most years under some warming scenarios with an inadequate increase in rainfall, drastically changing both natural and cultivated vegetation.

A good example of the potential significance of favourable changes in seasonal rainfall in a warmer world is the optimistic scenario for Australia produced by Pittock and Nix (1986). As the figure shows, they predict an increase of at least 20 per cent in productivity for the vegetation of over half of Australia – this assumes not only lower increases in mean annual temperature at lower latitudes (as predicted by global models), but that the increase in precipitation over the year of about 20 per cent is divided into an increase of 40 per cent in the summer and a decrease of 20 per cent in the winter. This is not inconsistent with concepts of changes in the strength of the monsoons, but the map would look far less optimistic if the summer increase were smaller.

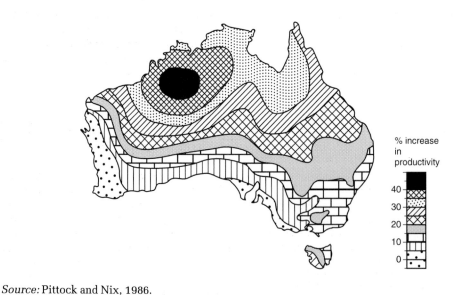

% increase
in
productivity

40
30
20
10
0

Source: Pittock and Nix, 1986.

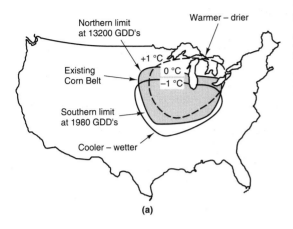

(a)

Unsuitable under all scenarios

Baseline suitability

2×2 CO$_2$ climate: maximum extension

(b)

Fig. 6.6 Maps of future crop distributions for (a) the USA and (b) NW Europe.
The maps are based on rather different assumptions to show how crop distributions will migrate northwards with future climatic change. In many cases, existing efforts of crop breeders to produce varieties which ripen more quickly will amplify these shifts. Less predictable is the impact of future agricultural policies. (GDD's = growing degree days) (Sources: Parry, 1990, and *Geographical Journal*, July 1993.)

difficult enough were nothing else changing, but the main effects on agriculture will not be the changing global environment, but the existing forces of economic policies and the rate of success of the plant breeders. The spread of maize into the UK has been the result of plant breeding, not of climatic change. The northern limit of the sunflower in France is similarly moving towards the English Channel as new varieties are developed. According to Parry (1990) every 1 °C increase in mean annual temperature will shift the current agricultural belts 300 km northward in Europe and 175 km northward in the USA even without the efforts of the plant breeders to improve crops still further (Figure 6.6)

Considerable effort will be put into the improvement of regional forecasts of climatic change (see Box 6.7). To the extent that we are committed to considerable future warming regardless of how quickly we act to try to stabilize current concentrations of atmospheric greenhouse gases, we need to discover where the most serious impacts will be. In this way threats to local food supply may be offset by understanding where higher productivity will be possible. The improvement of these predictions depends on developing 'nested' regional climatic models within the global models (an example developed for Europe is Figure 6.7), as well as improving the GCMs themselves. In particular, the representation of the oceans needs improving as does the coupling of the ocean model to the atmosphere. Other important refinements are the better representation of clouds and the feedbacks they cause. Even the chemistry of the atmosphere is being built into the more advanced models. To achieve all this will take at least ten years. That is too long to risk doing nothing in the meantime, hence the interest in the 'no regrets' strategies outlined in Chapter 17.

What might we do to reduce future global warming?

We have already seen that the discovery of the depletion of stratospheric ozone over Antarctica led in 1987 to the international agreement known as the Montreal Protocol. Although driven by the threat to the protective stratospheric ozone layer (which protects the Earth's surface from harmful ultraviolet radiation from the sun), the Protocol will have the effect of reducing the contribution the halocarbons make to the enhanced greenhouse effect. To some extent this will be

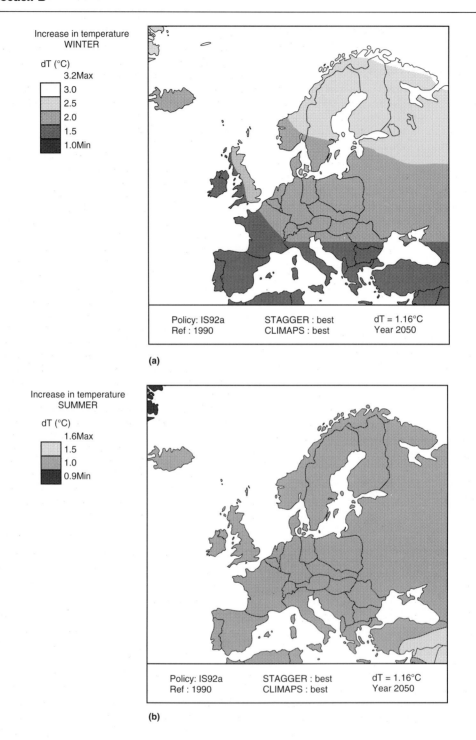

Fig. 6.7 Example of regional prediction for ×2 CO_2.
These maps are derived from detailed regional simulations of future climatic change. (Source: Rotmans *et al.*, 1994.)

offset by substitutes which are less chemically active in the stratosphere, but still possess greenhouse properties in the troposphere.

The immediate outcome of the UN Environment and Development Conference held in Brazil in 1992 was disappointing for those who hoped for early action to reduce our use of fossil fuels. In Chapters 1 and 20, the politics of the UN Framework Convention aimed at reducing non-CFC greenhouse gases is examined. In scientific terms, it is essential to understand the huge reductions that would be necessary to bring about an end to increased climatic forcing. The IPCC estimated the reductions shown in Table 6.1. At present most countries regard such reductions as unattainable, and likely to disrupt the world economy even more than global warming, so a compromise is likely to be sought. Currently the Canadian government is one of the most ambitious with a proposal to seek a reduction in carbon dioxide output to 20 per cent below its 1990 level by the year 2000. The EC aims at getting back to 1990 levels by 2000, though compliance will be difficult to establish since current measurements of CO_2 emissions are estimates and collected by several different methods. It could take up to ten years for the developing world to create the monitoring capacity for carbon dioxide which is needed if future output is to be managed in the light of international targets. Verifiable data collection is thus one of the most important contributions of the environmental sciences in the coming years across the whole spectrum of global change issues.

We need to understand that even were emissions higher than those of 1750 (i.e. the pre-industrial revolution level) to be eliminated tomorrow, there is a considerable 'commitment' to warming in the higher levels of greenhouse gases already in the atmosphere. The world is not in equilibrium with the higher levels of today; it is warming and that warming will continue for some time until equilibrium is reached. Similarly, where the lag between forcing and change is longer, as is the case with sea-level, then the commitment will continue for longer and be larger in amount. Figure 6.8 shows that if international efforts were to succeed immediately sea-level will continue to rise for at least another hundred years, passing 18 cm higher than today before the end of the next century. In other words, even early action on increasing atmospheric CO_2 levels will still leave the next three or four generations coping with changes brought about by the 20th century consumption of fossil fuels. Yet to take effective action and incur the social and economic costs involved in change is difficult when we are still discuss-

---

Box 6.9 The politics of climate science

Warrick and Rahman (1992) observe that four-fifths of the accumulated anthropogenic CO_2 emissions have arisen from the developed world, and about three-quarters of the deforestation-induced CO_2 have come from forest removal outside the third world. Yet a country such as Bangladesh, with 2 per cent of the world's population is currently faced with the gravest danger of sea-level rise, though it adds only 0.06 per cent of global warming. This raises some important ethical issues. Box 6.5 presented the index of global warming attributed to various greenhouse gases. But can a unit of CO_2 emitted by a powerful commuter car in Los Angeles be equated with a unit of methane emitted by a bullock that pulls a plough on a small Indian farm? Is it right that the US, responsible for almost one-quarter of all greenhouse gas emissions, should itself require the assimilative capacities of the global commons of ocean and forest? If trade agreements push more industry powered by electricity towards the lower-cost labour and weaker environmental controls of the Third World, should the additional CO_2 produced in providing this electricity be taxed at the same rate as the declining CO_2 emissions from the industrialized world with its legacy of freedom to emit without restraint or tax until now?

Here is where science, politics, the law and ethics interact. The shaping up of response measures such as forest sequestration, carbon taxes, and coastal flood defence should take note of the fact that greenhouse gases are not emitted by nations into a fair or equitable world. This is why good environmental science has to be both interactive and politically sensitive – yet true to its own traditions and standards.

---

ing an uncertain future change; 'Let's wait and see' is a popular call. Yet others would argue to play for safety and do something now rather than later – the precautionary policy described as 'no regrets'.

Recently one comparison (Pachauri and Damodaran 1992) of the choice between early precautionary action ('no regrets') and 'wait and see' (and adjust if needed) has shown how important the economic models used are in suggesting the outcomes. Here is an interesting analogy of the issue tackled by the IPCC – the initial variation in the prediction of complex models all based on the same physical principles and the same mathematical rules. They found that draconian measures would retard economic development, but that there were ways in which the open

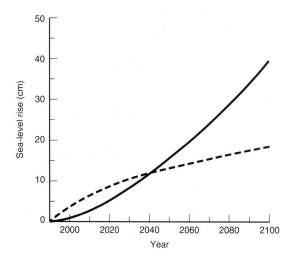

Fig. 6.8 Commitment to future sea-level rise
Even if we were to stop adding fossil fuel CO_2 to the atmosphere tomorrow, the lag of the effects of past global temperature rise on the ocean volume and on glaciers and ice sheets would cause sea level to continue to rise for several decades. The dashed line is the existing *commitment* of past changes. (Source: Warrick and Rahman, 1992.)

dissemination of information about future change could improve areas such as energy efficiency and forest preservation for the benefit of the world's economy, as well as mitigating future rates of climatic change. A carbon tax seemed to be an important part of such policies. But they also found that whether the world acts now or waits to see, global warming will have both 'winners' and 'losers' – in other words the costs of inaction will be as unevenly spread as the costs of action. In particular the divergencies between policies and possible threats between the North and South emphasize the difficulties in getting early agreement on a truly global basis about what, if anything, should be done. Even the attribution of 'blame' for the present, less stable, state of our global environment provokes wide disagreement and the 'facts' about greenhouse gas emissions can be presented and analysed in many different ways.

All this goes to show the central theme of this text, namely that the environmental sciences exist in a world of power, prejudice, wishful thinking and unjustified alarm. Above the level of the individual scientist, there is no independent evaluation of the evidence and no truly objective collection of facts. Data are framed by the models, the computer power, the collection

methods and the agency mandates of those who present the information for public choice. This is *not* to say that there is no place for rigorous science: very much the opposite. Without the networks of self-critical scientists in panels such as the IPCC there would be no credible consensus on which to base international action. The environmental sciences remain imperfect, and there is still much research to be done before complex global systems are adequately understood, but even our current knowledge is vital in world affairs.

Can the predictions be improved?

If the 'precautionary principle' is adopted we can wait patiently for the science of global change to become more precise, confident that we have begun to adopt appropriate measures which over a long period of time will reduce the rate of change and could eventually stabilize the global heat balance. Unfortunately, there is room to argue that the precautionary principle is premature, given the uncertainties in current forecasts of change and the evidence that the present tendency is for more careful analyses to reduce forecasts of the rate of future warming. There are even signs that scientists, convinced of the inevitability of future change and the need to act, are willing to slow down the process of enquiry and withhold revision of estimates of future warming for fear of losing the world's interest in the urgency and reality of the problem.

Clearly such a politically motivated science cannot be allowed to develop. The success of the IPCC has been its achievement of virtual unanimity through the improvement of the quality of the science. What is likely to happen is that at the global level better understanding of the role of the oceans, of the various atmospheric feedbacks (such as changes in cloud cover) and the increasing evidence for a 'CO_2 fertilization' feedback, estimates of the rate of warming will continue to decline. However, at the same time, powerful GCMs are being developed that allow more detailed and thus more realistic analyses of changes at a regional level. We may expect these to provide improved regional forecasts of temperature and precipitation change, and from these future water balance forecasts can be developed. It is very likely that despite the overall increase of rainfall implied by a warmer world, seasonal changes, coupled with higher evapotranspiration from warmer and longer seasons, will cause adverse changes in some areas. These will quickly impact on the strategic thinking of the governments concerned, and in the case of the less adaptable economies of the developing world, on those developed nations which fear instability and its knock-on effects.

Thus we may expect that it will be increasingly easy for developed nations to argue that for them adaptation is an effective strategy, except where regional forecasts imply changes in water balance which may be harder to accommodate than changes in temperature. At the same time, the increased reliability of regional forecasts for developing countries (where temperature changes are expected to be less than at higher latitudes) may well imply changes in water balance which threaten the existing precarious balance between population and food supply. The resolution of these issues is going to take far longer than the early reactions to the first IPCC forecasts suggested. The issue of global climatic change and the appropriate measures to counteract it will not go away, but it will not be limited to the simple doom or dismiss scenarios of the last few years. It will become increasingly complex and increasingly more intertwined with other global and regional issues, including population growth and the many issues surrounding the concept of sustainability. These points are developed, both in Chapter 1 and in Chapter 20.

References

Gleick, P.H. (1992) Effects of climatic change on shared water resources. In I.M. Mintzer (Ed.) *Confronting climatic change: risks, implications and responses.* Cambridge: Cambridge University Press.

Hammond, A., E. Rudenberg and W. Moonmaw (1991) The greenhouse index. *Environment*, **33** (1), 10–15, 33–5. (See also the responses to this article in *Environment*, **23** (2), 3–5, 42–3).

Hoffert, M.I. (1992) Climate sensitivity, climate feedbacks and policy implications. In I.M. Mintzer (Ed.) *Confronting climatic change: risks, implications and responses.* Cambridge: Cambridge University Press.

Houghton, J.T. (1991) Scientific assessment of climate change: summary of the IPCC Working Group 1 Report. In Jäger, J. and H.L. Ferguson (Eds) *Climate change: science, impacts and policy. Proceedings of the Second World Climate Conference.* Cambridge: Cambridge University Press, pp. 23–45.

Houghton, J.T., G.J. Jenkins and J.J. Ephraums (Eds) (1990) Climate change. IPCC scientific assessment (report prepared for IPCC by Working Group 1). Cambridge: Cambridge University Press.

Houghton, J.T., B.A. Callender and S.K. Varney (1992) *Climatic change 1992: the supplementary report to the IPCC scientific assessment.* Cambridge: Cambridge University Press.

Hulme, M. and P.M. Kelly (1993) Exploring the links between desertification and climatic change. *Environment*, **35** (6), 4–11, 39–46.

Kowoloh, M.E. (1993) Common threads: research lessons from acid rain, ozone depletion and global warming. *Environment*, **35** (6) 12–20, 35–8.

Pachauri, R.K. and M. Damodaran (1992) 'Wait and see' versus 'No regrets': comparing the costs of economic strategies. In Mintzer (Ed.) *Confronting climatic change: risks, implications and responses.* Cambridge: Cambridge University Press, pp. 237–52.

Pittock, A.B. and H.A. Nix (1986) The effects of changing climate on Australian biomass production – a preliminary study. *Climatic Change*, **8**, 243–55.

Rotmans, J., M. Hulme and T.E. Downing (1994) Climate change implications for Europe: an application of the ESCAPE model. *Global Environmental Change* (in press).

Warrick, R.A. and A.A. Rahman (1992) Future sea level rise: environmental ands socio-political considerations. In I.M. Mintzer (Ed.) *Confronting climatic change: risks, implications and responses.* Cambridge: Cambridge University Press, pp. 97–112.

Wigley, T.M.L. (1989) Possible climate change due to SO_2-derived cloud compensation media. *Nature*, **339**, 365–367.

Wigley, T.M.L. (1991) Could reducing fossil-fuel emissions cause global warming? *Nature*, **349**, 503–6.

Wigley, T.M.L. and S.C.B. Raper (1992) Implications for climate and sea level of revised IPCC emissions scenarios. *Nature*, **357**, 293–300.

Wigley, T.M.L., G.I. Pearman and P.M. Kelly (1992) Indices and indicators of climate change: issues of detection, validation and climate sensitivity. In I.M. Mintzer (Ed.) *Confronting climatic change: risks, implications and responses.* Cambridge: Cambridge University Press, pp. 85–96.

Further reading

Jäger, J. and H.L. Ferguson (Eds) (1991) *Climate change: science, impacts and policy. Proceedings of the Second World Climate Conference.* Cambridge: Cambridge University Press.

Mintzer, I.M. (Ed.) (1992) *Confronting climatic change: risks, implications and responses.* Cambridge: Cambridge University Press.

Netherlands, Ministry of Housing, Physical Planning and Environment (1990) *CFC action programme: cooperation between government and industry*. The Hague.

Nilsson, A. (1992) *Greenhouse earth*. Chichester: John Wiley.

Parry, M. (1990) *Climate change and world agriculture*. London: Earthscan.

Parry, M.L. and M.S. Swaminathan (1992) Effects of climatic change on food production. In I.M. Mintzer (Ed.) *Confronting climatic change: risks, implications and responses*. Cambridge: Cambridge University Press, pp. 113–27.

Smith, P.M. and K. Warr (Eds) (1992) *Global environmental issues*. London: Hodder and Stoughton.

Warrick, R.A., E.M. Barrow and T.M.L. Wigley (1990) *The greenhouse effect and its implications for the European Community*. Commission of the European Communities, EUR 12707 EN, 30pp. (also available in French).

CHAPTER 7

River processes and management

RICHARD HEY

One of the less publicized aspects of environmental modernization has been the slow but steady 'greening' of the professions. Engineering was one of the earliest to recognize that natural processes actually perform engineering work, so it is wiser to design alongside such processes than against them. In the course of time, engineers have been followed by accountants, investment analysts, chartered surveyors, land agents and, most recently, by the medical profession with its grudging acceptance of complementary medicine.

Richard Hey surveys the progress made in ecological engineering for river management. It is of interest to examine how this wider perspective entered into the mindset of river engineers. There have always been ecologically minded visionaries in the trade, but their voices have not been heard until recently. One cause is simply the costly mistakes of ignoring natural processes when designing dams, levees, channel stabilization and flood protection schemes.

Another factor was the rise of the environmental impact assessment. This was introduced in the US National Environmental Policy Act in 1969. Through this remarkable piece of legislation, which incidentally argued for a productive harmony with nature across all US federal policy, the formal environmental impact statement, or account, was born. The outcome was a generation of engineer-designers who simply had to know about ecology, soil sciences, environmental economics and ethics, and planning and land-use change. This was a slow process, and even today too many environmental impact assessments (EIAs) are 'cook-book studies', done in-house by shadowy teams to fulfil a legal obligation. Only recently has there been a move to improve the quality control of the various environmental science consultancies that have sprung up since EIAs became commonplace the world over. A study of EIAs in the UK showed that less than half were adequate and only a quarter could be regarded as comprehensive. There is a good job market in high quality environmental assessment within which the well-trained environmental scientist is an attractive employee.

A third propelling force was the rise of statutory duties of environmental care imposed on water management organization by 'green' legislation. In the UK this clause is sometimes referred to as the *amenity clause* because it arose out of an earlier duty on electricity companies to have regard for the desirability of safeguarding natural beauty in the pursuit of their responsibilities. Natural beauty in legal parlance means both wildlife and habitat as well as scenic splendour and public appreciation. It also covers both geological and physiographical features, not simply biological organisms and processes.

The late 1980s saw the emergence of more privatized utilities in the UK, notably in telecommunications, gas, water and electricity. As the legislation was being prepared, there was a cry from the environmental groups for proper safeguarding clauses for natural beauty. This resulted in a strengthening of the legal wording from the very discretionary phrases of the 1950s to concepts such as 'furthering', 'balancing' and 'harmonizing' economic activity with a respect for the existence of natural processes. The private water companies in the UK, together with the publicly funded regulatory body known as the National Rivers Authority, both have a 'furthering' duty towards the natural environment and conservation of natural beauty. This is taken seriously by the companies and agencies concerned because of the scope for judicial review of any ministerially determined strategy on, say, flood protection or river bank stabilization that did not show that such a policy had been actively pursued.

The New Zealand Resource Conservation Act of 1991 provides the image of times to come. This states as its purpose the promotion of sustainable management of natural and physical resources. Section 6 requires that all persons managing any resource must recognize the need to safeguard key sites, including sites important through Maori cultural traditions and property rights. This is a formal duty akin to the public trust doctrine outlined in Chapter 1. Furthermore, resource managers are expected to pay particular regard to the Maori notion of *Kaitiakitanga* or the exercise of guardianship and stewardship, efficiency of use, the maintenance and enhancement of amenity, and of environmental quality generally, and the intrinsic values of ecosystems. These are slightly more discretionary obligations, but they do demand a formal statement of intent and of response for any resource management proposal. The extension of such legislation to the northern hemisphere would place a clearer burden on the developer to be environmentally accountable.

Finally, the emergence of ecological economics has begun to show that designing with nature is not only cost effective, but can be justified on the basis of the social valuations of wildlife and habitats or accessible amenities saved or reconstructed. So contingent valuation studies of the kind outlined in Chapter 3 are beginning to appear on the cost benefit analysis of river management schemes and flood protection strategies.

Acceptance of social values as benefits has to be discounted on low time preference rates. Arguably, the benefit stream is much longer than the normal 40 year time horizon for engineered projects. This tends to encourage the use of lower discount rates to take into account the longer time horizon of gains. But such a strategy is looked on very warily by finance ministers. There is a lively tussle between the old and the new cost benefit analysis these days, just as there is still in the engineering fraternity between creative but multi-disciplinary river engineering and the older, more simple, ways of designing with concrete and steel to impose human will on turbulent nature. The 'green' modernization pendulum continues to swing favourably.

Introduction

For centuries we have harnessed rivers for our own purposes. They have been dammed for water resource development and hydroelectric power production, dredged, widened and straightened to aid navigation, improve land drainage and alleviate flooding, and stabilized to prevent the loss of buildings and bridges or to protect farmland. These works change the natural character of the river, which can lead to major instability problems unless the river is heavily engineered (Raynov *et al.*, 1986). All this can seriously impair the conservation and amenity value of the riverine environment.

Environmental impact legislation in the European Community, the USA and many other countries now makes it mandatory to carry out formal impact assessments of any major scheme likely to alter river systems. This includes dams and channel realignments. While this enables least damaging options to be identified and in some cases to be implemented, conservation bodies are advocating the adoption of more environmentally sensitive solutions that aim to preserve natural-type channels using bioengineering methods. Such approaches are certainly laudable, but arbitrary modifications to a river are likely to be no more than a temporary palliative. Poorly thought out, such alterations may actually jeopardize design objectives.

Major problems arise when unnatural conditions are imposed on a river and it follows that more sympathetic approaches should be based on an understanding of the processes that control river morphology and its dynamic adjustment to changed conditions. By designing with nature, stable and environmentally sensitive solutions can be achieved. This maintains a natural range of instream and bankside habitats, which are required for fisheries, flora and fauna, preserves visual amenity and ensures that subsequent maintenance requirements are minimized. Environmental approaches are, therefore, likely to be more cost effective in the longer term than traditional methods.

In order to understand why many traditional engineering works have caused instability and environmental degradation, and to identify more appropriate design procedures, consideration needs to be given to the factors controlling the shape and size of alluvial channels.

Natural channel processes

Basic research in river mechanics has identified the factors controlling the morphology of alluvial channels. Essentially they adjust their overall, bankfull, width, depth, slope, plan shape and velocity in response to discharge, sediment load, calibre of the bed and bank sediment (gravel, sand, silt or clay), the bank's vegetation (grass, shrubs or trees) and the slope of the valley. Change in any one of these variables through flow regulation or land-use change, or by directly modifying the river, can destabilize the channel and promote erosion and deposition.

Empirical equations, based on field measurements and statistical analysis, which have been developed to predict the dimensions of stable alluvial rivers, can be used to identify the direction of change (Box 7.1).

If changes increase the sediment transport capacity of the river, then instability, manifested as either bed scour or fill and associated bank failure, is propagated upstream. Alternatively, if there is a rapid local change in sediment supply, instability will migrate downstream. Once initiated, a sequence of scour and fill phases will occur, each being of progressively smaller magnitude. Eventually a new equilibrium condition will be achieved, provided the controlling factors stabilize.

The principal design requirement for river engineering works is, therefore, to maintain the natural sediment transport regime of the river. This will prevent instability occurring and will obviate the need for expensive remedial works and long-term maintenance commitments.

In order to preserve or enhance fisheries and the conservation value of the river, it is essential that engineering works should, wherever possible, maintain or recreate natural channel features including pools, riffles, meander bends, point bars and natural steep banks. Where heavier engineering works are required, habitat improvements should be implemented to increase diversity. These need to be sensibly located as arbitrary modifications to a river are unlikely to be enduring.

Sufficient is now known about the hydraulic and sedimentary processes operating in meandering alluvial channels for ecologically appropriate measures to be incorporated into engineering design. Essentially this identifies the large-scale erosion and deposition processes which are responsible for the formation of meanders, pools, riffles and bar deposits and for bank failure (Richards, 1982; Hey, 1986).

Box 7.1 Stable channel dimensions and prediction of channel change

Empirical equations that define the dimensions of stable alluvial channels can be used to predict channel change. These equations are specific to a particular river environment, for example, gravel, sand or silt/clay bed rivers, and should not be used out of context. For gravel-bed rivers the following equations have been developed based on UK field data (Hey and Thorne, 1986).

Cross section

Bankfull top width			
	$W = 4.33\ Q^{0.5}$ (m)	Vegetation type I	(1)
	$W = 3.33\ Q^{0.5}$ (m)	Vegetation type II	(2)
	$W = 2.73\ Q^{0.5}$ (m)	Vegetation type III	(3)
	$W = 2.34\ Q^{0.5}$ (m)	Vegetation type IV	(4)
Bankfull mean depth	$d = 0.22\ Q^{0.37}\ D_{50}^{-0.11}$ (m)	Vegetation types I–IV	(5)

Longitudinal section

Bankfull slope $S = 0.087\ Q^{-0.43}\ D_{50}^{-0.09}\ D_{84}^{0.84}\ Q_S^{0.10}$ Vegetation types I–IV   (6)

Plan section

Sinuosity	$p = \dfrac{S_V}{S}$	Vegetation types I–IV	(7)
Meander arc length (riffle spacing)	$Z = 6.31\ W$ (m)	Vegetation types I–IV	(8)

where Q = bankfull discharge (m³/s); Q_s = bankfull bedload discharge (kg/s); D_{50} = median bed material size (m); D_{84} = bed material size, 84% finer (m); Vegetation type I = bankside trees and shrubs absent; Vegetation type II = 1–5% trees and shrubs; Vegetation type III = 5–50% trees and shrubs; Vegetation type IV = greater than 50% trees and shrubs; S_V = valley slope.

River response to changed conditions can be identified by considering the direction of the imposed change on the river (increase +, decrease –) in the above equations. To achieve a new stable condition the river must adjust the other variables in each equation (+ or –) to accommodate the imposed change.

For example, dam construction cuts off sediment supply to downstream reaches and reduces flood discharges (i.e. Q and Q_s decrease). Disruption to the sediment transport regime of the river causes erosion downstream from the dam with the following consequences:

From equation (6)

$$S\ \overline{Q} \propto \overline{Q_s}\ D_{84}$$

(imposed change)

(responses)

- channel slope reduced to point where bed material can no longer be transported (i.e. S decreases);
- fine bed material will be preferentially eroded leaving a coarser residual (i.e. D_{84} increases).

The remaining equations indicate that

- width is reduced;
- depth is reduced, in spite of incision, since higher banks are unstable;
- sinuosity increases provided valley slope does not change.

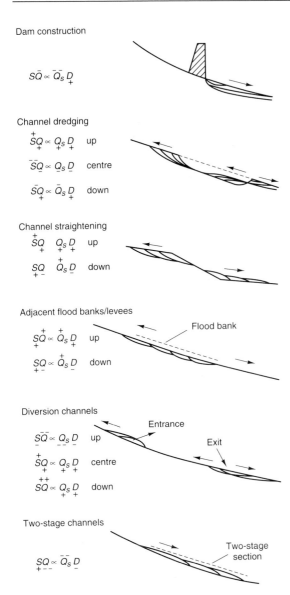

Fig 7.1 Channel response to construction of flood alleviation schemes (+, increase; – decrease; above line, control; below line, response).

Flood alleviation schemes

Floods can be alleviated either by storing flood waters in specially constructed storage reservoirs or by modifying the river to accommodate the flood flows within the bank.

Construction of flood storage or detention reservoirs can provide adequate safeguards in the immediate vicinity of the reservoir, but their effect is reduced as the percentage of uncontrolled catchment increases. They are often employed to prevent flood run-off from urbanized areas, motorways and car parks. For large river basins, numerous reservoirs would be required in the headwater valleys or a number of major reservoirs on the main river if a significant reduction in flood flows were to be achieved in the lower reaches of the basin.

Reservoirs, by modifying the flow and sediment transport regime downstream from the dam, can cause significant bed degradation as releases from the dam are relatively sediment free. Regime equations (Box 7.1) indicate that the decreased sediment load causes erosion and an associated reduction in channel gradient and an increase in the size of the bed material (Figure 7.1) until a new equilibrium is achieved. For example, on the Colorado River, USA, the bed has been eroded by 4.6 m immediately below Parker Dam and 50 km further downstream by 2.6 m. Degradation has been observed for 125 km below the dam (Figure 7.2).

Recent plans to construct major flood storage reservoirs at Serre de la Fare on the River Loire, on the Allier at Le Veurdre, and on the Cher at Chambonchard to alleviate flooding in the Upper and Middle Loire have been turned down or deferred as a result of sustained environmental lobbying because cost-effective alternatives were shown to be possible without any associated environmental degradation (Purseglove, 1991).

Increasing in-bank flows was commonly achieved by widening and dredging the river (Figure 7.3). The aim was to increase the cross-sectional area of the channel in order to increase 'in-bank' discharge capacities. Much of lowland England has been affected by this course of action. Agricultural improvement schemes to drain low-lying flood plain land required the bed of the channel to be dredged by up to 1 m to lower the water-table, and widened to increase flood capacity. Much of this work was carried out in the early to mid-19th century, although this has been maintained and developed subsequently, particularly during the 'Plough for Victory' campaign in the Second World War. On these lowland rivers the riparian and instream habitats were decimated, with adverse effects on invertebrates, fisheries, flora, fauna and bird life. Subsequent maintenance dredging in a 5–10 year cycle has maintained these artificial channels

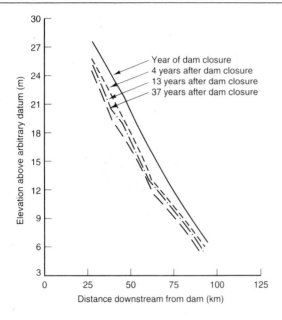

Fig 7.2 Longitudinal profile of Colorado River downstream form Parker Dam at dam closure and 4, 13 and 37 years later. (Source: Williams and Wolman, 1984.)

from siltation, which, inevitably, prevents ecological recolonization.

On rivers transporting considerable bed-material load, often upland rivers, such a course of action can seriously destabilize the river as well as adversely affecting the riverine environment. Application of the regime equations (Box 7.1) indicates that erosion will occur at the head of the dredged section, because of increased gradients, and progress upstream (Figure 7.1), while much of this eroded material will be deposited in the lower part of the undredged reach where the gradient has been artificially reduced (Figure 7.1). Should sediment loads downstream from the dredged reach be reduced, then further degradation could result (Figure 7.3). These sequence of changes have been observed on a dredged and widened section of the River Usk at Brecon (UK). Although headward erosion is prevented by a weir, 5000 tonnes of material have to be removed annually from the dredged section to maintain its design capacity (Figure 7.4). Even then erosion is occurring further downstream.

Channel straightening has also been carried out to enhance flood capacities since flow velocities are increased in the steepened reach. What has happened to the Mississippi is a classic example of how channel stability can be initiated by channel straightening.

After serious flooding in 1927, sections of the lower river were altered to reduce navigation distances and enlarge flood capacities (Figure 7.5). The increased gradient resulting from channel straightening promoted bed erosion in the engineered section and this progressed upstream and also affected tributary rivers (Figure 7.1). Enhanced sediment loads resulting from headward erosion subsequently caused serious sedimentation in the straightened sections as the river attempted to recreate a meandering channel (Figure 7.1). Billions of dollars have since been spent dredging the river to maintain navigation depths and flood capacities, and building spur dykes to prevent bank erosion and bed sedimentation (Winkley, 1982). Significantly, the natural river required relatively little maintenance (Table 7.1)

Similar problems have been experienced in the UK. The Ystwyth in west Wales was regularly straightened to increase its gradient and enhance its flood capacity but the meandering channel quickly re-established itself. In order to maintain the artificially straightened channel, some form of heavy revetment would be needed to stabilize the banks. This could be achieved by masonry walls, sheet piling, cellular concrete blocks, stone-filled wire baskets (gabions) or large blockstone slabs. Inevitably this is visually very intrusive and can completely destroy the bankside environment.

Another traditional approach to flood alleviation is to construct flood banks or levees adjacent to the river (Figure 7.3). The natural channel is left intact and flood control is achieved by allowing overspill from the channel but curtailing its extent. Usually the banks are constructed close to the river to maximize the protected area. Such measures can adversely affect channel stability on upland type rivers as they locally increase the bed load transport capacity of the river (Figure 7.1). On lowland type rivers, channel stability can be maintained and bankside habitats enhanced. Visually, however, they can be quite intrusive as they restrict views of the river across the flood plain.

Conservation groups strongly criticized the ecological and aesthetic devastation wrought by the construction of flood alleviation schemes. This is part of a general trend favouring ecologically based engineering that can be seen in coastal management and in the design and routing of motorways. Much of this is influenced by the kind of ecological economics outlined in Chapters 2 and 3, and subsequently incorporated into modified cost benefit analysis. All this has led to the development of alternative approaches which were considered to be environ-

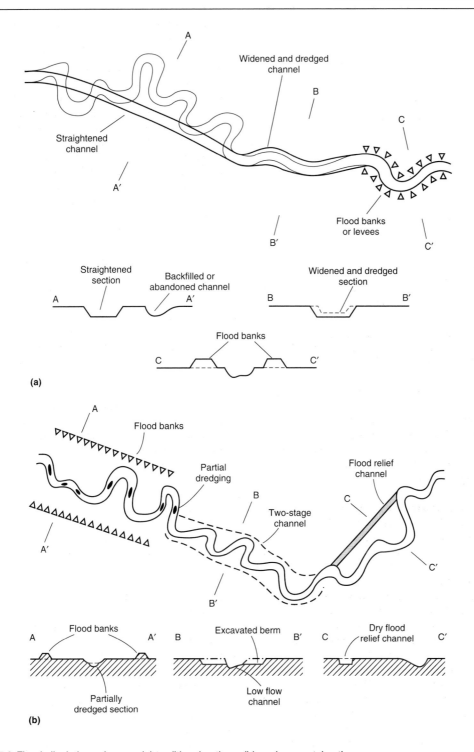

Fig 7.3 Flood alleviation schemes: (a) traditional options; (b) environmental options.

Fig 7.4 Flood alleviation scheme, River Usk, Brecon, Wales. This river has been dredged and widened to increase its flood capacity, which has reduced its ability to transport sediment and has created a sediment trap. Regular maintenance dredging is required to preserve its flood capacity. Note the masonry wall to prevent mass failure of the heightened bank.

mentally sensitive (Lewis and Williams, 1984). These include bypass or diversion channels, where flood waters above a certain flow are overspilled into a separate flood channel and the natural channel is left intact, flood banks set back from the river at the edge of the meander belt, and two stage channels in which the top section of the flood plain is dredged to create a flood channel, leaving the natural low flow channel untouched (Figure 7.3).

Diversion channels have been successfully implemented on lowland rivers, as, for example, at Exeter on the River Exe (UK), without adversely affecting the conservation and fisheries value of the original river or its channel stability. However, on upland type rivers the regime equations indicate that they would promote deposition at the entrance to the diversion and erosion at the exit (Figure 7.1). Similarly, two stage channels are appropriate on lowland sites especially as they can increase plant diversity. The flood berm would need to be managed to prevent it becoming overgrown, with consequent loss of flood capacity, and could form a linear park in built-up areas. On upland sites, two stage

channels would cause severe aggradation, as the transport capacity is significantly reduced (Figure 7.1).

Flood banks set back at the edge of the meander belt afford the best solution for flood alleviation as the natural channel is not disturbed (Hey *et al.*, 1990). Even on upland type rivers the natural sediment transport regime will not be modified. In many cases, particularly for urban schemes, space limitations may preclude the adoption of such designs and alternative solutions will

Table 7.1 Maintenance dredging record: Greenville Reach, River Mississippi

Period	Volume dredged (m^3/km/yr)
Pre cut-off	137
Cut-off – 1950	10 360
1951–64	29 835
1965–73	62 833
1974–77	39 695

Source: Winkley (1982).

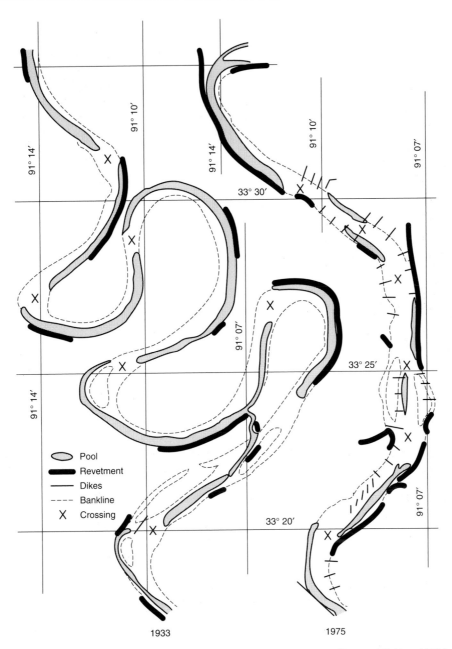

Fig 7.5 Comparison of Greenville Reach of lower Mississippi in 1933 and 1975. (Source: Winkley, 1982.)

be necessary. For lowland sites, two stage channels are a possibility provided they are properly managed, but even these require additional space. On upland sites, or where space is at a premium on lowland rivers, flood walls may need to be built to contain flooding. In these circumstances it is essential that they have architectural merit and that instream structures, such as weirs, should be incorporated in the design to ensure that the sediment transport regime of the river is not disrupted and that habitat diversity is maintained.

Decisions regarding the implementation of a flood alleviation scheme are based on cost benefit analysis. Environmentally sensitive approaches, by designing with nature rather than trying to impose man's will on the river, are inherently more stable, and hence relatively maintenance free, and can actually enhance the riverine environment. Consequently, they are likely to be less expensive than traditional approaches in both monetary and environmental terms. Techniques based on those outlined in Chapter 3 are now widely used. The recreational public are prepared to pay an identifiable extra price for an aesthetically pleasing river design.

River stabilization

Rivers become unstable if there is an imbalance between the sediment load supplied to a reach of river and its ability to transport it. Regional instability refers to large-scale and systematic long-term degradation and aggradation resulting from natural or man-induced changes.

Reduced sediment supply due, for example, to dam construction or land-use change, or increased transport capacity resulting from a fall in sea-level, raised land levels or channel straightening amongst other things, causes channel incision. Eventually a new equilibrium is achieved with the river flowing in a new, lower level flood plain. The original valley is normally left as a terrace. To control erosion and to prevent it spreading to adjacent reaches it is necessary to reduce the transport capacity of the river. This is best achieved by reducing the channel gradient by constructing a series of weirs or drop structures in the affected reach and at the head of the incised section to prevent further headward erosion (Figure 7.6). Typically these structures are designed and located in order to ensure that no bed material transport can occur or that the material supplied to the reach from further upstream can be transmitted through the affected reach without any erosion or deposition.

A geomorphological approach offers an alternative procedure for determining the requisite number of weirs. Measurements taken at sections that have evolved to a quasi-equilibrium condition enable a simple equation to be developed for predicting the gradient of the stable reach. The size, location and number of grade control structures can then be determined to provide the requisite gradient (Schumm *et al.*,

1984). Many streams and rivers in northern Mississippi have become dramatically unstable as a result of channel straightening for flood control purposes. Incision into the fine flood plain alluvium has increased channel widths from 2–3 m to over 40 m and depths from 0.5 m to upwards of 10–15 m. Grade control structures have been constructed to stabilize these rivers, and calculations for Oaklimiter Creek indicate that a smaller number of weirs would be required using the geomorphologically based calculation procedure (6 weirs) than the more traditional methods (15–20 weirs) and, hence, would be more cost effective.

Increased sediment loads can choke the river with material and promote braiding, which is manifest as a series of sediment bars and islands with multiple interconnected channels. The elevation of the river bed and its valley are raised in the process and a new flood plain is created. Such channels can be stabilized by controlling the sediment supply to the reach from upstream, through the construction of grade control structures or afforestation programmes. Alternatively, the river can be engineered to transmit the sediment supplied from upstream. This is generally achieved by increasing stream power to enable the river to transmit the sediment load, by maximizing the channel gradient and flow depth by straightening and narrowing the river into a single channel. In order to maintain the river in this unnatural state, the banks of the river have to be constructed of blockstone, or similar, to prevent bank failure (Figure 7.7). The formerly braided Alpine Rhine

Fig 7.6 Grade control structure, Goodwin Creek, Mississippi, USA. This has been constructed to prevent headward erosion. The stilling basin lined with rockstone and baffle board dissipates energy below the weir.

Fig 7.7 River stabilization, Alpine Rhine, Switzerland. The original braided river has been stabilized by narrowing, deepening and straightening the river. The banks have been protected by blockstone to prevent erosion and maintain a straight channel.

in Switzerland was extensively trained in the 18th century in this manner. Inevitably the natural river with its diverse habitats is replaced by a uniform canalized channel of limited conservation and environmental value.

A more environmentally acceptable alternative would be to create an irregular sinuous channel. This would be designed to transmit the sediment supplied from upstream on a slightly reduced gradient to accommodate a meandering pattern. By creating a meandering channel with a variable bed geometry, a range of instream habitats could be created which are beneficial to flora, invertebrates and fisheries. Although harder bank protection measures would be required to stabilize the outer bank in meander bends, softer procedures, particularly those involving vegetation, could provide a more sympathetic approach elsewhere which is aesthetically more pleasing and provides cover for fish.

On a more local scale, instability problems are generally concerned with the prevention of bank failures and the maintenance of channel plan form. Tradition-

ally, eroding banks have been protected by lining the bank with some form of protective cover to prevent both surface scour and mass failure. In extreme cases this can take the form of a concrete or masonry wall, for banks exposed to extreme hydraulic loading, through cellular type blocks, stone-filled wire baskets and stone rip rap to geotextile mats and willow, reed and grass cover as loadings decrease. The softest possible options need to be chosen for each site according to local circumstances, and guidelines and flowcharts have been developed, based on field experience which enables this to be achieved (Hey *et al.*, 1991).

All the aforementioned methods provide protection by increasing the erosional resistance of the bank. An alternative solution is to modify the flow adjacent to the bank such that the hydraulic loadings on the bank are reduced and bank failure prevented. This effectively would treat the cause of the problem, rather than the symptoms, and would enable the bank to remain in a natural state.

For meander bends, submerged vanes or hydrofoils

can be installed on the bed of the river to generate secondary currents, or cross flows, which oppose the main helicoidal cell which results from flow curvature in the bend (Figure 7.8). As a result, downwelling of faster surface water, which normally occurs adjacent to the outer bank causing bed scouring, bank steepening and failure, now occurs inside the line of the hydrofoils (Figure 7.8). Bed scouring is now relocated in the cross section and scoured material refills the pool adjacent to the bank. As a consequence the toe of the bank is stabilized and further bank failure prevented. Should deposition cover the hydrofoils, the original secondary flow pattern would become re-established. As associated scouring would re-expose the hydrofoils, the system is self-regulatory. The systems have been successfully deployed for bank erosion control on the East Nishnabotna River, USA (Odgaard and Mosconi, 1987), and on the River Roding, Essex, UK (Paice and Hey, 1989 and Figure 7.9).

Knowledge of river mechanics can also be used to prevent local bed scour problems at bridge piers. Re-cent bridge failures on the River Towy at Glanrhyd (Wales), on the River Ness at Inverness (Scotland), on the Route 90 bridge over Schoharie Creek (USA) and on the River Inn at Innsbruck (Austria) have high-lighted the need for improved methods of scour con-trol. Traditionally, scour holes have been refilled with large stone rip rap, but this is rarely successful as it effectively increases the size of the bridge footing, mak-ing the bed more prone to scour. In time the stone is either washed away or buried. Observation of scour processes in scale models indicated that scouring oc-curred because of faster flowing surface water descend-ing the upstream face of the pier which significantly increases near bed velocities. It is the latter that is responsible for eroding the bed material adjacent to the pier. By installing a group of four cylindrical piles in a diamond-shaped formation into the river bed immediately upstream from the pier, the velocities at the pier are significantly reduced. Consequently, downwelling at the pier face is less pronounced and bed scour is reduced. Scale model tests indicate the local

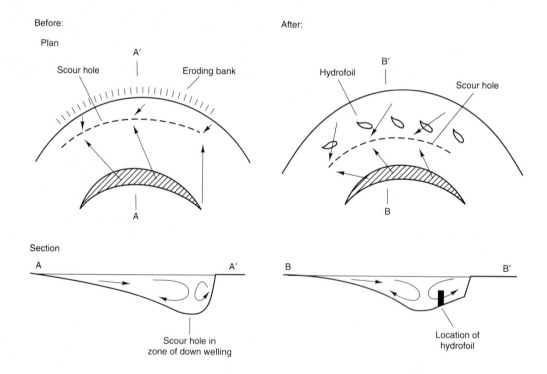

Fig 7.8 Bank erosion control with hydrofoils. Here submerged hydrofoils reduce hydraulic loading against the bank, by suppressing development of secondary flows which direct faster flowing water against the bank, and prevent bank erosion.

scour can be reduced by up to 70 per cent (Figure 7.10) and field trials to evaluate the method further are currently being carried out on the Tavy viaduct across the Tavy estuary at Plymouth, the Over viaduct across the River Severn at Gloucester, (Figure 7.11), and the Coton viaduct crossing the River Tame at Tamworth (Paice *et al.*, 1993).

River restoration

River engineering works have, over the centuries, adversely affected hundreds of kilometres of rivers (Brookes, 1988; Purseglove, 1988). A post-project appraisal of flood alleviation schemes indicates that unsympathetic engineering treatments consistently reduce plant species richness, when compared with natural channels, while environmentally sensitive approaches actually increased richness by creating a greater range of habitats (Hey *et al.,* 1990). The requirement, therefore, is to reinstate natural channels, provided that engineering objectives can be maintained, or to rehabilitate reaches that require a heavier engineering treatment.

Non-structural approaches refer to the reinstatement of natural features within a reach that had previously been dredged and/or straightened. It could involve, *inter alia*, the restoration of meanders, pools, riffles, vertical banks and dead zones. On upland type rivers there is generally only one restoration solution, which is prescribed by the controlling variables (Box 7.1). With lowland type rivers, because flows are generally below bed material transport thresholds, there is more flexibility in the choice of restoration procedure.

A geomorphological survey of the reach is required in order to ascertain the nature of the existing channel morphology and substrate characteristics. This, together with old maps and aerial photographs of the site, enables the natural, pre-engineered and existing conditions to be compared.

For lowland rivers that have simply been straightened, it should be possible to reinstate the original meander pattern, with associated pools at meander bends and riffles at inflexion points between bends. Channel widths and depths can be determined from appropriate design equations (Box 7.1), or from the survey of adjacent natural reaches. Several lowland rivers in Denmark have been successfully reconstructed to recreate natural type meandering channels using these techniques (Figure 7.12).

Fig 7.9 Hydrofoil installation to prevent bank erosion in meander bends.

On rivers that retain their natural meander pattern but have been widened and the riffles removed, it is necessary to reinstate riffles and pools and to narrow the channel at strategic locations to accelerate natural accretion processes. Provided the riffles are drowned out during bankfull flows, the flood capacity of the river is unimpaired. This type of approach has been successfully carried out at Lyng on the River Wensum (UK) as part of a fish habitat improvement programme (Figure 7.13).

For channels that have been straightened and the bed elevation significantly lowered (by up to 1 m) by dredging, more drastic action is required. Simply recreating the meandering channel would produce a river that was too deep. Backfilling the channel to re-establish the pre-engineered bed elevations is not a viable option as it would raise the water-table by a corresponding amount and adversely affect local land drain-

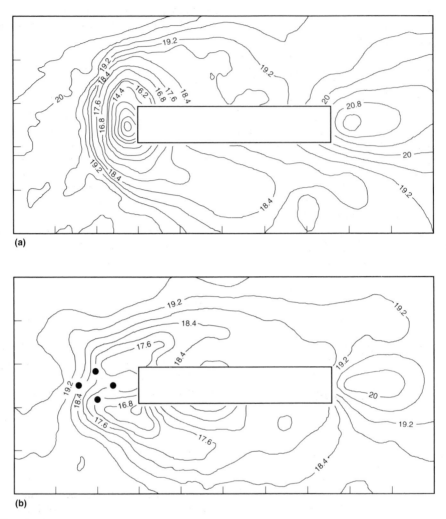

(a)

(b)

Fig 7.10 River bed scour at model bridge piers (blunt nosed): (a) unprotected, local scour 80 mm, Q = 0.03 cumecs; (b) protected by pile group, local scour 33 mm, Q = 0.03 cumecs. Contours in cm, initial bed level 20 cm. (Source: Paice and Hey (1993) The control and monitoring of local scour at bridge piers. In Hsieh Wen Shen, S.T. Shu and Feng Wen (Eds) *Hydraulic Engineering '93*, **1**. Reproduced by permission of ASCE.)

age. The solution is to excavate a corridor in the existing flood plain, by an amount the river bed has been lowered by dredging, to create a new low level flood plain. The width of the corridor is determined by the amplitude of the meander pattern that is to be reinstated. Although the river will have a lower gradient than the straightened engineered channel, since it is sinuous, and a smaller cross section, as the depth is reduced, its overall flood capacity is maintained within the new flood plain.

The River Blackwater in Norfolk (UK) was exten-

sively dredged and canalized in the early to mid-19th century. In order to extend flood plain gravel workings, the opportunity was taken to restore the river to its precanalized condition. Maps of 1790 showed that the river was then much smaller and quite sinuous, and a geomorphological survey indicated that the river bed had been lowered by 0.8 m. A new low level flood plain was excavated, 15–20 m wide and 0.8 m deep, containing a small sinuous channel, maximum width 5 m, with pools and riffles (Figures 7.14, and 7.15). Calculations showed that low water levels would not be raised, flood

Fig 7.11 Bridge pier scour control, Over Viaduct, River Severn, Gloucester, England. A pile group has been installed upstream from the pier to reduce flow velocities and prevent scouring of the river bed. At this bridge, the width of the pier necessitated the use of six piles set in triangular shaped formation.

capacity below the existing flood plain level would be preserved and the channel would remain stable. Effectively it recreates the precanalized river and its natural diversity will significantly improve the fisheries potential of this chalk-fed stream.

With river restoration on upland type rivers it is necessary to ensure that the sediment transport regime of the river is not impaired by the planned restoration works. The design of the diversion is, therefore, critical and it should be based on current design constraints, since the pre-engineered condition refers to an earlier situation which may not currently prevail. A geomorphological survey of the reach to be restored and adjacent natural sections will define existing conditions and

this, in conjunction with appropriate design equations (Box 7.1), will enable the new channel to be sensitively designed.

River diversions are similar to restoration schemes in terms of design procedures. Often engineers would advocate the construction of straight diversion channels where a river had to be moved to accommodate a new road. As this would locally increase the sediment transport capacity of the river, instability would result. It is necessary, therefore, to reinstate a natural-type diversion and, in particular, to maintain the channel length, and hence gradient, to avoid instability problems. Where the original channel is heavily engineered, opportunities should be taken to create a more natural channel.

River diversions on the River Neath, south Wales (UK), have been designed using these principles (Hey, 1992). A typical geomorphological map and design for part of one diversion is illustrated in Figure 7.16.

Structural methods, involving the installation of artificial instream structures, can be deployed to promote local aggradation or degradation, create ponded reaches and diversify substratum types. They are particularly useful for increasing habitat diversity in more heavily engineered sections of river. Before installing any structures, it is important to ensure that they are correctly located to enhance local instream processes and that they do not impair the sediment transport or flood capacity of the river. By locally harnessing the energy within the flow, either by overspill on weirs, by concentrating flows with deflectors, or by generating secondary flows with submerged vanes, erosion and deposition can be encouraged. These structures are particularly useful on lowland type rivers where stream power is generally insufficient to cause bed scour without some assistance. On upland rivers they are best deployed for stabilizing and creating habitat diversity in heavily engineered reaches. Non-structural methods are preferable on more natural channels.

The range and type of structures are illustrated in Figure 7.17. Submerged vanes are less intrusive than the other structures and also have the benefit of not trapping floating debris or adversely affecting the flood capacity of the river. They were originally developed for pool creation and maintenance (Hey, 1992), but they can also be deployed to cause bank erosion and meander initiation. A range of vanes have been successfully installed on the River Wensum (UK) at Fakenham and Lyng.

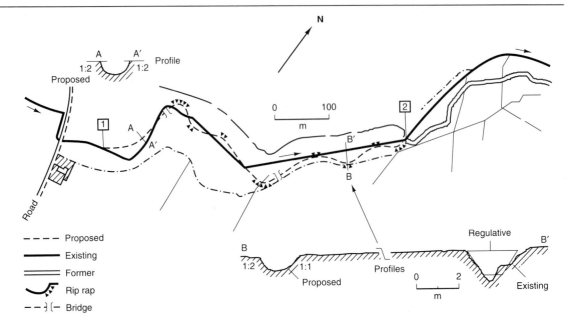

Fig 7.12 Restored course of Stensbaek stream in southern Jutland, Denmark. (Source: Brookes, 1987.)

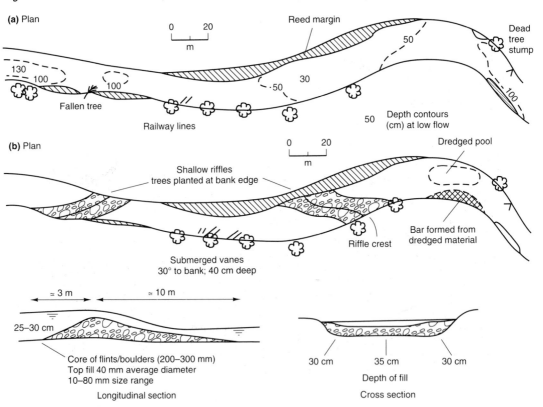

Fig 7.13 Recreation of pools and riffles at Lyng, River Wensum, England: (a) geomorphological map of original channel; (b) proposed riffle-pool sequence. (Source: Hey, 1992.)

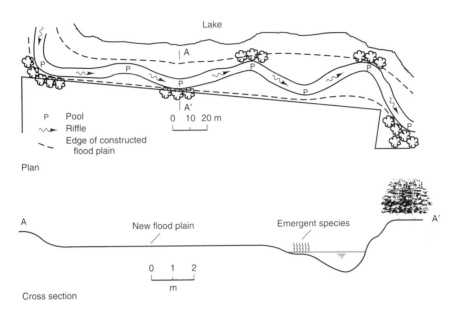

Fig 7.14 Design of diversion at Reymerston, River Blackwater, England. (Source: Hey, 1992.)

Fig 7.15 River diversion, River Blackwater, Reymerston, England. This plate shows the recreation of a small sinuous channel within a new low level flood plain. A variety of habitats had been restored which have since been colonized by instream and bankside vegetation.

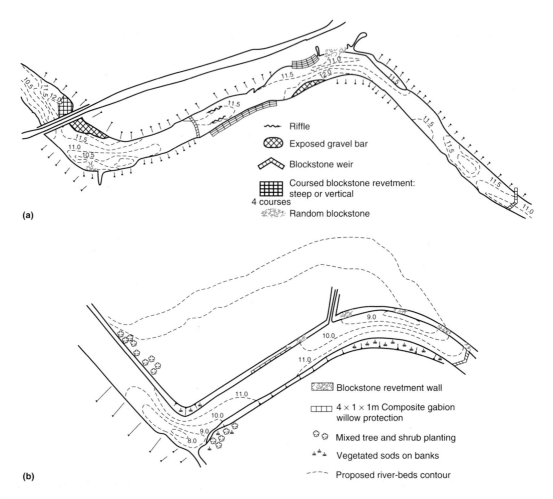

Fig 7.16 Design of diversion for section of River Neath, south Wales: (a) geomorphological map of original channel; (b) proposed diversion. (Source: Hey, 1992.)

Conclusions

Attempts to impose an unnatural condition on a river will, on upland-type channels that transport considerable amounts of bed material load, create major instability problems and long-term maintenance commitments. On lowland-type rivers that transport relatively little bed material, instability may not be a problem, but the creation of uniform, sterile, canalized rivers totally destroys the riverine environment.

This brief review illustrates the key role of fluvial geomorphology in river management. It indicates that basic understanding of natural channel processes is a prerequisite for successful environmentally sensitive engineering design.

References

Brookes, A. (1987) Restoring the sinuosity of artificially straightened stream channels. *Environmental Geology and Water Science*, **10**, 33–41.

Brookes, A. (1988) *Channelized rivers, perspectives for environmental management*. Chichester: Wiley.

Hey, R.D. (1986) River Mechanics. *Journal of the Institution of Water Engineers and Scientists*, **40**(2), 139–58.

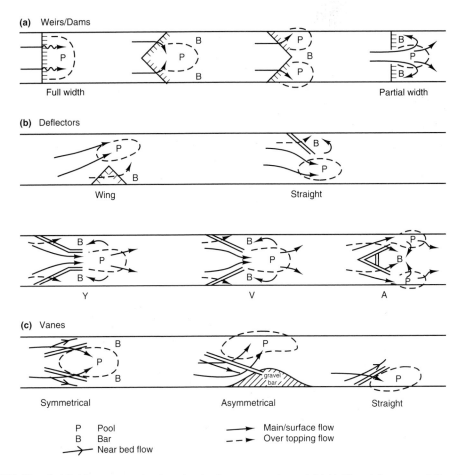

(a) Weirs/Dams

Full width　　　　　　　　　　　　　　　　　Partial width

(b) Deflectors

Wing　　　　　　　　　　　　　　Straight

Y　　　　　　　　　　　V　　　　　　　　　　A

(c) Vanes

Symmetrical　　　　　　　　Asymmetrical　　　　　　　Straight

P　　Pool　　　　　　　　　　⟶　Main/surface flow
B　　Bar　　　　　　　　　　- - ►　Over topping flow
⟶　Near bed flow

Fig 7.17 River habitat improvement using structural measures. In part (b) Y, V and A represent the shapes of the deflectors. (Source: Hey, 1992.)

Hey, R.D. (1992) River mechanics and habitat creation. In K.T. O'Grady, A.J.B. Butterworth, P.B. Spillett and J.C.J. Domaniewski (Eds) *Fisheries in the year 2000*. Nottingham: Institute of Fisheries Management, pp. 271–85.

Hey, R.D. and C.R. Thorne (1986) Stable channels with mobile gravel beds. *Journal of Hydraulics Division, American Society of Civil Engineers*, **112**(8), 671–89.

Hey, R.D., G.L. Heritage and M. Patteson (1990) *Design of flood alleviation schemes: engineering and the environment*. London: Ministry of Agriculture, Fisheries and Food.

Hey, R.D., G.L. Heritage, N.K. Tovey, R.R. Boar, A. Grant and R.K. Turner (1991) *Streambank protection in England and Wales*, R&D Note 22. Bristol: National Rivers Authority.

Lewis, G. and G. Williams (1984) *Rivers and wildlife*

handbook. Sandy: Royal Society for the Protection of Birds.

Odgaard, A.J. and C.E. Mosconi (1987) Streambank protection by submerged vanes. *Journal of Hydraulic Engineering, American Society of Civil Engineers*, **113**(4), 520–36.

Paice, C. and R.D. Hey (1989) Hydraulic control of secondary circulation in meander bend to reduce outer bank erosion. In M.L. Albertson and R.H. Kia (Eds) *Design of Hydraulic Structures 89*. Rotterdam: Balkema, pp. 249–54.

Paice, C. and R.D. Hey (1993) The control and monitoring of local scour at bridge piers. In Hsieh Wen Shen, S.T. Shu and Feng Wen (Eds) *Hydraulic Engineering '93*, **1**. New York: American Society of Civil Engineers, pp. 1061–6.

Paice, C., R.D. Hey and J. Whitbread (1993) Protection of

bridge piers from scour. In J.E. Harding, G.A.R. Parke and M.J. Ryall (Eds) *Bridge Management 2*, London: Telford, pp. 543–52.

Purseglove, J. (1988) *Taming the flood*. Oxford: Oxford University Press.

Purseglove, J. (1991) Liberty, ecology, modernity. *New Scientist*, 28 September, 45–8.

Raynov, S., D. Pechinov, Z. Kopaliany and R.D. Hey (1986) *River response to hydraulic structures*. Paris: UNESCO.

Richards, K. (1982) *Rivers*. London: Methuen.

Schumm, S.A., M.D. Harvey and C.C. Watson (1984) *Incised channels: morphology, dynamics and control*. Littleton, Colorado: Water Resources Publications.

Williams, G.P. and M.G. Wolman (1984) *Downstream effects of dams on alluvial rivers*. Washington, DC: US Government Printing Office.

Winkley, B.R. (1982) Response of the Lower Mississippi to river training and realignment. In R.D. Hey, J.C. Bathurst and C.R. Thorne (Eds) *Gravel Bed Rivers*. Chichester: Wiley, pp. 659–81.

Further reading

This chapter briefly illustrates how knowledge of natural channel processes can be used to design environmentally sensitive river engineering works. Space precludes a full coverage of river mechanics principles which underpin the design of these schemes. Consequently it was not possible to provide detailed design guidelines.

For further information the reader is referred to the following books and papers.

Rivers: Processes and Form

Hey (1986).

Knighton, D. (1984) *Fluvial forms and processes*. London: Edward Arnold.

Morisawa, M. (1985) *Rivers*. London: Longman.

Richards (1982).

Appraisal of Engineering works and Environmentally Sensitive Design Procedures

Brookes (1988).

Hey, R.D. (1990) Environmental river engineering. *Journal of Water and Environmental Management*, **4**(4), 335–40.

Hey, R.D. (1993) Environmentally sensitive river engineering. In P. Calow and G.E. Petts (Eds) *Rivers Handbook II*. Oxford: Blackwell pp. 337–62.

Hey, R.D. and G.L. Heritage (1993) *Draft guidelines for design and restoration of flood alleviation schemes*, R & D Note 154. Bristol: National Rivers Authority.

Hey *et al.* (1990).

Paice and Hey (1989).

CHAPTER 8

Coastal processes and management

KEITH CLAYTON AND TIMOTHY O'RIORDAN

The coast is an amazingly awkward zone to manage. Yet it is of crucial significance for economic activity, leisure and natural restoration processes. Over two-thirds of marine biological activity takes place at or near the coast, and most especially in estuaries. In crucially significant nutrient-rich zones such as the Waddensee in the eastern North Sea, well over half the commercial fish population spawn and develop in their formative life cycle. To lose that area would be a major blow to North Sea marine ecology. Mangrove swamps in the coastal tropics play indispensable roles in regulating tides and floods, trapping nutrient-rich sediment and providing refuges for fish and invertebrates. They are under threat, as are the equally valuable coral reefs, from coastal mismanagement – everything from poaching of coral for commercial sale, to polluting discharges from hotels and coastal residences to altering marine currents as a result of port, road or marina developments.

The coastal zone is awkward to manage because it covers three 'territories', three administrative 'regions' and three 'styles' of management. The territories are:

- the offshore waters, beyond low tide and within national territorial jurisdiction;
- the coastal margin between low and high water tides and including estuaries;
- the littoral landward zone, including headlands, beaches and coastal settlement.

Normally, though not in every country, these zones are administered by different agencies reporting to a variety of government departments. In the UK, for example, the offshore is run by the agriculture departments, the shore by the crown and environment departments, and the littoral area by local authorities answerable to environment departments. Coastal protection is the responsibility of local government with all their heavy budget restrictions imposed by threats of rate 'capping' by central government, while flood defence is the responsibility of the National Rivers Authority answerable to the agriculture departments.

In other countries the mix is different, but the potential for conflict between competing administrations is ever-present. In the chapter that follows a case is made for *shared governance* of this zone, the sophisticated administrative marriage of local, regional and national authorities, coupled with regulatory agencies for planning, coastal defence, offshore minerals and fisheries management. In no country yet has there been a successful union of the triple alliance of land-use planning controls, offshore management controls and integrated coastal protection utilizing ecological-geomorphological principles.

This takes us to the third difficulty facing any much-needed reform in the management of the coastal zone. The management styles are so very different. Offshore, the long reach of formal planning regulation and full environmental impact assessment is often just beyond grasp. Marine gravel extraction, offshore pipelines and port developments, marinas beyond the coastline – all of these can elude the gambit of both strategic and local planning. Management here tends to be more pragmatic, alleviating problems of extraction and development by fairly aggressive measures according to tradition and influence.

On the actual coast, as the chapter that follows reveals, there is a persistent tension between the 'eco' orientated management measures, which are pro-active and exploratory, and the 'techno' style of build and be damned. This tends to be reactive, waiting for evidence of crisis or failure in protective structures, carried by the howl of protest from residents and property owners who have been allowed to move into vulnerable zones. They believe they are entitled to protection by a publicly financed agency whose remit is to safeguard. Similarly, on the landward part of the coastal triad of zones, the management style is primarily facilitative, allowing development to proceed with regard to flooding and possible sea-level rise, but by no means fully taking into account the special demands of the 'eco' protective approach of safeguarding sacrificial headlands, permitting coastal retreat of salt marshes into areas that should be specifically zoned against developments and designing new dunes in locations where development should be sympathetic and tourism appropriately limited. The tools are there in the planning kitboxes: as yet they have not been deployed as sensitively as they should.

This raises the perennial issue in environmental management, namely that of *policy integration*. Despite years of interdepartmental, interstate and intersectoral co-ordination the coastal zone is still a policy battleground in the USA. Subsidies encourage the overuse of chemicals that provide the coastal arena with nutrients and toxins, destroying shellfish and creating tourist-repelling algae. Flood insurance schemes promote insensitive waterside development, that is subsequently backed out by federal subsidies when the next hurricane strikes. In South Carolina, for example, Hurricane Hugo struck Folly Island, off the coast of Charleston, destroying or damaging 89 of 290 properties. Despite legislation to limit rebuilding, the act was changed to enable reconstruction in zones known to be subject to erosion and inundation. The flood insurance programme will cover such property. Federal tax provisions do not take into account environmentally sensitive economics, so it pays to develop wetlands, and receive a tax deduction in so doing, while the social value of the marsh is lost, because there is no tax subsidy for its survival.

These policy conflicts are very troublesome. They are rooted in the administrative history of the managing agencies, they create beneficiaries who lobby hard and successfully to protect their interests, they establish precedent that can be supported by the courts on technical rather than moral grounds, and they weaken the resolve of would-be reformers because the hurdles are not just high, but are also unpredictable. The chapter that follows offers a number of ways forward, building on the principles that guide this text as a whole.

Be aware: there is an administrative revolution taking place on the coast. For example, in the UK about half the coastal district authorities now co-ordinate planning and development in the coastal zone. Some have detailed inter-agency strategies backed by project officers and participatory steering groups. As yet, all have insufficient powers and resources, but their presence is influential.

The prospect of sea-level rise is likely to stimulate innovation and adaptation even more. Humans, like all organisms, are capable of responding to environmental change. But unlike their non-human comrades in the evolutionary game, humans make a fuss about it.

Further reading

R. Platt, T. Beatley and H.C. Miller (1991) The folly at Folly Beach and other failings of US coastal erosion policy. *Environment*, **33**(9), 6–9, 25–32.

Coastal zones are both vulnerable and populated. More than half the world's inhabitants live within 60 km of the coast. By 2020 this figure could be 70 per cent, many of whom will be concentrated in cities or densely packed agricultural areas. The rise of international tourism and the permanent lure of the beach has also created a new style of settlement and breed of resident in coastal areas, packed into resorts and expensive homes. The coast is both attractive and dangerous. It is constantly undergoing physical and biological alteration, yet habitation continues almost as if the zone was peaceful and stable. Coasts also contribute about 25 per cent of total biological productivity, supporting over two-thirds of the world's fisheries and nine-tenths of the shellfish industry.

The coastal zone has always proved a problem to manage. In the introductions both to this section and to this chapter the point is made that both institutions and policies usually fail to coincide for compatible and anticipatory management of this vulnerable and unstable area. The trouble is that the coast is too much in demand for it to be left to nature to determine its fate. Sea-level rise presents more of a formidable problem than is generally realized because it threatens wealth, property protectionism, powerful economic interests, it can swing political votes and it further reinforces the status of an engineering fraternity that does not like to be beaten. It is no wonder that the coast is such an administrative battleground, full of agency jealousies, ill-matched budgets and suspicious tiers of government.

In this relative state of managerial anarchy, powerful interests can gain ground. Engineers of the 'old school' delight when crisis creates a serious threat, even if they are very concerned about the suffering and the distress thereby caused. In the wake of a coastal disaster, the tendency is to reassert an engineering-dominant approach, almost as if it is a mission in itself. The true adjusters are those prepared to relocate, to identify and enforce strict zones of managed retreat, which should have considerable recreational and wildlife advantage, and to establish sound budgets for compensation for those deliberately left vulnerable in the face of a managed retreat management regime. All this will take great vision, much public involvement, steadiness of nerve and extremely effective communication. These are all qualities of good interdisciplinarity in applied environmental science.

Coastal processes

Coasts are formed by waves and currents. Waves in turn are generated by wind, which converts its kinetic energy to the sea surface. The longer the fetch or distance of wind-disturbed sea, the more powerful the waves. Surfing is always most popular on open ocean coasts. As waves approach shallow water they dissipate their energy in sediment disturbance, erosive power and broken water. The shape of the coast influences the pattern of energy. Converging orthogonals, the force of energy at right angles to the wave crest, focus wave power, while diverging orthogonals disperse it. With satellite technology it is possible to map potential wave energy for different wind directions, and thus to explain the pattern of erosion and accretion zones for subsequent planning purposes. By adding an understanding of the processes at work to historical records of coastal change, this allows the recognition of persistently hazardous coastal sectors. How far that will in time be converted into planning restrictions will depend on the credibility of the science and the political influence of planning and management agencies.

As waves usually approach any beach at an angle, part of their energy is converted into lateral movement of sediment. Even where wind patterns are diverse, the importance of fetch will ensure that this drift will be predictable and often significant, for example beach sediment moves southward along the California coast at a rate of about 300 000 m^3 each year. Severe storms, maybe occurring with a probability of once in 10 or 20 years, will account for an extraordinary amount of sediment disturbance. Whole beaches can form or disappear overnight. This episodic convulsion not only gives rise to much property loss and human suffering; it is the very essence of coastal formation. Figure 8.1 shows how the coast of England and Wales has prograded and eroded over the past 100 years.

In addition to wave-generated sediment movement, tidal currents sort sediment and help to shape the geomorphology of the coastline. This is dominant in deeper areas offshore and especially important in estuarine areas protected by offshore bars or spits. From a management point of view, estuarine tidal-induced sediment movement will offset dredging and can move toxic material buried below the surface. In densely populated areas where river waters may carry sediment from polluting industrial zones, such as the Rotterdam harbour at the mouth of the Rhine, this can be a severe problem – so severe that the Dutch government is

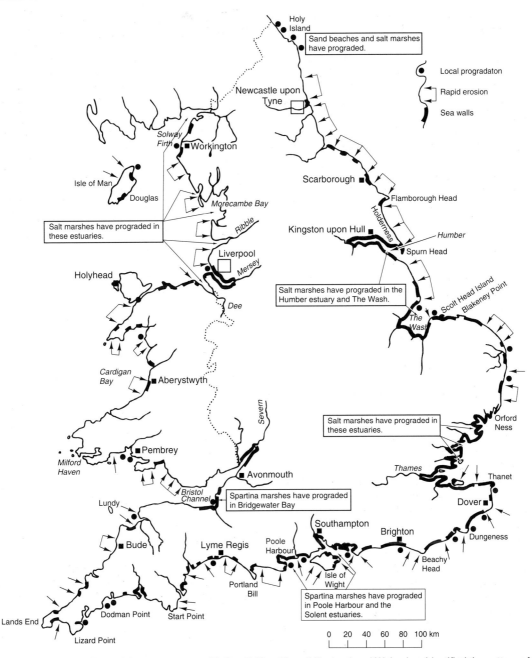

Fig 8.1 Comparison of late 19th century maps with the 1980 outline of England and Wales has identified the pattern of coastline changes shown here.

contemplating an ingenious variant of a tradeable permit. The proposal is to establish a property right in effluent discharge by issuing a covenant to the polluting firm. This is a form of voluntary payment by the identified polluter to pay for sediment removal, or stabilization, in lieu of court proceedings and the possibility of a heavy fine. The scheme relies on proof of effluent discharge and sediment transport. 'Finger printing' by coding indicator chemicals of particular effluents together with sound modelling can provide this service.

Beaches are forever readjusting. Their prime function is to buffer the coast from wave and tidal energy. Without this protection, soft coastlines would disappear very rapidly. Beaches form from a 'sediment store' collected from the sea floor, from eroded headlands or from riverborne materials. Shingle tends to be found where wave energy is concentrated, and sand or mud where it is more dispersed. Figure 8.2 describes coastal terminology. Dunes are especially important in this arrangement for they feed beaches when they erode, but re-establish naturally during periods of relative calm. Dunes may be stabilized by long-rooted grasses such as marram. This not only binds the sand, forming a thin organic soil on the surface, it also lowers wind

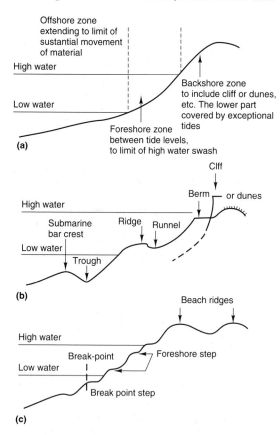

(a)

(b)

(c)

Fig 8.2 Coastal terminology: (a) The beach in profile; (b) composite sand beach profile; (c) composite shingle beach

speed, thereby encouraging greater sand settlement.

Dunes can be damaged more by the trampling of visitors than by natural factors: hence the need for tough dune management schemes to keep people off vulnerable or damaged areas. More often than not wardens and public information programmes are necessary to ensure that trampling is kept to a minimum. Better public understanding of the ecological and geomorphological role of dunes in beach formation and coastal protection has to be actively promoted. This will become even more of an issue as dune reconstruction and new dune construction is undertaken as part of the strategic response to sea-level rise. In the Netherlands, for example, dune protection is a major component in coastal management. All existing dunes are safeguarded by law and by sympathetic management practice. Dune restoration zones have also been identified. The cost benefit justification of this programme includes estimates of the recreational value of the dunes using the travel cost method as outlined in Chapter 3, and economic-ecological approaches as presented in Chapter 2. Without these techniques, it would have been a little more difficult to invest in the restoration programme. They are even used as sources of fresh groundwater supply.

Salt marshes are found in sheltered coastal regions where wave energy is dissipated by offshore bars or barrier beaches or alongside estuaries. The marshes themselves are efficiently flooded and drained by an intricate web of tidal creeks, bordered by vegetation that traps the mud and builds the marsh slowly above to the level of the highest tides. The marshes themselves are important converters of sulphur, and sequesterers of nutrients and toxic sediment. Their bio-geo-chemical role in the ocean–atmosphere interface is nowadays a focus of much scientific research. Early findings suggest a self-regulating ability to maintain carbon, sulphur and methane generation. Not only do such marshes protect soft coasts and flood banks from wave action, they may have an important role to play in accommodating the rising fluxes of carbon and sulphur. In addition, salt marsh habitats are extremely valuable for bird-life. Wading birds can be found in great numbers, as for example on the Waddensee and the North Norfolk Coast around the North Sea and the Carolina–Delaware estuaries of the eastern United States. Many salt marshes are protected zones for conservation and amenity purposes, with a social value so large as to justify their extension by carefully managed controlled retreat, i.e. the removal of flood banks from in front of reclaimed former marshes.

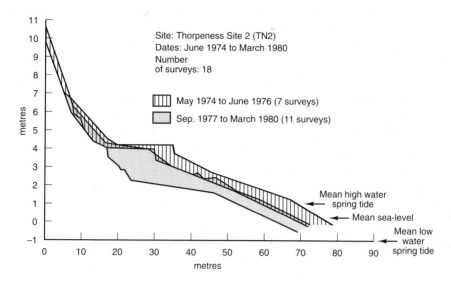

Fig 8.3 Cross-section illustrating the sweep zones.

Figure 8.3 illustrates a typical set of beach profiles. The profile has an enormous influence on the erosion potential of a beach, as well as on the likely shape of the beach during a period of persistent sea-level rise. Under what is known as the Bruun Rule, as devised by a Norwegian engineer:

$$\text{shoreline erosion}\,(R) = \frac{\text{Profile width} \times \text{sea–level rise}\,(s')}{\text{profile depth}\,(z)}$$

as illustrated in Figure 8.4.

The rate of erosion can be modelled as follows:

- record wind direction and speeds over as long a time as possible;
- model the relationship between wind speed and direction and wave height from both observation and wave tank experimentation;
- in turn, model wave diffraction on the basis of the beach profile, using Snell's Law of wave refraction.

Persistently eroding coastal cliffs provide an important supply of beach material. They involve an erosive offshore zone and at the coast an efficient littoral drift. Offshore sand and shingle banks in areas of relative stability act as sediment stores and can prove invaluable as buffers for exceptionally high tides. Zones which are relatively self-regulating in this regard are sometimes referred to as coastal cells. These are forever changing, but can be used to measure sediment erosion, transport and deposition. Figure 8.5 shows how this technique can be used to reveal the sand budget of the East Anglian coast. The role of 'feeder cliffs' as sources of continual replenishment is of the utmost importance, especially in lowlands where rivers do not deliver sand and shingle to the coast. Such areas should be protected from any form of development and deliberately allowed to continue to erode.

Sea defence and coastal protection

In the UK the responsibility for managing the coast falls to two ministries and two political jurisdictions (see introduction to this chapter). The coast itself is the responsibility of the Ministry of Agriculture, Fisheries

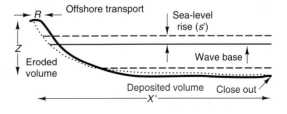

Fig 8.4 The Bruun Rule: in 1962, Bruun described a concept that attempted to explain the development of an equilibrium coastal profile during landward movement of the shoreline as a result of sea-level rise. Bruun assumed that there were no long-term changes in energy input and sediment volume.

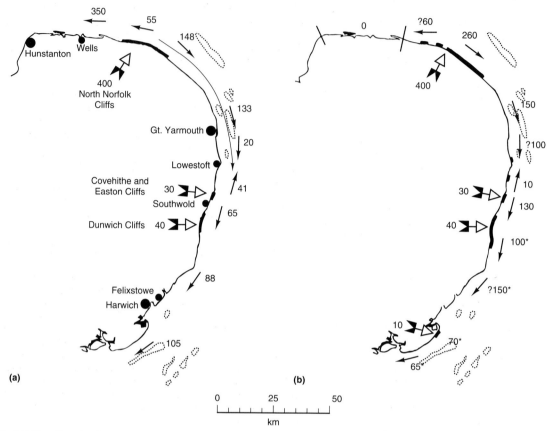

Fig 8.5 The East Anglian sand budget. Cliff inputs and littoral drift values in 1000 m³/yr. (a) Computed net longshore sand transport values over 13 years (1964–76). (b) Most probable values derived from examination of gross values and net values for longshore transport over varying periods of time, using both computed values and those calculated from wave observer observations, 1974–79. These are regarded as relatively reliable values (over a period of 20 years or more), but for those marked ? the value remains uncertain, although the direction is certain. The asterisks note theoretical values not reached due to lack of sand and/or lack of exposed beach at all states of tide. The main offshore banks are indicated on both maps.

and Food (MAFF) and its agency, the National Rivers Authority (NRA). The NRA is divided into ten regions, and directed in its work by local flood defence committees. These are composed, for the most part, of landowners in flood-prone areas and local authority councillors, more often than not, representing coastal constituencies. The coastal zone landward of the sea is the responsibility of the Department of the Environment (DoE), and through it, the district councils bordering the coast. They aim to control erosion and to stabilize the coastal zone. They receive grants for approved coastal protection schemes from the MAFF, but generally have to meet the cost of repairs themselves.

Cash bottlenecks are also common for flood protection schemes known as sea defence. In the UK the county councils must contribute about a quarter of the NRA sea defence capital works programme. That money eventually comes back from the DoE a year later. In the meantime the county councils must levy their council taxpayers for the capital when they also have to raise revenue for a host of other requirements, such as the police, social services and roads. The formula on which county spending is assessed does not take into account specific sea defence needs. Consequently, the counties are regularly faced with a bill that exceeds their actual spending allocation. Even though

Box 8.1 The Venice Lagoon

By any standards Venice is both priceless and imperilled. Its maritime dominance in the 13th to 16th centuries endowed it with the stability and wealth to construct a magnificent city on a series of islands lying within a lagoon, feebly protected by an offshore bar. Over the centuries the bar has been breached for commercial shipping, the lagoon has been dredged for access and landfill, and much of the 'barriers' or ecologically rich mudflats has disappeared, or has been marginalized. Yet Venice is subject to periodic storm surges, bursts of exceptionally high tides pushed by strong winds on the eastern flank of a southerly moving alpine depression. On 4 November 1986 the tide reached 194 cm compared with an average high tide of 50–60 cm. The famous St Mark's Square was flooded to over a metre, and over 70% of the city was under water. Nowadays, tides of 100 cm occur five or six times per year: a sea-level rise of 30 cm would mean that St Mark's Square would flood nearly every day. These tides are not only a great nuisance to the tourist and to commerce generally: they corrode the foundation of the buildings and increase both odour and mosquito problems.

In 1992 the Italian government allocated $1–2 billion to the preparation of a plan to place hydraulic barriers across the four entrances to the Lagoon. These structures will consist of 79 flap gates, each one of which is designed to rise to an angle of 50° against the rising sea. The gates can operate independently, allowing tides of a modest height to enter through one gate so as to increase the flushing capacity of the Lagoon itself, which is heavily polluted with nutrient and agricultural run-off. In addition, the Lagoon will be manipulated by four schemes designed to restore its capacity to absorb high waters:

1. Reconstruction of the coastal marshlands, presently only half their original extent of 100 km^2. This is being undertaken via a series of experimental schemes of salt marsh reconstruction.
2. Maintenance of the complex hydraulic network of the Lagoon, presently altered by erosion and dredging, to permit greater water circulation to coastal marshes.
3. Replanting the marsh vegetation in shallow areas both to stabilize the muds and colonize the mudflats for ecological reasons.
4. The construction of sand bypasses to recapture part of the sediment carried by the marine currents, presently deflected by the inlet jetties.

The Venice Lagoon Project is well analysed on paper, but a long way from actual completion. Part of the problem lies in the multiple jurisdictions between local, regional and national governments. But a major difficulty is the obtaining of agreement amongst local governments to fund sewage treatment works, removal of nutrients and reduction of agricultural fertilizer application. Ironically the success of the physical barrier to control tides could seriously damage the morphology and ecology of the Lagoon unless the Project is designed and managed as an integrated whole.

the money is eventually returned, this is of little consequence if the county is restricted in its total spend by central government allocations based on theoretical spending assessments.

There is thus a tug of war between the coastal counties and the local land drainage committees, in which they are well represented, and the specific needs of the NRA. Engineering works rarely receive funding to the degree to which finances are required, and each year of short-fall builds up a capital spend backlog that can prove politically embarrassing.

Behind the facade of busy engineering activity there is much political and economic turmoil. In no country is there administrative cohesion over managing the coast. New Zealand passed the Resource Conservation Act that provides for a single coastal agency: but the landward position is still administered by two tiers of local authorities. In the USA conflicts abound between federal, state and local agencies, especially over land-use planning controls and the protection of vulnerable beach-funding areas and wetlands. The Venice Lagoon project has been static for many years because of an inability to co-ordinate regional and national priorities for spending, despite the increasing threat of *'aqua-alta'* (high tides) and an administrative committee designed to co-ordinate the various responsible parties (see Box 8.1).

Clearly it is in the best interests of all to build durable and cost-effective coastal protection works. The question is, what is durable and what is cost effective when it comes to coastal defence?

The commonest form of defence is the shingle or clay bank, or seawall. These are usually designed to withstand a high tide of 1 in 20 years' recurrence for small areas of farmland, 1 in 50 years' recurrence for roads and rail communications, and 1 in 200 years' recurrence for commercial and residential property. These structures rarely last more than 40 years, and

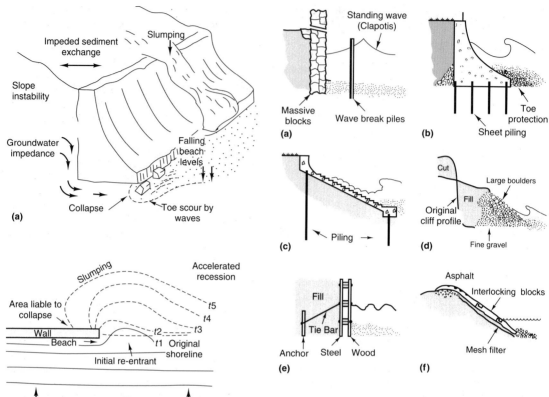

(a)

(b)

Fig 8.6 Some environmental problems relating to seawalls: (a) falling beach levels, poor drainage and impeded sediment exchange lead to both undercutting and overslumping; (b) at the end of the wall 'flanking' is common, with an erosional re-entrant forming and eventually scouring behind the wall causing collapse. t_1 to t_5 represent progradation over time.

Fig 8.7 An energy-based sequence of shore protection designs (high to low, a–f): (a) vertical seawall constructed of resistant interlocking blocks; (b) curved seawall with toe protection; (c) curved and stepped wall secured by piling; (d) rubble-mound armouring plus regrading of the coastal slope; (e) bulkhead of wood or steel; (f) revetment made of armour blocks, gabions or asphalt.

some fail quite soon after construction if the coastal geomorphology is not fully understood. Figure 8.6 shows how inadequate drainage protection can undermine a cliff floor wall, partly because the cliff is not allowed to erode. This causes a loss of feed to the beach. Also, where a seawall or groyne system ends there may be additional erosion on what might otherwise have been a relatively stable coast.

Figure 8.7 shows more clearly how various coastal defences operate. The main problem with most of these designs is that they cause wave reflection, and hence greater erosion of the beach, thereby exposing the foundations to more erosive force and seepage. Revetments, or wood structures designed to dissipate wave energy, are equally damaging if fully planked. The better design should be to allow some seawater to pass through with shore or cliff sediment to a controlled extent. Similarly groynes, or wood structures built at right angles to the coast, should be widely spaced to allow for the accumulation of sediment. This means that beach material should rest between the upper and lower sections of adjacent groynes, rather like a continually filling bathtub with a controlled outlet. The correct spacing is a matter of trial and error, knowledge of wave patterns and intensity, and calculations as to trapping ability and groyne effectiveness. Figure 8.8 describes the sequence of calculations. It is also essential that sand or shingle is placed between newly constructed groynes and not 'stolen' from the natural littoral drift.

Integrated coastal zone management

Integrated coastal zone management is the ideal arrangement for which everybody strives, but few attain. Essentially it is the recognition of four principles:

1. That natural processes of defence and protection should be encouraged, costed properly and fully incorporated into any plan or management scheme.

2. That natural zones essential to this purpose, such as headlands, dunes, salt marshes and wetlands, should be adequately protected by law, cleared of existing settlement, with compensation if necessary, and carefully monitored for their continuing role.

3. That coastal defence works should always be designed sympathetically and encourage the retention of a natural beach, and that cost benefit analyses should recognize the essential linkage between the two.

4. That land-use planning formally take into account the vulnerable areas of coast subject to sea-level rise and increased storminess, so that no new settlement or economic activity is permitted in such areas, and, where possible, existing buildings are left unprotected, again with compensation where necessary.

These are tough and controversial requirements. One can readily see why they would not easily be met even in cohesive administrations. But in the case of jealously protected governmental levels, where cost benefit has not yet come of age in terms of the ideas promoted in Chapters 2 and 3, it is easy to understand that the politics of coastal protection confound integrated management.

Box 8.2 The Broads flood alleviation strategy

The Norfolk and Suffolk Broads (lakes) in eastern England are one of the most important wetlands in North Western Europe. The 20 000 ha region is essentially the drained and undrained valleys of three rivers which converge at Great Yarmouth. The whole area is below the level of high tides, and is very vulnerable to storm surge tides carried by northerly winds on a depression running south-east across the North Sea. At present, the coastal defences are relatively sound, having been built and rebuilt since the great storm surge of 1 February 1953. Ten years ago, the justification of any scheme to upgrade the slowly sinking river walls and to block the rising sea by a barrier at Yarmouth required some heroic calculations of improved agricultural output in the drained marshes. Since cereals were both heavily subsidized and in surplus, this justification simply would not be made in the face of criticism by environmental groups anxious to retain the historical grazing marsh landscapes and the diverse aquatic plantago of the drainage dykes.

Nowadays the whole region is designated as an environmentally sensitive area. This means that the UK Ministry of Agriculture pays about £2.5 million annually to farmers to retain unprofitable grazing and to recreate the ecologically diverse drainage systems. This investment provides the basis for an ecologically biased cost benefit analysis along the lines discussed in Chapter 2. The conservation interests in the region believe that a combination of a barrier on the Bure river along with washlands to absorb tidal surges on the southern rivers would provide adequate levels of protection and a much more diverse ecology. The local land drainage com-

mittee prefers a single barrier on the inner Yare with no washlands but with a much higher level of protection for all the valleys. Current government guidelines to give priority to the protection of urban areas suggest an outer barrier at the Yare mouth which would protect Great Yarmouth as well as the Broads. For navigation-related reasons, however, this option has been ruled out. The matter is still to be resolved, but it seems likely that neither a barrier on the Yare nor a smaller barrier on the ecologically sensitive Bure will prove cost-effective. This is the case even with liberal use and contingent valuation studies in the case of the Yare barrier. Therefore a program of bank strengthening along with planned localized washlands, coupled to land set-aside schemes for surplus agricultural land for local tidal relief schemes is being prepared, along with a scheme to augment low river flows by freshwater injection from boreholes. This should keep saltwater intrusion to the less ecologically sensitive lower reaches.

The Broads story reveals the intricate politics of land versus soft engineering styles, the changing role of cost benefit analysis as agricultural profitability and land-use decline, and the scope for extending a biodiversity component of agricultural extensification as part of a total approach to flood protection. This is a case of integrated coastal management, permitting the scope for controlled retreat work on protective scheme that is both desirable and flexible. But the compromise took three years of intense argument and counter argument to achieve. Antagonistic attitudes of mind were not noticeably altered by the process.

Integrated coastal management is not a single-minded outcome. It is a process with many possible pathways, depending on the physical, institutional and political circumstances of coastal protection. It would be most unwise to lay down a blueprint planning guide. Three criteria can be used to assist the evaluation of good performance in integrated coastal management:

1. *Optimization of multiple objectives.* Multiple objections cannot be met without some losing while others gain. The aim of integrated coastal management should be to create structures of administration and public involvement geared to achieving agreement. This may mean sub-optimal realization of objectives for each special interest group, but at least respect for and support towards a common goal. It also means flexible and adaptive management geared to shifts in information, scientific experimentation and shifting public interest demands as all this innovation proceeds. Clearly this also indicates the need for imaginative and innovative cost benefit analysis backed by informed public support (see Box 8.2).

2. *Maintenance of life-support processes.* A well-managed coastal project should demonstrably enhance the life-support systems of the coastal zone, by empathetic design, by creating and protecting habitats, and by ensuring that there is room for ignorance because of the necessarily limited understanding of ecological resilience. This requires a sound scientific basis of the workings of the coast, good ecological and hydrological modelling as far

as knowledge allows, and honest acceptance of the limits of knowledge. Uncertainty is not an ogre if it is properly taken into account.

3. *Responsive management.* The 'cost' of any coastal zone scheme must be seen in terms of its success in balancing inherently contradictory objectives and in guaranteeing ecological viability. Where these objectives are evident, the 'benefits' are partly measured by the procedures that achieve such success. Responsive management translates into the satisfaction of trust in a scheme that is well grounded, well monitored and well communicated to those who have a stake in its outcome. Participation is not a democratic symbol: it should be a process of guidance and continual readjustment to a changing set of optimized objectives that become compatible only by the revelation of shared interest (see Box 8.3).

Still, progress is being made. There has been a steady shift amongst all engineering organizations in favour of a mix of beach nourishment and the concept of controlled retreat along with conventional revetments, seawalls and groynes. There is much talk of 'soft engineering' and of 'working with nature'. This is an important step forward, for the cost benefit analyses have to incorporate some measure of recreational benefit (using the travel cost method) and amenity provision (using contingent valuation).

Secondly, the precautionary principle is now being applied more readily to such aspects as safeguarding coastal wetlands, controlling polluting emissions, notably nutrients, and placing more of the burden of an

---

Box 8.3 The Australian coastal zone inquiry

Throughout 1992 to 1994 the Resource Assessment Commission of the Australian Commonwealth government held hearings and developed position papers on the management of the whole Australian coast. The Commission concluded along the following lines:

- *Coastal zone management.* There is a need for much better co-ordination of commonwealth, state and local government, with pooling of both objectives and budgets, and a full acceptance of the principle of shared governance. This means establishing legally supported administrative co-operatives headed by project co-ordinators on a sub-regional basis for structures of waste.
- *Precaution in pollution and land-use planning.* Coastal pollution is already excessive and wor-

rying. The precautionary approach, coupled to ecological economics, should be applied to sewage treatment clean-up, control of agricultural wastes and estuary clean-up programmes. Tourist developments should be strictly controlled, with safeguards for key habitats, and the polluter pays principle should be extended to a tourist impact tax to fund sustainable tourism projects.

- *Involvement of indigenous peoples.* In many parts of northern and western Australia indigenous peoples have *de facto* property rights in fishing, tourism development, marine parks management and the protection of cultural and sacred sites. These requirements should be built into the coastal management co-operatives.

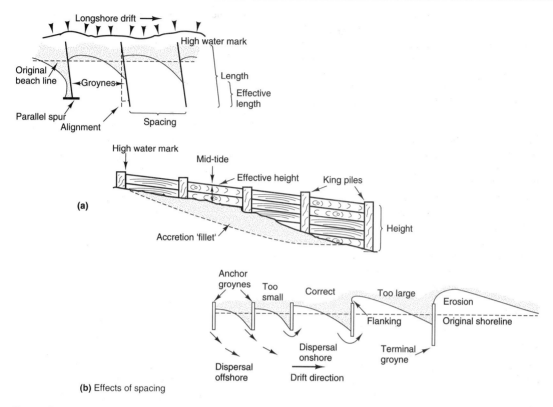

Fig 8.8 Groyne design and spacing. (a) Groynes should be designed to trap and retain sediment, but all too often this is not accomplished. Trapping ability and groyne effectiveness can be assessed by knowing the amounts of material moving in and out of the groyne field. The accretion 'fillet' in the middle diagram may occupy only a small proportion of the inter-groyne volume. (b) Correct spacing of groynes is probably a function of wave parameters. Relatively small spacings promote flanking. Terminal groynes are often responsible for downdrift erosion. Trapping ability (%) = volume retained × '100'/(length × spacing × height); groyne effectiveness (%) = (volume input − output (downdrift)) × 100/volume input (updrift).

acceptable environmental assessment on the shoulders of developers. In addition, strategic environmental impact assessment is becoming in vogue. This is the meshing of coastal management policies over nature conservation, pollution control, tourism restraint and water use limitation with long-term plans to shape the coast to accommodate sea-level rise. To date, achievements in this area have been modest, because policy integration is still a distant vision. But at least the matter is getting a hearing in this period of local level Agenda 21s, natural sustainable development strategies, and increasing pressure on governments to incorporate environmental thinking into all aspects of resource management policy.

Sadly all this will come too late for many populated and vulnerable coasts. The low-lying islands of the Pacific and Caribbean are extremely vulnerable even to modest sea-level rise, yet they cannot obtain insurance cover for flooding to existing property, including resort hotels, let alone any compensation for property removal. The consequences for future economic development are potentially severe, yet no compensation is in the offing. In every country battles are looming over the denial of taxpayer-financed protection for property in the wave firing line, especially after a flurry of storm damage. The politics of property wealth coupled to post-disaster sympathy usually combine to protect such areas just when controlled retreat would prove a better option. Despite all the huffing and puffing, EIAs are not particularly effective in safeguarding wetlands and other vital national zones on the coast. Nor is the revamped cost benefit analysis a particular safeguard.

As the IPCC gathers its strength in identifying more comprehensive approaches to coastal zone management, so one hopes that some of these deficiencies will be overcome. The omens are not good, when seawater is lapping at the door, and the cry is to protect rather than to retreat. One possible breakthrough might come with the strengthening of national strategic coastal management plans, on the back of the Agenda 21 exercise, and cash for compensating the removal of protection of property on coasts that should be returned to natural processes. That money could come, in part, from a carbon tax. After all, sea-level rise is arguably 60 per cent due to carbon dioxide. This opens up the Pandora's box of directional revenue from environmental taxation. When all these jigsaw pieces fit into place, integrated coastal management might just come of age.

Further reading

A good start can be made in R.W.G. Carter (1988) *Coastal environments: an introduction to the physical, ecological and cultural systems of coastlines* (Academic Press, London). For the geomorphological story see K.M. Clayton (1979) *Coastal geomorphology* (Macmillan Educational Books, London). A useful perspective on how various countries approach this topic is given in Organization of Economic Cooperation and Development (1993) *Coastal zone management: integrated policies* (OECD, Paris). For a perspective on ecological planning see R.V. Salm and J.R. Clark (1984) *Marine and coastal protected areas: a guide for planners and managers* (International Union for the Conservation of Nature, Gland, Switzerland).

CHAPTER 9

Predicting sea-level rise and managing the consequences

KEITH CLAYTON

As we saw from the previous chapter, the coast can be both ecologically sensitive and highly populated. Many coastal areas are vulnerable to sea-level rise. Nowhere is this more so than the thirty or so small island states, mostly in the Pacific or Indian Oceans, whose highest points do not exceed one metre above sea-level. Should eventual sea-level rise exceed this height these whole nations would disappear. No wonder they have formed an association that vigorously defends the precautionary principle. Yet even today it is very unlikely that the international insurance industry will provide cover for any major development on the coasts of these tourist-dependent islands. This means that either the island economies have to provide their own insurance support against coastal flooding, or the scope for more overseas currency from new tourist resorts will be severely limited.

The small island state dilemma raises a number of points about the management of sea-level rise. First of all, how much rise should be planned for? Clearly this in turn depends on how far the global community is prepared to reduce its greenhouse gas emissions. For example to hold sea level rise at about 20 cms for example, by stabilizing CO_2 to 1990 levels by 2000 and keeping the total CO_2 concentration steady at 400 ppmv thereafter, could cost $15 trillion dollars. To allow the seas to rise by say another 10 cm, to stabilize CO_2 at 500 ppmv would cost possibly $6 trillion. These are guesstimates based on still relatively early modelling but they provide an order of magnitude for the kind of global expenditures necessary to restrict the associated damage attached to sea-level rise (see Kay *et al.* 1993 for a full summary). For the USA, however, the cost of sea-level rise of 30–40 cm would be in the range of $5–10 billion or 0.2 per cent of GDP. The programmes of defensive walls, set back schemes and imaginative coastal redesign would create jobs and rearrange tourist resorts and holiday home complexes. Arguably the US could 'absorb' sea level rise, albeit with important adjustments for the water supplies of deltaic cities such as New Orleans.

But the picture would be vastly different for the small island states and the great swathes of agricultural lands of the Third World river deltas, notably in Bangladesh and Pakistan but also Indonesia and South-east Asia generally. Here the people, many of whom are landless and desperate, are marginal and so extremely vulnerable to sea-level rise of even a few centimetres. The USA and Europe (including the former Soviet Union) are all big emitters of CO_2: how far do they care about the additional centimetres of sea-level rise, when their economies are already strained by political manipulation of budgets, trade and industrial policies? The connections do not seem that clear to hard-pressed politicians.

The UN Commission on Sustainable Development, introduced in Chapter 1 and discussed further in Chapter 19, could address the political and ethical aspects to these issues via its analysis of sustainable development strategies and its attention to integrated coastal management. There is a middle way, both to adjust to sea-level rise as well as to curtail the emissions that heighten the sea unnecessarily. Environmental sciences can do much to develop the proper relationship between preventative coastal planning and precautionary reduction of greenhouse emissions.

Recent sea-level history

Sea-level is changing all the time with a twice-daily tidal cycle on many coasts and the change with each phase of the moon from the limited range of neap tides to the larger range of spring tides. Nevertheless, it is possible to extract an average sea-level over a period of time and this is done by analysing the complex record at a gauging site. Such tide gauges are not particularly common, for example there are only about a dozen long and reliable records available in the UK, though in recent years interest in sea-level changes and in the risk of tidal inundation during storms has led to the establishment of new gauge sites.

Even the North Sea gauges show that the relationship between the levels of land and sea is a complex one. In southern Britain, and indeed along most of the east coast of England, the long-term trend is for sea-level to rise, at a rate of one or two millimetres each year. But in Scotland and Norway the tide gauges show a long-term fall in sea-level (Figure 9.1). A similar pattern occurs in the USA, with rising sea-levels from New York southwards and falling sea-levels along the coast of New England and in Alaska. The reason is the same in each case: the record of the northern gauges is affected by the continuing recovery of the Earth's crust following the depression caused by the huge ice sheets, two or more kilometres thick, which accumulated during the last ice age some 18 000 years ago. Although these melted away between 14 000 and 8 000 years ago, the crust is still slowly easing back into its balanced position without the ice load. In addition, some of the gauges are also affected by the additional load of sea-water which has been imposed as the same melting ice sheets returned water to the oceans and caused sea-level to rise from about −130 m 18 000 years ago to close to current levels about 5 000 years ago.

We cannot determine a very reliable trend for average sea-level from these few gauges, but if we select a wider sample of gauges from around the world and try to eliminate those that are in areas of post-glacial uplift or of current subsidence (e.g. on river deltas), we discover that global sea-level is rising at a little over a millimetre a year. This rate of rise seems to have been going on for at least the past century, but we do not know when it started. Most probably it is a response to the natural global warming which has followed the Little Ice Age of the 17th to 18th centuries.

Box 9.1 Coastal vulnerability and flood hazard

The coast is a hazardous zone, so why do so many people live there and why has it been used for urban and industrial purposes in so many places? In a few cases, of course, industries and other activities must be at the coast, whether for sea access for fishing or other ports, or for cooling water as for nuclear and conventional power stations. And seaside resorts can hardly be anywhere else, though they need not be located on eroding coasts or land liable to tidal flood. But most coastal development falls outside these requirements and need not be at hazard.

The reasons people will live and build in hazardous areas are complex, but they can be related to the themes of risk assessment outlined in Chapter 16:

- The benefits of enjoying the coast are real and continuous, but the dangers are uncertain and very episodic. So people tend to play down the risks and play up the benefits.
- Coastal defence works are built by agencies who get state cash to do the job because there is property to defend. So it follows that the more defences are built, the more people will wish to move in behind them to a potentially dangerous zone. And the more houses are built, so the case for an even better coastal defence scheme increases – and so the cycle continues.
- For some very poor people the dangerous coast may be the only land available to them for settlement. The landless are the most vulnerable to disease or disaster, as in the Ganges–Brahmaputra delta of Bangladesh. Paradoxically, those most likely to suffer from coastal erosion or flooding are the very rich in the developed countries and the very poor in the developing world.

The response of the coast to current sea-level rise

Surveys of beaches around the world show that sand loss from beaches and consequent landward movement of coastlines is very widespread. While there is no single reason for this tendency, it is a response we would expect from persistent sea-level rise. The reason that sea-level rise leads to erosion is that deeper water gradually allows higher energy waves to reach the beach, and these will erode it, seeking to restore equilibrium by moving the beach landward, so stabilizing the wave energy reaching the coast.

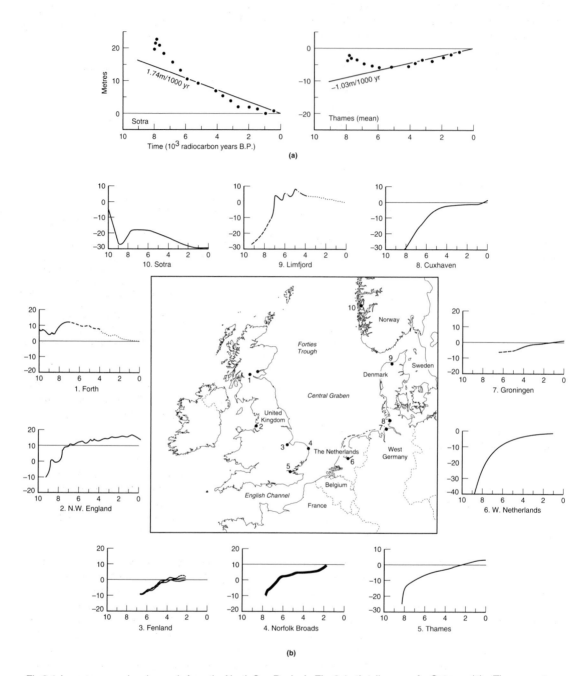

Fig 9.1 Long term sea-level records from the North Sea Basin. In Fig. 9.1a the diagrams for Sotra and the Thames estuary show the generalized trend of local land movements by allowing for the change of sea-level as the ice sheets of the world melted. The sloping line shows a fall due to isotopic uplift at Sotra and a rise, due to local subsidence, in the Thames estuary. The graphs around the map in Fig. 9.1b show the record of sea-level change against the land over the last 10 000 years. Note how the relatively stable southern sites record the recovery of sea-level as the ice melted, the more northern sites record the interaction of the overall rise of sea-level with the recovery of the land after the ice melted.

If we did not seek to make use of the coastal zone, there would be few problems as a result of the erosion that is occurring. However, over the last 150 years almost all societies have developed their coastal zones, using them for agriculture (with flood banks and drainage systems to allow this) and increasingly for urban settlements. Indeed, many of the major cities of the world such as London, New Orleans and Bangkok are already at risk of flood and will be at increasing risk in the future.

There are, of course, some activities that must go on in a coastal location, such as ports and those industries requiring direct access to the sea for transport or cooling water (Box 9.1). The development of the coast for recreation has also led to urbanization of the coastal zone, though this has been greatly increased by the common pattern of retirement to coastal towns in the developed world, adding large resident populations to those actually needed to service a tourist industry. As a result we have built up and developed this littoral hazard zone and from time to time tidal flooding and cliff erosion take their toll. Even the developing world faces increasing problems as coastal areas are developed for tourism, whilst some small island states (especially oceanic coral islands) have no high ground at all and feel particularly vulnerable.

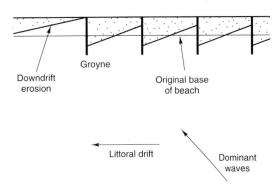

Fig 9.2 How an effective groyne works.
Although groynes dam the movement of sand along the beach by littoral drift, their impact on littoral drift through the reorientation of the beach within each groyne bay is more important. Thus if the beach is reasonably close to being normal to the approach of the dominant waves (usually those of longest fetch), the reorientation can bring the littoral drift close to zero, so conserving beach volume. However, if the beach is more than about 15 ° from the alignment normal to the dominant waves, then although the groynes hold back some sand, at the same time they divert much of it so far offshore it is lost to the beach system. A good example of effective groynes is seen in the photograph in Box 9.2.

Engineers and the stabilization of the coastline

As in all cases of natural hazard, the most common reaction has been to build engineering structures that are designed to eliminate the threat to life and property. In the early days, such structures seemed almost entirely beneficial; they reduced the threat of overtopping and consequent flooding and stopped erosion where this was occurring (Figure 9.2). However, as the natural processes that were causing the erosion continued to operate seaward of the structure, offshore deepening and/or beach retreat continued. If the beach could not move landward because the top was fixed by a wall, then the beach level fell; this soon exposed the wall to increasing wave attack, and with reflection of waves from the wall, beach sediment loss was accelerated. As a result, walls found themselves without adequate foundations and they collapsed. Even more serious has been the effect of engineering works on coastal stability. Where natural sources of beach sediment have been eliminated by protective works, beaches further down

the coast lose volume and cease to provide a good buffer against wave attack. Rivers carrying sediment from California to the Nile have been dammed, trapping the sediment that used to reach the beaches or deltas in the reservoirs. The result is increasing coastal erosion as the perturbed system attempts to come back into balance. In other locations, shingle beaches have been steepened to raise their crest and eliminate wave overtopping: the resulting steep beach face loses sediment offshore and beaches that have survived for thousands of years have been destroyed in decades (Box 9.2).

By the second half of the century the extension of engineering defences along the coast of Britain had passed the optimal level. We know, for example, that at the time of the 1911 Royal Commission on Coastal Erosion and Afforestation, measurements commissioned from the Ordnance Survey showed that although some 200 acres (80 ha) were lost each year by coastal erosion, 1600 acres (650 ha) were gained through the reclamation of salt marshes, sand spits and other areas of natural coastal accretion. The large volume of sediment produced by eroding high cliffs was being moved round the coast and was building out quite large areas at or just above sea-level. However,

Box 9.2 Why the best form of coastal defence is a beach

The common response to coastal erosion or flood risk is to build strong walls with deep foundations, but this does nothing to eliminate the loss of sediment from the beach and nearshore zone that accompanies erosion. In addition, walls are reflective and cause the waves to scour hollows in the beach, so making matters worse. Groynes may retain a wider beach where the natural sediment supply is adequate, but they can do no more than retain part of the natural sediment supply. They, too, can increase sediment loss by driving the sediment further offshore as it moves round the seaward ends of the groynes. Another problem with groynes is that by retaining sediment, they make conditions even worse further downdrift – this is often called the 'terminal groyne problem'. About the only effective measure is beach feeding – placing sand dredge from offshore on the beach, often with groynes to aid its retention. This has the double benefit at seaside resorts that the existing investment in the wall and promenade is made safe, whilst at the same time the recreational value of the beach is retained or even increased. The beach at Cromer (Norfolk, England) shown below urgently needs restoration by adding sand dredged from offshore.

today rather more land is being lost than is gained; our interference with natural processes around the coast has cut off too many natural sources of sediment and speeded up loss of sediment from too many beaches by attempting to fix their position. We have also discouraged the accumulation of sediment by reclaiming large areas of salt marsh that can no longer benefit from natural accretion, while damage to sand dunes also means that these important natural stores of sand are no longer rebuilt quickly after storm damage – yet if they can rebuild they can stand ready to supply large quantities of sand to the beach to offset the erosive power of storm waves.

This sorry picture has been repeated in a number of countries, including the USA (see Box 9.3). Indeed, the Dutch are one of the few nations who through good national planning and much careful scientific research have managed to stabilize a large part of their coast without deleterious effects. But the cost is large (and will continue to be large since much of their coasts relies on beach nourishment), though fully justified by the large area of the country below sea-level (Figure 9.3).

Box 9.3 The barrier islands of the Atlantic coast of the USA

Along the Atlantic coast of North America, the low barrier islands have proved attractive for summer residences and, as so often happens in such areas, these are increasingly occupied the year round. Indeed, in such places as Ocean City, Maryland, high rise structures house hundreds of families, many of whom have retired to the coast. This coastline has a history of erosion and of severe flooding during surges induced by hurricanes moving. At high value sites such as Ocean City huge sums may justifiably be spent on maintaining a stable beach through repeated feeds of sand, but this cannot be justified for more scattered housing. So most of these islands will roll landward and the residents will live from one evacuation to the next until a major storm destroys their home. In the past they have then rebuilt, often with private insurance or public disaster relief to help. The question for the future is how long can this continue, or should coastal zone management preclude the rebuilding of damaged property and forbid the further development of these vulnerable islands?

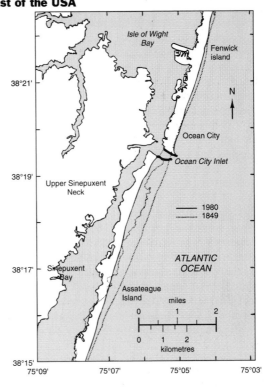

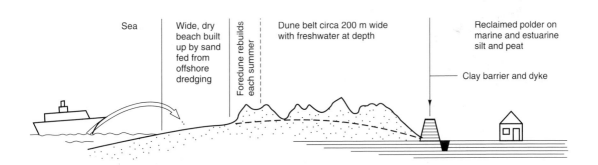

Fig 9.3 The Netherlands: cross section of typical coastal defences. (Source: After Rijkswaterstaat, 1990).

We have built so many fixed structures in areas liable to coastal flood and coastal erosion that long sections of the developed coasts of the world have become totally dependent on continued investment in engineering works. Unfortunately, as more and more of the coast is modified in this way, the natural sediment balance becomes so disturbed that we begin to lose the natural landforms along the coast, including beaches, salt marshes and shingle storm ridges. As we have seen (Box 9.2) this creates an unstable coast which may erode more quickly than the natural coast did before the engineer started work. All too often societies have come to believe the engineer and assume that the coastline can be fixed by technology and that coastal hazard can be eliminated. But any coastline is a dynamic natural environment, in balance between sediment supply from erosion and its loss into beaches, dunes and salt marshes, or to nearshore banks. The more of the coast that can be left to evolve naturally, the better.

As the 1911 data showed, this does not imply the abandonment of 'small' islands such as Britain to persistent destruction by the sea. As a result of these observations, coastal engineering is shifting its emphasis, and has in particular come to appreciate the import-
ant role of beaches and other natural coastal landforms in the stability of the shore. Most modern designs seek to retain wide and high beaches in front of engineering structures, to improve the volumes of sand retained in dunes, and to maintain wide salt marshes in front of flood banks. In low latitudes, coral reefs and mangrove swamps play similar roles and deserve equal protection. Sometimes it is a matter of designing with greater attention to the retention of a good beach, in other cases so much sand may have been lost that recharge (beach feeding) is required. This is not a panacea as the volumes required are large and the sand may disappear even more quickly than the natural beach the feed is designed to replace, but it is increasingly adopted as an element of coastal defence, especially in the USA and the Netherlands.

This reassessment of the limitations of an engineering 'solution' to coastal problems has also led to the same conclusion as reached in the study of the mitigation of flooding along rivers: land-use controls in the hazard zone are even more important than the adoption of 'structural' measures such as the construction of flood banks. We will examine how this can be achieved later in this chapter. However, the large areas

Fig 9.4 Typical storm damage, US Atlantic coast barrier islands.

of coastal land liable to flood that have been built up also means that warning and evacuation systems are as important as structural defences constructed by engineers. Thus along the low barrier islands of the Atlantic coast of the USA and along the North Sea coast of England and the Netherlands and north-west Germany, storm warning systems are in place (Box 9.4). They are designed to eliminate the risk of loss of life, but can do little to reduce the damage caused when tidal flooding occurs (Figure 9.4).

Just as we do not always manage to forecast tomorrow's weather correctly, so there are limitations to the precision with which scientists can warn against coastal storm surges. Indeed the American Meteorological Society has warned that the difficulties in predicting the precise landfall of hurricanes on the Gulf and Atlantic coasts of the USA will continue to require evacuation of three times the length of coast eventually affected, and thus two evacuations out of three will not have been needed. It is difficult to maintain a good response in these circumstances. In addition, large coastal cities take longer to evacuate than the warning that can be given; it is hoped to solve this problem by using high, strong buildings for 'vertical evacuation' (see Box 9.5). A similar problem arises in the UK where those in two-storey houses are safer upstairs than leaving the building – though those in single-storey bungalows which are very common near the seaside will only be safe if they have a ladder that can be used to reach their roof-space. All warning and evacuation schemes depend on a well-educated public, aware of the risks and knowing what to do when the siren sounds. This is not easy to achieve, but knowledge and response is better in the USA than in Britain where there are fewer public warnings and less education of those at risk.

Forecasting future sea-level rise

As is discussed in Chapter 6, the probability of future global warming as a result of changes in the composition of the atmosphere (the so-called 'greenhouse' gases) is very high. Although we cannot be sure that we should attribute the sea-level rise over the last 150 years to global warming (the world has warmed a little more than half a degree Celsius over that period), we are certain that if future warming does occur, it will cause sea-level to rise. Whatever the case, the rather marked warming of the last decade and a half is likely to have an effect on sea-level over the next 40 years. Table 9.1 shows how estimates of the different contributions of sea-level rise which result from the rise in mean global temperature can be shown to match the sea-level rise over the past century and are thus a reasonable basis on which to estimate future changes given forecasts of future temperature rise.

Our current best estimates of future sea-level rise is around 13 cm by 2030 (when the carbon dioxide equivalent of the 'greenhouse' gases reaches double its 1750 level) and around 21 cm by 2050 (Figure 6.5). It is unlikely to exceed half a metre until after 2100. These are not large figures, though they are best guesses involving a number of assumptions and 'high' estimates may turn out to be correct. But even these projections are not insignificant. After all, we suffer coastal flooding today and are not doing particularly well in our efforts to stabilize the coast – yet sea-level has risen only 10–15 cm over the last 100 years. Thirteen cm in the next 40 years is a much faster rate; indeed the annual rate of rise must soon increase from just over 1 mm/yr to between 3 and 6 mm/yr. That increase of three or four times will increase the tendency of beaches to move landward, will increase greatly the rate of beach loss in front of fixed walls, and will increase the rate of erosion along some undefended eroding coasts.

Adjusting to future sea-level

It is important to realize at the outset that future sea-level rise, at least while it remains below one metre above current mean sea-level, will bring no new problems to those countries already attempting to stabilize their coasts and to reduce the risk of tidal flooding. However, it will exacerbate all our existing problems and require more critical examination of some of our existing techniques. It is already bringing more serious interest in the broader approach implied in coastal zone management, where the control over land use near the coast is seen as of equal importance to the management of the beach system.

In some places, indeed along many developed coasts, we shall have no option but to intensify existing efforts to keep the sea at bay. We shall have to improve the strength and quality of design of our engineering structures and go to greater lengths to keep sand on the beaches in front of them. We shall no doubt resort to beach feeding on an increasing scale. All this can be done, though it will be very costly. Current coastal defence schemes often cost over £5 million per

Box 9.4 How the British North Sea storm warning system works

As the figure shows, a storm surge develops within the southern North Sea when a small depression (low) moves eastwards or south-eastwards from Scotland towards Denmark. This gives south-westerly winds in advance of the low which push the water northwards, giving unusually low tides (a negative surge) which pose a navigational risk to supertankers and other large ships. The slope of the sea surface is increased by the rise of sea-level below the deep low pressure centre; the sea-level will rise 5.5 cm for each millibar fall in barometric pressure. The figure may not seem particularly large, but consideration of the area of sea surface affected will show that a considerable volume of water is involved. As the low moves towards the continent, the northerly winds in its rear reverse the stress on the sea surface, pushing water southwards, back into the southern North Sea. This process, too, is aided by the increase in pressure as the low moves away, pushing the sea surface in the north back down. Thus a surge of water raising levels up to 2.5 m above normal tidal heights moves in an anti-clockwise direction, down the east coast of England and then (since it cannot escape through the narrow Straits of Dover) back northwards past the Belgian, Dutch and German coasts. This is the same pattern of movement as the tides, though the speed of the surge is not exactly the same as that of the tidal wave.

The warning system is triggered by the prediction of the movement of a low pressure system across the northern North Sea. This is then updated and the possible surge is modelled using a computer model of a North Sea surge, verified against past events. This allows the issuing of an early 'stand by' warning. Officials, both nationally and locally (the Ministry of Agriculture, Fisheries and Food (MAFF) and the National Rivers Authority (NRA)) are thus alerted, and the disaster response organizations of the local authorities are also placed on stand-by. The actual surge can be monitored from tide gauges as it moves down the east coast of Scotland and England. Thus the computer can amend and improve its forecast of the timing and level of the surge (which is critical since where it arrives at high tide problems will be at their worst) as it begins to move around the North Sea basin. Telex or fax is used to print out forecast surge additions to predicted tides at gauges along the British coast, and NRA officials can then compare water levels over time at their gauge with the forecast, still further to refine the prediction of the local surge level. Where they fear inundation, the police are informed. It is the police who have the responsibility to deliver the warning to the public, using local radio and TV and a series of coastal sirens under their control. They are also responsible for advising and securing evacuation if this seems necessary. In recent years local householders have been told by leaflet of the surge danger and how they should react, and in a few cases people have been evacuated from areas of particular hazard, though not always to a site above potential flood level. However, in general the actual delivery of the warning to individuals at risk is not rehearsed or tested.

The loss of life along the coast in 1953 was over 300 in England and over 3000 in the Netherlands. The warning system ought to prevent a recurrence, but since there has been no restriction on further building (including many single storey houses) in the intervening period, there are now many more people at risk than in 1953 and serious loss of life in a future surge cannot be ruled out given the limitations of the delivery of the present warning system. The science of prediction is excellent, the social science of education, warning and the appropriate public reaction is less secure.

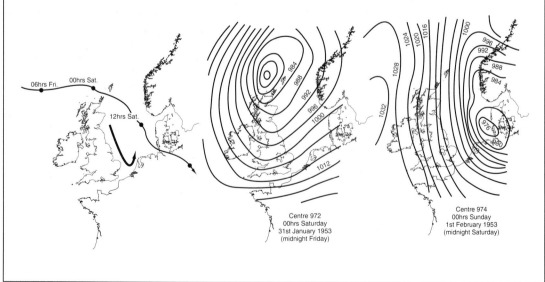

Centre 972
00hrs Saturday
31st January 1953
(midnight Friday)

Centre 974
00hrs Sunday
1st February 1953
(midnight Saturday)

Box 9.5 The American Meteorological Society warns of the limitations of science

In 1986 the American Meteorological Society published a statement with the title 'Is the United States headed for hurricane disaster?' It began,

> We are more vulnerable to hurricanes in the United States than we have ever been before. Millions of people have been attracted to our beautiful coasts, exposing a large population to the threat from hurricanes and the storm surge associated with them. Unfortunately, the rate of improvement in achieving greater forecast lead times is not keeping pace with the time requirements for evacuating an ever-increasing coastal population.

The immediate problem they describe is the fact that good warnings, reliable enough to avoid evacuating people needlessly, cannot be given more than 12 hours ahead, yet evacuation commonly needs 24 hours, far more for big cities. Yet action on earlier warnings means that, owing to the uncertainties associated with both the speed of movement and the future path of hurricanes, two out of every three evacuations will be unnecessary – wasteful, dangerous and liable to reduce the likelihood of appropriate action next time a warning is received. Equally significant is that most of those affected neither understood the problems of accurate prediction, nor were able to realize just how long evacuation took.

The fundamental problem which was not fully addressed is that even if we spend far more money and develop ever-more sophisticated observational systems, it is unlikely we shall be able to improve our prediction of the time and place of landfall of a hurricane by very much; certainly there is no current hope of improving the length of reliable warnings. Thus at least for some time vertical evacuation and planning policies which decrease the numbers at risk are required. But even in the long term it is likely that the chaotic and complex nature of global weather systems will retain a random and thus an unpredictable aspect to hurricane movement. It is important that scientists explain that underlying problem as well as seeking credit for the sophistication and relative reliability of their forecasting and warning systems. It is equally important that non-scientists understand the hazardous nature of the coastal zone and the importance of controlling and managing development to reduce the numbers of people and their property at risk.

Table 9.1 The main factors contributing to sea-level rise

Contributor	Estimates (cm)[a]		
	Low	Best	High
Over the last century			
Thermal expansion of the oceans[b]	5.5	3.7	2.7
Melting of alpine glaciers	1.5	3.9	7.4
Greenland ice-sheet	1.0	2.5	4.0
Antarctic ice-sheet	−5.0	0.0	5.0
Modelled total	3.0	10.1	19.1
Observed total	10	15	20
1990–2030			
Thermal expansion of the oceans	6.0	8.0	12.6
Melting of alpine glaciers	1.7	7.2	18.8
Greenland ice-sheet	0.4	1.9	5.1
Antarctic ice-sheet	−0.6	−0.6	0.0
Modelled total	2.6	16.4	36.5

[a]Note that 'best' and 'high' correspond to global mean temperature change estimates and do not necessarily give the low, best and high estimates for the various sea-level rise components.
[b]The larger thermal expansion for the low estimate (and vice versa) is due to the combination of the model parameters used in the warming model and the tuning for a temperature increase of 0.5 °C.
Source: Wigley and Raper (1992).

kilometre and can run much higher than this if construction is combined with beach recharge. Topping up beaches will have to be done more frequently in the future and/or repairs to damaged structures will also be more frequent. Higher structures can be much more costly because they are more massive and require larger foundations.

We shall have no option but to spend more money in quite a number of places. No one in the Netherlands can contemplate allowing the sea to overrun the country, and with a large proportion of the land area below current sea-level, existing policies will be maintained (Figure 9.3). Where reliance on wide beaches and associated dunes is not feasible, massive structures have been built, most notably in the bank reclaiming the former Zuider Zee (now the Ijssel Meer) and in the recently completed delta scheme which separates the whole of the complex distributary system of the Rhine Delta from tidal influence. This has enough height to cope with sea-level rise for some time, but a programme of steady improvement and enhancement will still be required. In the UK, barriers capable of cutting off the sea from long estuaries are being built; the largest is on

Fig 9.5 The Thames Barrier, England. (Courtesy of the National Rivers Authority, Thames Region.)

the Thames and protects the whole of London from the danger of tidal flood. These barriers are very costly, but are able to provide high levels of protection – London is protected against a 1000-year flood; for most coastal cities behind seawalls, a 200-year level is the highest that can be justified (Figure 9.5).

If these problems seem considerable, consider the case of Bangladesh. Built on the delta of the Ganges–Brahmaputra, this desperately poor country suffers regular flooding from the rivers; in wet years well over half the country is submerged. But the land quickly recovers from freshwater flooding and though disease is a problem, the population survives largely unscathed. Storm surges brought by hurricanes in the Bay of Bengal are a different matter. The speed of onslaught, the great difficulty of giving adequate warning, the lack of safe refuges, the great depth of tidal flooding, the strong winds and waves and the salt water all threaten people, cattle and crops. Indeed in 1970 an estimated 300 000 people died, and another 100 000 in 1990. Warnings are now given, and usually received since radios are now common enough, but on the low-lying islands of the deltas refuges above flood level have to be built for people and cattle and these are still few and far between. Engineering schemes to reduce the risk have been devised but they are all extremely costly and most, if not all, have major environmental disadvantages. In the meantime the population continues to grow, and every new low island in the delta is colonized, increasing the numbers at risk and the problems of providing adequate refuges that can withstand surge conditions. Poverty and landlessness, representing a complete lack of power to settle in safe areas, mean that more and more people are vulnerable to coastal storms even when they fully realize the danger. Inequality of income and opportunity breeds inequality of safety. Managing the coastal zone often highlights these tragedies of modern societies. Even in developed countries such as the UK flood defence schemes may be designed to preserve extensive areas treasured for the nature conservation value, yet ignore the very real risk of poor urban people nearby!

The concept of coastal zone management

In recent years, the need to do better than merely defend the line of the existing coast has led to the development of the concept of coastal zone management (CZM) – the combined use of land-use controls and decisions about the particular measures to be taken to defend (or to leave to nature) the actual coastline. This approach has the advantage of recognizing the coastal zone as one of natural hazard where appropriate non-structural measures can be taken alongside the more common structural mitigation of hazard. It also allows an appropriate place for warning and evacuation measures, again an appropriate response to many natural hazards. The CZM approach is also far more long term than the essentially short-term approach adopted by engineers: most schemes are designed with a life of between 20 and 40 years and cost benefit approaches maximize the more immediate benefits of such schemes and discount long-term problems or effects.

It is easy to propose the CZM approach, but to put it into effect requires definition of a coastal hazard zone and the combination of responsibility for coastal protection (and/or sea defence), with the power of land-use control and provision of a warning and evacuation system. These duties are generally defined in national legislation and commonly held by very different bodies, so that legislation may be required to establish effective CZM. For example in England sea defence (i.e. against tidal flooding) is the responsibility of a regionalized public body, the National Rivers Authority; coastal protection (i.e. against erosion), of the district authorities; planning (in the immediate sense of development control) lies also with the districts; whilst broad (structural) planning policy and the oversight of the warning system lie with the county. In addition, it may not be the situation that planning (zoning) policies take account of hazard: in England there are relatively strict planning controls, yet if you are refused permission to build a house on the top of a cliff the reason is likely to be preservation of a rural view, not the risk that your house may fall down the cliff in a few years' time. Recently, central government directives have introduced the concept of hazard from landslide, coastal erosion or flood as reasons for withholding permission for development, but it remains to be seen how far this voluntary set of guidelines can be put into effect.

In some countries the position over response to haz-ard is more satisfactory. Thus in the eastern USA it is common to find the requirement that living floors must be above flood level, though at the same time the general controls over development through zoning are far more local and ineffective than in the UK. However, it is also possible to own land down to the low water mark in the USA, allowing houses to be built on beaches and in other exposed positions. In the UK all land between high and low water marks is owned by the public body known as the Crown Estate Commissioners who are thus in a position to control the misuse of beaches. They also allow easy public access to the shore and free passage along it, whereas the lack of such rights of access is a major problem in many parts of the USA and becomes a role of public land such as National and State Parks.

The provision of a land-use management system that will eliminate hazard at the coast, an adequate warning system, a management structure that preserves most of the coast in a natural (and thus dynamic) state, and that provides a very high standard of coastal defence at sites where it is required is not easy. All the signs are, from knowledge of various national patterns of management, that it requires a single, strong, central authority. Indeed, only where responsibility for the coast is placed at a national level do we find an effectively managed system. Any effective system of CZM should have both the power and the determination to refuse applications for development and must also decide to allow extended lengths of coast to evolve naturally. This implies decisions which individuals will find disheartening and individually very costly, so they must be enforceable by law and/or brought about by appropriate compensation.

As always, it is tempting to try to find a compromise between a strongly centralized system of CZM and a pattern that allows for regional differences and the involvement of local people in decision making. Certainly at the very least any centralized system must understand the physical contrasts of coastal sediments, wave energy and the nature of landward development pressures between major coastal sectors. As explained in Box 9.6, the British system is typical of those that seek to involve local communities in decisions about their local coastline, whilst using central funding, in particular, to impose some common standards and techniques. As is also quite common, the degree of local involvement is only strong on eroding, upland coasts and the arrangements for tackling defence against coastal flood are far more centralized and bureaucratic. The extreme situation is in those countries, which

---

Box 9.6 The UK structure of coastal zone management

The *coastline* is divided between low coasts, liable to tidal flooding, which are the responsibility of the National Rivers Authority, and high coasts which are the responsibility of district councils. Works carried out on low coasts to reduce the risk of flooding are called sea defences, works carried out on high coasts to reduce coastal erosion are described as coastal protection. Both are grant-aided in approved cases by central government through the Ministry of Agriculture, Fisheries and Food (MAFF) which pays 60–80 per cent of the capital cost of schemes. Repairs are regarded as a recurrent cost and fall on the local authority. In addition to the central government contribution, support also comes from county councils from local taxation, as well as from local taxes in the case of the district councils.

The *intertidal* and *offshore zones* are administered by the Crown Estate Commissioners. They grant or withhold licences for the extraction of sand and marine aggregates offshore and generally prevent their extraction from the intertidal or nearshore zone. Indeed most permissions for extraction are granted at least 3 miles (5 km) offshore and always to the seaward of the nearest bank to the coast which is seen as having the greatest effect on wave energies at the shore.

The *littoral zone landward of the coast* is not formally defined. It obviously includes all low-lying land liable to tidal flood, and also those coastal areas liable to erosion over some future period. In the few places where this has been defined by the responsible authorities for structural plans (county councils) this has been defined as the zone at risk from erosion over the next 75–100 years. One local authority has already drawn up plans in order to presume against permission being granted in the zone at risk from erosion and the zone so defined is almost 1 km inland in the area of most rapid current erosion. Development control rests with the district councils, so that on high coasts liable to erosion, both coastal protection and planning control are in the same hands. Advice on the granting of planning permission in zones liable to flood or erosion (or coastal landslip) comes from central government (the Department of the Environment). In addition, the NRA has to be consulted over all applications to develop on land liable to flood, though its advice is rarely, if ever, taken by the local authority which usually regards development as requiring a higher level of protection from the NRA, not that it should be avoided. There should be some change in this attitude following stronger advice from central government and greater publicity about future sea-level rise. Coastal defence works also require planning permission – this is always readily granted.

There is no legal basis in the UK by which *compensation* may be paid to property owners were a decision taken not to proceed with coastal protection or sea defence schemes.

---

include the USA, where it is common for individual coastal landowners to construct their own defences against erosion – their limited success and adverse visual impact is testimony to the need to plan on a much larger scale.

One of the very few countries with a strong and centralized system is the Netherlands and we have already admired the quality and effectiveness of its coastal management scheme. This suitably ambitious and well-funded national scheme is described in well-produced documents and updated from time to time. It receives public discussion and amendment before adoption and no doubt could be considered in a wide-ranging public enquiry if controversy arose. Thus certainly there can be democratic public involvement in the establishment of the principles whereby the coast should be managed and the aims and methods to be used. But as is true of local decisions permitting or refusing development, some wider community-linked decision-making body governed by rules or laws and

supported by an independent administration is required if long-term choices are to be made about the management of individually owned land. This is especially true if decisions are to be taken which condemn that land to continuing erosion or frequent tidal flooding.

The USA has (on the whole) very weak zoning laws and houses are more likely to be moved vertically (to comply with legislation governing the elevation of living floors in relation to tidal levels) than horizontally, away from the zone of immediate risk. There is central design of coastal defence and recharge schemes (by the US Army Corps of Engineers), but they are by their nature prejudiced in favour of structural solutions to coastal problems. Coastal management runs from local federal involvement on public land and in National Parks, to state, township and even individual responses. There can be few developed countries with so many kilometres of *ad hoc*, individually constructed defences, visually damaging and by their local and amateur nature of no long-term value as a means of stabilizing the shore. The equally complex and equally ineffective UK scheme is described in Box 9.6.

Facing up to difficult choices: selectivity in CZM

It seems likely that over time a coastal zone approach to the management of the coastal area liable to flood or future erosion will be adopted in many countries. Indeed the more rapid changes as sea-level rises more quickly will accelerate the implementation of such an approach. However, it is easy to write about a more flexible coastal management policy, or to suggest that smaller areas will be defended to a higher standard whilst others are let go. Bringing that about is an exercise in practical politics which requires good scientific understanding of the coast, strong planning policies, rational processes of cost benefit and other methods of comparative analysis, and some method to compensate those who are disadvantaged in the wider interests of society and the long-term protection of coastal areas.

As has already been implied, in many cases existing efforts to keep the sea out of low-lying land, or to prevent the erosion of coastal ports and seaside resorts, will continue. However, even in these cases it is likely that much greater efforts will be made to maintain natural elements of a coastline as part of the defence against marine attack; salt-marshes or sand dunes in front of coastal embankments, beaches in front of seawalls. Techniques allowing this already exist, but most either rely on importing sediment (which can be very costly) or require the maintenance of a natural supply of sediment from a river rising in high ground or from eroding cliffs. Thus there are likely to be pressures to allow sediment to travel down major rivers (which means the cessation of further dam construction) and to allow the cliffs (or 'feeder bluffs' as the Americans call them) to erode. Where a system of CZM brings these responsibilities together it should be easier to get rational decisions. Where, as for example in the UK at the moment, the cliffs come under one authority and the low-lying coast under another, the potential for conflict and inaction is high. To some this will suggest that coastal sediment cells should become the basis of coastal planning, and certainly they should not be ignored in the way that coastal engineers have come to disregard beach stability and the sediment sources on

which this depends. On the other hand, many countries now have high levels of investment in the areas landward of their coasts, and CZM needs to take the level of landward development into account in deciding the appropriate level and style of protection. We would seek to protect the whole of a coastal city or a major low-lying agricultural plain to the same standard, whatever the pattern of sediment cells along the adjacent coastline.

As they face up to the increasing problems that sea-level rise will bring, many countries are moving away from a situation where engineers take the decisions about what should be done to maintain coastal stability, towards one where the presumption will be that if at all possible the coast should be left to evolve in a natural way. This will of course only be possible if strict controls are brought in to reduce development in areas that are at risk. But if we do stop new building (and even the major refurbishment of ageing structures) there will then be much less at risk if (or when) the sea does move in. This action will in time have an effect on the arithmetic of cost benefit assessments and so reduce the economic pressures for coastal defence schemes. One problem with such an approach is the time-scale involved. Sea defences can be built and provide protection, or at least some amelioration of coastal hazard, for periods of 1–30 years. A coastal land-use policy will only begin to show its effectiveness over periods from 20 to 300 years. These are very long lead times on which to base decisions about the form and location of development and which require the aspirations of many landowners to be overruled.

Nonetheless, there are real advantages in a radical shift in our attitude towards the natural (and potentially natural) coast. We would return to a situation where we value the natural features of a coast for their role as natural buffers against marine attack as well as for their aesthetic value. This will make them more attractive to society and thus more likely to be properly valued and protected. In many places the costs of such a shift of attitude will be small, indeed the sums may show a benefit in the long term over existing policies. The reason for this is that the total shift of natural coasts even under conditions of rising sea-level is likely to be rather small, provided we continue to allow the erosion of the adjacent cliffs and so maintain an adequate sediment supply (Box 9.7). Where we cannot (yet?) allow cliff erosion (though maintaining strict control on cliff-top development) we may have to supplement the natural sediment feed to help maintain coastal stability (Figure 9.6).

Box 9.7 How dynamic is the natural coast?
The popular conception that unchecked the sea has the power to sweep large distances inland is inaccurate; if the beach shifts a few tens of metres landward, the effect on the nearshore slope is considerable and rapidly attenuates the power of wave attack. Only where removal of sediment from the nearshore zone is highly efficient (either off-shore or along the shore by littoral drift) will coastline shift be persistent, and such eroding zones have often already developed into eroding cliff lines, as, for example, the (English) Holderness cliffs north of the Humber (average retreat rate 2 m/yr) and the Norfolk cliffs (average retreat rate 1 m/yr). Where these cliffs are topped by agricultural land, they can safely be left to erode: the area lost is of no national significance in terms of production, whilst the simplest calculation will show that the conversion of fields to sediment on the beach is highly cost effective.

On low coasts, the main aim will be to reverse the reclamation of salt marsh which has now affected up to 80 or 90 per cent of the salt marshes of developed countries. As we have seen, salt marshes are of great value because of their ability to keep pace with sea-level rise, whilst their value as nature reserves is also considerable. As with cliffs, the removal of agricultural land from production is no problem in developed countries, so it may seem a simple matter to remove the flood banks and let the sea take over. In land management terms this is true, for seeds quickly re-establish salt marsh vegetation, although for some very low-lying areas the resulting mudflats may have to be built up before salt marsh can be re-established. However, the farmers will not be happy unless compensated and this is often not possible without changes in national legislation. The tensions are well shown by the reluctance of managers of nature reserves (and especially bird reserves) on reclaimed salt marsh along the coast to see those areas returned to marsh. Yet in principle they are as appropriate a sacrifice as agricultural land. The cost and benefits of these decisions are complex, for many intangible assets must be valued. Thus, whilst it is easy to announce fall-back as an adjustment to future sea-level rise, it is difficult to achieve it without conflict. Some of the valuation issues are aired in Chapters 2 and 3.

The contribution of the geomorphologist to CZM is to show that along the coast we have a series of land-forms that are naturally adjusted to sea-level and will remain in adjustment even if sea-level rises. These include beaches (of sand and of shingle), sand dunes and salt marshes. One aim of coastal management must be to allow these to develop in as natural a way as possible, for if they do, they will keep pace with sea-level rise, by accretion or by relatively limited landward movement. We shall have to recognize that in some cases we have already modified these landforms so that they cannot develop naturally. Sand dunes may be cut off from the beach (and the beach from the dunes) by a wall, beaches are cluttered with groynes, salt marshes have frequently been greatly reduced in width by the reclamation of the landward areas for agriculture. Not surprisingly, such modified systems no longer function well and we shall have to consider if we can restore them to their natural state. Only then can we leave them to evolve naturally, keeping pace with sea-level rise free of charge.

Thus in some coastal areas we shall have to reverse the decisions of past years and return reclaimed land to

Fig 9.6 House on edge of collapsing coastal cliff, California, USA. (Source: Platt *et al.*, 1992).

Fig 9.7 Dune management, planting marram grass, Fenwick Island, Barrier Island coast of the Atlantic, USA.

the coastal regime. Where areas are small and still in agricultural use this should not prove too contentious, though we may have to develop ways of encouraging the reversion of reclaimed land to salt marsh – unless we discover that nature does that for us effectively enough. Where houses have been built the choice will be more difficult and it may be that time will have to elapse before it becomes both economic and politically feasible. The improvement of coastal dunes will be another priority; all too often these are subject to intense trampling pressure and in many areas summer cottages are scattered across them. The improved management of dunes has already been tackled at some coastal sites, by English Nature in nature reserves within the UK, by Sefton District Council along the Lancashire coast of England, and by the US authorities at many sites on the barrier islands of the Atlantic coast (Figure 9.7). But the lead here has been taken by the Dutch who value them not only for sea defence and (controlled) recreation, but also for their role in water supply.

The long-term management of the coastal zone

Future CZM under rising sea-level will be co-ordinated, will integrate the spatial relationships of the coastal zone (such as matching eroding cliffs with the maintenance of adjacent beaches and salt marshes), and above all will take a long-term view of the problem. It will be selective: many areas will always require major expenditure on measures to ensure coastal stability and effective defence against even the worst tidal floods. But this expenditure will be balanced by reducing the money at present spent on the protection of small communities and some of the smaller areas of agricultural land. We shall reverse the pattern of the past 150 years by increasing the areas of salt marshes and of active coastal dunes. We shall provide an improved hazard warning system with far better education of those at risk of the appropriate action when surges occur. Above all we shall learn to live with

Box 9.8 Land-use planning in the coastal zone

Land-use planning in the littoral zone will become much more significant as a long-term policy measure, requiring strong legislation and enforcement. Individuals will always make out a case for short-term occupancy of hazardous zones for the perceived advantages of a coastal location and a sea view. Yet society must look ahead with a clear vision if investment now is not to embarrass future generations. It will take time to convince people that continuation of present attempts to stabilize coast-lines is not the best option. No one should believe that stating the desirability of coastal zone management in the coastal zone will bring good hazard management quickly; it is likely to be a long battle to change public opinion, and no doubt we shall still be building new groynes and even extending sea walls for another generation. Some idea of a comprehensive approach was given in the proposals for North Carolina (Owens, 1985).

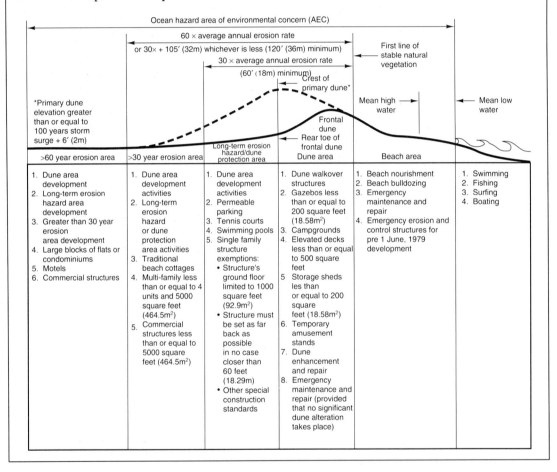

>60 year erosion area	>30 year erosion area	Long-term erosion hazard/dune protection area	Dune area	Beach area	
1. Dune area development 2. Long-term erosion hazard area development 3. Greater than 30 year erosion area development 4. Large blocks of flats or condominiums 5. Motels 6. Commercial structures	1. Dune area development activities 2. Long-term erosion hazard or dune protection area activities 3. Traditional beach cottages 4. Multi-family less than or equal to 4 units and 5000 square feet (464.5m²) 5. Commercial structures less than or equal to 5000 square feet (464.5m²)	1. Dune area development activities 2. Permeable parking 3. Tennis courts 4. Swimming pools 5. Single family structure exemptions: • Structure's ground floor limited to 1000 square feet (92.9m²) • Structure must be set as far back as possible in no case closer than 60 feet (18.29m) • Other special construction standards	1. Dune walkover structures 2. Gazebos less than or equal to 200 square feet (18.58m²) 3. Campgrounds 4. Elevated decks less than or equal to 500 square feet 5 Storage sheds les than or equal to 200 square feet (18.58m²) 6. Temporary amusement stands 7. Dune enhancement and repair 8. Emergency maintenance and repair (provided that no significant dune alteration takes place)	1. Beach nourishment 2. Beach bulldozing 3. Emergency maintenance and repair 4. Emergency erosion and control structures for pre 1 June, 1979 development	1. Swimming 2. Fishing 3. Surfing 4. Boating

nature along the coast and not to assume that we have a duty to spend money on timber and concrete to keep the sea in its place. Wherever possible we shall allow the sea to find its own place; even at a time of rising sea-level that need not be too hard to manage. But it will emphasize the case for adopting measures to reduce future global warming sooner rather than later.

In many countries the coast remains largely natural, with only short lengths modified for industry or tourism. It is to be hoped that the very unsatisfactory situation in many developed countries will be noted by those who have yet to experience widespread modification and development of their coastal zones. Even in heavily populated countries, the coastal margin can remain a zone where natural processes can continue

Box 9.9 An example of potential change on a low coast – Norfolk, UK

The low coast of North Norfolk is marked by barrier islands and spits. It is stable or accreting at present, though being a low and mobile coast, this includes local sites where erosion is occurring, even today. Over half of the salt marsh has been reclaimed for agriculture, including areas of grazing which have become bird reserves, and one area of sand dunes is used as a golf course. With sea-level rise there will be some adjustments on the unprotected coast, but the main problem will be that the reclaimed salt marsh will be increasingly vulnerable to flooding because it will not build up by the accretion of mud at high tides. Money will no doubt be spent to try to improve the protection of such coastal villages as Cley and Wells, though some of the smaller villages such as Blakeney, Salthouse and Brancaster Staithe will suffer more frequent and deeper flooding in the lowest areas. But reclaimed agricultural areas including Holme (1), Brancaster (3), Burnham Overy (5), Holkham (6), Morston/Blakeney (7, 8) and Salthouse (9) will not justify expenditure on improvements and

ought to be returned to natural salt marsh. Smaller areas will go first as the value defended will certainly not justify work on the surrounding banks, but eventually it is doubtful if any of the limited areas of former salt marsh reclaimed for agriculture should survive. This may be politically easier than returning what appear to be natural bird reserves such as Titchwell (2) and Cley (9) to salt marsh, though in the long run they cannot easily be defended against inundation. Golf courses on cliffs as at Sheringham (10) will suffer increasingly rapid attrition by cliff erosion; those on sand dunes as at Brancaster (4) can only be defended if sand is fed to the beach – which *may* be justified through a combination of the recreational values of the golf course and the adjacent holiday beach. But in the long run, low coasts such as this are best left to nature except where small settlements can be protected by improved banks set well back so they are protected from wave attack by salt marshes and/or sand dunes.

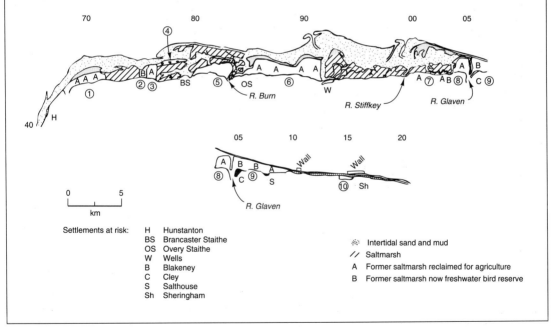

Settlements at risk:
- H   Hunstanton
- BS   Brancaster Staithe
- OS   Overy Staithe
- W   Wells
- B   Blakeney
- C   Cley
- S   Salthouse
- Sh   Sheringham

- ☷   Intertidal sand and mud
- //   Saltmarsh
- A   Former saltmarsh reclaimed for agriculture
- B   Former saltmarsh now freshwater bird reserve

and the natural environment can be enjoyed. The coast with its dunes, beaches and shallow sea is of great importance in recreation, and whilst urbanized tourist resorts are one way it is utilized, these need to lie alongside unspoilt areas. Such a juxtaposition, such a balance, is perhaps the most appropriate way of utiliz-

ing coasts both today and with future sea-level rise (Box 9.8). Above all, the majority of the coast must be left to adjust without interference to the daily, seasonal and longer-term changes in sea-level. It should be no more than a minor proportion which is urbanized, and dominated by man. Even there, the maintenance of high beach levels is the only long-term way of safeguarding the developed coast (Box 9.9).

References

Clayton, K.M. (1992) *Coastal geomorphology.* London: Nelson.

Hicks, S.D., H.A. Debaugh Jr. and L.E. Hickman Jr. (1983) *Sea-level variations for the United States, 1955–1980.* Rockville, MD: NOAA.

Owens, D.W. (1984) Erosion rates and hazard mapping in coastal resource management. In: *Preventing coastal flood disasters: the role of the States and Federal response,* Proceedings of a National Symposium, Ocean City, Maryland, May 23–25, 1983, 137–148, **Special Publication No. 7,** Boulder, Colorado: Association of State Floodplain Managers and the University of Colorado, Natural Hazards Research and Applications Information Center.

Owens, D.W. (1985) Coastal management in North Carolina: building a regional consensus. *Journal of the American Planning Association,* **51,** 322–9.

Platt, R.H., H.C. Miller, T. Beatley, J. Melville and B.G. Mathenia (1992) *Coastal erosion: has retreat sounded?* Monograph 53. Boulder: University of Colorado, Institute of Behavioral Science Program on Environment and Behaviour.

Raper, S.C. and T.M.L. Wigley (1991) Short-term global mean temperature and sea level change. In C.M. Goodess and J.P. Palutikov (Eds) *Future climate change and radioactive waste disposal. Proceedings of International Workshop,* Nirex Safety Studies, **NSS/R257,** 203–13.

Rijkswaterstaat (Dutch Ministry of Transport and Public Works) (1990) *A new coastal defence policy for the Netherlands.* The Hague: Netherlands Ministry of Transport and Public Works

Shennan, I. (1987) Holocene sea-level changes in the North Sea region. In M.J. Tooley and I. Shennan (Eds) *Sea-level changes.* Oxford: Blackwell.

Further reading

Anon (American Meteorological Society) (1986) Is the United States headed for hurricane disaster? A statement of concern by the American Meteorological Society as adopted by the Council on January 12, 1986. *Bulletin American Meteorological Society,* **67**(5), 537–58.

Bird, E.C.F. (1985) *Coastline changes: a global review.* Chichester: Wiley.

Bruun, P. (1962) Sea-level rise as a cause of shore erosion. *Journal of the Waterways and Harbors Division, American Society of Civil Engineers,* **88,** 117–30.

Clayton, K.M. (1989) Sediment input from the Norfolk cliffs, eastern England – a century of coast protection and its effect. *Journal of Coastal Research,* **5,** 433–42.

Clayton, K.M. (1990) Sea-level rise and coastal defences in the UK. *Quarterly Journal of Engineering Geology, London,* **23,** 283–7.

Davies, J.L. (1980) *Geographical variation in coastal development* (2nd edition). London: Longman

Houghton, J.T., G.J. Jenkins and J.J. Ephraum (Eds) (1990) *Climate change: the IPCC scientific assessment.* Cambridge: Cambridge University Press.

Intergovernmental Panel on Climate Change, Response Strategies Working Group, Coastal Zone Management Subgroup (1992) *Global climate change and the rising challenge of the sea.* (*Report prepared for IPCC by Working Group 3*). The Hague, The Netherlands: Directorate General Rijkwaterstaat.

Kaufman, W. and O.H. Pilkey Jr. (1983) *The beaches are moving: the drowning of America's shoreline.* Durham, NC: Duke University Press.

Kay, R.C. (1990) Development controls on eroding coastlines: reducing the impact of greenhouse-induced sea-level rise. *Land Use Policy,* **17,** 169–72.

Penning-Rowsell, E.C. *et al.* (1992) *The economics of coastal management. A manual of benefit assessment techniques.* London: Belhaven Press.

Royal Commission on Coast Erosion and Afforestation (1911) *Third and Final Report,* Volume III (Part I) Cd. 5708. London: HMSO.

Warrick, R.A., E.M. Barrow and T.M.L. Wigley (Eds) (1993) *Climate and sea level change: observations, projections and implications.* Cambridge: Cambridge University Press.

Warrick, R. and G. Farmer (1990) The greenhouse effect, climatic change and rising sea level: implications for development. *Transactions of the Institute British Geographers,* **15,** 5–20.

Warrick, R. (1993) Slowing global warming and sea-level rise: the rough road from Rio. *Transactions of the Institute British Geographers,* **18,** 140–8.

Wigley, T.M.L. and S.C.B. Raper (1992) Implications for climate and sea level of revised IPCC emissions scenarios. *Nature,* **357** 293–300.

Williams, S.J., K. Dodd and K.K. Gohn (1991) *Coasts in Crisis.* US Geological Survey Circular 1075, p. 32.

CHAPTER 10

The oceans from space

KAREN J. HEYWOOD

We are just beginning to realize how important the oceans are in regulating the Earth. Karen Heywood reveals how modern satellite imagery coupled to detailed oceanographic investigation and sophisticated modelling tell us how much the ocean mirrors the atmosphere. It is full of turmoil, with megacurrents carrying energy and carbon dioxide over huge expanses of the oceanic Earth. Cold and warm pools form, dissipate, reform and stabilize across the ocean surface. These are energy sinks and energy sources with great significance for the climate and for the production of biologically induced atmospheric gases that control cloudiness and precipitation. Plankton densities are enormously affected by sunlight, by water clarity and temperature, and by current movement.

The seas may be even more of a temperature regulator of the Earth. The action of sunlight on the water vapour evaporated off the ocean surface produces the hydroxyl radical (OH). This is responsible for scavenging methane from the upper atmosphere, and may play a major role in controlling other greenhouse gases, such as the chlorofluorocarbons. The OH production varies considerably in space and altitude: we still know very little about its moderating roles. The oceans are slowly yielding their secrets to science: the voyage of discovery is still in its infancy.

It is little wonder that one of the next major themes for international attention is the planetary management of the oceans. A UN convention on the oceans is due to be signed in 1996. That convention will be very dependent on the kind of science and understanding of ocean–atmosphere coupling outlined by Karen Heywood in the chapter that follows. Work is being done on the possible impact of increased ultraviolet radiation on the phytoplankton of the southern and northern oceans. This is an area where empirical evidence is desperately required. Only the analysis of relatively short time series data will be available, so possible fluctuations in primary productivity at the ocean surface will have to be modelled in the context of the precautionary principle. It is possible, too, that global warming will increase the desert-like qualities of much of the ocean surface in favour of marginalizing plankton in the upwelling zones of the coastal margins and estuaries. This in turn could limit the extent of oceanic cloudiness generated by the dimethyl sulphate aerosols produced by certain phytoplankton. Such a reduction of marine cloud cover may more than offset the possible increase of cloudiness caused by sulphate aerosols created by industrial pollution and automobile exhausts.

But then, it may not: all of this is still speculation. Either way could produce reinforcement or dampening of any tendency towards warming. No wonder that we should proceed slowly and adaptively, rooted in the precaution principle. The issues raised in the editorial introduction to and content of Chapter 8 are vitally relevant here. Integrated coastal zone management is as much an ethical necessity as it is a scientific requirement. To tamper further with the oceanic margins could be great folly: yet this is precisely the zone still undergoing the most unco-ordinated transformation.

Whatever the outcome, oceans will forever be studied for what they are – great reservoirs of vital bio-geo-chemical and physical processes on almost unimaginable scales, the significance of which we can barely comprehend. This is no substitute for painstaking scientific research – systematic record-ing of temperature, salinity, current movement, gaseous exchange, depth dynamics and physiochemical links to the atmosphere. This work is already well in hand in the World Ocean Circulation Experiment along with its sibling studies financed by international and national scientific programmes. This information will be of the utmost significance.

The trouble is that it will take decades of collaborative evidence, numer-ous workshops and conferences, and expensively networked scientific teams to do the job. Once started, such endeavour simply cannot be subject to the vagaries of political mood, science budgets as determined by politically inspired budget cuts, and impatience at incomplete results. Research of this kind is utterly dependent on reliable funding, continuous recording and stable research networks. Maybe there needs to be something equivalent to the IPCC for oceanographic research. Let us hope that this is one of many outcomes of the UN Conference and its subsequent international conven-tion.

International scientific collaboration of this kind is an endangered species if science budgets are threatened by whim and by prejudice. Like all endan-gered species, the future of such sophisticated networking should be safe-guarded by devices that are politics-proof, though always subject to independent auditing of quality and reliability. That does not mean that politicians should be kept out: quite the opposite. For oceanographic science to flourish, it must be made both politician- and people-friendly. Obviously one should be careful not to misunderstand that call. Science need not be disadvantaged by popularization: it should be enhanced. With modern graphic display techniques, the scientific discovery of the planetary stabiliz-ing role of the oceans can literally be brought into the living rooms of those whose job it will be to safeguard this mysterious phenomenon.

Introduction

Of the surface of our planet, 70 per cent is covered by water, yet we still do not understand how the physics, chemistry and biology of the ocean interact. How then can we manage this resource? The global oceans are used as a source of food from krill to fish and whales; as a means of transporting goods by world-wide shipping; as the site for extracting natural resources such as oil and gas; as a means of recreation and tourism. We shall also see that they have an important influence on our climate, both locally and globally.

Meteorologists are able to predict the weather with reasonable accuracy, since there exists a global network of observing stations measuring atmospheric parameters several times every day. Oceanographers have no such network, and until now have had to hope that the measurements made almost in isolation from a small but expensive ship in the middle of the ocean would be the same in other years or in nearby areas. Poorer countries are often unable to support such shipborne surveys, yet their local ocean may be of special value in assisting development. The provision of relatively cheap, remotely sensed oceanographic data is one way in which we can all share in the responsibility for managing a shared resource – after all, water which is today in the Indian Ocean may in a few decades be flowing in the North Atlantic.

The launch in 1978 of the first dedicated ocean-observing satellite, Seasat, revolutionized the study of the oceans. For the first time, thousands of square kilometres of ocean surface could be observed on a daily basis to a resolution of a few kilometres. In July 1991, the European remote sensing satellite ERS-1 was launched (Figure 10.1). Further ocean-observing satellites are planned for the next few decades. Maybe satellites will at last provide the tools needed to understand the mysterious oceans:

- How and why do their current systems vary from season to season, or year to year?
- How does the ocean contribute to the transport of heat from equator to poles, and thus to potential changes in our climate caused by excess greenhouse gases?
- How does the productivity of the ocean (from plankton to fish) depend on the physical processes?

In this chapter we will see how recent developments in remote sensing are helping us to improve our under-

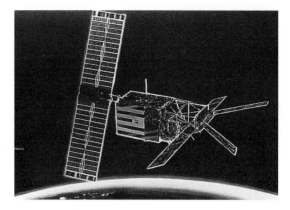

Fig 10.1 An artists's impression of the ERS-1 Earth-observing satellite launched in 1991.

standing of how the oceans work. We will explain how the currents in the oceans are driven, and how satellites can measure these currents in more detail than ever before. We will see how the distribution of biological productivity can be measured from space, and how it links with physical processes such as eddies or fronts. We will learn how the ocean interacts with sea ice, and the implications of this for our climate.

Satellite altimetry: The role of ocean circulation in climate

Ocean currents, both near the surface and near the sea-bed (about 4 km depth), play a large part in transporting heat from equatorial to polar regions (Box 10.1). If the ocean and atmosphere did not transport heat away from the equator, the Earth would get warmer in tropical regions where there is a net warming by the sun, and get colder in polar regions where more heat is lost than is gained. It is believed that the ocean transports approximately half of the heat needed to maintain the Earth's climate in equilibrium – the other half is transported by the atmospheric circulation. There are several ways in which the ocean achieves this:

- Warm surface currents (such as the Gulf Stream – part of the North Atlantic subtropical gyre) take water to cooler regions where the heat is given up to the atmosphere (this is why the climate of northern Europe is milder than that in Canada, yet both are on the same latitude).
- Cold, dense waters formed in polar regions sink and

Box 10.1 What drives the ocean circulation?

The surface currents in the ocean (see the figure) are driven by the atmosphere in two ways:

1. Directly by the wind (the *wind-driven circulation*).

2. Indirectly by variations in the distribution of heat and salt (the *thermohaline circulation*) due to solar heating, evaporation, precipitation and other air–sea fluxes.

In general, surface currents along the equator flow from east to west, while immediately to the north and south are large-scale circulations called the *subtropical gyres*. These gyres are anticlockwise in the southern hemisphere and clockwise in the northern hemisphere – that is, they are anticyclonic. The main current in the Southern Ocean flows from west to east and is the only means of transporting water between the Pacific, Atlantic and Indian Ocean basins. In the northern Atlantic and Pacific, smaller cyclonic *subpolar gyres* provide a second circulation, complicated by interchanges with adjacent seas such as the Greenland Sea, Labrador Sea and Arctic Ocean.

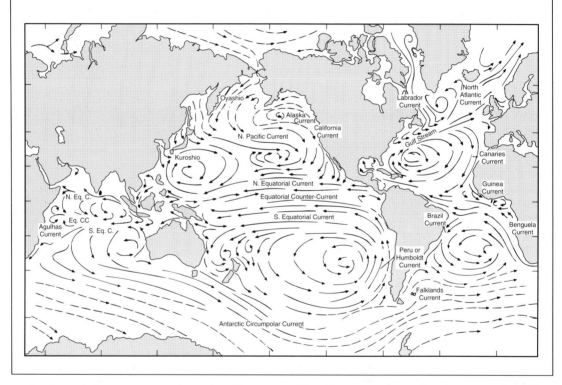

flow towards the equator near the sea-bed (they are dense because they are both cold and salty – colder water is denser than warmer water, and more saline water is denser than fresher water).

- Eddies can be shed by ocean currents and move away from their source region.

We cannot expect to model climate (and therefore to predict warming due to the increase of greenhouse gases) until we understand how to include in our computer models oceanic processes such as mixing by eddies, flow over topography, air–sea transfer of heat, momentum and freshwater, and water mass formation and circulation.

Until the advent of oceanographic satellites, the only cheap and regular determinations of ocean surface currents were obtained by measurement of the deviations of ships from their intended course after correction for windage. Since coverage was mainly confined to shipping lanes and therefore relatively sparse, particularly in the southern hemisphere, data were averaged over large areas (tens of kilometres) and long time

Most currents in the ocean are known as *geostrophic*, meaning that the Coriolis force due to the Earth's rotation is balanced by a pressure gradient acting horizontally in the water (Figure 10.2). This horizontal pressure gradient arises because the sea surface is higher on one side of an ocean current than the other. For example, the Gulf Stream flows northwards along the eastern coast of the USA as a narrow jet less than 100 km wide with speeds of at least 2 m/s. The sea surface on the eastern side can be as much as 2 m higher than the western side. These changes in height (sea surface topography) are associated with all ocean currents – if one can measure the slope of the sea surface, one can calculate the current speed.

intervals (tens of years). In other words, oceanographers were measuring the 'climate' of the ocean – the mean currents. Now we would like to look at the oceanographic 'weather' – the eddies, and the changes in the large-scale currents, which previously required specialized equipment on a research vessel. How can satellites many hundreds of kilometres above the ocean surface measure the current speed?

Instruments carried by satellite cannot directly measure the speed at which the water is travelling, but an instrument called an *altimeter* can measure slopes in the height of the sea surface. If the current is geostrophic (see Box 10.2), then measuring the sea surface slope will tell us the speed of the current.

The radar altimeter carried on a satellite orbiting the Earth emits a pulse of microwave radiation which is reflected back from the sea surface (Figure 10.2). By precisely timing the return of the pulse, the distance between the satellite and the sea can be measured. If the position of the satellite's orbit is known, the height of the sea surface, and hence the geostrophic current, can be deduced. This technique was proven during the three month Seasat mission in 1978. Since then, altimeters have been carried on other Earth-observing satellites such as Geosat (1986–89), ERS-1 (launched in 1991) and TOPEX/POSEIDON (launched in 1992), and are planned for future missions such as ERS-2 and any polar orbiting platforms.

During the 1990s, intensive large-scale measurements are being made to determine the causes of long-term changes in the ocean gyre system as part of the World Ocean Circulation Experiment (WOCE). It is thought that seasonal changes in the ocean circulation depend mainly on the variation of the surface wind, whilst thermohaline processes (i.e. the formation of

cold water masses in polar regions which then travel slowly all around the world ocean) are important on a decadal time-scale.

An example of long-term atmosphere–ocean interaction is the 'great salinity anomaly'. In the North Atlantic during the 1970s freshwater of Arctic origin travelled round the subpolar gyre. This may have affected fisheries and local weather, but it has also pointed to a possible feedback to the world's climate which might have a catastrophic effect. Low salinity surface water in the North Atlantic may act to prevent deep convection and subsequent formation of the cold North Atlantic deep water. This is because fresher water is less dense – it stabilizes the water column and prevents the mixing by the wind and by surface cooling which is essential to form the cold and saline North Atlantic deep water. North Atlantic deep water is important not only because it is cold and therefore part of the transport of heat away from equatorial regions, but also because it is believed to be instrumental in taking carbon dioxide down into the oceans. Some people believe that the climate has two 'states' – one with North Atlantic deep water being formed (i.e. the

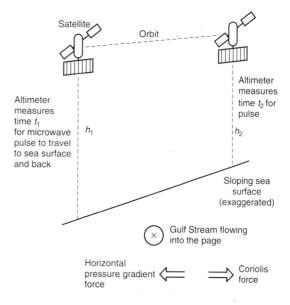

Fig 10.2 The measurement of a geostrophic current using a satellite altimeter. The horizontal pressure gradient force due to the sloping sea surface is balanced by the Coriolis force acting at 90° to the right of the current in the northern hemisphere. h_1 and h_2 are heights of the satellite above the sea surface at two points on its orbit. They are deduced from measurements of the times t_1 and t_2 respectively and knowledge of the speed of electromagnetic radiation.

present climate) and one where this process was stopped. If this were to happen (as it may have done previously on the geological time-scale), our climate would be very different – North Europe would no longer have relatively mild winters, for example, because heat would no longer be released to the atmosphere by the convection processes. Although the measurement of salinity from space is still under development, satellite altimetry offers the opportunity to monitor the changes in surface currents over time-scales from seasons to decades.

Climate variations in Northern Europe have been correlated with sea surface temperature (SST) anomalies in the North Atlantic; this has been termed the North Atlantic Oscillation. This is analogous to ENSO – the El Niño Southern Oscillation phenomenon in the Pacific Ocean. We have learnt that the occasional cessation of upwelling of nutrient rich waters off Peru (which causes catastrophic failure of the local fishing industry) is associated with a pulse of warm water travelling across the equatorial Pacific – seen both in altimetry and in remote sensing of sea surface temperature.

Between 1978 and 1980 a change in the currents of the North Atlantic subtropical gyre was measured. It is not known whether the whole gyre changed in strength, or whether the gyre system moved slightly or changed in shape. Shipborne observations are now underway to determine the gyre scale response to forcing on seasonal time-scales. There is an inevitable compromise between surveying a large enough area to provide a good spatial average to remove effects of meanders and eddies, yet a small enough area to ensure observations are synoptic compared with the time-scale of changes to the gyre. Long-term ocean climate change can only be comprehensively monitored using remote sensing, since a shipboard survey cannot provide the temporal and spatial coverage.

Infrared radiometry: ocean eddies and coastal upwelling

The satellite altimeter is an *active* sensor, because it sends out a pulse of radiation and records the reflection of that pulse. *Passive* sensors, on the other hand, pick up the radiation which is emitted naturally by the Earth itself. The intensity of the radiation in the infrared wavebands tells us the temperature of the surface emitter (the sun is so hot that it emits radiation in the visible

wavelengths, whereas the much cooler Earth emits radiation with peaks in the infrared and microwave bands). Sensors such as the Advanced Very High Resolution Radiometer (AVHRR) carried on the US National Oceans and Atmosphere Administration (NOAA) series of satellites during the 1980s and 1990s showed that differences in sea surface temperature of less than a tenth of a degree Celsius could be detected from space, with absolute values of sea surface temperature being accurate to a degree. This temperature is that of the top few millimetres of the ocean.

You may have wondered why the sea off California (the west coast of the USA) is much colder than off Florida on the east coast. This is due to coastal upwelling (see Box 10.3), a process driven by the prevailing wind. Satellite images of sea surface temperature have shown that the upwelling does not occur in a uniform band along the coast, but consists of jets and filaments of cold water extending offshore for many kilometres. Their position may be controlled by headlands or points along the coast. Coastal upwelling influences local climate – a particular example is the sea fogs that occur sometimes in summer on the west coast of the USA. These happen because the cold upwelled water cools the air rapidly and the water vapour carried by the atmosphere condenses.

The upwelled water is also nutrient-rich, so these regions are very productive, maintaining important fisheries. Knowledge of when, where and under what conditions these cold, highly productive regions will occur is important for prediction of fishery yields. In this way relatively cheap and frequent remotely sensed sea surface temperature images can assist in the management of local fishing industries, particularly important for developing countries. Some fishing fleets are even receiving infrared satellite images on their boats in real time, to enable them to move to the likely locations of fish shoals.

AVHRR imagery is also helping us to understand the structure and evolution of eddies. These eddies are important both for heat transport and for biological processes, since they can carry nutrient-rich water into a less productive area, providing an oasis for the growth of plankton. Some particularly dramatic eddies are formed in the Gulf of Tehuantepec, on the Pacific coast of Mexico, in response to atmospheric forcing (Barton *et al.*, 1993). A large area of cold water (some 10 °C cooler than the surrounding water) extends several hundred kilometres offshore, caused by an intense offshore wind jet known as a 'Norther'. This intermittent wind event occurs regularly during the winter

Box 10.3 How the wind causes coastal upwelling

Owing to the action of the Coriolis force, a wind blowing in the northern hemisphere will tend to induce in the surface layer a current 90° to the right of the wind (to the left in the southern hemisphere). If a wind blows parallel to the coastline as in the figure, the water will be forced away from the coast. To maintain equilibrium, water must come from somewhere to fill the gap – it upwells from underneath, and must flow in towards the coast beneath the water flowing away. The upwelling water is cooler than that which it displaces. This is the situation along the eastern boundaries of the Pacific and Atlantic oceans – for example, Peru, California and Portugal.

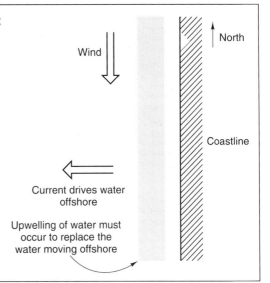

Wind

North

Coastline

Current drives water offshore

Upwelling of water must occur to replace the water moving offshore

months, due to a build-up of atmospheric pressure over the North American continent and subsequent sudden release through the only gap in the Sierra Madre mountain range, at the Isthmus of Tehuantepec.

Figure 10.3 shows the sea surface temperature observed during a Norther in January 1989 using AVHRR. Superimposed are arrows showing the wind velocity observed from a research ship. The wind leaves the coast near Salina Cruz, and fans out over the Gulf, with maximum speeds in excess of 20 m/s. A combination of upwelling, surface cooling and mixing by the wind leads to a reduction in the sea surface temperature in the centre of the Gulf, from 28 °C to 16 °C.

A large eddy forms to the right of the wind jet, as is shown by the curving round of the white area. Remnants of an eddy formed by the previous Norther can be seen to the south. The AVHRR imagery allows the shape and extent of the eddy to be determined – it would take a ship several days to survey the eddy, during which time its structure would have changed. Furthermore, AVHRR images in the days following the event have enabled researchers to study the decay and dynamics of the eddy as the wind jet abates.

The launch of ERS-1 offers even more accurate determination of sea surface temperature (to about 0.1°C) using the along track scanning radiometer (ATSR). This has two beams, one pointing forward and one pointing directly below the spacecraft. Since each area on the Earth's surface is observed twice, correction can be made for the absorption of the infrared radiation by the atmosphere.

Ocean colour sensing: ocean productivity

The colour of seawater is determined by the sediment carried in it (in coastal waters) and by the phytoplankton living in it (in open ocean or coastal waters). Phytoplankton are microscopic plants containing chlorophyll *a* and other pigments which absorb the sunlight they need for photosynthesis (Box 10.4). Being usually green, the phytoplankton absorb light in the red and blue wavelengths. The surface primary productivity can therefore be estimated from the wavelengths of the light being emitted from the sea surface, and this can be measured from space. This light has been scattered from the phytoplankton in the upper tens of metres (or from sediment in the upper few metres in coastal waters, where light cannot penetrate so deeply).

The Coastal Zone Color Scanner (CZCS) was a radiometer carried by the US National Atmospheric and Space Administration's (NASA) Nimbus-7 satellite from 1978 to 1986. Measuring the radiance in several different visible wavelengths, algorithms to determine the phytoplankton concentrations were developed. In tropical waters where sunlight is not a limiting factor, the greatest primary productivity is in regions where the surface wind field induces upwelling of nutrient-rich water from hundreds of metres below the surface (for example, the Gulf of Tehuantepec). Generally this is on the eastern boundaries of oceans, such as the coasts of north-west Africa, Portugal and

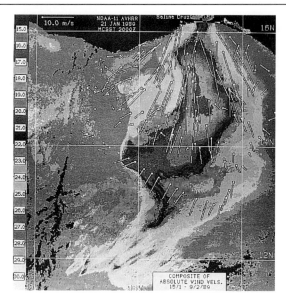

Fig 10.3 An AVHRR image of the Gulf of Tehuantepec, Mexico in January 1989 showing a cold eddy forced by a strong wind event. Wind vectors are superimposed.

California (Figure 10.4). In extratropical oceans such as the North Atlantic, primary productivity occurs when the sunlight reaches a sufficient level after winter mixing of nutrients into the surface layers so there is a spring phytoplankton bloom. These blooms are often

---

Box 10.4 The role of phytoplankton in bio-geo-chemical cycling

Phytoplankton remove carbon dioxide dissolved in seawater and emit oxygen. As well as sunlight, their growth requires nutrients such as nitrogen. They are therefore an important component of the global bio-geo-chemical cycles of carbon, nitrogen and other elements. The phytoplankton are grazed by zooplankton, whose faecal pellets then fall to the sea-bed as an amorphous substance known as *marine snow*. Thus the carbon dioxide, originally an atmospheric gas, is packaged up and sent to the sea bed – we believe that this removes substantial amounts of CO_2 from the atmosphere for long periods. Greater understanding of the carbon cycle is necessary to determine whether increased concentrations of man-made carbon dioxide are warming our climate. Satellite ocean colour sensors are now allowing us to determine the magnitude and variability of primary productivity. A major international project to do this, the Joint Global Ocean Flux Study (JGOFS), is now underway.

---

patchy, the phytoplankton distribution depending on eddies and other physical processes. Knowledge of plankton abundance in real time from ocean colour satellites enables us to direct a research vessel to the bloom areas to study the biological processes. The chlorophyll content determined from the CZCS has been shown to be directly related to large numbers of tuna and associated high catches off California.

Ocean colour is also valuable in revealing physical processes such as fronts and eddies, because phytoplankton are advected by the currents. These features do not always show up on infrared images of sea surface temperature, because the fronts may only occur in salinity, or because they may be capped by a surface layer masking temperature differences below. However, it is often the case that the two water masses either side of a front differ in their productivity and are therefore visible in ocean colour imagery.

Eddies are usually spun off from regions of strong current shear. For example, in the Agulhas Retroflection south of South Africa, where the currents flowing south-westwards down the east coast are turned back eastwards by the strong Antarctic Circumpolar Current, eddies of warm Indian Ocean water are formed. These travel round the Cape of Good Hope into the Atlantic Ocean, and are significant in transporting heat and water mass characteristics between the oceans. They have also been seen on satellite altimetry tracks travelling as far as the equatorial Atlantic. It has been suggested that the heat transported in these rings or eddies contributes to the warm climate of northern Europe, but we do not yet know how significant this heat transport is for global climate.

Gulf Stream Rings are another example of discrete eddies of one water mass being spun off into another. They form when meanders in the Gulf Stream pinch off (Figure 10.5). They may be 100–300 km in diameter and can exist for months, rotating once every few days.

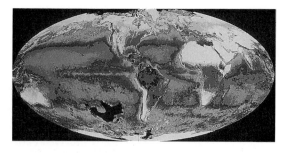

Fig 10.4 Global ocean productivity measured from the Coastal Zone Color Scanner.

The inshore waters to the north are cool and fresh, and are high in productivity because tides and winds mix nutrients up from below the surface, and nutrients are input from rivers. The waters of the Gulf Stream and Sargasso Sea are warm and more saline, and are low in productivity, being depleted of nutrients. Therefore the Rings are clearly visible on satellite images of both ocean colour and sea surface temperature (Figure 10.6), which together give us the tools to follow the lives of the Rings from pinching off, through advection along the Gulf Stream, to gradual mixing into the surrounding waters.

A successor to CZCS will be SeaWIFS, to be launched in 1995. This is in orbit at the same time as other ocean-observing satellites such as TOPEX/ POSEIDON, ERS-1 and ERS-2. The synergistic use of data from several different sensors is one of the greatest challenges and areas of excitement for ocean scientists.

Microwave radiometry: polynyas

Every winter, sea ice covers a large area of the Southern Ocean adjoining Antarctica, behaving like a blanket, insulating the ocean from the cooling effect of the wind. Polar regions are the sink for the excess solar radiation received at the equator, and therefore air–sea interactions there are crucial to maintain the global heat balance. If we wish to predict changes in climate, we need to determine the role of ice and snow and the interannual variations in the sea ice extent.

Mapping ice extent and revealing seasonal changes were not possible until the advent of microwave sensors on Earth-observing satellites. Visible wavelengths are

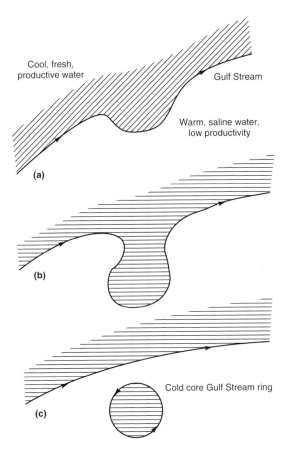

Fig 10.5 The formation of a Gulf Stream Ring. (a) The Gulf Stream marks the front between shelf waters to the north and ocean waters to the south. Like many fast currents, it can become unstable and begin to meander; (b) the meander often becomes more exaggerated and grows; (c) eventually the meander is pinched off and an isolated eddy of shelf water remains to the south of the Gulf Stream. The Gulf Stream itself has now become smoother.

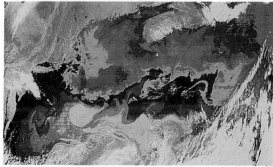

Fig 10.6 Ocean colour (top) and sea surface temperature (bottom) showing a Gulf Stream Ring.

not suitable because of cloud cover and long hours of darkness in polar winters. However, microwaves are emitted continually by the Earth's surface, their intensity dependent on its temperature, and have the advantage of passing through cloud. The intensity of radiation emitted by ice and by the open ocean is quite different so microwave scanners can be used to determine the thickness and distribution of the sea ice.

When the first microwave sensors were flown in the early 1970s, exciting discoveries were made concerning the sea ice distribution. Large areas of ice-free water, *polynyas*, were revealed, existing even during winter (Figure 10.7). The Weddell Sea polynya appeared several years running in the same position, implying that some kind of preconditioning prevailed which remained during the summer months. We do not yet understand why the polynya forms in some years but not in others (see Box 10.5).

The existence of a large polynya may affect the climate locally and even globally. The water in the polynya will be warmer than the sea ice around it, so its presence increases the transfer of heat from ocean to atmosphere, as the wind blowing over the water is warmed. In addition, this wind picks up moisture from the exposed water, and finds the surface of the water is smoother than that of the ice, so is slowed less by the surface friction. Satellite images show that cloud cover may be greater downwind of the polynya, where the increased moisture in the air condenses out. It has also been suggested that carbon dioxide would be carried into the deep ocean by the convection cells in open ocean polynyas. This would remove the gas from the short-term climate system, since it might be hundreds of years before the carbon dioxide was again at the sea surface. Other negative feedback effects stabilizing the climate include increased evaporation from the polynya leading to more precipitation over the ice cap so the total ice amount may not vary significantly. It is possible that polynyas may be part of nature's way of staying in equilibrium in the event of increased atmospheric carbon dioxide. Some of these points were made in Chapter 6 during the discussion of uncertainties in climate warming models.

Conclusions

It would be misleading to present remote sensing as the answer to all ocean-related questions. There are many problems that it cannot address – the identification and

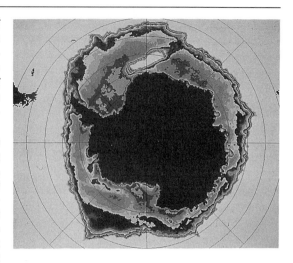

Fig 10.7 Passive microwave image of Antarctica showing the Weddell Sea polynya.

distribution of animals in the sea, the study of sea-bed sediments, determination of contamination by industrial waste or the measurement of deep ocean currents, for example. In general, satellites can only detect surface phenomena – at most in the upper hundreds of metres (e.g. ocean colour or surface geostrophic currents), and sometimes only in the top millimetres (e.g. infrared measurements of sea surface temperature). It is still necessary to go to sea in ships to collect water or sediment samples or marine organisms. Furthermore, many of the sensors described here are still under development and it is necessary to take shipborne measurements to calibrate and validate the satellite measurements. However, remote sensing is a valuable new tool poised to give people of the 21st century unprecedented information on the global ocean, without even getting their feet wet.

In this chapter we have seen a glimpse of the questions that oceanographers are tackling in order to understand the oceans. The sea has always held a fascination for mankind, quite apart from the practical problems of exploitation or climate. It is often said that we know more about the surface of the moon than the deep ocean! Many countries' economies depend to a large extent on their fishing fleets, yet we do not fully understand the complex food web from nutrients and phytoplankton, through zooplankton to larger species. The oceans are used for transport and as a site for extraction of fossil fuels, and our ability to use them without endangering lives depends on our understanding of this hostile environment. It is not surprising that the world's oceans will be the subject of a global management convention, along the lines of the UN Framework Convention on Climate Change, in 1995 or 1996. Preparation for this conference will depend enormously on the results of scientific discovery summarized in this chapter.

We have learnt how the use of satellite remote sensing techniques promises a leap forward in oceanography, as the scientists, engineers and managers suddenly find available vast amounts of data, more abundant in both space and time than ever before. Phenomena such as fronts and eddies, which are thought to have a significant influence on plankton distributions, are being revealed in areas previously thought to have smooth flow. For the first time, we are able to look at the variability in ocean currents, and monitor their changes over seasons, years and decades. This is of particular relevance to those concerned about the in-crease in greenhouse gases and possible effects on our climate. Changes in atmospheric forcing could alter the formation of bottom water, for example, which could completely alter the circulation of the world's oceans. However, not enough is known about the interaction of ocean and atmosphere to enable scientists to predict these effects with any certainty.

It is therefore important that we learn more about the oceans – and that this is a multidisciplinary effort. Remote sensing will increasingly become a standard tool alongside shipborne measurements, enabling us to reveal the fascinating processes occurring in the oceans.

Box 10.5 Formation of polynyas

There are two types of polynya caused by different forcing mechanisms. The first are coastal polynyas (shown below), formed by the action of katabatic winds flowing out from Antarctica driving the sea ice offshore, leaving open water where new ice can form. When sea ice forms, it is fresher than seawater and so the water left behind is more saline (*brine* solution) and therefore denser. This dense water sinks and forms a source of the water mass known as Antarctic bottom water, a cold saline water which spreads out over the sea-bed in areas of all the world's ocean basins. This water mass is an important component of the global heat budget, since it provides a significant fraction of the necessary poleward heat transport by taking cold water from the Southern Ocean to equatorial regions. This is a focus of attention for the World Ocean Circulation Experiment (WOCE) which hopes to quantify the heat transport by such bottom currents.

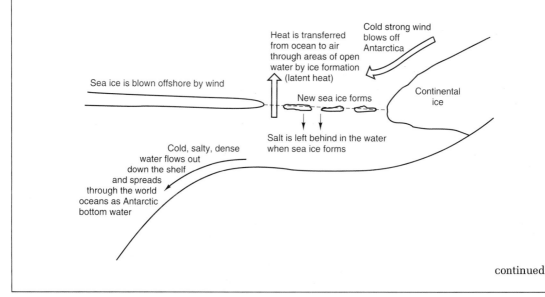

Heat is transferred from ocean to air through areas of open water by ice formation (latent heat)

Cold strong wind blows off Antarctica

Sea ice is blown offshore by wind

New sea ice forms

Continental ice

Salt is left behind in the water when sea ice forms

Cold, salty, dense water flows out down the shelf and spreads through the world oceans as Antarctic bottom water

continued

Box 10.5 continued

Deep ocean polynyas (shown below), of which the Weddell Sea polynya is an example, are larger and more persistent, occupying hundreds of square kilometres often for several successive winters. The polynya is thought to be maintained by convective cells some 10 km across, bringing warm water from below to the surface where it is cooled and sinks again. The salinity of the water is important since in polar regions it determines the density stratification – colder fresher water overlies warmer, more saline water. The salinity stratification will determine whether a polynya forms or not – if the surface salinity is high because overturning in previous years brought salty water to the surface, then a polynya is more likely to form since only a small amount of cooling will make the surface waters denser than those below, setting off convective cells. These convective cells cause melting of the ice by sensible heat flux (conduction) and therefore an area of open water appears. The location of the polynya is thought to be related to the bottom topography which can help to precondition the area. For example, during the 1980s a large polynya recurred over the Maud Rise near Antarctica, which may have been aided by upwelling. The injection of cold water into the deep ocean is thought to contribute to Antarctic bottom water by mixing with the very saline waters from the coastal polynya.

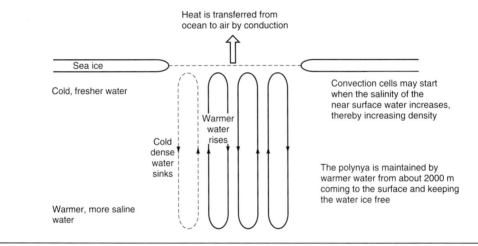

References

Barton, E.D., M.L. Argote, J. Brown, P.M. Kosro, M.L. Lavin, J.M. Robles, R.L. Smith, A. Trasuiña and H.S. Velez (1993) Supersquirt: the dynamics of the Gulf of Tehuantepec, Mexico. *Oceanography*, **6**, 23–30.

Other relevant papers include D.J. Ellett (1993) The north-east Atlantic: a fan assisted storage heater *Weather*, **48**(4), 118–26; A.L. Gordon (1988) The Southern Ocean and global climate, *Oceanus*, **31**(2), 39–46.

Further Reading

Those who wish to learn more about satellite oceanography should read I.S. Robinson (1985) *Satellite oceanography: an introduction for oceanographers and remote-sensing scientists* (Chichester: Ellis Horwood) which explains in detail how each sensor works, together with examples of oceanographic phenomena. There are many good textbooks in which the physics of ocean circulation and air-sea interaction are explained. A series recent enough to include remote sensing applications is published by the Open University (1989), *Ocean Circulation* (Oxford: Pergamon).

The classic paper in which altimeter data from Seasat were used for the first time to obtain global maps of mesoscale variability is that by R.C. Cheney, J.G. Marsh and B.D. Beckley (1983) Global mesoscale variability from collinear tracks of Seasat altimeter data, *Journal of Geophysical Research*, **88**, 4343–54. More recently, a special issue of the *Journal of Geophysical Research – Oceans* (March 1990) was devoted to results from the US Navy's altimetric satellite Geosat, which flew from 1986 to 1989. The scientific background of the international World Ocean Circulation Experiment

(WOCE) is discussed by J.D. Woods (1985) The world ocean circulation experiment, *Nature*, **314**, 501–11. Recent changes observed in the circulation of the North Atlantic, in particular the 'great salinity anomaly' of freshwater which travelled round the North Atlantic during the 1970s, were described by R.R. Dickson, J. Meincke, S.A. Malmburg and A.J. Lee (1988) The great salinity anomaly in the northern North Atlantic 1968–1982, *Progress in Oceanography*, **20**, 103–51. Exiting new results showing the eddy structure in the Gulf of Tehuantepec may be found in Barton *et al.* (1993).

CHAPTER 11

The land from space

KEITH CLAYTON

In 1980 nobody had any clear idea of how much tropical forest was being removed, nor the extent of land degradation. These are two intertwined schemes of the utmost importance to global environmental well-being. Evidence was collected by national agencies, independent scientists and by international organizations. This was inevitably patchy, with great variation as to the criteria employed for defining loss and degradation. This was the 'old geography' soundly rooted on the ground, well meaning and immensely valuable for providing a synoptic picture, and at least surveying something close to a culturally varied but global picture.

Today much of this task is overtaken by remote sensing from satellites whose original purpose was military surveillance. The military inheritance has meant that the quality of the technology is orders of magnitude higher than might have been the case if the original motive had been entirely scientific and geographical. Resolution of detail to remarkable levels of clarity is an outcome of a need to identify a missile site or a strategic radar operation within densely wooded areas. Nowadays, there is just about enough money in the science budgets, helped enormously by more environment-friendly space agencies now that both military and extra planetary surveillance is less popular, to release the inventiveness of space technology on the assessment of land-use change and global environmental impact. For relatively modest cost, the geographical information systems databanks are becoming available to a host of research institutes across the world.

This is important, but at the same time one should be wary. The importance lies in data sets of change that would not be possible without armies of analysts swarming over inhospitable terrain. The estimation of tropical forest losses has been clarified to be almost twice that which was originally believed to be the case even in the mid-1980s. Any sincere effort by a biodiversity-conscious nation to restrict the extent of the loss can also be recorded. Clearly the technology has profound significance for monitoring compliance of any level of international agreement or management innovation. In this regard it is an indispensable accompanist to any protocol or restrictive covenant.

For example, the gain or loss to habitat under the UN Biodiversity Convention can now be organized in a systematic manner. Similarly the physical extent of desertification (though not its cultural significance) should be recordable in time for the UN Convention on Desertification. Changes to coral, to coastal ecosystems and to vulnerable upland habitats caused by tourism, recreation and inappropriate development are all now recordable for national and international organizations and NGOs. In the UK the set-aside scheme and the environmentally sensitive area programme both involve detailed compliance by landowners and occupiers before money is paid. This is the case for set-aside, namely the removal of land from production for periods of up to 20 years on a permanent or rotational basis, throughout the European Community. Satellite surveillance is essential to 'prove' that the objectives of the schemes are met. Farmers get paid by evidence on computer printouts as much as from their own records. One can foresee that the surveillance and verification component of satellite and GIS technology will become ever more significant in the applied environmental sciences.

This is where scientific capacity building comes in. Providing computers, datasets and image recorders will not always work in developing countries where power failures can disrupt computer disks, where training rarely keeps up with innovation, and where the supporting research services are too expensive to establish or maintain. The Agenda 21 demand for more scientific capacity building needs to marry high technology with good science, extra-terrestrial recording with ground truthing, digitized mapping with ethnobotanical understanding and culturally sensitive economic analysis. There is no doubt that the information revolution is still in its infancy. As it evolves the role of remote sensing and GIS will help enormously in the preparation of a more accurate global audit of environmental change.

The trick is to link this effectively and consciously to culture-specific adaptation measures and institutional realignments on the ground. A beginning has been made by the science training programme, START, promoted by the International Biosphere Geosphere Programme of the International Council of Scientific Unions. Further development can be foreseen by the extension of a modest project, promoted by the United Nations University, of critical environmental zones. This combined geographers with ecologists and anthropologists to identify areas of the globe which were especially vulnerable to environmental stress, and where the inherent capabilities of the societies involved were overwhelmed making them unable to adjust. The scheme highlighted how a combination of aggregated data of environmental change can be coupled to detailed assessments of institutional failure and capacity overload to reinforce vulnerability and marginality (the first being a physical notion, the second a socio-cultural one) in the areas most at risk from both globally induced, and locally created environmental stress. Much more of this work should form the basis for the flourishing of sustainable development experiment and achievement, continent by continent.

Further reading

Kasperson, R.E. (Ed.) (1993) *Critical environmental zones*. Tokyo: United Nations University Press.

The peculiar advantages of a vertical view of the Earth's surface from a considerable height were first apparent when the early balloon and later aircraft ascents were made. Here was a plan view, more cluttered and less easy to read than a map, yet with patterns that could not be perceived on the ground and often of features that were not shown on any map. One of the earliest systematic uses of this approach was the archaeological survey of Salisbury Plain, on the chalklands of southern England, which discovered wooden precursors to Stonehenge and many other fascinating and significant patterns which recorded the early colonization of the land by prehistoric man.

Remote sensing from satellites

With the launch of the first spacecraft in the 1960s, cameras and other more sophisticated sensors were used to study the Earth's atmosphere, oceans and land surfaces. The first camera shots from the US Apollo spacecraft showed patterns of land and sea that had until then only been visible in an atlas. They showed, too, patterns of land cover that were related to vegetation patterns, most of them natural, some of them agricultural in origin. Some of these were expected and familiar, seen in a new clarity, such as the pattern of irrigated agriculture within the desert of Egypt in the Nile delta and as a narrow thread along the Nile itself. Some of the largest man-made patterns, such as those of the Gezira irrigation scheme in the Sudan, or the circular centre-pivot irrigated fields of the American south-west or the Libyan desert were on no normal map. Urban areas and other signs of man's habitation or transport systems were not easy to find.

The serious business of surveying the land from space began with the launch of the Landsat series of satellites in the early 1970s. Indeed the series remains the single most important source of data obtained from space for the world as a whole. Thus the sensors chosen and developed over time for Landsat are central to the business of recording and interpreting features on the land surface of most of the Earth. Only the highest latitudes remain uncovered by this sequence of Earth recording satellites, though areas frequently covered by cloud (high latitudes and equatorial zones) are inevita-

bly less well known than deserts and other seasonally dry zones. In the latter case dry season coverage is easier by far to obtain than wet season cover which is sometimes entirely missing. Thus observations requiring frequent repeated coverage or data from a particular season can be hard to find for some areas of the globe.

Passive and active sensors

Sensors in a satellite may be used to detect and measure three types of energy (Figure 11.1). The first is the reflected solar energy from a surface, whether it be water, a leaf, a roof or a cloud. This will in principle encompass the whole wavelength range of solar energy, but it practice the atmosphere absorbs so much of some energy bands that little can be detected. Between these absorption bands are 'windows' where energy passes through the atmosphere relatively easily, and these are the preferred wavelengths for remote sensing purposes (Figure 11.2). Secondly, sensors may detect energy radiated from the surface – this is principally the thermal infrared wavelength. These two are passive sensors and dominate because they do not require a source of energy other than the sun, or the radiation from the earth's surface – thus thermal IR may be measured at night. Active sensors involve an energy source on the spacecraft which is directed at Earth and the reflected energy is then measured back at the satellite – the main method uses radar wavelengths.

The data explosion

One aspect of the collection of data from the Landsat series and now from the French SPOT (Système Probatoire de l'Observation de la Terre) and other satellites which deserves comment is the sheer volume of available material. These systems are recording data digitally and the reflectance is recorded for rectangular areas known as pixels. These pixels are arranged side by side in rows as the satellite moves above the surface of the rotating Earth (Figure 11.3). Each Landsat scene on the original MSS (multi-

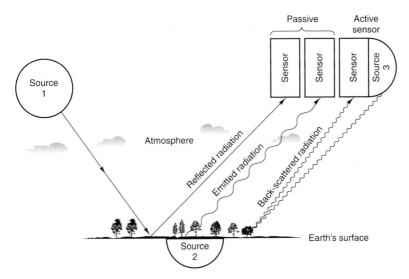

Fig 11.1 The three main sources of satellite data. For passive sensors, the main source of energy is the sun, and both reflected energy and radiated energy may be detected. Active sensors have a source in the satellite and the reflected radar waves are detected by an appropriate sensor. (Source: Curran, 1985, Fig. 2.1.)

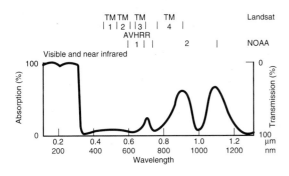

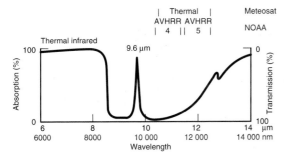

Fig 11.2 The atmospheric 'windows' utilized by satellite systems. In addition to the visible and near-infrared wavelengths, various parts of the infrared waveband penetrate the atmosphere successfully and are utilized by the sensors indicated. For details of satellites and sensors see Box 11.3. (Source: Harris, 1987, Fig. 2.5.)

spectral scanner) format had 2340 scan lines with 3240 pixels per line, giving 7.5 million pixels per channel and 30 million pixels for each scene with four channels. The newer TM (thematic mapper) format consists of data for seven wavebands with a higher resolution (30 m for all but the thermal IR, compared with 79 m for Landsat MSS) and thus with about 100 million pixels per scene. Each scene is collected in 25 seconds, so that even the early Landsat system was capable of filling 30 million computer tapes each year. The result of this capacity to fill magnetic tapes with data is that not all scenes are recorded, and very many of those that have been collected have never been used. Thus we have over-provision of data (in fact, as well as potentially) for some areas; yet for other areas it is hard to find a cloud-free scene, and for some countries none is yet available for the wet season.

A related problem is the availability of information. Most work has been done using the US Landsat series of platforms, and one of the most important reasons is the availability of this material from a central source and at subsidized prices. Any system that attempts to recover the full costs of a satellite platform will produce such expensive data that use will be small. In addition, poorer countries will find it difficult to invest in the data and the means of interpretation, both human and the necessary equipment. In particular, the computer

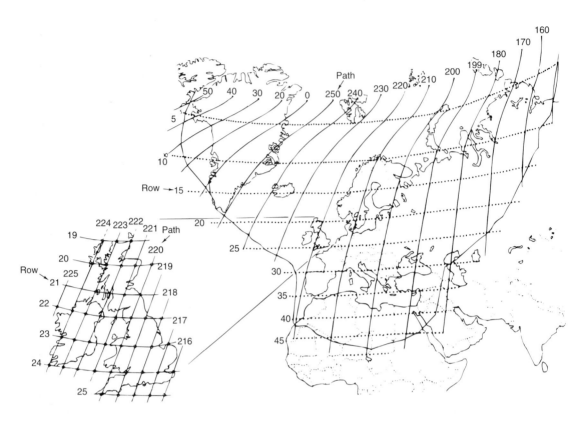

Fig 11.3 The path and row system of reference of orbiting satellites. The path and row system is used to identify the 180 × 180 km scenes of the Landsat MSS system. Successive paths are displaced westwards by the Earth's rotation and each path is revisited every 18 (later every 16) days. (Source: Curran, 1985, Fig. 5.20.)

analysis of satellite images requires considerably more training, and has considerably more pitfalls, than mapping from aerial photographs. It is partly for this reason that, while there is much current research using satellite images, their routine use in mapping, monitoring and data collection remains rather limited, especially in developing countries where they offer most potential. It will require a considerable further development in training and in analytical systems for the full potential of satellite data to be realized across the world. For those satellites without on-board recorders, it will also require further receiving stations (Figure 11.4).

Box 11.1 gives further details of satellites and sensor systems.

Pictures or digital data?

Many writers carelessly refer to satellite scenes as photographs. A few are. The early Apollo series of spacecraft carried handheld Hasselblad cameras which took coloured photographs of the Earth, and very pretty they are too (Figure 11.5). They are usually obliques and bring a reality to the large-scale abstractions of the atlas map which never ceases to impress. However, most black and white or coloured reproductions are made by producing grey-scale images from the digital pixel by pixel data recorded and transmitted by the satellite, just as a newspaper picture is made up of thousands upon thousands of small dots produced by 'screening' the original, higher resolution, photographic image. There are so many pixels, the texture cannot be seen unless (as rather often happens) whole

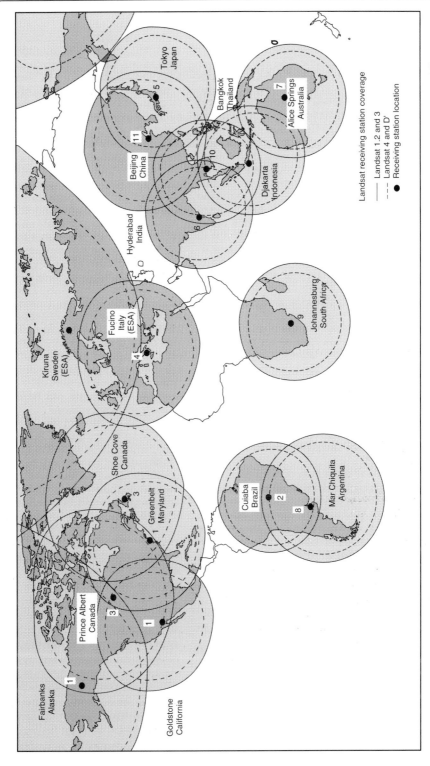

Fig 11.4 The location of Landsat receiving stations around the world. The areas which are not covered by a ground station can only be covered if scenes are successfully recorded on the on-board tape recorder and downloaded later. Note that coverage is poor in the developing world and that polar latitudes are not seen from these satellites. (Source: Curran, 1985, Fig. 5.18.)

0

000

000

Box 11.1 Satellites and sensor systems

The lowest altitude at which a satellite can circle the Earth for an adequate period of time without being brought down by atmospheric drag is a little over 700 km. This is the altitude which most of the Earth observing satellites use, in order to maximize resolution. The earliest Landsat satellites (from 1972) orbited at about 900 km and like most of their successors were designed to follow a sun-synchronous path, i.e. they crossed the equator at the same time each day, chosen to be relatively early in the morning, giving adequate illumination, good shadows and avoiding the tendency for cloud to increase during the day. The progress of the orbit round the world gave repeat coverage every 18 days, a figure reduced to 16 days from Landsat 5 (launched 1984).

The other preferred position for a satellite is at least 35 000 km from Earth. By placing such a satellite in the plane of the equator and setting up its direction of rotation in the same direction as the rotation of the Earth, it will appear in a geostationary position, i.e. it will stay above the same point on the globe. By keeping at least three such satellites in position, complete global coverage is achieved, primarily for providing data for weather forecasting, but increasingly these geostationary satellites have been provided with sophisticated instruments capable of observing far more than cloud patterns and temperature throughout the atmosphere. The only disadvantage of the distant position is the reduction of resolution. Typical resolution for the lower orbiting satellites is in the range 10–70 m per pixel, whereas 1–10 km is characteristic of the stationary satellites.

The observations made from these platforms are necessarily limited to wavelengths which are readily transmitted by the atmosphere. These wavelengths are referred to as spectral windows and are shown in Figure 11.2. The spectral data can be divided into narrow or broader bands (see also Box 11.3). The original MSS (multispectral scanner) of the Landsat series utilized four bands (numbered from 4 to 7 because the RBV (return beam vidicon) system had bands 1–3), three of them in the visual range and one in the near-infrared, a band reflected by healthy vegetation and strongly absorbed by water. The succeeding thematic mapper (TM) system utilized seven bands, three in the visual range and rather similar to those used in the MSS, together with four in the infrared. One of these is affected by healthy vegetation, one is moisture sensitive, one gives good geological discrimination (Band 7, 2.08–2.35 μm) and the last (Band 6) is in the thermal infrared. To obtain adequate energy, the pixel size for Band 6 covers four pixels for the other bands. Other sensors that may be carried by orbiting satellites include radar, whilst the more technically advanced meteorological satellites carry a wide range of specialized instruments. The one of most relevance to surface observations is the very effective Advanced Very High Resolution Radiometer (AVHRR) which has a number of spectral channels. This collects radiance data daily with a resolution of 4 km on a global basis, the daily coverage allowing use of all cloud-free days. By observing the spectral range most strongly absorbed by plants, an estimate of green leaf biomass can be made and thus an estimate of photosynthesis.

The transmission of data from the satellite to Earth is by radio, though the Landsat and SPOT satellites carry tape recorders to allow delay in the transmission of scenes until the platform is over a ground receiving station. The higher resolution systems do not collect all possible scenes, selection being made in terms of land/sea, cloud cover and research requirements.

lines of data are recorded above or below the average values for neighbouring lines. Large colour images (which can be purchased at scales such as 1:250 000) are produced from the Landsat MSS by using three of the four bands and the three primary colours, blue, green and red. The normal convention is to print the near IR (e.g. Band 7 of Landsat MSS) in red, the red end of the visual spectrum in green and the blue-green part of the spectrum in blue. The result is what is known as a 'false-colour' image, with healthy vegetation in red and deep water almost black.

The visual interpretation of printed satellite images is of considerable value and as users become adjusted to the scale of the imagery and the inclusion of wavebands beyond the visual range these can be very useful and are increasingly used as illustrations in books and on TV (Figure 11.6). Thus night IR cloud images are commonly displayed during the TV weather forecast and accepted without question by viewers who never wonder how clouds can be 'seen' when it is dark! However, most precise work (e.g. even as simple as the measurement of areas) is best done direct from digital images, and computer software capable of handling and analysing satellite images in several bands is widely available for desktop computers. In most cases the images are handled as if they were on a square north–south and east–west grid (they are in fact skewed) but the more sophisticated software packages are able to

Fig 11.5 An early space photo of southern Saudi Arabia. This oblique shot was originally in colour and shows a huge wadi system in the Hadramawt Plateau of the Saudi Arabian desert. Clouds obscure the far view; it is not obvious whether these lie over the desert or the sea of the Persian Gulf. (Courtesy of NASA.)

transform the images and resample them on true grid co-ordinates.

In the rest of this chapter the methods described will generally involve the computer manipulation of digital data, rather than visual interpretation. Some examples of the programs available are described in Box 11.2. Since this chapter does not seek to replace the detailed guides to remote sensing available in various excellent texts, it is taken for granted that the images will already have been corrected for geometric errors, for sensor

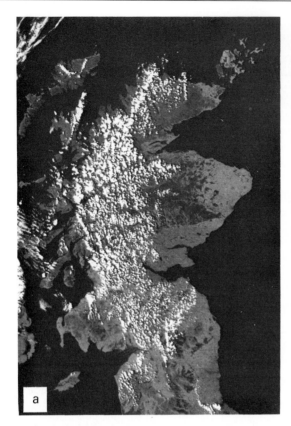 

Fig 11.6 Visible light and thermal infrared images of Scotland. The image on the left shows white clouds reflecting sunlight and a dark, light-absorbent sea. That on the right could as well have been taken at night, and the clouds are cold and thus dark, contrasting with the warm land and the cooler sea (the image was taken in May). A negative image would show white clouds as convincing as those in the visible image. (Courtesy of NASA.)

problems (e.g. by removing striping) and for atmospheric distortion (e.g. haze affects shorter wavelengths more than longer). In practice, tapes obtained from official and commercial sources have usually had such corrections applied.

Resolution

In general, the Earth Resources type of satellite has gradually improved its resolution over two decades by reducing the pixel size, partly through improvements in instrumentation, partly by putting the satellite into a lower orbit, the latter shift also reducing the gap between passes. Thus the original Landsat series had a pixel size of 79×79 m, the TM series has a pixel size of 30 m (except for the far IR band) and Spot achieves

about 10 m. Many researchers and potential users of satellite data have pressed for these improvements, since they allow more effective discrimination of small areas (such as fields) and thus more accurate classification. But since even better resolution can be achieved for considerable areas by air photography, it is not always obvious that the very large amount of additional data that has to be handled is worth the additional precision.

For many users, the wide area overview of the satellite image is of great value, allowing a scale of study difficult even with small-scale maps and effectively impossible with thousands of aerial photographs. Thus while the move towards greater precision in the wavebands utilized (and the concomitant increase in the number of spectral bands) is to be welcomed, improved resolution is a mixed blessing. Indeed, at the other extreme, some important work has been done utilizing the very poor (1–10 km) resolution of the

---

Box 11.2 Computer programs used to analyse digital images

When the first Landsat satellite was launched, computer programs had to be written to analyse the data. These required large mainframe computers to run, a tendency that persisted even with faster computers as more complex algorithms were developed to classify multispectral images. In the last decade, it has become possible to display and analyse images using software packages developed for the purpose such as the early PCIPS or the more sophisticated IDRISI. More recently, these have been combined with various levels of geographical information system (GIS) to allow the integration of satellite and other spatial data.

Almost all orbiting satellites use an inclined orbit, so the combination of the satellite pixel data with geometrically correct mapped data requires rectification of the satellite image, usually also involving resampling of the data to generate pixels which are aligned with the map grid. This requires considerable computing power, so that in the past it was performed as a separate process on a large computer, the rectified image then being utilized on a desktop computer. With ever-more powerful desktop machines, these processes can now be carried out by the same machine using a program such as ERDAS. Thus we have moved from a stage where the desktop user found it easier to distort the map to match the computer-captured complexity of the satellite data to a fully integrated (if inevitably rather more complex) system capable of combining classified satellite images with a fully developed GIS.

As with most computer software packages, the level of understanding required of the user is limited. This has its advantages and dangers. It is marvellous to be able to utilize sophisticated algorithms which use maximum likelihood and related techniques to secure optimal classification of the multispectral data. But without some understanding of what is being done, and of the data being used, some rough and ready results can be produced. The optimal selection of bands and of training areas requires proper understanding of the multispectral data and what it is recording. Scale is also important. In some areas a high proportion of the pixels will lie within single fields (and thus perhaps single crops) or record uniform vegetation cover. In other areas (especially those with small fields or the complex patterns typical of built-up areas) most pixels will sample a mixed cover. Both types will classify in much the same way, yet the meaning of the classes produced will be very different.

When interpretation is seeking more subtle levels of information such as soil type, moisture levels or the solid geology, then the computer interpretation of digital images requires a proper insight into the reasons the different spectral bands may be affected and a higher level of ground-based data to check on the interpretation made.

---

stationary meteorological satellites (Figure 11.7). Indeed, for some purposes involving the monitoring of global change, the analysis of stationary satellite data is of particular value and methods exist to integrate separate observations of the surface as clouds move across the view. It may also not be obvious that success in classifying images tends to improve as resolution declines; as an example we might cite urban areas that are relatively easy to separate out unless the pixels are so large that we start getting a patchwork of buildings, streets, trees and gardens, in which case we have to group the pixels in some way to get the overall effect of a typical built-up area.

At the high resolution end of the range, there are military satellites using specialist techniques which can yield images comparable to those from aircraft. They are effectively taking aerial photographs from space, so are only appropriate where ground access is denied. They can also involve recovery of the recorded image by physical means, rather than the transmission of an image in digital form.

There is also the important issue of spectral resolution. The narrowing in the width of the bands used in successive sensors of Landsat MSS type can be noted from the table in Box 11.3. This also shows an increase in the spectral range utilized, particularly beyond the longer end of the visible range in the infrared. Several of these adjustments were made with specific aims, thus the late addition (as its position in the sequence shows) to the TM of Landsat D (and subsequent satellites with the TM sensor) reflected the view that it was of particular utility in the mapping of geology. Indeed, just as the MSS was unproved before it flew on the first Landsat satellite, and was nearly omitted in favour of the RBV (return beam vidicon) which did not work at all well, so the TM system was nearly omitted from Landsat D. The competitor was a solid state system known as the multilinear array which was subsequently adopted for Spot. This can achieve higher resolution but can also be used to collect spectral data across a very large number of narrow channels. This additional information can in principle be used to improve on the

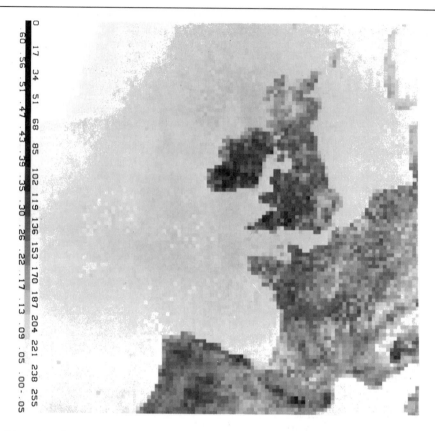

Fig 11.7 A cloud-free view of the vegetation of Europe. This image was built up over seven days in March 1983 to map a vegetation index using the AVHRR data. Despite the poor resolution, the overall pattern is usefully clear, and by acquiring areas that were cloud free on successive days an image is built up which could never be seen at a single time. Part of this scene would be cloud-covered every day of every year. (Courtesy of NOAA.)

classification and recognition of Earth surface detail. The difficulty is that it requires simplification through combination or omission of information if it is to be analysed by conventional programs, or new algorithms if the time taken for numerical analysis by computer is to be kept to tolerable levels.

It is interesting to note that the original MSS system was maintained alongside the TM from Landsat 4 on. This is in part because of its proven technology and thus reliability, but also to allow similar images to be used in the detection of change over time. It also allows established interpretation routines to continue in use, an important consideration in the many countries where the costs of data acquisition and interpretation are an important constraint on the utilization of satellite images.

Radar

So far we have reviewed satellites utilizing visible and IR wavebands derived from the reflection of the sun's energy. These are known as passive sensing systems. The other important group uses an active sensor which emits energy. The most important of these uses radar wavelengths, usually in the form of SLAR, sideways-looking airborne radar, where the impulse from the equipment on the plane or satellite is reflected with varying effect from the Earth's surface and received back at the radar source where the reflected energy is recorded. One cunning aspect of this is that the distance between source and receiver is offset by the distance travelled by the satellite while the radar wave travels to the Earth's surface and back; and this shift of position can, with the aid of sophisticated data processing, in

Box 11.3 Multispectral sensors in successive satellites

The reader is referred to the many textbooks on remote sensing (see references at the end of this chapter) for a full list of satellites and their sensors. This selected list includes those which have been most widely used in the interpretation of Earth land surface features.

Name and country	Sensor	Wavebands[a]	Resolution	Repeat cover
Landsat 1–5 (USA)	MSS			
	Band 4	0.5–0.6	79 m	18 days[b]
	Band 5	0.6–0.7	..	..
	Band 6	0.7–0.8	..	..
	Band 7	0.8–1.1	..	..
Landsat 4–5 (USA)	TM			
	Band 1	0.45–0.52	30 m	16 days
	Band 2	0.52–0.60	..	..
	Band 3	0.63–0.69	..	..
	Band 4	0.76–0.90	..	..
	Band 5	1.55–1.75	..	..
	Band 6	10.4–12.5	..	..
	Band 7	2.08–2.35	..	..
SPOT (France)	HRV (High Resolution Visible) Scanner			
	Panchromatic	0.51–0.73	10 m	≥ 4 days[c]
	Multispectral mode:			
	Green	0.50–0.59	30 m	as above
	Red	0.61–0.69	..	..
	Near-infrared	0.79–0.89	..	..
TIROS/NOAA (USA)	AVHRR			
	Channel 1	0.55–0.68	1.1 or 5.5 km	12 hours
	Channel 2	0.725–1.1	..	..
	Channel 3	3.55–3.93	..	..
	Channel 4	10.5–11.5	..	..
	Channel 5	11.5–12.5	..	..

[a]For simplicity of comparison, all wavelengths are in micrometres (μm).
[b]16 days for Landsat 4 and 5.
[c]Using oblique view.

effect be used as a giant receiving aerial. By this means, the satellite system is able to achieve a resolution that is independent of the altitude of the source; thus satellite SLAR has as good a resolution as that from an aircraft and typically about 30 m. The other advantage of SLAR is that neither visibility (e.g. clouds or night), nor the absorption of particular wavelengths by the atmosphere affect it (Figure 11.8); for this reason it is of particular value in tropical latitudes where cloud cover arises early every day. The disadvantage is that the image is even more removed from a visual light image than multispectral images, and some training is needed for effective and accurate interpretation of the imagery.

Geographical Information Systems

Over the last few years computerized systems for handling spatial data on computer have been developed, known by the initials of Geographical Information System, GIS. These can allow the operator to combine map and statistical data, to measure values within boundaries of various types (political or physical) and to study spatial patterns or the degree of spatial correspondence between different variables within the GIS system.

These systems generally hold information as vectors, i.e. in an x, y type of co-ordinate system. Many programs are available on a wide variety of machines. Most of these will also allow the integration of satellite

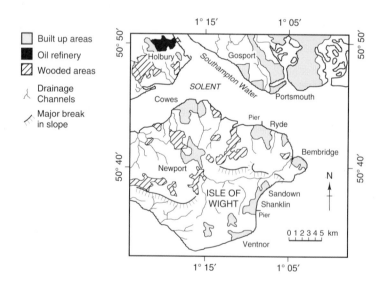

Fig 11.8 A SLAR image of the Isle of Wight. Note that the detail includes the pattern of waves at sea as well as many features on land. This image comes from the Seasat satellite which operated for just 100 days in 1978. (Courtesy of Space and Communications Department, DRA, Farnborough, UK.)

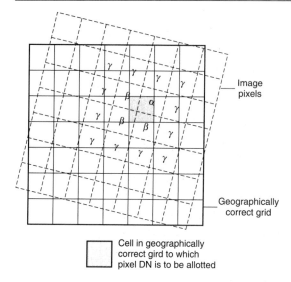

Cell in geographically
correct gird to which
pixel DN is to be allotted

Fig 11.9 Resampling procedure used to rectify and resample a satellite image. The image has to be corrected for the oblique skew and for distance north-south and east-west. The new pixels can either be given DN values corresponding to the old pixel which covers most of the new one (nearest neighbour method i.e. value of pixel α), by the weighted average of the four pixels concerned (bilinear interpolation, i.e. proportionally from values of α and β), or by the proportional weight of the 16 nearest pixels (α, β and γ), known as cubic convolution. Computing time required for each process goes up from relative values of 1 through 10 to 20 for the cubic convolution. (Source: Curran, 1985, Fig. 6.16.)

data so that the reflectance values may be related to a map, to digital elevation data (DTM or digital terrain model), to administrative boundaries, etc. The integration also allows data in the GIS to be used to aid in the classification of the satellite scene. For example, considerable improvements in the classification of forest cover can be achieved if the varying illumination of different slopes can be allowed for by incorporating relief information from a DTM.

Utilization of satellite data requires the rectification of the image, usually to correct its skew orientation and to achieve correct scale in both east–west and north–south directions (Figure 11.9). This requires the identification of several points on the image in terms of ground co-ordinates (e.g. map grid or latitude/longitude). It is then possible either to resample the rectified image to achieve a new system of pixels which conforms to the map grid, or alternatively to transform the raster data of the original scene into the vector co-ordinates of the GIS system. In some cases, all that may be

Box 11.4 The Large Area Crop Inventory Experiment (LACIE) program sponsored by NASA.

This joint programme was established in the USA by NASA (the National Aeronautics and Space Administration), the NOAA (National Oceans and Atmospheres Administration) and the USDA (Department of Agriculture) and aimed to establish crop-recognition techniques which could be used to inventory acreages and yields over the main grain-producing areas of the Earth including the former USSR. It assumed that 'spectral signatures' could provide unique identification of crop type and thus the establishment of areas sown. The yield was to be estimated from the growth of the crop (primary productivity from colour, i.e. chlorophyll) and from climatic and other information about the conditions under which the crop had grown.

The programme rested on the assumption, now largely discarded, that a library of crop 'spectral signatures' could be built up from known areas and that these could be successfully applied in other locations. A particular problem was that images gathered in mid-summer in the American midwest showed considerable confusion between mature and ripening crops. This meant that a time series of images was required for more accurate measurements and this implied both the regular availability of multiple images, year on year, and additional time (and thus money) spent on image classification. The LACIE research programme is a good example of the optimism which surrounded the launch and early utilization of Landsat data. By the 1980s the project had been discontinued (without producing any crop data of value in agricultural planning). Rather little progress has since been made. Feasibility studies continue, but the Italian AGRIT scheme designed to measure annual crop inventories and to forecast production on a national scale was reported in 1986 as still experimenting with the use of TM data to map durum wheat in the Puglia region. Among the difficulties were the many scenes required and the difficulty of obtaining cloud-free cover of similar date for the whole area, together with the vast number of images to be examined and the cost and difficulty of obtaining adequate ground truth for the many training areas required (Ascani, 1986). Many ambitious national schemes run into these persistent problems which are at the heart of the effective utilization of the vast output of space images of the Earth.

required is the ability to overlay some map variable such as the pattern of roads, of administrative boundaries, or even a coastline. In this case it may be preferred

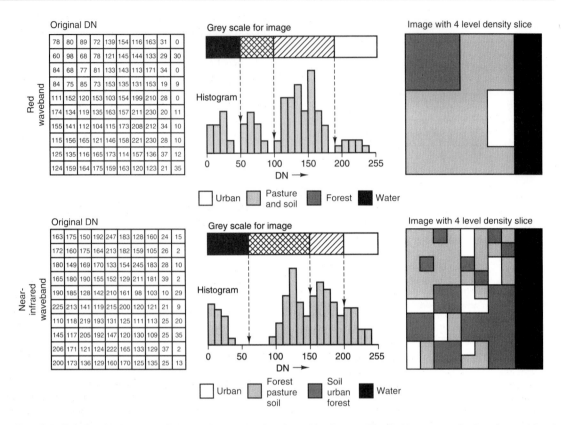

Fig 11.10 Relationship between digital numbers in two bands and land cover. The limiting range of values for each land cover type for these two bands is shown in the centre diagrams. By combining two or more different bands which are poorly correlated with each other, more accurate decisions may be made. (Source: Curran, 1985, Fig. 6.28.)

to project this on to the resampled raster image since then the standard procedures of numerical analysis available in the image-processing package can still be used. In other cases, the classified image may be resampled and overlaid as a variable within the GIS package.

The potential uses of satellite images

Data on the multispectral or radar reflectivity of the Earth's surface can be used to identify land cover. This may be natural vegetation, crops, urban or industrial areas, water, etc. In many cases this information will have characteristics (intensity, pattern, changes over time) that allow secondary interpretation of features, often with great precision. In this way information on landforms, soils, geology, surface processes (e.g. floods or landslides) or crop disease may be derived. As we

shall see, some of this secondary interpretation is of great use, for example in the location of major ore bodies or the management of major natural hazards such as severe floods. However, it is also possible to derive either details of little value from images or data that cannot be securely interpreted. For example, much early classification produced complex tables which on inspection might be found to include six or seven different classes of water (clear, muddy, eutrophic, patchy, continuous sheet, deep, shallow). More serious is the step required to turn land cover information into data on land use. Just as you cannot tell if sheep are being kept primarily for wool or meat by looking at them, so fields of 'grass' in spring may represent grazing, hay, a public park, a sports field, young cereals or just unploughed weed. Some of these classes may be determined from other features or by looking at changes over the seasons (though this is only possible where limited cloud cover allows repeated coverage).

Box 11.5 'Ground Truth'

Only limited inferences may be made from satellite data alone. Some types of land cover are clear enough from the spectral data, such as areas of water which can usually be recognized securely using the near-infrared band alone (e.g. Landsat MSS Band 7). In some areas, general knowledge of the crops grown may be used to infer what various classes represent, indeed even some knowledge of the relative proportions by area of the main crops can aid this process.

Most detailed classification of images requires accurate information on land cover for small areas which are then used as 'training areas' to set the spectral range for each type. The extent to which this classification may safely be extended should then be checked by further areas where the cover is known and which were not used in the classification. This also allows an estimate of the level of accuracy of the classification of the whole image. Extrapolation to adjacent images may be insecure, extrapolation over time is usually quite unsafe. Unfortunately, very little of what is commonly called 'ground truth' is actually obtained at the moment of the satellite overpass. To achieve that would require a level of organization and a financial commitment that are not normally available. In places such as the UK or the eastern USA, it would also involve the abortive deployment of scientists on days when the satellite obtains no data because of cloud cover. Thus various surrogates for ground truth in the strict sense are used. These include land-use surveys made before or after the overpass, statistical data on land use, aerial photographs with detail allowing more confident interpretation of ground cover, and so on.

Often the acquisition of adequate ground truth to allow effective classification of satellite data is a large part of the cost of the work. It is also often the least satisfactory part of the project. The need to collect enough data to check the interpretation is also not always met. Yet to assume that an interpretation based on reliable training areas has done its job is naïve. For example, reliable training areas for moorland on the uplands of northern England allow the rapid mapping of upland vegetation, but the spectral range of moorland is precisely matched by the major urban areas around our northern hills. Thus without some knowledge of the disposition of urban areas and their exclusion from the classified image, a map with major errors and of no practical value is produced.

More commonly, the interpretation of land use rests upon other information about the location of the scene and the range of farming practices, or on national or local survey data on crops or farm enterprises. This may also be true of soil or geology. A dissected sheet of basalt may be recognized by a skilled interpreter, but whether it belongs to the local Jurassic or Tertiary lava series is sure to require some other source of information. One of the most ambitious programmes was called LACIE, and it aimed to use satellite data to forecast crop yields in the main temperate grain-growing areas. It is described in Box 11.4.

Land cover classification from remotely sensed data

The most common approach to land cover classification is to use areas that can be classified from ground data, map sources or in other independent ways, and then use these to erect classification rules which may then be applied to the entire image. These areas of known land cover are called training areas. They can be classified in various ways. At the simplest level, we might discover that on Band 7 of Landsat, a known area of water is below DN (digital; number) 10, in which case we might feel confident to recognize all other areas DN 1–10 as water. However, there would then be a risk that very steep areas in deep shadow, or even areas shadowed by large, high buildings, were insufficiently illuminated to reflect more than 10 in Band 7, and these would then be misclassified as water (Figure 11.10). We can get over this problem by using the power of the computer to classify a larger number of spectral bands, usually using all available (e.g. four on Landsat MSS, seven on TM). Well-lit water will then show quite high values at the blue end of the spectrum, and a range of values for each waveband will be established from the training areas. When the whole image is classified on this basis, deep shadow will not be classified as water, since although it may satisfy the criteria for Band 7, it will fall short of the normal range for the other bands, and particularly the bands at shorter wavelengths (e.g. Landsat Band 4).

There are various ways in which these calculations may be performed, and the different algorithms carry different names. Some are accurate mathematical descriptors of the process (e.g. parallelepiped) and others are popular representations of the same process (i.e. 'box' or 'boxcar' classifier). Given the speed of modern computers, even desktop machines, it is possible to use sophisticated algorithms, such as the maximum likelihood classifier. As a result, provided the training areas are well chosen, quite high levels of accuracy can be achieved when the classified images are checked against further knowledge of actual cover.

However, despite this, the accuracy of land cover classification is never total and often errors of 20 or 30 per cent are regarded as inevitable. Whether these errors are high enough to limit the utility of remotely sensed data depends on the use to which the classified images will be put. If comparison is being made with crop estimates from earlier years, it may be that the rogue cover forms a constant proportion of the total, and thus recorded increases or decreases can be regarded as real. In another case, areas of apparent change may have a spatial pattern which may suggest either that the land cover has been correctly identified, or perhaps if some of the 'wheat' fields are consistently along the coast, that a cover such as mature salt marsh has been misclassified. In some cases, an image from a different season may show continuity for some areas and the loss to another cover type of others. Thus winter wheat should classify as 'grass' in winter and early spring, but be clearly separable from pasture by the time of harvest. Yet while this is obvious enough, the separation depends on the ability to obtain a cloud-free image at the vital summer season, and in areas such as the British Isles this will not be possible every year (Box 11.5).

In an earlier section we noted that classification accuracy tends to improve as resolution declines. An exception to this is agricultural land, where the ideal resolution is one that picks up individual fields. These vary in size across the world, so it is a matter of selecting the appropriate imagery (or the way in which classification is managed) for each area. Thus the huge fields and rotary-irrigator features of the American West are readily viewed on Landsat MSS, whilst even the TM resolution is inadequate for most areas of cultivation in Africa. Here only a resolution such as SPOT is able to separate individual fields. A further factor is the nature of field boundaries. Fences do not contribute any problems, but hedges can obviously complicate the classification of small fields, since they are not wide enough to fill any pixel but will be included in quite a high proportion of pixels where fields are not much larger than one or two pixels. Some comment on this and related problems will be found in Box 11.6 (mixed pixels)

Relief

Remarkably little work has been done extracting topographical information from satellite images. Indeed, the effects of slope and aspect are regarded as confusing classification, for example of vegetation, and techniques have been developed to use information on relief available from maps to compute the effect of slope angle and aspect on illumination and thus on the reflectance of energy back to the sensor in the satellite. In principle this information can be used in reverse to infer slope, and it has been shown that this can be done, but no extensive interpretation of relief from computer images has been undertaken.

In the visual mode, the combination of selective illumination of slope according to angle and aspect combines with the variation of vegetation with altitude to give a remarkably clear impression of relief as can be seen on a space image of any hilly area. This is obviously most true in mountainous areas where relief is at a maximum, but even rather level areas can be 'etched' by a clearly visible river pattern, again carrying an effective image of relief to the human mind.

Geology

Except where there is no soil and vegetation cover, it is only possible to map geological outcrops indirectly, and actual exposure of solid rock is rare except in some desert and steep mountain areas. Nevertheless, there are many examples where geological features have been identified from satellite images, usually through their indirect effect on vegetation. This includes some quite specific effects of rocks with particular ores of economic value, and search for possible sites has undoubtedly been aided by the overview achieved with satellite cover. As much as any type of interpretation, success depends on some ground truth information to classify the image in a relevant way. However, for example, in a country such as Australia where vegetation cover is limited by the arid climate, known ore bodies can be used to establish 'spectral signatures' which may then be sought across extensive, remote and little-known areas.

Other geological aspects which may be mapped include outcrop patterns indicating structures. Thus anticlinal domes which might be acting as oil traps, or bringing deeper rocks to the surface can be located.

These sites may then be investigated in more detail using aircraft (e.g. magnetic survey) or by ground traverse (e.g. seismic techniques).

Snow and ice

Snow cover can only be mapped over wide areas by satellite, either by daylight using reflected light or by IR at night. The ephemeral nature of individual falls and the need to be able to map areas most frequently and continuously covered are both well served by satellite imagery provided periods without cloud cover are available. The continual monitoring possible from stationary meteorological satellites allows mapping of both snow and ice on land and ice cover over the oceans. Year on year variations can be detected and a level of detailed knowledge of winter ice cover achieved which is unmatched by any historical observations. Indeed, it is worth recalling that in the late 1940s no one knew whether Hudson Bay froze over completely in winter or not, and only the initiation of air photography on a national scale by the Canadian government answered that and other questions of considerable importance to the understanding of the arctic climate. Today, year on year variations in the date of freeze-over and in the location of the southern limit of pack ice in the North Atlantic and North Pacific Oceans are known from remotely sensed data. Even ice thickness can be measured by radar. Another useful aspect is the tracking of icebergs, both for the information it yields about ocean current patterns, and to warn shipping of potential danger.

The advance and retreat of glaciers in response to variations in precipitation and especially temperature are of considerable interest. Stored ice volume and its release on melting in spring and summer is the basis of water availability for many hydro-electric and irrigation schemes. Over longer time-scales of decades or more the general advance or retreat of glaciers is an important indicator of global warming and has a direct influence on sea-level. Models of future sea-level rise require some understanding of the link between global temperature and ice volumes if confident predictions are to be made of future effects. The lower limits of mountain glaciers can readily be mapped from Landsat images whenever cloud-free passes are available and changes over time established. Altimetric data from satellites can be used to map the surfaces of our large ice sheets, and in time these will allow far more accurate

computations of mass balance changes. Currently these are difficult to make and there is, for example, no agreement in the literature on whether the Antarctic ice sheet is in negative or positive balance. Over the next decade, altimetric data of sufficient precision should allow measurement of the changing volume of the Greenland ice sheet, and once a platform is launched which will cover latitudes above 82 °S, changes in volume of the Antarctic ice-sheet can be detected. Currently the plan is for the European Space Agency (ESA) Polar Platform, POEM-1 to carry an advanced terrain-tracking altimeter to carry out this and other tasks.

Oceans

In many senses, apart from the literal one, the oceans remain the great 'terra incognita' of our world. Gathering data from surface ships, floating buoys and various submersible probes is slow, and necessarily observations made at different locations are separated in time. Many aspects of the world ocean can be monitored by satellite, with coverage of immense areas at virtually the same moment in time. Among the variables readily measured are surface temperature (from which current patterns became visible), wave height and alignment and surface roughness (from which wind speed and direction can be determined), colour (e.g. chlorophyll indicating plankton blooms), turbidity (pollution, coastal erosion and river plumes), rainfall over oceans and of course ice cover. It has been proposed that oceanic primary production can be measured from the interpretation of chlorophyll patterns based on ocean colour (Platt and Sathyendranath, 1988). Satellite-borne altimeters can map sea surface altitude with considerable precision, allowing the measurement of tides, even in mid-ocean. Surface slope can also be related to wind stress and to ocean currents. Pollution episodes such as oil spills can be detected and followed over time. These points were exemplified in the previous chapter.

In coastal regions passes at different tidal stages can be used to prepare very detailed maps of elevation on low coasts, as has for example been carried out for the Danish Waddensee (Folving, 1984). That same publication also maps vegetation in the intertidal zone and sediment types in the lower part of that zone. The changing nature of coastal zones, whether through natural evolution or the acts of man (e.g. reclamation of intertidal land or mangrove clearance for prawn farming) means that the synoptic overview of successive passes allows the monitoring of change.

Box 11.6 The mixed pixel problem

The concept of a spectral signature and of the classification by spectral range over a number of spectral bands using a box or maximum likelihood classification rest on the simplification that each pixel of a scene covers a single land cover class and thus measures reflectance (and atmospheric transmission) in that spectral band. Where pixels are relatively small, as in the TM or in SPOT, then this simplification will be true for quite a large proportion of the pixels. But inevitably there will also be many pixels, and perhaps very many on the MSS, which include at least two cover types. In this case the digital number recorded by the satellite will be a weighted average of the reflectances of the surfaces concerned. If there are few such pixels, then misclassification will be relatively rare, but with more, the proportion of the scene correctly classified will decline.

We can illustrate the point by using the simple example of a lake surrounded by broad-leaved woodland in summer when leaf growth is active. Pixels which record lake reflectance in Band 7, MSS (or any near-infrared band recorded by another multispectral scanner) will record low values, probably below 15, whilst those entirely covering the woodland will record high values, perhaps around 100. Along the boundary between the lake and the woodland, individual pixels will include anything from a few per cent by area of water, to 95 per cent water. Thus there will be a range of values between 15 and 100 depending on the proportion of the area covered by water and the proportion covered by wood. A pixel neatly split into two equal halves by the shoreline will record about 57. If in places the lake has a sandy shore, then some pixels will be built up from three separate reflectance values.

In general such mixed pixels will neither be classified as water, nor as woodland, whilst though they may match other land covers in Band 7, they are unlikely to match another land cover class in all the bands being analysed. Thus they tend to remain unclassified, even if the two main classes of water and woodland are being mapped. However, if generalization is greater still (e.g. on a geostationary satellite scene) then all pixels will be mixed and a classification will pick out classes with a similar mixture of cover types. An example of the effect of

Digital values and land cover. These two (greatly enlarged) Landsat MSS images cover part of the Thames valley in England; the river can be seen on the lower (Band 7) image and bare fields are pale on the upper (Band 5) image. The Thames is about as wide as one pixel, but only a few of the pixels are mainly water in Band 7 and thus dark. Most are paler shades of grey depending on the proportion of water within each pixel, but the water makes almost all of them darker than the adjacent land, so the line of the river can be seen. (Source: Curran, 1985, Fig. 6.19.)

different proportions of land cover in adjacent pixels will be seen in the figure. The River Thames can be picked out quite easily in the lower image (Band 7, near-infrared), but the darkness of the pixels (lower values are darker) varies with the proportion of each pixel occupied by water.

There are simple ways to detect edges (boundaries) in scenes, generally by smoothing the image and then taking away the values of the smoothed image from the original image. This can pick out edges such as field boundaries and shorelines and may help in the interpretation of zones of mixed pixels.

Weather and climate

As every viewer of a television forecast is aware, satellite imagery is of considerable value in weather fore-

casting (Figure 11.11). This includes not only the changing patterns of cloud cover, but the detection of wind speed and direction over oceans (using the scatterometer on the ERS-1 satellite) and of rainfall over oceans. Most of the data are utilized by GCMs

Fig 11.11 View of the Earth from the geostationary satellite GOES east in the visible waveband, 12 March 1980. The pattern of North and South America can be seen between the cloud patterns. The rotating low pressure systems of the higher latitudes north and south of the equator are clearly seen. (Courtesy of NOAA.)

(numerical computerized global circulation models) which have a large grid pattern for their analysis, so the rather coarse resolution of the very distant geostationary meteorological satellites is no disadvantage.

In recent years increased attempts have been made to utilize satellite sensors in the detection of climatic change. The accurate measurement of sea surface temperature has greatly added to our knowledge of ocean temperatures across the world, including areas of the southern hemisphere where few ships go and thus little past data have been obtained. This in turn aids the computation of global average temperature, an annual variable basic to studies of the enhanced greenhouse effect. It was a satellite-borne sensor which confirmed the extent of the annual Antarctic 'ozone hole', first detected from ground-based observations.

Downward-looking sensors on satellites are able to measure temperature at different pressure levels within the atmosphere. Thus upper atmosphere (including stratosphere) temperature measurements can be made,

as well as at levels representative of surface values. Careful analysis of a decade-long series of these measurements for the middle troposphere (Spencer and Christy, 1990) claimed a precision for each average monthly temperature measured on a global basis across land and ocean of 0.01 °C. Large variability on time-scales from weeks to several years were found, but no trend over time.

Correlation with the two main global temperature series based on surface measurements by thermometers showed better agreement with the time series of Jones and others than that of Hansen and Lebedev. Unfortunately there are physical reasons why the agreement should be poor over the oceans – and this is where better data are urgently needed. A longer time-scale allowing greater and eventually more persistent temperature change is needed to establish if the Earth is warming over time.

Raval and Ramanathan (1989) claimed that they were able to measure the greenhouse effect over the world's oceans, i.e. the measurement of the IR radiant energy trapped by atmospheric gases and clouds. The radiation escaping to space has been measured since 1985 by the spaceborne Earth Radiation Budget Experiment (ERBE) for areas of 35 × 35 km. Data are separated for clear skies and for cloud cover when the greenhouse effect is greatly increased. Ocean surface temperature data (themselves in part based on satellite data) were used to calculate the surface-emitted flux, and when the energy escaping to space is subtracted, the balance is that retained in the atmosphere by the greenhouse effect. Once measured and averaged over the oceans for a sufficient time, later measurements on a similar basis will detect changes in the greenhouse absorption. The data analysed show the rapid increase with water vapour which was expected, but also show that the greenhouse effect for both clear sky and cloudy conditions increases rapidly at high surface temperatures, such as those characteristic of the tropical oceans.

The utility of the space radar altimeter (such as Seasat and the altimeter on ERS-1) in climatic research has been explored by Rapley (1991). Among situations where climate change could be detected by accurate altimetric measurements, he lists changing sea-level, ice-sheet topography (and thus mass balance), lake levels, related to river discharge, and the mapping of wetlands such as the Sudd where two-thirds of the water which leaves Lake Victoria by the White Nile is evaporated.

Global change

As long ago as the spring of 1983, NASA set up a working group to design an Earth Observing System (EOS) for the 1990s. This became 'Mission to planet Earth', NASA's contribution, planned for the mid-1990s, to the US global change programme (Asrar, 1990). The approach was to design sensors and establish methodologies to measure the main aspects of the energy, water and bio-geo-chemical cycles of Earth. Measurement of the flux of solar energy through the atmosphere is not possible directly (though the net balance can of course be measured) so that observation of such controlling variables as cloud cover is required with modelling to convert data on cloud cover and key cloud-top properties to obtain the amount of energy transmitted through clouds. Other variables that may be measured by remote observation include the height

of the boundary layer on a global basis and both sensible and latent heat flux. The latter overlaps with measurements designed to establish the pattern of the global hydrological cycle. Variables here include evapotranspiration, rainfall, water vapour in the atmosphere and snow cover. Several of these can only be assessed on a global basis if satellite data are available, given the limitations of our current land-based observatories and the limited number of observations made from ships at sea. Some, such as the pattern of evaporation from oceans, will be determined for the first time.

The bio-geo-chemical cycles of interest include the carbon budget, as yet unbalanced in terms of current observations. The four central biochemical processes involved are photosynthesis, autotrophic respiration, aerobic oxidation and anaerobic oxidation. Direct measurements of these from space are not feasible, but some of the controlling variables can be established with improved precision by satellite observation. The improved understanding of ocean circulation, sea surface temperature, sea surface roughness and biotic activity coming from space observations will all help to improve the precision of our estimates of the net uptake of CO_2 by the oceans. The EOS system is designed to measure the distribution, in time and space, of primary production with temperature, wind, turbidity and sunlight in the context of the global pattern of ocean circulation. A better fix on the net balance of the terrestrial biosphere–atmosphere exchange of carbon requires improved estimates of the effect of tropical forest clearance, and the productivity of the systems that are replacing the cleared forest. It also requires better understanding of the extent of soil disturbance and the implications that this has for carbon and also for methane and nitrous oxide. Clearly progress will require the effective combination of surface measurements and their extrapolation on a global scale; neither can improve our understanding without the contributions of the other.

Natural hazards

As global population grows, the toll of damage, death and injury from natural events such as floods, earthquakes and volcanic eruptions grows remorselessly. Some reduction can be achieved by improved forecasting and warning systems and there are ways in which these might utilize space observations. Thus changes in the surface temperature of volcanoes can be monitored, and flood events in the upper reaches of rivers can be observed and their downstream propagation forecast. However, these techniques can only be effective if the imagery or other data are reported promptly, and obtained on a reliable basis. This places a premium on the constant monitoring of the geostationary meteorological satellites, since the cycle of cover from orbiting satellites is rather long for effective warning systems and in any case is all too frequently obscured by cloud. This is obvious if floods are being monitored, since they result from heavy rain and thus widespread cloud cover.

Detailed observations from orbiting satellites are of more value after the event in establishing the extent of flooded areas, the area impacted by volcanic eruption, or the extent of earthquake damage. Indeed, after the Nicaragua earthquake, radar imagery of the entire country was flown by aircraft to establish the extent of damage. Again, it is easy to overestimate the utility of such techniques. As is always the case with such imagery, the collection of the information is rapid and efficient, but utilization depends on interpretation and mapping of the results and few countries have the capability or can maintain an adequate pool of skilled interpreters with the necessary equipment to provide an adequate response when a large area has been devastated by earthquake or flood. This is a facility which, together with temporary housing, would be a better response by the international community than the despatch of specialized teams to search the rubble for buried victims.

Developing countries

Although more countries are covered by adequate topographical maps than is popularly supposed to be the case, and may even have good air photo coverage, up-to-date information on land use, vegetation cover, settlement and forest clearance is usually lacking. Much of this information can be mapped from space images, allowing the progress of change to be followed and thus better national planning for agriculture, food supply and so on. Change may be impelled by population growth or even rural decline due to urbanization, by changing economic circumstances, by climatic fluctuations (especially drought) or by various combinations of these. Cash crops disturb the pattern and place of traditional rural systems. Vegetation clearance and

field enlargement encourages soil erosion. Increased grazing, population growth, vegetation clearance and drought all encourage a general deterioration often summarized by the term desertification.

Examples of the utilization of space images in such areas are many. One good example is work carried out from Belgium in Burkina Faso. This classified Landsat MSS data to map land cover in areas where the pattern and extent of cultivation was unknown. Five types of land cover were distinguished: fields and bare ground; duricrust and degraded soils; bushy savanna; wooded savannas and dry woodland; and seasonally flooded lowlands. Distinctive patterns were found in different areas, each of which could then be sampled to determine population densities and the level of food self-sufficiency. Change over time could also be monitored, to see whether the areas with duricrust at the surface were growing or were stable. Similar sampling techniques combined with remote sensing images at several scales can be used to build up a good picture of agricultural production year on year. Landsat MSS allows the broad location and internal patterns of habitation and especially of cultivation to be established. Individual sample villages can be identified and located accurately, and these sample areas can then be examined in more detail with high resolution data, TM or SPOT. These systems can distinguish individual fields and thus individual crops. With the aid of ground survey, field crop statistics with an accuracy of up to 85 per cent can be obtained, a good deal better than the existing statistical data available for most countries.

The pattern of work is more complex than this model suggests. The best estimates for biomass and thus grain productivity are obtained, not from SPOT, but from the AVHRR on the US NOAA satellite. This can provide 'local-area-coverage' (LAC) data, but at a low resolution which necessarily integrates biomass over wide areas. However, the ability of this instrument to measure changes day by day is what allows the extraction of data for a crop such as sorghum. The low frequency coverage offered by the higher resolution satellites means that without the temporal continuity, signals from different crops become confused and yield estimates are unsatisfactory. Add to this the many different crops grown in such areas and their interplanting in many cases and it will be clear that there are limitations to the detail that it is feasible to obtain. On the other hand, given the current inadequacies of official agricultural statistics, the broad-brush picture painted from the satellite information is of great value.

The Belgian study in Burkina Faso has revealed

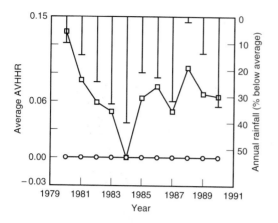

Fig 11.12 The relationship between rainfall and vegetation cover in the Sahel of Africa. Average vegetation indices derived from the NOAA AVHRR for the zone with an average rainfall in the range 200–400 mm/yr and the Sahara desert (the baseline). The broad agreement between vegetation productivity and rainfall can be seen; the very dry year of 1984 brought the vegetation of the desert south into the normally wet savanna. (Sources: AVHRR values from Tucker *et al.*, 1991; rainfall anomalies (departures) from M. Hulme, personal communication.)

considerable information about the rate of modification of forest and wooded savanna, especially around the larger settlements. Wood for fuel is being brought in over ever-increasing distances, even up to several hundred kilometres in some cases. The increasing difficulty of providing growing towns with wood or charcoal means that the cost of fuel now accounts for 15–20 per cent of the typical household budget. This in turn makes increasing exploitation of available woodland viable, even at great distances from the towns. Since these patterns can readily be obtained from Landsat MSS data and, since dry season images are now available for a 20 year span, changes over time can be established.

The clearance of woodland for fuel is one part of a pattern of increasing pressure on the land resources of much of Africa. The decadal oscillations in Sahel rainfall bring serious famines to the region which have received much public attention (Figure 11.12). The impact of drought on vegetation can be monitored and areas of particular stress can be identified. This is not to suggest that famine is simply a matter of the onset of drought. Quite apart from the impact of internal unrest and civil wars which have exacerbated the problems triggered by drought, the people who live in the Sahel have developed their own ways of coping with

drought, by storing food and through episodic migration. Thus even in this case, satellite information must be integrated with ground-based information on economic, political and social factors if it is to provide a reliable warning of impending famine. Another factor is that wetter years encourage the breeding of grasshoppers and locusts which then migrate with the winds to devastate potentially productive lands. Vegetation growth in potential breeding areas can be monitored by remote sensing and steps taken to spray the breeding insects. The preferred instrument is again the NOAA AVHRR, given its twice a day coverage and the lower costs of interpretation of its 1 or 4 km resolution. And as before, the interpretation is remote, carried out in the USA or Europe, and thus subsidized by the research funds of agencies and scientific groups in the developed world.

A topical issue where space data is of great value is the clearance of the tropical rainforest. The largest area of forest is in the Amazon Basin and its role in the global carbon cycle, together with its internal feedbacks of significance for both rainfall and soil fertility, make the monitoring of change a high priority. Skole and Tucker (1993) report on the extent of deforestation and habitat fragmentation between 1978 and 1988. Reported rates of deforestation range from 21 000 to 80 000 km^2/year. They used computer classification of Landsat TM images (200 in all) which they found compared well with the visual interpretation of TM and the more detailed SPOT images. The data were organized by a GIS, because of the large number of images involved. Their analysis revealed a cleared area of 230 000 km^2, and additionally that an estimated 341 000 km^2 were affected by the 'edge effect' of nearby clearance. Comparison with 1978 required the analysis of MSS data and from this a figure of 152 000 km^2 of cleared, formerly closed, forest was measured, an annual rate considerably below most published estimates and representing by 1988 6 per cent of the total closed forest area. However, the extent of forest affected by clearance by isolation and edge effects was very much greater.

An earlier study (Green and Sussman, 1990) on the more limited forest area of Madagascar utilized Landsat imagery and combined this with maps from 1950 derived from air photography to establish rates of change over 35 years (Figure 11.13). This estimated the original extent of rainforest at colonization as 1120 km^2, of which 760 m^2 remained by the map of 1950. By 1985 the area was down to 380 km^2, most of it on steep and rugged land unsuited to agriculture. The

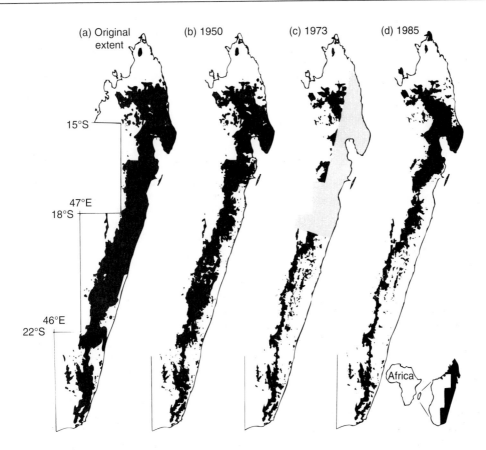

Fig 11.13 Forest clearance in Madagascar to 1985. The map on the left is a reconstruction of the area of forest prior to colonization. The 1950 map was compiled from aerial photography. The 1973 map uses Landsat images, as does that for 1985. Note that the 1973 map is incomplete because cloud-free images were only available for two-thirds of the area. Correlation with the topographical map shows that the surviving, uncleared forest is on steep land that is not suited to cultivation. (Source: Green and Sussman, 1990, Fig. 1.)

pattern of clearance is closely correlated with population density, emphasizing that it is the need to clear land for food production that has driven forest clearance.

One problem when more detailed land cover information is sought is the issue of national sovereignty. The low resolution of the AVHRR is not seen as a threat to national security, but in post-colonial Africa the availability of imagery such as SPOT, which allows recognition and mapping of roads, tracks, villages and fields from space, is seen as a threat. For this reason, the French will not sell SPOT data of countries to any user without the permission of the nation involved. We might note that similar problems have arisen over the deep sea drilling programme, especially where the investigation of continental shelf areas has been proposed. If detailed imagery is available to a neighbour, to what use might it be put? But it is equally unacceptable for it to be available without control to a developed country, which might be using it to search for raw materials or other resources which might give it further economic advantage. Most developing countries remain disadvantaged by the cost of the raw imagery and the further investment in training and equipment required for its effective interpretation and utilization. With time this will be overcome, and the cost of the computers required to run efficient image-interpretation and GIS programs has already fallen to acceptable levels.

References

Ascani, F. (1986) AGRIT-program: the operation use of remote sensing for wheat and corn production forecasting at national level. *Proceedings of the 20th International Symposium on Remote Sensing of Environment*, Vol, 1, pp. 287–92. Environmental Research Institute of Michigan. Michigan: Ann Arbor.

Asrar, G. (1990) Mission to planet Earth: a global change programme. *Remote sensing & global change*, Proc. 16th Annual Conference of the Remote Sensing Society, pp. i–v. Environmental Research Institute of Michigan. Michigan: Ann Arbor.

Curran, P.J. (1985) *Principles of remote sensing*. London and New York: Longman.

Drury, S.A. (1990), *A guide to remote sensing: interpreting images of the Earth*. Oxford: Oxford University Press.

Folving, S. (1984) The Danish Wadden Sea: thematic mapping by means of remote sensing. *Folia Geographica Danica*, **15(2)**, 4–56.

Green, G.M. and R.W. Sussman (1990) Deforestation history of the eastern rain forests of Madagascar from satellite images. *Science*, **248**, 212–15.

Hansen, J. and S. Lebedeff (1987) Global trends of measured surface air temperature. *Journal of Geophysical Research*, **92**, 13 345–13 372.

Harris, R. (1987) *Satellite remote sensing*. London & New York: Routledge & Kegan Paul.

Jones, P.D. (1988) Hemispheric surface air temperature variations: recent trends and an update to 1987. *Journal of Climatology*, **1**, 654–660.

Meier, M.F. (1980) Remote sensing of snow and ice.

Hydrological Sciences – Bulletin des Sciences Hydrologiques, **25**, 307–30.

Paul, C.K. and A.C. Mascarenhas (1981) Remote sensing in development. *Science*, **214**, 139–45.

Platt, T. and S. Sathyendranath (1988) Oceanic primary production: estimation by remote sensing at local and regional scales. *Science*, **241**, 1613–20.

Rapley, C. (1991) The ups and downs of climate change. *Earth Observation Quarterly*, **34**, 1–6.

Ravel, A. and V. Ramanathan (1989) Observational determination of the greenhouse effect. *Nature*, **342**, 758–61.

Skole, D. and C. Tucker (1993), Tropical deforestation and habitat fragmentation in the Amazon: satellite data from 1978 to 1988. *Science*, **260**, 1905–10.

Spencer, R.W. and J.R. Christy (1990) Precise monitoring of global temperature trends from satellites. *Science*, **247**, 1558–62.

Tucker, C.J., H.E. Dregne and W.W. Newcomb (1991) Expansion and contraction of the Sahara desert from 1980 to 1990. *Science*, **253**, 299–301.

Further reading

Cracknell, A.P. and L.W.B. Hayes (1991) *Introduction to remote sensing*. London: Taylor and Francis.

Houghton, J.T. Cook A.H. and H. Charnock (Eds) (1983) *The study of the ocean and the land surface from satellites*. Proceedings of a Royal Society Discussion Meeting. London: The Royal Society.

Massom, R. (1990) *Remote sensing of polar regions*. London Belhaven Press.

CHAPTER 12

Soil erosion and land degradation

MICHAEL STOCKING

The Rio Conference was criticized by many developing countries for being hijacked into concentrating on climate change and biodiversity losses. The poor nations believe that the wealthy commandeer these issues because they have a vested interest in long-term climate stability, and have a huge guilt trip over their prolonged period of greenhouse gas emissions. As for biodiversity, well, that begins abroad. Biodiversity enhancement in nations with a long history of land transformation is yet to be recognized as a high priority.

This is obviously a simplistic analysis of a sophisticated argument. For the world's poor, health, soil erosion, loss of fuelwood supplies, inadequate sanitation and reduction of cultivable land area are the major environmental concerns. Arguably land degradation is the single most pressing current global problem. As a result of remote sensing evidence we know that since 1945 1.2 billion ha, an area roughly the size of China and India combined, have been eroded at least to the point where their original biotic functions are impaired. At the very least it will be costly and time consuming to rehabilitate them. Of this area, about 9 million ha are very severely damaged, to the point of unreclaimability, and 300 million ha are so damaged that cultivation is all but impracticable. Much of this is in regions that are already overpopulated in relation to food production capacity.

Agenda 21 placed a lot of emphasis on re-establishing sustainable livelihoods for the 1–2 billion who are impoverished by the lack of water, land cover, soil fertility and fuelwood. This is a critical issue of both human care and environmental well-being. The long-term consequences of removing land cover from huge areas of the tropics and semi-arid lands are frankly not known. But one can be sure that there will be cumulative catastrophic failure of both the land and its peoples if these processes are allowed to continue.

Agenda 21 argued for both capacity building and the promotion of ecologically and culturally sensitive schemes of land restoration. Capacity building means expanding the vernacular science of local knowledge and tradition with the western science of soil and water management, monitoring of rainfall and groundwater movement, and analysing changes in soil fertility following different treatments. This is slow work, long in preparation, involving scientists who are as much anthropologists and communicators as they are soil specialists, hydrologists or ecologists. There is no blueprint for land restoration. The process will always be dictated by the rhythms of cultural experience, political expectation and investment capital from aid agencies and philanthropic foundations.

There is also a body of thought that regards soil erosion and land degradation as a process of continual negotiation between culture and the land. Careful monitoring of the tree or savanna margins in semi-arid areas reveals a fluctuating interface, punctuated by changes in rainfall, movement of people and shifts in agricultural techniques and cropping patterns. Soil erosion is not a purely physical phenomenon. It cannot solely be measured by sediment movement, nutrient status and surface seepage. True, these are measures of physical status; but they may have limited cultural meaning for societies that prefer to co-operate only when the need arises, that share property as well as food in times of need or plenty as part of established peer group ritual, and which appreciate systems of water harvesting that rely on low technology coupled to communal action. Such responses are not unusual. It is always dangerous to generalize. This is why the land degradation theme is so dependent on both vernacular science and capacity building for local land managers and community leaders.

That is not a straightforward matter. It will require labour-intensive training, a great number of carefully monitored experimental projects, and much international co-operation. It is still a moot point whether Agenda 21 really derived any reliable means for financing and administering such arrangements. This will be a costly enterprise, involving both consultative and educational schemes and long-term commitment of resources for managing and monitoring. The non-governmental aid agencies are poised to assist, though arguably they need the support of the environmental NGOs as well as the international science community. The trick is to devise schemes that promote integrated community-land development, yet that do not alienate the machinery of local government at national administrative agencies in agriculture, forestry conservation, tourism and regional planning. This will not be easy. Experimentation on a modest scale, but tried out in a host of circumstances, may be the best bet.

It will also be fertile training ground for integrated environmental science. The economics of soil degradation were covered in Box 1.4. Recent estimates suggest that in the absence of remedial action, Ghana could lose up to 7 per cent of its GNP, and Nigeria 17 per cent because of soil loss, water contamination and removal of vegetative cover. Land degradation is an economic as well as an environmental haemorrhage. With surprisingly modest resources, but with supreme mobilization at local levels, this particular tragedy is avoidable. Now we know what is happening and why, there is less of an excuse for inaction. The success or failure of the forthcoming UN Convention on Combatting Desertification will be a test case of global commitment.

Further reading

Norse, D. (1992) A new strategy for feeding a crowded planet. *Environment*, **34**(5), 6–11, 32–9.

Introduction

Soil is basic to life. It is the primary means of food production, directly supporting the livelihood of most rural people and indirectly of everyone; it is an essential component of terrestrial ecosystems, sustaining their primary producers (all living vegetation) and decomposers (microorganisms, herbivores, carnivores) while providing major sinks for heat energy, nutrients, water and gases (Wild, 1993). That soil in physical terms is merely the unconsolidated material on the Earth's surface yet is the hub for a host of life-supporting processes is testimony to the marvels of the natural environment.

This beguiling semblance of complex harmony is, however, a challenge to the environmental manager because the integrity of the world's soils is under threat. Soil quality is diminishing (Box 12.1). Crop production is becoming more difficult and more expensive as soil fertility, water-holding capacity and depth decline. Badlands are increasingly evident in vulnerable places.

Soils can be restored, even quite quickly, with large technical inputs. Productivity declines can be masked by ever-increasing applications of irrigation, fertilizer and other chemicals. These cost money and, worse still, render land use reliant on outside inputs. Likened to the drug addict, farmers are beholden to the pushers of chemicals and of high technology. Yet, in theory the soil can provide all necessary ingredients at minimal environmental cost, providing self-sufficiency for the land user and security for society. The fundamental question is how to employ technology to maintain the quality of the soil resource at an acceptable cost without having to resort to the treadmill of excessive inputs.

This chapter examines the processes of soil degradation, looks at the extent of soil erosion and the ways it may be assessed, and concludes with an overview of management responses to the degradation threat. *Soil degradation* is defined as a decrease in soil quality as measured by changes in soil properties and processes, and the consequent decline in productivity in terms of production now and in the foreseeable future. *Soil erosion* is one of the main processes of degradation and consists of physical detachment of soil particles by wind and water and their transport elsewhere in the landscape, to rivers and water storages or to the sea. *Land degradation* is a composite term describing the aggregate diminution of the productive potential of the land, including its major uses (rainfed arable, irrigated, rangeland, forestry), its farming systems (e.g. smallholder subsistence) and its value as an economic resource.

Box 12.1 Resource sustainability: land degradation

According to assessments made possible by satellite telemetry and improved ground investigation, about 1.2 billion hectares, or 11 per cent of the Earth's vegetated and potentially cultivable surface, has been moderately or severely degraded. Some 300 million hectares are so badly damaged that they have essentially lost their biological function. Rehabilitation would be slow, difficult and far more expensive than farmers can afford. While world agricultural production is at an all-time high, for 64 countries future food production increases will enable less than half the projected year 2000 population to be fed (World Resource Institute, 1992; Norse, 1992).

Areas of moderate to excessive erosion (millions ha)

	Water erosion	Wind erosion	Chemical degradation	Physical degradation	Total
Africa	170	98	36	17	321
Asia	315	90	41	6	452
South America	77	16	44	1	138
North and Central America	90	37	7	5	139
Europe	93	39	18	8	158
Australasia	3	–	1	2	6
Total	748	280	147	39	1214

Source: Oldeman *et al.* (1990).

Soil as a resource

The soil resources of landscapes vary widely in their suitability for use (Table 12.1). Each soil type has its limitations, and each agro-ecological zone its climatic factors restricting crop-growing seasons (FAO, 1978). For example, in the humid tropics plant stresses are mostly the result of nutrient deficiencies exacerbated by leaching and surface removal rendering the soil acid and nutrient-poor. In contrast, in the vast areas of seasonal tropics of South Asia, Africa and South America, where rainfall is concentrated into part of the year only, plant-available water capacity is the major handicap. Indeed, soil degradation may manifest itself in many forms. What often masquerades as drought is

Table 12.1 Land use by classes of productive potential in millions of hectares, 1975 and 2000

	Land classes of productive potential				
	High	Medium	Low	Zero	Totals
1975 Actual					
Cropland	400	500	600	0	1 500
Grassland	200	300	500	2 000	3 000
Forest	100	300	400	3 300	4 100
Non-agricultural	0	0	0	400	400
Other land	0	0	0	4 400	4 400
1975 totals	700	1 100	1 500	10 100	13 400
2000 Predicted					
Cropland	345	745	710	0	1 800
Grassland	170	320	510	2 000	3 000
Forest	30	100	230	3 140	3 500
Non-agricultural	0	0	0	600	600
Other land	0	0	0	4 500	4 500
2000 totals	545	1 165	1 450	10 240	13 400

Source: Buringh and Dudal (1987).

nothing more than a reduction in the ability of soils to contain sufficient water for plant growth between quite normal gaps in rainstorms.

Estimates of the productive potential of land are difficult to make because of the enormous variety of land uses, levels of technology, land management standards and population pressures. The largest study of its kind, entitled '*Potential population supporting capacities of lands in the developing world*', was conducted by the UN Food and Agriculture Organization (FAO, 1982). Although a little dated, its predictions are widely used and give a measure of the global scale of the degradation threat. At the base year 1975, 54 developing countries with a total population of 460 million did not have land of sufficient quality at low levels of inputs to feed their own populations. Overloading of some lands was estimated to be threatening 2450 million hectares or 38 per cent of the total land area. For the future, according to Norse (1992), 64 of 117 countries surveyed would be unable to support more than half their year 2000 populations on current technologies, while 18 countries remain critical even at the highest projected levels of agricultural inputs (Box 12.2).

The entire potentially cultivatable land of the 117 less-developed countries would be sufficient in aggregate to support 1.6 times their expected year 2000 populations if every piece of land were used for food. The two major changes between 1975 and 2000 are the interrelated factors of population increase and declin-

ing quality of the soil resource base. From the same FAO database, Buringh and Dudal (1987) calculate that 25 per cent of all highly productive land will be lost because of erosion and other soil degradation processes (Table 12.1). Forest and grassland will decrease by 24 per cent and the most productive land class by 33 per cent. It is this last item that is unambiguously the result of soil degradation, describing a process of the increasing marginalization of land and people. As productivity and the per capita productive land declines, farmers are forced on to unsuitable or vulnerable land – steep slopes, wetlands, tropical forests (Figure 12.1). Land

---

Box 12.2 Projected decline in potentially cultivable land, 1990–2025

Apart from a few vast countries with somewhat small but nevertheless expanding populations, such as Brazil and Zaïre, most developing countries have essentially reached the limit of new cultivation – at least with the technologies, resources and costs they can afford. As populations grow, therefore, so the amount of cultivable land per capita will fall. In sub-Saharan Africa this will drop from 1.6 to 0.63 ha per person by 2025 according to official estimates. Comparative figures for West Asia and North Africa are 0.22 down to 0.16 ha per capita, 0.20 down to 0.12 ha for the rest of Asia excluding China, and 2.0 to 1.17 ha for Central and South America.

Source: Norse et al. (1992)

Fig 12.1 Decline in potentially cultivable land leads farmers to cultivate steeper and steeper slopes. On this 60% slope in the Hill Lands of Sri Lanka small farmers displaced by major new reservoirs are trying to grow crops with hillside ditches and lock-and-spill drains as the only form of soil conservation.

Box 12.3 How people see soil degradation: an example from Tanzania

The Burungee people of Kondoa district, Dodoma Region, Tanzania do not 'see' soil degradation in the same way as you do. Even though the signs of erosion are everywhere, the evidence before their eyes leads them to very different conclusions as to what is happening. In common with much of semi-arid Africa, gullies punctuate extensive sheet eroded pediments. Arable lands give meagre crops and the range supports emaciated cattle. How do the Burungee perceive their environment?

A Swedish anthropologist, Wilhelm Ostberg (1991) collected these observations.

How soil is created:

> If it rains heavily, it results in thick layers of soil, if the rains are poor the soil layers become thin. Have you not held a hailstone in your hand and allowed it to melt? Do you not get small particles of soil in your hand? There you can see that the rain contains soil.
>
> When rain falls, water sinks to the ground. It reaches a point where it cannot go further down. Water accumulates there forming a soil layer as it dries up. This layer will be stained by the colour of the water. . . . The soil layer moves up, and next time it rains a new soil layer will form below the one that was last created. In this way, new layers of soil are continuously being formed.

Why the surface is littered with stones:

> Look the land is coming up.

Land has life:

> If you cut the branch from a tree, it is dead. But put it back into the soil and it will grow again. It draws its life from the land.

---

quality rapidly diminishes and the cycle of soil degradation and the pauperization of the peasantry continues ever faster. Plenty of evidence exists to show that the FAO's predictions are being realized (Box 12.3). It is not an appealing prospect.

Consequences of soil degradation

The best demonstration of soil's value as a resource is to monitor what happens when it degrades. On site, soil productivity is affected and this may be assessed in a number of ways. First, nutrients are lost in sediment and run-off. Generally, those nutrients associated with organic matter (N and P) and the cation exchange of soil colloids (K and Ca) are most at risk. Nutrients in sediment are approximately ten times the quantity of those dissolved in run-off. Values may be attached to lost nutrients via the equivalent cost of fertilizer containing the same amounts of elemental N, P or K (Box 12.4).

Secondly, water is lost to the soil and to plant growth in run-off. As soil degrades, its infiltration capacity worsens. Typically, with surface sealing and crusting on a tropical soil, water losses in run-off may increase from 20 to 50 per cent of total rainfall. For a farm in, say, the rainfed maize zone of Zambia (800–900 mm mean annual rainfall), this is equivalent to moving the farm to a semi-arid rainfall regime (400–500 mm)

Box 12.4 The cost of soil erosion in Zimbabwe

Concern about soil erosion is world-wide but only rarely do we have the opportunity to attach financial values to the sediments being lost.

Over five years, 2000 storm soil loss events on four soils in Zimbabwe were monitored, and losses of nitrogen, phosphorus and organic carbon measured. Extrapolating these losses to all soil types and the major land use systems, it was calculated that Zimbabwe loses annually 1.6 million tonnes of N, 0.24 million tonnes of P and 15.6 million tonnes of organic C.

If the value of N and P were to be translated into money by the cost of the equivalent amount of fertilizer (at 1984 prices) containing those nutrients, Zimbabwe's annual financial drain because of erosion amounts to US$1.5 billion.

On a per hectare basis, the financial cost of eroded nutrients varies according to actual erosion rates:

- $20–50 per ha per year on arable lands;
- $10–80 on grazing lands.

Arable lands alone lose by erosion about three times the N and P which is applied as fertilizer each year.

There are large physical and economic assumptions behind these calculations, but nevertheless the potential loss is staggering compared to Zimbabwe's GNP. It amounts to a cost per person of about US$200 – an unsustainable drain on the resources of any country, let alone a poor one.

Source: Stocking (1988a).

Pimentel *et al.* (1993) set a typical scenario: at least 7 cm of topsoil have been lost throughout the midwest USA. This is equivalent to a cumulative erosion of 900 tonnes/ha, a total easily attained without soil conservation on arable lands in two to three decades. A 6 per cent maize yield reduction per centimetre of soil loss is a conservative estimate of erosion's impact on production. Inputs can then be costed to maintain yield levels, although for fertilizer in particular it is known there are diminishing returns on increased use of it. Assuming, however, a linear relationship and an average US maize yield of 6.5 tonnes/ha, yields would drop in the scenario to 2.73 tonnes, a direct production loss which can be costed in producer price of maize. Alternatively, fossil energy inputs of 2.5 million kcal/ha (or 10 500 MJ), based on the 920 kcal of inputs expended in the USA per kilogram of maize produced, would be required to restore yields to pre-erosion levels. Again this could be costed at current energy prices, or could be considered as the energy required to keep one person alive for 1000 days. By any of the calculations, the financial loss attributable to 7 cm soil loss is in the range US$500–1000 per hectare.

Although on-site damage to soil resources is quantitatively most significant to land users, off-site impacts have received wide publicity because of disruption to society. In the USA it is estimated that sediments derived mostly from agricultural lands cause damage to canals, water storages, irrigation schemes, ports and hydro-electric power plants. Of new reservoir storage capacity, 10–25 per cent is built to accommodate sediment rather than water (Clark, 1985). Damage in developing countries can be equally serious. Five major dams in the Hill Country of Sri Lanka, built with aid-donor finance, supply electricity to Colombo and water to the dry-zone irrigation schemes of Mahaweli. Not only has the erosion of fertilizers from the rich tobacco crops of the catchment caused eutrophication, but also damage to the turbines has caused power cuts, incurred economic costs in lost production and reduced the credibility of the government. The Mahaweli irrigation systems have been threatened with water shortages at critical growing periods as the Polgolla Diversion Barrage at Kandy repeatedly fills with sediment. Ironically, such impacts are made worse by the water storage investments themselves. People displaced by the reservoirs now have little choice but to farm steep lands in the catchment, while others, seeing the opportunity of wage labour and better access to water, have also flocked to the area, thereby increasing land pressure and encouraging further erosion.

suitable only for low-value crops such as millet. Relative land prices could be used to attach a cost to this degradation.

Finally, because water erosion is selective of the finer, more fertile fraction of the soil, the eroded sediments are usually always richer in nutrients and organic matter than the soil from which they were taken. Known as the *enrichment ratio* (ER), a measure of the relative degree of concentration of key nutrients indicates the proportional seriousness of the decline in soil quality. Average values of 2.5 for the ER of several soil types in Zimbabwe show that soil erosion involves fertility losses that are very much more than the removal of a topsoil slice.

How do these on-site physical processes affect crop production and what are the economic consequences? Most data derive from the USA where yield reductions and associated costs have been closely monitored.

Processes of soil degradation

Six processes of soil degradation are usually recognized (Box 12.5). Definition and measurement of the degradation processes pose problems for the environmental manager because of difficulties of gaining the data, interrelationships between the processes and errors inherent in measurement methods – see next section for soil erosion assessment. Table 12.2 gives the most commonly accepted measures and FAO classes of severity of degradation. These processes act such that soil degradation will challenge plant productivity in a number of ways simultaneously. For example, sodication is the greatest single factor in the tropics rendering soils erodible: when dry, the soil becomes massive and hard; when wet, it loses cohesion and erodes alarmingly. Similarly, water erosion results in loss of structure, surface sealing and breakdown of water-stable aggregates; on high clay soils in Zimbabwe, once organic carbon content goes below a threshold of 2 per cent, erodibility suddenly increases. Such interrelationships underline the vulnerability of many soils and farming systems, especially in the tropics, to soil degradation. On a few deep soils with large reserves of weatherable

Box 12.5 Processes of soil degradation

- *Water erosion.* Splash, sheet and gully erosion, as well as mass movements such as landslides.
- *Wind erosion.* The removal and deposition of soil by wind.
- *Excess of salts.* Processes of the accumulation of salt in the soil solution (salinization) and of the increase of exchangeable sodium on the cation exchange of soil colloids (sodication or alkalinization).
- *Chemical degradation.* A variety of processes related to leaching of bases and essential nutrients and the build-up of toxic elements. pH-related problems such as aluminium toxicity and P-fixation also included.
- *Physical degradation.* An adverse change in properties such as porosity, permeability, bulk density and structural stability. Often related to a decrease in infiltration capacity and plant-water deficiency.
- *Biological degradation.* Increase in rate of mineralization of humus without replenishment of organic matter.

minerals (e.g. Vertisols and Nitisols), the impact of degradation may be slight. However, on soils that lose their fertility quickly through intensive cropping without artificial replenishment of organic matter and nutrients, the impact can be disastrous with knock-on effects to adjacent lands which have to take up the pressure of feeding the population. Figure 12.2 compares two soils (A and B) and how degradation over 40 years interacts with management of the soil to give yields above and below that which is economical.

Take the sandy, easily worked Alfisols (FAO classification: Luvisols) of the savanna zones of Africa, South Asia and South America. They provide for much of the subsistence smallholder farming, where hand tools are used for cultivation and chemical inputs are scarce. Nutrients are concentrated in the top few centimetres. Consequently, erosion has a devastating impact on crop production. In the example from West Africa in Figure 12.3, shallow soils are especially vulnerable on low angle slopes because of restricted rooting depths and fertility concentrations in the topsoil.

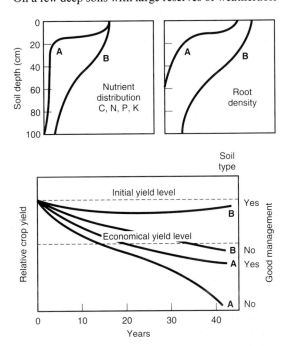

Fig 12.2 Soil productivity (crop yield) in relation to different soils (A and B), level of management and soil degradation over 40 years.

Assessment of soil erosion

Erosion assessments are usually made from standard soil loss and run-off plots (Figure 12.4). Nearly every

Table 12.2 Soil degradation processes, units and classes according to the FAO *Methodology of Soil Degradation Assessment.*

Degradation process	Code	Definition	Units of measurement	Classes			
				None to slight	Moderate	High	Very high
Water erosion	E	Soil loss	t/ha/yr or mm/yr	<10 <0.6	10–50 0.6–3.3	50–200 3.3–13.3	>200 >13.3
Wind erosion	W	Soil loss	t/ha/yr or mm/yr	<10 <0.6	10–50 0.6–3.3	50–200 3.3–13.3	>200 >13.3
Excess of salts salinization	Sz	Increase of electrical conductivity of saturated paste at 25 °C in 0–60 cm layer	mmho/cm/yr	<2	2–3	3–5	>5
sodication	Sa	Increase in exchangeable Na% in 0–60 cm layer	% per year	<1	1–2	2–3	>3
Chemical degradation acidification	Cn	Decrease of base saturation in 0–30 cm layer, if: (a) BS less than 50% (b) BS greater than 50%	% per year	<1.25 2.5	1.25–2.5 2.5–5	2.5–5 5–10	>5 >10
toxicity	Ct	Increase in toxic elements in 0–30 cm layer	ppm per year	not yet used – not mappable at 1:5 m			
Physical degradation	P	(a) Increase in bulk density in 0–60 cm layer Initial level (g/cm^3): <1 1–1.25 1.25–1.4 1.4–1.6	% change per year	<5 <2.5 <1.5 <1	5–10 2.5–5 1.5–2.5 1–2	10–15 5–7.5 2.5–5 2–3	>15 >7.5 >5 >3
		(b) Decrease in permeability Initial level: rapid (20 cm/h) moderate (5–10) slow (5)	% change per year	<2.5 <1.25 <1	2.5–10 1.25–5 1–2	10–50 5–20 2–10	>50 >20 >10
Biological degradation	B	Decrease in humus in 0–30 cm layer	% change per year	<1	1–2.5	2.5–5	>5

Source: FAO (1979).

country has some of these plots on agricultural research stations in order to test the erosion hazard of different permutations of cropping system, soil, slope and management. Dimensions vary from country to country but the length of bounded plots ranges from 6 to 10 m and the width from 1.5 to 3 m. Sediment and run-off are caught in a downslope trough and led to a set of storage tanks. To cope with the exceptionally heavy storm that causes the greatest erosion, there are usually two or more tanks, separated by a divisor system by heavy thunderstorm they have huge quantities of water

which only a proportion of the run-off is taken to the lower tanks. Run-off is measured by the level of water in the tanks, and soil loss by taking a thoroughly stirred sample of water and sludge from each tank followed by drying and weighing. Errors are frequent and the sampling method for sediment is known to underestimate actual soil loss from the plot because of inadequate stirring. To obviate this, the scientists at the Institute of Agricultural Engineering in Zimbabwe use a total weighing technique, but this does mean that after a and sediment to handle.

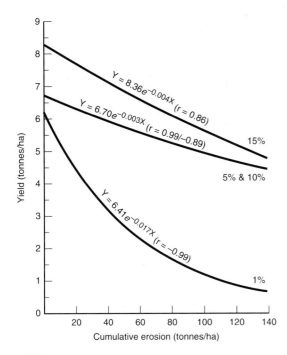

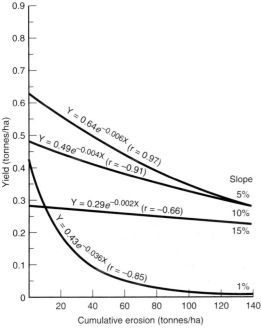

Fig 12.3 Maize yield loss with erosion in Nigeria. (Source: Lal, 1984.)

Other erosion assessment methods are also used. Geomorphologists commonly employ erosion pins and measure the lowering of the ground surface. Gerlach troughs, of the approximate dimensions of a hand dustpan, catch soil and run-off as they move downslope. At a broader scale, small catchments of 0.5–2 ha can be monitored using a flume and sediment sampler. Hydrologists often measure sediment loads from large catchments by sampling, followed by extrapolating total sediment loss from the stream hydrograph and then quoting the result as sediment loss per unit area of catchment. More sophisticated methods use fluorescent or radioactive tracers, or monitor the concentration of isotopes such as caesium 137. What is, however, crucial to note is that the measurements from one technique to another give different results because they assess different things.

The commonest error is to forget the scale effect. Small, bounded plots give the highest measured soil losses per unit area. This is because each soil particle that is detached by erosion and starts to move is caught and weighed. As the area for assessment increases, there is a greater likelihood of storage of sediment within the bounded area (and hence there being no recording of its movement at the downslope end of the plot). In real field conditions as much as 90–95 per cent of eroded soil is redeposited elsewhere within the landscape. Consequently, catchment sediment yields are typically only a small fraction of measured losses from field plots. Hydrologists express this as the sediment delivery ratio. For the environmental manager it means that all measurements of soil loss must be treated with extreme caution, and both the technique and the scale of measurement must be quoted. In the following discussion all rates of soil loss will be from the standard field plot as shown in Figure 12.4.

Plot studies show the immense variability in measured rates of erosion. Just removing a complete cover of vegetation increases erosion by about three orders of magnitude (1000 times or more). The USA and Australia have the largest record of plot results displaying the effect of land use and site condition on soil loss (Table 12.3). Specific losses in exceptional events can be much larger, such as the single storm in Western Australia falling on freshly seeded ground where 350 tonnes/ha soil loss was recorded. The type and degree of canopy cover is the single most influential factor in determining erosion rates. Inevitably in cropping systems, the land is bare or inadequately covered for the early part of the season. If storms occur, not

Table 12.3 Selected soil loss rates from plot experiments in the USA and Australia

Land use	Location	Soil loss rates (t/ha/yr)
USA		
Cropland	Average of all	18.1
	Midwest, deep loess	35.6
	Southern high plains	51.5
Australia		
Bare	New South Wales	31.3–87.0
Cropland	New South Wales	0–16.0
	Queensland	7.0–36.4
Pasture/range	New South Wales	0–1.9
	Queensland	0–21.1
Mine sites	Hunter Valley, NSW	0.4–11.8
	Jabiru, NT	20–102

Sources: Pimentel *et al.* (1993); Edwards (1993).

only will the rate of erosion be high but the potential impact on productivity will also be high.

In tropical environments where almost all developing countries are located, there is good evidence that soil loss rates in agricultural systems are even higher (Figure 12.5). From an experiment in Java to measure the impact of erosion on hill rice, 900 tonnes/ha of soil were eroded in just over a year. Similar alarming figures are available from throughout the humid tropics where the natural vegetation on steep slopes has been replaced by annual cultivation. In the seasonally wet-and-dry tropics, rates of 100–200 tonnes/ha are common. Again, there is significant variability and, with a good cover of foliage, erosion rates reduce to less than 1 per cent of the rate without vegetation – an aspect crucial when considering soil conservation.

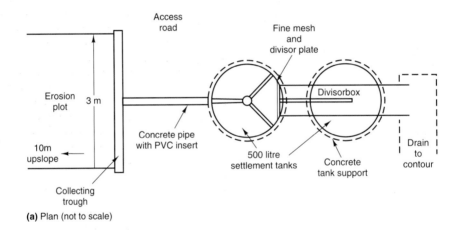

(a) Plan (not to scale)

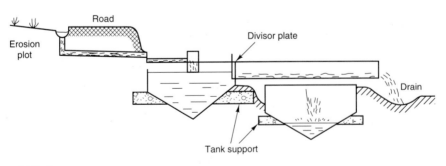

(b) Section

Fig 12.4 Soil loss plots as used at the Institute of Agricultural Engineering, Harare, Zimbabwe, to measure eroded sediments and run-off.

Fig 12.5 Soil loss rates on the Loess Plateau, China, are reputed to be the highest in the world. Extensive bench terraces barely control the erosion.

Prediction and explanation of soil erosion

An analysis of erosion rates and immediate site causes demonstrates that a number of factors can explain the variations. *Soil type* is a determinant of soil erodibility. In the tropics especially, erodibility is greatly enhanced not only by the physical and chemical properties of the soil, but also by management factors which allow the soil to crust, increase in bulk density or reduce in organic matter. *Topographic factors* such as slope steepness, length and shape are also influential. Physical measures such as contour bunding – which cuts the slope into shorter lengths – or terracing – which alters the effective slope steepness – are ways that the influence of topography may be reduced in land use. *Rainfall* is an important factor giving rise to erosivities varying according to amount, intensity and seasonality of storms. The only way to protect the soil from the erosivity of rainfall is to ensure a *cover of vegetation* to intercept the kinetic energy of raindrops and absorb it harmlessly into leaves and surface organic matter.

These factors may be combined into empirical models to predict rates of erosion under any combination of soil, rainfall, slope and vegetation. One such model, used by the conservation services in southern Africa for more than a decade, is shown in Figure 12.6. Predictions are only as good as the database used to give physical values to the control variables. In developing countries this places severe limitations on the use of more sophisticated models that need large research resources to support the required experiments.

It is tempting to stop at the site factors to explain soil erosion. We may justify the use of prediction models to calculate how changes in land use or management may alter the erosion hazard. Most technical studies and consultant reports only take these obvious, tangible site factors into account. The socio-economic, cultural and

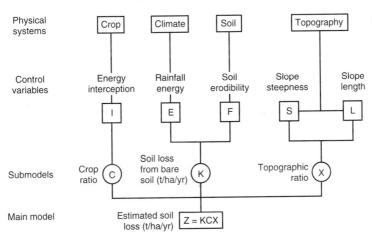

Fig 12.6 The soil loss estimation model for southern Africa. (Source: Elwell and Stocking, 1982.)

Box 12.6 Why does soil conservation so often go wrong?

A classical approach to soil conservation
or
How easy it is to blame the farmer

In his youth Watch Mafuta worked at the mines. Now, at age 40, he is tired, and his yearning for his communal ancestral home has brought him back to the family '*shamba*'. . . . A thriving home garden supplies vegetables . . . Watch cultivates cotton and maize on an extensive plot. . . . Declining yields force him to plough more land each year. Weeding is a real problem on the extra land. . . . Concerned because of reports of land degradation, the government agricultural officer, a local extension assistant, and a foreign aid worker call on the Mafutas.

What was the outcome?

1. *Identification of the problem:* these technicians see the degrading arable land, the overgrazed range, the poor crop stands . . . and not a single measure they could call 'conservation'. . . . Erosion is confirmed as serious; soil conservation and land reclamation are urgently needed!
2. *Planning of control measures:* soil loss rates are calculated and packages of remedial measures designed to reduce degradation. . . . 'We only need co-operation from the community now', they say.
3. *Implementation of the plan:* the plan is explained to the Mafutas. Encouragement and persuasion, even subtle threats are employed. Typically, the household is shown photographs of eroded land, statistics on soil loss, and embellished descriptions of the dire consequences of allowing erosion to continue. Appeals based on patriotism, their custody of the land for future generations and the security of the state are launched. Demonstration plots and field days show what can be done. Hoe in hand, the Mafutas set to.

Successive stages in the scenario appear as headlines in the press:

Soil conservation project hits teething problems
Targets not met in conservation plan
Government minister urges unity to fight menace of erosion
Lazy farmers blamed for erosion
Heavy rains destroy contour terraces
Aid agency pulls out

The innocent and guilty are thus exposed. Foremost among the innocent is the aid agency. Didn't it do its best? The government minister and the experts too are blameless. Didn't they warn of erosion's dangers? Watch Mafuta, his family and the millions of households like theirs that failed to heed the warnings and do the necessary work – they are the guilty; they now suffer the consequences. If nothing else, justice at least is done.

Lessons

The Mafutas demonstrate how small is the room for manoeuvre of farmers and how easily blame can be pinned to the least powerful in society. At a global level, economic and political forces encourage developed country aid agencies to channel some money – many say far too little – to developing countries. But the agency wants its say in how the money is spent. Capital goods (bulldozers, tractors), technical inputs (professional experts, chemicals) and training (advanced techniques, often in a developed country institution) are the easiest aid items to mobilize and the preferred means of addressing the erosion problem. The immediate problem is not, however, a lack of machinery or experts or even knowledge – it is that the Mafutas have too little land, not enough labour, a difficult environment and precious few resources to enhance their livelihood. Working harder, digging contours and drains, and being told they are lazy/ignorant/uneducated are not solutions.

Source: Abridged from Stocking (1988b).

---

political contexts are, if considered at all, merely complications or externalities that may marginally modify the core technical analysis. This view of the importance of site-specific, technical analysis has potentially un-fortunate side effects. Because several of the variables can be controlled by land users and because soil conditions and vegetation cover are very much affected by mismanagement of the land, prediction models are not only useful in designing conservation strategies, but are also, by implication, able to point the finger of blame for erosion at the land user. If that person is a resource-poor farmer, gaining a subsistence on a steep slope, poor soils and deficient vegetation, so much the better – the culprit for erosion is all the more obvious (the Mafuta family in Box 12.6 is so blamed). But is this a fair or even adequate explanation for erosion?

No. Explanations of soil erosion and land degradation are possible at a number of levels. For example, a valid question is why should farmers erode their soil when many know full well that their practices jeopardize their future well-being? Part of the answer lies in the decision making and prioritization of income opportunities of different households. For developed country farmers, it may not be economically worthwhile to undertake soil conservation. The immediate investments may be too costly in contrast to benefits in future production which may only accrue in succeeding generations. A change to organic farming can be extraordinarily demanding in labour and may depress initial yields, even though the long-term benefit is reduced production costs, a premium on market prices for the produce and a lessened dependence on inputs. If society wants the comfort of knowing its land resources are in caring hands, then the land user cannot be expected solely to take the burden. For resource-poor farmers in developing countries, the issue may be starker. It may rest between a choice of starvation now or starvation in the future. Usually, however, it is less dramatic. The 'reproduction squeeze' described by Blaikie (1989) is a good example of how rural peasantry may be caught between maintaining current livelihoods and looking after conservation works – livelihood will usually win. Typically a small farmer must produce primary products for sale to purchase commodities for production (e.g. a hand hoe) or for consumption (batteries for the radio). As the relative value of local production falls in comparison to the cost of purchases – a world-wide phenomenon – the small farmer must reduce the cost of production and/or increase primary product output. The result is an impoverished peasantry working ever-harder on poorer, degraded and more distant soils. Labour essential for investment in soil improvement or maintenance of conservation structures must be diverted to the immediate goal of primary production.

A further valid question is how have this world's economic and political systems developed to the state that it is the rational choice of land users to degrade their land? In such a milieu, market prices, the terms of trade, the structure of agrarian society, international economic relations, competing political interests and global politics become parts of the explanation of why the Mafutas (Box 12.6) struggle, and, despite their valiant efforts and the arguments of well-meaning professionals, they fail to conserve their soils.

Explanation of soil erosion thus involves a wider political economy and a complexity of non-technical issues. Blaikie (1989) provides a model, a 'chain of explanation', to combine these issues into an analytical framework (Fig. 12.7) which can relate why a gully in

---

Box 12.7 Resilience and sensitivity: a matrix for environmental managers

- *Resilience:* a property that allows a land system to absorb and utilize change; resistance to a shock.

- *Sensitivity:* the degree to which a land system undergoes change due to natural forces, following human interference; how readily change occurs with only small differences in external force.

Examples

1. The deep loess soils of the midwest Corn Belt of the USA. They erode easily (cf. Dust Bowl) but because of good reserves of nutrients and the availability of fertilizers and irrigation, they are quick to restore. High sensitivity; high resilience.
2. Oxisols in the Cerrado (savanna) of Brazil. They have an open structure and excellent physical properties. But the intensive use of machinery eventually collapses structure and renders them extremely hard and erodible. Low sensitivity; low resilience.

		Sensitivity	
		High	Low
Resilience	High	Easy to degrade, but responds well to land management that restores capability	Only suffers degradation under very poor management and persistent mismanagement
	Low	Easy to degrade, unresponsive to land management and should be kept in as natural a condition as possible	Initially resistant to degradation, but after severe misuse land management has great difficulty in restoring capability

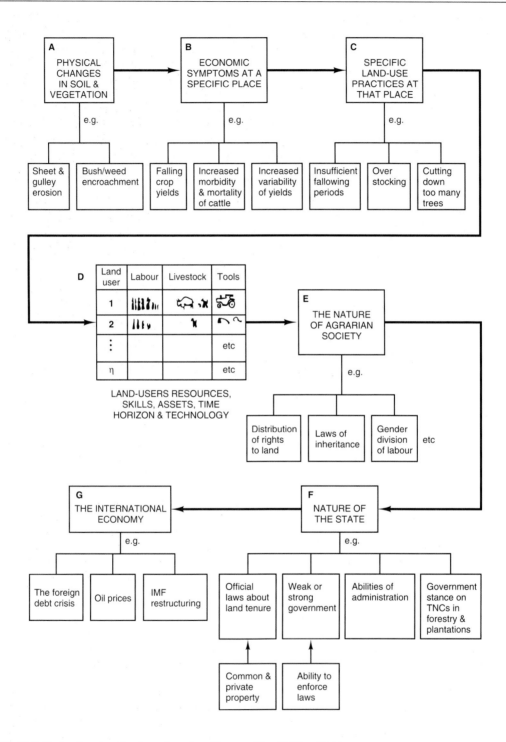

Fig 12.7 Chain of explanation for soil erosion. (Source: After Blaikie, 1989.)

Fig 12.8 Bench terraces are a principal means of controlling water erosion throughout South-east Asia. They are costly to construct and require continual maintenance.

Africa could be linked to a desk-bound bureaucrat in Brussels. The finger of blame turns to a broad sweep of the hand.

For the environmental manager inevitably some explanatory issues can be addressed and some cannot. Where natural systems of soil, water and vegetation are resilient, only major disturbances may cause degradation that has a substantial impact on production. This natural resilience can be assessed. If this is coupled with relatively stable economies in societies that are not only willing and able to subsidize land users to ensure conservation, but also have a high degree of empowerment and local decision making, then land management is relatively easy. But in a poor developing country with inequitable access to resources, corruption and many other pressing problems, it would be a brave land manager who might contemplate tackling international economic relations. Nevertheless, an understanding of the varying levels of explanation for soil degradation will enable purely technical solutions to be set in a real world context and will allow assessment of the likelihood of innovations being acceptable to the land user. An explanatory framework also provides alternative avenues to address the soil erosion problem – a manipulation of producer prices, perhaps, to favour good cover crops; or subsidies and incentives to implement conservation practices; or a change in rights of access and ownership of land. All these may, in the right circumstances, have the potential to change a situation of increasing degradation to one of rehabilitation. A matrix of guidance to the land manager is offered in Box 12.7 using two useful terms – resilience and sensitivity – each of which can be considered in both physical and human terms.

Soil and water conservation

The response of society to land degradation is *soil conservation*, defined as any set of measures that controls or prevents soil erosion, or maintains soil fertility. *Water conservation*, especially in drier zones, is very closely related such that many techniques of soil conservation achieve short-term benefit through increasing plant-available water rather than through saving soil (Figure 12.8). The objective of soil and water conservation is to achieve consistent and lasting production from land while keeping soil loss at or below the soil's rate of renewal. Since subsoil formation rates are in the region of 0.5–1 tonne/ha/year – which is equivalent to natural rates of soil erosion – soil conservation strategies should not allow greater soil losses than those occurring under a complete natural vegetation. Because any disturbance of the soil causes an increase in soil loss, we have a dilemma: all agricultural and land-use systems are theoretically unsustainable. In practice, therefore, 'tolerable' soil losses are taken to be either some arbitrary figure which is known to be achievable in practice (the US approach where soil loss tolerance values are quoted in the range 5–10 tons/acre/year: c.10–25 tonnes/ha/yr) or the level at which soil fertility can be maintained with inputs of technology in the medium term, say up to 30 years. The latter approach to setting target levels of allowable soil loss in a conservation programme is gaining ground. It recognizes that topsoil formation rates can easily reach ten times subsoil formation rates, it acknowledges that farmers utilize their soil 'capital' of nutrients at certain times, restoring them later by fallowing (see Box 12.8) and it allows for the role of the land manager in compensating for nutrient and organic matter losses by specific interventions such as green manuring, cover crops, fertilizer and so on. Nevertheless, a nagging doubt remains. The implication of the current state of knowledge on erosion and soil formation rates is that overall soil depths will decline, even if the quality of the topsoil may remain.

Soil and water conservation is nothing new. Civilizations have been based on water harvesting and soil management technologies (Mesopotamia and the Andean Incas, for example) and Homer, Virgil and Plato make passing reference to environmental problems and the need for conservation. Nevertheless, it is only comparatively recently that soil conservation has been recognized as a necessary strategy for restoring degraded lands and protecting production. The American Dust Bowl conditions of the early 1930s were the trigger that set in train the largest single institution of its kind, the Soil Conservation Service (SCS) of the US Department of Agriculture and its associated Agricultural Research Service (ARS). The influence of SCS-ARS has been large, leading to similar organizations in other countries, notably Australia, and to a high technology/high input/research-based approach to erosion control.

Partly in response to the difficulty of applying high cost solutions in resource-poor environments, an understanding of indigenous responses to land degradation has developed along with a recognition of the

---

Box 12.8 Sustainability quotients: a way of analysing land use

Sustainability quotient (SQ)

The fraction of present net farm income per hectare of all land including fallow that is *not* obtained at the expense of extracting soil nutrients. It expresses that part of production obtained from renewable sources (e.g. nitrogen fixed by lightening) and that part of income not reliant on using the soil 'capital'.

An example from Mali

Agricultural practices in southern Mali are contributing to a severe decline in soil fertility. Different cropping systems and application rates of fertilizer are being tried, not only to maintain yields and farmer income but also to restore soil fertility.

How far can fertilizers contribute to sustainability? The two main nutrients, N and K, that are being depleted could be restored by a maximum of 27 and 12 per cent respectively if fertilizer application were doubled. If erosion were to be reduced by half, the N and K deficits would reduce by 20 and 33 per cent. In other words, in this dry environment soil conservation is at least as effective as increasing fertilizer use. And this does not take account of increased production through water conservation which comes along with soil conservation practices.

What are the differences between land uses?

- Overall: SQ = 0.57, i.e. 43 per cent of farmers' income is based on monetary value of nutrients (N, P, K, Ca, Mg) leaving the soil through erosion, leaching, cropping and not being replaced by artificial or natural inputs (e.g. fertilizers, N-fixation).
- Recommended cotton–maize–sorghum rotational package: SQ = 0.95.
- Actual cotton–maize–sorghum package as practised by farmers: SQ = 0.73.
- Traditional groundnut–millet–millet rotation: SQ = 0.39.
- Traditional millet–fallow rotation, the cycle for which is under threat because of increasing population: SQ = 0.01 – or 99% of farmer income through 'mining' the soil.

Source: van der Pol (1992).

Fig 12.9 An intensive biological approach to soil conservation in Sri Lanka, using live fences of leguminous shrubs, grass strips and ground surface mulch.

conservation value of many traditional systems in developing countries (Figure 12.9). Tables 12.4 and 12.5 contrast the two principal approaches to soil and water conservation, the differences between which can be summarized as:

- developed country v. developing country;
- subsidies/incentives from society v. farmer pays;
- introduced technology v. indigenously developed technology;
- erosion control v. erosion prevention;
- structures and mechanical measures v. biological means;
- bulldozers and tractors v. hand hoes and seeds;
- high cost v. low/no cost.

These differences between countries should not be exaggerated. Small farms arise in developed countries where low cost biological methods of soil improvement are appropriate; large-scale estate and commercial production occurs in developing countries where machinery and conservation structures are the obvious first choice of land managers. Clashes between the approaches do, however, happen where an attempt is made to force a conservation strategy developed in one set of resource, human and environmental circumstances on quite another situation – the Mafuta family's circumstance in Box 12.6 is a classic example.

The term 'land husbandry' has recently been coined to try to overcome the different perspectives of those attempting conservation and to get over the realization that soil and water conservation is really only a part of agricultural production and environmental management. Rather than seeing conservation as a separate strategy with its own approaches and institutions, land husbandry fosters the idea that integrated, grass-roots approaches to the land involve the total production cycle, land users' constraints and opportunities, access to land, labour and capital, as well as the technical appropriateness of solutions. Although lauded as a new philosophy by Hudson (1992) – and perhaps it is for agricultural engineers – land husbandry does not, therefore, directly address soil erosion. Another of the new conservation strategists, Francis Shaxson, calls it 'conservation-by-stealth' on the grounds that land

Table 12.4 Examples of modern techniques of soil and water conservation

Technique	Description	Resource implications
Tillage practices		
Strip tillage	Conditioning soil along narrow strips in or adjacent to seed rows, leaving rest of soil undisturbed.	Special equipment; possible crusting/infiltration problems in untilled parts.
Basin listing, or tied ridging	Formation of contour bunds (earth banks) with constructed 'ties' or banks between bunds. Listing done by machinery and tied ridging usually by hand.	Need for dedicated machinery and/or considerable extra labour. Danger of water-logging.
Conservation tillage	Technique of light harrowing and retention of crop residues at surface.	Special machinery. Crop residues not available for other uses, e.g. forage, fuel.
Minimum/zero tillage	Use of herbicides, then direct drilling into residues. Very little disturbance to the soil.	Expensive chemicals and machinery. Danger of pollution and soil compaction. Saving on conventional tillage costs.
Land formation techniques		
Contour bunds	Earth banks up to 2 m wide across slope to form barrier to run-off and break slope into shorter segments. Varieties: narrow or wide-based; contour or graded.	Additional labour and/or equipment. Varieties have different costs, e.g. narrow-based loses about 14% of plantable area.
Terraces	Earth embankments and major re-formation of surface. Three main types: diversion, retention and bench terrace.	Large labour and equipment requirement. Continual maintenance.
Terracettes	Small constructions usually to harvest water. Known by many local names, e.g. fish-scale terraces in China for rows of perennial crops; eyebrow terraces for tree planting in semi-arid zone.	Labour and continuing maintenance requirement.
Stabilization structures		
Gabions	Stone and rock-filled bolsters to protect vulnerable surfaces, e.g. bridges, culverts.	High cost, transport of stone, continual maintenance.
Gully control dams	Usually constructed of brushwood across a gully.	Materials, labour and maintenance. Often fail in heavy storms.

users will practise conservation if it is perceived to be in their individual interest. Their primary concerns are production, risk-minimization and livelihood-security: if these are achieved by whatever means (improved seed; new soil management techniques; intercropping; agroforestry; contour bunds, etc.), then soil conservation automatically follows. It is an appealing prospect – simple in theory, but extraordinarily difficult to practise.

In the final analysis, soil and water conservation is one of the major challenges of our time to counter what many see as the single most immediate threat to the world's food security, land degradation. Other threats – global warming or environmental pollution, for example – catch the catastrophists' imaginations. But not only have soil erosion and land degradation been known for centuries but people have also adjusted their lives and practices to accommodate a declining resource base caused by these human-induced accelerated processes. Erosion is difficult to see; it is insidious and incremental. Technology has provided a buffer, buying time for society, making it easier for rich, developed nations to delude themselves into believing they hold the key to future production, but sooner or later the soil 'capital' must run out. It has run out in some places: parts of the Rif Mountains of Morocco are

Table 12.5 Examples of indigenous soil and water conservation techniques from Africa

Country		Rainfall (mm)	Technique
Burkina Faso (SW)		1000–1100	Stone bunds on slopes; network of earth bunds and drainage channels in lowlands
	(Central)	400–700	Stone lines; stone terraces; planting pits (*zay*)
Cameroon	(North)	800–1100	Bench terraces (0.5–3 m high), stone bunds
Nigeria	(Jos Plateau)	1000–1500	Stepped, level benched stone terraces, rectangular ridges (*sagan*), mound cultivation
Mali	(Central)	400	Large pits
		500–650	Cone-shaped mounds, planting holes, terrace basins, stone lines, low walls, millet stalk trash lines
Sierra Leone		2000–2500	Sticks and stone bunding on fields; gully drainage
Tanzania	(Uluguru Mts)	1500	Ladder terraces (trash contour ridges)
	(SW)	1000	Matengo pits: 1–1.5 m diameter
	(Ukara Isl.)	1500	Earth and stone terraces, tied ridging, stone barriers

Source: IFAD (1992).

almost entirely depopulated because of land degradation; the problems of the Sahel regularly hit the headlines; less well known are the abandoned commercial farms in hilly areas of the USA, the so-called marginal lands where erosion renders agricultural land use uneconomic; Australian rangelands where wind erosion has stripped topsoils in some parts and covered formerly productive areas in sterile sand. The likely scenario is that such 'hot spots' of degradation will increase in number. This will place added burdens on adjacent lands, whose resilience will be sorely tested. To compensate for declining production, inputs will have to increase more and more on the remaining lands.

What is the way out from the vicious circle? Frustratingly, the techniques are there for the asking. There is no shortage of measures for all permutations of environments, land uses and societies. Part of the answer may well lie in better matching of solutions to situations, but probably the only long-term answer is to allow soil resources to get worse and worse so that people are forced to change. After all, indigenous responses to land degradation have usually developed in the face of starvation and the crisis circumstance. Developed and developing countries alike will have to develop their responses, as indeed they already are; land use will inevitably change; technologies will come and go; people will migrate; and some may die. Meanwhile, environmental managers may adjust their armouries of techniques, develop new methods of analysis, find persons with the resources to heed their warnings and castigate those who ignore them. There is only one certain thing: soil erosion and land degradation are bound to get worse before they get better.

References

Blaikie, P.M. (1989) Explanation and policy in land degradation and rehabilitation for developing countries. *Land Degradation and Rehabilitation*, **1**, 23–37.

Buringh, P. and R. Dudal (1987) Agricultural land use in space and time. In M.G. Wolman and F. Fournier (Eds) *Land transformation in agriculture*, Scope 32. Chichester: Wiley, pp. 9–43.

Clark, E.H. (1985) The off-site costs of soil erosion. *Journal of Soil and Water Conservation*, **40**, 19–22.

Edwards, K. (1993) Soil erosion and conservation in Australia. In D. Pimentel (Ed.) *World soil erosion and conservation*. Cambridge: Cambridge University Press, pp. 147–69.

Elwell, H.A. and M.A. Stocking (1982) Developing a simple yet practical method of soil loss estimation. *Tropical Agriculture*, **59**, 43–8.

FAO (1978) *Report on the agro-ecological zones project*, Vol. 1, *Methodology and results for Africa*, World Soil Resources Report 48. Rome: Food and Agriculture Organization of the United Nations.

FAO (1979) *A provisional methodology for soil degradation assessment* (with mapping of North Africa at a scale of 1:5 million). Rome: Food and Agriculture Organization of the United Nations

FAO (1982) *Potential population supporting capacities of lands in the developing world*, Technical Report FPA/INT/513 and mapping at 1:5 million. Jointly with UNFPA and IIASA. Rome: Food and Agriculture Organization of the United Nations.

Hudson, N.W. (1971) *Soil conservation*. London: Batsford.

Hudson, N.W. (1992) *Land husbandry*. London: Batsford.

IFAD (1992) *Soil and water conservation in sub-Saharan Africa. Towards sustainable production by the rural poor*.

Report prepared by the Centre for Development
Cooperation Services, Free University, Amsterdam.
Rome: International Fund for Agricultural
Development.

Lal, R. (1984) Productivity assessment of tropical soils and
the effects of erosion. In F.R. Rijsberman and M.G.
Wolman (Eds) *Quantification of the effect of erosion on
soil productivity in an international context.* Delft:
Hydraulics Laboratory, pp. 70–94.

Norse, D. (1992) A new strategy for feeding a crowded
planet. *Environment,* **34**(5), 6–12, 32–9.

Norse, D., C. James, B.J. Skinner and Q. Zhao (1992)
Agricultural land use and degradation. In J. Dooge
(Ed.) *Agenda for science for environment and
development into the 21st century.* Cambridge:
Cambridge University Press.

Oldeman, L.R., R.T.A. Hakkeling and W.G. Sombroek
(1990) *Global assessment of soil degradation.*
Wageningen: International Soil Reference Information
Centre.

Ostberg, W. (1991) *Land is coming up. Burungee thoughts on
soil erosion and soil formation.* EDSU Working Paper
11. Stockholm: School of Geography, Stockholm
University.

Pimentel, D., J. Allen, A. Beers *et al.* (1993) Soil
erosion and agricultural productivity. In D.
Pimentel (Ed.) *World soil erosion and conservation.*
Cambridge: Cambridge University Press,
pp. 277–92.

Stocking, M.A. (1988a) Quantifying the on-site
impact of soil erosion. In Sanarn Rimwanich
(Ed.) *Land conservation for future generations.*
Bangkok: Department of Land Development,
pp. 137–61.

Stocking, M.A. (1988b) Socio-economics of soil
conservation in developing countries. *Journal of Soil
and Water Conservation,* **43**, 381–5.

Van der Pol, F. (1992) *Soil mining: an unseen contributor to
farm income in southern Mali,* Bulletin 325. Amsterdam:
Royal Tropical Institute.

Wild, A. (1993) *Soils and the environment: an introduction.*
Cambridge: Cambridge University Press.

World Resources Institute (1992) *World resources 1992–93.*
Oxford: Oxford University Press.

Further Reading

The standard text looking at degradation from a non-
technical perspective is P. Blaikie and H. Brookfield
(Eds) (1987) *Land degradation and society* (Methuen,
London). Chapters on measurement, colonialism,
common property resources, enterprise and economic
costs and benefits. Not for the faint-hearted.

J. De Graf (1993) *Soil conservation and sustainable land
use: an economic approach* (Royal Tropical Institute, Amsterdam) is a 190-page book that sets conservation
technologies into clear economic context with guidance
on ways to include social and economic costs and benefits,
as well as external effects. Many useful examples from
developing countries.

N.W. Hudson (1992) is a *mea culpa* of an engineer
and author of the standard text (1971) on soil conservation who now admits we have been treating the
symptoms, not the cause, of degradation. Land husbandry means the care, management and improvement
of land resources. It is still a technical approach to
resource management but encompassing a wider range
of factors including biological control. Old dogs can
learn new tricks!

An excellent account of participatory resource management is IFAD (1992) which puts particular emphasis on local knowledge and the pitfalls of attempting to
impose high-technology solutions to land degradation
in resource-poor societies. D. Pimentel (Ed.) (1993)
World soil erosion and conservation, Cambridge Studies
in Applied Ecology and Resource Management, (Cambridge University Press, Cambridge) has an ambitious
title. Some excellent country review chapters, especially
on relationship of land degradation and famine in
Ethiopia. Pimentel gives a useful account of relationship of soil erosion and agricultural productivity.
Finally M. Tiffin, M. Mortimore and F. Gichuki (1994)
More people, less erosion: environmental recovery in Kenya
(Wiley: Chichester) gives fascinating detail on how local
society adapts to declining soil recources. Look especially at photographs of 1937 Machokos, degraded
hillsides, compared to the lushness of 1990.

Pollution, risk, health effects and energy generation all connect through uncertain science and institutional failure. Pollution is a function of inappropriate property rights, a regulatory regime that is always subservient to capitalism, whether of the state or private kind, and of sincere difficulty in proving effect from cause. Despite the lack of some kind of citizens' environmental right, the best arrangement so far is legislation such as the Michigan Environmental Protection Act of 1972 which permits citizens' groups to take action against a polluter or a regulatory agency in the cause of protecting their health and peace of mind. In the event, such legislation encourages the regulators to be tough and aggressive, rather than spawn a host of citizens' law suits.

In the modern world of pollution control, important changes are taking place:

- *Information* is more widely available as a result of regular state-of-the-environment reports nowadays produced by most countries in the northern hemisphere, and through information networks provided by the UN Environment Programme. The creation of a European Environmental Agency by the European Community, long delayed because of a wrangle over location, should help to standardize the collection and publication of scientific data on environmental quality. This is an important development, although eventually all countries should create independent and competent bureaux of environmental statistics.
- *The definition of environmental harm* is steadily widening to include the integrity of ecosystems and not just human health. Though this is by no means the equivalent of an environmental right, it does provide the regulator with a more ecologically based interpretation of environmental quality, and provides more scope for the precautionary principle to be put into effect.
- *Environmental quality standards*, regulatory assessment levels, *de minimis* risk levels – all ambient or regional scale yardsticks of healthy environments – are becoming more commonplace and unified as a basis for determining emissions and waste disposal tolerances. The concept of critical load, namely the threshold value of ecosystem absorption of pollutants, is also in vogue. These are not easy standards to set. But science has an important role to play in providing advice on what levels to set, even though inevitably there is still much guesswork involved.
- *Arms' length regulatory agencies* and negotiating practices depend very much on the culture of regulation and the actual regulatory guidelines used. In the USA and Germany, the practice is usually more formal and target-driven, with the regulator acting somewhat as an ecological police force. In the UK and southern Europe, as well as in Scandinavia, a more discretionary approach is taken to environmental standard setting, with the use of the words 'reasonable' or 'practicable' to soften the blow of strict enforcement. In practice, however, most regulatory officials do negotiate around a set of possible actions so long as there are technological or managerial options to best practice, so long as the managers are willing to comply, and so long as the levels of emission reduction are not excessively demanding in too short a time period for an impoverished polluter already in economic difficulties. One can see how, inevitably, there is room for compromise.

- *Up the pipe regulation* is a phrase to indicate that firms are increasingly looking to restructuring their product lines, creating new products from what was formerly waste, and seeking the stimulation of more efficient technology in the reduction of pollution. So the regulator does not seek to control the emission just at the point of discharge. With new environmental management systems such as the EC Environmental Management and Auditing System (EMAS) eco-audit for industry (and eventually government), the UK BS 7750 and the US risk prevention programme of the US Environmental Protection Agency (US EPA), so management is beginning to incorporate environmental safeguards into the very core of business innovation.
- *Charging* for polluting discharges, for the cost of providing licences and to encourage the return of used material to proper disposal sites (deposit refund schemes) is becoming more popular. This is partly a reflection of a changing political ideology that favours the customer, rather than the taxpayer, as the source of revenue for services. It is also a reflection of the prevailing mood to reduce the burden of public spending by forcing the consumer to pay via indirect taxation. But, to be fair, it is also a sign of the new mood favouring environmental taxation as an incentive to direct behaviour towards sustainability, and to create revenue for precautionary investment.

All these developments require the reconstruction of institutions, economies and science around a more socially responsive and anticipatory approach to resource management and pollution control. The very nature of these changes also helps to alter the political climate favouring such reforms. Thus, as international action is more and more needed to cope with cross-border transfers of pollutants of all kinds, so countries look to the extended science of participation and communication to determine standards, support enforcement and justify charging for services supplied.

In all of the chapters that follow there is also a legitimate concern over the appropriate cut-off point between the amount of technology, effort and investment spent in reducing pollution or risk, compared with the resulting gains in ecological vitality and human health. Understandably the scientist as economist is often put on the spot in such calculations. No matter how inexact the scientific modelling and weighted judgements, some measures of benefits ought to be set against the costs. These points were touched on in Chapter 2, and reappear in the discussion of risk benefit calculus in Chapter 16 and in the multi-attribute displays introduced in Chapter 17. The difficulties of identifying health effects of environmental change are examined in some detail in Chapter 18.

In the UK, the integrated pollution control agency known as Her Majesty's Inspectorate of Pollution, HMIP (1993), is grappling with these problems in an intriguing way. HMIP recognizes that the regulatory assessment levels cannot be fixed from existing scientific knowledge so it resorts to in-house research, expert judgement and international equivalents, where formal standards do not exist. These form the basis of action levels, which is where regulatory enforcement is mobilized. To be safe from pushing overall environmental detriment too close to the regulatory assessment levels, HMIP judges that the action level should be about one-tenth of the quality standard of the ambient or assessment level.

The point at which costs and benefits are determined is set in the context of what HMIP terms a best practicable environmental option (BPEO). This is derived in three stages:

1. First, a *substance tolerability quotient* (TQ) is derived for each substance being emitted into either air, water or land. This is the sum of the emission of the actual substance together with the background concentration of the substance divided by the environmental quality standard (EQS) or the regulatory assessment level (RAL):

$$\text{TQ (substance)} = \frac{\text{ambient conc.} + \text{plant contribution}}{\text{EQS or RAL}}$$

2. Second, a *medium tolerability quotient* is derived by summing the medium specific substance TQs:

$$\text{TQ(medium)} = \text{TQ}(a) + \text{TQ}(b) + \text{TQ}(c) \ldots \text{TQ}(i)$$

where (a), (b), (c), etc. are environmentally significant substances emitted into air, water or land.

3. Third, a BPEO index is constructed by adding the medium TQs for the site in question. If a range of abatement processes are considered in this way then the best environmental option would be that with the lowest BPEO index. This can be set against an annualized cost of abatement for any of the alternative options studied and compared for cost effectiveness.

This approach is still very much at an early stage of development. A preliminary case study has indicated that more expensive abatement options for a coal-fired coal plant do not create significant improvements in the BPEO index. Thus the best available techniques not entailing excessive costs need not be the very best techniques, but the best for a given BPEO target index.

It is likely that the pressure groups will view this approach with misgiving because it will explicitly move HMIP away from the best available technology approach found in the USA and Germany. There is also a difficulty in that any given environmental option being considered is not automatically optimal unless the TQ for substances is used to identify some optionality of removal. Finally, the benefits are not in any way marginal benefits, but simply a surrogate measure based on somewhat crudely defined environmental quality standards. Nevertheless, this is a valuable start in trying to determine a robust yardstick against which to measure the cost effectiveness of pollution control and, in time, risk reduction.

Further reading

The HMIP document in question is Her Majesty's Inspectorate of Pollution (1993) *Environmental, economic and BPEO assessment: principles for integrated pollution control* (HMIP, London). A good review of the changing politics of pollution is A. Weale (1993) *The new politics of pollution* (Manchester University Press, Manchester). For an assessment of integrated pollution control, see N. Haigh and F. Irwin (Eds) (1987) *Integrated pollution control* (The Conservation Foundation, Washington, DC).

CHAPTER 13

Groundwater pollution and protection

KEVIN HISCOCK

Groundwater pollution could become one of the scourges of the age. Much depends on the spread of toxic and persistent chemicals from agricultural intensification the world over, from salt extrusion in disturbed dryland soils, and from the rain contaminated with the fugitive emissions of millions of tiny sources, each one of which may be almost impossible to detect and to monitor. The natural repository of all these chemicals is the soil, groundwater and estuaries filling with toxic sediments; of these the most insidious is the contamination of groundwater by pathogens from the discharge of sewage works, nitrate pollution from excessive or inappropriate fertilizer use, heavy metals from rainfall, oil discharges from illegal dumping, solvent discharges from poorly managed waste disposal sites and sedimentation of rivers and estuaries from which seep all manner of stored pollutants.

Hydrogeology is coming into its own as a discipline and as a consultancy. Part of the reason is the steady growth in groundwater sources as new surface sources become opposed by amenity groups or for reasons of nature conservation as introduced in Chapter 7. An equally important factor is the change in the law of contaminated land to a more formal status of strict liability. In principle, an owner is responsible for anything that occurs from his/her land that damages the interest of a neighbour. In the USA, this problem has to some extent been overcome by the introduction of the Superfund legislation more formally known as the Comprehensive Environmental Response, Compensation and Liability Act 1980. This imposes a levy on all disposers of toxic waste into sites that could result in long-term groundwater pollution of mismanaged industrial premises. Because many sites are abandoned from a previous industrial age, the cost of risk assessment and clean-up of these deserted locales is borne by the Superfund. The hazard assessment process generates a hazard ranking score for each site, and the most dangerous are placed on a national priorities list. About 35 000 preliminary assessments and 20 000 site investigations have been completed. Possibly as many as 3500 sites may be placed on the national priorities list out of a staggering 300 000 sites that need attention. Though Superfund has frozen some $15 billion, it is very likely that all of this and much more will be needed to do the job. The estimate of the cost of clean-up depends in part on the skills of the hydrogeologist who has the tools to estimate where toxic pollution might enter the groundwater source if the site is not cleaned up. Similarly, any proposed landfill site will need the services of a trained hydrogeologist if the environmental impact assessment is to stand up.

An alarming development for both commercial companies and their financial backers in Europe is the probability of an EC directive on the civil liability of wastes. This directive will impose a statutory responsibility on the landowner to clean up any site that is contaminated, or to pay for any consequences arising from subsequent contamination arising from that site at any time in the future. Because the liability is both strict and severe, it will apply even when a landowner has been observing the pollution control regulations, and will extend to anyone who has a financial interest in the site. Understandably this has caused a flurry of activity in corporate boardrooms and amongst the insurance industry. Needless to say any contemplated purchase of an old gas works site or former electrical engineering plant would require the expensive advice of an experienced hydrogeologist before the site was acquired. It is not surprising that hydrogeology has become a lucrative source of environmental consultancy.

A recent court case in the UK highlights the significance of applied groundwater studies in the tortuous process of civil liability for pollution. Cambridge Water Company is a private body supplying water to the City of Cambridge and its environs. In 1976 it purchased a borehole from which it supplied about one-eighth of all the water it provided for a quarter of a million people. To distribute this water, the Company had to meet the EC drinking water directive. Among other requirements this directive expected wholesome water to contain not more than one microgram per litre (1 µg/l) of organochlorine compounds. But for the compound tetrachloroethane or perchloroethene (PCE), the maximum admissible concentration was to be 10 µg/l. When the company first assessed the borehole quality such regulations were not in place. But by the mid-1980s PCE concentrations were found to be 70–170 µg/l. The company was stopped from pumping, so looked for the source to seek compensation.

That source turned out to be a tanning company known as Eastern Counties Leather PLC. This firm degreased pelts with PCE. The PCE had been stored in drums on the site and presumably some of this had either leaked or accidentally spilled into the groundwater regime. The cost of the alternative borehole supply was close to £1 million and this formed the basis of the compensation claim against Eastern Counties Leather.

The Appeal Court found in favour of Cambridge Water Company, not on the grounds of strict liability but on the grounds of nuisance. Strict liability is a common law tort that places the onus of responsibility on a landowner to be careful about the management of the site irrespective of meeting regulatory requirements. Any discharge from a non-natural source, that is a source that would not be expected to arise naturally from the site, would form the basis of liability. The Appeal Court took another route and argued that Eastern Counties Leather was subject in nuisance in the sense that interference with a natural right of property is also a matter of strict liability. It is no defence to claim that pollution control standards only came into force after the spillage had occurred.

The case was finally settled in the House of Lords in December 1993. This is the highest court for matters of legal principle in the UK. Their lordships concluded that it was unreasonable to hold Eastern Countries Leather liable for activities undertaken so long ago and where the company had taken reasonable safeguards against spillage. The judgement turned on the forseeability of damage: because the storage of chemicals on an industrial site is an acceptable or natural use of land, spillage of these toxic substances was to be expected, so long as the spillages were kept small and appropriate safeguards were in place. In effect the Lords judgement returned the matter of liability to a narrower frame of reference, namely demonstrable and avoidable damage which any reasonable person would forsee, much to the relief of the insurance world. But their lordships also pointed out strenuously that surveillance and enforcement measures under the modern regulations for groundwater protection should be considerably tightened up. This ruling will place even more emphasis on good quality hydrogeological science in environmental regulation.

This case does not resolve the contentious legal disputes between strict liability *per se* and a strict liability interpretation of nuisance. But it does show that knowledge of groundwater hydrology is now essential if possible compensation claims of enormous magnitude are to be avoided. It is little wonder that a number of thoughtful insurance companies are avoiding cover for premises where there is any possibility of environmental risk. Indeed, cover generally for firms faced with environmental liability is increasingly difficult to obtain.

Introduction

Groundwater forms that part of the natural water cycle present within underground strata or aquifers. Unfortunately, groundwater is all too often considered out of sight and out of mind. Of the global quantity of available freshwater, more than 98 per cent is groundwater stored in the pores and fractures of rock strata. In England and Wales groundwater makes up 35 per cent of the total public freshwater supply, constituting approximately 75 per cent of all abstracted groundwater. Groundwater is also an important source for industry and agriculture as well as for sustaining rivers experiencing low flows. Groundwater is not only abstracted for supply or river regulation purposes, it also naturally feeds surface-waters through springs and seepages to rivers and is often important in supporting wetlands and their ecosystems. Removal or diversion of groundwater can affect total river flow. A reduction in either quantity or quality of the discharging groundwater can significantly influence surface-water quality and the attainment of water quality standards. Surface-water and groundwater are therefore intimately linked in the water cycle, with many common issues.

The protection of groundwater quality is of paramount importance. If groundwater becomes polluted, it is difficult, if not impossible, to rehabilitate. The slow rates of groundwater flow and low microbiological activity limit any self-purification. Processes which take place in days or weeks in surface-water systems are likely to take decades in groundwater.

The risk of groundwater pollution is increasing both from the disposal of waste materials and from the widespread use by industry and agriculture of potentially polluting chemicals in the environment. Pollution can occur either as discrete, point sources, such as from the landfilling of wastes, or from the wider, more diffuse use of chemicals, such as the application to land of fertilizers and pesticides and the deposition of airborne pollutants in heavily industrialized regions.

The volume and quality of groundwater must therefore be protected by proper management. It is better to prevent or reduce the risk of groundwater contamination than to deal with its consequences.

This chapter is concerned with groundwater contamination (see Box 13.1). This topic is dealt with from both a consideration of hydrogeological principles and from a discussion of two case studies, one from a developing country and one from an industrialized country. By the end of the chapter, the reader should have gained a general understanding of the science and issues involved in understanding groundwater pollution and in formulating protection measures.

Sources of groundwater pollution

Changes in groundwater quality may result from the direct or indirect influence of anthropogenic activities. Direct influences occur as a result of the introduction of natural or artificial substances into groundwater

Fig 13.1 Point source pollution arising from the inadequate storage and subsequent rupture of barrels of lubricating oil additives. Although perhaps not immediately recognizable as a source of groundwater contamination, such insidious release of industrial chemicals is a serious threat, particularly given that very low concentrations of synthetic toxic chemicals can render groundwater unfit for human consumption. In this photograph there is an apparently impervious hard surface, but in reality badly maintained concrete surfaces and surface drainage networks can permit direct access of aqueous pollutants to the groundwater environment. (Courtesy of R.P. Ashley.)

Box 13.1 Definition of contaminated groundwater

Contaminated groundwater is groundwater that has been affected by human activities to the extent that it has higher concentrations of dissolved or suspended constituents than the maximum admissible concentrations formulated by national or international standards for drinking, industrial or agricultural purposes.

Fig 13.2 An example of a pollution incident caused by the derailment of rail tankers containing oil. Noticeable warping of the tankers resulted from the ensuing fire. As with road transport accidents, runoff either by gravity drainage to local surface water courses or by interception to soakaways are possible pathways for groundwater pollution. (Courtesy of R.P. Ashley.)

derived from human activities. Indirect influences are those changes of quality brought about by human interference with hydrological, physical and biochemical processes, but without the addition of substances.

The main contaminants of groundwater are heavy metals, organic chemicals, fertilizers, bacteria and viruses. Figures 13.1 and 13.2 illustrate incidents giving rise to groundwater pollution. The enormous range of contaminants encountered in groundwater reflects the wide range of human economic activity in the world, as well as the incomplete measures for controlling pollution of groundwater the world over. The major activities generating contaminants are associated with the agricultural, mining, industrial and domestic sectors. Table 13.1 is a compilation of the sources and potential characteristics of groundwater contaminants. Box 13.2 discusses how contaminants are transported.

Groundwater pollution in developing countries

Groundwater is extensively used for drinking water supplies in developing countries, especially in smaller towns and rural areas where it is the cheapest and safest source. Often it is the willingness to pay for cheap and clean water that governs progress in providing better sanitation in poorer countries (see Box 13.3).

In developing countries, groundwater schemes consist of large numbers of boreholes, often drilled on an uncontrolled basis, providing untreated, unmonitored and often unconnected supplies. Shallower dug wells continue to be constructed in some cases. Better-yielding boreholes (10–100 l/s) are quite widely developed in larger towns to provide piped supplies. Even in these cases, raw water monitoring and treatment are often limited and intermittent. Generally, sources of groundwater pollution result from the widespread practice of

Box 13.2 Transport of contaminants in groundwater

The subsurface movement of a contaminant is influenced by the moisture content of the unsaturated zone and the volume of groundwater flow in the saturated zone below the water-table, both of which are determined by climatic and topographic parameters.

The fundamental physical processes controlling the transport of non-reactive contaminants are advection and hydrodynamic dispersion. Advection is the component of solute movement attributed to transport by the flowing groundwater. Hydrodynamic dispersion occurs as a result of mechanical mixing and molecular diffusion as illustrated in the figure.

The significance of the dispersive processes is to decrease the contaminant concentration with distance from the source. The next figure illustrates how a continuous pollution source will produce a plume, whereas a single point source will produce a slug that grows with time as the plume moves in the direction of groundwater flow.

The idea of a homogeneous aquifer, in which the hydrogeological properties do not vary in space, is a simplification of the real situation in nature. Heterogeneities within the aquifer lithology will create a pattern of solute movement considerably different from that predicted by the theory for homogeneous material.

Reactive substances behave similarly to non-reactive substances, but can also undergo a change in concentration resulting from chemical reactions that take place either in the aqueous phase, or as a result of adsorption of the solute to the solid matrix of the rock. The chemical and biochemical reactions that can alter contaminant concentrations in groundwater are acid-based reactions, solution–precipitation reactions, oxidation–reduction reactions, ion pairing or complexation, microbiological processes and radioactive decay. Adsorption attenuates, or retards a dissolved contaminant in groundwater.

The processes of advection, dispersion and retardation all influence the pattern of contaminant distribution away from the pollution source. If a pollution source contains multiple solutes and occurs within a heterogeneous aquifer, then there will be a number of contaminant fronts and the morphology of the resulting plume will be very complex indeed. Consequently, prediction of the pollution front will be very difficult.

In fractured media, aquifer properties are spacially variable and are controlled by the orientation and frequency of fractures. Information relating to contaminant migration in fractured rocks is limited. A common approach in field investigations is to treat the problem as if it were a granular medium.

As the third figure shows, when contamination occurs in fractures, there is a gradient of contaminant concentration between the mobile groundwater in the fracture and the static water in the adjacent rock matrix. Under this condition, part of the contaminant mass will migrate by molecular diffusion from the fracture into the matrix, so effectively removing it from the flowing groundwater.

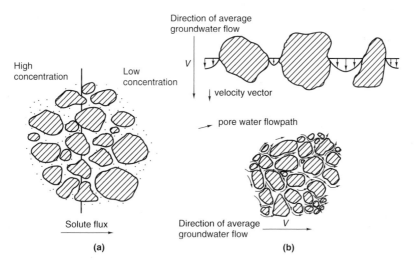

Diagrammatic representation of (a) molecular diffusion and (b) mechanical dispersion which combine to transport a solute within a porous medium by the process of hydrodynamic dispersion. Notice that mechanical dispersion results from the variation of velocity within and between saturated pore spaces and from the tortuosity of the flowpaths through the assemblage of solid particles. Molecular diffusion can occur in the absence of groundwater flow, since solute transport is driven by the influence of a concentration gradient, while mechanical dispersion occurs while the contaminant is being advected by the groundwater.

Box 13.2 continued

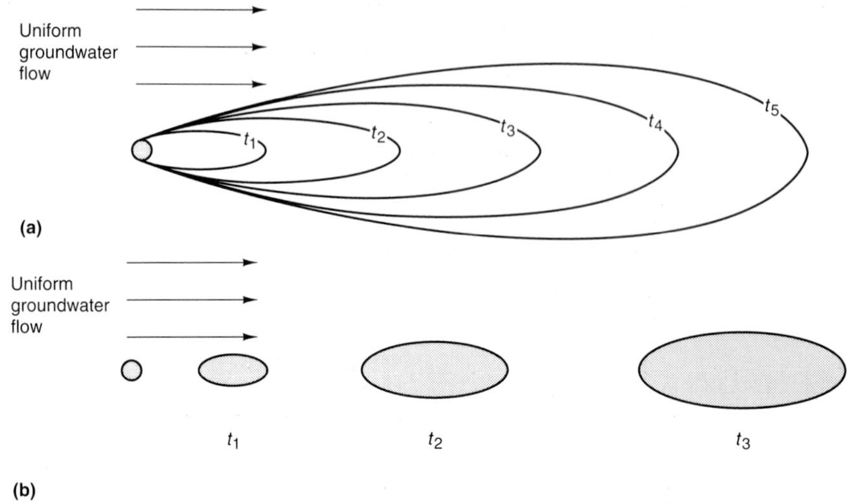

(a)

(b)

Dispersion within an isotropic porous medium of (a) a continuous point source of pollution at various times, *t*, and (b) an instantaneous point source of pollution. Spreading of the pollution plumes results from hydrodynamic dispersion, while advection transports the plumes in the field of uniform groundwater flow.

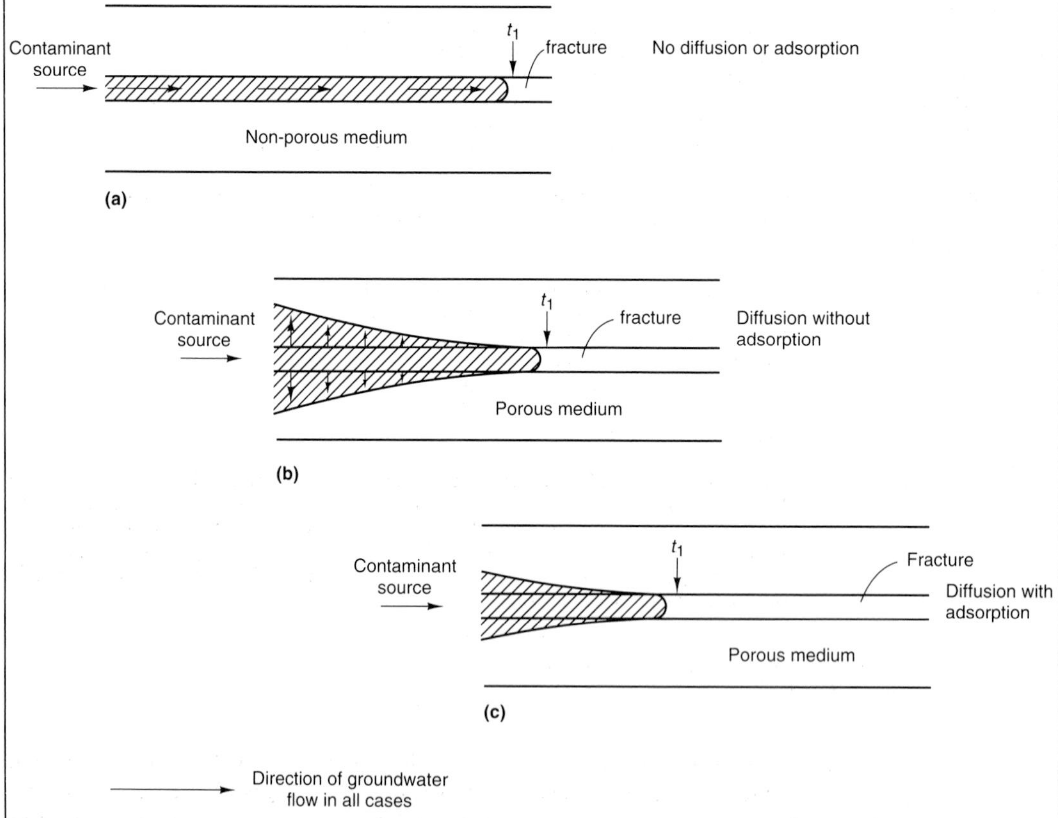

(a)

(b)

(c)

Contaminant transport within porous fractured media. In (a) the solute is advected, without hydrodynamic dispersion, with the groundwater flowing through a fracture where the matrix porosity is insignificant. In (b) the solute transport is retarded by the instantaneous molecular diffusion of the solute into the uncontaminated porous matrix. Further attenuation occurs in (c) where adsorption of a reactive solute occurs, accentuated by the greater surface area of contact resulting from migration of the solute into the porous matrix. The position of the leading edge of the contaminant front within the fracture is shown for time t_1 in each case.

Table 13.1 Potential sources of groundwater pollution arising from domestic, industrial and agricultural activities

Contaminant source	Contaminant characteristics
Septic tanks	Suspended solids 100–300 mg/l BOD 50–400 mg/l Ammonia 20–40 mg/l Chloride 100–200 mg/l High faecal coliforms and streptococci. Trace organisms, greases.
Storm water drains	Suspended solids ~1000 mg/l Hydrocarbons from roads, service areas. Chlorides or urea from de-icing. Compounds from accidental spillages. Bacterial contamination.
Industry	
Food and drink manufacturing	High BOD. High suspended solids. Colloidal and dissolved organic substances. Odours.
Textile and clothing	High suspended solids and BOD. Alkaline effluent.
Tanneries	High BOD, total solids, hardness, chlorides, sulphides, chromium.
Chemicals	
acids	Low pH.
detergents	High BOD.
pesticides	High TOC, toxic benzene derivatives, low pH.
synthetic resins and fibres	High BOD.
Petroleum and petrochemical	
refining	High BOD, chloride, phenols, sulphur compounds.
process	High BOD, suspended solids, chloride, variable pH.
Plating and metal finishing	Low pH. High content of toxic metals.
Engineering works	High suspended solids, hydrocarbons, trace heavy metals. Variable BOD, pH.
Power generation	Pulverized fuel ash: sulphate, and may contain germanium and selenium. Fly ash and flue gas scrubber sludges: low pH, disseminated heavy metals.
Deep well injection	Concentrated liquid wastes, often toxic brines. Acid and alkaline wastes. Organic wastes.
Leakage from storage tanks and pipelines	Aqueous solutions, hydrocarbons, petrochemicals, sewage.
Agriculture	
Arable crops	Nitrate, ammonia, sulphate, chloride and phosphates from fertilizers. Bacterial contamination from organic fertilizers. Organo-chlorine compounds from pesticides.
Livestock	Suspended solids, BOD, nitrogen. High faecal coliforms and streptococci.
Silage	High suspended solids, BOD $1–6 \times 10^4$ mg/l. Carbohydrates, phenols.
Mining	
Coal mine drainage	High TDS (total dissolved solids), suspended solids. Iron. Low pH. Possibly high chloride.
Metals	High suspended solids. Possibly low pH. High sulphates. Dissolved and particulate metals.
Household wastes	High sulphate, chloride, ammonia, BOD, TOC and suspended solids from fresh wastes. Bacterial contamination. On decomposition: initially TOC of mainly volatile fatty acids (acetic, butyric, propionic acids), subsequently changing to high molecular weight organics (humic substances, carbohydrates).

BOD is biological oxygen demand, TOC is total organic carbon, pH is $-\log_{10}(H^+)$
Source: Adapted from Jackson (1980).

on-site disposal of untreated domestic and industrial effluents to the ground, owing to the prohibitive cost of handling and disposal processes.

In developing countries, unsewered, ventilated and pour-flush pit latrines provide adequate excreta disposal in rural areas, villages and small towns, at a much lower cost than main sewerage systems. Consequently, the possibility of an expansion of excreta disposal into

It is evident that, where people have the choice, they are prepared to pay for clean water and good sanitation for reasons of health, convenience, privacy and stable property prices. Studies in poor countries in Africa show that urban people already pay about 2 per cent of family income on inadequate water and sanitation services. This is similar to the amount paid for electricity. Nowadays developers are being required to provide packaged sewage treatment services as part of a permit to construct housing even in the poorest country cities. A recent World Bank study showed that less than 10 per cent of sewage connections are actually being made, despite the regulations. The answers lie in widening the provision of low technology sewage provision, separating the regulator from the provider, ensuring performance cash bonds are paid beforehand to stop financial defaulting and enabling the private sector to bid for projects. In this way, health-debilitating groundwater pollution in many developing country cities can be reduced.

the ground is very real, especially in many Asian countries where many people are without any form of sanitation.

The natural soil profile can be effective in purifying human wastes, including the elimination of faecal microbes, and also in the adsorption, breakdown and removal of many chemicals. However, in some cases, for example where thin soils are developed on aquifer outcrops, there is the risk of direct migration of pathogenic microbes, especially viruses, to adjacent groundwater sources. The inevitable result will be the transmission of water-borne diseases.

A further problem with excreta is the organic nitrogen content which can cause widespread and persistent problems of nitrate in water, even where dilution and biological reduction processes occur. The problem is exacerbated in arid areas without significant regional groundwater flow to provide dilution.

Another source of pollution risk arises from the use of inorganic fertilizers and pesticides in the effort to secure self-sufficiency in food production. The use of irrigation to provide crop moisture requirements poses the risk of leaching losses of nutrients if not carefully managed, especially from thin, coarse-textured soils. The use of wastewater for irrigation may contribute to groundwater salinity and nitrate concentrations, and possibly micropollutants. Increases in chloride, nitrate and perhaps trace elements will result from excessive land application of sewage effluent and sludge or animal slurry.

In many developing countries, extensive urban areas are unsewered, yet it is these areas where an increasing number of small-scale industries, such as textiles, metal processing, vehicle maintenance and paper manufacture are located. The small quantities of liquid effluent generated by each will generally be discharged to the soil; especially in the absence of specific control measures and the prohibitive cost of treatment processes. Larger industrial plants generating large volumes of process water will commonly have unlined surface impoundments for the handling of liquid effluents.

Groundwater contamination in Sri Lanka

The Jaffna Peninsula of Sri Lanka is a low, flat area of 800 km^2 in the extreme north of the country. Rainfall totals about 1000 mm/year, and mostly occurs in association with the north-east monsoon. Large evaporative losses are associated with very high temperatures. The regional aquifer is composed of Miocene limestone, which varies from a mass of coral material to a massive cemented rock with interbedded coral debris. The aquifer is mantled by a thin layer of light-textured, well-drained soil, generally less than 1 m thick. There is no surface-water, except for ephemeral ponds and flood channels. The water-table varies from 2 to 10 m, depending on season and location.

The population of Jaffna Town is about 100 000. There is also a very high density and rapidly increasing rural population in many parts of the peninsula. There are probably more than 10 000 domestic dug wells, usually less than 10 m deep, used for potable supply, and perhaps a similar number of irrigation wells.

The urban areas are virtually unsewered. During the 1970s there was a major campaign for household pour-flush latrine installation, with a depth of typically 2 m and situated at distances of less than 10 m from drinking water supply wells. The latrines are thought to be the cause of widespread microbiological contamination and are believed to be the cause of a number of incidents of pathogen transmission.

Shallow groundwaters, as shown in Figure 13.3, contain in excess of 20 mg N/l and locally 30–50 mg N/l, mainly in the form of nitrate. These concentrations are very high when compared with the World Health Organization (WHO) guide value of 10 mg N/l. Latrines contribute to the increasing nitrate problem, but the suspected main source is irrigation of cultivated

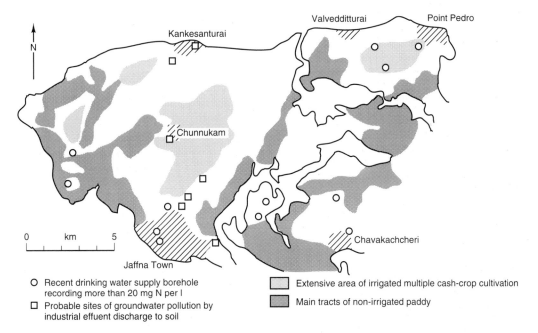

Fig 13.3 Distribution of land-use types in the western part of the Jaffna Peninsula, Sri Lanka. Problems of groundwater contamination resulting from agricultural and industrial activities are indicated, respectively, by boreholes recording greater than 20 mg N/l of nitrate and sites of probable industrial effluent discharge to soil. (Source: After Foster, 1985.)

land. Parts of the Jaffna Peninsula are amongst the most intensively cultivated and highest-yielding land in Asia. Major increases in chilli, onion and other cash-crop yields have been achieved with intensification to double or triple cropping. Such intensification has necessitated the use of inorganic fertilizers totalling 80 kg N/ha per crop, coupled with a similar quantity in the form of organic manure applied on seeding. Irrigation losses through the thin permeable soils are primarily responsible for the unusually high groundwater nitrate concentrations observed. A further problem results from increases in salinity in the shallow groundwater in years of below-average monsoon rainfall and associated groundwater recharge.

The urban areas of the peninsula have significant numbers of small-scale industries. Without proper effluent disposal, these industries also pose a groundwater pollution threat.

Groundwater protection in developing countries

Protection of groundwater supply sources requires a broad-based pollution control policy in the form of:

first, minimum separations, depending on the hydrogeological environment, between groundwater supply source and excreta disposal unit for microbiological protection; and second, dilution zones of modified land use to alleviate the impact of polluting land use activities.

The water laws and codes of practice of many countries require a minimum spacing between excreta disposal unit and groundwater supply source of 15 m under favourable hydrogeological conditions. Some countries have selected a greater distance, for example 200 m in Malawi water law. There is, however, considerable pressure to reduce this permitted spacing to as little as 5 m in some developing countries, such as Bangladesh and parts of India and Sri Lanka, often resulting from the lack of space in very densely populated settlements.

This one example of law governing the location of excreta disposal units demonstrates that criteria for groundwater pollution protection are rather arbitrary, based on limited or no technical data. In the future, a more comprehensive, flexible and widely applicable policy for groundwater protection is needed, specifically related to aquifer conditions and human activities.

A consistent, detailed procedure for the rapid

assessment of groundwater pollution risk needs to be defined. Definition should be based on the classification of: first, pollutant and hydraulic loading from specific activities; and second, aquifer pollution vulnerability. The procedure should be developed to encompass the presentation of results, and the formulation and implementation of pollution protection policy in relation to polluting activities. Intensive investigations, with or without careful monitoring of groundwater quality, in selected field situations in developing countries need to be promoted under the auspices of international organizations, in order to improve knowledge of, and focus attention upon, potential pollution problems.

The water quality criteria for the case of groundwater pollution protection in developing countries need more detailed examination. In the case of organic micropollutants, precise limits can only be set when there is adequate medical evidence of the toxicological effects. However, in other cases, the existing WHO recommendations are unnecessarily stringent in the light of the disproportionate cost of attaining such standards in relation to other public health risks. For example, the WHO guide value for nitrate in drinking water supplies in tropical countries is currently 10 mg N/l, but it is argued that concentrations up to 22.6 mg N/l are permissible under most circumstances.

Groundwater pollution in industrialized countries

The science of contaminant hydrogeology has largely been driven by both developments in analytical procedures for identifying pollutants and the need to formulate water quality standards and aquifer protection policies. This has promoted research effort in trying to understand contaminant behaviour in groundwater.

The pace of development also reflects the concerns of individual countries. For example, in the USA during the early 1970s, the public concern for hazardous waste sites and contaminated land led to the introduction in 1980 of the Comprehensive Environmental Response, Compensation and Liability Act: the 'Superfund' legislation. The legislation also embraced concerns about the deterioration of groundwater quality in states such as New Jersey arising from point sources of industrial pollution in situations, typical in the USA, of shallow aquifers with little protection.

In the UK, until the late 1970s, concern for ground-

water quality concentrated largely on the threat posed by pollutants of diffuse origin, in particular nitrate from agricultural sources. The stringent legislation initiated by the Commission of the European Community in 1980 and more sophisticated analytical equipment then began to focus attention on trace organic and inorganic contaminants in the UK.

In industrial societies, sources of pollutants include toxic chemicals such as chlorinated solvents, mineral oils and heavy metals. The behaviour of toxic chemicals in groundwater is complicated by the physical and chemical characteristics of the contaminants involved. Boxes 13.4 and 13.5 describe respectively the behaviour of non-aqueous phase liquids and heavy metals in groundwater.

Generally, many chemicals have had a long history of usage before becoming recognized as hazardous. During this time, handling and waste disposal practices have frequently been inadequate. Hence, it must be considered that any industrial site where hazardous materials have been used is now a potential source of groundwater contamination. Furthermore, the simple application of classical hydrogeological theory breaks down when investigating point sources of pollution.

Groundwater pollution problems can only be solved by careful analysis of actual ground conditions and infrastructure immediately below a site, followed by accurately positioned monitoring boreholes (or by the employment of rapid survey techniques such as soil gas analysis) to provide a detailed view of the spatial distribution of the pollutant. Even then, any pollution plume emanating from a point source may not be properly understood, particularly in strongly heterogeneous media or in situations where sub surface structures, such as building foundations, complicate the groundwater flow regime. Indeed, the carrying out of pollution investigations in built-up industrial areas is made difficult, almost by definition, by the presence of buildings and extensive paved areas.

Once the extent of pollution is assessed, clean-up of the site can commence, but again problems of non-ideal conditions and deciding at what point the aquifer is deemed to be restored arise. In future years, the legacy of past polluting practices will engage regulators and clean-up agencies in considerable lucrative work in locating and dealing with groundwater contamination.

Box 13.4 Non-aqueous phase liquid pollution of groundwater

Chlorinated solvents were developed in the early years of this century as a safe, non-flammable alternative to petroleum-based decreasing solvents in the metal processing industry. Until about 1970, trichloroethene (TCE) and tetrachloroethene (PCE) were predominantly used, the latter also in dry cleaning application. Both solvents were recognized early on as potentially harmful to humans in both liquid and vapour forms, and in the 1960s both began to be replaced by the less toxic 1,1,1-

result of careless handling, accidental spillages, misuse, poor disposal practice and inadequately designed, poorly maintained or badly operated equipment.

Chlorinated solvents are dense liquids that are volatile and of low viscosity, and consequently are more mobile than water in a porous medium. On entering the ground, solvents migrate downwards and through the water-table whereupon their migration is halted by the base of the aquifer, or by some other

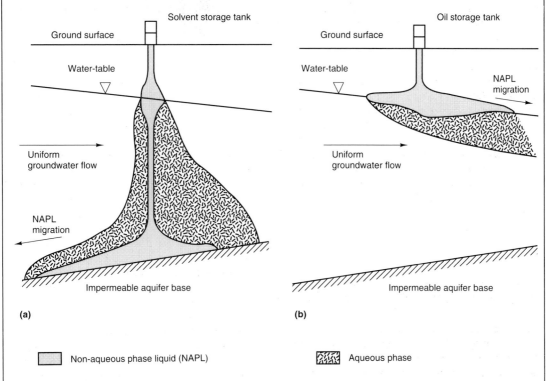

Behaviour of organic contaminants in groundwater. The chlorinated solvent contaminant shown in (a) has a density greater than water and so sinks to the base of the aquifer. Here, transport of the non-aqueous phase is controlled by the slope of the base of the aquifer, while the dissolved aqueous phase moves in the direction of groundwater flow. The hydrocarbon contaminant shown in (b) has a density less than water and so floats on the water-table. In this case, transport of the non-aqueous phase is controlled by the slope of the water-table, while the dissolved aqueous phase moves in the direction of groundwater flow.

trichloroethane (TCA) and 1,1,2-trichlorotrifluoroethane (Freon 113). From the mid-1970s concern was expressed about the potentially carcinogenic effects of TCE, PCE and carbon tetrachloride (CTC) at trace level concentrations in drinking water, and the WHO set guide values of 30 µg/l for TCE, 10 µg/l for PCE and 3 µg/l for CTC.

Sources of solvent contamination arise during the delivery of solvents to the works, through use and from the disposal of distillation sludge. Solvents escape to the subsurface environment mainly as a

intermediate impermeable barrier, as illustrated in the figure. Residual amounts of solvent are left in the pore spaces through which the solvent body has passed. TCE and PCE are not completely insoluble and the non-aqueous phase becomes surrounded by groundwater contaminated with dissolved solvent. TCE and PCE degrade extremely slowly, and some of the degradation products may be more toxic, soluble and mobile than the parent compounds. For

continued

Box 13.4 continued

example tetrachloroethane can be progressively de-halogenated, first to trichloroethane, then to dichloroethane, and finally to carcinogenic vinyl chloride.

Refined mineral oils include petrol, aviation fuel, diesel and heating oils. As a group, their physical characteristics are variable, particularly that of viscosity; but all have a density less than water, and a heterogeneous composition dominated by pure hydrocarbons. In the context of groundwater, regulation is aimed primarily at taste and odour control.

The WHO guide level is 10 mg/l. Sources of contamination include oil storage depots, cross-country oil pipelines, service stations, tanker transport and airfields.

Mineral oils behave in a similar manner to chlorinated solvents, except that, as shown in the figure, by reason of their density, they float on the water-table. In this situation, migration is controlled by the water-table gradient. Mineral oils are capable of degradation under aerobic conditions, although the rate of degradation is slow.

Groundwater contamination in Nassau County

Infiltration of metal plating waste through disposal basins in Nassau County on Long Island, New York, has formed a plume of contaminated groundwater since the early 1940s (Figure 13.4). The plume contains elevated chromium and cadmium concentrations. The area is within an undulating glacial outwash plain, and there are two major hydrogeological units: the Upper glacial aquifer of Late Pleistocene age; and the Magothy aquifer of Late Cretaceous age, which supplies all local municipal water supplies.

The Upper glacial aquifer is between 24 and 43 m thick, with a water-table from 0 to 8 m below ground level. The aquifer comprises medium to coarse sand and lenses of fine sand and gravel. Stratification of the

Box 13.5 Heavy metal pollution of groundwater

The heavy metals of concern in drinking water supplies are, to choose a few, nickel, zinc, lead, copper, mercury, cadmium and chromium. In the form of their reduced species and in acidic waters, heavy metals remain mobile in groundwater; but in soils and aquifers that have a pH buffering capacity, and under oxidizing conditions, heavy metals and readily adsorbed or exchanged by clays, oxides and other minerals.

Heavy metal pollution of groundwater therefore becomes a particular threat under extreme conditions such as in acidic mine waters, or in leachate beneath landfill sites where there is a high concentration of fatty acids. Other sources of heavy metals include, in general, the metal processing industries, particularly electro-plating works with their concentrated acidic electrolytes, and other metal surface treatment processes.

deposits means that the vertical permeability is up to five to ten times less than the horizontal permeability.

As part of the historical investigation in the South Farmingdale-Massapequa area, a number of test wells were installed in 1962, driven to depths ranging from 2.4 to 23 m below ground level. Water samples were collected at depth intervals of 1.5 m by hand pump during the driving operations. The results of this investigation are shown in Figure 13.4, and define a pollution plume that is about 1300 m long, up to 300 m wide, and as much as 21 m thick. The upper surface of the plume is generally less than 3 m below the water-table. The plume is thickest along its longitudinal axis, the principal path of flow from the basins, and is thinnest along its east and west boundaries. The plume appears to be entirely within the Upper glacial aquifer.

Differences in chemical quality of water within the plume may reflect the varying types of contamination introduced in the past. In general, groundwater in the southern part of the plume reflects conditions prior to 1948 when extraction of chromium from the plating wastes, before disposal to the basins, was commenced. Since the start of chromium treatment, the maximum observed concentrations in the plume have decreased from about 40 mg/l in 1949 to about 10 mg/l in 1962. The WHO guide value for chromium is 0.05 mg/l. Cadmium concentrations have apparently decreased in some places and increased in others, and peak concentrations do not coincide with those of chromium. These differences are probably due partly to changes in the chemical character of the treated effluent over the years and partly to the influence of hydrological and geological factors. A test site near the disposal basins recorded as much as 10 mg/l of cadmium in 1964. The WHO guide value for cadmium is 0.005 mg/l.

The pattern of movement of the plating waste is vertically downwards from the disposal basins, through the unsaturated zone, and into the saturated

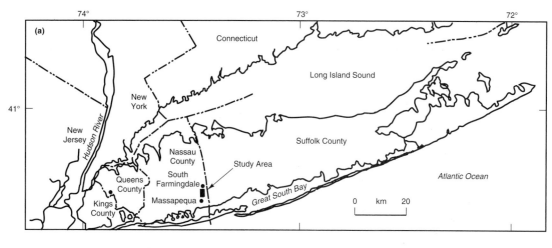

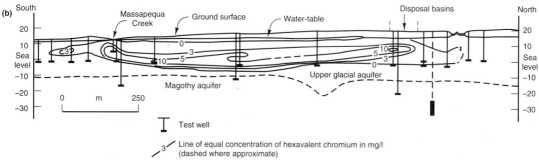

Fig 13.4 Groundwater contamination by metal plating wastes, Long Island, New York. The location of the investigation area is shown in (a) and a cross-section of the distribution of the hexavalent chromium plume in the Upper glacial aquifer in 1962, South Farmingdale-Massapequa area, Nassau County, is illustrated in (b). (Source: Adapted from Ku, 1980.)

zone of the Upper glacial aquifer. From here, most of the groundwater moves horizontally southwards, with an average velocity of about 0.5 m/day, and discharges to the Massapequa Creek. Solute transport computer modelling indicates that with complete cessation of all discharges, it would take 7–11 years for the plume to move out of the area.

Analysis of cores of aquifer material along the axis of the plume showed that the median concentrations of chromium and cadmium per kg of aquifer material are, respectively, 7.5 and 1.1 mg, and the maximum concentrations are, respectively, 19 and 2.3 mg. Adsorption occurs on to hydrous iron oxide coatings on the aquifer sands. The ability of the aquifer material to adsorb heavy metals complicates the prediction of the movement and concentration of the plume. Furthermore, metals may continue to leach from the aquifer material into the groundwater long after cessation of plating waste discharges, necessitating continued monitoring of the site.

Groundwater protection in industrialized countries

The adoption of a groundwater protection policy in an industrialized country, and to some extent a developing country, will be influenced by the hydrogeological characteristics of the aquifer. In particular a distinction can be made between those aquifers in which groundwater flow is predominantly intergranular, and those where fracture flow is significant.

In unconsolidated, porous, permeable sediments, groundwater flow velocities are such that groundwater protection areas, based on delay times of groundwater in aquifers, achieve realistic dimensions. The advantage of a delay time strategy is that it can be related to economic and technical factors, and also to the behaviour of contaminants underground. Differences between countries in respect of technical, socio-economic and legislative matters mean that an exactly uniform system of water supply protection cannot be achieved. An example of one such system, as applied in the Netherlands, is described here.

In the Netherlands, abstraction of drinking water supplies is concentrated within 240 wellfields tapping mainly uniform, horizontally layered aquifers of unconsolidated sands and clays. In principle, the entire recharge area in the vicinity of the wellfields should be protected, but this is unrealistic on socioeconomic grounds. In this situation, a system of zoning of the recharge area, or the protection area, is desirable. Zonation is dependent on soil properties and the behaviour of the contaminant, and also takes into account short and long-term objectives.

The zoning system used in the Netherlands is shown in Figure 13.5 and Table 13.2. The first zone is based on a delay time of 50 days to protect against pathogenic bacteria and viruses and rapidly degrading chemicals; it extends some 30–150 m from an individual borehole. For the sake of the continuity of water supply in the event of a severe pollution incident requiring remedial action, and in order to exclude public health risks, a delay time of at least 10 years is needed in the next zone. In many cases, even 10 years is not sufficient to guarantee the continuity of safe water supplies and, with associated economic reasons, a protection zone of 25 years is necessary. These two protection zones, extending to about 800 and 1200 m from the borehole, constitute the protection area.

The delay times should only be calculated for the saturated zone of the aquifer. Only when the purifying or attenuating properties, or the impermeable nature of any covering layers, are assured can the vertical delay time of the infiltrating polluted water be included in the calculation. Outside the defined protection area it is still important to legislate to protect the more remote recharge areas, especially against any severe or persistent type of contamination.

Although hydrogeological factors are important in groundwater protection, restrictions on land use and human activities are also required. The types of restriction and the criteria for their definition are interrelated. Historically, most attention has been paid to pathogens; but nowadays the tendency is to concentrate more on chemical pollutants. The source of pollution, whether point or diffuse, and its underground behaviour not only form criteria for defining the dimensions of the protection zones, but also dictate the types of restriction to be applied. The types of restriction, which become more severe as the borehole is approached, are illustrated in Table 13.2.

The European experience in the definition of protection zones based on minimum aquifer residence times (delay times) from either tracer tests or using groundwater computer models, or a combination of both, has proved effective, particularly in porous, permeable aquifers. A similar approach in fractured strata is less successful. The higher groundwater velocities and variable nature of such aquifers mean that protection areas will be large and irregular in shape. Typically, available data for defining the areas will often be poor and possibly conflicting. Very large protection areas will not suit other socio-economic interests since it will be perceived that the interest of water protection is being unreasonably favoured. On a world-wide scale, fractured strata probably predominate over non-fractured and so it is necessary to devise a rational system for approaching the problem.

A modified approach to groundwater protection is required based on an inner protection zone, a regional protection policy and individual investigations. This

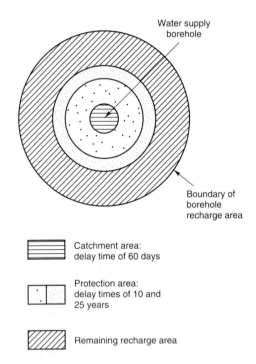

Water supply borehole

Boundary of borehole recharge area

Catchment area: delay time of 60 days

Protection area: delay times of 10 and 25 years

Remaining recharge area

Fig 13.5 A suggested zoning of land-use restrictions to form the basis of an aquifer protection policy. The methodology was developed in the Netherlands, and is suitable for porous, permeable strata where groundwater flow is predominantly intergranular. (*Source*: Adapted from van Waegeningh, 1985.)

Table 13.2 Restrictions in protection areas in the Netherlands

Catchment area	Protection area	Remaining recharge area
60 days' delay time	10 and 25 years' delay time	Rules on soil and groundwater protection practices
Protection against pathogenic bacteria and viruses and against chemical pollution sources	Protection against hardly degradable chemicals	
Only activities relating to water supply are admissible	Activities generally not admissible, e.g. • Transport and storage of dangerous goods • Industries • Waste disposal sites • Building • Military activities • Intensive agriculture and cattle breeding • Gravel, sand or limestone quarries • Waste water disposal	

Source: Adapted from van Waegeningh (1985).

combined approach, looking at the regional and site-specific aspects as part of one integrated exercise, strives to achieve a realistic balance of community interests while encompassing a wide range of hydrogeological situations.

In the inner protection zone, the high priority given to the protection of existing potable water sources requires that a protection zone is established based on a residence time of up to 50 to 60 days.

The remainder of the area should be divided into groundwater vulnerability classes which are defined to provide protection to the groundwater resources outside the inner protection zone. The vulnerability classes should be based on various hydrogeological, soil and geological criteria.

The value of regional maps based upon vulnerability classes is in their provision of information for policy and planning purposes. Properly used, they can encourage the development of potentially polluting practices in those areas where it will present least concern, allowing a balance of interests to be achieved. The regulation of diffuse pollution can be readily related to aquifer vulnerability zones.

The aquifer vulnerability map provides a regional picture, but is insufficiently detailed at a local scale to demonstrate whether or not an individual, potential pollution source is a threat to the groundwater resource. It does not, of itself, provide protection to the aquifer; but it does provide levels of concern. The protection comes through requiring scrutiny of all proposals of potentially polluting practices by individual investigations. Such investigations have traditionally relied significantly on tracer tests to prove a borehole connection and to measure travel times. In fractured media this approach is difficult, since flow paths are unpredictable. However, if the investigation is related to one specific pollution threat at a known location, it is much easier to undertake realistic tracer work to determine the limiting travel times to groundwater supply sources, springs or rivers.

Conclusions

The study of groundwater pollution is a multidisciplinary subject requiring skills in physical and chemical hydrogeology, theoretical and practical experience of pollution incidents, and the understanding of the activities and processes giving rise to the pollution. Knowledge of the surrounding environment, particularly soil type and climatic conditions, is necessary in predicting the vulnerability of any underlying aquifer to groundwater contamination.

In translating these skills and knowledge into policies aimed at protecting groundwater resources, the cost of protecting water supplies must be balanced against other socio-economic factors, and whether the protection policy is to be defined for a developing or an industrialized country. Importantly, and as demonstrated by this chapter, no groundwater pollution investigation or protection policy strategy should be undertaken or formulated without first having a clear understanding of the geology of a region. Geological properties are fundamental in governing the nature of groundwater flow. In particular, the flow mechanism, whether it be intergranular or within fractures, must be established, as well as the aquifer boundaries and groundwater conditions determined by geological structure. Such considerations should be uppermost in the minds of groundwater practitioners and administrators alike.

References

Foster, S.S.D. (1985) Groundwater protection in developing countries. In G. Matthess, S.S.D. Foster and A.C. Skinner (Eds) *Theoretical background, hydrogeology and practice of groundwater protection zones.* Hanover: Verlag Heinz Heiss, pp. 167–200.

Jackson, R.E. (Ed.) (1980) *Aquifer contamination and protection.* Paris: UNESCO.

Ku, H.F.H. (1980) Ground-water contamination by metal-plating wastes, Long Island, New York, USA. In R.E. Jackson (Ed.) *Aquifer contamination and protection.* Paris: UNESCO, pp. 310–17.

Van Waegeningh, H.G. (1985) Protection of groundwater quality in porous permeable rocks. In G. Matthess, S.S.D. Foster and A.C. Skinner (Eds) *Theoretical background, hydrogeology and practice of groundwater protection zones.* Hanover: Verlag Heinz Heise, pp. 111–21.

Further reading

There are a number of textbooks dealing with the physical and chemical principles of hydrogeology which also contain sections on contaminant hydrogeology. Of these, R.A. Freeze and J.A. Cherry (1979) *Groundwater* (Prentice Hall, New Jersey) and P.A. Domenico and F.W. Schwartz (1990) *Physical and chemical hydrogeology* (Wiley, New York) are comprehensive treatments of the subjects. C.W. Fetter (1993) *Contaminant hydrogeology* (Macmillan, New York) deals specifically with contaminant hydrogeology. A more easily understood text for those requiring a rigorous, yet immediately accessible, read is M. Price (1985) *Introducing groundwater* (Allen & Unwin, London). A discussion of the theoretical and practical aspects of aquifer contamination and protection, together with a compendium of case studies of groundwater pollution, is contained in a UNESCO publication edited by Jackson (1980). Lastly, the International Association of Hydrogeologists publish a volume, edited by G. Matthess, S.S.D. Foster and A.C. Skinner (1985) called *Theoretical background hydrogeology and practice of groundwater protection zones* (Hanover, Verlag Heinz Heise) and this is recommended for those approaching this topic for the first time, especially the chapter by Foster (Groundwater protection in developing countries) and H.G. Van Waegeningh (Protection of groundwater quality in porous permeable rocks).

Also see J. Briscoe (1993) When the cup is half full: improving water and sanitation services in the developing world, *Environment*, **35**(4), 6–10, 28–36; and Ku (1980).

CHAPTER 14

Marine and estuarine pollution

ALASTAIR GRANT AND TIM JICKELLS

Much of the chapter that follows is an exercise in exploration and discovery. The next major UN convention will be one on the protection of the oceans, because we now know that the oceans play a vital part in absorbing and emitting atmospheric gases, dissipating energy into the northern and southern latitudes, regulating bio-geo-chemical cycles, and providing vast reservoirs of life in complex food chains. The oceans are probably more important for regulating the biosphere than many realize, hence the need for continued scientific monitoring of the physics and chemistry of ocean–atmosphere relationships.

Yet monitoring marine ecology is fraught with difficulty. When unusual plankton blooms occur, as in the North Sea case reported in this chapter, it is very tempting to blame human agency. But unless there is good historical record, or unless we have comprehensive monitoring and screening, it is quite possible that plankton may have been subject to regular (or irregular) blooms, or that changes in the NE Atlantic or climate may be a significant cause of environmental variability. In short, we do not know. Toxicological studies of a chemical cost $10 000 just for measures of bioconcentration and acute toxicity, and $100 000 to $1 million for a fuller, but still incomplete, assessment. Clearly the toxicity of chemical interactions in food chains will only be partially understood.

Species interactions are so complicated, so rooted in relationships that are not well understood, that only an exhaustive and expensive monitoring programme could unravel all the connections. This is obviously impossible except in the most precious and confined of ecosystems. Ecologists tend to look for indicator or keystone species which provide a measure of conditions favouring or afflicting other species. But sadly few species are true indicators, and even fewer are indicators from place to place and over time. So the very basis of ecological monitoring is put in question. Add to that the subtle changes in environmental conditions caused by cyclical variations in energy, or chemical additions through human interference, and you will readily appreciate how troublesome ecological prediction is becoming. Finally, we are beginning to realize just how random, or chaotic, population fluctuations actually are. McGarvin (1994) cites a study of barnacles that indicated that the number of adults was determined by the number of larvae that survived their plankton stage and settled on the rocks. These populations vary widely every year and cannot be predicted with any accuracy without very large databases running for hundreds of years.

This has profound implications, not just for theoretical ecology, but also for pollution control policy and international co-ordination. For example, the variability of naturally occurring heavy metals is quite large, but not fully known. It makes no sense to identify threshold levels of anthropogenic inputs of these metals, because the thresholds, or critical loads, may never be known with any accuracy.

All this implies that even greater weight will be given to the precautionary principle in the years ahead. This will force pollution control agencies to adopt more rigorously the common burden principle of equivalence of effort, regardless of the 'scientific' justification for differential treatment. It will also place much more reliance on 'up the pipe' pollution prevention at source, utilizing techniques such as life-cycle analysis and whole firm environmental management services. The introductory essay to this section suggests a transition that has barely begun to run its course.

Introduction

Pollution of oceans, coastal waters and estuaries is an issue of great public concern. It ranks highest in public opinion surveys, with over 90 per cent of respondents stating that it is a serious or very serious problem. The subject was brought to the forefront of public attention, at least in Europe, by two phenomena which occurred in the summer of 1988, a viral epidemic that killed large numbers of seals and a bloom of toxic algae in Scandinavian waters.

In April of that year, near the Danish island of Anholt, nearly 100 pups of the common or harbour seal were born prematurely. Shortly afterwards sick adult seals were observed on the Danish and Swedish coasts of the Kategatt and dead bodies began to be washed up on beaches. The epidemic then spread rapidly round the Danish coast and along the Waddensee, reaching the UK in August, where the first cases were observed in the Wash. By October, dead and dying seals were being found along much of the UK coastline. The immediate cause of the deaths was a virus related to canine distemper and named Phocine Distemper Virus (PDV). More than 16 000 dead common seals were washed up on beaches and best estimates are that at least half the population of this species died. The grey seal was less severely affected, and only about 200 bodies were reported. The big doleful eyes of seals have always attracted public sympathy. Pictures of large numbers of bodies being removed from beaches were regularly featured on television news and the events achieved a very high level of public awareness. Fundraising appeals by newspapers in the UK and West Germany raised hundreds of thousands of pounds to save the seals, although whether the tabloid press had any viable proposals to tackle the epidemic was never evident.

On 9 May 1988, the owner of a rainbow trout farm in Gullmarfjorden near Götenborg on the west coast of Sweden reported that his fish were showing signs of stress. He observed a yellowish colour to the water which proved to be due to a small flagellated alga *Chrysochromulina polylepis*. Over the next three weeks, the algal bloom drifted north and west along the Swedish and Norwegian coasts, reaching the coast off Stavanger by 26 May. By mid-June the bloom had dissipated. The bloom caused the deaths of caged salmon and trout at several farms in Norway and Sweden, and divers reported extensive mortality of marine invertebrates. Some wild fish were killed, but in general these were able to avoid the bloom, which was concentrated in the surface layers.

The immediate assumption of many was that these two phenomena were the consequence of years of discharging sewage and other effluents to the North Sea. The bloom of *Chrysochromulina* was attributed to eutrophication, while the PDV epidemic was attributed to the action of polychlorinated biphenyls (PCBs) and other chemicals suppressing the immune systems of seals. In neither case is the evidence for a human-caused contribution strong, although the lack of causal proof does emphasize the need for detailed understanding of the complex coastal marine ecosystem and the effects of human activities upon it. Here we review some of these important issues. Many of our examples come from the North Sea. This is a shallow shelf sea and is largely surrounded by the land masses of eight wealthy and industrialized nations, so it is particularly vulnerable to pollution. It is also probably the most intensively studied area of coastal waters. Our conclusions are, however, of relevance globally.

Contamination and pollution

An important distinction is that between *contamination* and *pollution*. The most commonly used definitions of these terms are attributable to an organization called GESAMP (a UN group of experts in the field of marine pollution).

Contamination is the presence of elevated concentrations of substances in water, sediments or organisms.

Pollution is the

> introduction by man, directly or indirectly, of substances or energy into the marine environment (including estuaries) resulting in deleterious effects such as harm to living resources, hazards to human health, hindrance of marine activities, including fishing, impairing quality for use of seawater and reduction of amenities. (GESAMP, 1982)

Clearly all pollution involves contamination, but the converse is not necessarily true. Using these definitions allows us to divide the process of identifying pollution damage into two separate stages. The first problem is the chemical measurement of the contaminant. For various toxic substances the concentration may be very low, e.g. 1 atom in 10^9–10^{12} of water and salt. The second problem is to determine whether this contamination is having any deleterious effects on the environment, its biota or potential users. The first of these tasks is the simpler, although even that is not always straightforward. To be able to determine whether contamination with a particular chemical has taken place one needs to be able to define a baseline – the environmental concentrations before anthropogenic (human-derived) inputs began. For synthetic organic compounds, such as PCBs, artificial radionuclides and a number of other substances, the baseline is zero. Other substances, such as heavy metals and oil, occur naturally, and considerable effort may be required to define a baseline.

For contaminants in sediments, there are a number of options available. One option is to seek to identify environments that are comparable in all aspects except degree of human influence, then to use the pristine environments as a baseline for the contaminated ones. This is sometimes possible, but in some parts of the world there are very few areas that are untouched by humans, and it is always difficult to be sure that the different environments are truly comparable. Another option, used particularly for heavy metals, is to use concentrations in rocks which are assumed to have been deposited in similar environments. For example, concentrations estimated by geochemists for 'average shale' are often used as a baseline with which to compare estuarine muds. A final possibility is to try to obtain pre-industrial sediments from the area that is being studied by sampling former estuarine channels or areas of reclaimed land. This gives data that are most likely to be comparable with modern samples, but requires the assumption that there has been no change in metal concentrations after deposition.

The approach of using primitive sediments from the same environment to provide a baseline can be extended to the construction of entire contamination histories. In a few cases, samples have been collected at known dates in the past and stored (see Figure 14.1), but this is unusual. However, it is often possible to identify sites where sediment accumulation has taken place continuously since before the industrial period. Such sites occur in many estuaries and some distance offshore, where water is deep enough for the influence of waves to be minimal. An undisturbed column of sediment can be extracted from such sites by coring, then dividing into sections where each is analysed for concentrations of contaminants. When concentrations become constant below a particular depth, this is assumed to represent the baseline. If the cores can be dated (using radioisotopes, artefacts or pollen) then a dated contamination history can be constructed. Figure 14.2 shows an example of this for the Bristol Channel, UK, showing a marked

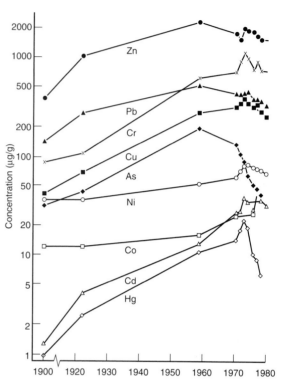

Fig 14.1 Metal contamination history of the River Rhine, based on analyses of sediments collected by Netherlands Institute for Soil Fertility. (Source: Salomons and de Groot, 1978.)

increase of lead concentrations during the 20th century.

For contaminants in surface-waters of the ocean and in biota, it is much more difficult to define baselines. As we shall describe below, there is a substantial input of many contaminants from the atmosphere, and this takes place even at sites well away from population centres. There are therefore no entirely pristine environments that can provide baselines. Consequently, it is difficult to be sure what the concentrations of metals or petroleum hydrocarbons in biota or seawater were before they were modified by human actions.

Ways of detecting pollution

The traditional approach to detecting the effects of pollution in the field has been ecological monitoring. Samples of the biota are collected from a large number of places, and concentrations of contaminants are also measured at the same sites. The biotic data are then

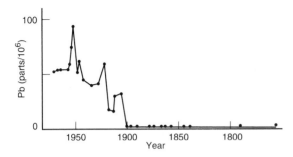

Fig 14.2 Lead contamination history of sediments in the Bristol Channel. Based on sediment core dated using ^{210}Pb chronology, with natural lead levels subtracted. (Source: Hamilton and Clifton, 1979.)

analysed to see if there are any signs of deleterious effects at any sites, and if so whether these are correlated with contaminant concentrations. This presents two sorts of problems. First, the marine environment can be very variable even in the absence of anthropogenic disturbances (see Figure 14.3 and discussion of eutrophication below). Second, the contamination at any particular site is a complex 'cocktail' of chemicals, so even if disturbed and undisturbed environments can be distinguished, it is difficult to establish which

contaminants are producing the effects. Correlations cannot prove causality, though they can be used to test hypotheses.

One approach is to carry out toxicity tests in the laboratory, then to try to extrapolate the results of these to the field. This extrapolation procedure is not straightforward, because the marine environment is far more complex than a laboratory glass dish in its physics, chemistry and biology. Contaminants may be complexed by organic compounds in the water or adsorbed by particulate matter. A pollutant may perturb the competitive interaction between species. It is difficult to predict which of these effects may be important in a particular situation and impossible at present to predict their consequences. The one thing which all the work on laboratory toxicity testing does allow us to say is that concentrations of contaminants are rarely high enough to cause acute toxicity (Figure 14.4). This means that we need to look for subtler 'sublethal' effects.

In recent years a variety of methods has been developed to look for these more subtle effects in the field. Most involve the measurement of biochemical or physiological indices and it is assumed that impaired performance on one of these indices reflects impaired ecological performance. Perhaps the most widely used

Box 14.1

Sampling marine pollution may involve collecting samples e.g. setting marine particles deep in oceans (left hand figure) or collecting deep ocean sediment (right hand figure). In both cases the critical research issues are the selection of the sampling frame and the accuracy of the measurement. The sampling frame has to recognize the variability of physical processes in both space and time under conditions

of uncertainty. Sampling therefore has to be carefully representative and subsequently averaged. Error bars are important to display 'freak data' which may turn out to be of crucial significance. Measurement accuracy is critical when concentrations of parts per trillion are being recorded. The avoidance of contamination is a major objective and requires meticulous preparation and replication.

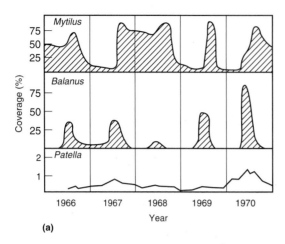

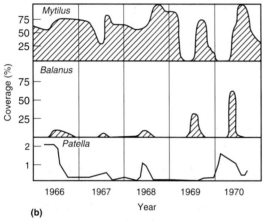

(a)

(b)

Fig 14.3 Natural fluctuations of numbers of marine organisms can be large. Data on percentage cover of mussels (*Mytilus*), barnacles (*Balanus*) and limpets (*Patella*) at two sites on the North Yorkshire coast, 1966–70. (Source: Lewis, 1972.)

of these is the effect on the *scope for growth* in the bivalve *Mytilus edulis*, namely the energy which an individual has left over to devote to growth after subtracting respiration and excretion. This involves determining the energy budget of individual animals by measuring feeding and respiration rates and assimilation efficiency. The assay can be used either by collecting animals from different sites, or by placing animals with a common origin at sites along a supposed pollution gradient (this can be done using cages attached to buoys when monitoring conditions in open water). The animals are then returned to the laboratory and scope for growth measured in standardized conditions. In

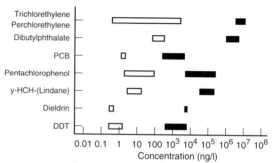

Fig 14.4 Environmental concentrations of most contaminants (open bars) are well below those necessary to cause acute toxicity (black bars). (Source: Ernst, 1980.)

uncontaminated seawater, scope for growth is relatively high, but its value declines in response to relatively low concentrations of contaminants either because respiration rate increases or feeding rate decreases. Unlike many other of the physiological and biochemical indices, this has the advantage that it seems to be measuring something of direct ecological importance.

Sources of contaminants to the North Sea

If we are to understand the environmental condition of a marine system it is first necessary to describe the inputs to that system. Only if these have been significantly perturbed is environmental change likely. Inputs to marine systems from land arise from many sources: here we attempt to document the major ones.

Rivers bring material to the seas both in dissolved and particulate phases and the balance between these two can change during mixing between marine and freshwaters due to the adsorption or precipitation of dissolved components or the desorption of components from particles under the rapidly changing salinity characteristics of estuaries. The nature of the mixing between fresh-and saltwaters and of many other processes (including primary production) is further influenced by rivers since the freshwater is less dense than seawater and will thus tend to float out over it unless turbulent mixing can overcome this stratification. Both dissolved and particulate fluxes in rivers are sensitive to change as a result of increasing inputs within the catchment from direct discharges or

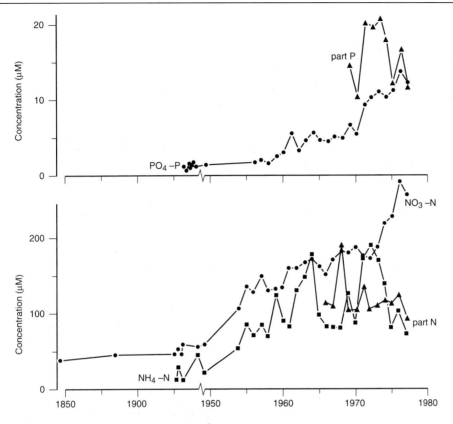

Fig 14.5 Increase of nitrate (NO₃⁻), ammonium (NH₄⁺), particulate nitrogen (part N), dissolved phosphorus (PO₄–P) and particulate phosphorus (part P) concentrations in the river Rhine. (Source: von Bennekrom and Salomons 1980.)

increased erosion, or decreasing inputs due to damming removing water, allowing settlement of solids or increased biological activity.

In Figure 14.5 the increase of nitrate, ammonium and phosphate in the Rhine over recent years is shown as an example of the effect of increasing inputs to river systems. In the case of nitrate the increase is thought to be the result of increasing use of land for agriculture and more intensive agricultural practices including deep ploughing and extensive, and relatively inefficient, use of fertilizers. This pattern is similar to that in most other European rivers (e.g. Figure 14.6) and results in current nitrate concentrations considerably higher than they naturally would be. By contrast, the effect of damming is illustrated by the Nile where the total water flows have been altered and, more dramatically, the peak discharge reduced. The dams have generated electricity, allowed irrigation and prevented flood damage but have also lowered fertility in soils dependent on the flood-deposited silt and reduced the

fisheries of the coastal waters off the Nile delta. Since river transport is episodic, with, for example, more particulate matter transported under high flow conditions, it is hard to obtain reliable estimates of riverine inputs to estuaries.

Atmospheric inputs can bypass the complex removal processes in estuaries and reach the open coastal and oceanic waters direct. The atmosphere can be an efficient transporter of dust and gases to coastal waters since many land-based activities release material to the atmosphere, including dust blown from fields, gases released from agricultural wastes, combustion processes of all kinds and many industrial activities. In addition, there is a large-scale natural cycle transporting material through the atmosphere and contributing to the inputs to coastal waters. In many areas of the world close to major source regions, it is now clear that human activity is discharging material through the atmosphere in comparable amounts to or even exceeding natural fluxes. Atmospheric concentrations vary

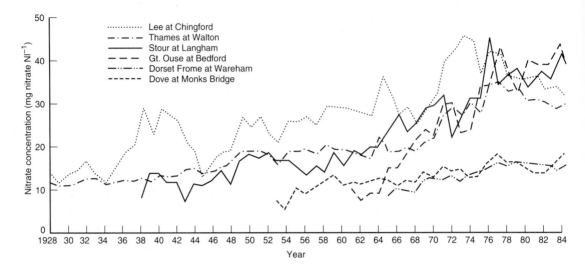

Fig 14.6 Increase of nitrate concentrations in several UK rivers. (Source: Royal Society, 1983.)

rapidly on short timescales owing to changes in wind direction and rainfall, making it very hard to obtain accurate estimations of average concentrations without extensive sampling. In addition, estimating inputs requires a knowledge of rainfall over the sea and/or dry deposition processes at sea. Both are poorly understood and monitored.

As well as these two major inputs, there is a wide variety of other inputs which are of significance in particular areas and for particular compounds. Some of these, such as direct industrial and sewage discharges and the dumping of sewage sludge and dredge spoil, are closely monitored in most industrialized countries and the amounts of material discharged are relatively well known. Others, such as losses from *in situ* corrosion and coastal erosion, are very poorly understood.

Despite the uncertainties involved, estimates of inputs to the North Sea from the various sources are available (Table 14.1) and they illustrate several important points. Firstly, despite the considerable attention directed towards them, direct discharges are not of great quantitative significance, though this is not to deny their considerable impact in the local area of dumping. The second point is the considerable importance of atmospheric inputs for many components. These, along with riverine inputs, dominate land-based sources.

For many of the components considered, including nitrogen and lead, emissions have indeed increased

dramatically in recent years, though for lead these are now decreasing even more rapidly as the use of unleaded petrol grows. The magnitudes of the fluxes of many synthetic organic components are poorly known but since there are no natural sources of these compounds, their very existence is testimony to

Table 14.1 Estimates of rates of input of selected elements to the North Sea (tonnes per year)

Input route	Element		
	N^a	Pb	Hg
Rivers	1 000 000[b]	920–980	20–21
Atmosphere	400 000[b]	2600–7400	10–30
Direct discharge	95 000[b]	170	5
Sewage sludge	11 700[b]	100[b]	0.6[b]
Dredge spoil	–[c]	2000[b]	17[b]
Industrial waste	–	200[b]	0.2[b]
Incineration at sea	–	–	Trace[b]
Inputs from transport of waters from offshore	7 705 000[d]		

[a]These N fluxes exclude nitrogen gas, because it cannot in general be utilized by algae, and are dominated by nitrate and ammonia.
[b]Maximum estimate.
[c]No data are available, but likely to be small.
[d]Nelissen and Stefels (1988).
Source: Department of the Environment (1987).

anthropogenic sources. However, there are still many elements and chemical species with large natural fluxes and relatively little interference from industrial activity (e.g. aluminium) for which the fluxes still approach their natural levels.

A final important point from Table 14.1 is that, while the riverine and atmospheric inputs of nitrate and ammonia have increased dramatically over the last 50 years or so, the input from offshore is still the major source, though a particularly difficult one to quantify.

In order to determine the effects of recent increases in inputs, it is necessary to know not only the size and form of all the inputs but also their location. Thus again considering nitrogen, the riverine inputs are centred in the southern North Sea where the big rivers discharge (Figure 14.7). The atmospheric inputs are less focused in this area but are probably higher in the southern area closest to industrial and urban sources. Thus the extra inputs are concentrated in the southern shallowest, least well-flushed regions, while the natural input from offshore is concentrated in the northern region. It is therefore no simple task to take input information alone and convert it into an assessment of the environmental condition of the North Sea, or indeed other coastal regions.

Environmental damage by specific chemicals

PCBs

PCBs are organic molecules with a structure that includes two linked benzene rings with a varying number of chlorine atoms attached. PCBs are very stable to heat and burning and have been used widely in electrical equipment, paints, plastics and adhesives.

PCBs are slow to be broken down once inside the bodies of organisms. They are also fat-soluble, so are readily absorbed into the body and then tend to accumulate in fatty tissues rather than being excreted. In animals, the majority of PCBs in the diet will be absorbed into the body. The majority of energy that an animal derives from its food is used to fuel activity and maintenance, and on average only about 10 per cent of the food is converted into body tissue. If all of the PCBs in the diet are absorbed, an animal will end up with concentrations of PCB in its tissues that are ten times those in its food. Food chains usually have several links

in them, so concentrations of PCBs in top carnivores, such as seals and seabirds, can become very high – a phenomenon known as bioaccumulation.

PCBs have been implicated as a cause of mass mortalities in seabirds, and in the decline of seal populations in the Baltic. However, the most convincing evidence of an impact by PCBs comes from the Dutch Waddensee. Between 1950 and 1975, numbers of the common seal *Phoca vitulina* in the western part of the Waddensee declined from more than 3000 individuals to fewer than 500. The production of pups by seals in Dutch waters also declined sharply in the same period. A comparison of body burdens of heavy metals and organochlorine compounds between the Dutch seals and those from the more northern parts of the Waddensee showed that only levels of PCBs differed significantly between the two. In an experiment carried out at Texel in the Netherlands, two groups of 12 seals were fed diets of fish containing different levels of PCBs. Seals fed on fish caught in the Waddensee that had high concentrations of PCBs showed reduced reproductive success when compared with the group fed on fish from the north-east Atlantic. So there seems good evidence that PCBs are having an adverse effect on seal reproduction in the Waddensee. However, in the PDV epidemic of 1988, the first seals to be affected were not those in the Waddensee, but those in the rather less contaminated Kattegatt, suggesting that PCBs were not an important contributary factor.

Tributyl tin oxide

If any hard substrate is placed into the sea, it is rapidly colonized by a range of animals and plants commonly labelled 'fouling organisms'. An analogy would be the way in which any piece of open ground on land is rapidly colonized by weeds. If the hard substrate is the hull of a ship, this colonization by fouling organisms replaces a smooth surface, which has relatively little friction with the water, with a much rougher surface. A well-developed fouling community reduces the maximum speed of a ship and increases fuel consumption considerably. To try to avoid this difficulty, the hulls of ships are usually painted with an antifouling paint, which prevents or reduces the settlement of fouling organisms. Traditional antifouling paints contained copper, arsenic and other highly toxic substances. In consequence, such paints required considerable safety precautions when being applied. In the 1960s a new

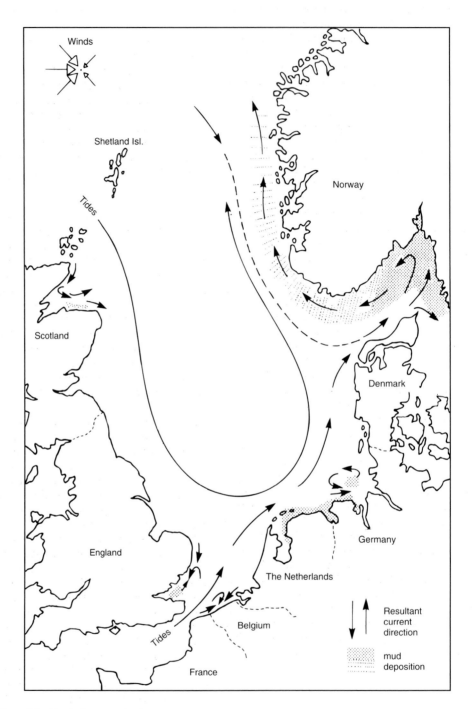

Fig 14.7 Map of the North Sea, showing main features of water circulation. (Source: Adapted from Eisma and Irion in Salomons et al., 1988.)

type of antifouling paint was introduced, with tributyl tin oxide (TBTO, or more usually just TBT) as the active ingredient. These new paints appeared to be of relatively low toxicity and rapidly gained a large share of the world market.

The first sign that these paints were not quite as innocuous as first appeared came in the early 1980s when evidence was found in the USA that TBT leaching from antifouling paints was causing females of the mud snail *Nassarius* to develop male secondary sexual characteristics. Shortly after this, French oyster growers began to find oysters with abnormally thickened shells. The oysters were unsaleable because of their deformed shells, and the effect was traced to TBT.

Some of the most detailed studies of the effect of TBT have been carried out on the dogwhelk *Nucella lapillus*. When exposed to TBT, females of the species begin to develop male secondary sexual characteristics, including the growth of a penis and blocking of the oviduct. The combination of characteristics has been given the name *imposex*. This prevents the females from laying eggs, and consequently populations decline. *N. lapillus* is completely absent around some marinas where there is a high concentration of TBT in water and sediments.

TBT has these effects at minute concentrations in the water. Shell thickening occurs in oysters exposed to 80 ng/l (80 parts in 10^{12}) and imposex in *N. lapillus* is induced by concentrations of only a few ng/l. Because the effect on *N. lapillus* is easily detectable and clearly attributable to TBT, it has been easier to establish cause and effect links here than in virtually any other case. There are some suggestions that TBT may have effects on the broader community, but these conclusions are based on correlations between TBT levels and community structure, so are subject to the difficulties facing all such studies (see the section on detecting pollution above). Since it became clear that TBT was so damaging to marine organisms, the use of TBT in antifouling paints is gradually being banned throughout the world. A ban on its use on vessels smaller than 25 m was introduced in the UK in 1987. Fortunately, TBT is less persistent in the environment than many other pesticides so concentrations in the environment have declined. There are signs that dogwhelk populations are recovering and oysters rapidly resume normal shell growth when no longer exposed to TBT.

Oil pollution

Oil discharges to the marine environment are often divided into two classes. The first, 'operational discharges', reflects the chronic low level inputs arising during transport, production, processing and disposal of oil products and dominates the total amounts of oil discharged, though they attract little attention. Improving pollution control measures and paying greater attention to minimizing discharges is resulting in declining inputs generally from this source. The second source of oil inputs is the occasional large-scale discharges from accidents such as shipwrecks, damage to offshore oil production facilities, broken pipelines or sabotage such as that during the Iraqi occupation of Kuwait. These occasional and often large-scale discharges attract great public concern and clearly do significant environmental damage. This damage arises because of certain specific features of oil as a contaminant. Oil, like some litter (see later), does not mix with seawater but instead floats and hence can not readily be diluted away by the vast volume of the ocean. After a spill, the oil spreads out as a thin surface film and consequently only does major damage to organisms that encounter this air–sea interface.

Oil itself is a complex mixture of thousands of different organic molecules dominated by aliphatic carbon compounds containing 1–24 carbon atoms, and this complexity makes it very difficult to generalize about the behaviour of oil. The toxicity of many of the individual compounds has been measured on some organisms, but it is difficult to extrapolate data from a few compounds and biological species to a real oil spill in the environment, where the species affected may be different and where the various compounds may act together to increase or reduce the toxicity of the individual compounds. Despite these complications, a few generalizations are possible. Aromatic and low molecular weight compounds are in general more toxic, but these compounds also tend to be those most rapidly lost from spilled oil within a few hours by evaporation and dissolution, because they are most volatile and water soluble. Such losses are of course temperature-dependent and will be much less important for oil spills in polar waters. Left alone, the remaining individual compounds in the oil will slowly degrade to CO_2, water and the other raw materials of oil on timescales ranging from days to centuries. The mechanisms of loss include photo-oxidation, dissolution and bacterial breakdown.

Oil is a natural product and bacteria capable of degrading it are present throughout the marine environment, albeit at low numbers. The capacity of an environment to disperse even large amounts of oil was illustrated by the *Braer* incident in the winter of 1993 off the Shetland Islands. A discharge of 87 000 tonnes of oil was relatively rapidly dispersed owing to exceptionally violent weather conditions with only modest local environmental damage. Thus the problems of oil pollution in the marine environment are short term (years) in contrast to persistent contaminants such as metals or PCBs.

After extensive degradation in the environment, the oil residue is tarry matter which forms tar balls floating on the sea. These are also released by tanker cleaning operations, being a residue of crude oil transportation as well. Tar balls have a residence time on the surface of the ocean of about a year and can cause considerable nuisance when beached in large numbers. However, the observation of many of these tar balls encrusted with fauna such as barnacles is testimony to the limited toxicity of these final residues of oil degradation.

As noted above, the chemical toxicity of oil is relatively low after a matter of a few hours in a warm environment, but the physical properties of the oil to coat and subsequently kill organisms persists as long as there is a coherent oil slick. Thus seabirds and intertidal communities are at high risk since these come into contact with the floating oil, whereas subtidal benthic communities are less at risk. The experience of beached oil spills suggests that the effects on intertidal communities can persist for several years, particularly in high latitude seas where low temperatures reduce the rate at which the oil degrades.

Experience over the last 30 years with major oil spills has suggested various strategies to minimize their environmental impact. If the slick is well out to sea and away from major bird communities, the most practical and economic action is to leave the natural processes of evaporation, dissolution and physical break-up to dissipate the slick. Nearer to land, however, it is often necessary to consider action to try to minimize the environmental damage from an oil spill. It is possible to use chemical dispersants which act as powerful surfactants (or detergents) to aid the dissolution of the oil. These have the effect of allowing much more effective dilution of the oil, but do expose biological systems, other than those that inhabit the water surface, to the oil. The first large-scale use of oil dispersants, during the *Torrey Canyon* incident, was a disaster with the dispersants proving to be more toxic than the oil.

Recently, less toxic dispersants have become available, but there is still reluctance to use this approach in many situations, and in addition the use of dispersants on large spills is logistically very difficult. During the *Torrey Canyon* incident, burning the oil was also attempted but then, and in subsequent attempts, this has proved a very inefficient and often counter-productive clean-up procedure. In calm waters it is possible to mop up the oil onto an absorbent solid or to skim it off the surface using specialized equipment, and these approaches are often used in harbours for small spills, since the waters are usually calm and equipment can be made available, if the eventuality of a spill is planned for.

If a large slick is heading for a shoreline it is possible to protect the area by using floating booms. These are only effective in calm waters since strong winds or tidal currents can force oil under the booms. In order to protect even a small area of coast, hundreds of metres of boom are needed, which must have been stored near to where it is needed since it is heavy, cumbersome, slow and expensive to move and deploy. Thus booming is best used across inlets to bays or estuaries where a relatively small boom can protect a long length of coast. Even then it is necessary to make choices about the coast to protect, since booming can never protect a whole coastline. This again illustrates the need for planning in advance for oil spill contingencies. Coasts can be categorized in terms of their sensitivity to damage from oil, the ease with which they can be cleaned and other factors such as amenity, fishery or economic value if appropriate. Thus, for example, cliffs and harbour walls are rarely affected by oil because wave patterns tend to keep oil away from then and oil that does reach them is readily removed by wave action or remedial cleaning. Sand and gravel beaches are much more readily impacted by oil as the oil tends to move deep into the beach, making it persistent and difficult to remove, and these areas may thus attract a higher priority than cliffs. However, such beaches may have low biological diversity but high amenity value so it is necessary to make value judgements at some stage. Sheltered rocky coasts, mud flats and marsh or mangrove communities are all sensitive to oil which would be difficult to remove and persistent, so these areas usually rate a high priority for protection.

Heavy metals

Metals are released to the marine environment from a multitude of sources. Once in the sea, they do not degrade although they may be removed by burial in sediments. Mercury is liable to bioaccumulate, particularly when incorporated into organic molecules such as methyl mercury. This was shown vividly in the Minimata pollution incident in Japan in the 1960s. A factory manufacturing vinyl chloride discharged large amounts of methyl mercury into the sea. Bioaccumulation led to large concentrations of methyl mercury being present in fish. The Japanese as a nation are rather fond of fish, and Minimata is a fishing community. Fishermen and their families were eating several kilograms of fish per week, and received large enough mercury dosages to produce neurotoxic effects. About 2000 people were affected, including 43 deaths during the epidemic and more than 700 permanently disabled. Discharges of mercury are now tightly regulated.

Cadmium also has a tendency to bioaccumulate, so is placed on most black or red lists of priority pollutants. It is, however, of relatively low toxicity to marine life and the strictness of most national regulatory regimes is such that damage to the marine environment by cadmium is unlikely to occur. Copper and silver are much more toxic to marine organisms, and are more likely to present a threat. Fortunately, the chemical composition of seawater reduces the environmental impact of heavy metals. The relatively high pH of seawater, coupled with its high carbonate content, mean that the solubility of many metals is low. Metal concentrations are generally several orders of magnitude lower than saturation, as a result of scavenging by particles and other processes. Consequently, metals

---

Box 14.2 Deoxygenation problems in estuaries

Traditionally, settlements grew up at the most downstream bridging point of estuaries because they offered sheltered harbours and improved communications. The development of London and Glasgow provides examples of this. We shall use London and the Thames estuary as an example of the problems that such development inevitably poses for the environmental health of the estuary. In trying to assess the environmental history of the Thames, scientific studies can only take us back a hundred years in history. Prior to that we must rely on qualitative descriptions from early writers and/or reconstructed histories based on records preserved in the sediments. For London there is an abundance of written material which provides some idea of how the people of the time perceived the state of the estuary. As early as the 14th century, for example, there are records of both parliament and the king discussing this problem.

The Thames within London remained in use as a drinking water supply until the beginning of the 19th century and at this time there was a flourishing fishery. However, the small streams draining through London to the Thames had become open sewers and indeed were subsequently paved over and used as sewers. During the first half of the 19th century the population grew rapidly and, with it, human and industrial waste inputs to the Thames grew. In addition, the development of the water closet and its connection to the sewage system allowed essentially all of London's sewage to flow directly into the estuary. The result of these well-intentioned and successful developments in public sanitation was a rapid deterioration of the Thames in London. After 1840 the smell from the estuary became a matter of comment in the Press and parliament. It seems safe to assume that the smell was of hydrogen sulphide. Decay of organic matter first uses up dissolved oxygen in the water. Then, in the absence of oxygen, bacterial communities develop that are able to decompose the organic matter using alternative oxygen sources. The first such sources utilized are nitrate, Fe(III) and Mn(IV). Once these are exhausted, sulphate is utilized with the subsequent production of hydrogen sulphide. Deoxygenation of the water severely reduces the diversity of invertebrates able to live in the river and prevents the passage of migratory fish such as salmon.

There were a number of cholera epidemics between 1830 and 1870 which were believed to result from contaminated water supplies from the Thames. By 1852 water abstraction for drinking was banned.

Spurred to action by the smell on their doorstep, the parliament created a Metropolitan Commissioner of Sewers and by 1852 main sewers were built to intercept existing sewers and convey the wastes below London to be discharged to the estuary on the ebb tide. This undertaking helped, but the condition of the river remained very poor, though subsequent improvements took place during the 1880s and 1890s because of better sewage treatment prior to discharge which removed some of the organic matter. From 1885 the first chemical measurements on the Thames become available and show a modest increase in oxygen levels to about 20 per cent of saturation from 1885 to 1895 and by 1890 there were once again fish in the river in London.

Box 14.2 continued

The population of London continued to grow rapidly with an attendant rapid increase in waste discharges which overloaded the new sewage system, resulting in a steady decline in the condition of the river from 1910, so by 1950 there was again total oxygen depletion and the appearance of hydrogen sulphide during the autumn as recorded by the now regular surveys (as shown in the figure).

In the early 1950s public and political opinion began to demand action to improve the Thames and the sewage works were subsequently upgraded to remove much of the organic load prior to discharge. Over the next few years there was a resulting dramatic improvement in the oxygen levels and by the mid-1960s fish and macro-invertebrate communities began to return to the Thames.

The history of the pollution of the Thames illustrates the interplay between public health, water quality and political decisions. In a confined water body, sewage is a very serious pollutant and its production is directly related to population numbers. However, sewage pollution is readily treatable given the political will and the financial resources. With appropriate reductions in inputs of organic matter, the adverse effects are almost entirely reversible.

The history of the pollution of the Thames by sewage-induced deoxygenation is particularly well documented, but there are many other similar cases including the Clyde estuary in Scotland, the Humber estuary in England, the Scheldt estuary on the Dutch/ Belgian border and New York and Boston harbour where a similar historical pattern can be traced.

(a) Average autumn dissolved oxygen concentrations in the tidal River Thames; (b) length of tidal river Thames with dissolved oxygen concentrations below 5% of saturation.

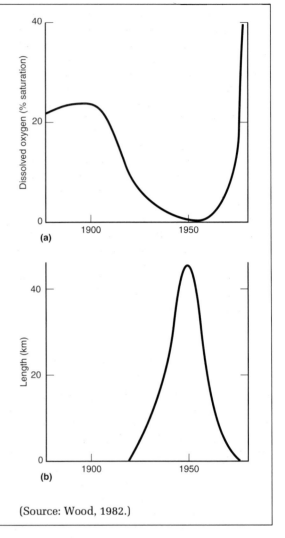

(Source: Wood, 1982.)

discharged to the marine environment are in general not readily bioavailable. High concentrations of metals in biota are only observed in rather anomalous situations such as estuaries receiving drainage water from metalliferous mines or effluents from smelters (e.g. Restronguet Creek in Cornwall and Sorfjorden in Norway). In the most contaminated sites, there are some signs of a reduction in faunal diversity, but this only occurs at concentrations well in excess of those found in normal industrialized estuaries.

Summary of specific effects

We have given some examples where we can be fairly certain that specific chemicals are having identifiable effects on the biota. Such cases are, however, rather few in number and the clearest examples of ecological damage are the result of deoxygenation caused by sewage discharges to estuaries. In general, field-based research has not provided us with a great ability to predict ecological effects of given concentrations of particular substances. As described earlier in this chapter, it is remarkably difficult to predict effects in the field from laboratory toxicity testing, so we cannot rely on that either. Regulation of discharges must therefore be done in a more arbitrary way. The legal regulation of the environmental release of individual chemicals in the EU places a high priority on reducing releases of substances that are toxic, persistent and liable to bioaccumulate. These are those substances that are most likely to cause long-lasting environmental damage, and discharge limits are usually set using uniform emission standards – an assessment of the lowest releases to the environment per unit quantity of product which it would be reasonable to achieve using the 'best available technology not entailing excessive cost'. In the UK, other substances are regulated using environmental quality standards. Discharge consents are set at levels that will lead to concentrations in the environment well below those that have been observed to cause an effect in laboratory tests. This approach takes into account the capacity of the receiving environment to dilute effluents, but precisely because of this it is more complicated to administer than uniform emission standards as consents have to be set on a case-by-case basis.

Eutrophication

In Box 14.2, the effects of the oxygen consumption arising from the breakdown of organic matter were discussed. However, if the breakdown of organic matter takes place after sufficient dilution so as to allow the rate of oxygen supply to exceed the oxygen consumption then the organic matter can be broken down to its constituent parts, carbon dioxide and nutrients including nitrogen (as the oxidized species nitrate or the reduced form ammonium) and phosphate, without deleterious effects on oxygen levels. These nutrients can then be reused by small unicellular free-floating algae called phytoplankton in their growth, thus forming new organic matter in a very efficient recycling process.

The phytoplankton form the basis of the marine food chain and their rate of primary production can be limited by either the availability of light (as often happens in the turbid waters of estuaries and during winter throughout much of the North Sea) or by the availability of nutrients. If nutrients are the limiting factor then increasing nutrient levels will increase primary production. At a modest level this can be beneficial in providing increased food supplies, but a large increase in nutrient supply can have several deleterious effects which are usually referred to as *eutrophication.*

The deleterious effects that are possible fall into two

groups: changes in species and increased oxygen consumption in bottom waters. The change of species arises because different algal species are adapted to different nutrient environments and a change in the nutrient status can favour certain species while disadvantaging others. As an example, some phytoplankton, the diatoms, require silicon to build their skeletons. Silicon is introduced to the marine environment primarily by weathering via rivers. If the nitrogen and phosphate inputs are increased without changing the silicon inputs then diatoms will be disadvantaged compared with other phytoplankton. The change in phytoplankton species can effect other parts of the marine food web because certain predator species are adapted to certain types of algal food, and changes in the species' composition can thus affect predators. In addition some phytoplankton species are apparently avoided as food supplies and some are actually toxic. In particular, certain dinoflagellates can form so-called 'red tides' with massive blooms which release toxins that can be accumulated by shellfish. Such blooms have been reported occasionally from the North Sea but are much more common in tropical waters where they regularly force the temporary closure of commercial shellfish farming operations. However, a clear link between eutrophication and such red tides has yet to be established.

The second problem that can arise from increased nutrient inputs results when the phytoplankton die and then sink into deeper waters. Here, if there is no light and hence no oxygen production by photosynthesis, the increased stock of dead phytoplankton represents an increased load of organic matter which requires oxygen to break it down. If the rate of oxygen consumption in the deep waters exceeds the rate of oxygen input, then oxygen concentrations will fall with subsequent deleterious effects as described earlier for sewage breakdown in estuaries. Several factors can act to exacerbate this situation, besides increased nutrients. Deeper waters tend to stratify, with warmer, less dense water forming a stable cap over the deep water and preventing transport of oxygen into the deep water. Thus under warm conditions the effect is increased, and in warmer situations there is both more light to drive photosynthesis in the upper water column and also increased rates of breakdown of organic matter throughout the water column.

There is evidence of eutrophication induced oxygen depletion in several coastal areas, including the Baltic and Chesapeake Bay on the north-east coast of the USA. In both cases nutrients have been considerably

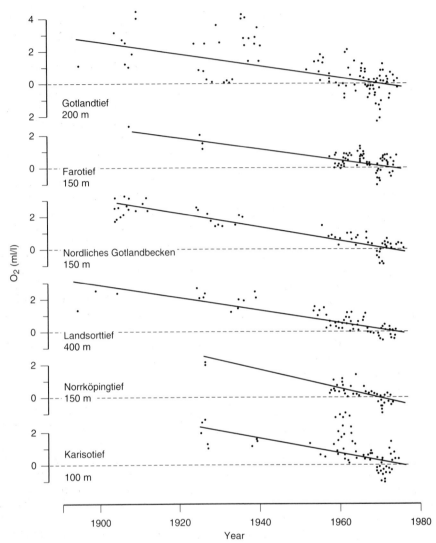

Fig 14.8 Decreases in oxygen concentrations in the bottom waters of the Baltic. Negative values indicate hydrogen sulphide production. (Source: Fonselius, 1982.)

enriched by human activity leading to increased algal activity. In addition, in both cases the estuarine system includes deep basins (about 100 m) with exchange with offshore waters restricted by shallow sills at the seaward end. This basin shape allows deep waters to be trapped for long periods during which time the settling organic matter is decomposed by bacteria and oxygen consumed. In Chesapeake Bay winter cooling allows the stratification to break down and deep water to mix with surface waters and replace the anoxic deep water by fresh, well-oxygenated waters, and the anoxia is

therefore seasonal. In the Baltic the winter mixing is inadequate to achieve such reoxygenation and the anoxic conditions can persist for many years until flushed out by exchange with the North Sea. The situation in the Baltic has been monitored for many years and there is a good time series of measurements documenting the increasing nutrient levels and declining oxygen levels (Figure 14.8).

In the southern North Sea the waters are generally shallow (less than 50 m) and well mixed by tidal action throughout most of the year. Under these conditions

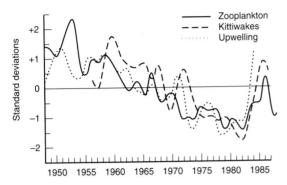

Fig 14.9 Synchronous long-term changes in populations of zooplankton and kittiwakes shown by data from the continuous plankton recorder. (Source: Adapted from Aebischer *et al.*, 1990 and Dickson *et al.*, 1988.)

bottom waters cannot become trapped and anoxic. In the south-east corner of the southern North Sea, regions of low oxygen have been observed intermittently since 1902. While increasing nutrient concentrations may contribute to this situation, a primary cause is probably the increased stratification in this area due to freshwater inputs. This stratification naturally traps the bottom waters and allows bacterial oxygen consumption to lower oxygen levels in the absence of a supply of fresh oxygen-rich water from above.

There has been much debate about whether increasing nutrient inputs to the southern North Sea are pushing the area towards eutrophication. However, there is considerable year to year variability in plankton stocks arising from climatic effects, so it is very difficult to identify subtle changes. Fortunately there is a record of plankton populations in the North Sea spanning more than 40 years. This record is collected using the 'continuous plankton recorder' (CPR) which is towed behind commercial ships. The record documents the considerable year-to-year variation but also suggests long-term changes that occur in all plankton groups throughout the North Sea and the North Atlantic (Figure 14.9). Changes of this magnitude cannot be the result of pollution effects over so large an area and also suggest a decrease in plankton rather than the increase that would be expected if eutrophication were occurring. It is now believed that the trend is the result of long-term climatic changes in wind strength and direction as illustrated by the decline in upwelling in parts of the North Atlantic. The trend is also seen in kittiwake numbers (the only exclusively open water feeding bird in this area), suggesting that the decline in their numbers may

reflect food shortages rather than pollution effects.

While the trend observed by the CPR is similar throughout the North Sea and North Atlantic, close to the European coast of the North Sea in areas not sampled by the CPR there is evidence of increasing levels of some algae, particularly *Phaeocystis*, a flagellate that releases large amounts of mucus into the water, resulting in the production of foams on beaches. These foams can lie over a metre thick on the beaches of the Netherlands, Germany and Denmark and fuel considerable public concern over the condition of the marine environment. The circulation of the North Sea acts to confine the inputs of the large European rivers such as the Rhine to the coast (Figure 14.7) and thus it is likely that the increasing algal levels very close to the coast are the result of increasing eutrophication, but this effect appears to be rather local. Exceptional blooms of algae have been reported on occasions throughout the North Sea sometimes with serious consequences, including the closure of fisheries during red tides and mass fish mortalities during *Chrysochromulina* blooms off the Norwegian coast (as noted earlier). However, the causes of these blooms are not well understood and there is at present no clear evidence to link them to eutrophication.

Bathing beaches

Seaside resorts are often large centres of population, and this may be increased by several hundred per cent in summer. As noted in our discussion of estuaries, the traditional UK approach to sewage disposal has been to discharge it into the sea with only limited treatment. This has been the practice of many coastal resorts, often involving the discharge of untreated sewage close to the low water mark on the most popular beaches, at best after primary screening and perhaps maceration. The sight of children swimming in the sea surrounded by what are euphemistically referred to a 'sewage-derived solids' causes at very least visual offence, and perhaps infection with sewage-borne diseases. Unless the sewage passes through a fine screen (preferably preceded by maceration), sea outfalls can also be significant sources of plastic litter.

A response to this has been the construction of long sea outfalls: rather than installing sewage treatment, simply build a longer pipe. The effluent is then diluted by the action of waves and tides and the organic matter can be broken down by bacterial action in a very similar way to the action of a land-based sewage treatment works. The greater distance between the point of discharge and the bathing beaches creates greater potential for dispersal of the effluent. Saltwater and sunlight also act as disinfectant. Provided long sea outfalls are properly designed, they avoid the gross fouling of beaches with faecal matter, although this does occur occasionally during periods of onshore winds. Standard methods of assessing sewage contamination which involve counting densities of sewage-derived bacteria in the water show that there is some increase in bacterial populations in bathing waters near long sea outfalls. The question is whether these increased bacterial populations carry any health risks.

There is persistent anecdotal evidence of bathers developing gastro-intestinal and ear infections, apparently as a consequence of sewage contamination. Until recently, the view of the UK regulatory authorities has been that a significant risk of infection occurs only when bathing waters are so contaminated with sewage as to be 'aesthetically revolting'. However, firm scientific evidence on the health risks of sea bathing is sparse. Experimental studies cannot be carried out because of the ethical difficulties in exposing people to something that may be harmful to health. Cohort studies are difficult because of the diverse geographical origins of people using a beach at any one time. The most detailed epidemiological studies have been in North America but these are based on freshwater bathing beaches, so there are some difficulties in directly applying the results to marine bathing. The main difference between marine and freshwater environments is likely to be in the rate of death of bacteria. If we assume that viable bacteria have the same probability of causing infection whatever the salinity of the water, then we can use relationships between bacterial counts and disease derived from freshwater as a basis for making predictions about the marine environment. The epidemiological studies indicate that in freshwater, there are measurable health risks at bacterial densities of 23 faecal coliforms/ml. This suggests that there are health risks involved in bathing in waters that fulfil the EC bathing water directive (which specifies a maximum of 2000 faecal coliforms/ml) and many bathing waters fall far short even of that standard. Further uncertainty is introduced by the fact that faecal coliforms are only being used as an indicator of the concentrations of human pathogens, as pathogenic organisms are rather more difficult to count. This is particularly true of viruses, which are able to survive for a substantially longer period in seawater than are sewage-derived bac-

teria. However, recent careful epidemiological studies of the effects of bathing in sewage-contaminated water do now suggest a clear link with the development of various symptoms.

Litter

Litter on land is a widely recognized problem, but the problem of litter at sea has a lower profile because fewer people see it. However, this changes when the litter washes up on beaches and it seems safe to assume that the composition of marine litter is similar to that of beached litter. The cleaning of beaches represents a considerable expense to the local community, though it is essential in tourist areas. Some of the beached material also constitutes a significant hazard.

Beach litter has been systematically studied by collecting and identifying all the material on a transect down a beach; the country of origin and the approximate date of manufacture can often be determined. The results of such studies indicate that litter on the beach appears to have three sources – sewage, visitor-dropped litter and material dumped at sea. The sewage-derived material is discussed above. In a series of studies of northern European beaches in the 1970s, 38–50 per cent of the identified material were household and lavatory cleaning bottles, emphasizing the importance of ship-derived litter (or the obsessive cleanliness of some beach visitors!). In the 1970s it was estimated (based on extrapolations from detailed studies on a few ships) that more than 6 million tonnes of waste were dumped annually by ships, though much of this was cargo related. Recent trends to increased packaging no doubt increase the total amount of dumped wastes and in particular the amount of floatable waste. Much of the dumped material will sink (bottles and tins) or be rapidly broken down (paper and food), but plastics do not degrade rapidly and float, so they cannot be diluted by the full volume of the sea. Ship dumping explains the cosmopolitan origins of the containers washed up on the beaches, the majority of which appear to be less than five years old. This age implies a relatively rapid removal process, possibly by beaching or physicochemical breakdown, though the details of the loss mechanism are unknown.

Some litter is obviously potentially dangerous. For example, pharmaceutical and hospital wastes are occasionally washed up on shore after dumping at sea or loss of cargoes. Other dangerous cargoes, including chemicals and munitions, are quite regularly reported washed up on beaches. While these rare incidents represent an acute hazard, the plastic debris represents a chronic insidious threat to marine life. When the stomach contents of birds from even remote regions of the world are analysed, they often contain plastic debris including pellets of a few millimetres diameter which are probably precursor material for plastics fabrication and which have been lost at sea or from coastal plastic manufacturing plants. Larger pieces of plastic can entangle birds and marine life, and ultimately kill them. This applies to waste plastics but perhaps more so to lost fishing gear, particularly large drift nets. These nets, often more than 10 km long, will, if lost, drift around for weeks or more still catching fish. The entrapped fish lure other fish and marine mammals to their doom in the nets.

The control of marine litter and fishing gear is clearly an international problem and a series of international agreements have now been implemented to try to control this problem. However, effective enforcement of such agreements at sea is impossible and compliance must therefore rely on public pressure to ensure that waste storage facilities are provided at sea and waste disposal facilities provided at ports. Then, as with terrestrial litter, it becomes a matter of public education to persuade people to use them. The fishing nets represent a rather different problem since the construction of robust drift nets, which will inevitably be occasionally lost, means that the problem is inevitable with this type of fishing and a ban seems the only solution.

Conclusions

There is lots of evidence for contamination throughout the marine environment and in coastal waters in particular. The evidence for ecological damage is thin on the ground, and limited to rather small areas or to the effects of a small number of persistent chemicals. This contrasts markedly with other sorts of anthropogenic impact in coastal waters. Fisheries have had a major impact on the marine environment, with most fish stocks being considerably lower than their unexploited numbers would be. Fishing can also have other environmental impacts. The whole bed of the North Sea is trawled over on average once a year, which ploughs up the sediment and has an uncertain effect on the benthos. Another anthropogenic impact has been on coastal habitats. Large areas of coastal marshland have

been reclaimed for agriculture and estuaries continue to be under threat from proposals to build tidal barrages and marinas. These areas are then lost forever to nature with uncertain effects, though their importance for bird life and as fish nursery areas is well documented. Furthermore, these estuarine and marsh environments represent one of the last truly natural areas in much of northern Europe and to fail to pass on this legacy intact will seriously diminish the environment of our successors.

References

Aebischer, N.J., J.C. Coulson and J.M. Colebrook (1990) Parallel long-term trends across four marine trophic levels and weather. *Nature*, **347**, 751–3.

Department of the Environment (1987) *North Sea Status Report.* London: Department of the Environment.

Dickson, R.R., P.M. Kelly, J.M. Colebrook, W.S. Wooster and D.H. Cushing (1988) North winds and production in the Eastern North Atlantic. *Journal of Plankton Research*, **10**, 151–69.

Ernst, W. (1980) Effects of pesticides and related organic compounds in the sea. *Helgoländer Meeresuntersuchungen*, **33**, 301–12.

Fonselius, S. (1982) Oxygen and hydrogen sulphide condition in the Baltic Sea. *Marine Pollution Bulletin*, **12**, 187–94.

GESAMP (1982) *The review of the health of the oceans.* GESAMP (United Nations Joint Group of Experts on the Scientific Aspects of Marine Pollution) Reports and Studies No. 15. Paris: UNESCO.

Hamilton, E.I. and R.J. Clifton (1979) Isotopic abundances of lead in estuarine sediments, Swansea Bay, Bristol Channel. *Estuarine and Coastal Marine Science*, **8**, 271–8.

Lewis, J.R. (1972) Problems and approaches to baseline studies in coastal communities. In M. Ruivo (Ed.) *Marine pollution and sea life.* London: Fishing News (Books) Ltd.

McGarvin, M. (1994) The implications of the precautionary principle for biological monitoring. In T. O'Riordan and J. Cameron (Eds) *Interpreting the precautionary principle.* London: Cameron and Day.

Nelissen, P. and J. Stefels (1988) *NIOZ Report 1988–4.* Texel, the Netherlands: NIOZ.

Royal Society (1983) *The Nitrogen cycle of the UK – A study group report.* London: Royal Society.

Salomons, W. and A.J. de Groot (1978) Pollution history of trace metals in sediments as affected by the Rhine River. In W.E. Krumbein (Ed.) *Environmental biogeochemistry and geomicrobiology*, Volume 1: The aquatic environment. Michigan: Ann Arbor Science, Ann Arbor.

Salomons, W.B.L Bayne, E.K. Duursma and U. Forstner (1988) *Pollution of the North Sea.* Berlin: Springer-Verlag.

von Bennekrom, A.J. and W. Salomons (1980) Pathways of nutrients and organic matter from land to ocean through rivers. In J.M. Martin *et al.* (Eds.) *River inputs to ocean systems.* Paris: UNEP/UNESCO.

Wood, L.B. (1982) *The restoration of the Thames.* Bristol: Adam Hilger.

Further reading

Abel, B.B. and V. Axiak (1991) *Ecotoxicology and the marine environment.* London: Ellis Horwood Series in Aquaculture and Fisheries Support.

Alexander, L.M., A. Heaven, A. Tennant and R. Morris (1992) Symptomalogy of children in contact with sea water contaminated with sewage. *Journal of Epidemiology and Community Health*, **46**, 340–4.

Clark, R.B. (1989) *Marine pollution*, 2nd edition. Oxford: Oxford Sciences Publication.

Department of the Environment (1987) *Quality status of the North Sea.* London: Department of the Environment.

Dixon, T.R. and T.J. Dixon (1981) Marine litter surveillance. *Marine Pollution Bulletin*, **18**, (68), 303–65.

Key, D. and A. McDonald (1986) Coastal bathing water quality. *Journal of Shoreline Management*, **2**, 259–83.

Newman, P.S. and A.R. Agg (1988) *Environmental protection of the North Sea.* London: Heinemann.

Wolfe, D.A. (Ed.) (1987) Plastics in the sea. *Marine Pollution Bulletin*, **18**(6B), 303–65.

CHAPTER 15

Urban air pollution and its consequences

PETER BRIMBLECOMBE AND FRANCES NICHOLAS

Air pollution is ubiquitous: even the once clear air of the Arctic is hazy (Soroos, 1992). The haze, composed of aerosols of human-generated chemicals, extends over an area the size of North America, and can have up to 25 different layers with a depth of 8 km. High ratios of manganese relative to vanadium suggest coal-burning plants in Russia and Europe are the main source. An unusually dense band of haze was traced 10 000 km from the North Alaska slopes to the Volga–Ural region of the Russian Federation.

The haze is rich in volatile compounds, many of which are carcinogenic at low concentrations. Sulphates also help to acidify ecosystems that are very susceptible to small changes in soil pH. Carbon specks accumulate on snow surfaces, accelerating melting and increasing the tendency towards warming by altering the reflectivity of the land surface.

Interestingly, little research was done on this problem before the mid-1970s because the Cold War precluded vital US–Soviet scientific collaboration. Now there is much co-operation and the prospect of an Arctic environmental regime (see Chapter 19 and Young and Osherenko, 1993). But there is precious little incentive for the beleaguered economies of the Russian Federation and its former European satellites to clean up for the Arctic. The science is certainly now in place, but it may take years for the necessary action to be co-ordinated. Only by linking aid to industrial renovation can this problem be solved. Realistically, one cannot expect the weak and emerging economies to do the job on their own. Offset pollution trading is a likely way forward, but sadly the Arctic will have to become demonstrably more polluted first.

Meanwhile the cost of air pollution control may be lower via economic incentives than by fixed targets and standards, the favoured approach of most regulatory agencies (Howe, 1991, p. 12). Studies by Tietenberg (1985) have suggested that conventional measures for our pollution control in the US are anywhere between 1.07 and 14.40 times as expensive as the estimated least cost approaches. This is one of the many findings that have led US regulatory authorities to look much harder at taxes and permit trading as ways of reducing pollution less expensively.

However, Howe (1991, p. 92) warns against an environmental economic revolution:

- Lawyers write the rules and prefer standards and targets plus enforcement as established, through court-interpretable, codes of practice.
- Legislators prefer the equivalence of treatment rather than the least cost outcome simply because it is perceived to be fairer.
- Some powerful US environmental groups resist economic instruments, mostly because they do not fully understand this approach, but also because they believe in property rights to clean and healthy environments.
- Firms already in an airshed like the competitive disadvantage of new firms entering a polluted area and having to clean up to the very highest (and unnecessarily costly) standards.
- The actual costs of best technology may not appear as high, especially if the technology has other advantages, than annual costs of environmental taxes and permits. Yet US air pollution control regulations cost some $15 billion annually yet provide at most $1 billion in gains nationwide. The system also fails to control transboundary pollutants which are transformed by solar radiation on other processes into new chemical formulations that are even more polluting. As yet there is little co-ordination too between US land-use control procedures and pollution control administration. If the delivery is inefficient and bureaucratic, all the good science in the world will not deliver clear air at least cost.

Historical background

Today everybody seems to be concerned about the foul air we breathe in cities. Although we still talk about the great black clouds of smoke that came forth from the 'satanic mills' of our past, nowadays we need to be interested in something far more subtle. The pollution we see in our cities today is very different from that of the past, so we must trace the way in which it has changed. Perhaps it is now better, perhaps it is worse, that is to be argued, but certainly it is different.

For almost as long as there have been cities they have been polluted, and before there were cities there were polluted huts and houses. In ancient Rome, where wood was burnt, Emperor Nero's tutor Seneca complained of the bad effect that smoke had on his health. The Roman courts even dealt with cases where factory smoke annoyed nearby residents.

In the London of the 13th century there was a particularly notable transition. The dramatic increase in population caused a fuel crisis and wood was replaced by coal in some industrial processes such as 'cement' making. The fuel change was so noticeable in terms of the smoke and smell that residents feared for their health, and popular protest led to attempts to restrict the use of coal.

However, by the late 17th century coal was well entrenched in England in domestic as well as industrial use. Later the development of the steam engine and more broadly the industrial revolution changed the focus of life by requiring large amounts of labour concentrated around factories. Thus the early part of the last century saw a great increase in the population of cities.

This rapid increase in urban population was accompanied by numerous social problems. In particular, the serious health effects of pollution, disease and sanitation were something that urban administrations had never had to cope with on any such scale before. There were very early laws governing the smoke from steam engines in Britain and France, so we know that smoke was a problem which engineers, stokers and officials had to grapple with. In fact most people were opposed to smoky cities, but smoke was generally seen as a necessary evil. While some argued against it, others saw that smoke was associated with wealth: 'Where there was muck there was money.'

Smoke

The concern about air pollution in the 19th century focused on smoke: smoke that soiled clothes, blackened buildings and ruined health by its presence in the urban atmosphere. In fact, smoke has dominated thought about air pollution almost through to the present day.

How was this smoke generated? Fuels and their combustion lie at the centre of the air pollution problem. Air pollution does have other sources too, but by and large it is combustion that has been the most important source. The fuels we use are usually based on carbon combined with small amounts of hydrogen, even though quite exotic fuels such as metals are known for special applications (e.g. as solid rocket fuels).

If we imagine a fuel such as coal or oil, we could write its combustion according to the equation:

$$'CH' + O_2 \rightarrow CO_2 + H_2O$$
$$\text{coal/oil} + \text{oxygen} \rightarrow \text{carbon dioxide} + \text{water}$$

Now this looks fairly harmless for the urban environment, as carbon dioxide (although being a greenhouse gas) is not really poisonous.

However, let us imagine that there is not enough oxygen during combustion. The equation might then look more like:

$$'CH' + O_2 \rightarrow CO + H_2O$$
$$\text{coal} + \text{oxygen} \rightarrow \text{carbon monoxide} + \text{water}$$

Now we have produced carbon monoxide. This is a rather poisonous gas which combines with red blood pigment and can kill by asphyxiation at high concentrations. Thus it is hardly a desirable constituent of the urban atmosphere. With even less oxygen we might get carbon, or we could simply say smoke:

Table 15.1 Sulphur content of fuels

Fuel	S (%)
Coal	0.2–7.0
Fuel oils	0.5–4.0
Coke	1.5–2.5
Diesel fuel	0.3–0.9
Petrol	0.1
Kerosene	0.1
Wood	very small
Natural gas	very small[a]

[a]Hydrogen sulphide is often removed from natural gases, but it may also be added as an olfactant

'CH' + $O_2 \rightarrow$ C + H_2O

coal + oxygen $\rightarrow$ ' smoke' + water

At low temperatures where there is relatively little oxygen, reactions may cause a rearrangement of atoms that can lead to polycyclic aromatic hydrocarbons. Typical of this class of compound is benzo(a)pyrene, B(a)P, a notorious cancer-inducing agent or carcinogen:

'CH' + $O_2 \rightarrow$ B(a)P + H_2O

coal + oxygen $\rightarrow$ benzo(a)pyrene + water

Thus, although the combustion of fuels would initially seem a fairly harmless activity, it can produce a range of pollutant carbon compounds. Now the early engineers saw that an excess of oxygen would help convert all the carbon to carbon dioxide. So they developed a philosophy of consuming smoke by burning it (often known as 'burning your own smoke'), though this required considerable skill to implement and was often not very successful in practice.

Gaseous pollutants

Although the air pollution problem and the smoke problem have been linked, there were always those who thought there was more to air pollution than just smoke. They were right, because fuels are not burnt in oxygen, as is suggested in the equations given above. They are burnt in air, which is a mixture of mainly oxygen and nitrogen. In flames molecules may fragment, and even the molecules of air can enter into a series of reactions:

$O + N_2 \rightarrow NO + N$

atomic + nitrogen $\rightarrow$ nitric oxide + atomic
oxygen   nitrogen

$N + O_2 \rightarrow NO + O$

atomic + oxygen $\rightarrow$ nitric oxide + atomic
nitrogen   oxygen

If we add these two reactions we get:

$N_2 + O_2 = 2NO$

nitrogen + oxygen = nitric oxide

Note that the second of the above reactions produces an oxygen atom, which can go back and re-enter at the first reaction. Once an oxygen atom is formed in a flame it will be regenerated and contribute to a whole chain of reactions.

Nitrogen oxides (NOx) in vehicle exhaust gases are generated in this way. They arise simply because we burn fuels in air rather than just in oxygen. Of course it must be admitted that some fuels contain nitrogen compounds as impurities, so that combustion products of these fuels may contain additional nitrogen oxides.

However, the most common and worrisome impurity in fossil fuels is sulphur. There may be as much as 6 per cent sulphur in some coals and this is converted to sulphur dioxide on combustion:

$S + O_2 \rightarrow SO_2$

sulphur + oxygen $\rightarrow$ sulphur dioxide

There are other impurities in fuels too, but sulphur has always been seen as the one most central to the air pollution problems of cities.

If we look at the composition of various fuels we see that they contain quite variable amounts of sulphur, as shown in Table 15.1. In the case of coal we see that the amount of sulphur can be very high. Also, the sulphur concentration in coal varies geographically. For instance, the coals of the eastern coalfields of the USA are rather higher in sulphur than those in the west. In Europe we find a similar situation, with Eastern Europe often having higher sulphur contents. When concern about pollution by sulphur compounds means that low sulphur coals become more valued, this can have economic repercussions.

If we look at the list of sulphur contents we see that the highest amounts of sulphur are found in coals, lignites and in fuel oils. These are fuels that are used in stationary sources such as boilers, furnaces (and traditionally steam engines), domestic chimneys, steam turbines, power stations, etc. As a simple rule one can thus associate sulphur pollution of the air with stationary sources.

Smoke, too, is mainly associated with stationary sources. Naturally, steam trains and boats caused the occasional problem, but it was the stationary source that was most significant.

For many people sulphur dioxide and smoke came to epitomize the air pollution problems of cities. Smoke and sulphur dioxide are called primary pollutants, because they are formed directly at the pollutant source, as we can see in the equations above. They then enter the atmosphere in this form. So in the case of primary pollutants it can be argued that given pollutants are clearly identified with particular sources. Thus the traditional air pollution problems experienced by cities have been associated with primary pollutants.

Smoke plus fog equals smog

Smoke can be seen, but sulphur dioxide is invisible. However, in the polluted city the combination of these two pollutants became very noticeable in smoke-laden fogs. Some people described these fogs as thick enough to spread on bread and butter. In the first years of the 20th century an air pollution expert with an enthusiasm for word play named this kind of fog smog, i.e. *smoke* and *fog*, and the word has subsequently been used to describe much urban air pollution.

The classical London smog forms under damp conditions when water vapour can condense on smoke particles. Sulphur dioxide can dissolve into this water.

$$SO_2 + H_2O = H^+ + HSO_3^-$$

sulphur + water = hydrogen ion + bisulphate
dioxide   ion

Traces of metal contaminants catalyse the conversion of dissolved sulphur dioxide to sulphuric acid:

$$2HSO_3^- + O_2 \rightarrow 2H^+ + 2SO_4^{2-}$$

bisulphate + oxygen → hydrogen ion + sulphate
ion   ion

Sulphuric acid has a great affinity for water so the droplet tends to absorb more water, it becomes bigger and the fog thickens.

Health and smog

The strange smells from combustion processes had always caused people to be concerned about the effects these 'vapours' might have on health. By the mid-1600s scientists were beginning to collect evidence of these effects. The higher death rates in London as compared with rural areas were sometimes blamed on the smoke from coal. In the areas around metal furnaces local industrial diseases were known and these were often attributed to toxic materials such as antimony, arsenic or mercury within the smoke.

Terrible fogs plagued London at the turn of the century when 'Sherlock Holmes' and Jack the Ripper paced the streets. Death rates invariably rose in periods of prolonged winter fog; little wonder considering that the fog droplets contained sulphuric acid. The medical experts of Victorian times recognized that the fogs were affecting health, but they, along with others, were not

---

Box 15.1 Air pollution in cities of the developing world.

In 1950 13 cities had more than 4 million inhabitants. Nowadays 40 cities fall into this category, two-thirds of which are in developing countries. By 2025 as many as 100 of the estimated 135 cities of 4 million people or more will be in developing countries. Poor controls on industrial emissions, especially state-owned establishments, and a rapid increase in ill-maintained vehicles has meant that the majority of Third World cities suffer from serious air pollution. In Shanghai, China, 146 days per year on average exceed the WHO guideline for SO_2, 104 days in Tehran, 87 days in Seoul and 68 days in Beijing. For suspended particulate material, Calcutta experiences 268 days on average when levels exceed the WHO health guidelines and Delhi 294 days. Beijing experiences 272 days per year with elevated particulate loads. Carbon monoxide concentrations in 15 cities studied by the UN Environment Programme (UNEP) in 1985 exceeded WHO guidelines. Mexico City smog alerts require motorists to stop driving by decree, although it has been exempt from controls so far. However, tough new control laws are enforced by only nine inspectors for the whole metropolis.

Sources: UN Environment Programme (1985); Humme (1991).

---

able to legislate smoke out of existence. Even where there was a will, and indeed there were enthusiasts in both Europe and North America who strove for change, the technology was far too naïve to achieve really obvious improvements. The improvements that did come about were often due to changes in fuel, location of industry, climate, etc. rather than changes in technology.

Such positive changes have not been nearly so evident in the developing world where there has been great pressure to industrialize and only limited resources for the abatement and control of air pollution (see Box 15.1).

In polluted conditions the respiratory system could not clear itself of the particles that were inhaled. The cilia that normally swept the respiratory passages clear became anaesthetized, and the particles penetrated deeper. Some people susceptible to respiratory diseases became ill. Others were apparently healthier, but the particles could still cause long-term problems. There were toxic trace metals on the surface of some of the tiny soot particles and others contained compounds such as benzo(a)pyrene, a potent carcinogen. These

---

Box 15.2 Health effects and air quality guidelines for major air pollutants

Pollutant	WHO guidelines		Effects
	Annual mean ($\mu g/m^3$ of air)	98 percentile ($\mu g/m^3$ of air)[a]	
Sulphur dioxide	40–60	100–150	Exacerbations of respiratory illness from short-term exposures
			Increased prevalence of respiratory symptoms, including chronic bronchitis from long-term exposures
Suspended particulate matter			
Black smoke	40–60	100–150	Same as for SO_2
Total suspended particulates	60–90	150–230	Combined exposure to SO_2 and SPM[b] may have pulmonary effects
Lead	0.5–1	–	Blood enzyme changes
			Anaemia
			Hyperactivity and neurobehavioural effects
Nitrogen dioxide			
1 hour	400	–	Effects on lung function in asthmatics from short-term exposures
24 hours	–	150	
Carbon monoxide			
15 minutes	100 000	–	Reduced oxygen-carrying capacity of blood
30 minutes	–	60 000	
1 hour	30 000	–	
8 hours	–	10 000	
Carboxy-haemoglobin	–	2.5–3%	

[a]The 98 percentile value stipulates that 98 per cent of the daily averages must fall below a given concentration. This means that less than 2 per cent, or less than 7 days per year, may exceed that concentration.
[b]Suspended particulate matter

These are the guidelines used by the World Health Organization and form the basis of air pollution control the world over.

---

may have contributed to a high incidence of cancer in smoky cities.

Box 15.2 shows health effects and air quality guidelines for air pollutants.

Other smoke damage

Smoke did not only affect health: its impact on the urban setting was easy to see. Even today, black encrustations on older buildings may be seen in many large cities. In the past, when there were virtually no effective controls on smoke emissions, the damage done by smoke was even more obvious.

Until the passage of the Clean Air Acts, smoke abatement enthusiasts were anxious to draw attention to the vast costs that were incurred by the presence of smoke in the atmosphere. Clothes were soiled, curtains and hangings blackened and the exteriors of houses spoilt. Much of the cleaning work fell to women, so it is understandable that they had strong views on the undesirability of smoke. It was they who had to wash the white shirts worn by businessmen, who sometimes had to change into a new shirt for the afternoon after the morning's issue had become soiled. Although it was not easy for women to make their views felt, records suggest that some of them saw the presence of smoke in the atmosphere as almost a moral issue. If cleanliness was next to godliness, then the smoke that made things so dirty might be seen as evil.

Smoke in the atmosphere may have led to interesting changes in fashions. The traditional umbrella may be black because inky soot-laden rain would have marked other colours. Women in urban England in past centuries avoided white as being a colour too easily affected

Fig 15.1 Winter evening pollution in Stirling 1976. Under dead calm conditions smoke from houses accumulates in the valley. This is typical of the kind of pollution many coal burning cities have experienced.

by smoke and favoured creams and off-whites. They wore pattens, rather thick iron soles, which kept the hems of long dresses out of the sooty mud on the London streets. Small industries abounded in the city for refurbishing clothes that had been badly 'smoked'.

Smoke could also affect the growth of plants. Gradually we have adopted, for agriculture, varieties that are more resistant to air pollution. City gardens too tend to be stocked with more resistant plants. In the past the trees around industrial centres became so blackened that light-coloured butterflies were no longer camouflaged. Melanic (dark) forms became more common because predators could see them less easily. Plants are also very sensitive to sulphur dioxide and one of the first effects seems to be the inhibition of photosynthesis.

Smoke was not confined to cities and their surrounding areas. It drifted long distances. In the southwest of England, countryfolk of the 1780s said that they could smell London when the wind blew from that direction. Upon the moors shepherds noticed that their sheep's wool was blackened by what they termed 'moor-groime'. In the highlands of Scotland and far away in Scandinavia the rain and snow were sometimes black because of smoke that had been transported over enormous distances in unusual winds. Such incidents still occur today.

As we have seen, smog contained sulphuric acid as well as smoke. Sulphuric acid is a powerful corrosive agent. It rusted iron bars and ate away the stone of buildings. Architects sometimes complained of layers of sulphate damage 10 cm thick on calcareous stone. Such building stone was attacked through the reaction:

$$H_2SO_4 + CaCO_3 \rightarrow H_2O + CO_2 + CaSO_4$$

sulphuric + calcium → water + carbon + calcium
  acid   carbonate   dioxide sulphate

This reaction would seem to be rather a good one because it gets rid of the sulphuric acid and converts limestone ($CaCO_3$) into another building material, gypsum ($CaSO_4$). However, gypsum is soluble and dissolves in rain. The other problem is that gypsum occupies a larger volume than limestone, so the stone almost explodes from within.

Smoke in the modern world

Smoke and smog are not just problems of the past. There are still many cities where coal is heavily used in poorly controlled furnaces and in domestic fireplaces (Figure 15.1). This is particularly true in the developing world. Shanghai, for example, uses vast quantities of coal and has great problems in trying to reduce the soot concentrations in its atmosphere. There are a large number of small furnaces to control, and switching the domestic user to less-polluting coal gas takes time.

However, in Western Europe and North America the problems of urban smoke have largely disappeared and sulphur dioxide levels are declining. This is partly due to changes in fuel use, especially domestically, from coal to 'cleaner' fuels such as gas or electricity. In the UK, the Clean Air Acts also contributed to the reduction of smoke. Where coal is used in developed countries today it tends to be concentrated in large plants often sited far from cities. These usually have good control on grit and particle emissions, so smoke is not a problem. However, sulphur dioxide removal is still a comparatively costly undertaking which some major emitter countries such as the UK, the USA, Poland, etc. are slow to implement. Increasingly, international agreements require that sulphur dioxide be removed from flue gases in order to reduce the subsequent acidification of rain and the environment downwind. As improvements come, the contribution of sulphur dioxide to acid rain declines and so the balance within acid rain shifts away from sulphuric acid towards nitric acid. An important fraction of this nitric acid derives from cars, whereas they do not contribute to atmospheric sulphuric acid.

Photochemical smog

The air pollutants that we have been discussing so far have come from stationary sources. The fuel is predominantly coal. This is very much the traditional type of pollution that has been experienced by cities for as long as coal has been burnt; or if we think of smoke alone, we might say for as long as fuel has been burnt.

However, this century has seen the emergence of an entirely new kind of air pollution. This pollution arises particularly when volatile liquid fuels are used and hence the motor vehicle has been a big contributor. However, most of the actual pollutants causing the

---

Box 15.3 Reactions in photochemical smog

As seen in the text, reactions involving nitrogen oxides and ozone lie at the heart of photochemical smog:

$$NO_2 + hv \text{ (less than 310 nm)} \rightarrow O(^3P) + NO \quad [1]$$

$$O(^3P) + O_2 \rightarrow O_3 \quad [2]$$

$$O_3 + NO \rightarrow O_2 + NO_2 \quad [3]$$

These may be imagined as being represented by a pseudo-equilibrium constant relating the partial pressures of the two nitrogen oxides and ozone:

$$K = \frac{[NO] \cdot [O_3]}{[NO_2]} \quad [4]$$

If we were to increase NO_2 concentrations (in a way that did not use ozone) then the equilibrium could be maintained by increasing ozone concentrations. This happens in the photochemical smog through the mediation of OH radicals (OH is an important radical present in trace amounts in the atmosphere) in the oxidation of hydrocarbons:

$$OH + CH_4 \rightarrow H_2O + CH_3 \quad [5]$$

$$CH_3 + O_2 \rightarrow CH_3O_2 \quad [6]$$

$$CH_3O_2 + NO \rightarrow CH_3O + NO_2 \quad [7]$$

$$CH_3O + O_2 \rightarrow HCHO + HO_2 \quad [8]$$

$$HO_2 + NO \rightarrow NO_2 + OH \quad [9]$$

Thus these reactions represent a conversion of NO to NO_2 and of an alkane to an aldehyde. Note that the OH radical is regenerated, so can be thought of as a kind of catalyst. Aldehydes may also undergo attack by OH radicals:

$$CH_3CHO + OH \rightarrow CH_3CO + H_2O \quad [10]$$

$$CH_3CO + O_2 \rightarrow CH_3COO_2 \quad [11]$$

$$CH_3COO_2 + NO \rightarrow NO_2 + CH_3CO_2 \quad [12]$$

$$CH_3CO_2 \rightarrow CH_3 + CO_2 \quad [13]$$

The methyl radical in [13] may re-enter [7]. An important branch to this set of reactions is:

$$CH_3COO_2 + NO_2 \rightarrow CH_3COO_2NO_2 \quad [14]$$

leading to the formation of the eye irritant PAN (peroxyacetylnitrate).

---

problems are not themselves emitted by motor vehicles. Rather, they form in the atmosphere. So they are called secondary pollutants – they are formed from the reactions of primary pollutants, such as nitric oxide and unburnt fuel, that come directly from the

Fig 15.2 Photochemical smog held under a high inversion in Vancouver. This is very typical of the situation found in Los Angeles or many of the cities along the West Coast of North America.

automobiles. The chemical reactions that produce the secondary pollutants proceed most effectively in sunlight, so the result is called photochemical smog.

Photochemical smog first began to be noticed in Los Angeles during the Second World War. It was unique but was initially assumed to be similar to the air pollution that had been experienced elsewhere. However, when conventional smoke abatement techniques failed to make any impression, it became clear that this pollution must be different, and the experts were really baffled. It was Haagen-Smit, a biochemist studying vegetation damage, who finally realized that the Los Angeles smog was caused by reactions of automobile exhaust vapours in sunlight.

How does this happen? The reactions are quite complicated, but we can simplify them by substituting a very simple organic molecule such as methane (CH_4) to represent the vehicle emissions:

$$CH_4 + 2O_2 + 2NO \xrightarrow{hv,\ sunlight} H_2O + HCHO + 2NO_2$$

methane + oxygen + nitric oxide → water + formaldehyde + nitrogen dioxide

Nitric oxide is a common pollutant from automobiles.

We can see two things taking place in this reaction. Firstly the automobile hydrocarbon is oxidized to an aldehyde (i.e. a molecule with a CHO group). In the reaction above it is formaldehyde. Aldehydes are eye irritants and, some have argued, also carcinogens. Secondly we can see that the nitrogen oxide has oxidized to nitrogen dioxide. This is a brownish gas. It can absorb light and dissociate:

$$NO_2 + hv \rightarrow O + NO$$

nitrogen + sunlight → atomic + nitric
dioxide   oxygen   oxide

This reforms the nitric oxide, but also gives an isolated and reactive oxygen atom that can react to form ozone:

$$O + O_2 \rightarrow O_3$$

atomic oxygen + molecular oxygen → ozone

It is this ozone that characterizes photochemical smog. Note the important fact that ozone, which we regard as such a problem, is not emitted by any major polluter: it is the product of the interaction of a number of pollutants in the atmosphere. The detailed reactions are rather more complicated than illustrated here. If you are interested, you can see them in Box 15.3.

Table 15.2 Comparison of Los Angeles and London smog

Characteristic	Los Angeles	London
Air temperature	24–32 °C	−1–4 °C
Relative humidity	<70 per cent	85 per cent (+ fog)
Type of temperature inversion	Subsidence, at a few thousand metres	Radiation (near ground) at about 100 metres
Wind speed	<3 m/s	Calm
Visibility	<0.8–1.6 km	<30 m
Months of most frequent occurrence	Aug.–Sept.	Dec.–Jan.
Major fuels	Petroleum	Largely coal
Principal constituents	O_3, NO, NO_2, CO, organic matter	Particulate matter, CO, S compounds
Type of chemical reaction	Oxidative	Reductive
Time of maximum occurrence	Midday	Early morning
Principal health irritation effects (SO_2/smoke)	Temporary eye irritation (PAN)	Lung diseases
Materials damaged	Rubber cracked (O_3)	Iron, concrete corroded

Source: R.W. Raiswell *et al.* (1980).

The smog found in the Los Angeles basin is very different from that which we have previously described as typical of coal-burning cities. There is no fog when Los Angeles smog forms and visibility does not decline to just a few metres as was typical of the London fogs. The Los Angeles smog forms best of course on sunny days. London fogs are blown away by a wind, but gentle sea breezes in the Los Angeles basin can hold the pollution in against the mountains and prevent it from escaping out to sea. The pollution cannot rise in the atmosphere because it is trapped by an inversion layer: the air at ground level is cooler than that aloft, thus a cap of warm air prevents the cooler air from rising and dispersing the pollutants (Figure 15.2). A fuller list of the differences between Los Angeles and London-type smogs is given in Table 15.2.

Effects of photochemical smog

Photochemical smog is quite unlike the smoky air typical of cities of old, so we would not expect thick crusts of soot to be growing on buildings. Petrol, unlike coal, contains relatively little sulphur, hence sulphate damage is not so likely to occur either. However, there are plenty of other pollutants that can damage materials.

Ozone is a particularly reactive gas. It attacks the double bonds of organic molecules very readily. Rubber is a polymeric material with many double bonds, so it is attacked very easily by ozone. Rubber exposed to ozone shows cracks, and tyres and windscreen wiper blades are especially vulnerable. Newer synthetic rubbers have the double bonds more protected by other chemical groups so they are somewhat resistant to damage by ozone. Many pigments and dyes are also attacked by ozone. The usual result of this is that the dye fades. This means that it is important for art galleries in polluted cities to filter their air carefully, especially where they house collections of paintings using traditional colouring materials that are especially sensitive.

Nitrogen oxides too are associated with photochemical smogs. They may also damage pigments. It is possible that nitrogen oxides may also increase the rate of damage to building stone, but it is not really clear how this takes place. Some have argued that nitrogen dioxide increases the efficiency of production of sulphuric acid on stone surfaces in those cities that have moderate sulphur dioxide concentrations. Others have suggested that the nitrogen compounds in polluted atmospheres enable micro-organisms to grow more effectively on stone surfaces and enhance the biologically mediated damage.

It is not just materials that are damaged by photochemical smog. Living things suffer too. Plants are especially sensitive to ozone and hence the early observations of damage that led to the research by Haagen-Smit. Ozone damages plants by changing the 'leakiness' of cells to important ions such as potassium. Early symptoms of such injury appear as water-soaked areas on the leaves.

Human health can also be affected by these gases. In general, oxidants such as aldehydes cause eye, nose and throat irritation as well as headaches. Ozone impairs pulmonary function. At high concentrations nitrogen oxides can do so too, especially in people with asthma. Eye irritation is a frequent complaint during photochemical smogs. This arises from the presence of a group of chemicals that form through a reaction of nitrogen oxides and various organic compounds in the smog. The best known of these eye irritants is peroxyacetylnitrate, or PAN, which is responsible for the particularly irritant quality of the Los Angeles atmosphere. The reactions that produce PAN are shown in Box 15.3, and World Health Organization guideline values for urban air pollutant concentrations appear in Box 15.1.

Other changes and their effects

Photochemical smog is not the only pollution problem created by vehicles. They are also associated with other pollutants such as lead and benzene. The success of lead tetralkyl compounds as anti-knock agents for improving the performance of automotive engines has meant that, in countries with high car use, very large quantities of lead have been mobilized. This lead has been widely dispersed, but particularly large quantities have been deposited in cities and near heavily used roads. Lead is a toxin and has been linked with a number of environmental health problems. Perhaps the most worrying evidence has come from studies which indicate a decline in intelligence among children exposed to quite low concentrations of lead.

Unleaded petrol was introduced in the USA in the 1970s so that catalytic converters could be used on cars. Since that time unleaded petrol has come to be used more widely. There is evidence that blood lead concentrations have dropped in parallel with the declining automotive source of lead. Nevertheless, a decrease in atmospheric lead may not be sufficient to reduce the risk in children to a satisfactory level. The high ratio of food intake to body weight among children means that they are likely to gain much of their lead burden from sources such as food and water (although some of the lead in these may have come from the atmosphere).

Benzene is a further worrying component of automotive fuels. It occurs naturally in crude oil and is a useful component because it can prevent knocking in unleaded petrol (the production process is usually adjusted so that the benzene concentration is about 5 per cent). However, benzene is a potent carcinogen. It appears that more than 10 per cent of the benzene used by society (33 Mt/year) ends up being lost to the environment. High concentrations can be found in the air of cities and these concentrations may increase the number of cancers. Exposure is complicated by the importance of other sources of benzene to humans, e.g. tobacco smoke.

Toluene is another aromatic compound present in large concentrations in petrol. Evidence would suggest that it is far less likely to be a carcinogen than benzene, but it does have some very undesirable effects. It contributes significantly to the production of ozone and formaldehyde in smoggy atmospheres. In addition it reacts to form a PAN-type compound, peroxybenzoyl nitrate, which is a particularly potent eye irritant.

Diesel-powered vehicles have been increasingly in evidence in Europe, and by no means all of them are large vehicles. Today, a substantial number of cars are diesel-powered, taking advantage of the lower fuel costs. Diesel fuels also have the advantage of being unleaded. On the other hand, the fuel injection process of the diesel engine leads to the fuel being dispersed as droplets within the engine. These may not always burn completely, which means that diesel engines may produce large quantities of smoke if not properly maintained. This smoke now makes a significant contribution to the soiling quality of urban air. In addition, the particles are rich in polyaromatic hydrocarbons (PAH), which are carcinogens. Diesel fuels have traditionally had a high sulphur content, but legislative pressures are set to lower that. There will also be increased attention in the future to lowering the emissions from the growing diesel fleet.

Solving the problem: the future

A solution to the problem of air pollution would seem relatively simple. We should emit less pollutants. Indeed that philosophy is inherent in laws such as the UK

Clean Air Act 1956. Here the aim was to reduce the amount of smoke by requiring smokeless fuels to be burnt in some areas. Later legislation in the UK and elsewhere sought to change the composition of some fuels – requiring them to have low sulphur or low lead contents.

Another solution was to attempt to disperse the pollutants from chimneys more widely through the use of tall stacks. This often has the effect of decreasing the pollutant concentrations locally while increasing them downwind. Consequently this approach is widely criticized, particularly in relation to the acid rain problem. However, it is hard to imagine that chimneys will vanish from our townscapes, and wisely used they probably represent an appropriate way to lower exposure to pollutants. But on large coal-burning plants tall chimneys need to be combined with other more active pollution abatement techniques.

When approaching the question of secondary pollutants we have to be aware that the problem is a good deal more subtle. In some cases stopping the emission of one pollutant can actually increase the secondary photochemical pollutant concentration in the air! Attempts to solve the pollution problems of cities with severe photochemical problems have not been a complete success. Los Angeles typically has great difficulty in meeting the US air quality guidelines.

One way of attacking the problem of secondary pollutants is to eliminate the 'catalyst' for their production. In this case we would wish to remove the hydrocarbons that lie at the heart of the photochemical reactions. These were represented as methane in our illustration (see Box 15.3), but in reality are usually somewhat larger hydrocarbon molecules. This approach was attempted through fitting cars with catalytic converters which destroyed the hydrocarbons in their exhausts. However, hydrocarbons still escaped by evaporation at filling stations or from hot engines while the cars were stationary. One solution to this is to design fuels of lower volatility so that less evaporates. Another possibility, although slower to implement, is to use a fuel such as methanol whose molecules have less tendency to enter into photochemical reactions. The difficulty is that methanol may actually increase the concentrations of formaldehyde in the urban atmosphere at the same time as lowering other photochemical pollutants. It has been seen by some as a rather expensive way to address the air pollution problem compared with lowering fuel volatility, using natural gas or adding catalytic converters.

These attempts to reduce secondary pollution assume that cities will continue to be filled with hydrocarbon-fuelled vehicles. However, the most obvious way of reducing vehicle emissions is to curtail the use of the private car. This would necessitate the creation of cheap, efficient and convenient public transport systems. Facilities for cyclists and pedestrians would also need to be improved, although a significant reduction in traffic would itself go some way towards making walking and cycling safer, healthier and more attractive. Incentives to encourage car sharing could contribute to reducing traffic, and the use of electric cars would cut down pollution in cities, though the pollution caused by the generation of the electricity cannot be ignored. Moving freight where possible from road to rail (which is generally more fuel-efficient) would also reduce emissions.

Ultimately, a lasting solution to the problems of urban air pollution may involve a change in lifestyle, perhaps with people living nearer their workplaces (or working from home) and buying more locally produced goods, and fuel economy being a priority in the minds of planners. Fuel economy also has advantages, of course, in terms of reducing resource use and curtailing the greenhouse effect.

However, vehicles are not the only source of urban air pollution. Incineration of waste, whether domestic or industrial, can cause considerable air pollution, and modern industrial processes can lead to the emission of a wide range of novel air pollutants. As most city-dwellers spend the vast majority of their time indoors, interior pollution can be a significant factor too. For instance, chipboards and insulating foam can release formaldehyde, gas cookers produce nitrogen dioxide, slow-burning wood stoves emit various carcinogens, and cigarette smoking produces a large number of harmful compounds including benzene and carbon monoxide. So the solution to urban air pollution problems no longer simply revolves around the reduction of smoke. Today if we really want to reduce human exposure to air pollutants we need to consider and regulate an enormous range of pollution sources.

References

Howe, C.W. (1991) An evaluation of US air and water policies. *Environment*, **33**(7), 10–15, 32–6.
Humme, R.P. (1991) Clearing the air: environmental reform in Mexico. *Environment*, **33**(10), 6–11, 26–30.
Raiswell, R.W., P. Brimblecombe, D.L. Dent and P.S. Liss

(1980) *Environmental Chemistry*. London: Edward Arnold.

Soroos, M.S. (1993) The odyssey of Arctic haze: towards a global atmospheric regime. *Environment*, **34**(10), 6–11, 25–7.

Tietenberg, T. (1985) *Emissions trading*. Washington, DC: Resources for the future.

UN Environment Programme (1985) An assessment of urban air quality. *Environment*, **31**(8), 7–13, 26–34.

Young, O. and G. Osherenko (Eds) (1993) *Polar politics: creating international environmental regimes*. New York: University of Columbia Press.

Further reading

For historical and literary background: P. Brimblecombe (1987) *The big smoke* (Methuen, London) and P. Brimblecombe (1990) Writing on smoke, in H. Bradby (Ed) *Dirty words* (Earthscan, London) pp. 93–114.

For air pollutants in the modern world: D.M. Elsom (1992) *Atmospheric pollution*, (Blackwell, Oxford).

For a study of the effects on health and plants: A. Wellburn (1994) *Air pollution and climate change*, 2nd edition (Longman, Harlow) and World Health Organization (1987) *Air quality guidelines for Europe*. (WHO, Copenhagen).

Regarding building and material damage see the special issue of *Atmospheric Environment*, **26B-2**, 1992, which includes papers from the International Conference on Acidic Deposition in Glasgow.

For the chemistry and photochemistry of smog see P. Brimblecombe (1986) *Air composition and chemistry* (Cambridge University Press, Cambridge) and Raiswell *et al.* (1980).

On a probable substitute fuel see C.L. Gray and J.A. Alson (1992) The case for methanol, *Scientific American*, **11**, 86–92.

Finally, looking at the present and the future, see 1st Report of The Quality of Urban Air Review Group (1993) *Urban Air Quality in the UK* (Department of Environment, London).

CHAPTER 16

Environmental risk management

SIMON GERRARD

Risk is now being regarded as a culturally framed concept that acts as a metaphor for individual feelings about loss of control, powerlessness and the drift of social change away from what is good for the Earth towards what seems to be bad. Risk is therefore a multidimensional notion. It is not separable into mechanistic structures of probability and evaluation. It is reflective of the changing social order regarding justice and opportunity.

Risk tolerance is quite different from risk acceptance. There may be no such thing as risk acceptance where the cause of the threat is suspected or disliked. Study after study has shown that the hard core of opposition to nuclear power believes as much that the industry cannot be trusted and is democratically unstoppable as it feels that nuclear reactors are inherently unsafe. Environmental groups exploit this by challenging the secrecy of the industry, exposing cover-ups in accident records, and revealing bribes or political connections between senior industry representatives and politicians. In a similar vein, opposition to genetically modified food products is fuelled by a despair that technology may produce endless arrays of 'unnatural' foods, while apparently nutritious natural varieties become commercially squeezed out of the markets.

This suggests that research into risk perception should integrate the psychometric approach with the cultural theory model. The former covers the relationship between judgements over the safety of products or processes and the level of safety actually provided, as far as is perceived by the respondent (Krimsky and Golding, 1992). The latter covers an array of ideas as to how people seem to accept technical judgements being made on their behalf. Some prefer a hierarchical model of society where an acknowledged élite take such decisions. This is common in the medical and legal professions, and in public views as to the credibility of doctors and lawyers. Others prefer more egalitarian perspectives where judgements are shared between professional and lay representatives on a negotiated basis where mutual respect guides the discourse (Rayner, 1992). There are many shades between. The point here is that risk tolerance is a function of a much wider view on how technical expertise should be handled in a society that is forever trying to flex its democratic muscles (see Schwartz and Thompson, 1990; Piller, 1991).

Behind this interesting academic analysis is an important argument about the changing role of science and peer review in modern society. These points have been touched on in the Introduction. In the risk management world the authority of regulation is very much dependent on the consent of the risk creator and the affected public. In the USA and to a lesser extent in Germany and in the Netherlands, the regulatory process tends to reflect clearly defined targets of public health and safety laid down by a mixture of political representatives, technical experts and pressure group opinion. These targets become enforceable standards which may or may not have the backing of evidence for public health studies. At times, such standards are not only technically demanding but can cause much economic hardship. Yet because these levels of presumed safety exist in law, they are defended by the regulatory culture and buttressed by pressure groups whose power rests in the statutory law.

In the UK, in France and in many Commonwealth countries based on UK legal and regulatory tradition, risk regulation is based much more on a self-policing approach. The role of the regulator is to set a broad zone of safety tolerability, based on discretionary phrases such as best practicable means, or as low as reasonably achievable, and then to offer the client a choice of meeting the requirements of this zonal range of safety options. This is clearly a more negotiative approach, where regulator and client dance around in arena of opportunity and persuasion. Because the law is also couched in discretionary terms, so the activist environmental and consumer groups have less room for judicial review over ministerial decisions.

For a while all this was changing. The Americans and the Germans began to favour a more consultative approach, the Germans having a penchant for corporatist structures where employees, shareholders, managers and local residents got involved. The British began to like more 'arm's length' and target-driven approaches to risk regulation, with a sense of formality in the proceedings rather than friendly cups of tea. More recently, the trend seems to have been reversed just at a time when industry is becoming much more consumer and environmentally friendly, and when regulation is taking on both an economic mode of taxes and tradable permits, and a more proactive negotiative stance.

Risk regulation is a function of social change and behavioural preferences for ensuring responsible action. As eco-auditing becomes more common in industrial management, as local Agenda 21s appear more ubiquitous in local government, as regulatory agencies become more sensitized to public opinion, and as representations of consumer and environmental organizations are incorporated into peer review panels, so risk regulation will adopt a more participatory role, mediating between various interpretations of safety propriety, fairness and technological change. Risk managers will have to become more adept at reading the social and political mood, and practising effective interdisciplinarity.

Further reading

The best available report on the changing world of risk management is that produced by the Royal Society Study Group in 1992 under the chairmanship of Sir Fred Warner, *Risk: analysis, perception and management* (Royal Society, London). For a good review of the basic social theories see S. Krimsky and D. Golding (Eds) (1992) *Social theories of risk* (Praeger, New York). For a fine analysis of cultural theory, see S. Rayner (1992) Cultural theory and risk analysis, in Krimsky and Golding (1992), pp. 83–117. On the matter of antagonism to technological development see M. Schwartz and M. Thompson (Eds) (1990) *Divided we stand: redefining politics, technology and social choice* (Harvester Wheatsheaf, Hemel Hempstead) and G. Piller (1991) *The fail-safe society: community defiance and the end of American technological optimism* (Basic Books, New York).

This world . . . is not a static entity populated by thinking ants who, crawling all over it, gradually discover its features without affecting them in any way. It is a dynamic and multifaceted entity which affects and reflects the activity of its explorers. It was once a world full of gods; it then became a drab material world and it will, hopefully, change further into a more peaceful world where matter and life, thought and feelings, innovation and tradition collaborate for the benefit of all.

The sentiment above from Californian philosopher Paul Feyerabend (1987, p. 89) echoes what many people with concern for the environment hope and feel. There are numerous similar writings within the environmental literature but few which actually go further to suggest how this 'new world' might be achieved. In a small way, this chapter attempts to provide an insight into an alternative system by which the environment might better be managed in the struggle for justice and equality. It describes an alternative decision-making framework through which environmental policy can be developed that goes some way to promoting the effective use of science and technology for the benefit of the majority.

Introduction: the concept of safety

In general, but not wholly, the development of modern society has regarded the promotion of safety as a good thing. The wish to reduce risks, particularly those associated with man-made technologies such as nuclear power and the motor car, is perhaps part of our underlying desire to promote life as long as possible. Whatever the precise reason, the process of managing risks, and thus increasing safety, involves a balancing act – that between the cost of reducing risk and the benefits arising from the amount of risk reduced. This chapter explores the whole concept of risk and examines some of the key issues associated with the management of risk, including its technical assessment, perception and communication. As Box 16.1 shows, these are the basic components of risk management. Box 16.2 provides some basic definitions.

The idea of management implies some form of decision making, often in an atmosphere of conflict between competing parties. Such conflict might be resolved simply by power, where the strongest party wins, imposing its rule and eliminating behaviour contrary to it. In this case there is little or no argument or discussion about alternative solutions to a problem. Conflict can also be resolved through the use of theory

Box 16.1 The risk management cycle

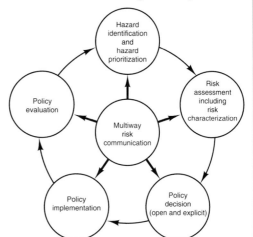

The risk management 'cycle'. (*Source:* Soby, Simpson and Ives, 1993.)

This shows the basic components of risk management. Note the importance of multiway risk communication throughout each of the stages and the feedback loop of policy monitoring back into the identification of hazards and problem definition.

where special groups, such as scientists, analyse the problem, develop systems representing the problem and provide guidelines for its resolution.

This approach has been the mainstay of the development of environmental policy in the UK, but suffers from a series of drawbacks. First, it assumes that only scientists and technical specialists are worthy of taking part in the debate and that, though they may not always agree, if consensus can be reached between scientists then society will benefit accordingly. Second, there are many examples where the adoption of a largely scientific approach, at the expense of the 'gut feelings' of individuals and groups within society, has led to disastrous consequences for certain people, or for ecosystems, and unnecessary human suffering. Examples include the failure to control persistent organochlorine pesticides that led to the death of birds of prey in the 1960s, the delayed lowering of occupational radiation exposure levels, which created widespread disease amongst workers using radionuclides, and the use of agricultural chemicals. In this last case the toxicological assessment of herbicides undertaken by the UK government's Pesticides Advisory Council (PAC) repeatedly stated that there was no scientific evidence, based upon laboratory studies, that the substances

---

Box 16.2 Definitions of the stages of risk management

Hazard identification: determines what can go wrong by identifying a set of circumstances.

Risk estimation: predicts how likely is it that a set of circumstances will arise.

Consequence analysis: determines subjectively the significance of the outcome of a hazard event.

Risk assessment: combines two-dimensionally the risk estimation and consequence analysis stages.

Risk evaluation: determines subjectively the tolerable level of risk.

Risk mitigation: considers how risks can best be avoided, reduced to tolerable levels and controlled.

Risk monitoring: provides feedback about the net effects of risk mitigation.

---

caused any harm to humans, despite large volumes of anecdotal evidence to the contrary provided by the farm workers themselves. Ultimately, in the face of mounting opposition the PAC were forced to qualify their original statement, acknowledging that there was no harm providing that the herbicides were produced and used under the correct conditions (Wynne, 1992). This apparently minor amendment to the scientific facts is crucial as it introduces the concept of management and operation into the safety debate – two points that we shall see are as important as the scientific and technical aspects of managing risks. In all of these cases, either the scientific assessments were flawed or the wider management and operational considerations had not been considered. In rather too many cases both kinds of misjudgement have been made.

An alternative method for resolving conflict lies in the free and open exchange of ideas between interested parties. This is not to say that conflict between parties will thus be avoided. But this approach recognizes that where conflict does occur it can be, and should be, a positive experience through which ideas are transformed into solutions. Increasingly, as people discover that Western ways do not offer the panacea that such ways once promised, they are beginning to realize that decisions concerning the value of science in the decision-making process are decisions about how we want to live; to feel; to think. If this is so then decisions about how to manage the environment should not rely wholly on scientific estimations but include the ethical and

moral considerations of other members of society. This can only be achieved by opening up the decision-making process, and the management of environmental risks provides one system by which this may occur.

This approach has two aspects. One involves the faithful multi way communication about dangers and tolerance to danger. The other provides a mediative or dispute-resolving mechanism for seeking common ground between interested parties. Environmental risk mediation is not particularly common in Europe or Japan, where more hierarchical structures of power operate. But in the USA and Canada and increasingly elsewhere, environmental mediation generally is becoming a valuable method of reaching consensus (for a good review see Bingham, 1986). This involves an element of power sharing between parties, and hence requires a more open, trusting and pluralistic approach to politics and power. Here is when environmental science in its interdisciplinary mode, as covered in the Introduction, can come into its own (see, in particular, Chapters 5 and 6 of the Royal Society, 1992, report on risk, and Krimsky *et al.*, 1992).

The concept of risk management

Historically the management of environmental risk has relied upon technical assessments designed to evaluate both the probability of particular events occurring, and the seriousness of the resulting consequences. However, this is only one part of the wider process of risk management. More recently the emphasis has shifted away from technical assessments towards consideration of the perception of risk. This has been generated, in part, from the communication of risk information within the wider process of developing publicly tolerable systems for managing the environment.

There are no universally accepted definitions of *hazard* and *risk*. As a consequence, some confusion can be found within risk literature as terms such as *hazard, risk, risk assessment, risk evaluation and risk analysis* are interpreted in different ways. This is in part a function of the relatively embryonic nature of the field, but, as we shall see, it can be argued that the lack of universal definitions for risk terms reflects the variety of the situations and the political systems in which the management of risk occurs. The definitions described below are those derived from modern Western society. It would be wrong to assume that similar definitions would be wholly applicable in other cultures. The fact that other non-Western societies may manage the environment, and the hazards it presents, in different ways is one of the major features of the concept of risk: indeed, its strength lies in this cultural pluralism. One only has to look at Western society's failed attempts to help in the environmental and economic development of other cultures to realize that our ways of thinking are not necessarily prescriptions for success elsewhere. For example, Western tobacco companies are actively promoting smoking in the Third World as their profit margins fade in more health-conscious and educated post-industrial societies. Yet the health risk assessments of smoking are now well established, though not necessarily well communicated to would-be consumers around the globe.

Within science it has been recognized that retaining a plurality of views is necessary. John Stuart Mill identified three reasons why this is advisable (Feyerabend, 1987). First, because to deny any view assumes infallibility – a dangerous assumption at any time. Second, because even if a view appears to be wrong, it may still hold a portion of truth. Any one view is rarely the whole truth. Third, a point of view that is wholly true but not contested becomes a prejudice. It is important to measure up these views against others even if the original view is retained because the meaning of any view cannot be fully understood unless contrasted with other opinions. We shall see that these are very important considerations for risk management.

Understanding hazard and risk

One of the most common confusions lies in the distinction between risk and hazard. Put at its simplest, the term *hazard* relates to the property of a substance, or an activity, to cause harm. The property or activity may best be described as a set of defined circumstances. For example, a substance such as cyanide is well known to be hazardous to human health if ingested or absorbed into the human body. However, if it is locked in a cupboard its hazard potential is negligible. In order for its hazard potential to be realized other circumstances must arise. For instance, there must be some escape route from the cupboard and a target, in this case a person, capable of ingesting the cyanide. Understanding the hazard as a set of defined circumstances, however simple or complex, is the key to developing systems to reduce the potential of the hazard to occur and thus to increase safety.

Defining the set of circumstances allows us to understand the nature and characteristics of the hazard. The next stage is to ask how likely is it that the set of circumstances will occur – to realize the hazard potential. Sometimes, but not always, it is possible to attribute a statistical probability to each of the factors within the set of circumstances. In the simple example above this would involve knowing about the likelihood that the cyanide would escape from the cupboard and the chance that a person would be exposed to it.

Most definitions of *risk* use terms such as probability, likelihood or chance which imply the potential of something occurring. Such an outcome is usually adverse – it is not usual to talk about the risk of benefiting from a particular outcome such as winning the national lottery or passing exams. Risk, then, is the likelihood, or probability, that a particular set of circumstances will occur, resulting in a particular consequence, over a particular time period. It is usually expressed as a frequency – for example the risk of being struck by lightning is about 1 chance in 10 million per year. This is based on the average number of people being struck by lightning each year divided by the total population. Clearly, this statistical probability is only an estimate and some people, for example golfers, will be at a greater risk than others. Traditionally, the time period used in calculating risks is one year, and the most common outcome or consequence of the risk event is human death, although environmental impairment would be equally valid.

Box 16.3 illustrates two common methods of identifying and organizing hazards. However, if defining sets of circumstances is often very problematic then the estimation of probabilities is even more so. First, there is the problem of how to frame the problem such that it is possible to undertake numerical analyses. Any framing must be balanced against the need to provide a sufficient level of comprehensiveness such that the majority of possible sequences are considered. Second, it is important to account for uncertainties within the system. These may be compounded throughout the analysis to the point where the numerical assessment of probability becomes meaningless. Third, it is important to consider the nature of the probability data itself, as the combination of data requires care and sensitivity.

Though this definition of risk implies a particular consequence, say, human death, it is only when the significance of the consequence is evaluated, in terms of societal judgement of the cost of the consequences, that a *risk assessment* is performed. Thus, a common definition of risk assessment would be the combination of a frequency estimation – a risk – with some form of

Box 16.3 Fault and event tree analysis

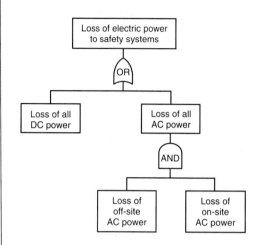

(a) Simplified fault tree on electric power. (Source: Rasmussen, 1990.)

These logic diagrams have been applied to engineering systems analysis since the 1960s. Each form of analysis attempts to identify the components of a system that may lead to a hazard being realized.

Event trees specify a range of possible outcomes of a hazardous event, such as a pipeline rupture. Each outcome is then linked to the main event by a series of circumstances known as an accident sequence. Probabilities of any part of the sequence occurring can be estimated and an overall probability of a particular outcome, say, a flash fire and explosion, can be calculated by multiplying the probabilities throughout the sequence.

Fault trees use the reverse process, beginning with the initial event. A 'top-down' analysis is then constructed using a series of formal statements or 'logic gates' which determine the relationship between the individual circumstances within the accident sequence. Such statements will identify whether circumstances are mutually inclusive ('AND' gates), whereby all circumstances must occur for the hazard to be realized, or whether the circumstances are mutually independent ('OR' gates)

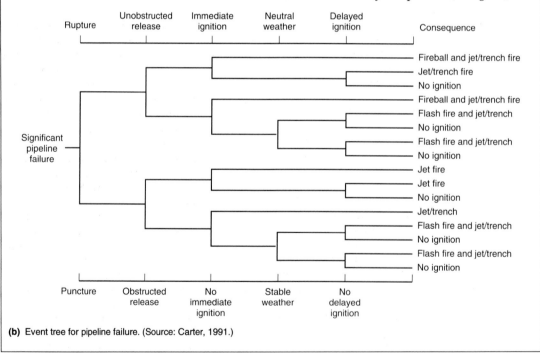

(b) Event tree for pipeline failure. (Source: Carter, 1991.)

consequence analysis – an evaluation of the seriousness of the consequences in question, such as of death, environmental damage or passing on a limitation of choice to future generations about the amount of fossil

fuels they can burn. This two-dimensional approach is what many people in the risk field understand by the term *risk assessment*. These two dimensions can be depicted graphically as is shown in Box 16.4.

Box 16.4 FN curves

Frequency – Consequence graphs, or *FN* curves, have been used extensively to depict and compare the risks from different activities. Where the consequences of an event vary over a wide range, this type of approach is particularly useful. However, a number of problems exist with *FN* curves. The calculation of fatalities is not always straightforward. For example, there is the difficulty of accounting for delayed deaths, those fatalities that occur long after the event. By considering only *fatalities* one omits to account for *fates worse than death*.

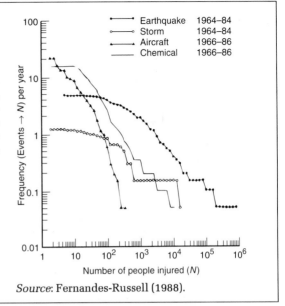

Source: Fernandes-Russell (1988).

Extending this definition further, risk management can be seen as a series of interlinked components with technical risk estimation at the outset, the assessment of that risk, and the development of some kind of policy response to that assessment. Thus, as Boxes 16.1 and 16.2 show, risk management involves much more than just the two-dimensional, probability/consequence assessment of risk. It also encompasses much broader factors such as public perceptions of risk, which may differ significantly from those of the experts, legal considerations regarding the style of regulation, and cost benefit analyses of various strategies for risk mitigation. These points are developed later in the chapter. Ultimately, the development of environmental policy, and the decision-making process through which policy is derived, faces the challenge of incorporating a wide range of concerns to determine what level of risk will be tolerable in any given set of defined circumstances. These include not only scientific evidence and probability estimates, but a cultural sense of fairness in the treatment of citizens and enterprise, the degree of trust in regulating agencies and the underlying feelings about how much manipulation of our lives we are prepared to tolerate when we have no means of avoiding certain outcomes, for example the extra ultraviolet radiation from ozone depletion.

How safe is safe enough?

The question of achieving sufficient levels of safety is one that has demanded much attention from risk analysts and decision makers. Determining acceptable or, more correctly, tolerable levels of risk has proved to be difficult for many reasons, not least because the answer lies not in scientific and technical assessment, but in economic, moral and ethical bases. Thus, the decision makers, the politicians, are forced to consider an array of much wider social concerns in order to achieve a tolerable level of risk. The simple fact that different groups within our democratic society adopt vastly different definitions of the term tolerable gives some indication of how complex a task this is. Decision makers have often been accused of trying to avoid criticism by concealing how decisions were reached, which has led to increasing public disquiet about the fairness of risk management, particularly in situations where a local public is asked to bear the brunt of the risks associated with an activity, when the benefits are shared more widely. Examples here include radioactive waste disposal and the incineration of industrial wastes, but the siting of high voltage transmission lines is also becoming a matter of controversy. The unequal distribution of risks and benefits is a feature of modern risk management that requires urgent attention, to the point that within the risk field the question becomes one of how fair is fair enough?

Box 16.5 Methods for evaluating risks

Risk benefit/cost analysis: based on the economic efficiency of introducing particular risk reduction measures.

Multi-objective approach: uses multi-attribute utility theory (MAUT) which evaluates different factors independently then combines these evaluations into some form of overall assessment.

Revealed preference: uses the tolerance of current risks as a basis for the introduction of new risks providing the benefits are similar. This method assumes that the degree to which people expose themselves to any danger reveals their willingness to tolerate the associated risk. This technique is based on actual evidence of behaviour and exposure.

Expressed preference: is more direct in that it measures risk by asking people what levels of safety and danger they are prepared to tolerate for certain classes of hazard. This may be done statistically or by comparative measures, for instance by determining how much more or less dangerous a hazard should be in comparison with another hazard. The difficulty here is to select comparable hazards. One cannot compare the risks of involuntary exposure, such as nuclear power, with voluntary risks, such as smoking. This method also assumes that people are well informed and it provides only a snapshot set of preferences at a given time.

De minimis: literally 'at the lowest level' assumes that some risks are too trivial to bother with, or that levels of safety are as high as they possibly can be. It seeks to establish thresholds below which risks are deemed acceptable. This suffers from the fallacy that background levels are thought of as 'natural', and therefore are 'normal', even to the extent of being considered moral. It is also couched in terms of discretion, that is the judgements of regulators as to what level of safety is tolerable are based on the extent of technological development, the economic circumstances of the risk creator and the likely public reaction.

Clearly there are a vast number of different types of risk that need to be evaluated. Some risks we cope with subconsciously on an everyday basis – where to cross the road, what to eat, which hobby to pursue. Others, the so-called societal risks, are evaluated for the benefit of society as a whole. It is on the latter that this chapter will concentrate. But first let us consider briefly how individual risks are judged. Why is it that some people choose to undertake dangerous activities, seeking relatively high levels of risk whilst others take extensive measures to avoid risk? One suggestion is that, as individuals, we each have an inherent level of risk at which we feel comfortable. Thus, if activities are made safer for us, we may strive to undertake them in a more dangerous way, compensating for the increased safety, and so restoring our chosen level of personal risk. An example of this concerns driving habits. The introduction of seatbelts was a safety measure designed to reduce the number of people killed in road accidents. The UK Department of Transport weighed up the cost of introducing seatbelts against the implied statistical value of the lives that seatbelts would save and concluded that it was cost effective to require car manufacturers to fit seatbelts to all new cars, and for drivers and passengers to use them. The net result of this was a reduction in the number of deaths to drivers and passengers. However, it has been suggested that one side effect of this reduction measure was to change the way in which some people drive. Not only do some people drive faster when wearing a seatbelt than when not, but they accelerate and brake more sharply to compensate for the increased safety that they perceive. This may be tolerable for those fortunate enough to be contained within the car, but for cyclists and pedestrians there is a net increase in risk. This example illustrates the complexity of managing risks, particularly when dealing with the transfer of risks from one group to another.

Evaluation of risks

There are a number of ways in which risks may be evaluated. In the example above the method used by the government was a fairly straightforward risk benefit/cost analysis based on economic efficiency. However, other methods are used, such as those shown in Box 16.5

It is tempting to view the technical assessment of risk as being somehow objective and rational whilst the wider evaluation of risk tolerability is filled with value judgements and internal and external biases. In reality, each of the components within the risk management process are subject to value judgements, biases and uncertainties. Risk management, although a very useful process, is not a precise science, nor is it a particularly well-developed art form. Some of the components of risk management are still embryonic in their development, though the path from hazard identification, through technical risk assessment to risk evaluation, mitigation and monitoring, has a broadly sequential

Box 16.6 The ALARP principle

ALARP, or as low as reasonably practicable, is couched in the British discretionary manner of determining safety. The onus of the safety case rests with the creator of the risk, who must satisfy the inspector that the ALARP principle has been followed in the management of industrial activities; that a safety culture is in place; and that action in the event of an accident is judged to be appropriate and fully intelligible to the nearby public. Finally, ALARP is based on a crude cost benefit comparison. Even for private concerns the benefits from a given technology or management approach may be only a tenth that of the costs. Yet the adoption of the scheme can be enforced on the bases of tolerance and precaution.

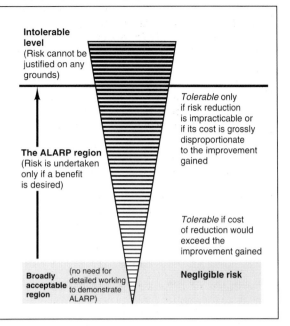

structure that feeds back into itself. All methods of risk assessment and risk evaluation suffer from unsound or tenuous assumptions. Open and honest scientific disagreement is therefore a valuable part of the process of developing risk policies. Proponents see these processes as rational, scientific tools providing accurate assessment and effective management, whilst opponents consider them deeply biased and inherently flawed. However, the portrayal of risk assessment and evaluation as scientific is not altogether useful. Even if risk assessment and evaluation were somehow miraculously objective, they would not be able to answer the wider question of how safe is safe enough, or to put it another way, what level of risk is tolerable?

Risk and tolerability

The notion of risk tolerability as opposed to acceptability emerged from the long-running Sizewell Inquiry into a major new nuclear reactor in East Anglia, UK, held between 1983 and 1986. The Inspector, Sir Frank Layfield, coined the term as it imparted more clearly the idea that people judge risks not only in terms of costs, but also benefits (O'Riordan *et al.*, 1987). He argued that if the benefits of a particular risk were considered to outweigh the costs then the risk would be tolerated, but never fully accepted. Whilst scientific

and technical assessments enable a clearer understanding of the nature of risks, the question of whether such risks are tolerable, is one for wider debate. This debate should include input not only from the scientific community, but also from other sections of society – not least the public itself. Clearly, opinions will differ. However, it is vital to realize that, despite the many and varied philosophies and world views supporting these perceptions, each has legitimacy. Facilitating open debate, where differing opinions are not only tolerated, but welcome, is the challenge facing risk management today.

Underlying the notion of tolerability are two fundamental principles. The first is that of ensuring that language assists communication, and is not a medium of dominance. The second is that of trust. The procedures through which risks are communicated have to be based on a mutual sense of respect for all positions of the interested parties. This in turn means applying some of the features of the precautionary principle outlined in Chapter 1, namely providing room for error, ensuring that the risk creator has to show that no unreasonable harm will occur, and guaranteeing some form of compensation in the event of unforseeable circumstances.

Risk regulation and the ALARP principle

In the UK the fundamental driving force behind risk assessment and management is the ALARP principle. This principle aims to reduce risks to as low as reasonably practicable and introduces the idea that, as zero risk is unachievable, efforts should be made to reduce risks only where they are either entirely intolerable, or where the cost of reducing them further still is reasonable given the extra risk reduction gained. Box 16.6 illustrates the basic concept of ALARP. Three areas exist: at the top of the diagram the level of risk is deemed to be entirely intolerable and risks have to be reduced *whatever the cost* or the activity terminated. At the bottom of the diagram the risks are deemed to be negligible where no reduction is necessary. The middle section, the ALARP area, represents risks that should be reduced if the cost of doing so is reasonable in relation to the activity concerned. The ALARP principle is designed to act as an ever-tightening risk reduction device such that, as new technologies are introduced, and novel pollution control systems become available, industrial risks are gradually reduced. This is a classic example of the UK approach to safety management. The aim is to place the burden of safety on the regulated who must negotiate ALARP for every piece of equipment and process. For its part the safety regulator will only grant a permit when the conditions of tolerability noted above are satisfied. In addition there is a rule of thumb about risk benefit calculations. In general, if the risk is relatively localized the benefit to cost ratio should be about 1 to 3. But if the risk is potentially catastrophic, the benefit to cost ratio may rise to as large as 1 to 1000 as is the case with radioactive waste disposal (see also the previous chapter on air pollution studies and public health).

Comparing environmental risks: the apples and pears problem

A clear problem emerges in comparing the relative merit of alternative, and sometimes competing, environmental risk management strategies. How is it possible to compare meaningfully between alternatives (such as apples and pears) that are not easily comparable? If we are faced with choices between different amounts and qualities of air pollution and water pollution which should we choose and, perhaps more importantly, how can we justify the decisions that we make? This problem is well known to risk analysts and is becoming better known to environmental policy makers, particularly those in search of the best practicable environmental option (BPEO) (see Box 16.7), or best available technique not entailing excessive costs (BATNEEC). These approaches were introduced in Chapter 2.

A key frustration to undertaking effective risk comparisons can be found at the very outset of performing risk assessments themselves – the significant uncertainties associated with deriving probabilistic estimates of particular events occurring. It is possible to identify five different levels at which information may be available for risk assessments and risk comparisons to be made. These points are highlighted in Boxes 16.8 and 16.9 and were also addressed in the Introduction, for they are an important part of vernacular science in the contemporary age.

1. Good, direct statistical evidence either from the historical record or from laboratory studies.

2. Direct statistical evidence is not available for the whole process, but is available for individual components within the process. Thus the whole process may be disaggregated using fault trees or event trees and aggregate probabilities for the whole process can be derived.

3. No good data are available for the process under consideration, but data are available for a similar process. These can be adapted and extended either directly or indirectly.

4. Little or no direct evidence exists but it is possible to use expert intuition to provide authoritative subjective judgement.

5. Little or no direct or indirect evidence exists and even the experts have trouble producing reliable or comparable subjective judgements.

Too often risk assessors are forced to base assessments on data derived from subjective sources. More often than not assessments cannot be based upon probabilistic estimates but must rely on expert guesses. Hopefully, as databases become larger and processes better understood it will be possible to undertake risk assessments more reliably. Until then, however, we are restricted to assessments of the likely hazards associated with a particular activity. Identifying the sets of circumstances that may give rise to adverse events is a necessary part of the risk assessment process, but risk managers should be aware that what is often called a

Box 16.7 Best Practicable Environmental Option (BPEO)

A major difficulty in modern risk management is getting consensus concerning outcomes that are not easily comparable. Take, for instance, a decision to dispose of toxic waste in landfill, or use ocean incineration as a waste disposal route. One issue is that of transporting the waste, either to the landfill or to the port. This will involve routes through different communities comprising different social groups. Once at the site there are the comparative problems of landfill leachate which may contaminate ground and surface-water courses and the potential for incinerator emissions to be bioaccumulated into the food chain. How does one compare the two? In its widest context BPEO is a technique that allows the best scientific and ethical weighting of systems based on asking particular groups for their judgements, set in the context of relative costs. In its more sophisticated form, this is what multi-attribute techniques try to do for complex environmental decisions.

Box 16.8 Data limitations: leukaemia in Seascale

Seascale is the community living near to the Sellafield nuclear reprocessing plant in Cumbria, northern England. For a long time it has been noted that the number of children suffering from leukaemia was larger than expected from a 'typical' village of this size. This has led to speculation that leukaemia 'clusters' are associated with nuclear facilities, supporting a differential risk for children linked to persistent exposure to low-level radiation. The controversy surrounds whether such clusters actually exist, and are not a matter of statistical juggling. Then there is a dispute as to the cause of leukaemia. It may not be due to radiation at all, but to the movement of migrant workers into an area carrying all kinds of diseases which in turn may affect the immune systems of youngsters. This could result in their genetic susceptibility to mutations leading to leukaemia. A recent study showed that children of workers exposed to radiation at the plant were no more likely to have leukaemia than children of workers who gave birth to them before moving to Seascale. This removes the theory that leukaemia is passed from an irradiated father to a child and tends to reinforce the immunity disruption thesis. But the data are simply not good enough to produce a scientific proof of cause. Hence the need to be very cautious about the claims of statistics and scientific method as the basis for determining risk tolerability.

risk assessment is in fact nothing more sophisticated than an exercise in hazard identification.

Where risk assessments are possible it is important that risk managers should realize that a meaningful risk comparison involves more than the accurate estimation of each option in isolation. Given the levels of scientific and technical uncertainty that exist within the development of environmental management policy, it seems appropriate to call for an opening-up of decision-making processes to a wider audience. In any case, those responsible for undertaking comparative risk evaluations should be wise to the following:

- Comparisons should include as wide a variety of options as possible. It is easier to exclude options after consideration than to include options once the evaluation process is underway.
- Comparative assessments must include geographical and technical parameters – a solution that is tolerable in one location may be intolerable elsewhere.
- Data limitations may require the extensive use of conservative assumptions, and methods for estimating environmental effects should err on the side of caution.
- Value judgements inherent within any assessment technique should be stated explicitly to avoid the danger of misinterpretation.

Environmental risk management: the prevailing philosophies

The regulation of environmental risk may occur in a direct form, as with the enforcement of technological standards, or through more informal channels such as the guidance provided by the series of Waste Management Papers published by Her Majesty's Inspectorate of Pollution and available from the Department of the Environment. Alternative approaches to risk regulation include voluntary compliance with best practice, incentives for hazard substitution, and economic penalties or taxation. Turner and his colleagues (1991) argue that environmental policy in the 1990s needs to be based upon a balance between the fragmented, piecemeal and expedient decision making and a more integrated, comprehensive type of approach. The gradual movement toward the latter will necessarily involve greater attention to 'analytic resources, a better understanding of the potentialities, limitations and institutional requirements of alternative conceptions' of such integrated systems. To that end, Turner and his associates conclude that an approach based on either a best available technique (BAT) or some such judgement comparison as BPEO may focus too much attention on technological solutions – indeed for a period of time BAT was regarded as applicable to technology rather than the more comprehensive term technique, which implies management and operation as well as the technology employed – rather than methods for eliminating dangerous and intractable substances by fundamentally altering the production processes. For example, certain industrial solvents cause low level air pollution in the form of ozone and microtoxic aerosols. The conversion to water-based solvents has helped to reduce emissions of volatile organic compounds (VOCs), but much more still needs to be done.

There are some very important geographical and technical limitations to a single option regulatory approach. For example, the disposal of sewage sludge has an obvious geographical dimension. In rural areas where sludges may not be contaminated, a BPEO study may result in land-based application to agricultural or forested areas. This may be a different strategy from that for sludges originating from more urban industrial areas where a BPEO study may point to incineration with associated power generation or heat recovery.

The remaining force – the precautionary principle – may serve only to frustrate this dilemma, in the short term at least. The essence behind precaution (and as with the concepts of hazard and risk, there are many interpretations) is to switch the burden of proof to the (potential) polluter, and in cases where significant uncertainty is present, to give the environment the benefit of any reasonable doubt. These points were more fully aired in Chapter 1. The implications for the widespread adoption of a precautionary approach, given the vast uncertainties that surround the relative environmental impacts of alternative waste management options, are a cause for some concern. Though it may be true that in the long term adopting a precautionary principle is intended to phase out the production, use, treatment and disposal of substances that are too difficult to manage in an environmentally tolerable manner, it can also be argued that decisions based primarily on political, economic or moral grounds will have different implications from those based on scientific data. First, a precautionary decision to terminate a particular activity will restrict scientific investigation into that activity and impede the development of a more comprehensive scientific understanding of its environ-

mental impacts. Second, should scientific evidence subsequently refute the basis for initial precaution, there is no guarantee that a reversal of policy will be possible. Changing political minds has been associated on may occasions with a loss of credibility, which can have very damaging results.

Precaution, waste and clean technology

The promotion of clean technology as a solution to the developed world's waste problem should reflect the potential for the transfer of environmental risks. Though several options exist, such as end-of-pipe add-on technology, internal alterations to existing plant, promoting waste minimization at source, reuse and recycling, changes to production processes, low emission strategies, and the fundamental redesign and substitution of products, it important to realize that the adoption of any of these does not guarantee that the potential for harm will decrease.

The tightening of environmental legislation in the USA has led to more and more wastes being classified as hazardous. This means that they are no longer acceptable for land disposal and alternative waste management options have to be found. In the longer term this will include waste minimization, increasing recycling, even the termination of production of some products that generate intractable wastes. However, in the short term these wastes exist and have to be managed. Stockpiling them until some form of novel technical fix is developed is one option, and the option favoured by some groups for the management of radioactive wastes. However, storage is by no means a low risk solution. Box 16.9 highlights the problems of particular wastes such as polychlorinated biphenyls (PCBs), associated with the electrical insulation of generating equipment. Current thinking is divided between using high temperature incineration as a destruction technique (euphemistically called thermal oxidation by some favouring the technology), bioremediation (which involves the use of specific microbiological organisms that 'digest' the PCBs) and those like the Australian government that favour waiting for a better alternative. In the UK, incineration is now regarded by the establishment as a 'better' alternative to landfilling, largely on the basis of greenhouse gas emissions and threats to ground- and surface-water quality (Royal Commission on Environmental Pollution, 1993).

The incineration versus landfill comparison shows

Box 16.9 The assessment of PCB and dioxin emissions from high temperature incineration

PCBs and dioxins are complex chemicals that are notoriously difficult to monitor. They are persistent bioaccumulators which have been shown to cause cancer in mice and rats, though no definitive link to human cancer has yet been proven.

The Environmental Risk Assessment Unit at the University of East Anglia has recently completed the first phase of what is probably the most comprehensive investigation into PCB and dioxin contamination in an area of South Wales close to a high temperature chemical waste incinerator. The study, commissioned by the Welsh Office, cost almost £500 000 and took 36 months to complete. It involved the use of several laboratories, each of which adopted slightly different techniques for determining the levels of PCBs and dioxins in air, grass, soil and duck eggs.

Ultimately the data showed that there were higher PCB and dioxin levels in the local environment than one would normally expect. When air concentrations were combined with measurements of wind direction, the results suggested that the major source of these emissions was the incinerator.

However, despite the intensity of the monitoring regime the study was not able to draw any conclusions as to how much of the contamination was related to past compared with recent operation. Nor could the study identify which part of the waste disposal process was the major contributor to the contamination. Much emphasis has been placed upon air emissions from incinerator stacks, but in this case fugitive emissions from other areas of the site might be equally, if not more, responsible for environmental releases. Further still, the study could not determine the significance of the contamination both in terms of the migration of PCBs and dioxins through the environment and, ultimately, of their effect on human health.

This state-of-the-art assessment represented a milestone in environmental monitoring. However, in terms of managing the problem, the lessons that can be drawn from the study are limited. No clear evidence has emerged about which parts of the incineration process require modification to reduce emissions. Those responsible for managing the plant have been forced to 'best guess' what form of risk management strategy should be implemented.

Though the nature and extent of the contamination has now been agreed by all parties, the local public remain unconvinced about attempts to clean up the incinerator and manage the risks that that particular industrial facility has imposed on the local community. Until further expensive studies are undertaken to determine human health effects it seems unlikely that residents immediately adjacent to the plant will feel reassured about the situation.

---

the advantages of environmental sciences in action. To begin with, the Royal Commission put the spotlight on the regulatory inadequacies of controlling the emissions of both landfill sites and incinerators constructed in a more lax age. By 1996 all municipal waste incinerators will have to meet tough EC air pollution standards created by the 1989 Directive. These standards reflect the risk aversion and tolerability themes already addressed. It is intimated that only a handful of the 30 incinerators will be upgraded to meet the new conditions.

But landfill sites have fallen prey to the UN Framework Convention on Climate Change, introduced in Chapter 6 and also discussed in Chapter 19. That forces the UK to cut methane and carbon dioxide emissions to 1990 levels by the year 2000. It is estimated that 40 per cent of UK methane emissions arise from landfill sites, but more work on this needs to be done. New municipal waste would release three times as much greenhouse gas as carbon dioxide equivalent in landfill as would be the case with incineration. Waste to power incineration has the ability to generate electricity which, given the new electricity generation arrange-

ments (see next chapter), would reduce the greenhouse gas budget further still as reliance on fossil fuel power can be reduced.

Environmental groups regard this conclusion as a licence to burn municipal waste and a frustration to the development of waste avoidance and minimization programmes. They advocate greater encouragement for waste recycling and reduction at source. This will be assisted by the introduction of a landfill tax and the proposal of an EC Directive that may force minimum levels of packaging. This illustrates the broad base of regulatory approaches – from global concerns to science trade-offs to pricing and commerce control. This is typical of the lively arena for interdisciplinary environmental science.

Thus, if we argue for a pragmatic approach to the development of environmental risk management policy then it becomes important to evaluate and, perhaps, to use a combination of options from end-of-pipe technology to complete redesign. Pollution control should not be restricted to a single option and we should be satisfied with progressively cleaner technology, rather than strive for immediate actions, involving the sudden termination of options. It must be remembered that once an option is terminated then reducing the scientific and technical uncertainties about its environmental risks becomes impossible. To a certain extent this has been witnessed with the termination of ocean incineration in January 1991. Whilst nobody could argue that ocean incineration had no environmental impact, the decision to terminate it was a wholly political one based upon the use of the precautionary and burden-sharing approach. Scientific evidence regarding the nature and extent of the impacts of fallout from ocean incineration vessels was largely inconclusive. Given that a net result of the termination of this practice has been the repatriation of wastes to North Sea member states which, in some cases, has contributed towards an increased demand for land-based facilities, there may be an argument for reconsidering ocean incineration as a waste management option for specific wastes. However, it must be said that such an argument would run into strong political opposition from environmental organizations. Risk tolerance is obviously not an objective phenomenon: it is very much a function of current practice, which in turn is a reflection of the changing balance of political power and moral responsibility in a modern age where environmental groups and industrialists are no longer so far apart. The point is that risk exposure is a function as much of regulatory issues and of social prejudices, rooted in the cultural lifeblood of a nation, as much as it is a feature of scientific uncertainty or lack of adequate data.

The movement towards a more comprehensive approach to environmental risk management is inhibited by four key impediments, sometimes referred to as institutional failures:

1. *Data limitations* are of two kinds, namely a lack of historical record on what to base current change, and the inadequacy of scientific understanding on which to base judgements about cause and consequence (see Box 16.8).

2. *Poor frameworks for analysis* impede the kind of comprehensiveness and decision making necessary to make informal judgements in the modern age. This is where multi-attribute analysis requires more attention.

3. *Inadequate regulatory principles*, which lay too much discretion at the door of the safety official, and which tend to lead to discrepancies in levels of safety provided for different groups in society

according to their environmental circumstances and income levels, i.e. the poor get higher levels of exposure whereas the wealthy are able to avoid industrial hazards.

4. *Insufficient consultation procedures* restrict the different interests that have a legitimate role to play in the final determination of risk. This has improved recently with regard to chemical plants and local communities, but remains a problem for more general consultation and involvement in the assessment of risks and the development of regulation.

A further frustration is that in most Western nations waste disposal is operated in part, if not completely, by the private sector. Like any other business enterprise, the disposal companies are under pressure to be profitable. This can lead to problems, particularly in recessionary times, when corners may have to be cut. This places real demands on the regulatory agencies to 'bend the rules' where wastes have to be disposed of, in spite of public opposition. One method to achieve this is to choose soft targets for siting where opposition is likely to be less vociferous; another is to 'bribe' communities to accept waste facilities. However, obtaining planning permission is becoming a significant problem. The development of highly complex waste treatment and disposal plant requires huge capital inputs. A typical high temperature, chemical waste incinerator now costs between £50 and £100 million. To be profitable it is necessary to plan an operation period of 20–25 years, so there is some validity in opposition arguments that such developments actually promote the production of wastes and wastefulness. However, the US Environmental Protection Agency has recently announced a package of new restrictions which goes much of the way to preventing the development of any further increase in high temperature incinerator capacity. In the UK it seems unlikely that waste companies will propose any further developments for the time being given the very uncertain outcomes of gaining planning permission. Box 16.10 outlines some recent criticisms of risk regulation in the USA regarding the inequalities of risk exposure in the siting of hazardous facilities.

Although alternative waste management options cannot be proven to be safe (indeed science cannot prove safety, only the degree of existing harm), regulatory agencies have continued to rely more upon technological design than on people to promote safety, simply because the former is easier to control. However, an over-bureaucratic regulatory system may ultimately remove responsibility for safety from de-

Box 16.10 Inequality in risk exposure

In the USA much attention has focused on the relationship between siting unwelcome and hazardous facilities and social injustice. A recent analysis prepared for the American Association for the Advancement of Science claimed that the US Environmental Protection Agency (EPA) rules reinforces injustice in its regulation of risk. This is because the EPA concentrates more on the saving of life as the criterion for tolerance rather than the reduction of morbidity (illness; reproductive defects; respiratory disease). Hence in communities where morbidity is higher due to poverty, eating habits, smoking, drinking and drug taking, the likelihood of establishing protection standards as high as for wealthy and healthy suburbs is much less. A US Greenpeace study found, for example:

- the racial minority population in areas of municipal incinerators is 89 per cent higher than the national average;
- communities where incinerators are proposed have 60 per cent higher racial minority population;
- average income in communities with incinerators is 15 per cent less than the national average;
- in communities where incinerators are proposed, property values are 35 per cent less than the national average.

Source: Costner and Thornton (1990).

signers to bureaucrats. The latter then focus on satisfying regulations through adherence to strict, rule book procedures. Experience in the USA shows that the serious legal implications of getting it wrong have led to the widespread use of standardized risk assessment methodologies, regardless of their validity and applicability, merely as a means of avoiding liability.

A direct relationship may exist between the seriousness of the consequences, the level of public anxiety, and the lack of bureaucratic rationality. Threats from hazardous wastes then become particularly difficult to manage because of the complex technical nature of the systems, the unknown (perhaps unknowable) threat that they pose, the willingness of the media to highlight governmental and scientific indecision or speculation, and the amplified fear of the public at large (see Box 16.11).

Risk communication

Returning to Box 16.1 it would appear that the central component of risk management is communication.

Disparities between the scientific and technical estimation of risk and public perceptions of risk were thought to be merely a question of education – that risk assessors were not getting the right message across. Thus, much effort was spent attempting to provide clear advice as to effective ways to make the public understand the science. Risk comparisons have been a favourite tool. This can be useful if presented in a meaningful way, using risks that are strictly comparable. But all too often rather spurious comparisons were made, comparing the risks of nuclear power to crossing the road, or smoking.

Most of these efforts failed, and appeared to reinforce the view that the factors that influenced public perception of risk lay in the statistical likelihood of death. Boxes 16.12 and 16.13 describe studies by psychologists which show this to be a simplistic assumption. Public perception of risk is influenced by a wide array of different concerns including the following:

- *The degree of familiarity and control.* Everyday risks such as smoking or driving are usually tolerated. Unfamiliar and uncontrollable dangers such as

Box 16.11 The management of genetically modified organisms

We are now in a position to swap genes at will. Designer technology can produce millions of variants of the building blocks of life, so it is now possible to create food that has special properties of disease resistance, colour or long shelf-life. In utilizing this technology there is a moral question as to how far it is right to manipulate food so boldly, and whether a future society may ultimately be deprived of purely 'natural' products. It is not easy to incorporate such moral concerns into the review structures that evaluate the risks of novel foods. One method is to add representatives of consumer groups and institutions such as the church into scientific review panels advising government on the introduction of such substances. This is becoming a more widespread solution, though problems with the (perception of the) ability of such groups to assimilate technical data have frustrated this process to some extent. Another solution is to label products clearly and comprehensively so that the consumer has a definite choice as to which products to endorse. A third is to encourage special interest groups to articulate contrary opinion in political forums, so that these wider moral and ethical arguments get a fuller airing. Though we have come a long way from purely scientific review panels there is still a long way to go.

Box 16.12 Psychological and sociological theories of risk perception

The call for increasing levels of public participation within risk management has echoed around the risk literature for over a decade. To satisfy this demand it is necessary to understand more clearly how lay perceptions of risk, which often differ from scientific and technical estimations, are developed. Initial attempts to understand public perceptions of risk focused on the determination of 'acceptable' levels. As it became clear that no single, standard level of risk could be called acceptable, psychologists began to realize that the nature of risk perceptions was far from simple. A complex web of factors that were thought to influence public perception was identified and tested through psychometric studies which involved the rating of different hazards either in direct comparison or in terms of different influencing factors such as controllability, familiarity, dread, novelty and catastrophic potential. The cognitive psychology approach introduced a whole range of qualitative factors that required some form of evaluation. One method linked risk perceptions to a variety of 'rules of thumb', or heuristics, of which the most obvious one was availability. This suggested that risk perceptions were driven in part by direct and recent experience of a particular event. Another approach used factor analysis to combine certain influences thought to affect risk perception on to two axes, from which a 'hazard map' could be drawn. Though this allowed comparisons to be drawn between different groups within the public (typically students), it became obvious that the psychometric approach was only painting part of the overall picture of risk perception. There were a number of disadvantages to the psychometric

approach. Studies tended to use small samples and these were mostly from the USA. Results could only provide a view of perception at the time that they were undertaken. When rating scales were used, these had a framing effect on the answers that respondents could give. More important, there was no easy way to extrapolate from small-scale psychometric studies to the population at large, and therefore it remained difficult to incorporate public perceptions of risk into policy making at a national level.

Partly in response to the failure of psychometric studies, in particular the way it tried to homogenize the population, a sociological approach to risk perception began to gain credence. Culture theory holds that there are a number of different biases that exist which can be characterized in two dimensions. The first relates to the extent that people are governed by bonded 'groups' in the way that they live their lives. The second is the extent to which social interaction is governed by rules ('grid'). The 'grid-group' theorists argue that views and values of life, and perceptions of risk, can be explained, in part, by the cultural bias that one exhibits. Culture theory offers a different insight into risk perception, but though much effort has been made to operationalize the theory through empirical research, it has failed to deliver a theoretical framework which can explain convincingly the concept of risk perception.

Whether the psychometric and cultural theories of risk perceptions will ever be unified remains to be seen. Some common ground is appearing in the recognition of the importance of trust as an influential factor in the perception and management of risk.

electromagnetic radiation from overhead power lines, or genetically modified organisms, are resisted.

- *The potential for catastrophe or irreversibility.* The more a danger is perceived to have the potential for causing a major, sudden disaster, or the more a possible hazard could realize a truly world-wide potential in its impact, the more it will be resisted.
- *The degree to, and the point at, which public opinion is seen to be taken into account.* This affects the willingness to tolerate the outcome of risk management. When regulators show that they require public opinions in order to make judgements about risk and safety, trust in the decision-making process is fostered, particularly if public opinion is sought early in the risk management process.
- *The notion of compensation should anything go*

wrong. This is also a vital element in risk tolerance. People need to feel that they will be protected by, say, long-term medical surveillance, in the light of a chemical hazard showing up in a nearby waste disposal facility. This is partly why the US Superfund Programme was set up in 1981, namely to levy a charge on chemical production to pay for the clean-up of old sites where the responsible party could not be identified. In practice Superfund is not achieving all that it might, but this is a result of administrative difficulties and not a fault of the principle itself.

More recent risk communication efforts have tended to focus on the necessity to address the fact that the public sees the world in a different way from the scientific and technical community – that is not to say that

---

Box 16.13 Risk aversion as stigma

Psychologists at the University of Oregon have sought to dig below the opposition of Nevada citizens to the proposed high level radioactive waste repository in Yucca Mountain. In a state-wide poll, over 80 per cent of the population rejected the proposal, virtually vetoing this technically suitable site as a disposal option. The psychologists found that people reacted to the notion of radioactive waste through fundamental underlying dislikes of danger, death and pollution. Over half of the weight of negative reactions were linked to these three images, which in turn are activated by a fear of nuclear weapons, a distrust of both the military and regulatory agencies, and a feeling of intense alienation over the way in which the decision was taken without democratic debate. The outcome was deep-rooted prejudice stimulated by mismanagement of the communication programme more than the actual threat of the radiation itself. Any further attempt to communicate with the public in this case would be set in the context of the deep resentment and suspicion already cultivated, and would therefore more than likely fail.

Source: Slovic *et al.* (1991).

---

scientific and technical people are not part of the public, but that a whole array of alternative rationalities exist. None can be wholly right, none wholly wrong, but they exist and, in our democratic society, they have a right to be considered in the decision-making process. So, risk communication has become a much more multi way process that is designed to make risk management more accessible to everyone. It attempts to promote mutual understanding, if not consensus, and, whilst nobody would argue that emphasizing risk communication is a one-stop solution for reducing conflict, it does offer an opportunity for people to become part of the solution and to gain a greater insight into how decisions are made, even if they do not necessarily agree with the outcome of the decision itself.

subjective and value-laden than citizens have realized or scientists themselves have admitted. Science and scientific analysis have been presented as rational and therefore logical and reasonable, even though within the scientific community many different and conflicting views and beliefs are held. For example, empiricists argue that it is irrational to retain views that contradict experimental evidence, whilst theoreticians regard it as irrational to change views at every flicker of evidence. Ultimately, and despite these conflicts, science has been built upon the idea that there is a single right way of doing things and that the world should be made to accept this.

The net result of this approach to scientific analysis has been to disenfranchise the citizen from the decision-making process to the point where, in our so-called democratic society, the citizen is often bypassed by the development of environmental policy and the management of environmental risk. We have reached a situation where the public are involved in decision making after the science has been completed and, in many cases, when the decision has virtually been reached. Public involvement in decision making in the UK, and in other countries like it, has sometimes served merely as a legitimation device, leaving the public exposed to risks largely without question, or branded as irrational opposition protecting self-interest at the expense of the benefit of society. Box 16.15 illustrates these points using the case study of radioactive waste disposal in the UK.

As Feyerabend recognizes, 'the reason of ordinary people trying to create a better and safer world for themselves and their children has very little in common with these ignorant and irrational dreams of domination.' He goes on, 'Unfortunately common-sense is too common an instrument to impress intellectuals and so [the experts] abandoned it long ago, replaced it by their own conceptions and tried to redirect power accordingly.' He concludes that 'we must restrict their influence, remove them from positions of power and turn them from the masters of free citizens into their most obedient servants' (Feyerabend, 1987, p. 102).

The role of experts in risk management

There is little doubt that the development of Western society has increasingly relied upon the judgement of scientific experts. This expert judgement is often more

Conclusions

Risk management is a tool for retaining a sense of the bigger picture. Over-reliance on the universality of scientific laws has led us to reject anomalies and idiosyncrasies that do not conform to the restrictive

Box 16.14 Superfund: the politics of environmental management

Superfund is the colloquial term for the innovative 'polluter pays' liability scheme for toxic waste clean-up established by the 1980 US legislation Comprehensive Environmental Response, Compensation and Liability Act (CERCLA) and its 1986 amendment. This statute authorized a levy on all producers of toxic substances to pay for the clean-up of some 1256 hazardous sites throughout the USA. The original allocation was $8.5 billion, though the likely total cost of remediation could well exceed $250 billion. This is mostly because the US public are acutely sensitive to hazardous waste in all its forms, but most especially old sites, created by a cowboy mentality in yesteryear, where seepage may be invisible, persistent and pernicious for generations. Risk adversity is fuelled by popular epidemiology (see Box 18.1), by a distrust of the independence and competence of the regulatory authorities and by media coverage that amplifies risk by innuendo, exposure of scientific fallibility and emotional human interest stories that become the metaphor for any innocently exposed household.

Superfund has been roundly criticized for being ineffective, litigation biased and unsympathetic to minority players who can get very hurt financially in protracted liability claims. In response the US Environmental Protection Agency points out that it can take many years to isolate and clean up a site. This is because groundwater contamination has to rely on the flushing out of soil or aquifer reservoirs of toxic substances (or 'time bombs') still above the groundwater level. Flushing may require six or more iterations, each carefully monitored by hydrogeologist. So far only 21 of 150 cleanup programmes have been declared safe – and even that may not be true if popular epidemiology remains buoyant. This is not to criticize public intervention, far from it. The point is that clean-up is a culturally famed concept

that requires communication and risk management practices in the round. It is certainly not, as EPA likes to believe, merely a matter of physical restoration.

The challenge over excessive legal fees is more problematic to refute. A RAND study found that 88 per cent of all superfund costs went in legal fees during the period 1980–90. The US EPA does not deny this, pointing out that companies which are not only expected to pay for all current toxic emissions are also required to pay for clean-up if there is any hint of culpability, naturally go to the courts to claim relief. Similarly insurance companies, fearful of open-ended financial chasms, litigate to ensure protection from any claims on coverage prior to 1986 when in good faith they were insuring outside a legal climate of strict liability. In many cases these expensive claims have been upheld, yielding little additional money for clean-up.

The plight of small polluters is now respected by a *de minimis* clause in the 1986 amendment. This allows EPA to settle for small sums, and quickly, so as to let the marginal contributor off the hook. Over 6500 parties have found satisfactory settlement in the past five years as a result of this initiative, very much a response to justified criticisms.

The Superfund story is bound to play on and on. It is the outcome of a highly bureaucratic approach to toxic waste clean-up spurred by spectacular stories of regulatory failure and time bomb fears. There is a real problem out there, but it is immensely worsened by heavy-handed management and incomplete community involvement at an early stage in the proceedings. Environmental sciences in the round provides a better route forward but what an expensive way to learn.

Source: Saillan (1993).

---

rationality of our scientific system. Yet rejection of them does not mean that they cease to exist and as has been shown on many occasions these idiosyncrasies can provide key information in the process of managing environmental risks.

At the same time, it is important to retain a sense of what risk management can provide. Efforts to develop the field of ecological risk assessment by the US EPA have met with resistance from some areas and as purse strings tighten in times of economic recession, so resistance increases. As yet, the benefits of being able to model complex ecosystems accurately do not appear to

outweigh the considerable costs of achieving this, particularly as less sophisticated hazard assessment techniques are able to highlight the majority of problem sites where some form of clean-up action is required. It makes no sense to prioritize all of one's limited resources to the understanding of environmental systems at the expense of being able to design, implement and monitor solutions. Similarly, it is unreasonable to expect to achieve success if policies are implemented without understanding to a certain extent the nature of the environmental system in question.

So, though risk management has an important part

Box 16.15 The disposal of low- and intermediate-level radioactive wastes

Since the early 1980s Nirex, the Nuclear Industry Radioactive Waste Executive, a company responsible for solving the radioactive waste disposal problem, has investigated and proposed a wide range of technical and geographical solutions. Initially low- and intermediate-level (LLW and ILW) radioactive wastes were to be disposed of separately; LLW in shallow trenches at Elstow in Bedfordshire, and ILW at a deep mine location in NE England. However, public opposition to these proposals, along with criticism from experts concerning the limited range of options considered, led to a first rethink of options.

In early 1985 it was announced that three additional shallow burial sites would be investigated along with Elstow. The formal announcement was made in the House of Commons, and as Nirex had been prevented from liaising with the local authorities in the three areas, it was no surprise that vociferous opposition developed. This opposition was fostered by the news that planning permission for investigation into the sites was to be granted by Special Development Order (SDO). This removed power over planning decisions from the local authorities and gave it to the House of Commons. Disenfranchized from the planning process, the local authorities in the three areas formed a political coalition against the proposals.

In the run up to the General Election in May 1987 another policy shift occurred. This time economic reasons were given for a move to combine the disposal of LLW and ILW to a deep repository. There was considerable scepticism about the timing of this policy reversal, not least because the four shallow burial sites were each in constituencies of prominent Conservative Members of Parliament.

In an attempt to pre-empt opposition to this latest switch in policy, Nirex launched a public consultation exercise to garner views from interest groups and the public at large. However, the history of administrative mismanagement served only to reduce the effectiveness of the exercise. The nine month consultation period generated over 2500 responses, and, though a small minority of the public invited Nirex to provide a 'short courtship and a large dowry', the vast majority felt that this novel policy of openness by Nirex was merely a 'Trojan horse'.

Following this exercise two deep disposal sites were identified: Sellafield, in Cumbria, England, and Dounreay in Grampian, Scotland. Both sites had existing nuclear facilities, housing communities with familiarity of radioactive issues and, perhaps more importantly, economic dependence on the nuclear industry. Since then, in part due to vociferous opposition from Scotland about the transport of radioactive wastes, Nirex has begun site investigations at Sellafield for a deep repository accessed from land stretching out under the Irish Sea. Technically Sellafield is proving to be a challenging site, but given the relatively low levels of public opposition the trade-off between technical suitability and political accessibility was considered to make Sellafield the prime choice.

For a thorough and entertaining discussion of the UK radioactive waste disposal story see Kemp (1992).

---

to play in the development of environmental policy, its primary value lies in the provision of a framework by which scientific and technical perceptions of risk can be integrated with those of other interest groups. In the UK and elsewhere, the Not In My Backyard (NIMBY) phenomenon is being gradually replaced by more informed and more active local public. Reactive campaigning is switching to pro-active education. Emphasis is moving from technical and geographic considerations to fundamental questions of need. In some cases this may lead to increasing tolerance of industrial activities, in others it may result in widespread resentment. Conflict between interest groups within the decision-making process is inevitable. The task is to create a positive atmosphere for conflict at the right time in the process such that, where at all possible, consensus can be reached.

Adopting a risk management approach to decision making serves two main aims. First, it encourages, even demands, communication between groups, which in turn promotes mutual understanding between, and mutual respect of, parties involved in decision making: collaboration does not need a shared ideology. Second, it opens up the decision-making process, making explicit the method by which decisions are reached. This does not guarantee satisfaction for all about the outcome of the decisions, but will allow interest groups to participate and understand how decisions are made, and give the decision makers some justification for the fruits of their labour.

References

Anon (1993) Major overhaul of US incinerator and waste reduction regs. *HAZNEWS International Hazardous Waste Management Monthly*, **63**, June, p. 16.

Bingham, G. (1986) *Resolving environmental disputes*. Washington DC: Conservation Foundation.

Carter, D. (1991) Aspects of risk assessment for hazardous pipeline containing flammable substances. *Journal of Loss Prevention Process Industries*, **4**, 68.

Costner, P. and J. Thornton (1990) *Playing with fire*. Washington DC: Greenpeace USA.

Fernandes-Russell, D. (1988) *Societal risk estimates from historical data for UK and worldwide events*. Norwich: University of East Anglia.

Feyerabend, P. (1987) *Farewell to reason*. London: Verso.

Kemp, R. (1992) *The politics of radioactive waste disposal*. Manchester: Manchester University Press.

Krimsky, S. and D. Golding (Eds) (1992) *Social theories of risk*. New York: Praeger.

O'Riordan, T., R. Kemp and M. Purdue (1988) *Sizewell B: an anatomy of the inquiry*. London: Macmillan.

Piller (1991) *The fail-safe society: community defiance and the end of American technological optimism*. New York: Basic Books.

Rasmussen, N.C. (1990) The application of probabilistic risk techniques. In T.S. Glickman *et al.* (Eds) *Readings in risk*. Washington, DC: Johns Hopkins University Press, p. 198.

Rayner, S. (1992) Cultural theory and risk analysis. In S. Krimsky and and D. Golding (Eds) *Social theories of risk*. New York: Praeger.

Royal Commission on Environmental Pollution (1993) *Incineration of Waste: Seventeenth Report*. London: HMSO

Royal Society (1992) *Risk: analysis, perception, and management*, Report of a Royal Society Study Group. London: The Royal Society.

Schwartz, M. and M. Thompson (Eds) (1990) *Divided we stand: redefining politics, technology and social change*. Hemel Hempstead: Harvester Wheatsheaf.

Slovic, P., M. Layman and J.H. Flynn (1991) Risk perception, trust and nuclear waste: lessons from Yucca Mountain. *Environment*, **33**(3), 6–9, 11, 28–30.

Soby, B.A., A.C.D. Simpson and D.P. Ives (1993) *Integrating public and scientific judgements into a toolkit for managing food-related risks*, stage 1 Literature review and feasibility study. Norwich: University of East Anglia.

Turner, R.K., D. Brown, I.J. Vickers and J.C. Powell (1991) *An assessment of the concept of BPEO by case studies*, Final report to ESRC and HMIP. Norwich: University of East Anglia.

Wynne, B. (1992) Introduction. In U. Beck, *Risk society: towards a new modernity*. London: Sage.

Further reading

Bromley, D.B. and K. Segerson (Eds) (1992) *The social response to environmental risk. Policy in an age of uncertainty*. Dordrecht: Kluwer.

Douglas, M. and A. Wildavsky (1984) *Risk and culture*. Berkeley: University of California Press.

Glickman, T.S. and M. Gough (Eds) (1990) *Readings in risk*. Washington, DC: Johns Hopkins University Press.

National Research Council (1989) *Improving risk communication*. Washington, DC: National Academy Press.

Jungermann, H., R.E. Kasperson and P. Weiderman (Eds) (1991) *Risk communication*. Jülich, Germany: KFA Research Centre.

Shrader-Freschette, K.R. (1991) *Risk and rationality: philosophical foundations for populist reforms*. Berkeley: University of California Press

The Royal Society report cited in the references is probably one of the most comprehensive statements of both the natural and engineering science and the social science aspects of risk management. For the US reader, Bromley and Segerson (1992) and Shrader-Freschette (1991) provide a primarily sociological-political interpretation of risk tolerance and response. The Glickman and Gough reader and the Krimsky and Golding volume take that material one stage further and provide a thorough examination of the social and cultural context of risk. The latter presents some insightful background material on each author which illustrates the many and varied specialisms that make up the risk field. The two volumes on risk communication published by KFA Jülich and the National Research Council provide an excellent coverage of the changing interpretations of this important topic. Both contain good examples from North America and Europe.

CHAPTER 17

Energy: hard choices ahead

GORDON EDGE and KEITH TOVEY

Of all the great challenges to sustainability, the expectation of sustainable energy use in anything like the foreseeable future looks the most formidable. Energy use is rooted in all societies as a manifestation of technology, consumption patterns, price distortions and land-use arrangements. Frankly it is extremely unlikely that energy production will ever become truly sustainable, by any definition offered in Box 17.1. Too many countries have fossil fuel resources and are too far down the development curve to withstand the pressures from their middle classes for more, low cost, subsidized energy to feed their voracious appetites.

What are the likely full social costs of energy? This involves a calculation of the so-called 'externality adders' attributed to the assorted environmental damages associated with the energy cycle. This is bound to be a matter of inspired guesswork coupled to some imaginative science and economic analysis. So any calculation has to be treated with circumspection. Estimates for SO_2 involve the damage to trees and buildings plus recreational side effects from diseased forests. Figures of 10–17 pence per kg of SO_2 have been suggested, and £14 per tonne of carbon (Pearce *et al.*, 1992). This would add about 1.06 pence to a kWh of 'old' coal (cf. 2–3 pence for the private price) 0.64 pence per kWh for 'new' coal (cf. 2 pence), 0.22 pence per kWh for gas (cf. 2–3 pence) and 0.03–0.28 pence per kWh for nuclear (cf. 4–5 pence). The range for nuclear involves the costs of possible accidents and some surcharge for risk aversion (see Chapter 16). Take your pick: this is early work, but a vital area for interdisciplinary environmental science.

The switch to renewables will soak up less than 10 per cent of future demand, and possibly no more than 6 per cent of future supply (McGowan, 1991). In any case, renewables are not without resource use implications or environmental impacts, so on sustainability grounds they still provide great problems. This is why there is a pressing need to improve the methods for allocating society's preferences for different energy – environment alternatives via displays of consequences and various trade-off games aimed at soliciting value preferences for different futures of energy economy and environment. Otherwise renewables will languish in the false economies of conventional power supply, or will grow through arranged marriages (with non-fossil fuel dowries) with energy management corporations.

To achieve energy conservation on a large scale would require a combination of sizeable and sustained price rises, possible only with the greatest political difficulties, especially if no redistributive funds are available for the poor, plus draconian standards of appliance use efficiency, building regulations, land-use planning controls and combined heat and power schemes. It is almost unthinkable that this combination of strategies would be politically tolerable except in highly advanced, wealthy and egalitarian societies such as Denmark or the Netherlands.

There is a big and compelling argument that existing energy prices should be adjusted to ensure that subsidies promoting non-sustainable fuel mix and uses should be removed. For example, energy prices in many developing countries are not supplied even at cost, let alone environmental burden. Between 1979 and 1988, average electricity tariffs in the rich countries rose by 3.5 per cent, but fell by 1.4 per cent in the poor world (World Bank, 1992, p. 117). Losses of electricity due to theft in transmission cost poor countries over $30 billion annually. The chronic underpricing of electricity in the developing world is summarized by the World Bank:

> Governments frequently intervene in the day to day operations of utilities, and they worry that price increases will exacerbate inflation. Utility managers and their boards have little say in pricing and investment decisions. Lack of accountability and transparency leads to poor management, either of the utilities themselves or of the state fund companies that frequently supply them. (World Bank, 1992, p. 117)

Analysis is one thing: curative action quite another. Unless all energy prices were to be reformed *en bloc*, there would be massive resistance to the hiking of prices if competitor nations did not follow suit. Unless energy prices are influenced by technology transfer for more durable energy supply, it is hard to see this highly distorted energy pricing structure changing very much. Given that, the prospects for really massive energy conservation efforts remain very bleak indeed, even though the technology is now on hand (Shipper, 1991).

The link between transport patterns and land use is now a matter of much research and policy interest. In Europe the notion of sustainable mobility within sustainable cities is slowly gaining political interest. At present there is virtually no relationship between transport investment and policy and land-use planning. But as local government is required to develop and implement local Agenda 21 plans, much more attention will be given to the connections between work, leisure, home and mobility, especially as the optical fibre, multi-information channel revolution looms, and it will be possible to conduct business and pleasure much more via highly energy efficient electronic means. The 21st century society may be less companionable, but much more energy efficient.

Introduction

All societies are dependent on energy. From the most remote tribes to downtown LA, fuel of some sort and quantity is being used. Where societies do differ in their energy use is in the *types* used and the *scale* of its use. As an illustration of the scale difference, Amory Lovins (1975) calculated that the world's energy use was equivalent to having 12 slaves for every man, woman and child on the planet. If these slaves were considered to be real people, the world population would have been 50 billion, of which the USA, using one-third of the world's energy, would account for 17 billion – by far the most populous country on Earth. The disparity in energy use is further shown by the calculation that the annual commute by car into New York alone uses up more oil than is consumed by the whole of Africa (barring South Africa). Apart from scale, industrialized societies differ from others in their dependence on forms of energy derived from our finite *energy capital* (fossil and nuclear sources) and not our inexhaustible *energy income* (direct or indirect solar energy). Societies dependent on these finite energy sources have difficult transitions away from these fuels in front of them, though not, as was feared in the 1970s, because of these fuels running out. The issue now is that the environment can no longer be assumed to have the capacity to act as a sink for the numerous pollutants produced by fossil fuels. Box 17.1 gives various energy definitions.

In 1990 the human population consumed the equivalent of 13 billion tonnes of coal, 4 times what it used in 1950 and 20 times more than in 1850 (see Table 17.1; Holdern and Pachauri, 1992, p. 103). In 1990, 77 per cent of this energy supply came from fossil fuels, 18 per cent from renewables and 5 per cent from nuclear

energy. The 1200 million people of the 'North' consumed over two-thirds of this energy; the rest was used by 4100 million people in the 'South'. The disparity of energy use is striking: so too are the environmental effects. In the poorer countries fuelwood is no longer available within easy reach of most households. Labour is needed to haul it increasing distances, while deforestation removes surface vegetative cover. Soils are eroded faster because soil-enriching dung is used as fuel rather than fertilizer. Particulate matter in the domestic environment and air pollution from inefficient fossil fuel power stations shorten the life expectancy of many in poorer countries. In the South, the environmental shocks from misallocated energy use are localized and immediate on health and economy. In the North, most effects are transboundary and delayed for the future to suffer.

At present rates of fossil-fuel use, world reserves of oil could sustain the world for about 70 years, for gas about 140 years and for coal nearly 300 years. These global figures obscure the important point that reserves in the developed countries are running low and they therefore will become increasingly dependent on the resources of the developing world (see Table 17.1). For instance, North America has oil reserves equivalent to about 7 years of its present usage, whereas Africa has reserves of about 50 years. The developed world will clearly wish to use the developing world's energy resources. However, as noted above, supply shortage is no longer the main issue: it is the use of the Earth's assimilative capacity – in soil, water and air – that is truly threatened by current consumption.

The use of fossil fuels is the source of the majority of CO_2 emissions, as well as being the source of SO_2, NO_x CH_4 and other pollutants (see Box 17.2). Other supply options have their own problems, such as the public

Table 17.1 Reserves and resources of fossil fuels (TWy)[a]

	Oil		Gas		Coal	
	Reserves	RURR[b]	Reserves	RURR	Reserves	RURR
North America	12.1	30	12.7	50	200	2000
Europe and Russia	24.3	50	58.3	120	290	3500
Middle East	114.0	140	43.0	80	0	0
Africa	11.6	20	7.1	20	60	200
Asia and Oceania	8.8	30	9.9	35	290	1000
Latin America	14.1	30	8.4	13	16	20
Total	184.9	300	139.4	318	856	6720

[a] 1 TWy = one terawatt year = 31.5 EJ.
[b] RURR = remaining ultimately recoverable reserves.
Source: Holdern and Pachauri (1992, p. 106).

Box 17.1 Energy definitions
Conversion factors

The basic quantity of energy is the joule. There are many other units in common use. These are related to the joule as follows:

1 kilowatt-hour (kWh)	= 3.6 MJ
1 megawatt-hour (MWh)	= 3.6 GJ
1 gigawatt-hour (GWh)	= 3.6 TJ
1 terawatt-hour (TWh)	= 3.6 PJ
1 terawatt-year (TWyr)	= 31.5 EJ
1 calorie	= 4.1868 J
1 kcalorie (or Kalorie)	= 4.1868 KJ
1 British Thermal Unit (BTU)	= 1.055 06 KJ
1 therm (100 000 BTU)	= 0.105 506 GJ

1 tonne coal equivalent (tce; composite units such as mtce (million tonnes coal equivalent) are in common use)   ~ 24 GJ (UK definition)

1 tonne coal equivalent (tce)   ~ 29.3 GJ (EC, excluding UK, definition)

1 tonne oil equivalent (toe)	~ 44 GJ
1 barrel oil equivalent	~ 6.8 GJ
1 litre oil equivalent	~ 42 MJ
1 Imperial gallon oil	~ 192 MJ
1 US gallon oil equivalent	~ 160 MJ
1 cubic metre gas	~ 38 MJ
1 tonne peat equivalent	~ 14 GJ
1 tonne wood	~ 20 GJ

The unit of *Power* or rate of using energy is the Watt = joules per second. (Units such as kilowatts per hour or kilowatts per year are generally meaningless.) Other units of power are:

1 horsepower	=	0.746 kW
1 BTU per hour	=	0.293 W

Primary energy, delivered energy, useful energy, energy service

Primary energy is a measurement of the energy content of a fuel as it exists in the ground or as growing biomass.

Delivered energy is the energy (in the form of gas, electricity, etc.) that is delivered to a consumer's premises. It differs from primary energy as it accounts for losses in extraction, processing, conversion and transmission.

Useful energy is energy in the form that is required by the user (i.e. the consumer requires heat, light, motive power, not electricity or gas). Useful energy differs from delivered energy as it accounts for the inefficiency of energy conversion by the end-use appliances.

An energy service is the function (e.g. heating a house) that useful energy performs.

Commercial fuels

This is a term used to distinguish between those fuels that are traded and those that are collected or found (such as fuelwood): the latter are sometimes called *traditional* fuels.

Energy efficiency, energy conservation

These are often used interchangeably, but are different things. Efficiency is the technical measure of how much useful energy is derived from the input fuel, stated as a proportion of the energy input. Energy conservation is the process of using less energy, either by making processes more energy efficient, or by reducing the demand for energy services. Energy efficiency is a necessary but not sufficient condition for energy conservation.

acceptability of nuclear power. Tackling the problems of energy use is an enormous job, since Western industrial economies are dependent on the use of fossil fuels and electricity and there is strong pressure in the industrializing world for increased commercial energy use. (See Box 17.3: there are other energy crises in the developing world, in particular the fuelwood crisis, but these are beyond the scope of this chapter.)

The growing evidence from environmental science that use of energy on the present massive scale is unsustainable has to be balanced against the undoubted benefits of energy use: basic provision for all can be seen to have social as well as individual benefits, such as reduced incidence of cold- or heat-related illness, which reduces the demand for health care. The desirability of the benefits of energy use ensure that upward pressure on energy demand will continue. Study upon study has shown that there is no direct link between energy use and economic growth. During the 1950s and 1960s, energy use was believed to be an essential precondition of economic growth; so much so that it was regarded as an indicator of economic performance. Nowadays that myth has been fully exploded. All industrialized countries have increased their gross

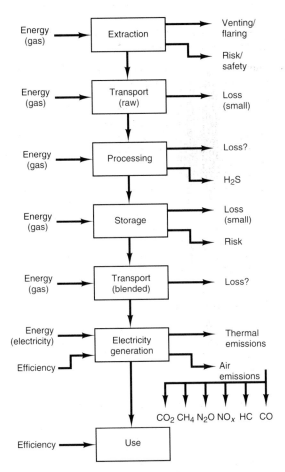

Fig 17.1 The gas to electricity fuel cycle, showing losses (left hand side) and environmental implications (right hand side).

has caused a switch from direct oil and coal burning to indirect electricity, which is more efficient at the point of use, sometimes outweighing the inefficiency in electricity generation.

- Regulations on energy efficiency standards supported by industry which sees the cost advantages of innovation and declining energy budgets.
- Threats of price increases because of environmental damage, notably the prospect of acid rain (for SO_2 and NOx) and carbon taxes. Though still only a prospect, such proposals have made industry and other manufacturers begin to economize.
- Disruptions in oil supplies in the 1970s revealed the dangers for the Western world of being too dependent on imported oil. This started a steady move away from oil profligacy in favour of coal (initially), then nuclear, now gas, and renewables in the future.
- Changes in the financing of the public sector to promote unit-based budgets (e.g. schools and hospitals). This is a necessary but not sufficient condition for the success of greater efficiency drives since efficiency requires decentralized management.

Governments will have to tread a fine line since they have now signed international agreements that imply that they will have to implement measures to curb the use of fossil fuels, but to do so they have to battle against strong political pressure for increasing energy use. The political balancing of the *potential* for catastrophic change against the very real social and economic upheaval necessary to deal with the problem is a tricky act. Integrating environmental information with other data when making decisions in the energy sector will therefore be very difficult; a difficulty compounded by the nature of the environmental problems and their interaction with energy systems.

A techno-social complex

A basic tool for understanding energy systems is the concept of the fuel cycle. This highlights the fact that there is a chain of activities between extraction of a fuel and its use, which is illustrated for the gas–electricity fuel cycle in Figure 17.1. It should be noted that fuel cycles are not circular, as the title implies, but linear. At each stage of the cycle, there is some loss of fuel, or some energy use which can be treated as a loss. These losses are multiplied by the downstream inefficiencies, which may make larger losses at a stage upstream less

domestic product while their use of energy per unit of output has declined. Japan leads the way with 2–3 per cent economic growth per year but with an increase of similar proportions in energy efficiency (see the second figure in Box 17.3). It is also the case that Japan has amongst the highest energy prices for OECD countries.

This decoupling of energy demand from economic growth is due to a number of factors:

- Changes in economic structure with the steady removal of energy-inefficient but demanding industry such as metal fabrication or shipbuilding.
- Improvements in technology encouraged by pollution control regulations and competitiveness of manufacturing processes. In many instances this

Box 17.2 Energy and environmental problems

Despite a vast increase in the use of commercial fuels since the end of the Second World War, there is still capacity for growth in the use of these fuels. The figure shows the growth in fuel use broken down by fuel type. This shows the huge growth in the use of liquid fuels, i.e. oil and its products, though this growth was checked by the oil crises of the 1970s. Use was still over four times higher in 1985 than 1950. Gas has also seen a large increase, though from a smaller base, showing an eight-fold increase. Coal demand, on the other hand, has merely doubled. The importance of this use of fossil

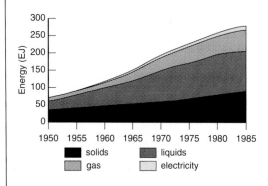

(a) World commercial energy use, by fuel type, 1950–85. (Sources: UN 1982; 1989.)

fuels can be seen in the second figure, which shows that 75 per cent of the anthropogenic emissions of CO_2 are due to the extraction and burning of fossil fuels. The difference in shares of energy used and amounts of CO_2 produced can be explained by the difference in carbon content of the different fuels, which leads to different levels of CO_2 emission when one unit of each fuel is burnt. The emission factors for the three basic types of fossil fuel are:

- bituminous coal – 89.7 kg/GJ;
- crude oil – 69.7 kg/GJ;
- natural gas – 50.6 kg/GJ.

Table 17.2 on page 325 shows how SO_2 and NOx emissions are unevenly distributed among activities in the UK. Anthropogenic SO_2 emission is almost entirely energy-related, and is concentrated in activities

that use fuels with a high sulphur content, which in the UK means burning British coal in power stations. NOx, which is formed in all high temperature combustion, is also widely spread. It is important to note that NOx contributes to different problems depending on where it is emitted from. If it comes from the tall stacks of power stations it may add to the problem of transboundary acid pollution, whereas if it is released at ground level in the urban environment, from car or heating system exhaust, then it will add to the problems of smog and tropospheric ozone.

Energy use is responsible for many other environmental problems: many energy installations are large and unsightly, hence being a visual pollution problem; nuclear installations are responsible for the contamination of the environment with small quantities of radioactive substances, though the effect of this is disputed; particulate emission from fossil fuel combustion, particularly coal, has been a problem, though with electrostatic precipitators capturing 99 per cent of particulates from power stations the situation is not so bad, though emissions of particulates from diesel engines are still a prob-

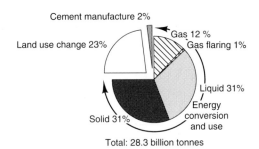

(b) Global emissions of CO_2, by emission source. (Source: World Resources Institute (1993) pp. 349–9.)

lem in urban areas; many energy installations have a high risk potential, for instance liquid natural gas terminals or nuclear power stations, posing a problem for the formation of policy towards such plant. Each of the many environmental issues, of which this is just a selection, pose their own individual problems, though CO_2 and acid emissions are the most intractable issues and certainly there are problems of control due to the scale of their effects.

important than smaller losses downstream (per unit throughput at a stage). This is especially true of electricity, where there is large inefficiency in generation, making it very important to ensure maximum efficiency at the point of use. That is why there is such a

potential saving to be made with even a small improvement in the efficiency of electric appliances such as refrigerators or freezers. For example, a 10 per cent improvement in the efficiency with which home appliances use energy in the UK alone would remove the

Box 17.3 Energy and growth

There is strong circumstantial evidence that economic activity and energy use are intimately linked. Indeed, it used to be regarded as axiomatic that energy was essential for economic growth. The first figure shows why this relationship was thought to be unbreakable, with a strong correlation between countries' GDP and their commercial energy consumption. In recent years, however, there has been

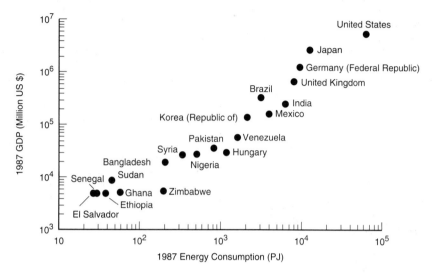

(a) Commercial energy consumption against GDP for 20 countries, 1987. (Sources: UN 1989; World Bank 1990.)

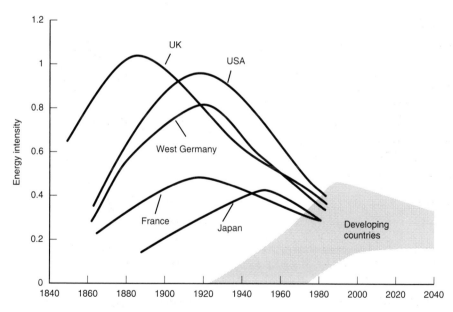

(b) Energy intensity versus time in industrialized and developing countries. In industrialized countries the energy intensity (ratio of energy consumption to GDP; the amount of energy (in equivalent tonnes of petroleum) consumed to yield $1000 of GDP) rose, then fell. Because of improvements in materials science and energy efficiency, the maxima reached by countries during industrialization have progressively decreased over time. Developing nations can avoid repeating the history of the industrialized world by using energy efficiently. We would add, however, that it may be unrealistic to expect the developing countries to reach very quickly an energy-efficient development path, given the capital constraints and industrial weakness these countries confront. (Source: Holdern and Pachauri 1992, p. 111.)

Box 17.3 continued

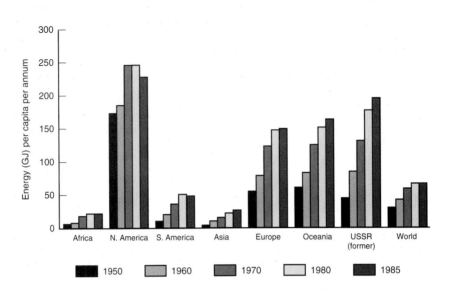

(c) Per capita energy requirement, GJ/capita/annum, 1950–85. (Sources: UN 1985, 1989.)

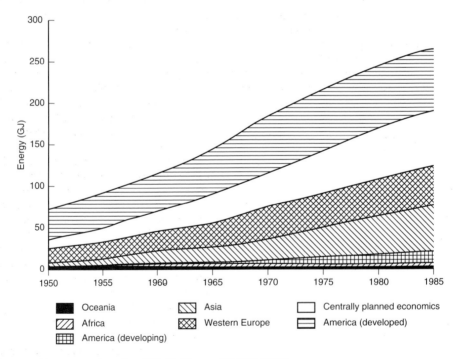

(d) World commercial energy use, by region, 1950–85. (Sources: UN 1982, 1989.)

Box 17.3 continued

talk of the 'decoupling' of economic and energy growth, with the performance of countries like Japan being pointed to as examples of a new phenomenon. The second figure shows how such countries reacted to the oil price shocks: in Japan, GDP continued to rise, while energy use rose by a relatively small amount. This decoupling was due partly to increases in the efficiency with which energy was used, but also to 'restructuring' of the Japanese economy, which, like most Western countries, moved away from heavy industry and towards service industries which are less energy intensive. The energy-intensive industries did not disappear, however, they went abroad, to wherever the energy needed could be obtained cheaply. The energy is still 'used' by the Japanese economy, in the form of embodied energy imported as products. The total world demand for energy is therefore not much affected by the 'export' of this energy use. Indeed, energy is expended in the transport of the goods made elsewhere, which may increase the total energy used.

If 'decoupling' is not feasible for developing economies (they cannot export their energy use), meeting their populations' energy demands will need an increase of the supply of energy. If they aspire to a Western lifestyle, then there will have to be a very considerable increase in energy use in the developing world. The third figure shows per capita energy use in the different regions of the world: there is clearly a large disparity in energy use between the developed and developing worlds. If per capita use in the developing world were to rise to Western levels, the rise in energy use over the last 50 years (fourth figure) would be dwarfed: Asia, Africa and South America use only roughly one-third of the world's energy while having three-quarters of the population, a situation which will become worse if present population predictions are realized: by 2025 it is expected that 85 per cent of the world population of 8.5 billion will live in Asia, Africa and Latin America. If present energy use is unsustainable, how will we cope if the poor of the world wish to copy the rich?

need to build a 2000 MW power station which would otherwise be necessary to meet that expanding demand.

When integrating the environment with other factors in decisions, the harm done at each stage should be related to units of the energy service provided (heating, lighting, etc.), or at the very least to units of delivered fuel (gas, electricity, etc.). This means that we are mixing uncertainty in the environmental science of estimating future impacts of, say, carbon emissions or wind

Table 17.2 UK emissions of SO_2 and NO_x, by emission source (thousand tonnes)

Source	SO_2	%	NO_x	%
Domestic	133	4	76	3
Commercial/public service	83	2	60	2
Power stations	2534	71	718	26
Refineries	115	3	37	1
Agriculture	8	–	4	–
Other industry	569	16	224	8
Offshore oil & gas	–	–	50	2
Railways	3	–	31	1
Road transport	58	2	1400	51
Civil aircraft	2	–	14	–
Shipping	61	2	133	5
Total	3565		2747	

Source: UK Department of Environment (1993).

generators on scenic hillsides or coastlines, with important assumptions about the operation of fuel cycles. This is one of the key themes covered in this chapter.

In order to analyse different courses of action for their environmental effects, many assumptions are implicitly made as to the operation of fuel cycles, assumptions which stem from a certain view of technological control over processes. If these assumptions about processes are not found in real life, then the analysis is flawed, and may be invalid. For example, engineers will calculate the likelihood of systems' failure in a nuclear power station, based on quality control studies of equipment manufacture and 'fault tree' estimates of multiple failure (as can be seen from the previous chapter). But there is no guarantee that such estimates will be believed by those who have to live next to the plant. This highlights that when technical and social systems interact, the complexity of perceptions and decision making in society can make purely analytical approaches to decision making inappropriate. This is reinforced by the ethical/political issues as to whether decisions about matters as vital as energy should be delegated to technocratic expertise with minimum political control.

If purely analytic routes are chosen, then ambiguities in environmental research present several difficulties, as can be seen from other chapters in this book. As environmental science cannot provide unambiguous evidence, important value judgements must be made by those assessing this evidence. Yet if technocratic routes are chosen, these judgements (not always conscious) are made by experts, and not by representatives of the people. When the environment is regarded as a technical arena, then this is an appropriate response, but if the environment is seen as an area for collective decision-making, then this may not be acceptable.

Responding to environmental problems

The traditional response to regulating the environmental consequences of energy generation and use has been the 'command-and-control' (c-and-c) strategy. With this policy, government passes legislation that allows specified regulatory bodies to limit the emissions from energy facilities to a set standard. This policy has some drawbacks: first, whilst everyone is required by law to limit their emissions, there is no incentive to reduce emissions below the standard, even when this may prove environmentally cost-effective along the lines outlined in Chapters 2 and 3; second, if there is no feasible means of removing the pollutant at the source, e.g. CO_2, then c-and-c amounts simply to fuel rationing; third, c-and-c cannot limit *total* emissions, only emissions from each point, and so if the number of emitters increases, the benefit of the emission standard may be negated (e.g. the increase in motor vehicles on the road may cancel out the benefits of catalytic converters).

Most legislation grants the regulatory authorities the powers to revoke licences and to reissue them to a tighter standard. But this normally requires an expensive and time-consuming appeal procedure, so has to be backed by political authority. This is why the modern environmental legislator looks to ambient quality standards in air and water so as to cap total emissions, and thence set the scene for possible trading of emission rights between emitters. Because of these drawbacks, and particularly c-and-c's inability to address the climate change issue equitably, other means of dealing with the problems have been sought.

The alternative to c-and-c most commonly put forward is the use of the tools of environmental economics, described in Chapters 2 and 3. By internalizing the costs imposed by energy use on the environment, the economy will come to a new equilibrium where the level of residual damage reflects the equation of the social gains of additional investments in pollution control and the costs of achieving these gains. The price signal is the means whereby individuals acquire information on the effects of their actions, which they can adjust accordingly. The most prominent of the tools proposed is the carbon tax, which, like general energy taxes with which it shares problems (see Box 17.4), is being looked at with much greater interest because of the belief that this is the most cost-effective way of reducing CO_2 emissions, as well as being a convenient means of raising revenue for beleaguered government budgets. Other forms of these economic tools are also starting to be used, such as the tradeable emission permits for SO_2 brought in by the US Clean Air Act of 1990.

The problem with these methods is that they rely on environmental science to give workable estimates of environmental damage, upon which values can then be placed. In the absence of these estimates, economists must use surrogate values derived from the cost of *controlling* emissions or *mitigating* their effects. Whether this approach can be ethically justified is a matter of some debate. Economists believe that honest approximations are much better than nothing; non-economists feel such calculations lose sight of the moral responsibility for reducing pollution and global damage generally to the lowest possible levels. As we discovered in Chapters 2 and 3, the two are not that far apart.

Despite these misgivings, it appears likely that market-adjusting tools will be used to deal with the problems of energy and the environment. To understand why, we need to look at the different ways that people view energy: different views set different limits on which policies are 'allowed'. The predominant view is that energy is seen simply as a *commodity*, one which is bought and sold on the open market like any other. In this view, the relationship between buyer and seller is essentially a private one, and any aspects external to this transaction have secondary importance. Other views acknowledge the wider meanings of energy: as an *ecological resource*, which would mean that the transaction between buyer and seller cannot be private but must involve some sort of environmental contract; as a *social necessity*, whereby access to minimum amounts of energy is seen as a right that citizens should not be denied; or as a *strategic material*, where energy use choices are seen to have implications for the security of nations. People who view energy in these last three ways have to lobby for their position to be included in

Box 17.4 Energy and carbon taxes: experience so far

With increasing pressure on governments to fulfil environmental commitments and balance the books, the idea of taxing resources, and particularly energy, is coming increasingly into vogue. The rough passage of proposals for such taxes does not bode well for the future of green fiscal measures, however.

One of the most ambitious schemes for the implementation of environmentally inspired taxes is the European plan for a mixed carbon/energy tax. In this scheme, a tax would be levied on fuels, half of which would be taxing its energy content, and half the carbon content. It would initially be set at 0.21 ECU/GJ plus 2.81 ECU/tCO$_2$, rising by a third of this amount each year to reach a level of 0.7 ECU/GJ plus 9.4 ECU/tCO$_2$ in the year 2000. (1ECU = US$1.2 in late 1992.) Small hydro and new renewable sources of energy would be exempt from the tax. The tax would be collected by the member states, the intention of the European Commission being that the revenue thus raised should be used to reduce the tax burden elsewhere by the same amount. (If this is the case, it will be a *revenue-neutral* tax.) Some energy-intensive industrial sectors will be exempt from the tax until such time as all the EC's major competitors have similar taxes.

Concessions made in order to make the tax acceptable to all the member states of the EC would dilute its effectiveness in reducing carbon emissions. Originally a pure carbon tax, the proposal was altered to be a mixed tax largely so that countries with a preponderance of nuclear power, i.e. France, will not gain undue advantage. (Nuclear power would not be subject to a carbon tax.) The sectoral exemptions were granted after much lobbying from industry, and will much reduce the efficacy of the tax. There has been little discussion of channelling any of the revenue from the tax into increasing the energy

efficiency of Europe's economies: this would offset some of the inequitable nature of the tax, which would fall disproportionately on poorer sections of the population.

The level of tax chosen had little to do with the estimates by economists of the possible damage costs of global warming: it was chosen so that the tax might be *politically* acceptable. There is also no attempt to quantify the other benefits of reducing energy use, such as the reduction in acid emissions, health cost savings, etc.

In order to gain agreement on the tax, not only have major concessions been made on the form of the tax itself, but other *complementary* policies have been cut back in the SAVE and ALTENER programmes (to promote energy conservation and alternative energy sources respectively) so that agreement might be reached on the principle of the tax. Even after considerable negotiation and compromise, however, agreement on a tax is, at time of writing, still far away.

The experience of President Clinton's energy tax has also been one of difficulty. Explicitly billed as a revenue-raising measure to fill some of the US government's budget deficit, it has also been sold on its general encouragement for energy efficiency. This 'BTU tax' (after the British Thermal Unit, a measure of energy used paradoxically in the USA and not the UK) would be raised simply on the energy content of a fuel, at a rate of 25.7 cents per million BTU, with an additional 34.2 cents per million BTU levied on refined petroleum products. Opposition from a supposedly sympathetic Congress has led to concessions for a number of special interest groups, which will reduce both the tax's revenue-raising potential and its effect on energy demand.

---

the dominant *laissez-faire* policy. Environmental economics is sometimes regarded as being consonant with the dominant view, in that the adjustment of prices for environmental externalities is secondary to the market price. If the view of energy as an ecological resource were dominant, limits would be placed on energy use through full price accounting and the implications for the economy would be secondary. Similarly, energy provision as a matter of social policy requires a radically different perspective on prices, tax regimes and political structures.

The dominant commodity view also moulds the institutional framework, and hence the responses possible. In the UK, successive governments have

dismantled the corporatist institutions built up during the post 1945 consensus period, and in their place are institutions based upon the premise of energy-as-commodity: the energy supply industries have been privatized, with arms-length regulation by the Offices of Gas Supply (OFGAS) and Electricity Regulation (OFFER). Interestingly, neither of these regulatory offices has applied any specific mandate to energy as an ecological resource, only to guarantee of competition and price protection for the customer. The Directors General of both offices regard any move towards environmental pricing purely as a government matter, to be imposed from the legislature.

Environmentally sensitive energy pricing is steadily

becoming a legitimate political objective. The problem is to define these prices in environmental science terms, then leave it to politicians to determine what is acceptable. This cannot be done by economists alone: hence the role for a more broadly based environmental science. Any new means of dealing with energy and the environment should incorporate social negotiation in order to balance the benefits of energy use with its effects on the environmental commons. Techniques from decision theory, such as multi-attribute utility theory, may be of use here: these methods allow the users of decision tools to consider how changing the weight put on different aspects of a choice would affect the outcome. This allows context-dependent choices to be made, which is important since the many dimensions of environmental problems will always differ in their relation from choice to choice. These dimensions need to be considered openly, not hidden behind a single environmental adder.

For instance, open decisions have to be made about the trade-offs between environmental risks, health risks, security of supply, meeting demand, and cost, to name but a few of the possible dimensions of energy policy choice. If a cost benefit framework is used, a lot of assumptions about such trade-offs are made in the *process* of producing final figures, before the report gets in front of someone with the political responsibility for making such trade-offs. Frameworks built around the assumption that these trade-offs are an integral part of a decision, such as an interactive decision analysis tool, can bring into the decision dimensions that CBA excludes.

In order to do this, a 'decision matrix' is needed, built up out of the various factors involved in a decision, from the cost of different options, through social implications, such as equity and impact on communities, to the environmental impacts. The information in this matrix will need to be in a form as close as possible to the raw data so that decision makers can judge the importance of each for themselves. Through an interactive process of education of the decision maker and the playing of 'what if?' games with the information in the matrix, preferred options can be identified, with a clearer understanding of the importance of the different dimensions.

For these sorts of tools to work, they have to have moral force behind them: people have to know that decisions made with these tools will be binding. They have to overcome the power of the 'bottom line' to dominate decisions, and since the moves in energy policy have been towards *strengthening* the profit

motive in the energy supply industries, the two would appear to be in conflict. Hence a move away from environmental economics would require a different concept of how energy industries are run.

But is an alternative necessary? Environmental economics has not yet been tested fully in practice, so can we determine whether it has a reasonable chance of success? To find out, we can consider an area of prime importance if our impact on the environment is to be reduced: energy efficiency.

No regrets: the example of energy efficiency

While the threat of catastrophe from problems such as global warming may eventually require societies to change fundamentally in order to avert the danger, there are policies that can be followed that do not challenge the basic 'rules' of society now in place. In fact, there are options that are justifiable for reasons other than their environmental benefit, and that are placed under the heading of 'no regrets' policies. For global warming, the relevant no regrets strategy mostly involves promoting energy efficiency. There is much evidence that there is scope for large reduction in total energy use through increasing the efficiency with which energy is used. This is particularly true for electrical appliances, since there is so much inefficiency in generating electricity from fossil fuels. On the face of it, there is large scope for saving energy (see Box 17.5), including many opportunities for saving money through investment in energy-saving equipment. But these opportunities are not taken up.

The reasons why are primarily institutional, that is they lie in the way that energy is perceived by the customer, regulated by bureaucracy and treated politically. In addition, as has been stressed, energy markets, while nominally 'free', are in fact largely unrelated to the social and environmental costs of energy production and use. Arguably prices should be doubled over the next ten years, stratified by their contribution to environmental degradation. In addition energy prices should have any in-built subsidy removed. In most Third World countries energy prices are half of what they should be even in non-environmental accounting because of deliberate subsidies to keep the powerful urban élites content (World Bank, 1992).

Grubb (1991) summarizes the main causes of this 'efficiency gap':

Box 17.5 The potential for energy conservation

Saving energy has, until recently, received much less prominence than the need to supply ever-increasing quantities of energy. Technology existed many decades ago that could have made substantive reductions in the amount of energy currently used. At the same time there has been the development of newer ideas, all of which have led to improved efficiency in energy use, with many leading to potentially large savings in energy. On the other hand there has been an unwillingness by both the individual and society as a whole to embrace many of these ideas. Part of the problem has resulted in some cases from increased initial costs even when substantive savings are possible. In other cases legislation or corporate interest has actively promoted options that are energy wasteful (e.g. the 1947 Electricity Act which specified that *electricity* (not energy) was to be generated as efficiently as possible). The problem needs to be tackled in three ways. Firstly in improvements in efficiency in energy conversion; secondly as improvements in end-use efficiency; and thirdly through a change in attitudes and behaviour.

Improvements in efficiency in energy conversion

Nearly two-thirds of the energy released when burning fossil fuels for conventional electricity generation is lost to the environment. Newer techniques using combined cycle gas turbines (CCGTs) can cut this loss to around 50 per cent representing a substantial saving in fossil fuels and substantial reductions in gaseous emissions of both CO_2 and SO_2. Older technologies such combined heat and power (CHP) have been used for a hundred years to reduce the loss further, and overall conversion efficiencies in excess of 80 per cent are readily achievable. However, while CHP technology is well established, its development has often been hampered by inappropriate political or corporate decisions. Thus for every unit of electricity generated, between about 0.8 units (in the case of CCGTs) and about 1.8 units (in the case of conventional power stations) of heat are generated and there must be a demand for such heat. CHP does reduce the amount of electricity generated from a given station, but it greatly increases the overall conversion efficiency of useful energy.

Two difficulties arise here. First, many power stations built in the last 30 years are very large (2000 MW) and a station of this size would provide heat sufficient to satisfy the demand for all the houses in the cities of Liverpool and Manchester combined. Second, the seasonal variation in heat demand for space heating varies to a greater extent than electricity demand, and unless there is a significant base load industrial demand there will be a limit on the maximum amount of electricity that can be generated in this way. The situation can be largely resolved by building smaller stations near the centre of cities where the heat and electricity demands can be matched more closely. This has local environmental implications, but with the development of the 'so-called green' (i.e. CCGT) stations, this is less of a problem.

Industrial CHP has been widespread for many years, but there is still further significant potential in this area. Many firms, despite having extensive CHP on their premises, nevertheless have an excess which is lost through cooling towers. Sometimes, adjacent firms which have a net requirement of heat can co-operate to give an overall improvement in efficiency, but in general there needs to be the infrastructure and planning control from a local authority or energy board to make effective use of such surplus energy.

Small-scale CHP units suitable for a single large building such as a hospital or a hotel are now becoming popular in the UK, and their numbers are likely to increase significantly in the next decade.

Improvements in end-use efficiency

Developments in technology have led to improvements in efficiency in appliances. Perhaps one of the most spectacular was the change from valve operated to solid state operated colour television sets in the 1970s. At the same time, the initial costs changed little. There was a 75 per cent reduction in the energy consumed, and this far outstripped the increasing use of televisions. In other areas savings have been more modest, and significant further improvements are possible only by increased capital outlay, but nevertheless with savings in running costs to compensate. Legislation could help to promote efficient appliances. Thus while there are thermodynamic limitations on the efficiency of some types of energy use (e.g. refrigeration), substantial savings (perhaps up to 40–50 per cent) can be made by improvements in the insulation to keep the 'cold' in. Power-factor correction devices which are now readily available in the domestic market can be fitted to fridges and freezers to save a further 10+ per cent.

The overall efficiency of motive power for transport can be improved to some extent, but additional savings are possible through the efficient design of the other components associated with transport, such as the weight of the vehicle, speed limits and to a lesser extent aerodynamic drag.

Box 17.5 continued

Low energy light bulbs use only around 20 per cent of the equivalent tungsten filament bulb, and newer fluorescent bulbs with more advanced control circuitry also offer significant savings. However, the substantive increased capital costs have been a deterrent to their widespread use despite pack-back periods as short as 1–2 years. Attitudes as to the aesthetics and light quality of low energy bulbs have hindered widespread exploitation of such devices.

Heat pumps have been used for most of this century and provide a particularly efficient method to provide space heating. Heat pumps, unlike power stations, work with thermodynamics to provide a particularly effective form of heating. Typically only one-third of the energy required as heat needs to be supplied as electricity. If gas is used to provide the motive power the potential savings are much larger.

Low temperature space heating constitutes up to 40 per cent of total energy demand in a developed country, and simple expediencies such as insulation, double glazing and cavity wall insulation can all substantially reduce energy requirements of a building. More sophisticated systems using ventilation heat recovery systems can make even further reductions so that new buildings could be built with little or even zero heat energy requirement.

Building regulations in the UK have been framed to encourage minimum compliance with regard to energy conservation measurements rather than to encourage conservation as such. The standard UK house built in 1993 will have an energy requirement only about one-half of a similarly sized house conforming to the 1976 regulations. At present rates of construction, the turnover rate in dwellings implies a lifespan of around 200 years. A tardiness in specifying more stringent regulations will mean that overall there will be little impact from such low energy houses for at least 10–20 years. This emphasizes the importance of specifying tougher regulations earlier rather than later.

In the last few years there has been a growing consensus among analysts that there is an 'efficiency gap': the known *economic* technologies for using energy more efficiently are not being installed, even when this would save the investor money. Where a potential for energy saving becomes an economical prospect is an unclear division. Much depends on assumptions made about energy prices, interest rates and other unknowables. What is clear, however, is that a proportion of our energy use is inessential and could be cut out with no penalty, frequently to our economic advantage.

Changing attitudes

Attitudes of the public and corporate bodies towards energy use can significantly affect the amount of energy used. Good energy management can readily lead to 10–20 per cent savings even if no technical measures are included at the same time. Record keeping of energy consumption and its analysis (to allow for weather, etc.) is essential to highlight areas of waste, etc. On the other hand, social pressures for additional appliances or the desire for greater mobility can outstrip any possible savings from technical means. Despite significant improvements in energy efficiency in cars over the last 20 years (15–20 per cent), any saving has been swamped not only by the increase in number of cars, but also in the number of miles driven per vehicle.

Options for energy conservation are often mutually exclusive: for instance, significantly improving the insulation standards in new buildings will reduce the viability of city-wide CHP schemes. A careful balance between options to effect the greatest overall efficiency in energy use is therefore needed.

Technical innovation and development are a necessary but not essential first step towards energy conservation; legislation and good management by corporate bodies are an important second step; individual responsibility and institutional change are the final step in energy conservation.

- *Lack of knowledge, know-how and technical studies.* Most consumers know little of the scope for energy saving and are not responsive to information alone. Unless there is a price signal, consumers simply do not bother to find out about the scope for efficiency.
- *Separation of expenditure and benefit.* In many local governments, and rented property, the nature of expenditure is not conducive to investing in 'up front' capital projects to reduce energy wastage. Local governments are often restricted in how much

they may borrow, but are less controlled on day-to-day expenditure. UK Treasury rules do not allow local authorities to hire energy consultants to advise on energy-efficiency schemes, even though such people can demonstrate that their advice is cost effective. Similarly householders or commercial tenants do not have the interest in insulating their premises or in changing the heating system, even though they should get their money back in 5–7 years.

- *Limited capital* particularly affects the poor who usually have the highest energy expenditure as a percentage of household budget (e.g. in the UK, the poorest 10 per cent of the population spend 4 per cent of their income on fuel, whereas the richest 10 per cent spend only 1 per cent of their income on fuel). Similarly, small firms simply do not have the funds to invest in energy-saving schemes given the demand for financial resources in more competitive areas.
- *Rapid payback* is expected and sometimes demanded of energy conservation investments – usually at rates of return of the order of 15 per cent, i.e. return within five years. Yet discount rates on energy supply may be only 10 per cent and sometimes 5 per cent, as was the case for nuclear for a long time.
- *Lack of interest in peripheral operating costs* because, for most industry and households, energy costs account for only 4–8 per cent of total expenditures. One fewer employee would probably save more than energy conservation for a smallish industry or a modestly sized school. Budget managers, as a result, do not always take energy seriously.
- *Impact of gas and electricity tariff structures.* These often are weighted in favour of a fixed charge which is payable irrespective of how much is used, and a variable charge which may be lowered if bulk demand is required. In many cases it pays for certain categories of energy users to waste as much as 10 per cent of their demand in order to get on a lower unit price tariff.
- *Tax regimes* usually favour energy supply over demand reduction. For example, in the UK there is VAT on energy conservation materials while some aspects of energy supply are zero rated. Recent changes in legislation now require VAT on domestic energy supplies, but this does not discriminate against the differential environmental consequences of the fuel cycle. Car taxation for companies still favours large mileage users, though tax changes have been made to reflect the performance of the vehicle, not its cost or engine capacity. Nevertheless there is no tax structure favouring energy-efficient vehicles.
- *Bureaucratic neatness.* Energy demand reduction means millions of decisions in thousands of ways. This is not easy to track and so it is regarded as much more bureaucratically tidy to look at supply aspects of energy management, not the demand-dampening element.

- *Energy management in the round* is not encouraged, though it is proving very effective in the USA. Most US utilities can gain commercial credit for reducing a customer's usage of power, not by supplying more. This approach has been attempted by private 'third party' financing in France, with some success. In the UK the privatized energy suppliers are steadily moving in this direction, but against the grain of legislation. Ideally new legislation is required primarily to reward them for being 'all round' energy managers, providing conservation and efficiency-promoting measures as much as supply side improvements.

The existence of these barriers means that users of energy are not responding to the price signals already available to them. In the economic view, the only reason that people would not respond to strong signals such as the waste of money represented by energy inefficiency is that they do not possess the information that would enable them to implement energy efficiency. This explains the reliance of governments on information campaigns to promote efficiency, eschewing more interventionist options such as setting high efficiency standards. However, the success of these campaigns is short-lived, and they do not address the barriers to efficiency described above.

The application of environmental taxes is supposed to alter behaviour by improving the price signal: consumers receive better information on the cost of using energy. If people are not responding to existing prices in the 'correct' economic manner, the imposition of carbon taxes and the like may not have the desired effect, and may increase social conflict over environmental policies.

If imperfections in the energy market make price rises a blunt tool for altering behaviour, very large rises may be necessary to get the desired effect. For example, to achieve a reduction of 15 per cent in total fossil fuel consumption in order to meet a practical objective of stabilizing CO_2 emissions in 2000 at 1990 levels, coal prices would have to rise by at least 80 per cent, oil by at least 60 per cent and gas by at least 10 per cent (Grubb, 1991). To stabilize CO_2 levels in the atmosphere by 2025 would mean a 6-fold increase in the coal price in the USA and a 90-fold increase in the coal price in China. Given that the current sensitivities in developed countries are inflation and factory competitiveness, such price increases are extremely unlikely. The European Commission has failed to get a modest energy-carbon tax of $3 per barrel of oil equivalent in

1993 rising to $10 per barrel of oil equivalent in 2000 (an average of about 60 per cent of the price of oil on present prices, but obviously susceptible to unforeseen changes in oil markets and prices). Yet Pearce and Frankhauser (1993) suggest that a carbon tax of $20 per tonne of carbon is a minimal estimate of the social costs of carbon for the period 1991–2000, rising to around $28 per tonne of carbon by 2030 on the most conservative estimates. This would almost double the price of the cheapest imported coal and add nearly 50 per cent to the price of subsidized domestic US and UK coal. In contrast, Haugland and his colleagues (1992) estimate that to stabilize CO_2 emissions at 1987 levels would require a global tax of $9 per tonne of carbon now, $19 by 2010 and $100 by 2025.

Reliance on market-influencing tools may be dangerous, therefore, as their implementation will be difficult. The singling out of the non-economic factors involved in the (mis)use of energy allows more effective and targeted policies to be formulated, but only if the narrow view of energy-as-commodity is abandoned will this be possible. The sort of policies necessary may also conflict with other objectives: product standards and certain taxes may run foul of the trend towards free trade. This is why some analysts such as Lovins advocate a c-and-c approach to energy regulation. Meeting energy-efficiency targets, whether in appliances, building standards or energy budgets in offices and industry, at least guarantees a particular emission reduction objective in a manner that everyone treats as even-handed. Economists rightly complain that this is highly inefficient, but it may be politically more acceptable.

If programmes for promoting energy conservation are to be successful, then they need to be designed carefully. If they are not, then they can be less effective than they might have been through inappropriate restrictions. A case in point is the loft insulation grant introduced in 1978 by the UK government. Homes with less than 30 mm of insulation qualified for the grant which would provide two-thirds of the cost of new insulation, and in some cases of particular need (e.g. pensioners) up to 90 per cent of the cost. This grant was available for several years. For typical post-1945 construction houses, this level of insulation would pay for itself in just over one year without the grant (assuming gas heating), a good payback which reduces to 4 months with the standard grant and only 5 weeks with the 90 per cent grant.

On the other hand, houses in which the occupants had previously installed 50 mm of insulation without the benefit of the grant would not qualify for the grant

if they wished to upgrade to the new standard of 100 mm. In this case, the pay-back time increases to well over 3 years, making this investment a far less attractive option than for the householder without any insulation. If in our example the standard installed was 150 mm of insulation and the second occupiers had previously installed 100 mm, occupiers with no insulation initially would see their payback rise to 7 months, but those who were installing only 50 mm extra would have a payback of 18 years.

This simple example illustrates several points. Firstly, without the grant, the energy conservation measure was much more cost effective for the person who had no insulation than was the case for the person who had been keen to initiate measures in the past. This type of approach will send the wrong signals to many people, for if they had only waited they would have got a grant, and this will act as a disincentive for the future. Clearly there must be a subsidy for the low paid in this area, but a fairer system and one that would act as an incentive for the future would be to allow tax credits for any such improvements in energy conservation. Secondly, it is apparent that incremental energy conservation in a situation like this is far less cost effective than the single action of installing the optimum level of insulation in one go.

Energy supply: a new approach

Whilst there is massive scope for energy saving, there will always need to be supply. An integrated strategy for sustainable energy use will include the shift of energy supplies away from fossil fuels and towards renewables, with gas acting as a transitional fuel. The move must be made away from using energy capital to using energy income: gas, being the least-polluting fossil fuel, will be an important stepping stone to a low or even zero emission energy supply, which will be necessary in order to avoid the risk of environmental degradation. It should be noted, however, that any positive moves in the area of supply may be negated if energy demand continues to grow, since absolute levels of emissions can rise even if per unit levels of pollution fall, because of the increased number of units. Substitution of one energy *supply* for another will therefore not be sufficient on its own, it will need to go in tandem with measures to curb *demand*. Energy supply is easier to regulate than demand, however, so it is likely that much government action will focus on this aspect.

However, the real change necessary in the energy industries is institutional: away from being oriented on the supply of fuels towards the supply of energy *services*. With different organizations supplying different fuels, matching of energy needs and supplies will be difficult: private utilities in particular will be pushing for maximum sales of their particular fuel over any consideration of whether that fuel is the right one for the use under consideration. For instance, electricity is used for domestic space heating, which would be a complete non-starter if companies were oriented towards providing energy services, and not promoting their particular fuel at the expense of their competitors. This perspective appears to point to a radical change in direction away from competition and towards planning and co-ordination, perhaps by publicly run local energy boards: at the very least it implies a much more active role for the regulation and direction of private energy utilities.

Moves in this direction are being made in the USA through the introduction of least cost planning (LCP). In order to bring the criteria for investment in supply and demand into line, some of the state electricity industry regulators have imposed restrictions on electric utilities which have led to these companies implementing LCP, which involves the use of demand side management (DSM). In LCP, investments in supply (new power stations or transmission capacity) are compared with investment in reducing demand (e.g. subsidizing or giving away low energy lightbulbs). In many cases, it is in the utility's own, private interest, *on present-day energy prices*, to invest in energy-efficient equipment on the customer's behalf, since this will obviate the need for new power plant.

It is debatable that utilities would have realized these savings without the threat of the regulators not to allow companies to pass through the cost of new plant automatically on to the consumer, showing how institutional inertia is another barrier to implementing energy efficiency. LCP forces utilities to think about how to provide energy *services* to their customers, a major shift away from their previous orientation of supplying energy *carriers* (i.e. fuels). It is important to note that LCP as implemented in the USA requires companies to be able to save the cost of investing in additional generation and transmission capacity by investing in efficiency instead. If, as in the UK, these expenditures are split between different companies, e.g. generators and distributors, then none of these companies can profit from the reduction in demand, and implementing LCP becomes much more difficult.

Conclusions

In this chapter, only a few of the many issues involved in orienting energy policies towards environmental compatibility have been discussed. The discussion has hinted at the conflict between sustainability on the one hand and present institutional arrangements and attitudes towards energy on the other. A wider question is begged here, however, and that is the extent to which the wastefulness of energy use in Western societies is 'built in' to the economic structures of those societies. Exemplars of this are the spread of electricity, demand for which has grown at a much higher rate than energy generally, and motorized transport, which will be a major environmental issue in the lead up to the millennium.

Electricity is the 'modern' fuel: clean, quiet, controllable. Unfortunately, it is also a highly wasteful form of energy, with up to two-thirds of the heat used to generate the electricity being thrown away. Economic pressures on industry to increase labour productivity lead to increased mechanization, which leads in turn to greater electricity use. Since electricity is generated away from the point of use, it allows an out of sight, out of mind attitude to develop, making environmental problems associated with electricity generation more acceptable than if the energy source was local.

The economic structures that make electricity so attractive also fuel the demand for mobility, which leads to the rapid spread of motor cars. The atomization of society and the pursuit of profits leads, for instance, to large out-of-town shopping complexes easily accessible only by car: unless the structures that promote these wasteful and polluting practices are changed, the rise in demand for mobility will continue.

Even though the outlook for such basic change is bleak, the technology nevertheless exists which would allow a low-impact society to develop. Renewable energy technologies can reduce the physical impact of energy supply, though perhaps at the expense of some aesthetic impact. Information technology has the potential to reduce the need for travel through teleworking and other ways of accessing information from the home. Cycles of resource use can be closed through recycling and generating energy from waste. These are just some of the possibilities that would allow lower energy use per capita without affecting quality of life, and also keeping societies economically sustainable.

The presence of these technologies means that conscious decisions need to be made about our resource use. Present economic structures force societies to bend more and more energy slaves to our will. Ivan Illich, writing in 1974, said 'The energy crisis focuses concern on the scarcity of fodder for these slaves. I prefer to ask whether free men need them.' Twenty years later, the environmental crisis may force this view back on the world agenda.

References

Carter, D. (1991) Aspects of risk assessment for hazardous pipeline containing flammable substances. *Journal of Loss Prevention Process Industries*, **4**, 68.

Department of the Environment (1993). *Digest of environmental protection and water statistics, No. 15, 1992*. London: HMSO.

Grubb, M. (1991) *Energy policies and the greenhouse effect, volume one: policy appraisal*. London: Royal Institute of International Affairs.

Haugland, T.H., O. Olsen and K. Roland (1992) Stabilizing CO_2 emissions: are carbon taxes a viable option? *Energy Policy*, **20**(5), 405–19.

Holdern, J. and R.K. Pachauri (1992) Energy. In J. Dooge (Ed.) *An agenda for science for environment and development into the 21st century*. Cambridge: Cambridge University Press, pp. 103–18.

Illich, I. (1974) *Energy and equity*. London: Calder and Boyars.

Lovins, A.B. (1975) *World energy strategies: facts, issues and options*. New York: Friends of the Earth.

McGowan, F. (1991) Controlling the greenhouse effect: the role of renewables. *Energy Policy*, **19**(2), 110–18.

Pearce, D.W. and S. Frankhauser (1993) *Cost effectiveness and cost–benefit in the control of greenhouse gas emissions* (Paper presented at the IPCC by Working Group 3), Montreal.

Pearce, D.W., R.K. Turner and T. O'Riordan (1992) *Energy and social health: integrating quantity and quality in energy planning*. CSERGE Working Paper 000 92–05. Norwich: University of East Anglia.

Rasmussen, N.C. (1990) The application of probabilistic risk techniques. In T.S. Glickman *et al. Readings in risk.*

Washington, DC: Johns Hopkins University Press, p. 198.

Shipper, L. (1991) Improved energy efficiency in the industrialized countries: past achievements, CO_2 emission prospects. *Energy Policy*, **19**(2), 127–37.

UN (1982) *1980 yearbook of world energy statistics*. New York: United Nations.

UN (1989) *1987 world statistics yearbook*. New York: United Nations.

UN (1985) *1982 yearbook of world energy statistics*. New York: United Nations.

World Bank (1990) *World development report 1989*. New York: Oxford University Press.

World Bank (1992) Energy. In *World Development Report 1992*. Oxford: Oxford University Press, pp. 115–27.

World Resources Institute (1993) *World resources 1992–93* Oxford: Oxford University Press.

Further Reading

Chapman, P.F. (1975) *Fuels paradise: energy options for Britain*. Harmondsworth, UK: Penguin Books.

Eastop, T.D. and D.R. Croft (1990) *Energy efficiency*. Harlow, UK: Longman.

Foley, G. (1987) *The energy question*. London: Pelican.

Lovins, A.B. (1977) *Soft energy paths: towards a durable peace*. Harmondsworth, UK: Penguin Books.

Patterson, W. (1976) *Nuclear power*. Harmondsworth, UK: Penguin Books.

Ramage, J. (1983) *Energy: a guide book*. Oxford: Oxford University Press.

Roberts, J.U., D. Elliot and T. Houghton. (1991) *Privatizing electricity: the politics of power*. London: Belhaven Press.

Stern, P.C. and E. Aronson (Eds) (1984) *Energy use: the human dimension*. New York: W.H. Freeman.

Thompson, M. (1984) Among the energy tribes: a cultural framework for the analysis and design of energy policy. *Policy Sciences* **17**(3), 321–39.

Vellinga, P. and M. Grubb (Eds) (1993) *Climate change policy in the European Community*. London: Royal Institute of International Affairs.

Preventing disease

ROBIN HAYNES

Health is increasingly being regarded as a holistic and socio-cultural phenomenon rather than a purely medical matter. This means that the four roles of health management – prevention, promotion, cure and rehabilitation – have to be integrated both into so-called 'complementary' medical procedures and into socio-economic development patterns that place the physical and mental wellbeing of people as first priority. We have already seen in Chapter 1 how there is a close link between health provision at a community level, better civil and economic rights for women, and a lowering of population growth. In the chapter that follows, rural development in certain areas, notably Central and East Africa and parts of South-East Asia may be critically influenced by the diminishing number of able-bodied young adults, whose siblings are infected by AIDS and by other debilitating and socially influenced diseases.

Health care is also very much a factor of service provision in a manner that is socially acceptable, readily accessible (in distance and money terms) and scientifically sound. Health provision need not require medical specialization at its primary level: much can also be done through community nursing, preventative health and welfare programmes, health education in the schools and adequate (but modest) funds to ensure satisfactory service. Much can be achieved through self-reliant measures that are interconnected with social and economic development programmes. Sadly this is still not the case. For the price of a couple of dozen high technology fighter aircraft per year, primary health care could be provided to over 90 per cent of the world's peoples with plenty of scope for job training and community employment. Yet after a decade of the international drinking water and sanitation supply effort of various United Nation agencies, over 1 billion people still do not have access to drinkable water, and nearly 1500 million are unable to enjoy minimal sanitation facilities (Bergstrom and Ramalingswami, 1992, p. 121).

The ideas are there; the practice usually fails. Chemical control of vector-borne diseases such as river blindness (onchocerciasis) and malaria are proving to be inadequate and expensive. In the case of river blindness, biological control via bacteria is being shown to be most successful and culturally accommodating. Mosquito protection netting, combined with environmental improvements of ecologically unnecessary water-pools, is also recognized as a better bet than extensive use of DDT or other inexpensive but non-systemic pesticides. Yet malaria claims 100 million clinical cases and at least 5 million deaths per year. In many frontier areas where forests are being removed, six out of ten young adults are infected.

Of interest to the modern epidemiologist is the consequence of migration for human health. At one level, disease is spread because individuals with unfamiliar ailments come into contact with people who have no natural resistance to these illnesses. As is well known, whole native populations have been wiped out because of colonization of disease as well as foreigners.

It is also possible that a similar pattern of immunodeficiency is being created by modern migration of people in very familiar circumstances. Port towns and military establishments attract the migrant and the distant traveller. As Robin Haynes suggests in the chapter that follows, leukaemia may possibly be caused by a virus, or it may be an outcome when an immature immune system is exposed to unfamiliar infections. Similarly there is much interest in the thesis, as yet unproven, that diseases such as asthma may now be more common because the illnesses that usually killed, namely cholera, smallpox and tuberculosis, are no longer doing so, leaving the immune system to cope with more subtle disease agents such as air pollution, ingestion of toxins and viral transmission.

Epidemiology is a science of both statistical inference and judgement. Rarely can cause and effect be clearly linked. Leukaemia clusters may not be clusters at all, and may not be attributed to human-created radiation. Yet in the suspicious public mind lack of scientific 'proof' can provide scope for prejudice and anxiety to gain ground through pressure lobbying. Environmental groups campaign successfully against lead in petrol and nitrates in water, because the formal scientific caution refused to lay blame on causes that were deemed unacceptable and removable. Just as is the case in the risk literature, so environmental health research and management is adopting a 'civic' form of science. This means ensuring that the very best scientific analyses are available, but ensuring a strong element of precaution where there is public alarm or avoidable danger, and incorporating voices of 'lay' science in advisory bodies and peer review mechanisms. The environmental health phenomenon is becoming a matter for the integration of ethical and medical values around socially significant themes such as preventative education, access to services and reinforcement of holistic approaches to human well-being.

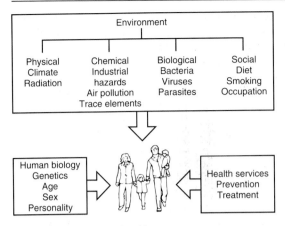

Fig 18.1 Influences on health.

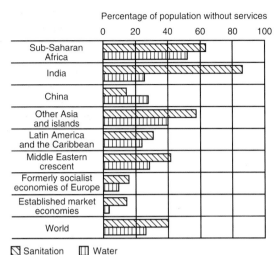

Fig 18.2 Population without sanitation or water supply services, 1990. (Source: World Bank, 1993.)

If 'the environment is everything that isn't me', as Albert Einstein is reported to have said, then the environment is largely responsible for human health and disease. Internal genetic factors certainly affect vulnerability to some diseases, but the environment generally has a stronger influence. Epidemiologists have estimated that 75–80 per cent of all cancers, for example, are caused by environmental conditions, which include diet and smoking. Figure 18.1 summarizes the main influences. Since many aspects of our environment are within our own control (unlike our genetic inheritance), much disease is preventable by changing the environment – in theory, at least. There are clear links between the work of the scientist investigating environmental associations with ill health and management of the environment to prevent illness and promote good health. This chapter illustrates some of the connections, but it will also sketch out the differing ethics and responsibilities of the scientist and the manager in areas where the causes of disease have yet to be established.

Clean water and sanitation

Since the early 19th century, death rates in Western industrialized countries have been falling, and they now stand at about half previous levels. The greatest improvements in survival have been in infants and children. Diseases which were rampant such as tuberculosis, cholera, dysentery, typhoid, typhus, smallpox, scarlet fever, measles, whooping cough and diphtheria are now eliminated or controlled. Environmental reforms such as the introduction of clean water supplies, sewerage systems, simple food hygiene, better housing and control of working conditions were responsible for much of the decline in the major endemic infectious diseases. The other important change was improvements in diet resulting from advances in agriculture, which enhanced resistance to disease. Medical interventions had very little effect until the 1930s, when sulphonamides were first used to treat infection, and, later, when antibiotics and improved vaccines were introduced. Now infectious diseases have been replaced by heart disease and cancer as the main killers in more developed countries. These do not respond positively to changes in the environment brought about by economic development. In fact, development and affluence have created new health problems.

In much of the Third World, diarrhoea, dysentery, cholera, typhoid, intestinal worms, tuberculosis and respiratory infections still dominate. Many of the gastro-intestinal disorders are transmitted via faeces, so the most effective first intervention is to improve water supplies and sanitation. Drinking water contaminated by excreta, food crops fertilized with human waste and fish from polluted waters are all health hazards that can be significantly reduced, but about 1.3 billion people in the developing world lack access to clean and plentiful water and nearly 2 billion people lack an adequate sewerage system (see Figure 18.2). The World Bank (1993) estimates that the cost of providing adequate water and sanitation services ranges from $15 per person per year for simple rural systems to $200 for urban systems with individual household taps and flush toilets. The benefits to be gained include increased productivity as well as improved health, so cost effectiveness is extremely high.

Air pollution

Air pollution and its various consequences are described in detail in Chapter 15. 'Smogs' used to be a frequent occurrence in industrialized cities where incomplete combustion of coal and oil produced soot, sulphur dioxide and sulphuric acid, which became lethal when trapped under a temperature inversion in stable winter weather conditions (Figure 18.3). Clean air legislation, smokeless technology and use of alternative fuels now protects the populations of most developed areas, but these advances have not yet occurred in former Eastern European countries. Parts of the Czech Republic, Poland and eastern Germany still suffer the effects of uncontrolled emissions of particulates and sulphur dioxide, and have high rates of respiratory illness and mortality. Air pollution is believed to be responsible for up to one-quarter of all respiratory morbidity in Czech children, for example (World Bank, 1993). Both human and economic costs are high.

In many cities elsewhere a different form of smog produced by motor vehicles and accentuated by sunny climates is now more common. Photochemical smog consists of ozone, carbon monoxide, hydrocarbons and photochemical decomposition products which induce a range of health problems, from eye irritation to severely impaired lung function. Motor traffic is also now a significant source of environmental lead. Lead poisoning is a well-known condition, but low doses of lead from car exhausts might affect blood pressure in adults and even the mental development of children living near congested roads. At national government level, motor vehicle policies that include incentives to improve fuel quality, enhance engine performance and reduce traffic volume have the greatest chance of success. Most industrial countries and some developing nations have set limits on lead levels in petrol and are using price differentials to encourage the use of lead-free petrol. Average blood lead levels in urban areas are declining in response.

Indoor air pollution is a much more significant problem in less developed countries. Burning coal and wood for cooking in poorly ventilated dwellings exposes

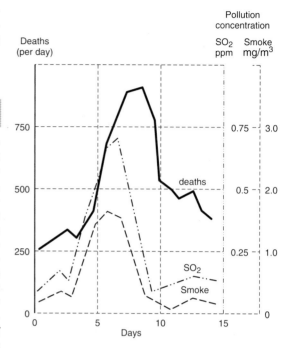

Fig 18.3 The London smog epidemic, December 1952. (Source: UK Ministry of Health, 1954.)

women and children especially to very high concentrations of particulates. Indoor air pollution contributes to pneumonia and other respiratory infections in children and chronic respiratory diseases including lung cancer in adults. It can even provoke stillbirths in women exposed during pregnancy. Reducing these effects will depend on providing not only information about the potential harm to babies and children but also alternative liquid or gas fuels at affordable prices.

AIDS

The HIV/AIDS epidemic was first recognized in 1981 and now covers almost the whole inhabited world. Its spread has been both rapid and volatile. Compared with cardiovascular diseases, gastro-intestinal diseases and cancer, AIDS (acquired immune deficiency syndrome) is not yet a major cause of death world-wide, but it is already a major killer in the most economically productive age group (20–40 years) in places as diverse as New York and much of Africa. AIDS has no effective vaccine or cure and a continuing geometrical

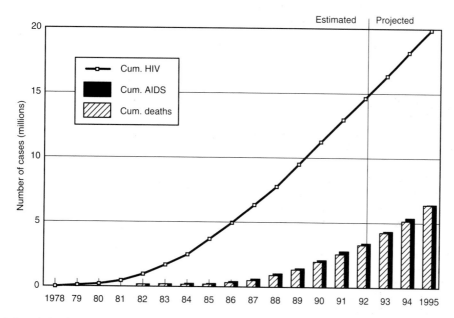

Fig 18.4 Cumulative HIV cases, AIDS cases and deaths world-wide, 1978–95. (Source: Mann *et al.*, 1992.)

increase is inevitable into the foreseeable future (Figure 18.4). So far, the largest numbers of cases have been in sub-Saharan Africa, followed by North America and Latin America, but the pattern is unstable. Preventative strategies have emerged from studies of the mechanisms of transmission and the social context in which transmission occurs.

HIV (human immunodeficiency virus) is a retrovirus which attacks the cells controlling the body's immune system, making the body very vulnerable to opportunistic infections. HIV is transmitted through sexual intercourse (most cases are from heterosexual intercourse), contact with contaminated blood in transfusions or shared hypodermic needles, and from mother to child before birth or through breast milk after birth. AIDS is diagnosed when a person carrying HIV develops an infectious disease which is rare in people whose immune systems are functioning. It was first recognised in San Francisco and New York when a rare cancer (Kaposi's sarcoma) suddenly appeared in apparently healthy young homosexual men. There is a long incubation period between becoming HIV positive and the onset of AIDS, typically 8–10 years. Antiviral drugs such as AZT might prolong this period somewhat, but they have serious side effects and are expensive. AIDS is always fatal.

In some cities in sub-Saharan Africa the prevalence of HIV is as high as 30 per cent and increasing numbers of babies are born with the infection. Infection through casual sexual encounters in the towns has spread to devastate family life in the rural villages. The illness of a young adult in a rural community leads to lower crop production and livestock yields, with a consequent reduction in income and nutrition for the family. When whole communities are affected, a spiral of decline is set in motion, with cash crops abandoned, food crops barely attended and ravaged by pests and a generation of orphans to be cared for. The challenge for the very poorly developed health services is to provide simple treatments with inexpensive drugs that alleviate the suffering of AIDS-related diseases. Prevention concentrates on programmes to promote condom use, and to control other sexually transmitted diseases which facilitate HIV transmission. In Uganda, some HIV testing centres have been established. AIDS awareness in Uganda is now so high that many people assume they are infected. Couples who are tested and found to be negative may now be motivated to be monogamous.

In other parts of the world, different cultural settings have created variations in the HIV/AIDS epidemic which call for alternative strategies. In Thailand, for example, there has been a rapid increase in HIV infection among drug injectors and commercial sex workers. Commercial sex is ingrained in Thai society, so high rates of infection in brothels can rapidly spread through the population. A national campaign through the mass media in Thailand is attempting to promote changes in sexual norms, but more effective in the short term is a new law enforcing 100 per cent condom use in sex establishments. In Romania, the problem could not be more different. Romania is unenviably a major centre of paediatric AIDS. During the Ceausescu regime, overthrown in 1989, many young children in orphanages became infected through contaminated blood transfusions and injections from re-used syringes. Blood for transfusions should be screened before use, but more radical action appropriate in all countries is to eliminate payments for donated blood (because paid donors tend to be people living in poverty, with a higher risk of HIV) and to reduce the need for transfusions by providing more effective early interventions. Sharing hypodermic needles is a particular risk for injecting drug abusers. In the United Kingdom there are local centres where drug users may exchange used needles for new ones, but there are enormous difficulties in enabling socially marginalized people with chaotic lives to make regular use of this service. In New York, tuberculosis has returned to scourge the poor and threaten the affluent. TB was largely eliminated from Western countries until the HIV pandemic, but now it is spreading again amongst the homeless, alcoholics and drug abusers. Prisons and shelters for the homeless are ideal breeding grounds and new, drug-resistant strains of TB have emerged. In New York, homelessness, drug use, AIDS and TB are inextricably linked, and what is needed is a broad programme to alleviate extreme urban poverty. There is clearly no single AIDS problem with a single solution anywhere in the inhabited world.

Ultra violet light and skin cancer

Concern over the depletion of stratospheric ozone as a result of man's activities has drawn attention to the current epidemic of skin cancer in Western countries. Ozone in the stratosphere absorbs ultraviolet (UV) radiation, and as the protective layer is progressively destroyed by chlorofluorocarbons (CFCs) and other products of human industry, more UV radiation is allowed to penetrate to the Earth's surface. In countries of the Third World the main effect of increased exposure to UV radiation will be an increase in cataracts and in the social and economic consequences of

blindness. In Western countries an increase in skin cancer is predicted.

There are two main types of skin cancer, both of which affect white-skinned people in particular. Non-melanoma skin cancer is relatively common and easily treated. It generally occurs on the most exposed parts of the body (the face, neck, arms and hands) and especially in people who work outdoors. Elderly people are more likely to suffer than younger people, and cumulative exposure to sunlight is thought to be the main cause. Melanoma, on the other hand, is rarer but more serious, with about one in seven cases proving fatal. Melanomas characteristically appear on women's legs and men's trunks, attacking young adults as well as the elderly. Office workers are more at risk of melanoma than outdoor workers, and it is believed that occasional high doses of UV radiation are to blame. UV radiation seems to have two effects: firstly, to damage the DNA in cells that have been badly sunburnt and, secondly, to suppress the natural immune system which normally would destroy unusual cells. The result is cancerous cells which are allowed to proliferate.

In most countries with white-skinned populations, the incidence of melanomas is increasing faster than that of any other major cancer, not because of ozone depletion (which is a recent phenomenon) but probably because of an increase in affluence and holidays in the sun. Queensland, Australia, where sunshine is abundant and beaches are inviting, has the highest melanoma rates in the world. In Australia public education campaigns have been used since the mid-1980s to alert the public to the dangers of sunburn and the symptoms of skin cancer. People are advised to wear protective clothing, such as a wide-brimmed hat, and to avoid the midday sun. Sunscreen lotions are helpful in that they reduce the risk of burning, but they may not protect against the immunosuppressive effects of UV radiation. Graphic posters displayed in drugstores have helped the early detection of melanomas before they become invasive, but the incidence rate has still not fallen. The main problem, of course, is that people enjoy sunbathing and a tan is considered to be attractive. Getting people to change their behaviour is a difficult and slow process, as experience with cigarette smoking has proved.

The depletion of ozone in the stratosphere will certainly intensify the problem. Ozone has natural fluctuations, but there is now compelling evidence that significant depletion has been occurring in recent years. A United Nations Environment Programme report

(1991) estimates that UV doses damaging to DNA have increased by 5 per cent per decade at 30 degrees north and south to 10 per cent at the North Pole and about 40 per cent over Antarctica. The same report predicts that a sustained 10 per cent reduction in ozone would produce at least 300 000 additional cases of non-melanoma skin cancer, 4500 additional cases of melanoma and 1.6 million extra cases of cataracts per year worldwide. These are conservative estimates. If the effects of UV radiation on the immune response system make us less resistant to infectious diseases, as some researchers claim, the consequences of inaction would be even more damaging to health.

Radiation

Nuclear safety is an issue of great concern. The accident at the Chernobyl nuclear power plant in 1986 caused immediate radiation sickness and early death for those exposed to high levels of radiation at the site and is expected to cause up to 7000 additional fatal cancers over Europe in years to come. But setting aside spectacular accidents, what are the dangers of living next to a nuclear plant operating normally? Much attention has been focused on childhood leukaemia as a possible consequence.

Leukaemia is a group of diseases of the blood, in which developing white blood cells fail to mature in the bone marrow, immature cells multiply and the body's defence against infection is eventually lost. Acute lymphocytic leukaemia is the commonest form of cancer in children, but it is still a rare disease. The causes of leukaemia are obscure, but exposure to ionizing radiation is known to be one, from studies of the survivors of the atom bombs dropped on Hiroshima and Nagasaki in 1945 (see Figure 18.5), studies of the effects of exposure to medical X-rays and studies of people exposed to high doses of radiation through their occupation. When a television programme in 1983 publicized the existence of a cluster of childhood leukaemias in the vicinity of the Windscale nuclear reprocessing plant (later renamed Sellafield) in Cumbria, the link between radioactive discharges from Britain's dirtiest nuclear plant and the disease appeared to be self-evident. Subsequent research has uncovered a more complicated story.

For a while, investigations concentrated on searching for clusters of childhood leukaemia around nuclear plants in the UK, and such clusters were found, with

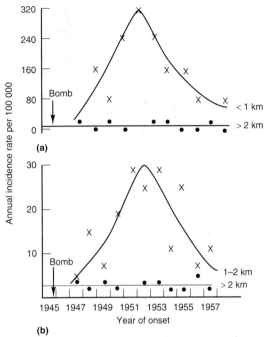

Fig 18.5 Annual incidence rate of leukaemia following the atomic bomb explosion among survivors in Hiroshima. (a) People less than 1 km from the hypocentre and (b) people 1–2 km from the hypocentre compared with people more than 2 km from the hypocentre at the time of explosion. (Source: Cobb *et al.*, 1959.)

the most significant (five cases) at Sellafield. Circumstantial evidence, however, is not proof of a causal relationship. The missing link in the argument was a demonstration that radiation doses received by children from nuclear plants was sufficient to cause the excess leukaemias, and careful calculations based on what was known about radioactive discharges, pathways of radiation into the human body and the relationship between the dose and the risk of leukaemia failed to account for the clusters. Another possibility was that the children's fathers had been exposed to high doses of radioactivity at work in the nuclear plant prior to conception, as was the case in Sellafield, but no supporting evidence could be found in other nuclear plants, or from studies of the children of Japanese atom bomb survivors.

The research team that had identified higher than expected childhood leukaemia rates near all nuclear plants in England and Wales must have been surprised when they investigated places earmarked as potential nuclear sites for the future. These places also had elevated childhood leukaemia rates, even though no nuclear facilities existed there yet. Perhaps childhood leukaemia is associated not with nuclear plants but with some unknown characteristic of people in the type of place where nuclear establishments are to be found. Remote rural areas, for example, have higher than average leukaemia rates, as do areas with rapidly growing populations, and both features are typical of nuclear sites. New towns built in rural surroundings in the 1950s which quickly grew in population had high childhood leukaemia rates. Perhaps a sudden mixing of population in a previously stable situation might be responsible for spreading the disease, as could occur, for example, if a virus were involved. A more sophisticated theory is that childhood leukaemia results when an insufficiently developed immune response system is challenged by sudden exposure to a range of infections. This might happen in a situation where children are shielded from infections at a very early age, only to be exposed later when infections are imported by migration. This and other hypotheses are under active investigation, but each new finding seems to complicate the story. Environmental influences on childhood leukaemia remain, for the time being, a mystery.

For most of us, exposure to natural sources of radiation far outstrips the danger from man-made radiation (see Figure 18.6). Radon, a radioactive gas produced by uranium decaying deep in bedrock, is the most important source of ionizing radiation exposure. The gas seeps up through fissures in the rock, through the soil to the surface, where it either disperses harmlessly into the atmosphere or collects in homes and other buildings. In the USA radon may cause up to 20 000 lung cancer deaths annually, and the current

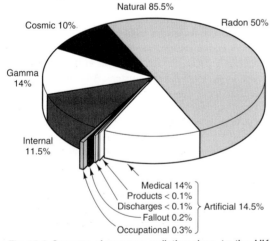

Fig 18.6 Sources of average radiation dose to the UK population. (Source: Adapted from Hughes and O'Riordan, 1993.)

estimate for England is 2000 extra lung cancer cases per year (National Research Council, 1988; National Radiological Protection Board, 1990). Such estimates are based on what is known about lung cancer incidence in uranium miners who received large doses of radiation from underground radon, and they are sufficiently alarming for most Western countries to have adopted 'action levels' of domestic radon gas concentrations. In areas with geology likely to produce high radon levels (Minnesota and North Dakota in the USA and Cornwall and Devon in the UK, for example) householders are encouraged to have their homes tested. Remedial measures are recommended if radon concentrations exceed the action level. Sealing the floor and ventilating the cavity under the house with a pipe and a fan are the main preventative measures.

Science and management

The major health problems of the less-developed world stem from poverty. The links between an impoverished environment and ill health are clear, and defeating the diseases of poverty depends on clean water supplies, proper sewerage systems, decent housing free from air pollution, better diets, safer workplaces and effective pest control as well as immunization programmes and basic health-care facilities. In the developed world the most obvious environmental hazards to health have been eliminated (with the exception of tobacco smoking), and the challenge now is to investigate insidious and rare effects. It may be, for example, that soft water is a risk factor for cardiovascular disease, that nitrates in the water supply could help to produce stomach cancer, that agricultural pesticides induce asthma, that lead released from petrol combustion could affect children's intelligence or that any one of the new chemical products being manufactured will create unforeseen problems in the future. Hypotheses are easily generated, but not so easy to prove.

There are several reasons. Firstly, there are problems of data accuracy. A high proportion of diagnoses are known to be inaccurate, even in countries with advanced health-care facilities, but much illness is never detected or reported to a doctor and does not even reach the diagnosis stage. Many diseases have a long latent period between exposure to the environmental agent that initiates the disease and the appearance of symptoms. Figure 18.5 illustrates this in the case of leukaemia. Lung cancer, to take another example, has

Box 18.1 Public campaigns

Woburn in Massachusetts is a town north of Boston which contains a toxic waste dump. In the 1970s the local residents were alarmed by cases of leukaemia that kept occurring and they lobbied for the wells that supplied the town water to be shut off. Subsequent investigation showed that the well water was contaminated with industrial wastes. The parents of children with leukaemia spent years in litigation against two companies. One company was found guilty of negligently dumping chemicals but the other was absolved. The evidence collected by the activists did, however, spur several official studies and contributed to the momentum of a national movement for better management of toxic wastes.

The Woburn case is typical of many public campaigns where ordinary citizens react against the complacency of companies or government agencies and seek to determine the nature and extent of health risks themselves. Campaigns usually begin with a few activists who note a strange pattern of ill health and contact the local doctor who is instrumental in providing data on local occurrences of birth abnormalities, skin rashes or whatever condition causes concern. The affected groups mobilize and stir up the media. Local health officials question the evidence, which they claim is inconclusive. The angered citizens bring in their own experts, take legal action and become generally confrontational. They press for official corroboration of their findings and file for adequate compensation. Campaigners face an uphill struggle, with access only to limited information. Their own consultant scientists may be branded as biased, and the weight

of scientific testimony seems to be loaded against them.

Why is it that evidence that appears so obviously to show a link between a pollution source and cases of illness is not acceptable as proof to a scientist? The scientist requires more than the existance of a 'cluster' because even randomly-occurring events sometimes cluster in a particular place just by chance. The scientist looks for confirmation that the suspected exposure happened before the illness, that the incidence of illness correlates with the amount and duration of the exposure, that there is a plausible biological mechanism for the pollution to cause the illness and that the same effect can be found in similar circumstances elsewhere. From a scientific point of view, evidence assembled to support a predetermined conviction is often one-sided and lacks an adequate comparison with a control group. However, as good studies are expensive to mount and may take years to deliver a conclusion, public frustration with science is understandable.

Satisfying strict scientific standards should not be a condition for taking precautionary action. Where doubt exists the real test is whether a reasonable person would expose themselves to the potential hazard. While public campaigns rarely prove that a source of pollution causes ill health, they do expose ignorance, complacency and inaction, and they are a powerful stimulant to provoke well-designed studies and government regulation.

Sources: Brown (1993); Crouch and Krollersmith (1992).

an average latent period of 20 years. Past smoking habits are known to be the major cause of lung cancer, but for conditions whose cause is unknown it is difficult to identify risk factors operating many years ago. Similarly, the effects of new pollution problems today will not be evident for many years. To add to the difficulties, most diseases are caused not by a single environmental factor but by a combination of many things, with perhaps different combinations triggering different stages of the disease. Confounding variables, such as age, sex, socio-economic circumstances, occupation, smoking and so on, are all very strongly related to health and must be properly controlled in an epidemiological study (see Box 18.2) so that their effects do not mask the effect being investigated. Then there is the problem of how to use what is known about the effects

of high doses of the pollutant to predict the health effects at low doses, a difficulty that besets studies of radiation effects, for example.

Many illnesses are comparatively rare events. A study population of 1 million people might be expected to produce between 10 and 20 acute lymphocytic leukaemias per year, and the infamous 'cluster' of childhood leukaemias near Sellafield consisted of just 5 cases, so any search for patterns of association is made difficult. Circumstantial evidence, such as the observation that childhood leukaemias occur near a nuclear reprocessing plant, does not prove that the cancers were caused by the plant, since both might be linked to another factor such as a sudden influx of population into a remote area when the plant was built. Other associations could be the result of pure chance, and

Box 18.2 Epidemiological methods

Epidemiology is the study of the distribution of disease in populations. While clinical doctors investigate disease in individual patients, epidemiologists look for patterns of occurrence in large numbers of people, in order to identify the causes of disease and to control health problems. There are three types of epidemiological study: descriptive, analytical and intervention.

Descriptive studies

The incidence of disease may vary with personal characteristics such as age, sex and occupation, it may fluctuate over time (as do epidemics of infec-

tious disease) or it may have a particular geographical distribution. Recognizing the pattern might generate new hypotheses about the cause, but it cannot by itself prove a causal association. For example, the incidence of lung cancer in some urban areas of the UK is almost twice that in rural areas, suggesting that ambient air pollution or industrial exposure may be causal factors. Further investigation would need to take the prevalence of cigarette smoking in previous years in both environments into account and to show that in cities those people most exposed to the hypothesized risk factors had the highest rates of lung cancer.

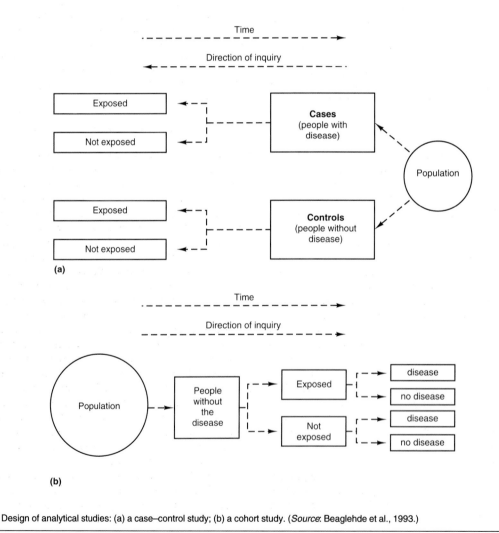

Design of analytical studies: (a) a case–control study; (b) a cohort study. (*Source*: Beaglehde et al., 1993.)

Box 18.2 continued
Analytical studies

Hypotheses are usually tested by studies designed for the purpose (see the figure). *Case–control* studies start by identifying a sample of people with the disease (cases) and a sample of people without the disease drawn from the same population (controls). Often the controls are selected so that some characteristics known to be associated with the disease, but not of interest to the study (such as age or sex), are 'matched' with the cases. The past history of both cases and controls is then investigated, to test whether the cases were more likely to be exposed to the suspected risk factor than the controls. A case–control study in south-west England is currently investigating whether lung cancer victims are more likely to have been exposed to high domestic radon levels than healthy controls.

Cohort studies start with a sample of healthy people, some of whom are exposed to the suspected cause and some who are not. Both groups are followed over a period of time (often several years) to determine which people develop disease. The long-term effects of methylisocyanate poisoning are the subject of a cohort study of residents around the pesticide factory in Bhopal, India, which was the scene of an major accident in 1984. Cohort studies take longer and are much more expensive than case–control studies, but they provide better information about the causation of disease and the most direct measurement of the risk of developing disease.

Intervention studies

Randomized controlled trials are experiments to study a new method of disease prevention or treatment. Subjects are randomly allocated to either a treatment or a control group and only the first group is given treatment. The results are assessed by comparing the outcome of the two situations. A randomized controlled trial was used, for example, to show that people with acute diarrhoea during a cholera epidemic in Bangladesh responded better to rice-based oral rehydration solutions than to glucose-based solutions.

---

here the methods of statistics are invaluable. If there is a probability of more than 5 per cent that any result could have been caused by chance, the scientist will reject the evidence as not being sufficiently strong. It is the scientist's responsibility never to claim more than the evidence allows, to be mindful of the complications and to be cautious in interpretation. Scientific scepticism ensures that investigations continue and do not stagnate.

The environmental manager, on the other hand, has a different responsibility: to safeguard public welfare in the light of current knowledge. Part of that responsibility is to make current knowledge more accessible to the general public: to make clearer, for example, the relative risks arising from natural as opposed to man-made radiation. Public concern needs to be alleviated by more effective communication when scientific investigation has determined that no serious threat exists, but scientific evidence is frequently incomplete and even contradictory. Like the scientist, the manager must err on the side of caution, but for the manager the cautious strategy in cases of doubt is to act as if the hazard were real.

Statistical significance is a criterion for accepting or rejecting evidence, but the manager is more concerned with public health significance, which is not necessarily the same. Statistical significance is in part dependent on sample size, so a result that is important for disease prevention could be overlooked because the study sample is not large enough for scientifically safe conclusions to be drawn. A real hazard might be so entangled with confounding effects that it is difficult to design the perfect study that isolates one particular relationship; but while the scientist grapples with methodological problems the public health consultant must decide what action to take. The precise effects of low doses of radiation are still open to scientific question, but few would argue with the principle of keeping human exposure to radiation as low as reasonably practicable. Defining what is reasonably practicable is an ethical minefield through which the manager must tread. Even when the scientific evidence is firm, as with the knowledge that fluoride in the water supply protects against dental caries, the question whether to add fluoride to the water supply in fluoride-deficient areas is not easy, for excess fluoride discolours teeth and may cause harmful effects not yet established. There are too many environmental changes occurring and new materials coming into use for each to be investigated, and, in the case of possible long-term effects, it would be unethical to wait until the damage has become obvious before taking action. Environmental management to protect health therefore requires a mixture of science and judgement.

References

Beaglehole, R., R. Bonita and T. Kjellstrom (1993) *Basic epidemiology*. Geneva: World Health Organization.

Bergstrom, S.K.D. and V. Ramalingswami (1992) Health. In J.C. Dooge *et al.* (Eds) *An agenda for science for environment and development into the 21st century*. Cambridge: Cambridge University Press.

Brown, P. (1993) When the public knows better: popular epidemiology challenges the system. *Environment* **35**(8), 16–20, 29–41.

Cobb, S., M. Miller and N. Wald (1959) On the estimation of the incubation period in malignant disease. *Journal of Chronic Diseases*, **9**, 385–93.

Crouch, J.R. and J.S. Krollersmith (Eds) (1992) *Communities at risk: Collective responses to technological hazard*. New York: Peter Lang.

Hughes, J.S. and M.C. O'Riordan (1993) *Radiation exposure of the UK population: 1993 review* (NRPB R263). Chilton: National Radiological Protection Board.

Mann, J., D.J.M. Tarantola and T.W. Netter (Eds) (1992) *AIDS in the World*. Cambridge, Mass.: Harvard University Press.

National Radiological Protection Board (1990) *Board statement on radon in homes* Documents of the NRPB No. 1. Chilton: National Radiological Protection Board.

National Research Council (1988) *Health risks of radon and other internally deposited alpha-emitters: BEIR IV*. Washington, DC: National Academy Press.

United Kingdom Ministry of Health (1954) *Mortality and morbidity during the London fog of December 1952*. London: HMSO.

United Nations Environment Programme (1991) *Environmental effects of ozone depletion: 1991 update*. Nairobi: UNEP.

World Bank (1993) *World development report 1993: investing in health*. New York: Oxford University Press.

Further reading

British Medical Association (1987) *Living with risk*. Chichester: John Wiley.

Farmer, R. and D. Miller (1991) *Lecture notes on epidemiology and public health medicine*. Oxford: Blackwell.

Rowland, A.J. and P. Cooper (1983) *Environment and health*. London: Edward Arnold.

Rodricks, J.V. (1992) *Calculated risks*. Cambridge: Cambridge University Press.

World Health Organization (1990) *Potential health effects of climate change*. Geneva: World Health Organization.

CHAPTER 19

Managing the global commons

TIMOTHY O'RIORDAN

Global change poses an enormous challenge for environmental science. We have already touched on the staggering scale, complexity and indeterminacy of many of the processes involved. In essence we are trying to fit two impossibly unfathomable systems together – the totality of processes that keep the Earth habitable and the totality of processes that determine human organization, culture and behaviour. Neither is modellable and the combination of the two is genuinely beyond our ken. Yet somehow we have to make some sense of the interrelationship if humanity is to survive as a civilized species.

This final chapter examines the critical need to create a sense of global citizenship in every household and human act. This is obviously a tall order, for at present only the faintest echoes of the beginning of creation beats in our breasts. To convert a modern, commercialized society to a commitment to sustainable consumption and a serious concern for the vulnerable and the offspring two generations hence is a hugely formidable task. Education is only partly the answer. The solution has to lie in wholesale acculturalization – we have to live and breathe sustainability. Since any major social change will take at least one generation, this places a heavy burden on environmental science in its popular forms leading the way towards a global citizenry.

One way forward is to amalgamate the truly international with the truly local – the major commons conventions, on climate, deserts, oceans, biodiversity, forests and population – with local agenda 21s. This would be the basis of community action and household involvement. So far it is proving difficult to persuade individuals to stop driving cars and recycle all wastes when they cannot see the gains of collective action, or feel the pain of communal disapproval when not meeting the codes of sustainable practice. Local agenda 21s are not that far off. Already a number of local authorities in the UK are experimenting with the approach. Much obviously depends on the tie in with the national Agenda 21s and their relationship to the global whole. The Rio Conference did begin a process of creating tiered A21s. Civic science should be able to flourish in this atmosphere, marrying not just the social, life and earth sciences but also embracing the humanities, the media and the church. There is still plenty for the young environmental scientist to get excited about, given the tools to serve the Earth.

We might . . . conclude that some severe problems result not from the evil of people, but from their helplessness as individuals. This is not to say that there aren't callous, even malicious, noise and waste and vandalism. . . . But some is unwitting; some offers little choice; and some results from the magnification of small incentives into massive results. (Schelling, 1972, p. 90)

On managing commons

We have already looked at the changing interpretation of the commons in Chapter 1. The original 'commons' were neither freely accessible, nor messily abused. Throughout history there have been lands and waters which provide resources of fertility, food, fuel or timber and which are not privately appropriated, but exist for people to use according to certain unwritten rules. The medieval village 'common' is but a fraction of the immense range of commons resources that still offer sustenance for many millions of people.

Commons provide a special quality of property right. Permissions of use are tempered by cultural, kinship or village membership, so there is no open house. Licences to use are also circumscribed by clearly defined custom and obligation to other users and to the well-being of the commons themselves. Anyone who abuses these privileges, in true commons, is subject to local condemnation and the odium of fellow commons users. For such people the presumption of being helped in time of need no longer holds. In a society that depends on sharing during periods of scarcity or pain, that is a far greater penalty than incarceration.

In modern times, however, international commons or common pool resources, and shared resources are destroyed, neglected, eroded or enclosed. For common property resources to suffer any or all of those fates, six quite specific conditions have to apply:

1. There is free access, without impediment, to anyone and everyone.
2. The assimilative capacity or critical load of the commons is finite and can be reduced or removed.
3. Individuals who enter the commons act in isolation from their neighbours: there are no rules of communal obligation and reciprocal support.
4. Individuals are unaware of the side effects of their use on others, partly because such effects may simply not be known, but partly because they do not take the trouble to find out, since they see themselves in competition, not co-operation.

5. Co-operation will only work when individual users know that *everyone* will do so, but unless there is an agreed management regime with a police force, in a 'pure' commons there will be some who prefer to deceive for advantage: this causes others to do likewise, so deceit and false reporting become widespread.

6. Individuals cannot change any of this on their own: their individual influence is too small, and the gains from citizens' action are very modest given the social and practical costs of taking such action in a pure and unregulated common.

Managing commons means controlling access, defining property rights, establishing codes of procedure that are accepted by all, enforcing compliance and ensuring that the whole management process operates on the practice of accountable consent.

So far we have been discussing commons in a general manner. This chapter looks at two special sets of commons, both of which involve intergovernmental co-operation, or international agreement. That is, their management cannot depend on the goodwill of a national democracy. There must be some sort of internationally agreed rules in order that the global interest is protected. These two kinds of commons are usually referred to as *international commons* and *shared resources*.

International commons are physical or biological systems that lie outside the jurisdiction of any one country, but whose services are valued by society as a whole. Examples include the biosphere generally and in particular the stratospheric ozone layer, the atmosphere, the diversity of natural species and their habitats on land and in water; also deep sea minerals, Antarctica, the electromagnetic spectrum, outer space and the biogeo-chemically active surface of the oceans. In some cases technological advance has created an interest in a commons where before no effective interest existed. Outer space, the geostationary orbit and the electromagnetic spectrum are obvious illustrations. In other instances, some former commons have been effectively nationalized, though subject to international rules. The coastal zone is a case in point where, for the most part, nation states have management rights over waters and minerals up to 200 miles (320 km) offshore under the principle of exclusive economic zones (Birnie, 1991).

For international commons the most cited forms of governance include:

* *world government*, in practice promoted by United Nations institutions;

- *extended national responsibility* by widening the basis of property rights to some sort of mutual obligation acquired by treaty or convention;
- *restricted common property* by imposing conditions of use on nation states through contractual obligations, bilateral agreements or international law.

Shared resources are physical or biological systems that extend across an international border, but which are geographically contained. Obvious examples include rivers, lakes or groundwaters that cross national boundaries, oil and gas reserves that underlie two or more nation states, migratory birds, fish or mammals (e.g. whales) that feed, breed or simply roost in one country while *en route* from another nation to a third national jurisdiction. The other major illustration is the regional sea, such as the North Sea (see Chapter 14) and the Mediterranean.

The common management solution to treating shared resources is the joint national agency either by co-ordination or some sort of multi-national regime (see Young, 1992, p. 250). Many of these arrangements are discussed by Birnie and Boyle (1992) in a most useful survey of international environmental law.

A third set of international commons problems is associated with the transfer of pollution or dangerous substances from one country to another. This is essentially a subset of shared resource management, for it includes such matters as acid rain, or nuclear explosions, or chemical contamination of international waterways. But *transboundary externalities* as they are called, do give rise to a number of vitally important principles for international environmental law:

- *Rights of sovereign action across a border.* When a neighbouring country causes environmental damage to its partner, what rights does the latter have over the former to stop the damage from continuing? Sulphur from the dirty coal-burning power stations in Ohio helps to damage the sugar maple industry of Quebec, just as toxic emissions from iron smelting plants of the Kola Peninsula in northern Russia adversely affect the sensitive ecosystems of Finland. What rights have the Canadians or the Finns to take preventative action against their neighbours?
- *Buying pollution rights.* The polluter pays principle suggests that those who cause damage should stop the source of the damage or pay for causing damage. But in practice where a poverty-stricken neighbour neither has the resources nor the political incentive to clean up, it may well pay a richer neighbour to

buy out the pollution in the form of aid assistance via political agreements or economic restructuring payments. Where this cost of clean-up in the polluted country is greater than the cost of removing the source of pollution, or environmental threat, then it may well be more sensible to invest in technological rehabilitation or process substitutes. Clearly this will require a good knowledge of cause and effect, a strong sense of the changing world of property rights, and a firm knowledge of environmental economics. There is a bright future for the lawyer trained in environmental science who is also blessed with imaginative negotiating skills.

All this takes us into the somewhat obscure field of international environmental law and diplomacy, and the changing role of science, economics, politics and ethics in what is probably the most critical and ill-developed area of applied environmental management. To this we now turn.

International environmental law

International law generally requires an enormous amount of trust, goodwill and collective determination to work. Essentially any agreement involving two or more countries, in effect, requires that both agree to co-operate, or alternatively that the international community is prepared to enforce this agreement by trade sanction or diplomatic pressure. Ideally there must be inter-party consensus within a framework of compliance.

International law is basically a set of principles, obligations and rules that bind international behaviour. Through various formal or informal arrangements the freedom to act as a sovereign state must be circumscribed by an obligation to respect the legitimate interests of other sovereign states. For this to have credibility three conditions should apply:

1. *Mutual advantage.* States have to accept that by co-operating and by compliance, all will be better off than if any one fails to play by the agreed rules. So states have to embrace a shared sovereign interest in collective agreements.

2. *Credible threat.* States have to be persuaded that non-compliance is not in their national interest. This requires supportive but believable science of the kind outlined in the Introduction, backed by an

independent scientific and technological review mechanism.

3. *Credible enforcement.* States equally must know that non-compliance will result in differential penalty. By some means or another there has to be enforced reporting of behaviour, of action to meet agreed objectives and of failure to achieve what is promised, by some sort of independently validated verification procedure, in order to provide an acceptable basis for international regulation and enforcement.

International environmental law is normally created by means of *treaties or conventions or protocols*, sometimes referred to as 'hard law', or by *custom and framework conventions*, based on more ambiguous wording and hence more feasible interpretation. This is sometimes termed 'soft law'. The distinction between hard and soft law is a dubious one, even though the two concepts sit side by side in the literature (Birnie, 1991, pp. 52–4). Hard law in international terms is probably best seen as regulations or enforceable targets of performance bound by treaty. These impose mandatory obligations on states which must subsequently enforce their commitments by national laws or regulations. An obvious example is the control of ozone-depleting substances under the Montreal Protocol (see Chapter 6). Here specific chemical formulations are being phased out over a clearly defined time period, and all new products have to undergo standardized tests for their ozone-depleting potential before they can be marketed anywhere – or at least amongst signatory states.

Soft law is for some a contradiction in terms. Law means rules and obligations which are entered into, or abided by, irrespective of original willingness or dissent. So there can be no true law that is so vague as to allow excessively flexible interpretation or endless delay in implementation without making a mockery of the notion of legal agreement. Others, however, see in the carefully written ambiguity of modern international environmental agreements an element of calculated persuasion. Some lawyers refer to this as *legal custom*, that is support for broad agreements that do not require a formal legal instrument. This allows signatories to accept the principle of sovereign consent, but also permits them to vary their interpretations of genuinely ambiguous terms such as sustainable development, precautionary principle, cost effectiveness and critical load analysis.

So soft law is a real phenomenon. Arguably it is of the greatest significance in the evolution of international environmental agreements aimed at managing the various global commons. One can say this for four reasons:

1. *Scientific doubt.* Where the science is supple or genuinely indeterminate, and where there needs to be regular updates on the state of knowledge, then phased commitments to tighter and tighter obligations (or the inverse, if the earlier scientific assessments were too pessimistic) are more likely to result in compliance.

2. *Freedom of action.* One of the great achievements of the EC has been to leave it to each member state to decide just how to meet an agreed target. This is the method by which all directives are agreed. On a global scale, it is the approach taken for the UN Framework Conventions on Climate Change and Biodiversity. Broad targets are set and each signatory party is free to find different ways of reaching these targets by means that are politically acceptable.

3. *Social learning.* Governments often learn by experiment and also from pursuing a course of action forced upon them by international commitment. This process of adaptation and reinterpretation of an earlier negotiating position is sometimes referred to as social learning. It is the collectivity of devices ranging from scientific discovery, popular alarm, international agreement and supporting institutional change that is the evolutionary element of governance. Soft law can be enormously influential in promoting this, at times, painful adjustment.

4. *Face saving.* At the start of difficult negotiations the parties may be implacably opposed to certain principles. Eventually, for agreement to be reached, wording has to be found that permits diplomats and their political masters to save face yet acquiesce to the outcome. Usually the wording agreed is a combining together of different aspects of the same principle. For example, Article 2 the Maastricht Treaty of the EU, finally ratified in late 1993, talks of 'harmonious and balanced development of economic activities [and] sustainable and non inflationary growth respecting the enviornment'. This is an amalgam of environmentally sustainable development and continuous economic growth. The result can be both meaningless or meaningful depending on the point of view of the parties involved. The UN Framework Convention on Climate Change talks of 'common but differentiated responsibility' in

reducing global greenhouse gas emissions. This could mean that every country must play its part, but some should do so much more than others. But it could also be interpreted as a matter of capability or practicality rather than moral principle or burden of contribution to atmospheric warming. For some time to come, different countries will respond to this wording as a cop out or a diplomatic lever, depending on the political and economic responsibilities involved in greenhouse gas reduction.

Soft law in action

A framework convention creates a legal atmosphere in which governments can work together. Tightly defined targets and mandated pathways for reaching these targets would create blocking resistance from the outset, especially if the science is fuzzy, and big economic sacrifices are in the offing. So the UN Framework Convention on Climate Change, signed at Rio in June 1992 which will ratified in early 1994, created a clever set of wording.

- It created an acceptable objective of stabilizing greenhouse gas concentrations at levels that would *prevent dangerous anthropogenic interference* with the climate system. This should be adopted in a time frame to allow *ecosystems to adapt naturally*. Both the emphasized phrases allow great latitude for interpretation. The early yardstick of 1990 levels stabilized by 2000 is simply not enough to prevent dangerous anthropogenic interference (see Chapter 6). Indeed it may do no more than delay the doubling of CO_2 concentrations by a few years and clip 1 cm off likely sea-level rise by 2100. So, as the science proceeds, signatories will have to examine tougher greenhouse gas removal regimes before 2000 for the period beyond 2000. But to do so now would be greatly counterproductive.
- Action by each nation should be carried out *in an equitable manner, according to historic responsibility, state of development and capacity to respond.* This builds in the concept of fairness, or ecological space, in the negotiations. The later developers, who potentially will become the main CO_2 and methane emitters in a generation's time, are being given a breathing space for ten years. This should allow for technology transfer, backed by incremental cost estimates (see Chapter 1) to allow China, India and

the Russian Federation to develop more energy-efficient technologies and lower CO_2 and methane emissions. This is where a restructured Global Environment Facility might utilize the application of 'joint implementation of carbon offsets'. This means rich countries financing the increased sequestration of CO_2 by planting trees (see Chapter 6) or offsetting CO_2 emissions by substituting lower CO_2-emitting strategies (switching to gas, creating energy-efficient technologies, assisting nuclear or renewables or clean energy from hydrogen). This is one of the most promising areas for international sustainability financing, and one of great need for attention by interdisciplinary environmental science.

Common heritage and global legal ethics

Within the notion of the international commons is a specific concept applying to the safeguarding of life-support and celestial processes which transcend the infinitesimally brief tenure on earth of the human species. This is the doctrine of *the common heritage for mankind* (for a discussion see Brown Weiss, 1989, pp. 48–9). The idea emerged in the 1930s and became incorporated in law in the 1950s. It has five principal elements, namely: non-ownership of the heritage; shared management; shared benefits; inclusive use for peaceful purposes; and conservation for humanity, including future generations. The significance of this doctrine lies in its obligation to current generations to act as trustees of the natural and human heritage so as to enhance the biological and spiritual life of its descendants.

The common heritage doctrine combines ethics with the law in a manner that is by no means agreed amongst international jurists. One view holds that no agreement can operate without the consent of national legislatures as part of formal ratification of treaties signed by ministers or heads of state. This is a conservative, but formally correct view that representatives of public opinion should bind nation states to shared action. The radical, or nonconformist, view holds that the law should have a moral or exhortatory character leading nations into uncharted waters on the basis of stewardship (wise management utilizing best practice) and trusteeship (handing on to future generations the legacy of what was given to the present generation). For example Allott (1990) believes that 'when law is not merely the multilaterization of individual purposes but the universalization of social purpose, it transcends self interest and becomes self creating of a society.' This body of thought believes that the International Court of Justice at The Hague in the Netherlands should have the power to declare general principles of natural justice for the sustainability of the Earth, as accepted by the conscience of concerned people. This should in turn set the stage for universal declarations for basic principles such as fundamental environmental rights of all matter and sustainable development.

The problem lies both in the concept and in the practice of ethical law and common heritage issues. If there is no consensus at state level, then all the declarations in the world will not help, for there will be no collective backing for enforcement and punitive sanction for wrongdoing. Soft law practices can help by creating Principles or Declarations for international consensus. In the environmental field are the Declaration of Principles arising from both the Stockholm and Rio conferences. To date these are exhortatory only with moral and some political persuasive support. The fact that they exist allows pressure groups to exert influence on future negotiations, places governments on the spot when new treaties come up for signature, and allows legislatures some room for critical surveillance.

Brown Weiss (1989, 148) believes this matter is so important that it should not be left to the pure UN machinery. She advocates the creation of a Commission on the Future of the Planet. This might be an amalgam of intergovernmental and non-governmental organizations. It would have to be backed by a UN Resolution on Human and Environmental Rights to give it moral force. Professor Brown Weiss suggests that such a body should have six functions:

1. *Symbolic*, emphasize global commitment to trusteeship.

2. *Cautionary*, warn of impending threats to any aspect of common heritage.

3. *Catalytic*, create new ideas by bringing together interests that may not have to force recognized collective self-interest.

4. *Advisory*, provide technical and scientific assistance to countries providing heritage as an act of trusteeship.

5. *Scientific*, investigate research issues of an interdis-

ciplinary nature to ensure that heritage is properly evaluated and given political support.

6. *Educational*, provide the necessary information and awareness to promote the cause amongst the public generally.

She also argues that the Commission would need some form of trouble-shooting support arm in the form of an ombudsman's office. This would take grievances from NGOs or even the general public where evidence of heritage damage would be shown to be happening or about to occur as a result of an existing or proposed course of action. The office, which might be regionalized on a continent basis, would also have powers to investigate complaints and would be responsible for the scientific and advisory roles suggested above.

What lies behind Brown Weiss's radical notions is a concept of international law and organization that promotes a broader cause of trusteeship for the planet than would happen if everything was left to politically driven UN organizations and states. Equally important from her vision is a principle of property right that embraces both a private and public responsibility embodied in the principle of trusteeship and companionship on an evolutionary journey that is life on Earth. Philosophers have coined the terms *deep ecology* or *transpersonal ecology* to reflect this very special application of property obligation. The two concepts are not quite the same. Deep ecology applies to a spiritual exploration of the inseparability of human consciousness and the sentience of the natural world (Box 19.1). Transpersonal ecology takes this one step further and seeks to establish a spiritual reincarnation between the purpose of day to day being and the exhilaration of being part of the creative energy that is evolution (see Box 19.2).

Another, very different approach to creating a fresh look at human relationships to the natural world is to examine scientifically the tight coupling of biota and the material existence of chemical and energy flows into a combined dynamic system that acts to retain life on Earth. This notion is termed *Gaia* (see Box 19.3). Its originator, James Lovelock, sees this totality of physical and biological processes as physiological or self regulating (Lovelock, 1992, 11). Lovelock believes in the interdisciplinarity of scientific investigation to learn more about the workings of Gaia. The diagnosis of the ills and therapies for this planetary medicine requires an extension of empiricist science based on the recognition of the inherent capacities of the earth as a whole to retain homoeostasis.

Box 19.1 Deep ecology

The philosophy of deep ecology was coined by the Norwegian Arne Naess to reflect the world of ever-more searching questions about the true nature of humans to the natural world. The 'deep' of deep ecology means asking deeper and more profound questions. Deep ecology is the ultimate in ecocentrism, the striving for equality with gaia or the biosphere, as part of organic totality with all creation, past, present and future. Deep ecology preaches egalitarianism, non-violence, animism and a non-dualistic appreciative attitude to the whole of the ecosphere. Deep ecology encourages compassion and benevolence to non-human beings, accords them with rights to co-existence with humans and calls on people to forego mindless consumerism. Deep ecologists believe that materialistic humanity is a slave to gratification, a passive actor in collective global destruction.

The philosophy has paradoxically been taken up by a growing number of ecoactivists, notably Earth First!, Sea Shepherd and the Environmental Liberation Front. Each of these groupings is shadowy, operating in cells of activism, forming, fragmenting and recreating as needs arise. They are the object of much intelligence surveillance, and continue to grow in number and activity. How far they will succeed in changing the order of things depends enormously on the culture of acceptance of ecological terrorism. The irony is that all these groups accept that violence and destruction of objects or processes that they believe are helping to destroy the planet are acceptable practices.

Source: Naess (1989).

Box 19.2 Transpersonal ecology

Transpersonal ecology is the brainchild of an Australian philosopher, Warwick Fox (1990). He was dissatisfied with the formality of deep ecology and looked instead for a more transcendentalist philosophy. This, he reasoned, should regard all objects in the world as part of a continuous and connected whole with innate sameness, or utter interconnectedness. He feels that the proper state is that of pure consciousness, that is, the experience of totality, of complete undifferentiatedness. Once we make distinctions in the world around us, by separating object from object, and emotional reaction from emotional reaction, then we lapse back into the realm of conscious contents. Thus, he claims, discreteness comes from mechanistic science, continuity reaches us from the 'new interactive sciences', and identity (or sameness) from mystical tradition. Transpersonal ecology is the middle way between the extended science of interdisciplinarity as outlined in the Introduction, and the totality of experience that comes from transcendentalism: the sense of utter nothingness, of complete loss of personal separateness, of spiritual engulfment in the comprehensiveness of creative evolution. This emancipated state, he believes, is the basis for education for sustainability.

Source: Fox (1992).

Lovelock and various colleagues have built up an impressive record of evidence to show how life and land work to retain a planet in active disequilibrium with its state, should there be no life at all on it. If only geophysics and geochemistry mattered, the Earth would be bathed in an atmosphere dominated by CO_2 with a mean temperature 20°C hotter. Like Mars and Venus there would be no ocean: the planet would be utterly inhospitable. Gaia changes all that. Lovelock and a growing band of adherents are revealing a host of life-preserving interconnections. For example, plankton in the ocean regulate cloud cover and atmospheric temperature by transforming sulphur and other substances into cloud droplets. Similarly CO_2 fluxes are controlled by plant growth affecting rock weathering

on a ten thousand year time scale, and by the 'pumping' of CO_2 into the oceans in a hundred year cycle. Humans can interrupt these sequences: the reduction in oceanic algae due to climate warming could remove a vital CO_2 sink. So too could the wholescale transformation of surface vegetation. Agricultural intensification could be one of the most devastating long-term threats to habitability on the planet, at least in the timeframe of human response.

Gaia is primarily a scientific notion that is growing in significance. It is introduced here to encourage the reader to reflect on the relationship between a holistic science, planetary physiography and societal responsibility for retaining the gyroscopes that maintain a habitable world. Despite his sincere attempts to separate any ethics out of gaia, Lovelock (1992,17) confesses that in studying gaia 'our collective attitude toward the Earth affects and is affected by the health of the planet'. The two approaches might do well to run abreast.

Box 19.3 The Gaia concept

The Gaia thesis is the product of an unusual mind – the non-establishment scientist. Jim Lovelock is a geochemist and an inventor who can earn his keep by designing and patenting an imaginative piece of machinery. But his true love is 'real science' – the 'wondering about how the world works and the design of simple experiments to test the theories that thus come to mind' (Lovelock, 1992, p. 15). Real science, like its companion artistic creativity, is best done quietly and inexpensively. He regrets the plethora of specialized environmental scientists, 'the brightly polished doctors of philosophy', who are most unlikely to achieve anything other than a secure and comfortable employment. Gaia is holist, not reductionist; integrative, not separatist; imaginative, not pedantic; open-ended, not closed.

Lovelock believes gaia is a form of planetary medicine similar to the folk medicine of the pre-scientific era. Keeping a healthy planet with an equitable climate is as complicated as maintaining a healthy body free of disease. The Gaian idea is to design a mode of existence to let the Earth live in a healthy fashion – where possible, to let nature be the guide and the gyroscope of homeostasis. To ignore gaia may mean that humans will have to live forever in a form of environmental conscription – looking after the planet as if it were on a kidney machine – functioning, but always circumscribed. Caring for Gaia means keeping a planetary healthy life – tending to the small things that accumulate across billions of thoughtful people into collective planetary health. This is gaian anarchy. We behave appropriately because we just know others are doing so. Gaianism is the transpersonal lifestyle of a sustained world.

Schneider (1990) concludes that the gaia notion is really five different ideas:

1. *Influential Gaia* simply states that biota have influence over the abiotic world, adjusting temperature and atmospheric chemistry.
2. *Co-evolutionary Gaia* believes that biotic and abiotic activities interact in a synergistic manner creating and sustaining the biosphere.
3. *Homeostatic Gaia* asserts that the co-evolutionary role is to maintain dynamic equilibrium of the biosphere, despite external or internal stresses.
4. *Teleological Gaia* holds that the atmosphere is kept in homeostasis not only by the biosphere but also for the biosphere.
5. *Optimizing Gaia* concludes that the biosphere operates in such a manner as to create conditions that are optimal for biological survival.

These are listed in order of interconnectedness. The first two are relatively weak notions. The latter three suggest a purpose in life on Earth, namely to maintain itself in near optimal conditions. Take your pick.

Sources: Lovelock (1992); Schneider and Boston (Eds) (1991); Schneider (1990).

Regime theory and sustainability

Regimes are sets of rules, norms and decision-making expectations that converge action around agreed principles and objectives, and that are based on a combination of international law, credible science and acceptable political custom. Regimes can only work if the parties involved recognize that their self-interest is best served by co-operation, mutual enforcement and collective action. The scope for *free-riding*, namely letting others conform while avoiding responsibility oneself and so benefiting from the commitment of others, has to be removed by some form of mutual coercion commonly agreed upon.

Three principal theories apply to the formation of regimes:

1. *Structural or hegomistic theories.* Here the regime is created and maintained by a single power, or small number of states, with the ability to influence or coerce the weaker members into its definition of acceptable action. With the break-up of the Cold War, and the growing relative dominance of the 'Group of 77' developing countries, this is now regarded as an out-of-date interpretation of international environmental action. In some senses too the USA has not taken a central role in international environmental negotiations, so its obvious diplomatic and military dominance has not been so apparent. It is interesting that the Rio conference achieved a Framework Convention on Biodiversity without US support, and set targets for greenhouse gas reduction against US opposition. It is even more interesting to note that the Clinton administration not only signed the Biodiversity Convention, it also agreed to the stabilization of US CO_2 emissions at 1990 levels by 2000. Admittedly this is a new

Box 19.4 Game playing and environmental diplomacy

Dasgupta (1992) has argued that it pays private resource managers not to know what damage they are creating. Ignorance is cost saving. There is of course a case for public investment in scientific knowledge, otherwise the victim has no basis for a claim, and the damager no incentive to be proactive. Game playing can be a means of overcoming this unique knowledge and power relationship so long as it is possible to alter the status quo.

In the so-called prisoner's dilemma, it pays players to assume non-co-operation, so a perverse outcome is the result. It is easier to try to 'free-ride' on the backs of others who comply; but of course all players take the same view with the consequence that all are worse off, in the absence of any kind of enforcing agreement.

Maler (1992) shows how this operates for sulphur dioxide reduction. Under normal competitive arrangements a country will emit SO_2, until marginal costs of abatement equal the marginal costs of damage from its domestic emissions. But where the SO_2 crosses borders, the marginal abatement cost for each country should equal to the total marginal damage in all affected countries. Maler shows that with 40 per cent abatement of SO_2, the total saving for all European countries is maximized at 6 billion DM. However, the main beneficiaries are the low sulphur emitters who get acidified from neighbouring emissions, for example Sweden.

The principal losers are those countries with little cross-border deposition such as the UK or Italy. In theory these countries have every incentive to free-ride an SO_2 agreement, unless compensated. Maler then shows that it would pay countries not to co-operate, thus negating any agreement except as forced through by dictate.

In practice, politics, morality and linkage to other foreign policy issues all intervene to create minimal scale international agreements. Nevertheless the incentives not to co-operate are very high, until the value of precaution, and the fuller ecological economic costs, are properly calculated. This is why good interdisciplinary environmental science is such a vital companion to international environmental diplomacy.

Sources: Dasgupta (1992); Maler (1992).

and expected utility is the combination of the likelihood of an outcome and the valuation of its benefit. Game theorists seek to calculate how negotiators manoeuvre to establish the best expected utility based on how they judge others will act. The 'game' becomes a clever guessing exercise on how much the other parties will sacrifice to get what they want, and how they judge the certainty or uncertainty of the outcome. Box 19.4 illustrates this approach. The tactic is best found with small groupings of negotiating nations and a clearly defined target (e.g. removal of sulphur and limitation of acid rain damage) or a regional resource (e.g. nutrient control in the southern North Sea).

3. *Epistemic communities*. This theory is based on the presumption that informed and influential people form international networks of expertise who share knowledge and undertake rigorous peer review to establish and maintain credibility. This aspect was outlined in the Introduction. The point is to establish mutual agreement amongst policy advisors regarding appropriate political action. Much depends on scientific consensus and a reasonable convergence of judgement as to likely outcomes of the policy measures, for example environmental taxes and their influence on jobs and income distribution, or pollutant removal as a precautionary measure and its benefit for specific ecosystems. The points raised in the Introduction are relevant here. Science needs both credibility and a broadly based political constituency before epistemic communities can prove successful. The Intergovernmental Panel on Climate Change is a good example of the epistemic science basis for regime formation.

In the contemporary world none of these theories is ideal for identifying negotiating regimes in environmental problem solving. There is no single most powerful actor; uncertainty in scientific analysis hampers both utilitarian and epistemic approaches. Linkage of environmental issues to trade negotiations, to regional conflict and security and to the migration of displaced persons (see Chapter 1) means that much of modern regime development is exploratory and revelatory. Indeed there is a good argument that bargaining over global commons issues is proving to be genuinely innovative and unique, exposing politicians to very different perceptions and placing them face to face with constellations of interests not encountered before. So negotiating regimes have to start small and evolve creatively within larger but supporting international structures.

political tenure in Washington, but it is also a sign of the significance of global commons regime.

2. *Utilitarian theories*. These are based on game-playing strategies. Utility is a measure of preference,

Box 19.5 Sequential diplomacy and the ozone hole

As is now widely known, ozone is a molecular form of oxygen composed of three atoms created by the fusing energy of sunlight. In the outer layers of the atmosphere, some 50km above the Earth's surface, oxygen molecules seeping out of the stratosphere are constantly converted into ozone. The ozone molecules are subsequently destroyed by the catalytic activities of minute concentrations of certain gases, in parts per billion or even parts per trillion (10^{-9} or 10^{-12}). These gases can 'steal' an oxygen atom to destroy ozone in what Warr (1991, 127) calls an 'atomic quadrille'. One such gas is nitric oxide (NO); its reaction with ozone is shown here:

$$O_3 + NO \rightarrow O_2 + NO_2$$
$$O + NO_2 \rightarrow O_2 + NO$$

Chlorine does a similar job, as follows:

$$O_3 + Cl \rightarrow O_2 + ClO$$
$$O + ClO \rightarrow O_2 + Cl$$

The catalytic nature of this process ensures that active chlorine radicals can remove ozone many times over; possibly as many as 100 000 molecules of ozone per free atom may be removed. For the most part, these free trace atoms are locked up in 'reservoirs' of inactivity. The chlorine rests as hydrogen chloride, and the nitrogen as chlorine nitrate.

All this is fine as long as the dynamic equilibrium is not disturbed. However, the source gases of chlorine and nitrogen atoms are being increased by human-induced activities. NO_x or various nitrogen oxides are created from fossil fuel burning, automobile exhausts, ammonia from manure and artificial fertilizer. Chlorine compounds are increasingly found in many chemical products from pesticides to solvents and bleach to plastics. Methane (CH_4) also plays its part as an ozone destroyer, and that too is on the increase. However, the most prominent of the new source gases is the chlorofluorocarbon series, a group of chemical compounds combining carbon, chlorine, fluorine and hydrogen. These gases were developed because they appeared to be inert and non-flammable and therefore could be combined with active agents for safety and security. In the stratosphere, the intense sunlight strips away a chlorine atom thereby adding to the stock of chlorine atoms. The length of time a CFC molecule remains active and the number of chlorine atoms it contains produces an index known as the Ozone Depleting Potential (ODP): a ratio compared to CFC-11 ($CFCl_3$), the most common of the CFC tribe. However if sufficient quantities are released, then even a low ODP may signal danger. Two examples illustrate this: methyl chloroform is a widely used dry cleaning agent with an output exceeding 500 000 tonnes annually, yet an ODP of 0.1 to 0.2. The hydrogen fluorocarbons, now being produced as substitutes to CFCs still contain chlorine atoms and so will add to ozone depletion. Both the HCFCs and the CFCs are greenhouse gases as well, contributing around 8 to 10 per cent of climate warming (see Box 6.5).

The polar regions, especially the Antarctic atmosphere, become very stable during the sunless winter months. Luminescent clouds of ice particles form in the intensely cold and stable atmospheres. On these ice particles chemical processes, as yet imperfectly understood, prepare the trace gases for liberation when energized by the first rays of spring sunshine. This is why the polar ozone 'holes' are so prominent in the spring, though the feature is much more marked over the Antarctic because of the scale of the polar icecap. Recent estimates suggest that the temporary loss of ozone in the Antarctic may be as high as 60 per cent and about 15 to 20 per cent in the Arctic. Overall the stratospheric ozone losses may be 1 to 2 per cent annually; even if all the additional trace gases were to be stabilized at pre-1990 levels it would take over 70 years for net ozone loss to cease.

The removal of stratospheric ozone exposes humans and plants to higher levels of the more intense ultraviolet solar radiation. Curiously, actual levels of UV-B, the band of greatest concern, have not been measured as increasing in the mid latitudes yet. This has led some to speculate that the whole CFC scare is a scientists' nightmare concocted to generate more research cash (see Kenny, 1994). The problem is outlined in the Introduction: measurement needs to be accurate, long term and very reliable before any trend in such a microscale can be recorded with confidence. Impatience is not a scientific virtue. Yet for political and very significant commercial reasons, it pays the big chemical companies to listen to, and to finance, scientists who are sceptical of the evidence. It is only since 1985 that instruments of sufficient accuracy have been designed to detect the changes in UV-B in the less polluted areas such as the southern hemisphere continents and Antarctica itself. Meanwhile the chemical manufacturers are making handsome profits out of new refrigeration technology using HCFCs and other lower ODP compounds. This is despite the fact that Greenpeace has championed a safe propane-butane refrigerator that is both inexpensive and entirely ozone friendly.

The sequential diplomacy concerns the negotiations surrounding the various protocols attached to the 1987 Montreal Protocol on Substances that Deplete the Ozone Layer. This is universally referred

Box 19.5 continued

to as the Montreal Protocol. In its 1987 version it committed every signatory state to reduce its use of certain CFCs by 50 per cent of their level of use in 1986 by 1999. In 1990 the London Amendments added more CFCs, halons and other substances, and widened the net of signatory nations to eighty. In 1992 the World Meteorological Organization reported that the 1994–1992 ozone 'winter' could be classified 'among those with the most negative deviation of systematic ozone observations . . . ' Estimates of skin cancer from increased exposure to UV-B alarmed many, as did reports of eye cataracts in humans and animals increasing in mountainous areas where thin clear air added to the radiation burden. Counter-balancing these scientific discoveries was the political and economic power of multinational chemical companies and nation states still dependent on the manufacture of high ODP compounds now in the firing line. Sequential environmental diplomacy is a cat-and-mouse game operating at many levels. The science is only one element: uncertainty is mercilessly exploited, as are the claims of environmental organizations that environmentally friendly substitutes can be manufactured profitably.

In November 1992 the fourth meeting of the Montreal Protocol agreed to phase out CFCs by 1996 with a 75 per cent reduction by 1994. However, 'essential uses' where no practicable substitutes are available can continue, as can CFC output in the developing world until 2006, so long as production is designed to meet 'basic domestic needs'. The scope for black market racketeering is considerable, though small scale manufacture of CFCs is not particularly profitable.

Nevertheless in a space of six years, environmental diplomacy has all but eliminated CFCs, halons, methyl chloroform and carbon tetrachloride. Yet the influence of the HCFC producers should not be underestimated. They managed to delay a phase out to 2030, to ensure that they would recoup the profits from their expensive research and development procedures. Rowlands (1993, 27) points out that the US chemical company Du Pont sent a delegation of seven people to the negotiations, a number that exceeded the delegations of all but six countries. The delayed phase out of HCFCs is in line with the demand by US business interests that our conditioning units in buildings be allowed to run their full forty year working lives.

Methyl bromide is also a known ozone depleting substance. Unlike the CFC group, it is used as a fungicide and is widely deployed in the Third World. Israel is a prominent manufacturer. Poorer countries successfully argued for a retention in the use of this substance with only a modest phase out subject to more scientific evidence. Sequential diplomacy will undoubtedly target this product as the science of ozone depletion improves. Poorer nations are seeking exceptions or grant aid from the Global Environment Facility to see them through the transition. In the ozone debate, as in many others, environmental science becomes enmeshed in the whirlpool of political economics.

All this puts considerable emphasis on constructive and coherent communication between the parties, and demands special skills of 'translation into the vernacular' for the *science entrepreneur*. This is a relatively new breed of scientist, trained in science, knowledgeable of the complexities and shortfalls of the trade, yet capable of summarizing in a faithful and intelligible manner. Such individuals are becoming half scientists and half politicians with great media talent for explaining and emphasizing according to the media needs of simple language, evocative illustration and memorable soundbites.

The UN Commission on Sustainable Development

As an example of contemporary regime formation at work, let us look at one of the principal organizational innovations of the Rio Conference, namely the establishment of a UN Commission on Sustainable development (UNCSD). This is a 53 member body with a mandate to receive national sustainable development strategies (SDSs), to provide guidance on the content and consistency of these strategies, and to implement Agenda 21. As such it is the major institutional focus for managing the whole global commons.

Haas and his colleagues (1992) suggest three criteria for evaluating the success of new institutional arrangements for managing the global commons:

1. *Focusing analysis*, by channelling discussion and research in policy terms and by enabling consensus positions to be reached.

2. *Creating international action* by aligning non-governmental interests into intergovernmental negotiating structures through bargaining and staged resolution.

3. *Promoting agreed national action* by enabling democratic national governments to adopt positions that stop or prevent environmental and social degradation even though initially this may not be perceived as primary national interest.

All this should promote a sense of mutual concern and shared action where none existed before; provide adaptable forums for achieving intercountry consensus; and build up national political and administrative capabilities for responding to these new challenges. This is very much the social learning component of regime formation.

The creation of the UNCSD has forced some important changes in the UN itself. First of all there is a Department of Policy Coordination and Sustainable Development in the Office of the Secretary General. This is designed to ensure that all UN agencies, including the financial institutions such as the World Bank, create and co-ordinate policies that promote the cause of sustainable development. Furthermore they will have to show to the UNCSD that they have done so by producing annual reports.

This process will not be confined to the major UN agencies, such as the Food and Agricultural Organization, the UN Environment Programme and the UN Development Programme. Reviews of how far these bodies have responded to the need for a more sustainable approach will be lively enough. The World Bank, the multilateral financing and aid agencies, and various trading arrangements, including the General Agreement on Tariffs and Trade (GATT) will also be subject to regular audit for their contribution towards sustainability. Since the UNCSD will contain representatives of the nine non-governmental stakeholder groups introduced in Chapter 1, such regular statements should create very lively debate.

These are very early days, so one should not get too excited. But in principle the whole apparatus of global development could become susceptible to a regular audit of performance in relation to the principles and practices of sustainability as outlined in Chapters 1 and 2, and enshrined in Agenda 21. This would be a major breakthrough if such is to be the outcome of the early manoeuvrings of the UNCSD. It would mean that for the first time the connections between trade, aid, debt and war could be assessed in terms of how far they were detracting from both national and local sustainable development strategies and initiatives. Obviously much depends on how the new structures are treated by the 'non-environmental' parts of trade, aid,

development and international finance. The 'greening' of all that will require thoughtful entry by environmental science. Environmental scientists may fare better by being accountants, financiers, diplomats and military attachés.

The potentially powerful UN Department of Policy Coordination and Sustainable Development is in turn advised by a panel of specialist advisers. This group is specially selected by the Secretary General to review all the policy papers in advance of each UNCSD meeting. These papers will look at the substantive elements of Agenda 21 in sequence – capacity building for science and management, health and environmental wellbeing, toxic waste and international exports, sustainable settlements, freshwater availability and energy. These will be handled in a series of intersessional meetings held between the annual review sessions of UNCSD. The aim is to avoid crisis response and prepare practical and programmed perspectives. To this end the UN Secretary General has created an Inter Agency Committee on Sustainable Development. This will seek to coordinate the thematic Agenda 21 elements into the programmes and budgets of all UN agencies and related institutions.

Meanwhile the UNCSD itself is encouraging and enabling national SDSs. Each of these will contain assessments of the intersessional agenda items, as well as a supposedly coherent national approach. In many countries local governments (one of the nine stakeholder groups) are creating local Agenda 21 strategies according to their capabilities and powers. It is worthy of note that in a number of federal countries, the constitution does not permit central governments to have power over purely local action. Even regional governments (state, provincial, *Länder*) may not hold powers over local communities. As the need for locally devised sustainable initiatives becomes more apparent, so these constitutional relationships will have to be carefully reassessed.

The aim, however, is to promote local initiatives, citizens' groups, carrying out the business of sustainability. In this way overlapping sequences of regimes are formed linking international commitments to global citizenship. No one knows how successful this will turn out to be: the stakes are as high as they can possibly be. But first we have to educate ourselves and become much more self-aware.

Education for a sustainable future

What is education for sustainability? It is the creation of a sense and a practice of global citizenship in all humanity. Arguably in the innermost recesses of every human conscience there is an echo of gaia. Humanity is a product of life's evolution on Earth. It is logical to surmise that, deep down, we are all basically global citizens, ready to share in the maintenance of Planet Earth. It is on this basis that education for sustainability has a chance to work.

The impediments to education for sustainability

The first impediment is *democratic short sightedness*. Paradoxically democracy is both the necessary vehicle for the transition to sustainability and the greatest obstacle. Democracy means informed consent. Without the support of the people no government can govern, whatever its cause. Understandably, democratic political institutions such as lobbying groups, regular general elections and media-generated public grievances against proposed actions thwart any long-term sustainability objective. Understandably too, a general ideology favouring self-interest and the prolonged survival of one's family may run against helping the less privileged and those yet to be born, unless the nature of the choices that have to be made can somehow be translated into transpersonal terms. So it is not so much democracy that is at fault, as the institutions that carry short-termism and selfishness in individual preferences, and political priorities that regard sharing and reciprocal aid as an anathema.

Language symbolism means that concepts such as self-interest and sacrifice have a nasty ring about them. The first implies 'me first', the second 'you last'. This is not the language of gaia. Yet in a truly gaian world self-interest is shared interest. The tropical forests will not remain unmolested by chance: if they are mostly cut down we all lose and all generations to come will be faced with a biologically impoverished world. The interest of the tropical forest dweller and tropical forest-owning country is served by all of us playing a part in the preservation and sustainable management of this magnificent resource.

So it is not a 'sacrifice' to give up some consumption today in order to have more tropical forest tomorrow.

Nor surely is it a 'sacrifice' to reduce a certain amount of demonstrably overconsumption today so that others can have their basic needs better met. Charity is seen as a middle class guilt trip. It should be a matter of emancipation and joy to help others so that we can all live in a sustainable world.

Yet we are *alienated from the knowledge of the consequences of our demands*. This inability to know what 'footprints' we are stamping on the life-support systems of the Earth is not just a matter of scientific ignorance, though certainly it is partly that. This separation of cause from effect is rooted in our ways of life, in our regulatory structures, in our economic lives as consumers, and in our political lives as voters. We allow non-sustainable economies to be perpetrated even when we know they are non-sustainable. We vote in governments that perpetuate our ignorance of demand and consequence. We tolerate packaging, advertisements, patterns of travel, routeways of roads that undermine sustainability at every turn. Education for sustainability should be about consciousness-raising and conscience-pricking. Empowerment is the recognition of the thousands of contradictions that govern our civil and personal lives. We may not be able to resolve all these inconsistencies but we should constantly be aware of them and ready, always ready, to recognize why they exist and are maintained in the economic and political structures that govern us.

Sadly, too, modern education provides *no entitlement in the curriculum for linking environment and development*, no common core of material that should be available to all youngsters whatever their schooling or vocation. In addition there is precious little *interdisciplinarity in the environmental sciences*. As noted in the Introduction interdisciplinarity is not a matter of integrating disciplines. It is much more a matter of relating science to various ways in which we all learn and feel about the world. These ways of knowing are in turn influenced by the social networks that influence us and the culture of the out-of-classroom learning that envelops us. Interdisciplinarity is the linkage of the scientific method to more vernacular ways of learning and experiencing. This helps to put science in its place – prominent, but not absolute.

All resources have a communal ownership element to them for they contain the essence of the lifeblood of the Earth – thus resources are the property of ecological processes and individual species as much as of the owners of the legal documents of proprietorship. It is this dual recognition of property right that forms the basis of true citizenship.

Maybe, too, we can twin our transitional experiences with sister settlements in the developed and developing world. What better way to generate an educational experience than to establish a bond across the globe in the move towards sustainability!

Finally we must open up the walls of our 'classrooms'. The 'classroom' is not the four walls of a school or higher education building. It is the confining cabin of all our day-to-day experiences; the anaesthetizing barriers of comfort and avoidance thus enable us to live non-sustainably against our gaian-driven consciences. So the 'classrooms' of the future should be the accumulation of local initiatives of the sustainable transition. These are the laboratories of both learning and training. If we try to show that we can begin to do it, maybe the politicians will come to believe that the 'classroom-less' school is the real political action field for the creation of a democracy ready and willing to make the long, arduous but ultimately rewarding journey to sustainability.

References

Allott, P. (1990) *Eunomia: new order for a new world.* Oxford: Oxford University Press.

Birnie, P. (1991) International environmental law: its adequacy for future needs. In A. Hurrell and B. Kingsbury (Eds) *The international politics of the environment.* Oxford: Clarendon Press, pp. 51–84.

Birnie, P. and S. Boyle (1992) *International environmental law.* London: Butterworth.

Brown Weiss, E. (1989) *In fairness to future generations: International law, common patrimony and intergenerational equity.* New York: Dobbs Ferry.

Dasgupta, P. (1992) The environment as a commodity. In D. Helm (Ed.) *Economic policy towards the environment.* Oxford: Blackwell, pp. 25–51.

Fox, W.R. (1992) *Towards a transpersonal ecology: developing new foundations for environmentalism.* Toronto: Shambhala Press.

Haas, P.M., M.A. Levy and E.A. Parson (1992) Appraising the Earth Summit: how should we judge UNCED's success? *Environment,* **34**(8), 6–12.

Kenny, A. (1994) The earth is fine: the problem is the greens. *The Spectator,* 11 March, pp. 3–7.

Lovelock, J. (1992) *Gaia: the practical science of planetary medicine.* London: Gaia Books.

Maler, K.G. (1992) International environmental problems. In D. Helm (Ed.) *Economic policy towards the environment.* Oxford: Blackwell, pp. 156–201.

Naess, A. (1989) *Ecology, community and lifestyle: outline of an ecosophy.* Cambridge: Cambridge University Press.

Rowlands, I. (1993) The fourth meeting of the parties to the Montreal Protocol: report and reflection. *Environment,* **35**(6), 25–34.

Sachs, W. (1993) *Global ecology: a new arena of political conflict.* London: Zed Books.

Schelling, T. (1972) On the ecology of micromotives. *The public interest,* **25**, pp. 61–78.

Schneider, S.H. (1990) Debating gains. *Environment,* **32**(5), 5–9, 30–32.

Schneider, S.H. and P.J. Boston (Eds) (1991) *Science of gaia.* Cambridge, MA: MIT Press.

Warr, K. (1991) The ozone layer. In P.M. Smith and K. Warr (Eds) *Global environmental issues.* Milton Keynes: Open University Press, pp. 121–71.

Young, O. (1992) International environmental governance: building institutions in an anarchical society. In IIASA, *Science and sustainability.* Laxenburg: International Institute for Applied Systems Analysis, pp. 245–369.

Further reading

There is now a great choice of books on international environmental politics and law as a result of the growth of interest in these topics. The following are recommended.

Birnie, P. and S. Boyle (1992). *International Environmental Law* London: Butterworth.

Hurrell, A. and B. Kingsbury (1992) *The international politics of the environment.* Oxford: Clarendon Press.

O'Riordan, T. and R.K. Turner (1983) The commons theme. In T. O'Riordan and R.K. Turner (Eds) *An annotated reader in environmental planning and management.* Oxford: Pergamon, pp. 265–88.

Porter, G. and J. Welsh Brown (1992) *Global environmental politics.* Bolder, CO: Westview Press.

Sand, P. (1994) *International environmental law.* London: Earthscan.

Sjostedt, G., U. Svedin and B.H. Aniansson (1993) *International environmental negotiations: process, issues and contexts.* Stockholm: The Swedish Institute of International Affairs.

Thomas, C. (1992) *The environment in international relations.* London: Royal Institute for International Affairs.

There is still precious little on education for sustainability. Some good material is being produced by the Forum for Education for Sustainability, International Institute for Environment and Development, 3 Endsleigh Street London WC1H ODD. See also Scottish Office (1993) *Learning for life: a national strategy for environmental education in Scotland* (The Scottish Office, Edinburgh).

List of journals

Environmental management advances through research. Peer review journals report the best of the new ideas and fresh perspectives. If you want to keep up with this rapidly changing field, it would be helpful if you look regularly at the following list of journals identified by the contributors.

Environmental policy and science

The standard scientific magazines *Nature, Science* and *New Scientist* carry regular features and news reports on environmental policy issues and the significance of new scientific findings. *Environment* is a monthly magazine that covers a wide range of environmental science reports and is well worth reading. Similarly *Ambio* maintains high quality science reports of interest to the general reader. *The Ecologist* covers both North and South environmental themes: it is cheerfully radical but always stimulating. The lead journal for global change issues with an interdisciplinary perspective is *Global Environmental Change. Environmental Politics* is a recent addition to the scene but covers a fine range of contemporary political analysis. It is also a repository of green environmental thinking, as is another newish journal, *Environmental Values.* This journal and *Environmental Ethics* provide excellent coverage for ideological and ethical issues.

Environmental economics and resource management

The most accessible journals are *Ecological Economics* and the *Journal of Resource and Environmental Economics.* Both of these cover applied environmental economics research reports. The *Journal of Environmental Economics and Management* is very advanced but of importance for serious specialists. The *Journal of Environmental Management and Planning* covers both the economics and management aspects of land use. For the specialist, *The American Journal of Agricultural Economics*, the *Journal of Agricultural Economics, Land Economics*, and the *American Economic Review* all contain material of substance. At a more accessible level, *Project Appraisal, The*

Environmentalist and *Environmental Management* provide plenty of excellent case studies in applied economics and planning. In a more lively format, *Town and Country Planning* and *The Planner* cover topical subjects in planning and environmental management generally.

Ecosystem management and environmental ethics

The main applied ecological journals are the *Journal of Biological Conservation*, the *Journal of Environmental Management, Biodiversity and Conservation*, and *Conservation Biology*. Each of these has case study material of great interest. At a popular level, especially for countryside management, read *Ecos, Land Use Planning* and the *Journal of Rural Studies*.

Oceans and coasts

The best journal for coastal research is *Marine Policy*, though this also has fine coverage of fisheries issues. *Marine Pollution Bulletin* is a lively journal with many topical articles. *Estuarine* covers coastal themes. At the basic level, *Ocean Challenge* is a readable magazine, while *Oceanus* is a colour magazine suitable for anyone interested in the oceans. For a journal covering new oceanographic theories and observations read *Deep-Sea Research*.

Soil erosion and land degradation

The three most useful journals here are *Land Degradation*, the *Journal of Soil and Water Conservation* and *International Agricultural Development*. Each offers good case studies from all over the globe.

Hydrology and hydrogeology

The *Journal of Hydrology* and *Water Resources Research* are the mainstream publications, though *Ground Water* and the *Journal of Contaminant Hydrology* are also good to consult.

Air pollution, energy and risk

Atmospheric Environment is a most important scientific journal. Subsidiary, but useful journals are *Environment and Technology* and the *Journal of Air and Waste Management Association*. *Risk Analysis* is by far the most comprehensive publication in the area of health and safety, as well as social perception. *Energy Policy* is the most reliable source for energy matters.

Environmental law

The Journal of Environmental Law is the most useful review of planning and law matters, but the *Journal of Environment and Planning Law* is invaluable as a source of commentary on recent legislation. *Environmental Policy and Practice* contains plenty of topical articles on environmental policy and management from a legal perspective. For international environmental law, two publications are suggested: the *Review of European Community and International Environmental Law* and *European Environmental Law Review* provide valuable coverage of European and international issues.

INDEX